Theology and Literature in the Age of Johnson

Theology and Literature in the Age of Johnson

Resisting Secularism

Edited by
Melvyn New and Gerard Reedy, S.J.

UNIVERSITY OF DELAWARE PRESS
Newark

University of Delaware Press
© 2012 by the University of Delaware Press
All rights reserved
Printed in the United States of America on acid-free paper
Distributed by the University of Virginia Press

ISBN 978-1-64453-097-9 (paper)
ISBN 978-1-64453-098-6 (ebook)

British Library Cataloguing-in-Publication Information Available

Library of Congress Cataloging-in-Publication Data

Theology and literature in the age of Johnson : resisting secularism / edited by Melvyn New and Gerard Reedy.
 p. cm.
 Includes bibliographical references and index.
 1. English literature—18th century—History and criticism. 2. Religion and literature—Great Britain—History—18th century. 3. Religion in literature. 4. Religious tolerance—Great Britain—History—18th century. 5. Great Britain—Intellectual life—18th century. 6. Secularism in literature I. New, Melvyn. II. Reedy, Gerard.
 PR448.R45T47 2012
 820.9'38287—dc23
 2012010679

Contents

Acknowledgments   vii

Introduction   ix
   Melvyn New

1. Novelistic Redemption and the History of Grace: Practical Theology and Literary Form in Richardson's *Pamela* and Fielding's *Joseph Andrews*   1
Donald R. Wehrs

2. *The Oxford Methodists* (1733; 1738): The Purloined Letter of John Wesley at Samuel Richardson's Press   27
John A. Dussinger

3. Henry Fielding Straddles a Moving Theme   49
Regina Janes

4. Samuel Richardson's *Clarissa* and the Problem of Heaven   71
E. Derek Taylor

5. The Intellectual Background to Johnson's *Life of Browne*: A Study of Johnsonian Construction   91
Robert G. Walker

6. "But Philosophy Can Tell No More": Johnson's Christian Moralism and the Genre of *Rasselas*   113
Patrick Müller

7. Johnson's Fallen World   131
Steven Scherwatzky

8	Aesthetics and Theology in Samuel Johnson's *Life of Isaac Watts* and *Prayers and Meditations* (1785) *Katherine Kickel*	147
9	Providence, Futurity, and Typology in Oliver Goldsmith's *The Vicar of Wakefield* *Nicholas Seager*	163
10	Divine and Human Love: Letters between John Norris and Mary Astell, Laurence Sterne and Eliza Draper *Geoff Newton*	183
11	*Tristram Shandy* and the Devil *Ryan J. Stark*	203
12	Methodists on the Move in *The Spiritual Quixote* *Brett C. McInelly*	219
13	"A Very Agreable Way of Thinking": Devotion and Doctrine in Boswell's Religion *Paul Tankard*	237
14	Bluestockings and Religion *Deborah Heller*	255
15	"Through a Glass Darkly": Edmund Burke, Political Theology, and Literary Allusion *Frans De Bruyn*	277
16	The Bible in the Dock: Thomas Erskine, Thomas Paine, and the Trial of *The Age of Reason* *Roger D. Lund*	293
17	The Novel as the Art of Secular Scripture: Mary Wollstonecraft's Feminist Gospel *Nathalie Zimpfer*	311

Selected Index	333
About the Contributors	347

Acknowledgments

The co-editors would like to acknowledge the generous financial support of Jesuits of Fordham, Inc., the always solid collegial advice of Robert G. Walker, and the astute editorial assistance of Gillian Hillis.

Introduction

Melvyn New

> Anyone who doesn't believe in miracles is no realist.
> —Paul Celan to Ilana Shmueli, February 5, 1970

The immediate impetus for this collection of essays was Jerry Reedy's suggestion that we undertake the project—his reaction to reading a draft entry on Anglicanism that I had written for a collection of "contexts" for Samuel Johnson. It seems appropriate, therefore, briefly to review a few of the salient points of that essay. Its epigraph, significantly enough, is Johnson's definition of Christian, "A professor of the religion of Christ," and its illustrative quotation, taken from Archbishop Tillotson, is "We *Christians* have certainly the best and the holiest, the wisest and most reasonable religion in the world." Perhaps unfairly the essay focused on the paradox I perceived in that sentence, the juxtaposition of superlatives ("best," "holiest," "wisest") with the word "reasonable," wherein I found a defining conflict inherent in Christianity between Truth and Peace.

After a century of religious warfare, unnecessary to rehearse to the audience for a collection of this nature, the eighteenth century was certainly fertile ground for privileging the Christian message of Peace over its equally pertinent message of Truth. For Tillotson—and for the latitudinarianism he represented as its most effective voice from the end of the seventeenth century to the very end of the eighteenth—this meant primarily a toleration of as many variations on Christianity as conscience could bear and politics could make possible. Tillotson envisioned an inclusive rather than exclusive congregation, one ever expanding because it envisioned itself always as a balancing, moderating, and mediating presence between extremes: Roman Catholicism on the one hand, Dissenters (non-Anglican Protestants, including, by Johnson's day, the new Methodist movement) on the other. It is telling that at the beginning of his career and even when he had reached the Anglican pinnacle as Archbishop of Canterbury, Tillotson was always under attack from both within and without the Anglican establishment—indeed, by every Christian for whom Truth remained more important than Peace. It is, in fact, much easier to believe that one has assigned equal measure to both than actually to achieve such a balance. To my mind it is, in fact, impossible; the capacity to put down one's own Truth to acknowledge the *equal* Truth of another is perhaps the most difficult lesson yet to be learned among the several lessons necessary to pacify the world. Needless to say, we are certainly no closer today to the ideal balance than we were in 1750.

In many ways, eighteenth-century Anglican theology represents an experiment testing whether or not it is possible ever to reconcile Peace and Truth, most especially when one embraces a religion that is "the best and the holiest, the wisest and most reasonable religion in the world." The predictable, perhaps inevitable outcome has been amply recorded and may be summarized thus: religious tolerance and an accepting attitude toward all belief systems is a wonderful idea if Peace is the final aim of religion; it is, however, a devastating blow to Truth. That in modern times we have read the history of Christian belief in eighteenth-century Britain as one long drift toward secularism is a direct result of the success of Tillotson and the latitudinarians; that we think of that drift as "enlightenment" and "progress" is equally attributable to them, but as failure rather than success. In winning the Peace, the eighteenth-century church seems to have lost the Truth.

Less metaphorically, if a Catholic priest or a Presbyterian pastor could argue that *his* system was the only true "religion of Christ" (to invoke Johnson's terse but telling definition), why would we want to practice a religion that refused to make a similar claim, and thus endanger our own salvation? On the other hand, if we are convinced, as Tillotson asserts, that ours is "the best and the holiest" religion, we have already joined with that priest and that pastor in maintaining our faith's superior claims to every other religion "in the world." Not only would we want to belong to the communion that worships "correctly," but we would want our faith to be invested in a church that was not second best. Moreover, Tillotson was not speaking of Christianity in general; his appeal to reasonableness—evoking the unreasonableness of Catholics and Dissenters—would have fallen on knowing ears from one end of the century to the other. The archbishop of the Anglican communion was stating, even while promulgating his brilliantly conceived religion of moderation, the absolute superiority of his own church as the true "religion of Christ." And of course, even Edward Gibbon had to admit, with his usual wit, that Christianity was not the only religion claiming absolute superiority; thus in a footnote to chapter 52 of *Decline and Fall*, he writes: "Among the Arabian philosophers, Averroes has been accused of despising the religions of the Jews, the Christians, and the Mohammedans. . . . Each of these sects would agree that, in two instances out of three, his contempt was reasonable."

To Tillotson's quite natural belief that his own religion was the one true faith, we must add the fundamental command of the New Testament: dutiful Christians should spread the Word and convert the unbeliever. Europe was actually still conducting crusades in the Middle East in the eighteenth century; closer to home, it was considered theologically uncharitable and unchristian to condemn the unbeliever to damnation. To be a good Christian meant working to convert the world—and, more practically, our wrongheaded neighbors—to our own beliefs; the evangelical mandate is a particularly pregnant marker separating the Old and New Testaments. This is the paradox that now confronted the eighteenth century, first manifested with the Glorious Revolution and culminating in the immensely paradoxical assertion one hundred years later, in the American Bill of Rights (1789), that the state, despite having a vested interest in the welfare of its citizens, cannot privilege one religion over another. To be "free" now meant having the freedom to condemn oneself to eternal damnation by practicing the *wrong* religion—the state could no longer impose *right* religion on benighted citizens. If political power, the only power left in the state, controlled one's earthly existence but withdrew completely from the business of how one would spend eternity, religious life would surely be weakened, if not entirely erased, for many; for others, it would be transferred from religion to the state itself. Truth now became the sole property of the state and its judicial system, and a new era of conflict between Peace and Truth was ushered into British consciousness with the events in France at the end of the century. Centuries of religious warfare were replaced by centuries of statist warfare—although perhaps we live today in the worst of all possible worlds, where we now seem to be fighting wars of state and of religion simultaneously. (Significantly, my epigraph originated not in Celan's love letter to Shmueli, but in David Ben Gurion's address to the Israeli army in 1948.)

To be sure, deists and freethinkers of widely varying degrees (a minute minority in the century, however one defines those who opted out of organized Christian communions) could argue that, as long as one believed in any sort of God and the promptings of a good heart, salvation would be assured. We inherited this argument from the "Enlightenment," and it underlies the religion of many today, both in and out of denominational systems. The problem is that the argument destroys most, if not all, of what had validated Christian belief for seventeen hundred years. The evangelical mandate is canceled, since the Word has now become simply words among words. Salvation is no longer particular to modes of ritual, sacrament, and communion, and one performs in church without any assurance at all that one is moving closer to God by one's practices—a much more acceptable service may well be taking place in a neighboring church.

Above all, trusting in one's "good heart" indicates a fundamental disbelief in the Fall in the Garden of Eden: a long tradition of Christian thought held that the heart was corrupted and rendered sinful by Adam's disobedience. Moreover, if the first Adam did not sin for us all, the "second Adam," Jesus Christ, had no reason to die on the cross; redemption from sin necessitates a belief that the human heart is in a state of sin and separated from God until thus redeemed by belief. John Locke, a figure certainly as important to the fate of Christian belief in the eighteenth century as was Tillotson, makes this the very first premise of his significantly titled *Reasonableness of Christianity* (1695): without the Fall in the Garden, Christ would have had no reason to come into the world, much less to be crucified; hence Christianity, the "religion of Christ [crucified]," would have no justification, no superiority, over any other belief system. A little more than a century after the armies of God killed one another over the finest theological points each side could muster, religion was discovered to be superfluous to mankind, replaced by the "good heart" of sensibility and sentimentalism among the secular ethicists, by the power of the state among the secular realists. Sterne's uncle Toby might embody both, but significantly enough, he is the creation of a satiric imagination; the reality was the revolution in France.

It is, to be sure, the imagination—satiric or comic or tragic—that is the second half of the dual interest of the essays in this collection, the inextricable relationship between theology and literature in the second half of the eighteenth century. Uncle Toby might well serve as an emblem for this relationship in so far as the "resisting" of our title invokes the warfare on his bowling green, for the unifying thesis behind all seventeen essays is that religion in the eighteenth century did not disappear from its literature but, quite the contrary, remained its dominant context. In the warfare between Peace and Truth, we might suggest, literature became a primary arena, one in which the truth content of Christianity was juxtaposed (but never reconciled) to its peace content by means of the literary imagination. Put another way, the literary imagination in the century defined itself by its infinitely varied, yet quite singular, attempt to resist secular thinking, at times in defense of Christianity and at times of literature itself. If all other human discourse, including religion, can be seen as efforts to resolve paradoxes, to make known the unknown, literature distinguishes itself by doing the opposite: it is the mode of discourse that dwells in paradox and that, rather than attempting to reconcile opposites (Truth and Peace, ultimately), forces us to acknowledge the untruthfulness and irritability behind each and every attempt to do so.

Of particular importance to the project of the political state in its displacing of religion as the center of human concern is the way it shadows religious thought, most pertinently for scholars of eighteenth-century literature, the paradoxical nature of Christianity and the attempt to resolve all paradoxes by finding solutions for them; the teleological (and perhaps moral) end of the state is, of course, the Final Solution. The decisive spiritual talent of Christian believers is, indeed, their ability to hold two conflicting ideas in their heads at the same time: that Christ is both human and divine; that God is omnipotent and omniscient, but that we nonetheless have free will; that the crucified man can rise from the dead; that God decided to save Europe, while leaving the rest of the world in spiritual darkness. In doing so, it might be argued that Christianity forged a link with literature unlike that of any other theology, enabling it to confront—even absorb—secularism with a flexibility that stretched but did not break its spiritual, otherworldly orientation. More specifically, during this era in Britain, the religious person, along with the political person, sought an intricate accommodation between piety and pragmatism, between an "Age of Reason" that (despite modernist critics) never did arrive and an "Age of Faith" that never did disappear. Thus, in the century, there is the rise of individual rights on the one hand, of Western capitalism and imperialism on the other. The century learned to live within a commercial society by invoking notions of God's providential care for those who worked hard, exercised thrift, and provided charity to the less fortunate, while prudently ignoring the impossible commercial advice to give up *all* material interests in order to follow Christ. Similarly, a pious pragmatism taught imperialists that its religion of peace justified its extension among the heathen, especially if one proselytized with a bit less violence than the Catholic imperialists of France and Spain.

Literature is often an expression of discontent with reconciliation, with holding opposite ideas in the mind; juxtaposition and reconciliation are quite distinct responses for the literary mind. In that the age moved quite steadily in the direction of imposing a much-needed, much-sought-after religious Peace by downplaying, perhaps quite ignoring, the Truth claims of an Anglicanism that was becoming the "state" religion in name only, literature served most often to impose a counterforce to the new domination of Peace over Truth, not by insisting on the truth of its own discourse, but rather by suggesting in a variety of ways how the reconciliation was inadequate and hypocritical, false, and—all too often—violent. It is worth keeping in mind that even as the age drifted more and more toward the secular, it was the desire to become "more Christian" that often produced this secularity. Anglicans intended only to strengthen their faith when, for example, they argued that the equality of souls formed the basis of equal rights for men *and* women—thus undercutting the authority of the patriarchal society the Church had abetted almost consistently since the epistles of Paul. Again, the abolitionist movement was headed not by secular thinkers but by Christians who argued that native societies had the same right to life, liberty, and the pursuit of happiness as their own. And when Anglicans suggested that it was best not to kill one another over differences of religious opinion, could they have predicted that the resultant loss of religious fervor would evolve over the century into tired indifference? The literature of the second half of the century, carefully read, helps us observe the wonderful interplay between Truth and Peace without assigning victory or defeat to either—nor to secularism, which has made its own foolish claims to both ideals.

Thus ran the argument of my essay on the Anglicanism that was one of many contexts being gathered for the reading of Samuel Johnson's canon. It was an argument with which Professor Reedy was already familiar, because it had been formulated and rehearsed over the twenty or more years of our acquaintance. Ours was almost solely a scholarly friendship, developed after our several publications had drawn each other's attention, but we soon discovered as well that, although never acquainted, we had grown up within five blocks of one another in the Yorkville section of Manhattan during the 1940s and 1950s. Our initial schooling separated us: Jerry had a Catholic education, I went to the colorfully named P.S. 190. I will note, however, that in that era the three Jewish children in the class sang "O Holy Night" with great gusto, if little understanding.

Thirty-five years later, when Jerry and I began our friendship, both of us were eighteenth-century scholars with a particular interest in Anglicanism. For a period we met annually, usually in Florida, where we discussed our mutual interests, sharing the scholarly "truths" we had arrived at but perhaps most admiring the "peace" that made our communion possible. We were, we would jokingly suggest, the only two scholars left in America—a Jesuit and a Jew—still interested in historical Anglicanism. Recall that this was the 1980s, when Truth had established itself in academe as far more important than Peace, and the war of "isms" was in almost total control of the hallways of English departments.

It was probably the control of department discourse at the University of Florida that tempted me, a silent observer of the scene, onto the bowling green to enact one tiny skirmish before retreating to my peaceful pursuit of commas and dashes in Laurence Sterne's texts and, at this time in particular, my work on an edition of Sterne's sermons. In order to annotate his forty-five surviving discourses, I was reading more seventeenth- and eighteenth-century sermons than any twentieth-century literary scholar should ever have to. A recreational break was called for, and what better way to entertain oneself in the 1980s than at an MLA convention? Having with that assertion clearly entered the world of make-believe, let me pursue my *Conventioneer's Progress* by envisioning a possible encounter between a typical MLA speaker of that decade and an atypical sermon-reading auditor. It was one of those early-morning sessions to which only the most dedicated seekers of intellectual entertainment would be drawn, but I had fortunately discovered in the program a most promising lecture on "Belinda's Hoops: Pope, Lacan, and the Pubic Square." This certainly sounded promising, and hither I hied to make the most of my 8 to 10 a.m. slot.

Unfortunately, in my haste—or perhaps directed by Providence—I ended up in Empire Room B rather than Empire Room A, and the lecture there was "Roxana's Hopes: Defoe, Habermas, and the Public Sphere" (as we all recall, titles were quite interchangeable in the 1980s—one author, one theory, one catchphrase). Needless to say, I would have left the room to find Lacan's Pope, but that would have reduced the typical 8 o'clock audience to one fewer than the number of panelists, so I politely snuggled into my chair and awaited the wisdom of Habermas's Defoe.

Now perhaps like pilgrims past, I may have nodded off a bit, when I felt myself abruptly jolted to attention by these words from the speaker, etched forever in my memory: "Near the end of her story Roxana longs for what the novel cannot provide—a confidante and a comforter." This assertion was supported by Defoe's own words in Roxana's mouth, which I have since copied into my notebook for future reference:

> as I had no Comforter, so I had no Counsellor; it was well as I often thought, that I was not a Roman-Catholick; for what a piece of Work shou'd I have made, to have gone to a Priest with such a History as I had to tell him? And what Pennance wou'd any Father-Confessor have oblig'd me to perform? Especially if he had been honest and true to his Office?

The lecturer's bold conclusion is also lodged in my memory, even thirty years later: "Roxana's interiority . . . is beyond institutional frameworks; no official discourse can encompass it."

Fully aroused by these assertions and obviously energized by my months of reading eighteenth-century sermons instead of Habermas, I started taking comprehensive notes, which I am now consulting, although they are already yellowed with age, in order to repeat here some additional provocative assertions. For example, Roxana is, thus, a "private person speaking wholly within the secularized confessional of the novel"; and another *truth*: Defoe is engaged in a "project of radical self-construction by a character who must operate from outside all existing institutional structures." Peace, serenity, and a good nap were no longer options, and as the lecturer drew to his heady conclusion, I became one of those conference boors we all most dread, the one with his hand in the air well before the wild applause of the four other listeners could die down. And of course, I did not have a question to open the Q&A session but, typically enough, a brilliant (and *true*) counter-assertion posing as a question—as already suggested, this is the way human beings are with ideas. Thus, I counterattacked, with great cordiality, I am sure: "This might be a plausible reading," I irenically suggested, "if 'Comforter' meant nothing but a security blanket and 'Counsellor' an evocation of summer camp or psychotherapy. But in the life of the eighteenth century, do not both words resonate profoundly within an institutional structure that you have ignored? Isn't the result a reading as misdirected as if you had failed correctly to translate words in a foreign language?" I then quoted a few scriptural verses and suggested, in my most *peaceful* tone, that "to read Defoe's sentence and not hear these echoes is equivalent, perhaps, to hearing the word 'Marxist' and not immediately calling to mind a privileged member of the academic community." With the words of Sterne's church lawyer Didius echoing in my head—"I have got him fast hung up . . . upon one of the two horns of my dilemma—let him get off as he can" (*Tristram Shandy*, V.26.)— I rose to my peroration, with a comment that might be considered an apt epigraph for this collection: "Unless one deals with Christianity as an aspect of the 'public sphere,' with what it means that public life in the eighteenth century intersects transcendence at every crux and crisis, one has little chance of understanding eighteenth-century 'institutional structures.' Above all else," I continued, gently poking my finger in his eye, "your concepts of 'inside' and 'outside' undergo radical transformation when the institution in question is deemed omnipotent; the strongest irony in *Roxana* is Roxana's absolute inability to find that 'outside,' summoned with so much ease by our secularist minds."

Reeling from this unexpected onslaught, the speaker first looked at my name tag to assure himself that I wasn't a spy sent by the *New York Times* to write its annual scathing account of the inanity of the MLA and its session titles—or worse, someone from an evangelical college—and then, after six more seconds in which he carefully weighed my arguments, he opened his own. First, however, he assured me of his own love of peacefulness by proffering a bit of Scripture for my contemplation: "A soft answer turneth away wrath." He assured the audience, now on the edge of their seats, that he took no offense at being accused of not knowing Scripture, and indeed would concede all I had said. And yet—and yet—he allowed himself reluctantly to continue, "I do begin to wonder if you have actually or at least recently read *Roxana* all the way through." A bit harsh, even by Old Testament standards, I thought to myself, but soon discovered that he had a great deal more to say: he had perceived, he informed me, a "totalizing instinct in my approach," manifested by my insistence on a "theological definition of Roxana's psychological state," by my assumption that "Defoe's (apparent) gloss on his narrative is the only possible one," and, most damning, by my "assumption . . . that the culture in which Defoe and Roxana moved was whole and utterly coherent, that Christianity . . . permeated and dominated everyone's consciousness" and was indeed "an enveloping institutional structure that offered transcendence as a possibility at 'every crux and crisis.'"

While the fit audience but few nodded (in 1980s agreement, or early-morning drowsiness, who can say?), he went on to assure me, continuing his *soft* answer, that my "confidence in coherence" was quite "misplaced and discredited, and in this particular case remarkably inattentive to the obsessive problematic in all of Defoe's novels surrounding moral values and social institutions." To be sure, I had myself written on *Roxana* some years before, highlighting its "obsessive problematic . . . surrounding moral values and social institutions," but in the obscure journal *PMLA*, and so the speaker had obviously not had occasion to see it. By now, he truly had me on the ropes (or, allegorically, head over heels in the Slough of Despond), and he moved in for the metaphorical kill (*peace* being one thing, but *truth* quite another): I was guilty, moreover, of "an historical positivism of an uninteresting and extremely limited kind"—a powerful left hook. And then another left; it was, in fact, a "literal-minded, narrow historicism" that I seemed to be sharing with Defoe and "many readers," all of us trapped by a form of "nostalgia" for the irrecoverable past. His own reading, he assured me with a left-right combination, was "licensed by our [i.e., modern] experience in its fullness of a disjunction between the private and public spheres of experience that for the early eighteenth century was only emerging."

Needless to say, I was down for the count, and I stayed down for the next thirty years. Indeed, only after reading several sentences in a recent review in *TLS* (September 16, 2011, p. 28) did I feel sufficiently inspired to set forth again on my pilgrimage. They were written by Bernice Martin, reviewing a book with the most unpromising title *A Sociology of Religious Emotion*:

> A powerful myth of our time claims there is a peculiar difficulty in justifying a role for religion in the public sphere and a voice in democratic debate. Religion alone is routinely pilloried for being dangerously emotional, impervious to the dictates of reason and a unique source of violence. . . . The godfather of the myth is Jürgen Habermas. . . .
> The curious thing about this argument is less its jaundiced view of religion than its supposition, especially after the lessons of National Socialism, that politics is, or could be, an arena in which detached participants are forever poised to concede to superior evidence and argument. . . .
> [If this book's] arguments and its proposals for research are heeded, it might ground the wrangles about the proper place of religion in something more solid and balanced than a Habermasian castle in the air where rational politics pleases and only religion is vile.

Here finally, thirty years too late, was what I had wanted to say to that MLA speaker, who was so absolutely certain—as were so many theoretical approaches of the last decades of the twentieth century—that narrowness was all on the "other" side of the debate, that his own approach was the all-encompassing one. Hence, although he firmly believed that his Marxist approach included the theological (but reduced to its *proper* dimension), religion's actual dismissal from his intellectual system was inherent in this one slighting phrase that I found heavily underscored in my notes: "Roxana's despair is more than *simple* alienation from [God]." In the intervening thirty years, some wonderful scholarship has taken place on which, I am certain, the authors of *A Sociology of Religious Emotion* have relied, but even then I should not have let that assertion pass; my only excuse, to end my parable of a lost soul in the middle of an MLA session in the 1980s, is its moral: "In a world of fugitives, / The person taking the opposite direction / Will appear to run away."

Concomitant with the certainty that a modern materialist psychology opens vast fields of inquiry unavailable to reactionaries interested only in a "simple" (simple-minded) notion that human beings are alienated from whatever it is they conceive as an ideal, a priority, a source beyond themselves ("beyond being," in Emmanuel Levinas's telling phrase), is the belief that a theological view is, of necessity, a tired one, a relic of our past, a worn-out historicizing by someone who has not read Habermas. The value, however, of keeping one's response in one's drawer for several decades is perhaps the perspective it provides on "worn-out historicizing"; has any concept from the 1980s been more worn and worn-out by eighteenth-century scholars than the public and private spheres? The primary role Habermas has played thus far in the twenty-first century, it seems, is as a whipping post for those who have found sufficient explanatory gaps in his sociological generalizations through which to drive a coach and six. He might indeed be taken as evidence today that the pervasive materialistic and secular narrowing of the study of literature that took place in the last decades of the twentieth century has begun to broaden itself again.

This collection as a whole maintains that the eighteenth century cannot be understood without a reeducation in the theology that was indeed the dominant and pervasive atmosphere in which the age lived. That some few found a space outside that atmosphere cannot be gainsaid, but for most, the struggles of life—of psychology and economics, social standing and scientific inquiry, and above all, politics and the arts—took place inside rather than outside the realm of religious conviction. To quote a passage of Scripture as elucidating a passage of literature in no way posits a monolithic church dominating the century with a totalizing or controlling vision of the world; as the essays herein clearly demonstrate, the century began and ended in conflicts most often defined by religious issues or, if not defined by them, necessarily resorting to a language and an ethical code shaped by Scripture and the commentary (theology) surrounding it. Without doubt, Defoe was a newly enfranchised economic man, but he became so by means of a worldview and moral system permeated with the language, laws, and bylaws of a pervasively Christian society.

In the domination of secular theorizing that marked the study of literature from the 1960s to the beginning of this new century, it was important to replay all intellectual pursuit as an Enlightenment struggle, whereby wisdom (modernity) was opposed to superstition (nostalgia), materialism to spirituality, the new and untraditional to the old and tired. Now, with the wisdom of hindsight, perhaps, we might suggest there is a tired nostalgia invoked by the name of Habermas (or Derrida or Foucault or Lacan) or any of the other "gods" at whose altars scholars knelt for the moment, before passing on to other idols of the marketplace. But one need not denigrate the achievements of the present moment (and all those mentioned contributed something, without doubt, to our understanding of literature and culture) in order to recognize that for someone who believes the alienation between Christians and their God is a simplistic reduction of "reality," the eighteenth century is a totally foreign country. If Habermas is correct in finding a "disjunction" between private and public spheres of experience, how much greater must the disjunction be between those for whom that alienation is the very measure of their lives, and those for whom it is a dull event of nostalgic concern only?

It helps when in a foreign country for a person first to learn its language, even if one plans to impose on that country the ideology or ism we carry as our necessary baggage wherever we travel. And without doubt, foreign countries can be subdued; in this regard, we are all imperialists, and it would be foolish to deny that this is our way of dealing with other times and other places (with otherness, in the modern idiom): to reduce them to the dimensions of our own particular (and narrow) time and space. Even after we learn the language of the natives, we will speak it with an accent and use it within the understanding fostered by our own native tongue. Still, the effort might be made, and in making that effort, we might learn not only the words but something of the world those words created. The eighteenth-century literary world was enormously different from our own—a difference created, I would suggest, because it emerged from a context in which, to be reductive, the alienation between God and mankind was the primary subject of its literary discourse, from its profound epic poem for the elite to its equally profound allegory for the masses. It was the single most important subject about which their most-read book concentered and their most frequent public activity (churchgoing) revolved. To read modern culture without regard to television, film, and the Internet would be analogous to reading the eighteenth century without the sermon literature that dominated its popular culture and without the church calendar that shaped and chronicled its public and private life. It can certainly be done, but both cultures are violated by a grasp that fails to account for their primary centers of intellectual and emotional life.

In soliciting essays for this collection we asked for contributions that reflected theology as both a serious and continuing concern for writers in the "Age of Johnson"—that is, in the second half of the British eighteenth century. We provided no other guidelines, and the range of figures and subjects covered suggests both the breadth and depth of theological concerns in the period—from Fielding to Wollstonecraft, with many figures in between. Most interesting, and perhaps unexpected, is that while we received essays on the "usual suspects" for a volume on this subject (Richardson and, obviously, Johnson), we also received essays on Sterne, Boswell, Paine, and Wollstonecraft—hardly a nostalgic, backward-looking quartet. The seventeen essays herein also exhibit the value of paying close attention to the theological underbrush of the century; whether biographical or bibliographical, historical or critical, the essays manifest an awareness of the intricacies of the age that clearly and cogently belies any indictment of monolithic Christian belief. Instead, we are reintroduced to the many subtleties of faith among eighteenth-century writers in the age and, as well, perhaps, to the subtleties of faith among the contributors.

This is readily apparent if we compare the two essays on Fielding, or the two on Sterne, or the essay on the Bluestockings alongside the essay on Wollstonecraft. If eighteenth-century theology shaped itself first and foremost around the latitudinarian thinking of Tillotson, South, Clarke, and the other irenic theologians of the late seventeenth century, the commentary in this collection seems to have taken its cue from them as well. Not that Peace is ever more important than Truth to a scholar, but rather that the theological context makes one ashamed to impose one's beliefs, at this distance in time and space, on the beliefs of others. This promotes, I would suggest, a rewarding willingness to listen to the voices from the past, to try to adjust one's own preconceptions to their conceptions, and above all, to eschew colonization of eighteenth-century texts, since the refusal to impose our own religious beliefs on others is the particular theoretical virtue we seem to have derived from the eighteenth century, and perhaps more from its clerics than from its enlightened *philosophes*. Moreover, any sense of monolithic belief among eighteenth-century Christians quickly disappears when we take careful note of the age's many different, disruptive, and disturbing meanings emerging from the discourse between religion and literature. This attentive reading is made possible, I would argue, because, rather than ironing out differences with the mangle of Marxism (or any less alliterative *ism*), a certain lack of aggressive belief in any Judeo-Christian theological truth allows us more clearly to place each work of literature under discussion alongside the historical moment of theology it entails.

I do not at all mean to imply that the essays herein are quite free from errors, or that they are embodiments of Truth as opposed to those written under a different mindset, but only that scholars of theology and literature in the eighteenth century have a model before them of an age in which the never-ending struggle—indeed warfare—between Truth and Peace was, at least in the arena of religion, decided in favor of Peace. In the quiet fostered by Peace, one can listen for the voice of others, one can hear the voice of others. What one listens to and what one can hear in the eighteenth century, if the noise of Truth does not interfere with its boisterousness, is a world still at prayer, a world still in awe at its creation, still in grief over separation from its Creator, still in exaltation at its redemption. If a Jesuit and a Jew can hear those voices, they surely must be available to every attentive ear.

Chapter One

Novelistic Redemption and the History of Grace

Practical Theology and Literary Form in Richardson's Pamela *and Fielding's* Joseph Andrews

Donald R. Wehrs

To gauge what concerns Fielding theologically about *Pamela*, we may consider here one thread in Richardson's novel. Imprisoned in Mr. B.'s Lincolnshire, Pamela famously resists the conscription of her body into Mr. B.'s designs by asserting an identity located in textual spaces alien to those that Mr. B., Mrs. Jewkes, and a host of other characters assume must circumscribe her. Because rebellion takes the form of aggressive, even ostentatious subordination to authoritative cultural discursive models, she at once baffles the efforts of her oppressors to label her resistance as "egotism" and articulates an assertive individualism that variously touched, galvanized, and scandalized her first readers. Claiming at once to possess her own "proper" selfhood as inalienable property and to bear in her personhood an absolute significance, Pamela may be seen as exemplifying the conjunction of emancipating and imperializing aspects of modernity.

For Fielding, the imperializing aspects embodied in Pamela's conception of herself are abetted by what he sees as fashionable confusions of Christianity with antinomianism, a heretical conviction that those saved are not bound by law, whether moral, natural, or positive. While Fielding sees George Whitefield's Calvinistic Methodism, which he associates with Pamela, as especially egregious in reinterpreting orthodoxy in antinomian directions, he is acutely aware that persons attempting to counter such tendencies by stressing the indispensability of ethical conduct for grace are apt to be charged with advocating Socinianism, the heretical view that to follow Christ's vir-

1

tues is to be saved. In linking theological and aesthetic criticism of Richardson's fiction and in presenting his own work as a conjoined rectification, Fielding places the theological challenge of avoiding both antinomianism and Socinianism at the forefront of concerns for the new genre of novelistic fiction.

In *Pamela*, on the one hand, a politically revolutionary association of human dignity with autonomous interiority not only generates a new genre, the novel, but demands of literary art generally that it emulate Pamela's letters by becoming an instrument of conversion—transforming the interiority of readers through making transparent to them, via a printed scripture, that ethical universalism, the unconditional obligation to accord any human being ethical consideration, constitutes the law of God written on the human heart. This aspect of Richardson's project, unappreciated by Fielding and remote from antinomianism, though perhaps not inconsistent with Socinianism, claimed the emulative imitation of Rousseau and Diderot.[1] Arguably a first fruit of this textual, conceptual revolution was the unprecedented popular mass movement to abolish the slave trade that swept Britain four decades after *Pamela*'s publication.[2] On the other hand, the sheer seriousness with which the self in *Pamela* takes its interiority to be inviolable property opens the door to limitless self-aggrandizement, loss of a sense of proportion, and a sense of the ridiculous integral—for writers like Fielding and Sterne—to a sense of sin, and so may be taken, consistent with Fielding's critique, as giving birth to peculiarly modern forms of idolatry and imperialism.

Moreover, anticipating a logic that Hegel would later codify, Richardson's novel discloses, perhaps unintentionally, how easily the self's demand for recognition leads to conceiving the world as properly interpreted only when it affirms the Idea that the self has come to have of itself.[3] Thus, after her betrothal to Mr. B., Pamela moves from insisting that others recognize her inviolable sanctity to organizing her relations with others and her ongoing narrative of self to ensure that no surprise, mortification, or unsettling growth is conceivable; in doing so, she passes out of the sphere of the novel. It is unsurprising that this view of the self might suggest, and be suggested by, Whitefield's understanding of the regenerated soul as "inwardly wrought upon and changed by the powerful operations of the Holy Spirit."[4] The inviolability of such a self may become conflated with insularity of consciousness in ways that colonize others, allowing them to be "good" only insofar as they affirm an Idea of self that is—as Hegel will explicitly state—coincident with one's Idea of God.[5] The unease that Pamela's triumph evokes arises not simply because her cataloging of her social ascent seems to conflate material and spiritual goods, but also because her tone assumes, for all its insistence on humility, accents of complacent, even giddy self-sufficiency. One comes to suspect that Pamela's idea of her self cannot include the possibility that she might benefit from modifications to it. Thus, Pamela's verses praising humility are not entirely persuasive, being introduced by her recording Mr. B.'s extravagant praise: "I admire that beautiful simplicity which in all you do, all you write, all you speak, makes so distinguishing a part of your character."[6]

Richardson is not blind to the dangers inherent in entanglements of assertive individualism and ethical universalism, but evading them is no slight matter, as Pamela's rewriting of the 137th Psalm underscores. Likening her imprisonment to that of the Jews in Babylonian exile confers divine sanction on her resistance and positions her innovative conduct as adherence to an authoritative model, but as Pamela's displacing of the psalm's plural pronouns with singular ones indicates, national, communal travails are rewritten in terms of personal anguish and affronts in ways that both assert the importance of the individual and encourage the subject's preoccupation with herself. Subjective life becomes the site where formerly political, national dramas are now enacted. This both sanctifies everyday, affective life and positions it as a possible object of idolatry. Offense to our feelings, our sense of self-worth, comes to assume attributes not just of insensitivity or boorish violence, but also of blasphemy. Flirtation with novel forms of idolatry, however, is the price that the ethical universalism integral to Richardson's generic innovation exacts, even as that universalism moderates (or sublimates) the imperiousness it fosters. Written out of Pamela's recasting of the psalm, as Mr. B. notes, is the original's ferocious conclusion—an anticipation of Babylon's destruction and bloody revenge on its people.

The metrical version that Richardson has Rev. Williams read is sobering enough:

> Ev'n so shalt thou, O Babylon!
> At length to dust be brought:
> And happy shall that man be called,
> That our revenge hath wrought.
> Yea, blessed shall that man be called,
> That takes thy little ones,
> And dasheth them in pieces small,
> Against the very stones. (352)

This sing-song evocation of child murder, however, mutes the cold bloody-mindedness of the King James Version: "O daughter of Babylon, who art to be destroyed; happy *shall he be*, that rewardeth thee as thou hast served us. Happy *shall he be*, that taketh and dasheth thy little ones against the stones" (137:8–9; original emphasis). By contrast, Pamela wishes only repentance for her oppressors. Her version reads:

> E'en so shalt thou, O wicked one,
> At length to shame be brought;
> And happy shall all those be called,

That my deliv'rance wrought.
Yea, blessed shall the man be called
That shames thee of thy evil;
And saves me from thy vile attempts,
And thee, too, from the d—l. (352–53)

Here Richardson's novel would seem as far from antinomianism as Fielding could wish. Even as Pamela equates herself and her plight with that of God's people, she places the psalm in the service of a discourse that insists we discover the law of ethical universalism inscribed on the heart because God has written it there, making any imitation of the psalm's final two verses morally intolerable—and thus rhetorically impossible. Pamela's rewriting constitutes a silent correction that makes ethical universalism the standard against which even authoritative cultural discourse is measured, thus authorizing the refashioning of scriptural models to speak unequivocally against customary or institutional exploitation of individuals.

Paula Backscheider notes that Mr. B. "compliments [Pamela] on turning the 'heavy curses' of the conclusion of the psalm into a hope for his repentance and salvation, thus replacing an Old Testament structure of feeling with a New Testament one."[7] But Pamela's dissociating of her typological reading from the psalmist's sentiments altogether, rather than transposing them to a different realm, reflects more than the pious hope that anyone not yet dead might be converted—it indicates (tacit) ethical repudiation of the model. Richardson thus aligns the religion underlying Pamela's revolt with the mode of sacred hermeneutics pioneered by Erasmus and made integral to the Anglican *via media*—in which any conflict between revealed discourse and an ethical sense reflective of the universalism that Christ is understood to have enjoined was reconciled through allegorical or historical interpretation. For Erasmus and the tradition that followed, it was an article of faith that divine discourse could not scandalize human ethical sense, and thus any literalism so tending had to be transposed into a morally acceptable figural or poetic meaning.[8] For this reason, the association of natural law with universal human moral intuitive insight, attested in such texts as Romans 2:14 ("For when the Gentiles, which have not the law, do by nature the things contained in the law, these, having not the law, are a law unto themselves"), was central to the Anglicanism of Hooker, Tillotson, and Joseph Butler.[9]

For religion distinguishing between "law" and "the things contained in the law" in this manner, religion suspicious of the "letter" that "killeth," the assertive individualism that Pamela embodies avoids pharisaic smugness only through binding itself to an ethical universalism resistant to the subjective imperialisms that emancipating individualism seem to bear within itself.[10] If the "poor in spirit" are "blessed," both forms of typological understandings of Babylon invoked in Pamela's rewriting of the psalm are problematic. As Michael Austin notes, "Typologically, the biblical empire of Babylon has always been interpreted in two equally supportable ways—either as Israel's tormentor, which deprived the Jews of their God-given homeland and condemned them to an unrighteous captivity, or as Israel's scourge, which forced the corrupt and idolatrous chosen people to acknowledge their God, reconsider their heritage, and forge their identity."[11] Austin argues that Pamela's original composition of the poem configures Mr. B. and Mrs. Jewkes in terms of the first typology of Babylon, associated with the books of Jeremiah and Isaiah, whereas the reciting of the poem in the presence of Rev. Williams and others, under the direction of Mr. B., constitutes a "strategic reinterpretation" that palliates Mr. B.'s earlier reprehensible conduct, and thus justifies Pamela's willingness to marry him, by "recasting [him] as the Babylon of Ezekiel—an instrument of divine will that acted for the long-term good of a chosen people" (509). As Austin observes, Richardson presents "two conflicting understandings of virtue"—"virtue as a function of intention and virtue as a function of outcome" (513). Were Mr. B. judged by his intent, Pamela's marrying him would indeed make her a Shamela, but, Austin claims, Mr. B. "encourages the reader to adopt a teleological standard of morality emphasizing the fact that everything that happened contributed to the long-term happiness of the heroine" (513).

This reinterpretation maintains undiluted, however, the association of Pamela with Israel and so retains the transposition of national history into personal story, spiritual redemption into vindication of one's conception of self. Mr. B.'s reinterpretation maintains Pamela's emphatic correspondence between political control of sacred space (the land of Israel but especially the Temple, the dwelling place of God), and proprietorship over bodily space, sacred because it is the mark of subjective sovereignty, one's absolute identity before God and one's idea of oneself. This equation of Israel and the self draws on long-standing Christian typological associations of Israel with the soul, but returns "Israel" to this-worldly frames of reference: rather than Babylon being "sin" that threatens to "capture" the soul-Israel, Babylon again denotes other people, and liberation from captivity does not mean escape from sin but restoration of bodily self-possession and divine vindication in the here and now. Equating the self with Israel confers absolute significance on any individual's well-being and happiness, thus making all manner of appropriation, for profit or pleasure, the equivalent of the Babylonian destruction of the First Temple—a damnable refusal to recognize the sacred. Thus, Pamela's insistence that Mr. B. recognize that his servant-maid *is* Israel prepares the reading public to view all forms of denying inalienable self-possession to others, such as Africans traded as property, as at once unethical and irreligious—irreligious *because* unethical—in ways no sanction by custom or law can render acceptable to conscience. The politically progressive potential of such novelistic religious hermeneutics is arresting.[12]

The equation of Israel with self rather than soul also has the effect, however, of authorizing a narrative of self in which others assume identities of mere typological significance, becoming meaningful in ways that naturalize the egocentric structure of intentional consciousness. In both the Jeremiah-Isaiah and Ezekiel readings, Babylon matters only because of its effects on Israel; without significance in itself, its actions can only be "good" to the extent that they contribute, however unwittingly, to Israel's renewal. The assertive individualism unleashed by casting *oneself*, not Britain generally nor a soul at war with itself, as the new Israel effectively organizes intersubjective space around the self as Ego-Ideal to such an extent that narrative perspectives reflective of the self-preoccupations of a fifteen-year-old become fused with the perspective that the narrative would make normative for the reader. Louis Dupré and Ullrich Langer trace how nominalist conceptions of God as a subject constrained only by what His freedom willed restructured Western reflection on human subjectivity.[13] Selfhood, once narrowed to "individual solitude," Dupré argues, "reduces the other to the status of object," for a "theoretical egocentrism inevitably leads to a moral one."[14] Identifying God with unconstrained voluntarism leads to thinking of subjects as "ordaining" their own identity in ways that mirror the unconditioned freedom of a voluntarist God.[15] Indeed, the world as Pamela encounters it is constantly reiterating her own importance, as when her departure from the first country house occasions Mr. B.'s servants, "all of them," to stand "in two rows" to bid her farewell (132), not because even a few of them find in Pamela's travails equivalents of their own grievances, but because all function as satellites moved by her goodness, reflecting back her own light. Here, Fielding's attribution to Pamela of the same blasphemous egoism he attributes to Whitefield's religious subjectivity seems to have some warrant.

More problematically, if Pamela acquiesces in Mr. B.'s reinterpretation of his place in her story, in which he functions at once as Ezekiel's Babylon and Ezekiel's God, she does so because "a teleological standard of morality" that makes "the long-term happiness of the heroine" the equivalent of "the long-term good of Israel" has been implicit in her narrative from the start. She insists more than once that the ultimate danger of sexual exploitation is being "tricked out of herself" so as to lose everlasting happiness in the life to come. To the extent that hope of future "rewards" regulates present "virtue," the equation of "long-term good" with "long-term happiness" allows material well-being or worldly enjoyment to function as metaphor for, or prefiguring of, spiritual well-being, thus opening the text to the charge of crassly figuring the pleasures of Heaven in terms of those of being a squire's wife.

But Pamela's rewriting of the psalm sets the terms for an even more far-reaching critique. On the one hand, her correction of the psalmist implies that any sort of typological reading of others betrays a deficiency of ethical universalism, reducing them to props in our stories, which, of course, is exactly how Mr. B. sees Pamela at the time of the poem's composition; on the other hand, Pamela's very assertion of her similitude to Israel affiliates her deepest sense of self, the basis for her assertive individualism, with the psalmist's typological imagination. The same audacious self-importance that empowers us to challenge slander and stare down would-be rapists encourages us to view the world's reformation in terms of its coming around to our way of thinking, accommodating our desire for happiness without qualification or end.

If, as the notorious tonal dualities of Pamela's discourse suggest, liberating individualism is accompanied by imperialistic egotism, then something like the Lacanian Other inflects and distorts speech, contaminating expressions of piety with accents of sanctimoniousness. While Fielding seems to view Pamela (and Richardson) as willfully blind to self-aggrandizing implications of her discourse and action, what may connect unease with Richardson's religion, as implied in *Pamela*, to reservations about his novelistic craftsmanship in readers more sympathetic than Fielding is suspicion that while the text presents good religious and psychological grounds for Pamela's abiding internal dissonance, the notion of "reward" for "virtue" structuring the narrative cannot wean itself of the psalmist's naïve and unethical notion of happiness—although the text implicitly recognizes the need to do so. The struggle to resolve tension between emancipating and imperializing aspects of assertive individualism characterizes much novelistic discourse in the decades following *Pamela*'s publication, often with the consequence that readers are invited to identify with drearily deferential heroines while glorying in vicarious enjoyment of their passively attained rewards. The combined ethical and generic problems that Pamela's rewriting of the psalm raises revolve around how assertive individualism may draw on ethical universalism for a sense of what is due to one as a human being, without lapsing into an idolatrous romance of self and a typological reduction of others. Indeed, the more the narrative and protagonist embrace such typological reductions, the more both seem to naturalize egocentric modes of intentionality that psychologically, if not doctrinally, partake of the self-complacency at the heart of antinomianism.

Aspiring to create a countergenre of narrative fiction to the one devised by Richardson, Fielding in *Joseph Andrews* (I.xvi–xvii) carefully locates his quixotic hero, Parson Adams, within a theological terrain marked by John Tillotson and Benjamin Hoadly—the first noted for his articulation of the latitudinarian position on grace, the second for advancing a highly controversial account of the sacraments.[16] In doing so, Fielding suggests that Tillotson's and Hoadly's theological critics, like Adams's antagonists, knowingly or not confound orthodoxy with a denial of the bearing of ethical life upon salvation, a denial that, by freeing the pursuit of self-interest from conscience, blocks receptivity to grace. Such a "Doctrine . . . coined in Hell"

(82), Adams declares, effectively reduces Christianity to antinomianism, which he takes to be the consequence of Whitefield's teachings. The latter's writings, a bookseller assures Adams, are the one species of religious discourse for which there is assured demand.

In both *Shamela* and *Joseph Andrews*, the Pamela figure is associated with Whitefield. In a letter to Shamela, Mrs. Andrews moves easily from observing that "seeing you have a rich Fool to deal with, your not making a good Market will be the more inexcusable" to praising her daughter for reading "good Books," to which end she encloses "one of Mr. Whitefield's Sermons."[17] The implication is that Whitefield's theology owes its popularity to its supporting reductions of moral language and sentiment (avoiding what is "inexcusable") to imperatives of maximizing self-interest. As Shamela's comments on Parson Williams's sermon indicate, depriving the ethical of significance in relation to grace denies it the status of good-in-itself, deprives it of its own meaning and authority, and so prevents it from opposing an alternative system of value to that which egoistic self-promotion and aggrandizement put into play.[18] Because "doing good to one another . . . is one of the greatest Sins we can commit, when we don't do it for the sake of Religion," Shamela declares, "'tis not what we do, but what we believe, that must save us" (253). If such theological views clear the way for upward social mobility through mercenary prudence, they also allow the material fruits of such self-assertion to be taken, complacently, as effects of grace. So Pamela, in advising Joseph to abandon Fanny, remarks, "I am now this Gentleman's Lady, and as such am above [Fanny]—I hope I shall never behave with an unbecoming Pride; but at the same time I shall always endeavour to know myself, and question not the Assistance of Grace to that purpose" (302). For Fielding's Pamela, grace assists us to know ourselves sufficiently to enjoy undisturbed as many worldly benefits as possible.

Both of Fielding's works highlight how theological discourse, in silencing conscience and natural feeling, may totalize the language and values of a predatory modernity, unleashing an individualism that is paradoxically illiberal in its discounting on principle all claims upon the self not reducible to "the sake of Religion," in which "Religion" is understood to denote self-promotion. By contrast, Eliza Haywood's *Anti-Pamela*, where the mother is equally bawdlike and the Pamela figure an equally adroit marketer of sexual capital, treats the characters as entirely secular in their motivations and self-understandings. The mother declares, "[M]y Girl there is a wide Difference between *Love* and *Liking*; the chief aim of the *one* is to make the *beloved Object* happy. That of the *other*, only to gratify *itself*.—Now your Business is by an artful Management to bring this *Liking* up to *Love*, and then it will be in your power to do with him as you please."[19] While Haywood's text juxtaposes (tongue-in-cheek?) moralistic lamentation over female cunning with exposition of the material-social conditions that render it rational, Fielding's texts underscore the entwinement of material and intellectual corruption, the way religious doctrines help free the desiring subject from impediments of conscience. Such religion "usefully" induces the self to identify totally with an assertive, possessive individualism in whose name every aspect of human life—commerce, domestic and erotic life, social relations, the state and church—may be recast as spheres within which antinomian cunning may display exploitive prowess.

At the heart of Fielding's agitation over *Pamela* and its popularity is his conviction that its religious core is fundamentally wrong, generating bad morality and bad art. Dissociating salvation from works, one denies that the ethical is self-legitimizing and autonomous in its significance, that natural law has a universal purchase that *grounds* rationality. Such denials, in Fielding's view, lead to modes of narrative and characterization that, being morally insensible and religiously skewed, can only be aesthetically debased. To counter what he sees as the religious-moral derangement of a modernity that celebrates Pamela, Fielding offers as antidote a narrative that dramatizes the autonomous significance and meaning-making agency of the ethical. The narrative will make inescapable to readers the claims of ethical perception on their own judgments, affections, and interpretations to such a degree that human susceptibility (and so answerability) to natural law will become self-evident, will be brought home involuntarily through the process of reading. By having the ethical disclose its adjudicating, interpretative authority within the semantic negotiations that his narrative's ironic prose stages, Fielding hopes to demonstrate that the ethical constitutes what Charles Taylor calls an "inescapable framework" of human consciousness and intelligibility.[20] If the ethical is not a luxury, option, or something secondary, then any attribution to God of insensibility to the ethical is likely to make Him appear less good than what He created. Such theology will be exposed as perverse and blasphemous, undercutting all discourse encouraging a marginalization of the ethical on grounds of divine disdain for what Shamela terms "mere morality."

However, in aligning Adams with Tillotson and Hoadly, Fielding could not be unaware that the theological premises of his own literary discourse are subject to challenge as heterodox. Any claim that ethical action and disposition necessarily have weight or significance within a scheme of grace is subject to the charge of incipient Pelagianism. Whereas Augustine's anti-Pelagian texts focus on demonstrating that the will is incapable of reforming itself,[21] the stress on divine sovereignty introduced by fourteenth-century nominalist theology associated depreciation of divine power with *any* suggestion that God might be "moved" by actions or actualities not originating in His own unconditioned will. Protestantism's nominalistic versions of Augustinianism led to broadening the Bishop of Hippo's critiques of Pelagius to claims that human merit could have no influence on a grace dependent on either faith alone (Luther) or determined from the beginning by divine will (Calvin).[22]

Fielding underscores Adams's approval of Hoadly's argument on sacraments, which he views as "calculated to restore the true Use of Christianity" (I.xvii.83). Fielding thus places Adams within the currents of latitudinarianism most likely to incur charges of Pelagianism. Hoadly's understanding of sacraments as means to attain moral dispositions and practices, rather than as vessels bestowing a supernatural power (which Adams summarizes), went beyond general latitudinarian doctrines on the absolute significance before God of ethical life and humans' natural creaturely intuition of natural law. Hoadly's argument implied not only that salvation was possible outside a church claiming apostolic succession (like the Anglican), but that a life outside Christianity, if it realized the moral goods that sacraments were ordained to foster, was more pleasing to God than a life in which the sacraments were received and formally believed in, but remained without moral fruit.[23] Adams paraphrases Hoadly in declaring, "[A] virtuous and good *Turk*, or Heathen, are more acceptable in the sight of their Creator than a vicious and wicked Christian, tho' his Faith was as perfectly Orthodox as St. *Paul's* himself" (82).[24] Hoadly's separating the transmission of grace from the diffusion of the Holy Spirit through apostolic succession undercut Anglican claims to institutional authoritativeness and exceptionalism. This precipitated a convulsion over doctrine and authority known as the Bangorian controversy.[25]

Hoadly's larger claim, that the primacy of the ethical, for God as for humans, might make a non-Christian receive grace where a Christian might not, opened him to the charge of Socinianism. The argument of Whitefield and other dissenting Protestants, as well as the argument of anti-Hoadly Anglicans—acknowledged within *Joseph Andrews* by the bookseller's decline of any interest in Adams's sermons or any "Book which the Clergy will be certain to cry down" (83)—is that heterodox denial of divine sovereignty follows from insisting that the ethical is self-signifying and self-authorizing, a natural law that is a law unto itself.[26] Such argument, it is claimed, courts deism by effectively reducing God to a figure for morality. Whitefield insists that grace involves a qualitative transformation of "the natural man" incommensurate with any scale of progressively increasing virtue; while Christianity "includes morality, . . . if we are only mere moralists, if we are not inwardly wrought upon and changed by the powerful operations of the Holy Spirit, and [if] our moral actions [do not] proceed from a principle of a new nature, however we may call ourselves Christians, it is to be feared we shall be found naked at the Great Day."[27] Within this intellectual climate, where distinguishing religion from "mere morality" becomes a fraught nexus of ideological, institutional, and psychological anxiety, the more ethical sense is affirmed as regulating the articulation of significance, the more predicating rationality upon ethics appears to imply Socinianism. Though Fielding is quick to charge Richardson with antinomianism, he anticipates being accused of Socinianism, and so is concerned to fashion generic means of delineating narrative confluences of the ethical and religious that will square orthodoxy and realism.

Like Hoadly's arguments that religious terminology escapes mystery and superstition only to the extent that it enters a rationalism predicated on ethical regulation of sense and language, Fielding's work makes the dislodging of the self from its position of privilege, from any resemblance to the nominalist God, the precondition for receptivity to grace. He presents such dislodging not as the effect of (self-interested) concern with salvation, but rather as the consequence of self-forgetting concern for others. Fielding's celebrated notion of "good Nature" (I.iii.23), a core disposition of benevolent regard toward others, belongs to the theological tradition running from Abelard through Hoadly. If we view created nature as so impressed by divine love that human nature, in its genetic responsiveness to natural law, is made susceptible to the workings of grace, then to argue that people may by will and habit cooperate with grace, may make their own exertions a party to the work of redemption, need not fall into Pelagianism or Socinianism, for the aspects of ourselves that are agents in redemptive labor have their origins in the grace informing natural law, which gives creaturely determinateness itself the shape of love. W. M. Spellman points out that latitudinarian receptivity to Abelard's "moral influence" argument, the notion that God "empowers us to change our hearts" and that "Christ binds us to himself by love," issued in "Restoration Anglican divines insist[ing] that men must turn their hearts to God once the experience of regeneration through Christ had begun."[28]

The moment at which Fielding's prose departs from mock-epic satire and becomes somehow "novelistic" is commonly identified with the scene, midway through the first book of *Joseph Andrews*, in which a stagecoach-full of passengers all seek to evade the significance communicated by Joseph's mute, beaten, naked body. While the episode reenacts the parable of the Good Samaritan, its authority does not rest on typological associations; rather, literary communication of spontaneous, autonomous ethical sense underscores *why* the parable has authority, how it speaks to a human ethical sensibility woven into natural law so as to be empowered by divine moral influence. Fielding's delineation of the symmetrical egoisms of the lady who would rather leave Joseph to die than "ride with a naked Man," the lawyer concerned with liability if Joseph is left behind, and the coachman weighing desire for payment against fear of prosecution can be appreciated as comically reprehensible, and so enjoyed aesthetically, only to the degree that the moral significance of the postilion's conduct is felt: "a Lad who hath been since transported for robbing a Hen-roost . . . voluntarily stript off a great

Coat, his only Garment, at the same time swearing a great Oath, (for which he was rebuked by the Passengers) 'that he would rather ride in his Shirt all his life, than suffer a Fellow-Creature to lie in so miserable a Condition'" (I.xii.53). Fielding's tone both elicits and assumes an ethical sense—shared recognition between writer and reader of the moral impossibility of indifference to another's suffering—which allows Fielding's ironic indirection to bring home to the reader what is not said: female modesty and regard for the law as displayed here, and in the later prosecution of the postilion, are not goodness but its affectation, which is, Fielding's preface assures us, the "true Ridiculous" (7).

Just as spontaneous laughter at the ridiculous discloses the ethical constitution of human subjectivity and significance, so the ubiquitous recourse of Fielding's selfish, vain, and foolish characters to affectation denotes, despite their best efforts, the inalienability of ethical consciousness. To appreciate, or even to process cognitively, Fielding's narration of the stagecoach scene requires us to simulate within our own minds how the impress of ethical significance and obligation upon consciousness *feels*, as revealed through the postilion's exasperated charity and through the affectation and evasion displayed by the gentry passengers. The "gaps" that Wolfgang Iser famously identifies in Fielding's ironic narration—the "blanks" and "negations" that the reader "fills up" with his own "disposition"—mostly prompt readers to simulate ethical consciousness, or to simulate being waylaid by ethical significance's unexpected and insistent pressure. Thus the reader's ethical consciousness, as well as what Iser calls his "habitual disposition," becomes both a "theme for observation" and an object of "correction" through Fielding's crafting of aesthetic-ethical "discoveries."[29] For Fielding, these discoveries attest to grace's loving influence behind the ethical orientation of human perception and communication.

We sense a generic transformation at this point in *Joseph Andrews* because earlier the narrative had been organized around lucid negative work, unmasking as moralistic claims affecting to be moral. When Joseph proclaims that regard for his Virtue precludes his entertaining Lady Booby's advances, accents of narcissistic self-congratulation undermine his discourse. Fielding underscores how easily what claims to be moral may lapse into self-love and serve as a vehicle for a coldly proprietary self-assertive individualism. Says Joseph:

> Madam . . . that Boy is the Brother of Pamela, and would be ashamed, that the Chastity of his Family, which is preserved in her, should be stained in him. If there are such Men as your Ladyship mentions, I am sorry for it, and I wish they had an Opportunity of reading over those Letters, which my Father hath sent me of my Sister Pamela's, nor do I doubt but such an Example would amend them. (I.viii.41)

Fielding's narration becomes novelistic once it moves beyond an unmasking that may be satirically adroit, but that seems marked by a lack of articulacy about the good. Indeed, Fielding associates precisely such inarticulacy with amatory fiction, as is apparent from his parody of the genre, "The Tale of Leonora," within *Joseph Andrews*.[30] Leonora, having preferred the shallow Bellarmine to the solid Horatio, is rejected with worldly banter masking crass self-interest. Leonora withdraws from a society full of Bellarmines, while the alternately pathetic and worldly tone of the narration shares the characters' lamentation at folly and treachery, and cultivation of self-indulgent dramatics. These are substituted for the ballast that the ethical gives discourse: Leonora "retired to that House I shewed you when I began the story, where she hath ever since led a disconsolate Life, and deserves perhaps Pity for her Misfortunes more than our Censure, for a Behaviour to which the Artifices of her Aunt very probably contributed" (II.vii.129).[31] The narrative voice here conflates being ethically deficient and having played one's cards badly enough to have lost at the game of securing comfort and respectability.

Fielding's prose becomes novelistic as he discovers means of making the actuality of the ethical sensible to readers in ways that work against co-options of the moral by the moralistic and interested. In dramatizing the embedding of the ethical in human sensory life and intellection, Fielding's work strongly intersects with current "turns" in philosophical and scientific discourse that suggest the West's efforts to cordon the ethical off from human subjectivity in general—whether in the interest of theological doctrines of natural degeneracy, philosophical postulates of abstract cognitive rationality, or psychologies of will, self-interest, desire, or power—have, despite their hegemony over the centuries, been fundamentally wrong-headed. Indeed, the comic aptitude of Fielding's characters at shrugging off responsibilities to others betrays their grudging or involuntary awareness of those responsibilities' unwelcome presence. Such shirking and evasion is thus symptomatic of how, in Emmanuel Levinas's words, "the unlimited responsibility in which I find myself comes from the hither side of my freedom, from a 'prior to every memory,' an 'ulterior to every accomplishment'"—making the "duty overflowing my being" inescapable, "like a Nessus tunic my skin would be."[32]

Taking the success of verbal indirection in communicating ethical significance as a measure of grace's influence on human nature, supporting the theological tradition that runs from Abelard to Hoadly, rather than opposing traditions advocated from Bernard of Clairvaux to Whitefield, Fielding suggests that the internal dynamics of literary form have determinate theological consequences. The success of Fielding's narration, however, is double-edged. Recent work on mirror neurons suggests a physiological basis for such inherence of the ethical within consciousness as his prose brings to the fore. When we see or imagine what another does or experiences, neurons that would fire if we were performing the action or undergoing the experience activate spontaneously. Such neural "mirrorings" allow—indeed, impel—our brains to "simulate" what others do and feel. While this phenomenon appears, neuroscientist Marco Iacobini argues, "essential for building social ties, . . . [m]ore abstract forms of empathy may rely less on somatic mirrorings and more on affective mirrorings," as in simulating what particular other people placed in certain situations are apt to experience psychologically as well as physiologically.[33] Narrative fiction holds our attention by engaging our curiosity or concern about what determinate others are likely to think or feel situated within various determinate circumstances.[34]

Although Levinas and cognitive science may help us account for the peculiar realism generated by Fielding's techniques for rendering the presence of the ethical sensible (an accomplishment all the more remarkable given Fielding's stylized characterization, diction, and running metafictional commentary), this very aesthetic success may be viewed as problematic given Fielding's theological aspirations for his narration. The more compellingly a literary text bears witness to the abiding agency of the ethical within human consciousness, the more its "gaps" are filled by simulations or memory-images of spontaneous ethical orientations of our own consciousnesses, the more doctrinal assertions about degenerate human nature may appear disjunctive with what the reading process discloses about each of us. The extraordinary success of novelistic discourse in bringing home the felt immediacy of the ethical, so striking to the first generation of Richardson's and Fielding's readers,[35] connects the somatic impress of the ethical with realism itself in ways that may seem to confirm the proximity of novelistic discourse, or modern culture, to Socinianism.

Fielding implicitly anchors the actuality of human goodness in divine grace along lines established by Abelard and Erasmus. Abelard argued that the Holy Spirit's loving-kindness constituted creation's ultimate structuring principle, from which it follows that human nature and reason, issuing from divine love, are marked by elemental desire for the good and native ethical sense,[36] as borne out by the phenomenon of virtuous pagans.[37] In stressing the redemptive agency of Christ's words and example, Abelard bestows ethical-spiritual agency on affective, sensuous dimensions of human experience, making susceptibility to affect, the body's hospitality to *passiones* (*pathos*), not just crucial to language's intelligibility (as he does in his hermeneutics), but also integral to a "saving" transformation of intellection (*nous*). Similarly, in contesting Luther's understanding of grace as a divine force breaking apart "the prudence of the flesh," Erasmus insists that "[Christ] does not extinguish the good he finds but perfects it; he does not destroy nature but completes it."[38] For all the bondage of will to sin, there is something in divinely created human nature to which grace may "speak" and so may transform: "If reason struggles against emotions that are prone to immorality, then it must needs be that to some degree it discerns and approves of what is moral" (592).

Tillotson, working consciously out of this tradition, argues along similar lines. In a series of sermons on "the Nature of Regeneration," he insists that "nothing will avail to our justification and acceptance with God, but the real renovation of our Hearts and Lives" and that to become a "new creature" through grace is properly understood as "a metaphorical expression" for "a mighty change both in . . . inward Principles and outward Practice; it darts a new light into their [humans'] Minds, so that they see things otherwise than they did before, and form a different judgment of things from what they did before," and "this inward change of their Minds necessarily produceth a proportionable change in their Lives and Conversations."[39] Such change, Tillotson argues, echoing Erasmus, need not "be effected in an *irresistible* manner," nor should we be "*altogether passive* in this Change," nor need the work "be done *in an instant* and admit of no degrees."[40] Like Erasmus and Abelard, Tillotson postulates that receptivity to grace must be part of human core dispositions. Otherwise, the logical consequences would be "unreasonable": if grace entailed "an *irresistible* act of Divine Power," repentance would be a matter of submission to "meer Force and violent Necessity" and so devoid of "Virtue"; if humans were incapable of receiving grace unless worked on by God *irresistibly*, then impenitency could not be blameworthy, for the "impossibility of the thing" in light of human "utter disability" would render divine reproof to the unrepentant at once absurd and unjust.[41]

Tillotson's fellow latitudinarian divine, Samuel Clarke, similarly maintains, "The *Practice of Virtue, or Living soberly, righteously, and godly*; is the *End* and *Design* of all Religion. . . . By the Light of *Nature and Reason* therefore, men are bound to the Practice of these Virtues," but that men might do what they know implicitly, intuitively, that they should, we are given "the *Example* of *Christ*, in his Life, and in his Suffering; the *Assistances* of his *Spirit*; the Assurance of a *Reward for Virtue*."[42] Clarke's teachings are in line with expressed views running from Abelard to Parson Adams: "Men are saved *by Grace*, because without God's gracious Assistance and Acceptance of their imperfect Endeavours, they could not of themselves attain unto Salvation; and at the same time 'tis no less true, that they *work out their own Salvation*, because without their leading a life of Virtue and Obedience through a diligent Use of those means which the Grace of God affords them, the *Grace of God* alone will in no wise force them to be saved."[43]

Human sociality, highlighted by Christianized Aristotelian thought such as Joseph Butler's, in pointed opposition to the naturalized possessive individualism of Hobbesian-Mandevillean subjectivity,[44] attests to the primordial orientation of the human to the ethical, or the writing of the law upon the heart. Indeed, one current of recent Aristotle studies stresses the inseparability of ethics from ontology and epistemology.[45] But for Fielding and the tradition in which he works, sociality constitutes a potential that receptivity to grace's work alone can bring to realization. Moreover, the strikingly uneven distribution of good nature within Fielding's fictional world (epitomized in the contrast of Tom Jones and Blifil) suggests the ease with which humans (prompted by original sin or egocentrism in collusion with debased social norms) denature themselves in turning away from the bent that God has given nature, but also the extent to which some hearts seem prone to hardness. Grace, while in principle open to all, nonetheless seems, for reasons that Fielding intimates are impenetrable to human intelligence, to have primed some souls for enactment of goodness more than others, making more arduous for some tempers than others the dispositional and habitual labors that facilitate grace's transformation of the soul.[46]

Yet by having Adams paraphrase Hoadly on virtuous Turks and heathens, Fielding pushes the theological tradition he evokes to go beyond claims that belief in Christian doctrine allows the saving disposition toward goodness and charity woven into human nature to realize itself, to reform seeing *and so* feeling and acting (as Tillotson and Clarke explicitly declare). Instead, Fielding implies, in line with Hoadly's teachings on sacraments, that positive doctrine has a real significance to the extent it is resolvable into ethical-rational sense. All that cannot be so resolved is metaphor, and metaphor misunderstood, hypostasized, is mystery or superstition, which serves institutional tyranny (identified with the Church of Rome) or the spreading of needless fears and discord (identified with Protestant dissenters). Hoadly assumes that coming to see in the ways that positive doctrine generally induces may be productive of the work of grace; however, he argues that what matters is the ethical fruit of such seeing, not the doctrinal claims themselves. These are, like the bread and wine of the Lord's Supper, means to ends, rather than ends as such. Thus, the ethical fruit of doctrine is what induces a moral-spiritual condition that finds favor with God, and this may be realized by nature or conscience. Possibly such a spiritual condition could be realized within non-Christian religious traditions, though both Hoadly and Adams seem to imply that the saving virtue of Turk or heathen emerges despite rather than with the assistance of their formal beliefs.

In any event, grace may work on a soul independently not only of communion within a church the spiritual authority of which derives from apostolic succession, but also independently of conscious acceptance of Christian doctrine. For Tillotson and Clarke, belief in Christian doctrine creates metaphysical convictions that have transformative consequences on affections and actions so as, in time, to make one a new creature reborn in grace: a "new Light" in the mind changes "judgment of things," which "necessarily produceth a proportionable change in . . . Lives and Conversations"; "the *Example* of *Christ*, in his Life, and in his Suffering; the *Assistances* of his *Spirit*; the Assurance of a *Reward for Virtue*" induce changes in understanding that yield changes in feeling and conduct. While the feelings and practices, rather than the understanding, constitute what is saving for Tillotson and Clarke, these are taken to flow from correct understanding. For Abelard and Erasmus, however, the example of Christ touches and reforms our feelings, awakens an emulative, imitative love responsive to divine love that *then* reconfigures understanding.[47] The working of the image of Christ's love on our affections engenders a responsive imitative love that transforms understanding and perception.

For Hoadly and Adams, divinely constituted receptivity to the image of Christ may be operative whenever the ethical-rational sense communicated by that image (unconditional love and responsibility to others grounding significance and constituting what is good and most real) is operative within our souls, even if the exterior form assumed by that communication within Christian teaching and history remains unknown. Just as doctrinal assertions need not induce the spiritual-ethical condition that denotes grace, so the saving spiritual-ethical condition may be realized apart from doctrinal assertions, not only because what people do and are is frequently disjunctive with what they say, but also because that which is redemptive within us is neither bounded nor signified by intentional consciousness, as is driven home by the novelistic presentation of the postilion. The more he is moved out from himself in preoccupation with the needs of another, the more are his affections and actions structured in *unconscious* imitation of divine example (as his unwitting enactment of the Good Samaritan's role attests). Thus third-person narration, Fielding implies, is theologically preferable to epistolary fiction, as genuine goodness and the self-regard of first-person testimony seldom converge.

Indeed, Fielding suggests that even good people, to the extent that their thinking is bound up with conceptual-metaphysical aspects of traditionally conceived piety, undermine the influence of ethical sense on them, and so work against the prime means that grace-infused nature gives us to participate actively in our own redemption. Through the influence of his university education and a certain prideful credulousness toward authorities and conventions, thinking "a Schoolmaster the greatest Character in the World, and himself the greatest of all Schoolmasters" (III.vi.232), Parson Adams is connected, surprisingly, to such theological adversaries as Barnabas, the cleric scandalized by Adams's championing of Hoadly. The degree to which Adams is theoretically impaired in doing justice to his own intuitions and best self (articulating a neo-Stoic detachment belied by his warm feelings and visceral empathy), helps explain why Joseph, naturally bright but innocent of learning and the chauvinism of a privileged guild, rather than the parson, is the novel's central hero. When Barnabas seeks to prepare the supposedly mortally wounded Joseph for death, Joseph acknowledges that "there was one thing which he knew not whether he should call a Sin; if it was, he feared he should die in the Commission of it, and that was the regret of parting with a young Woman, whom he loved tenderly as he did his Heartstrings" (I.xiii.59). Barnabas conventionally assures him that "any repining at the Divine Will" is a great sin and that he "ought to forget all carnal Affections, and think of better things," which here denotes, devastatingly, that Joseph should think of "better things" for himself personally by having a proper understanding of his interest (as positive religion articulates it). Joseph replies that "neither in this World nor the next," could he "forget his *Fanny*," and though the thought of parting from her was "grievous," it was "not half so tormenting, as the Fear of what she would suffer when she knew his Misfortune" (59).

Erotic love saves Joseph from being the male analogue of Pamela by opening him to concern for another that displaces and disrupts egoistic intentionality, making imitation of another's exemplary love (here Fanny's) the mainspring of one's identity. Fanny's image within Joseph's psyche does the grace-diffusing work that Abelard and Erasmus attribute to the image of Christ. In opposition to Barnabas's suggestion that other people are to be dismissed from consciousness so the self can properly preoccupy itself with its everlasting extension, Joseph insists that he can never forget Fanny because what he *is* is inseparable from responsiveness to her. Concern for her suffering is more real to him than what concerns only himself could ever be. Erotic love, whose robust component of sexual desire Fielding constantly underscores, breaks apart the self-love natural to self-assertive individualism and the delusive autarky that a subject modeling itself on the nominalist God might assume and prize. In sexual desire's conversion of *cupiditas* into *caritas*, in the idealized beloved's assumption of a Christlike agency in the moral-spiritual life of the lover, marriage becomes the privileged arena of enacted piety or practical theology. Barnabas, oblivious to the ethical-religious significance of Joseph's discourse, urges him to "divest himself of all human Passion, and fix his Heart above" (59), for the very idea that desire might be independent of self-interest, irreducible to the ego's cupidity, is beyond his imagination.[48]

After such a depiction of Barnabas, Adams's later echoing of elements of his discourse is all the more arresting. After the roasting squire's minions have kidnapped Fanny and tied up Joseph and Adams, the parson attempts to comfort Joseph by drawing on the *consolatio* tradition to argue that "it is the Business of a Man and a Christian to summon Reason as quickly as he can to his Aid; and she will presently teach him Patience and Submission" (III.xi.264). After painting the dangers to Fanny in terms that make Joseph cry out, Adams sketches a picture for the understanding: "you are to consider you are a Christian, that no Accident happens to us without the Divine

Permission, and that it is the Duty of a Man, much more of a Christian, to submit" (265). The entanglement of manliness in piety, and the association of both with impassivity, suggests the influence of Stoic and Neoplatonic notions of happiness as self-sufficiency on Christian metaphysical discourse and imagination. Indeed, Adams insists that we should not complain because of our "Ignorance": "that which first threatens Evil, may in the end produce our Good"; if the misfortune is punishment for sin, this "may be esteemed as a Good, yea the greatest Good" (265). Joseph interrupts to say that while all this is no doubt true, it brings no comfort, as only assurance of Fanny's rescue could do that, to which Adams rejoins, "[I]f you are wise, and truly know your own Interest, you will peaceably and quietly submit to all the Dispensations of Providence" (266).

While the text invites laughter at Adams's naïve confidence that people will really act in ways that theoretical discourse prescribes, it also pointedly calls attention to the egocentrism underlying the understanding that Adams would have regulate feeling: if Joseph could realize that he cannot really be hurt, that his interest need not be imperiled no matter what transpires, he should then, in reason, be comforted despite being forced to leave Fanny to her fate. Adams cannot grasp that since for Joseph Fanny's well-being is inseparable from the good, feelings arising from his bond with her cannot be modified by any understanding organized around a privileging of self-concern. The implication of Adams's well-meaning obtuseness is that traditional Christian conceptuality unreflectively theorizes humans in terms uncomfortably close to those of self-assertive individualism, which makes the intentionality promoted by positive religion perhaps more of an impediment than an aid to the workings of grace on affections and action. Indeed, Christianity's signature focus on salvation becomes problematic in ways Levinas highlights: "There is a vulgarity and a baseness in an action that is conceived only . . . in the last analysis, for our life. . . . Even a sublime need, such as the need for salvation, is still . . . the anxiety of the I for itself, egoism."[49]

Restrained a bit by the thought that not giving way to despair might influence God to help Fanny, Joseph deflects the vulgarity and baseness, the anxiety of the I for itself, that mars Adams's kindly meant importunities by having recourse to Macduff's lament for wife and children, "Yes, I will bear my Sorrows like a Man, / But I must also feel them as a Man. / I cannot but remember such things were, / And were most dear to me—" (267). It is a mark of Adams's limitations that he does not know and cannot appreciate Shakespeare, and that only more conventional and reassuring literature, Addison's *Cato* and Steele's *The Conscious Lovers*, can interest him. Moreover, the movement of the text from traditional philosophical-religious discourse to that of a realistic literature tied to a disruption of convention suggests that, for Joseph and us, coming to appreciate how nature opens us to grace may be better facilitated by a new kind of literary culture than by reiterations of traditions that are not just timeworn and hackneyed, but as apt to consolidate as to chasten forms of intentionality screening us off from our best selves.

The dubious effects of such screening are implied in the case of Adams, who, as Joseph remarks, shows himself quite properly insensible to Stoic-Christian consolatory tropes when he imagines that his young son has drowned (IV.viii.309–11). When Adams stubbornly insists that a man should love his wife "with Moderation and Discretion" and Joseph replies that he "shall love without any Moderation, I am sure" (310), Fielding implies that traditional teachings of the priority of the other world over this, of not valuing attachments here overmuch, are, however abstractly defensible, in practice contaminated by associations of happiness with personal self-interest and immunity from pain. While pursuit of such happiness (transposed from another life to this) becomes the central preoccupation of the new paganism darkening assertive individualism, the best people, through grace, are only "theoretically" captive to such thinking. So Mrs. Adams declares,

> I hope, my Dear, you will never preach any such Doctrines as that Husbands can love their Wives too well. . . . Besides, I am certain you do not preach as you practise; for you have been a loving and a cherishing Husband to me, that's the truth on't; and why you should endeavour to put such wicked Nonsense into this young Man's Head, I cannot devise. Don't hearken to him, Mr. *Joseph*, be as good a Husband as you are able, and love your Wife with all your Body and Soul too. (311)

Because we mercifully are not coextensive with our ideas, much of what we consciously believe is only a matter of talk or abstract opinion.

While Richardson's interfusion of self-assertion and ethical universalism may unite Pamela's claim to ownership of her own interiority with acknowledgment of each individual's claim to a sanctity akin to that of ancient Israel, it also suggests a prioritizing of the self and its way of seeing that tends to construe others as actors in one's own plot and tie justification to the unassailability of one's intentionality—and all this may be viewed as at best theologically and psychologically naïve. In practice, abiding interest in Richardson's great fictions largely hinges on the tensions between principled integrity and (unwitting) self-serving constructions of self that mark his protagonists' letters. For Fielding, however, grace places our best self outside the regulation of an intentionality that invariably abstracts and distorts what we are. The theological consequences are far-reaching. Not only is doctrine radically deemphasized, but the entire conceptual-metaphysical inheritance of premodern Western thought is also made problematic *within* a Christian framework. When Mrs. Adams enjoins, "[L]ove your Wife with all your Body and Soul too," she unconsciously echoes the principal Christian injunction: "love the Lord thy God with all thy heart, and with thy soul, and with all thy mind" (Matthew 22:37). On the one hand, there is some irony in what she thinks due herself and other wives, some connection of Mrs. Adams with what Fielding sees as Pamela's modern and dubious drift toward self-deification. On the other hand, the novel presents Parson Adams as well rebuked by his wife (and spiritually lucky in having a wife who, despite her limitations, has the virtue of telling him off and treating his theorizing as male nonsense). We see grace operative in Adams precisely to the extent that his conduct transgresses his ideas, and his ideas become sound or not to the degree that they reflect his actual practice and moral feelings. Redemption, however, the novel implies, entails imitating Joseph in taking the Other as the trace of the divine sufficiently to incarnate love of God in heart, soul, and mind through love of another in body and soul. In becoming responsive to what exceeds us, what comes from outside to re-form us, we receptively participate in undoing, ethically-spiritually, all affiliation with the pride or arrogation of self-sufficiency that—following Hoadly's ethical-rational understanding of religious language—Pelagianism and Socinianism must promote to be heresies.

If Fielding is highly conscious that his narrative representations can only gesture toward what life reformed by such grace might entail, that there is absurdity or pomposity in all claims to depict ideality, his ironic narration nonetheless aspires to exercise faculties engaged in receptivity to grace by demanding that we mirror the narrator's susceptibility to the ethical if we are to register the actual sense of his words. Attunement to narrative irony allows aesthetic experience to function much as phenomenological experience does for Levinas, as the basis for making conceptual, interpretative claims answerable to an ethical presence understood as unconditioned and inescapable. When Fielding has Adams argue that "a good and virtuous Turk, or Heathen, are more acceptable in the sight of their Creator, than a vicious and wicked Christian" (I.xvii.82), he is not simply venting his religious opinions, but acknowledging religious claims that his texts' embrace of autonomous ethical-aesthetic significance and meaning-making both presuppose and entail. In doing so, Fielding intimates that the culture of modernity, to which his fiction mightily contributed, can be neither theologically indistinct nor neutral.

NOTES

1. Rousseau understood himself to be imitating Richardsonian epistolary fiction in *La Nouvelle Heloïse*, and Diderot argues that because the reader, despite himself, participates in Richardson's work ("on se mêle à la conversation, on approuve, on blâme, on s'irrite, on s'indigne"), "Richardson sème dans les coeurs des germes de vertus qui y restent d'abord oisifs et tranquilles," virtue being understood as "un sacrifice de soi-même," so that "on se sent porter au bien avec une impétuosité qu'on ne se connaissait pas. On éprouve, à l'aspect de l'injustice,

une révolte qu'on ne saurait s'expliquer à soi-même. C'est qu'on a fréquenté Richardson." (*Éloge de Richardson*, in Denis Diderot, *Oeuvres esthétiques*, ed. Paul Vernière [Paris: Classiques Garnier, 1959], 30, 31).

2. While noting that abolitionist advocates wanted to argue that in the long term free labor would prove more productive than slave labor, Seymour Drescher, perhaps the most influential contemporary historian of British abolitionism, stresses that slavery was "massively challenged on moral grounds," and that morally motivated "mass abolitionism," not elite intellectual arguments about productivity, governed the pace and direction of emancipation (*The Mighty Experiment: Labor versus Slavery in British Emancipation* [Oxford: Oxford University Press, 2002], 5, 7).

3. See G.W.F. Hegel, *The Phenomenology of Mind*, trans. J.B. Baillie (New York: Harper & Row, 1967), esp. "Lordship and Bondage," 228–40, "The Unhappy Consciousness," 240–67, "Absolute Freedom and Terror," 599–610. On the connection between desire for self-recognition and totalizing thought, see Alexandre Kojève, *Introduction to the Reading of Hegel*, trans. James H. Nichols Jr. (New York: Basic Books, 1969).

4. George Whitefield, "The Nature and Necessity of Our Regeneration or New Birth in Christ Jesus," in *Whitefield and Wesley on the New Birth*, ed. Timothy L. Smith (Grand Rapids, MI: Francis Asbury Press, 1986), 75.

5. Hegel, "Absolute Knowledge," in *The Phenomenology of Mind*, 789–808: "It is that part of the embodiment of self-assured spirit which keeps within its essential principle and was called the 'beautiful soul.' That is to say, the 'beautiful soul' is its own knowledge of itself in its pure transparent unity—self-consciousness, which knows this pure knowledge of pure inwardness to be spirit, is not merely intuition of the divine, but the self-intuition of God Himself" (795).

6. Samuel Richardson, *Pamela: or, Virtue Rewarded* (Harmondsworth: Penguin, 1980), 514. Hereafter cited in text.

7. Paula Backscheider, *Eighteenth-Century Women Poets and Their Poetry: Inventing Agency, Inventing Genre* (Baltimore: Johns Hopkins University Press, 2005), 132.

8. For the line of descent from Erasmus to Hooker to Chillingsworth to the Cambridge Platonists to the latitudinarians, see esp. W.M. Spellman, *The Latitudinarians and the Church of England, 1660–1700* (Athens: University of Georgia Press, 1993), esp. 11–32, 112–31; B.W. Young, *Religion and Enlightenment in Eighteenth-Century England: Theological Debate from Locke to Burke* (Oxford: Clarendon Press, 1998), 19–44. In *Institutio Principis Christiani* (1516), to cite one example, Erasmus warns that a good prince should "learn that the wars of the Hebrews, the bloodshed and cruelty to enemies, must be interpreted allegorically, or such reading is destructive (*pestiferam*)" (*Opera Omnia Desiderii Erasmui Rotterodami recognita et adnotatione critica instructa notisque illustrata* [*ASD*] [Amsterdam: North Holland, 1969], IV-I, 182; cited in Shimon Markish, *Erasmus and the Jews*, trans. Anthony Olcott [Chicago: University of Chicago Press, 1986], 32).

9. See esp. Richard Hooker, *Of the Laws of Ecclesiastical Polity*, "The Fyrst Book: Concerning Lawes, and their severall kindes in generall," in *Works of Richard Hooker*, gen. ed. W. Speed Hill, vol. 1., ed. Georges Edelen (Cambridge, MA: Harvard University Press, 1977), ch. 8, "Of the naturall finding out of lawes by the light of reason to guide the will unto that which is good," and ch. 9, "Of the benefit of keeping that lawe which reason teacheth," 81–93, 93–95; John Tillotson, "The Wisdom of Being Religious" and "Of the Tryall of the Spirits," in *Three Restoration Divines: Barrow, South, Tillotson: Selected Sermons*, ed. Irène Simon, Bibliothèthique de la Faculté de Philosophie et Lettres de l'Université de Liège (Paris: Société d'Éditions "Les Belles Lettres," 1976), 363–416, 433–53; Joseph Butler, *The Analogy of Religion, Natural and Revealed* (London: George Bell and Sons, 1889 [1736]), esp. 98–161, 275–327; Butler, "Two Brief Dissertations: I. Of Personal Identity, II. Of the Nature of Virtue," 328–343; Butler, "Sermon I–III.—Upon Human Nature," "Sermon V.—Upon Compassion," "Sermon XI–XII.—Upon the Love of Our Neighbour," 385–414, 425–43, 484–511. For links between Erasmus, Cambridge Platonism, and early eighteenth-century "moral sense" philosophy, see Charles Taylor, *Sources of the Self: The Making of the Modern Identity* (Cambridge, MA: Harvard University Press, 1992), 248–65; Spellman, *The Latitudinarians and the Church*

of England, 54–88. For Richardson's relation to the late Cambridge Platonist John Norris, see E. Derek Taylor, *Reason and Religion in* Clarissa: *Samuel Richardson and 'The Famous Mr. Norris, of Bemerton'* (Aldershot, UK: Ashgate, 2009).

10. Frank Ardolino, in "Richardson's *Pamela*," *Explicator* 66, no. 2 (2008): 78–82, argues, "Whereas Pamela's comparison of herself to the ancient Israelites in Psalm 137 emphasizes her active role in gaining freedom from bondage and in conquering her captors through charity and good example, the Old Testament figure of Ruth serves as a more fitting biblical parallel to Pamela's rise from humble station to social preeminence as the result of her spiritual exaltation" (78). However, as Ardolino notes, it is Pamela's father who proposes the Ruth analogy, while Pamela chooses the 137th Psalm.

11. Michael Austin, "Lincolnshire Babylonian: Competing Typologies in Pamela's 137th Psalm," *Eighteenth-Century Fiction* 12, no. 4 (2000): 501–14, 504 cited. Hereafter cited in text.

12. See for example Quobna Ottobah Cugoano's argument in *Thoughts and Sentiments on the Evil of Slavery* (New York: Penguin, 1999), 38, 43.

13. See Louis Dupré, *Passage to Modernity: An Essay in the Hermeneutics of Nature and Culture* (New Haven: Yale University Press, 1993), 42–144; Ullrich Langer, *Divine and Poetic Freedom in the Renaissance: Nominalist Theology and Literature in France and Italy* (Princeton: Princeton University Press, 1990), 3–24, 84–148.

14. Dupré, *Passage to Modernity*, 119. Also see Taylor's discussion of Descartes and moral philosophy in *Sources of the Self*, 143–58.

15. See Dupré, *Passage to Modernity*, 140.

16. Henry Fielding, *Joseph Andrews*, ed. Martin C. Battestin (Middletown, CT: Wesleyan University Press, 1967), 70–85. Hereafter cited in text. For Fielding's relation to latitudinarian theology, see Martin C. Battestin, *The Moral Basis of Fielding's Art* (Middletown, CT: Wesleyan University Press, 1959); *The Providence of Wit: Aspects of Form in Augustan Literature and the Arts* (Oxford: Clarendon Press, 1974); Martin C. Battestin with Ruth R. Battestin, *Henry Fielding: A Life* (New York: Routledge, 1989), 199–200, 273–74, 305–6, 332–35; Patrick Müller, *Latitudinarianism and Didacticism in Eighteenth-Century Literature: Moral Theology in Fielding, Sterne, and Goldsmith* (Frankfurt: Peter Lang, 2009), 229–79. For Tillotson on grace, see esp. John Tillotson, "Of the Nature of Regeneration, and its Necessity, in Order to Justification and Salvation," "The Fruits of the Spirit, the Same with Moral Virtues," and "The Necessity of Supernatural Grace in Order to a Christian Life," in *Three Restoration Divines*, 515–68, 569–83, 585–96. Also see Spellman, *The Latitudinarians and the Church of England*, 89–111. On Hoadly and the sacraments, see Benjamin Hoadly, *A Plain Account of the Nature and End of the Sacrament of the Lord's-Supper*, 8th ed. (London: Robert Horsefield, no. 22, 1772).

17. Henry Fielding, *An Apology for the Life of Mrs. Shamela Andrews*, in Eliza Haywood, *Anti-Pamela*, and Henry Fielding, *Shamela*, ed. Catherine Ingrassia (Toronto: Broadview, 2004), 245. Hereafter cited in text.

18. Fielding has Williams advocate what, in a 1739 anti-Whitefield sermon by Dr. Joseph Trapp, is presented as the alarming theological consequences of Methodism. See *Shamela*, 253n3. On anti-Methodist polemic and satire, see Albert M. Lyles, *Methodism Mocked: The Satiric Reaction to Methodism in the Eighteenth Century* (London: Epworth Press, 1960).

19. Eliza Haywood, *Anti-Pamela*, in Eliza Haywood, *Anti-Pamela*, and Henry Fielding, *Shamela*, 66.

20. See Taylor, *Sources of the Self*, 3–52.

21. See Saint Augustine, *Four Anti-Pelagian Writings: On Nature and Grace; On the Proceedings of Pelagius; On the Predestination of the Saints; On the Gift of Perseverance*, trans. John A. Mourant and William J. Collinge (Washington, DC: Catholic University of America, 1992).

22. See esp. Martin Luther, "Two Kinds of Righteousness," in *Luther's Works*, vol. 31, ed. Harold J. Grimm (Philadelphia: Muhlenberg Press, 1957), 297–306; *The Bondage of the Will*, in *Luther's Works*, vol. 33, ed. Philip S. Watson (Philadelphia: Fortress Press, 1972), esp. 212–29; Jean Calvin, *Institution de la religion chrestienne, livre troisième*, ed. Jean-Daniel Benoit (Paris: Libraire philosophique J. Vrin, 1960), chapitre XXI, "De l'élection éternelle: par laquelle Dieu en a prédestiné les uns à salut, et les autres à condamnation," 404–16.

23. Hoadly stresses that he wants to clear away "great Errors, or great Superstition," that have induced unwarranted "Fears and Terrors" among those desiring to be "truly Religious" by showing that the value of communion is moral, not supernatural, for as "the End of this *Institution* was the *Remembrance* of Christ; it must follow from hence that to *eat* and *drink*, in the Lord's Supper, must be, To *eat* and *drink* in a sense consistent with the Notion of this *Remembrance*" (*A Plain Account*, 1, 22).

24. Battestin cites Hoadly, "The Good Samaritan," from *Twenty Sermons* (1755), 332, in *Joseph Andrews*, 83n.

25. For the implications of claims that access to grace is mediated by a church organized around apostolic succession, see Robert D. Cornwall, "Politics and the Lay Baptism Controversy in England, 1708–15," in *Religion, Politics and Dissent, 1660–1832: Essays in Honour of James E. Bradley*, ed. Robert D. Cornwall and William Gibson (Burlington, VT: Ashgate, 2010), 147–63. On the historical and conceptual relation between such positions as Hoadly's to those of Blackburne and late-eighteenth-century divergences between Unitarianism and conservative reaction, see Martin Fitzpatrick, "Latitudinarianism at the Parting of the Ways: A Suggestion," in *The Church of England, c. 1689–c. 1833: From Toleration to Tractarianism*, ed. John Walsh, Colin Haydon, and Stephen Taylor (Cambridge: Cambridge University Press, 1993), 209–27; Young, *Religion and Enlightenment in Eighteenth-Century England*, 45–80.

26. See for example Stephen Taylor, "The Bowman Affair: Latitudinarian Theology, Anti-Clericalism and the Limits of Orthodoxy in Early Hanoverian England" and "Philip Doddridge and the Formulations of Calvinistic Theology in an Era of Rationalism and Deconfessionalism," in *Religion, Politics and Dissent, 1660–1832*, 35–50, 65–84.

27. George Whitefield, "The Nature and Necessity of Our Regeneration or New Birth in Christ Jesus," 75.

28. Spellman, *The Latitudinarians and the Church of England*, 103–4.

29. Wolfgang Iser, *The Act of Reading: A Theory of Aesthetic Response* (Baltimore: Johns Hopkins University Press, 1978), 218.

30. See esp. Scott Black's "The Adventures of Love in *Tom Jones*," in *Henry Fielding in Our Time: Papers Presented at the Tercentenary Conference*, ed. J.A. Downie (Newcastle upon Tyne: Cambridge Scholars Publishing, 2008), 27–50.

31. Contemporary approbation of both Richardson's and Fielding's works appears connected with viewing them as distinct from the narratives of amatory intrigue by Behn, Manley, and Haywood, widely perceived as encouraging uncritical identifications with unprincipled characters. See William B. Warner's discussion of Fielding's reading of *Pamela* and other "anti-Pamela" critiques in *Licensing Entertainment: The Elevating of Novel Reading in Britain, 1684–1750* (Berkeley: University of California Press, 1998), 208–24; also Tom Keymer, "Jane Collier, Reader of Richardson, and the Fire Scene in *Clarissa*," in *New Essays on Samuel Richardson*, ed. Albert J. Rivero (New York: St. Martin's Press, 1996), 141–61; Sarah Fielding, *Remarks on Clarissa* (London: Robinson, 1749), rpt. in *The Augustan Reprint Society*, no. 231–32 (Los Angeles: William Andrews Clark Memorial Library, University of California Press, 1985); Francis Coventry, *An Essay on the New Species of Writing Founded by Mr. Fielding* (London: W. Owen, 1751), rpt. in *The Augustan Reprint Society*, no. 95 (Los Angeles: William Andrews Clark Memorial Library, University of California Press, 1962).

32. Emmanuel Levinas, *Otherwise Than Being, or Beyond Essence*, trans. Alphonso Lingis (Pittsburgh: Duquesne University Press, 1981), 10, 109. For a succinct summary of Levinas's argument that ethical significance constitutes the inescapable horizon of human consciousness and somatic experience, see Levinas, "Ethics as First Philosophy," in *The Levinas Reader*, ed. Seán Hand (Oxford: Blackwell, 1989), 76–87. For discussions of the significance of Levinasian thought to literary criticism, see esp. Steven Shankman, *Other Others: Levinas, Literature, Transcultural Studies* (Albany: State University of New York Press, 2010); *Levinas and Nineteenth-Century Literature: Ethics and Otherness from Romanticism through Realism*, ed. Donald R. Wehrs and David P. Haney (Newark: University of Delaware Press, 2009); Elizabeth Kraft, *Women Novelists and the Ethics of Desire, 1684–1814* (Aldershot, UK: Ashgate, 2008); *In Proximity: Levinas and the Eighteenth Century*, ed. Melvyn New (Lubbock: Texas Tech University Press, 2001).

33. Marco Iacobini, *Mirroring People: The New Science of How We Connect with Others* (New York: Farrar, Straus & Giroux, 2008), 124.
34. See esp. Patrick Colm Hogan, *Cognitive Science, Literature, and the Arts: A Guide for Humanists* (New York: Routledge, 2003), 87–114, 140–90, and Blakey Vermeule, *Why Do We Care about Literary Characters?* (Baltimore: Johns Hopkins University Press, 2010). For the complementarity of Levinasian ethical phenomenology and neuroscientific research, see Joel W. Krueger, "Levinasian Reflections on Somaticity and the Ethical Self," *Inquiry* 51, no. 6 (2008): 603–26.
35. Sarah Fielding notes in 1749 that "the Author may thank himself for" Clarissa's being "treated like an intimate Acquaintance by all her Readers" (*Remarks on Clarissa*, 14). Similarly, Diderot in 1761 argued that Richardson's "personnages ont toute la réalité possible" and claims, "J'ai entendu disputer sur la conduite de ses personnages, comme sur des événements réels" (*Éloge de Richardson*, 31, 37). Also see Coventry, *An Essay on the New Species of Writing Founded by Mr. Fielding*.
36. See John Marenbon, *The Philosophy of Peter Abelard* (Cambridge: Cambridge University Press, 1997); Constant J. Mews, *Abelard and Heloise* (Oxford: Oxford University Press, 2005); Thomas Williams, "Sin, Grace, and Redemption," in *The Cambridge Companion to Abelard*, ed. Jeffrey E. Bowers and Kevin Guilfoy (Cambridge: Cambridge University Press, 2004), 258–78.
37. See Abelard, *Theologia christiana*, Book Two, in Petrus Abaelardus, *Opera*, ed. Victor Cousin (Hildesheim and New York: Georg Olms Verlag, 1970), 2:404–46; *Commentariorum super S. Pauli Epistolam ad Romanos*, in Petrus Abaelardus, *Opera*, esp. prologue, 2:153–56, where Abelard draws parallels between Paul's discourse and Cicero's *De inventione*, II.56, and Book One, 172–82.
38. Erasmus, *Hyperaspistes*, Book II, trans. Clarence H. Miller, in *Collected Works of Erasmus* [*CWE*], vol. 77, ed. Charles Trinkaus (Toronto: University of Toronto Press, 2000), 592. Hereafter cited in text.
39. Tillotson, "Of the Nature of Regeneration, and its Necessity, in Order to Justification and Salvation," in *Three Restoration Divines*, 519, 522, 524. For the role of such arguments within early latitudinarian theology generally, see Spellman, *The Latitudinarians and the Church of England*, 100–11.
40. Tillotson, "Of the Nature of Regeneration," 528. For Erasmian analogues, see *Hyperaspistes*, Book II, in *CWE*, 77:596, 624, 732.
41. Tillotson, "Of the Nature of Regeneration," 529.
42. Samuel Clarke, Sermon XXIX, "Of the Grace of God," in Samuel Clarke, *The Works* (New York and London: Garland, 1978), 1:183–84.
43. Clarke, Sermon XXX, "Of the Grace of God," in *The Works*, 1:189.
44. See Butler, "Sermon I–III. Upon Human Nature," 385–414.
45. See Claudia Baracchi, *Aristotle's Ethics as First Philosophy* (Cambridge: Cambridge University Press, 2008); Christopher P. Long, *The Ethics of Ontology: Rethinking an Aristotelian Legacy* (Albany: State University of New York Press, 2005); Deborah K.W. Modrak, *Aristotle's Theory of Language and Meaning* (Cambridge: Cambridge University Press, 2001); Troels Engberg-Pedersen, *Aristotle's Theory of Moral Insight* (Oxford: Clarendon Press, 1983).
46. Engberg-Pedersen argues that in Aristotle "the rational cognitive state of *phronêsis* presupposes the *desiderative* state of non-rational moral virtue" (161), and Fielding suggests that differential susceptibility to such a desiderative state reflects varying workings of grace, for which human responsiveness is in part but not entirely responsible.
47. See Erasmus, *The Paraphrase on the Epistle of Paul the Apostle to the Romans*, trans. John B. Payne, Albert Rabil Jr., and Warren S. Smith, in *CWE*, vol. 42, ed. Robert D. Sider (Toronto: University of Toronto Press, 1984), 51–52; Donald R. Wehrs, "Touching Words: Embodying Ethics in Erasmus, Shakespearean Comedy, and Contemporary Theory," *Modern Philology* 104, no. 1 (2006): 1–33, esp. 9–12; Manfred Hoffmann, *Rhetoric and Theology: The Hermeneutics of Erasmus* (Toronto: University of Toronto Press, 1994); Marjorie O'Rourke Boyle, *Christening Pagan Mysteries: Erasmus in Pursuit of Wisdom* (Toronto: University of Toronto Press, 1981).

48. The distinction between desire as desire for the Other, desire exceeding signifying economies of self-interest, and traditional Western notions of desire as need is a key theme in Levinas's thought. See Levinas, *Totality and Infinity: An Essay on Exteriority*, trans. Alphonso Lingis (Pittsburgh: Duquesne University Press, 1961), 33–35, 179–80, 256–66, 304–5; "Meaning and Sense," in *Basic Philosophical Writings*, ed. Adriaan T. Peperzak, Simon Critchley, and Robert Bernasconi (Bloomington: Indiana University Press, 1996), 51–54.

49. Levinas, "Meaning and Sense," in *Basic Philosophical Writings*, 51.

Chapter Two

The Oxford Methodists (1733; 1738)

The Purloined Letter of John Wesley at Samuel Richardson's Press

John A. Dussinger

> If any is so needlessly curious as to enquire from what Hand they come, they may please to know, that it is not good Manners to ask, since the Title-Page does not tell them: We are all of us sufficiently Vain, and without doubt the Celebrated Name of Author, which most are so fond of, had not been avoided but for very good Reasons: To name but one; Who will care to pull upon themselves an Hornet's Nest. 'Tis a very great Fault to regard rather who it is that Speaks, than what is spoken; and either to submit to Authority, when we should only yield to Reason; or if Reason press too hard, to think to ward it off by Personal Objections and Reflections.[1]

This eloquent advice about anonymous writing seems especially apt for *The Oxford Methodists: Being some Account of a Society of Young Gentlemen in that City, so denominated . . . In a Letter from a Gentleman near Oxford, to his Friend at London* (1733; 1738), hereafter *OM*, which has traditionally been attributed to William Law (1686–1761) and followed by ESTC, the British Library, the Bodleian Library, Cambridge University Library, and most American libraries. Yet L. Tyerman, the great Victorian biographer of John Wesley, gave a full summary of *OM* without attributing it to anyone.[2] Similarly, Alexander Gordon's *DNB* article on Wesley (1899) avoided any attempt at naming its author. In his *ODNB* article on John Wesley, Henry D. Rack observes that this pamphlet was "often accredited erroneously to William Law," but he does not explain why it is a wrong attribution.

A lapse of historical imagination may have been the root cause for bringing William Law into the picture. From simply the evidence that in July 1732 Wesley made the pilgrimage to Putney to introduce himself to Law, John S. Simon jumped to the conclusion in 1921 that Law was the "Gentleman near Oxford" who wrote this account to his friend in London.[3] Since Putney, Law's residence at this time, was more than fifty-six miles from Oxford, and thus hardly "near" for eighteenth-century stagecoach travelers, Simon might have hesitated before taking the fictional framework of this pamphlet at its face value.[4]

Oddly overlooked, twelve years before Simon's attribution, the "standard edition" by Nehemiah Curnock of *The Journal of the Rev. John Wesley* contains a note that quietly mentions *OM* as an unauthorized printing of Wesley's "Preface."[5] Apparently such early Wesley scholars as John Simon and J. Brazier Green[6] missed seeing Curnock's important identification. The passage in Wesley's "Preface" that Curnock annotates is as follows:

> 3. I have prefixt hereto a Letter wrote several Years since, containing a plain Account, of the Rise of that little Society in *Oxford*, which has been so variously represented. Part of this was publish'd in 1733; but without my Consent or Knowledge. It now stands as it was wrote; without any Addition, Diminution, or Amendment: It being my only Concern herein, nakedly to *declare the thing as it is*.[7]

Wesley's words "without any Addition, Diminution, or Amendment" are significant, and as my analysis below will indicate, it will become clear that for reasons of his own the editor of *OM* took considerable liberties with Wesley's original text.

Since the middle of the last century Samuel Richardson has always been identified as the printer of the first edition of *OM*, and recently of the second edition of 1738 as well. The printer's ornaments indicate that the third and final edition of 1738 was also from Richardson's press.[8] The fact that Richardson was the exclusive printer of this pamphlet may help provide the scenario for its provenance, beginning with the question of who may have provided him with Wesley's "Preface." Although transcripts may have been in the possession of many members of the "little Society in Oxford," it is not unlikely that Samuel Wesley Sr. made a copy available to Richardson for the purpose of printing something in answer to the censure in *Fog's Weekly Journal*. Gordon's *DNB* article on Wesley almost implies this equation:

> Their proceedings were attacked in 'Fog's Weekly Journal' . . . and a defensive pamphlet was issued by an outsider, 'The Oxford Methodists' (1732; 2nd edit. 1738). Samuel Wesley, the father, visited Oxford in January 1732–3 to learn 'what his sons were doing,' encouraged them to persevere, and helped them from time to time by his advice.

Richardson may have shared the printing of a pamphlet that was partly written by Wesley Sr.: *Two Letters from a Deist to His Friend, Concerning the Truth and Propagation of Deism, in Opposition to Christianity, with Remarks* (London: Printed for James Roberts in Warwick-Lane, 1730). According to ESTC, a Nicholas Stevens wrote the letters, and Samuel Wesley (1662–1735) wrote the Remarks.[9] It seems plausible that during this visit to Oxford, Wesley Sr. obtained the manuscripts of his son's journal relating to the "Holy Club" activities. Then, in the following month, Richardson printed *OM*. It was advertised in *The Daily Journal* (February 14, 1733), a newspaper that Richardson was also printing at this time.[10]

As the following argument should make clear, the question raised here concerns more than merely identifying the author of this little pamphlet but rather its significance to the early Methodist movement and Richardson's affinity with this movement. He appears to have been entrusted with getting into print a defense of Wesley's religious vocation during his years at Oxford. But from Wesley's own testimony, Richardson's role was not simply as a printer; not content to reproduce this religious leader's "Preface," the anonymous author took liberties with his received material to give it a new spin. He crafted a fictional letter from Wesley's original manuscript letter to Richard Morgan in the form of advice from an impartial observer to a nervous parent of a son intended for Oxford. In defending the early "Methodists" against charges of religious fanaticism, this pamphlet stresses their public service in attending the poor, the sick, and the imprisoned. To charges of reviving morbid puritanism, the anonymous writer emphasizes their faith as the only means of worldly happiness. In light of similar views not only in other anonymous pamphlets from his press but also in his novels written years later, Richardson's revamping of Wesley's "Preface" for *OM* was a crucial step for defining himself as an "editor" of moral "histories."

Wesley's "Preface" was initially written as a letter to a family friend, Richard Morgan, the father of William, who died of consumption in his twentieth year in August 1732. William was one of the first and most zealous students in the "Holy Club"; after he fell seriously ill, his father wrote a letter scolding him for his religious fasting and other ascetic practices as well as for arousing controversy at Oxford. On October 18 of that same year John Wesley wrote a letter to the father to explain why the religious discipline of their little group had nothing to do with his son's death. The letter reconciled him to the society, and he even submitted his younger son, Richard, to Wesley's care at Oxford.[11] In contrast to Wesley's original purpose of reconciling himself with William Morgan's family, however, *OM* is primarily aimed at refuting the charges raised by the anonymous writer of the letter published in *Fog's Weekly Journal* (December 9, 1732).

What is missing in the pamphlet account is Richard Morgan's change of heart after receiving Wesley's letter. Even if there was too little time to include this information in the first edition, the editor might have updated the Morgan story for the second and third editions. Surely Morgan's altered view of these devout students would have strengthened the case against the author of the letter to *Fog's*. Perhaps Richardson never knew about the father's reconciliation with the Wesleys. In any case, this omission appears to support John Wesley's claim when producing his Journal in 1740 that *OM* was published in 1733 "without my Consent or Knowledge." It may well be that the reprinting of this pamphlet in 1738 even prompted him to publish his own account of the Oxford religious society two years later.

The narrative frame of *OM* is in the form of a letter of advice by someone living near Oxford to a close friend in London, whose son is planning to study at Oxford. This unnamed father has presumably sent a copy of the letter in *Fog's* to the narrator to inquire into the controversy over the activities of this religious society. Without having any previous knowledge about the matter, the narrator is at pains to offer a perfectly unbiased account based on diverse witnesses at the university and also on some transcripts obtained from an unidentified student member of this religious society.

The situation here of a counselor sending advice to a father worried about sending his son to a university where students are self-destructive in their religious zeal is exactly the reverse of the situation in a pamphlet that Richardson had compiled and printed two years earlier: *The Infidel Convicted: Or, A Brief Defence of the Christian Revelation. In Which The Excellency of the Christian Morality is fully shewn, and the Consistency of Revelation with human Reason proved* (London: Printed for J. Roberts, at the Oxford-Arms in Warwick-Lane, 1731).[12] In a letter signed "W.B.," first published in *Fog's Weekly Journal* (September 26, 1730) and now reprinted in the postscript to *Infidel Convicted*, a student was represented as having committed suicide after supposedly first being seduced to deism and despair by reading a popular and subversive tract. Observing how pamphlet wars tend to depend on some published incendiary catalyst, I think it more than a coincidence that both *The Infidel Convicted* and *OM* were written in response to anonymous letters to *Fog's Weekly Journal*; in any case, these letters take exactly opposite positions about the impact of religion on a student's education. In the first, a father describes the physical decline and death of his son at the Inns of Court after having succumbed to the supposedly rampant infidelity there; in the second, the writer is warning against the "Enthusiastick Madness and superstitious Scruples" among the society of "Methodists" at Oxford. Both anonymous letters to *Fog's* are the occasion, then, of the larger epistolary framework that comprises narratives about the dangers of deism and free-thinking, on the one hand, and about the exemplariness of the behavior of the Oxford society in an age of depravity, on the other.

Only a year after *OM* appeared, Richardson repeated in much the same language a jeremiad about his times when compiling his manual for young tradesmen:

> The present Age, by a strange Fatality, which I know not to what to ascribe it, is so lamentably over-run with Atheism, Deism, and Infidelity, that it is a matter of no small Concern, that it should be necessary to caution a young Man on this Head: For is it not a sad thing to reflect, that after Upwards of 1700 Years, in which Christianity has triumphed over all its Enemies, converting Principalities and Powers from Paganism to the Light of the Gospel, we should now have our most Holy Religion to defend?[13]

With already a number of moral guidebooks to his credit, it is not surprising that in 1740 Richardson was asked by the booksellers Osborn and Rivington to prepare a letter manual that answered the requirements of a wide range of domestic situations: *Letters Written to and for Particular Friends, on the Most Important Occasions* was published on January 23, 1741, and is usually known as *Familiar Letters*. Although intended for an audience in the laboring and middling classes by contrast to the focus on university and law students in *OM* and *The Infidel Convicted*, respectively, *Familiar Letters* contains ten letters addressed to fathers. Two are particularly concerned with a son's education: Letter I, *To a Father, against putting a Youth of but moderate Parts to a Profession that requires more extensive Abilities*, and Letter CXXX, *To a Father, on his Neglect of his Childrens Education.*[14] It seems likely that when these booksellers commissioned Richardson to produce this letter book they were well aware of his earlier manuals of advice to parents and children.

As a way of reconstructing the provenance of *OM* from its sources and contexts, I have provided two appendixes comparing the various texts involved in this inquiry. The first shows the relationship between Wesley's original letter to Richard Morgan and *OM*. The second concerns the more general comparison of *OM* to Richardson's known writings.

Even though Richardson had John Wesley's letter to Richard Morgan in his possession, he did not simply reprint it as the first part of *OM*. Rather, the editor/narrator of the pamphlet scrambled the evidence so that sometimes it is unclear whether he is actually quoting something heard or paraphrasing Wesley's transcript. Despite this difficulty, it seems fair to say that of the approximately 4,650 words comprising the first eighteen pages of *OM*, the narrator contributes only 40 percent of the text, the remainder being drawn from Wesley's letter. The rest of *OM*, pages 18–32, is commentary on the letter in *Fog's*.

In contrast to Wesley's letter, *OM* completely avoids naming the various members of this religious society, even to the extent of alluding to Wesley Sr. only as a "near Relation" of one of the students. William Morgan's initiating role is glossed over, and his death only vaguely mentioned. Wesley's name never appears and his specific references to himself and his family become "three or four serious young Gentlemen," the Bishop's Chaplain becomes simply a "Gentleman," Samuel Wesley's letter and his reference to his two sons at Oxford are obscured, and the direct threat from the Oxford Censors to the "Holy Club" is diluted by the passive voice (appendix 1. 1, 2, 3, and 8).

One important detail gleaned from a comparison of Wesley's "Preface" and *OM* is that while Wesley only sparingly alludes to Morgan's scolding letter to his son in March 1732, the editor of *OM* quotes it directly at length. Hence, we may infer that Richardson had access to a transcript of the letter and made more extensive use of it than would have been relevant to Wesley's purpose of mollifying his friend's grief. By contrast, the editor of *OM* wanted to emphasize the wrath of the father over his son's supposed religious enthusiasm. His almost obsessive concern with absolute deference to parental authority, even if that authority may be in error, has a familiar ring in Richardson's writings.[15]

Although doubtless aware of the letter to *Fog's*, Wesley did not feel threatened by such journalistic slander. The editor of *OM*, however, wanted to make capital of it, and even while admitting that it would have been better to ignore it ("for the Writer's Sake, it were much better it were intirely forgotten" [*OM*, 19]), he nevertheless proceeds in the second half of the pamphlet to condemn the letter-writer as if the future of Christianity were at stake. Yet, despite the bluster about this critic of the young "Methodists," under the guise of being impartial the editor/narrator of *OM* allows the possibility that these students may have brought on themselves the ridicule of their peers because of their indiscretion. In general, the editor of *OM* has three major objectives in denouncing the letter to *Fog's*: (1) to refute the claim that the Oxford "Methodists" were reviving a puritan religion; (2) to stress their benevolent actions on behalf of the poor, sick, and oppressed; and (3) to justify their religious devotion as no more than following the rules of the Church that in the present age of pervasive freethinking appear to many to be enthusiastic madness. Appendix 2 allows us to compare the narrator's objections to the "scoffer" in *Fog's* to similar contexts in Richardson's writings.

Concerning the first charge, of reviving a puritan religion, the narrator denies that "Methodists" resemble the ascetic Pietists in Saxony and Switzerland or the Essenes among the Jews. He rejects categorically that this is a gloomy sect reviving the old puritanism and renouncing all pleasure and sociability (*OM*, 20–22). A basic tenet in Richardson's writings is against the idea that "Religion was design'd to contradict Nature" (*OM*, 23); he emphasizes instead that it is the only way to fulfil our imperfect nature. In his third novel, while trying to reconnect the word *prude* with its derivative *prudence*, Harriet Byron remarks: "I own myself one of those who would wish to restore it to its natural respectable signification, for the sake of virtue; which, as Sir Charles himself once hinted . . . is in danger of suffering by the abuse of it; as Religion once did, by that of the word Puritan."[16] While recognizing the difficulties of restoring positive moral terms in the wake of overreaction to the puritan past, Richardson "threw in his mite" as both printer and writer.

Far from being "disconsolate or gloomy," true religion, we are to understand, is "the most chearful thing in the World" and the means to "Serenity of Mind" (appendix 2.23). Pamela's conversation with Lady Davers about religion and social behavior seems to be identical to the narrator's position in *OM*:

> We return'd to the Gentlemen as soon as Supper was ready, and as chearful and easy, as Lady Davers observ'd, as if we had not been present at so solemn a Service; And this, said she, after the Gentlemen were gone, makes Religion so pleasant and delightful a thing, that I profess I shall have a much higher Opinion of those who make it a regular and constant Part of their Imployment, than ever I had. But I have seen, added her Ladyship, very humorously, such wry Faces, and such gloomy Countenances, among some of your pious Folks, in and after a solemn Office, that quite disharten'd me; for I thought, after such an Exercise, that it would be a Sin to go to Bed with a Smile upon one's Face, or without sighing and groaning at such a Rate, as must rob one of all the Comforts of Life.[17]

Even more surprisingly, Lovelace himself advises Belford that a spiritual conversion does not necessarily mean becoming a Puritan:

> Dost thou not know, that Religion, if it has taken proper hold of the heart, is the most chearful countenance-maker in the world?—I have heard my beloved Miss Harlowe say so: And she knew, or nobody did.[18]

When the *Fog's* "scoffer" insinuates that the "Methodists" were guilty of unspeakable practices like incest and other sexual perversions, the narrator affects a delicacy similar to that of the narrator in *Clarissa* regarding Lovelace's libertine fantasies (appendix 2.15).

Given the perceived infidelity of the age, the narrator censures the *Fog's* "scoffer" for choosing the wrong time to attack any rare example of religious devotion (appendix 2.17). The "unseasonableness" of an action is a familiar stance in Richardson's writing: no matter what the merits of a plea, it must depend on the time and circumstances of making it. When deism seems to be infecting the whole society, there is no good reason at this moment for attacking young students devoutly following the rules of the Gospel. With the same logic, the narrator impugns any reader not in agreement with his position for having been "tainted" by the supposedly pervasive "Scepticism and Infidelity" (appendix 2.22). In the conclusion of the *Apprentice's Vade Mecum* (1734), for example, Richardson advises his readers how to avoid the dangerous circumstances of falling into the company of freethinkers:

> Let the Young Man therefore, if he should be solicited to enter into the Clubs and Societies that are, as we are inform'd, erected to propagate Infidelity, determine to avoid such Company, as the Bane of his future Peace and Welfare. If he is oblig'd to converse with any of them, and has any thing suggested to him, which he cannot answer, and which makes him doubt, let him preserve his Modesty, and his Desire to be inform'd; and, by proper Application to learned and pious Persons, or to Books, he will be set right, and taught not to be sham'd out of his Religion by a prophane Jest, or rally'd out of his Faith by a lewd Scoffer, and not to doubt, where he ought, and may be assur'd: For Doubt, or Uncertainty, of all Circumstances in Life, is certainly the most uneasy; and to a serious Person, Religious Doubts are of all others the most affecting, and yet this is all that these Persons pretend to bring you to; for they cannot be sure they are right, and if they should be wrong, how dreadful will be the Mistake![19]

The basic idea is Pascal's famous wager—why gamble? If the freethinkers prove to be wrong in the end, "how dreadful will be the Mistake!" On a more practical level than the various chance circumstances that may threaten a young mind's religious faith, as a printer and businessman Richardson was in the habit of continually weighing the odds for publishing books in the marketplace.[20]

The editor's second purpose in *OM* is to stress benevolence and the pleasures of religion. In his "Preface," Wesley makes clear that it was William Morgan who took the initiative of visiting the poor, sick, and oppressed.

> In the Summer following Mr. *M.* told me he had call'd at the Goal, to see a Man who was condemn'd for killing his Wife; and that, from the Talk he had with one of the Debtors, he verily believed it would do much Good, if any one would be at the Pains, of now and then speaking with them. This he so frequently repeated, that on the 24th of *Aug.* 1730, my Brother and I walked with him to the Castle. We were so well satisfied with our Conversation there, that we agreed to go thither once or twice a Week; which we had not done long,

before he desired me, to go with him to see a poor Woman in the Town who was sick. In this Employment too when we came to reflect upon it, we believed it would be worth while to spend an Hour or two in a Week. ("Preface," iv)

In the paraphrase of this passage in *OM*, William Morgan is simply identified as "the Gentleman who proposed this (who, it seems, is since dead)," and John Wesley as "one of his Friends":

> The following Summer one of these Gentlemen having called at the Gaol out of Curiosity to see a Man condemn'd for killing his Wife, told his Companions, that from the Talk he had had with one of the Debtors there, he verily believed it would do much Good, if a sober Person would now and then take the Trouble to talk to them: That upon his pressing the Matter, two of his Companions walk'd down with him to the Castle; and they were all so well satisfy'd with their Conversation there, that they agreed to go thither once or twice a Week. The Gentleman who proposed this (who, it seems, is since dead) soon after desir'd one of his Friends to accompany him in a Visit to a poor Woman in the Town, who was taken sick: And finding their Advice well receiv'd, this induc'd them now and then to pass an Hour in such charitable Visits to poor People, who were taken ill. (*OM*, 3)

Although Wesley offers only a dry account of these charitable offices, the *OM* narrator extols their good works as the most positive aspect of their religion: "What can inspire a nobler and more exalted Pleasure, than to see, by what is spared from our Luxury and Superfluities, the Hungry fed, the Sick relieved, the Naked cloathed, the oppressed Mind chear'd and made glad?" Such lyricism about the immediate rewards of charity is foreign to Wesley's terse report: "Whether we shall not be more happy hereafter, the more Good we do now?" ("Preface," x).

Where Wesley carefully accounts for all their precautions against offending the Church authorities while making their rounds, the *OM* narrator stresses the immediate gratifications of doing good as opposed to "Whether we shall not be more happy hereafter." But the *OM* narrator's hedonism does resemble Pamela's triumphal testimony: "Indeed I know nothing so God-like in Human Nature as this Disposition to do Good to our Fellow-Creatures" (appendix 2.9). The *Fog's* letter-writer "knows nothing of the Seraphick Pleasure of having cheared the drooping Spirit." Again, in Richardson's prose, "Reason and Religion will come in seasonably with their powerful aids, to raise the drooping heart" (appendix 2.12). The *OM* narrator's major argument against the "scoffer" in *Fog's* concerns the ultimate pleasures from religion in having a consciousness of having done well. In both his letters and fiction Richardson never tired of stressing the enormous advantage of having the means of *giving*, and the implicit embarrassment of having to be on the *receiving* end.[21]

When in the summer of 1730 William Morgan paid that first visit to one of the debtors in the Oxford castle, it may be that he had been inspired by reading one of the various books devoted to prison reform at this time. One anonymous item—signed with the teasing initials of "W. M."—was printed by Richardson, *The Case of the Unfortunate Truly Stated*, and provides ample statistical evidence as well as biblical grounds for demanding a change in the criminal system regarding the punishment of debtors.[22] Given the information from Wesley himself that it was William Morgan who began the visits to the prison at Oxford and subsequently encouraged the rest of the "Methodists" to follow suit, it is not unthinkable that he might have been the author of this "small Treatise" (6).

The question raised in Wesley's "Preface," "Whether we can be happy at all hereafter unless we have according to our Power, *Fed the Hungry, Cloathed the Naked, Visited those that are Sick, and in Prison*, and made all these Actions subservient to a higher Purpose, even the saving of Souls from Death?," paraphrases Matthew 25:35–46. The author of *The Case of the Unfortunate Truly Stated* quotes at length this same Gospel passage while questioning whether the British government's cruel imprisonment of debtors can be justified in a Christian society (10–11). In the dedication to King George II, this pamphleteer is deeply aware of arousing the resentment of authority but humbly begs that his "Majesty may cast an Eye of Pity and Compassion on the Unfortunate" (6). Rather than breathe the slightest hint of the need to change the system, however, the editor of *OM* simply alludes to Matthew 25 as a means of glorifying the self-rewarding acts of benevolence by the rich to the poor. For Richardson's Pamela, daughter of a peasant, presumably one of her dangers after the sudden good fortune of her marriage into the gentry class is a nervous breakdown from having so much power all at once to bestow benefits to the needy (appendix 2.9).

By contrast to such emphasis on the creditor's pleasures, however, in *Familiar Letters* Richardson highlighted the human toll involved in a legal system that makes criminals out of hard-working people who suffer misfortunes beyond their control, become incarcerated, and see their families end up as burdens on the parish. Letters CVI to CXXIV, 147–61, cover a variety of situations involving the subject of loans and the failure to repay them. While recognizing that many debtors are simply irresponsible and could have prevented their ruin, Richardson mainly commiserates with those farmers, for instance, who had bad luck with their crops and deserve compassion while trying to pay their debts to the landowners. In such a manual one would not expect to find the polemical edge of *The Case of the Unfortunate*, but Letter CXIII's rendering of the agony of a prisoner who prefers a friend's soothing visit to his distraught wife's coming to his cell offers a vivid recognition of the debtor's plight:

> As to your kind Offer, my dear Friend, I will beg to see you as often as may not be detrimental to your own Affairs. I care not how seldom I see my dear Wife: Neither her Heart nor mine can bear the Grief that oppresses us when we think of our happier Days and Prospects, and see them all concluded within these Bars and Bolts, and Lattices; so that we sink one another still lower every doleful Visit the dear good Woman makes me. But your Visits, my Friend, will be of singular Use and Comfort to me (as your Presence and kind Advice will be to *her*, as often as you can), to save us both the Mortification of seeing one another so often as my Affairs will otherwise require her to come to this dismal Place.[23]

While avoiding any political agenda, Clarissa's public humiliation after having been raped in a brothel and subsequently imprisoned for debt by Mrs. Sinclair shows amply Richardson's agreement with the author of *The Case of the Unfortunate* that "this Hell on Earth, is worse than the Hell in a future State; and I wish every hard-hearted Creditor here, doth not prepare a future Hell for himself, by making one here on Earth."[24]

In addition to the arguments that the "Methodists" were not reviving gloomy puritanism but rather promoting a euphoric evangelical activism on behalf of the poor, sick, and oppressed, the *OM* narrator impugns the *Fog's* letter-writer for being so much a part of the pervasive deism and infidelity of the age as to warrant condemnation as a lunatic enthusiast. Given the pervasive scepticism of the present age, however, the narrator admits that these young students were perhaps heedless of how their peers would perceive their activities:

> But after all, Sir, between Friends, I cannot help saying, that I wish these young Gentlemen have not, at their first setting out, fallen upon too great a Refinement in some small Points, which their Friends might have wish'd, that proper Regard to the Censure of the World (which is so necessary to augment their Numbers, and to prevent Ridicule) had made them avoid. I am entirely satisfy'd with their Scheme in general, and think it worthy of a more primitive Age; but if the dispensing with such Points, if there are any such, as they in Conscience think might be dispensed with, would have taken away the Occasion of any Part of that Obloquy, which a misjudging World is so ready to fix upon all good Designs, I wish they had done it; that they might have had less Difficulties to encounter, and more Hopes of Success in propagating so worthy a Scheme. (*OM*, 26–27)

This declamation on the depravity of the age and the need to protect oneself from "a misjudging World" is Richardsonian boilerplate (appendix 2.4).

As a businessman he was cautious about extreme conduct of any kind. He stressed the positive effects of religious zeal, but also recognized the need for knowledge and guidance by more experienced paternal figures (appendix 2.21). It may have been that the "Methodists" were partly to blame for the public outcry, but the perfection of one's religious beliefs and behavior takes time (appendix 2.18). As a novelist in later years, Richardson showed a similar restraint toward the Methodist movement. He was always careful, however, to temper his criticism of these "overdoers" who "make religion look unlovely, and put underdoers out of heart."[25] Despite their excesses, Richardson still admired the Methodists for reaching out to the poor and morally lapsed; and he admitted that the regular Anglican clergy seemed ineffective in their duties because of their lack of such zeal.[26]

Yet he also recognized that excesses of religious enthusiasm could result in madness. Because of his inherent benevolence, the titular hero of his last novel can barely bring himself to condemn the woman he loves for her sincere piety:

> I hastened into the garden, greatly dissatisfied with myself, yet hardly knowing why. I thought I wanted somebody to accuse, somebody to blame—Yet how could it be Clementina? But the words Narrow zeal!—Sweet Enthusiast!—as if I would find fault with her religion, involuntarily slipt from me to myself.[27]

If Richardson knew about William Morgan's mental collapse in the remaining months before his death, it may be that this Oxford student was a prototype of Clementina's "Enthusiastick Madness" in the Roman Catholic culture. Sir Charles's pronouncements "Narrow zeal!—Sweet Enthusiast!" imply a need for reason, prudence, and judgment while devoting oneself to the religious "rules." Presumably a sturdy British Protestant character as opposed to the Italian counterpart is needed to protect oneself against this dangerous excess of religious zeal.

Prudence governed Richardson in all his ideological commitment. After the storm of protest against Parliament's passing of the so-called "Jew Bill" on July 7, 1753, and the vociferous Tory opposition that led to its repeal in 1754, Richardson decided that it would be better if the Jews gave up their quest for citizenship rather than cause so much division in the society.[28] Similarly, his asking Lady Bradshaigh in 1756 how he should respond to an invitation from the Moravians, who had fallen out of favor in England by that time, betrays his habitual wariness of exposing his religious and political sympathies. Thus, the *OM* narrator's slightly equivocal support of the young Oxford enthusiasts seems typical of Richardson's own "divided mind."

Despite the advertisement on the title page of the second and third editions, "With very great Alterations and Improvements," the three editions, except for a few textual changes, are remarkably similar. There are some variants among the accidentals of the text, but the only substantial variants are the addition of the dedication to George Whitefield and two omissions.[29]

By 1737, after Wesley had left for Georgia, Whitefield had become a prominent religious force at Oxford; and Richardson printed two of his sermons at this time: *The Benefits of an early Piety* and *The Nature and Necessity of our New Birth in Christ Jesus*.[30]

When "altering and improving" the second and third editions, the editor may have decided to delete the report from a "celebrated" Oxford college administrator[31] because it drew attention to a specific individual rather than to the issues involved. Perhaps the editor came to see that this statement was too much of a concession to the idea that a profligate life was usually a first step to eventual rebirth and devout faith. But what is still worse, the paragraph implied that these students had indeed been guilty of too much religious zeal and thus contradicts the view held elsewhere in the pamphlet that they were model Christians. And perhaps the editor deleted the reference (originally made by the letter-writer in *Fog's*) to Dr. Willis's cap because it was too obscure. But even if the readers knew that it was a device intended as a remedy for mental illness, it may have seemed too harsh of an ad hominem.[32]

William Sale insightfully remarked on Richardson's conflicted disposition of being a successful printer and businessman but nonetheless a deeply disgruntled participant in his society:

> That his financial success should have brought a degree of complacency is to be expected, and some of that complacency is reflected in his fiction. But Richardson wrote his novels because he had not—and indeed could not—come completely to terms with his age. . . . His professional career gives little hint of what his novels so clearly show—his refusal to accept his age; his unwillingness to follow his contemporaries in finding a place into which to fit everything, and for everything a place into which it might be fitted.[33]

In light of the numerous titles from Richardson's press that have been found since Sale's groundbreaking work, however, I would suggest that this printer's professional career already during the 1730s shows signs of the same reforming spirit found in his novels. This sympathetic account of the "Methodist" struggle against all odds in even Oxford, that bastion of conservative Christianity, is yet another testimony to Richardson's sense of urgency about the depravity of his time

APPENDIX 1

Table 2.1. Comparison of John Wesley's "Preface" to *The Oxford Methodists*

Wesley's "Preface"	The Oxford Methodists
1. "In *November*, **1729**, at which Time I came to reside at *Oxford*, **your Son, my Brother, myself, and one more, agreed to spend three or four Evenings in a Week together**. . . . provided the Minister of the Parish, in which any such Person was, were not against it," p. iii (lines 27–29)–p. iv (line 25).	"In the latter End of the Year **1729, three or four serious young Gentlemen agreed to pass certain Evenings in every Week together**. . . . Design of preaching to the Prisoners once a Month, if his Lordship approv'd of it," p. 3 (lines 14–37)–p. 4 (lines 1–11).
2. "[The Bishop's Chaplain] **approv'd** of it. He much commended our Design, and **said he would answer for the Bishop's Approbation**, to whom he would take the first Opportunity of mentioning it. It was not long before he informed me he had done so, and that his **Lordship not only gave his Permission, but was greatly pleas'd with the Undertaking**, and **hoped it would have the desir'd Success**," p. vii (lines 20–26)–p. viii (line 2).	"The Gentleman, for his own Part, **approv'd** the Design, and **undertook that the Bishop would do the same**; and soon after signify'd his Lordship's Permission, and great Satisfaction in the Undertaking, and hearty **Wishes for the good Success** of it," p. 4 (lines 11–16).
3. "**I am afraid, lest the main Objection you make against your going on in the Business with the Prisoners. . . . to obtain the Direction and Approbation of your Bishop**," p. vi (lines 3–30)–p. vii (line 1).	"**I am afraid, lest the main Objection you make against your going on in the Business with the Prisoners. . . . to obtain the Direction and Approbation of your Bishop**," p. 5 (lines 8–30).
4. "I have the highest Reason to **bless God**, that he has given me two Sons together at Oxford . . . **expect the Crown which fadeth not away**," p. v (lines 9–19).	"— **I bless God**, who has given you Grace and Courage . . . **expect the Crown which fades not away**," p. 5 (lines 31–35)–p. 6 (lines 1–4).
5. ". . . **this Evening in our Course of our Reading, I thought I found an Answer** that would be more proper than any I myself could dictate. . . . **will both accept, esteem and reward you**," p. viii (lines 15–28)–p. ix (1–24).	"— **This Evening, in our Course of Reading, I thought I found an Answer** to yours. . . . **will both accept, esteem, and reward you**," p. 6 (lines 9–35).
6. "**Upon this Encouragement we still continued to sit together as usual** . . . **(which is here once a Week**;)," p. ix (lines 25–29)–p. x (line 1).	"**Upon these Encouragements, the young Gentlemen continued to meet together** . . . **which at Oxford is once a Week**," p. 7 (lines 22–27).
7. "The **two Points**, whereunto by the Blessing of GOD, and your Son's Help, we had before attain'd, we endeavour'd to hold fast. . . . **To these . . . we have added a third**," p. xviii (lines 3–13).	"There are **Three Points** to which these Gentlemen think themselves oblig'd to adhere," p. 8 (lines 7–36).
8. ". . . some of the Men of Wit in *Christ-Church* enter'd the List against us. . . . This much delighted our **Gay Opponents**. . . . it was soon reported, that . . . **the Censors were going to blow up the Godly Club**," p. xiv (lines 6–30)–p. xv (lines 1–18).	". . . they met with too many Discouragements . . . from several Men of Wit in *Chr—Ch*—and *M—n* . . . great Matter of Triumph to their **gay Opponents** . . . that it was given out thereupon, that **the Godly Club was to be blown up**," p. 9 (lines 25–34)–p. 10 (lines 1–6).
9. "**To the Law and to the Testimony we appeal**, whereby we ought to be judged. . . . **if the Neglect of known Duties be the one Condition of securing our Reputation, why fare it well**," p. xviii (lines 23–30)–p. xix (lines 1–6).	"That they appealed to the Law and to the Testimony, by which he conceived they ought to be judged . . . That if the Neglect of known Duties were to be the Condition of securing their Reputation, fare-it-well," p. 10 (lines 4–14).
10. "**A pretty while after the Date your's came to my Hand. I wav'd my Answer till I had an Opportunity of consulting** your Father, who	"**A pretty while after the Date, yours came to my Hands. I wav'd my Answer till I had an Opportunity of consulting** . . . who, upon all

upon all Accounts is a more proper Judge of the Affair than I am. . . . yet should you have the Concurrence of their proper Pastor, your good Offices would be more regular, and less liable to Censure," p. xv (lines 25–29)–p. xvi (lines 1–36).

11. "'He frequently went into poor Peoples Houses in the Villages about *Holt,* call'd their Children together, and instructed them the Necessity of private as well as publick Prayer, and provided them with such Forms as were best suited to their several Capacities; And being well appriz'd how much the Success of his Endeavours depended on their Good-will towards him, to win upon their Affections, he sometimes distributed among them a little of that Money, which he had saved from Gaming, and the other fashionable Expences of the Place,'" pp. ii–iii. Wesley's paraphrase of Richard Morgan's letter to son, March 1732.

12. ". . . his Eyes are open, and he sees clearly whether it was 'Blind Zeal and a thorough Mistake of true Religion, that hurried him on the Error of his Way,'" p. xix (lines 12–15). Paraphrase of Richard Morgan's letter to his son.

13. ". . . they would be contented that their *Lives too should be counted Madness, and their End thought to be without Honour.* But the Truth is, their Title to Holiness stands upon much less stable Foundations; as you will easily perceive when you know the Ground of this wonderful Outcry," p. iii (lines 18–25).

14. ". . . these, or the like Questions: I. Whether it does not concern all Men of all Conditions, to imitate Him as much as they can, *who went about doing Good?* . . . Whether we may not, as we have Opportunity, explain and enforce these upon them, especially with Respect to publick and private Prayer, and the blessed Sacrament," p. x (lines 7–28)–p. xiii (lines 1–8).

15. "I do not remember that we met with any Person who answer'd any of these Questions in the Negative, . . . so that the more Persons we propos'd our Designs to, the more were we confirm'd in the Belief of their Innocency, and the more determin'd to pursue them in Spight of the Ridicule," p. xiii (lines 9–22).

Accounts, is a more proper Judge of the Affair than I am. . . . yet should you have the Concurrence of their proper Pastor, those good Offices would be more regular, and less liable to Censure," p. 11 (lines 18–36)–p. 12 (lines 1–16).

"'You can't conceive what a Noise that *Ridiculous* Society, that you have engag'd in, has made here. Besides the Particulars of the great Follies of it at *Oxford,* which, to my great Concern, I have often heard repeated, it gave me sensible Trouble to hear that you were noted for going into the Villages about *Holt,* entring [sic] into poor Peoples Houses, calling their Children together, teaching them their Prayers and Catechism, and giving them a Shilling at your Departure,'" p. 12 (lines 16–26). Direct quotation from Richard Morgan's letter to son, March 1732.

"'I could not, says he [Richard Morgan], but advise with a wise, learned and pious Clergyman: He told me, That he had known the worst of Consequences arise from such *blind Zeal,* and plainly satisfied me, that it was a thorough Mistake of true Piety and Religion. — He concluded with saying, That you was young as yet, and that your Judgment was not come to its Maturity: But that, as your Judgment improv'd, and on the good Advice of a true Friend, you would see the Error of the Way you was in, and think (as he does) that you may walk uprightly and safely, without endeavouring to out-do all the good Bishops, Clergy, and other pious good Men of the present and past Ages,'" p. 13 (lines 1–15). Much fuller quotation, hence, SR had access to Richard Morgan's original letter.

". . . they would be well content, he said, that their Life too should be counted Madness, and their End thought to be without Honour: But the Truth is, continu'd he, our Title to Holiness, stands upon much less stable Foundations, as you will perceive when you reflect upon the Ground of this wonderful Outcry," p. 14 (lines 9–16).

". . . these or the like Questions. . . . I. *Whether it does not concern all Men, of all Conditions, to imitate Him, as much as they can, who went about doing Good? . . . Whether we may not, as we have Opportunity, explain and enforce them, especially with regard to Publick and Private Prayer, and the Sacrament?*" p. 14 (line 36)–p. 17 (lines 1–10).

"He said, They never met with any Person, who answer'd any of these Questions in the Negative. . . . the more we were confirm'd in the Belief of its Innocence; and the more determin'd we were, of consequence, to pursue it, notwithstanding the Ridicule and Derision wherewith we were more and more loaded," p. 17 (lines 11–27).

APPENDIX 2

Table 2.2. Comparison of *The Oxford Methodists* to Richardson's Authorial Contexts

The Oxford Methodists (1733)	Richardson's Writings (References are to Chadwyck-Healy Eighteenth-Century Fiction)
1. "to be able to answer to the Desire of so good a Friend, and **so sincere a Man**," p. 1 (lines 6–7).	"This makes me half afraid to ask you, If you think you are not too cruel, too ungenerous shall I say, in your behaviour to a man who loves you so dearly, and is so worthy and **so sincere a man**?" *Clarissa*, 1st ed. (1748), 2:137.
2. "I have **Time upon my Hands**," p. 2 (line 4).	"I Have so much **Time upon my Hands**, that I must write on to employ myself," *Pamela*, 1st ed. (1741) 1:195. "having a little **Time upon my Hands**, to see your Chapel," *Pamela*, 2:173. "I long for the full particulars of your story. You must have but too much **time upon your hands**, for a mind so active as yours, if tolerable health and spirits be afforded you," *Clarissa* (1748), 6:83.
3. "they were so **diffident of themselves** . . . that they took Advice from . . . a venerable Gentleman," p. 4 (lines 10–13).	The evidence that these students "were so diffident of themselves" as to seek out this Wesley patriarch for counsel has a parallel in SR's emphasis on "diffidence" as an ideal feminine quality: "that bashfulness, or **diffidence of a person's own merits**, are but other words for undoubted worthiness." SR to Sarah Wescomb (27 August 1746), Barbauld, 3:244.
4. "this little Society; for a large one I doubt, considering the Opposition they meet with, and the **Depravity of the Age**, there is little Room to expect or hope it will ever be," p. 8 (lines 12–14).	"The present Depravity of Servants is a general Complaint in the Mouths of all Masters of Families; and it must be allow'd, there is but too much Reason for it. It were easy to assign several Causes to which this Depravity is owing, and, besides the Degeneracy of the Times, and the Prophaneness and Immorality, and even the open Infidelity that is every where propagated with Impunity, something perhaps might be too justly laid at the Door of the Complainants themselves," *The Apprentice's Vade Mecum* (London, 1735), p. v. "In **this general depravity**, when even the Pulpit has lost great part of its weight, and the Clergy are considered as a body of interested men, the Author thought he should be able to answer it to his own heart, be the success what it would, if he threw in his mite towards introducing a Reformation so much wanted. . . ," *Clarissa*, 3rd ed. (1751), Postscript, 8:279.
5. "the **Circumspection** wherewith these young Gentlemen had proceeded, in this Affair," p. 12 (lines 10–11).	"altho' I must call myself a lost creature, as to this world, yet have I this consolation left me, that I have not suffered either for **want of circumspection**, or thro' credulity, or weakness," *Clarissa* (1748), 6:32.
6. "Opinionatry," p. 19 (line 6).	Although the *OED* offers only one example of this usage, an important one occurs in a writer familiar to SR: Cf. "for Age increases Opinionatry in some, as well as it does Experience in others." Mary Astell (1668–1731), *Some Reflections upon Marriage* (London: printed for William Parker, 1730), p. 46. On the basis of Maslen's system of

7. "shews as much Zeal **in a bad Cause**, as those Gentlemen express **in a good one**," p. 19 (lines 11–12).

"We shall soon find that all the monstrous Absurdities that have assum'd the Name of Religion in the different Regions and Ages of the World, are owing intirely to this proud, this boasted Reason, for which our present wise and modest Scepticks so zealously contend," *The Apprentice's Vade Mecum* (London, 1735), p. 65.
"it is but glossing over one part of a story, and omitting another, that will **make a bad cause a good one** at any time. What an admirable Lawyer should I have made!" *Clarissa* (1748), 7:102.
The Chadwyck-Healey database of Eighteenth-Century Fiction indicates twelve instances of "bad cause," and ten are from SR. But only SR invokes this dichotomy between a good and a bad cause.

8. "the *Simplicity* of their *Diet*, and *Regularity* of their *Life*; by which, as ***Josephus*** witnesses, (*cap. viii. De Bell. Jud.*) it was usual for many of that Sect to attain to an hundred Years of Age," p. 20 (lines 4–6).

SR cites **Josephus** in *Clarissa* (1748), 4:84, and 6:254.

9. "What can inspire a nobler and more exalted Pleasure, than to see, by what is spared from our *Luxury* and *Superfluities*, the *Hungry* fed, the *Sick* relieved, the *Naked* cloathed, the *oppressed Mind* chear'd and made glad, the *Prisoner* enlarged, and the Mouths of even the *Profligate* taught **to overflow with Praises**, and to sing Thanksgivings to **that gracious Providence which has put it into the Hearts of these generous Youths to comfort and relieve them. . . ?**" p. 20 (lines 31–37)– p. 21 (lines 1–3).
See Matthew 25.

"Indeed I know nothing so God-like in Human Nature as this Disposition to do Good to our Fellow-Creatures; for is it not following immediately the Example of **that gracious Providence which every Minute is conferring Blessings on us all, and by giving Power to the Rich, makes them but the Dispensers of its Benefits to those that want them?**" *Pamela*, 3:50.
"Take care, take care, my best Beloved! that the Joy which **overflows your dear Heart**, for having done a beneficent and a noble Action, to a deserving Gentleman, does not affect you too much," *Pamela*, 3:300.

10. "I am sorry the Letter-writer is unable to judge of it, that there is more true and solid Satisfaction arising to a generous Mind, from the doing a kind and **beneficent Action** to his Fellow-creatures that want his Assistance," p. 21 (lines 8–10).

"I know how much you despise riches in the main: But yet it behoves you to remember, that in one instance you yourself have judged them valuable — 'In that they put it into one's power to lay obligations; while the want of them puts a person under a necessity of receiving favours; receiving them, perhaps from grudging and narrow spirits, who know not how to confer them with that grace, which gives the principal merit to a **beneficent action**,'" *Clarissa*, (1748), 2:10.
"when such persons are brought to taste the sweets of a generous and **beneficent action**, they are able to behave greatly," *Sir Charles Grandison*, 1st ed., (1753–1754), 5:17.

11. "Who can hear the **lisping Children** of the Poor taught to acknowledge the God that made them, and to instruct, by the Repetition, even their abject and untaught Parents in the principal Duties of the Christian Religion, without being affected with Joy and Transport," p. 21 (lines 4–10).

"I am sure, I, and my Wife and Children too, tho' three of them can but **lisp their Prayers**, shall, Morning, Noon, and Night, pray to God for his Honour's Health and Prosperity, as well as for you and yours; and to enable me to be just to his Expectations," *Familiar Letters*, Letter CVIII, p. 149.

12. "He knows nothing of the Seraphick Pleasure of having **cheared the drooping Spirit**, and comforted the desponding Heart," p. 21 (lines 21–24).

"Nature will have way given to it (and so it ought) till sorrow has in a manner exhausted itself; and then Reason and Religion will come in seasonably with their powerful aids, to **raise the drooping heart**," *Clarissa*, (1751), 8:84.

identifying the printer's ornaments, we may safely conclude that SR printed this edition of Mary Astell's work. It contains the following ornaments: R382, R046, R332, R511, R480, R177, R465, R176, and R275.

13. "the base and mere **conjectural Foundation**," p. 23 (line 14).

"Spare, therefore, my dear uncle Selby, all your **conjectural constructions**," *Grandison*, 1:261.

14. "They do not think their Way of Life either *disconsolate* or *gloomy*; but as **Religion itself**, as is before observ'd, **is the most chearful thing in the World**, both as to Cause and Effects, so they enjoy so happy a Serenity of Mind, that even the undeserved Calumnies of such an Adversary, and the unprovoked Ill-treatment of their more significant Opposers, cannot disturb it," *OM*, p. 25 (lines 21–29).

"I said, that this **Over-gloominess was not Religion**, I was persuaded; but either Constitution or Mistake; and I was sorry always when I met with it; for tho' it might betoken a pious Mind, it certainly shew'd a narrow one, and I fear'd did more Harm than Good," *Pamela*, 1st ed., 3:264.

"Nor is it to be doubted, had life been spared her, that the sweetness of her temper, and **her chearful piety, would have made Virtue and Religion appear so lovely**, that her example would have had no small influence upon the minds and manners of those who would have had the honour of conversing with her," *Clarissa*, (1751), 8:221.

15. "**too shocking to be repeated**," p. 26 (line 8).

"Here Mr. Lovelace lays himself under a curse, **too shocking to be repeated**, if he revenge not himself upon the Lady, should he once more get her into his hands," *Clarissa*, (1748), 4:324.

16. "As to the Character into which he resolves the Matter at last, to wit, of *Enthusiastic Madness*, of **superstitious Scrupulousness**," p. 26 (lines 15–17).

"Not one offensive Word, or Look from me, shall wound your nicest Thoughts; but pray try to subdue **this Over-scrupulousness, and unseasonable Timidity**," *Pamela*, 2:160.

"You will now see, that you have nothing left, but to overcome all **scrupulousness**, and marry, as soon as you have opportunity," *Clarissa*, (1758), 3:262.

No other novels in the Chadwyck-Healey database of Eighteenth-Century Fiction use the word "scrupulousness."

17. "I need make no Reflection **on the particular Unseasonableness** of making such an Outcry against [a supposed Excess in] Religion at *this* Time," p. 28 (lines 10–11).

"*St. John*, as you most properly call him, has raised against his Work many Writers. I almost wish, that they had been left to the noble Discourses of Sherlock, **so seasonably publish'd** (tho' not levelled at their Author) and to Leland," SR to Thomas Edwards, 30 December 1754, Carroll, pp. 316–17.

"If this be not one of those proper Opportunities, forgive, dearest Sir, **the Unseasonableness of your very impertinent, but, in Intention, and Resolution**," *Pamela*, 4:387.

"Their answers, if they vouchsafe to answer me, will demonstrate, I doubt not, **the unseasonableness of this rash man's presence at our church**," *Clarissa*, (1748), 1:192.

The title of a pamphlet that A.D. McKillop attributed to Richardson again emphasizes the timeliness of a publication: *A Seasonable Examination of the Pleas and Pretensions of the proprietors of, and subscribers to, play-houses, erected in defiance of the royal licence. With some brief observations on the printed case of the players belonging to Drury-Lane and Covent-Garden Theatres* (London, 1735). See McKillop, *JEGP* (1954), 53:72–75. Eaves and Kimpel believe that it is probably by SR, p. 54. Maslen, 751.

18. "If we suppose Indiscretion in some Part of these young Mens Conduct; how can it well be otherwise, in the first setting out? **Perfection is a Work of Time and Experience.** But where might we expect proper Help and Direction for young Beginners, if not at *Oxford?*" p. 28 (lines 21–26).

"Some people **reach perfection sooner than others**; and are as swift in their decay." *Grandison*, 5:280.

The Oxford Methodists *(1733; 1738)* 45

19. "Can they be Friends to the *Thing* itself, who raise greater Clamours at *Zeal for Religion* (whatever Indiscretion there may be supposed) than at all the horrid and barefaced **Insults of Blasphemy** and *Profaneness*?" p. 28 (lines 15–20).

"But what will your Leaders think of their senseless Ridicule, when they are reminded, that even their very *Blasphemy* and *lewd Banters* on the **Christian System**, are a strong Proof of the Truth of that Dispensation which they are so resolutely bent to deny; and that THEY are the abandon'd Wretches who single out themselves for the Completion of a Prophecy of St. *Peter* (2 Ep.iii.3.) *That there shall come in the last Days* SCOFFERS?" *Infidel Convicted*, p. 14.
"Yet this, we cannot but observe, is the *same* Law, and the *same* Saviour, that are become the Subject of the *profane Scoffs* and *Banter* of the **Infidels of this** *enlighten'd* **Age**!" *Infidel Convicted*, p. 47.

20. "This shews how necessary it is that *Zeal* should ever be attended with *Knowledge* . . . a double Advice: Not only to *Novices* and Beginners in a Religious Course, that they ought to put themselves under the Conduct and Direction of some knowing Guide," p. 29 (lines 11–15).

"O dear! — to be so angry, an't please me, for his zeal — **Yes, zeal without knowledge**, I [Anna Howe] said — ."
Clarissa, (1751), 4:154–55.

21. "Were the Rules, by which these young Gentlemen are acted, known as well to the World, as they are to me, in Virtue of the Enquiry I have made, other Thoughts would be conceived of them by all serious Men, and by such as have not **a strong Taint of Scepticism and Infidelity**, and are not bad, if one may so say, upon Principle," p. 30 (lines 18–25).

"No wonder that the Yoke it [Christian Religion] imposes should gall the Necks of wicked Men, whose Actions and daily Pursuits, have a Tendency so directly opposite to its holy Rules," *The Apprentice's Vade Mecum* (London, 1735), pp. 64–65.
"The Reason why I address myself not only to the British Youth in general, but particularly to You, Gentlemen, of the Inns of Court about this great City, is, because 'tis too justly to be apprehended, that many of you have **taken a very deep Taint of this Infection of Infidelity**; insomuch, that many of you affect servilely to repeat, at every Coffeehouse Table where you frequent, to the great Offence of all sober Minds, the **senseless Buffoonery and lewd Scoffs of the most virulent Apostate** that has appear'd since the Time of the Emperor Julian." Anonymous. *The Infidel Convicted*, p. iii.

22. "you will excuse my **Prolixity**," p. 32 (line 3).

"Shall I not own, that your Ladiship's Hint of **Prolixity** in my Writings, was the more sincerely felt, as perhaps I was conscious of having justly incurred the friendly, the lively Censure? Nineteen or Twenty Vols. Closely printed! A Man of Business too!—Monstrous!—Reflecting upon my now [habitual] unconquerable Reluctance to the Pen, I wonder [myself] at my enormous Luxuriance."
FC XI, ff. 190–1, To Lady Bradshaigh (9 Oct. 1756), Carroll, p. 329.

NOTES

1. Mary Astell, *Some Reflections upon Marriage*, 2nd ed. (London, 1703), sig. A2 recto–A2 verso.
2. *The Life and Times of the Rev. John Wesley, M.A., Founder of the Methodists*, 2 vols., 3rd ed. (London: Hodder and Stoughton, 1876), 86–88.
3. *John Wesley and the Religious Societies* (London: Epworth Press, 1921), 97.
4. Gerda J. Joling–van der Sar recently criticized my essay "'Stealing in the Great Doctrines of Christianity': Samuel Richardson as Journalist," *ECF* 15, no. 3–4 (2003): 451–506, for assuming (on page 479 of my article), that Law was the author of this pamphlet. See her article "The Controversy between William Law and John Wesley," *English Studies* 87 (August 2006): 457. In the introduction to her article, Joling rightly points out that Simon offered no evidence whatsoever that Law was the author of this pamphlet.
5. *The Journal of the Rev. John Wesley, A.M.*, ed. Nehemiah Curnock, 8 vols. (London: Robert Culley, [1909]), 1:86.
6. *John Wesley and William Law* (London: Epworth Press, 1945).
7. A facsimile of the "Preface" from the first edition of Wesley's *Journal: An Extract of the Rev. Mr. John Wesley's Journal From his Embarking for Georgia To his Return to London* (Bristol: Printed by S. and F. Farley [1740]), Curnock, 1:84.
8. William M. Sale Jr., *Samuel Richardson: Master Printer* (Ithaca, NY: Cornell University Press, 1950), 183, identified two of Richardson's ornaments for the first edition of *OM*, no. 124A. In his greatly expanded study based on Sale's pioneering work, Keith Maslen has listed all the ornaments for the first edition and also for the second edition of *OM*. See *Samuel Richardson of London, Printer: A Study of his Printing Based on Ornament Use and Business Accounts* (Dunedin, NZ: University of Otago, 2001), 100, books numbered 413–14. The third edition contains the following ornaments in the order of their occurrence according to Maslen's system of identifying them: R060, R448, R055, R451, R081. Despite these different ornaments, the pagination is identical to that of the second edition, but a collation shows minor alterations in the text of the third.
9. This pamphlet has an ornament that closely resembles the Richardson ornament R297 on the final page, 37, sig. F 3 recto. For the connection of this pamphlet to his anonymous pamphlets during this period, see John A. Dussinger, "Fabrications from Samuel Richardson's Press," *PBSA* 100 (June 2006): 273–74.
10. Maslen, *Samuel Richardson of London, Printer*, 29.
11. For a detailed account of William Morgan and the aftermath of his death, see L. Tyerman, *The Oxford Methodists* (New York: Harper and Brothers, 1873), 4–23. Despite quoting at length Wesley's sources that were also included in *OM*, as well as carefully outlining *OM* in *The Life and Times of the Rev. John Wesley, M.A.* (86–88), Tyerman failed to see any direct connection between Wesley's letter to Morgan and this pamphlet.
12. Dussinger, "Fabrications from Samuel Richardson's Press," 268–75.
13. [Samuel Richardson], *The Apprentice's Vade Mecum: Or, Young Man's Pocket-Companion* (London, 1734), 555–56. See also Appendix 2.4, 7, 22.
14. *Letters Written to and for Particular Friends, On the most Important Occasions. Directing not only the Requisite Style and Forms To be Observed in Writing Familiar Letters; But how to Think and Act Justly and Prudently, in the Common Concerns of Human Life. Containing One Hundred and Seventy-three Letters*, 4th ed. (London, 1750), 1–5 and 168–70, respectively.
15. The narrator's stress on the students' exemplary deference to this patriarchal authority is characteristic of Richardson's later role as "Papa" among his circle of female correspondents. The evidence that these students "were so diffident of themselves" (*OM*, 4) as to seek out this Wesley patriarch (Samuel Sr.) for counsel has a parallel in Richardson's emphasis on "diffidence" as an ideal feminine quality: "that bashfulness, or diffidence of a person's own merits, are but other words for undoubted worthiness" (Richardson to Sarah Wescomb [August 27, 1746], *The Correspondence of Samuel Richardson*, ed. Anna Laetitia Barbauld, 6 vols. [London, 1804], 3:244). For Richardson, Father always knows best: "I would not have Children

provoked to Wrath. I would have them complied with in every reasonable Request. Only, that Parents should be the Judges, not the Children, of the Fit and Reasonable" (Richardson to Frances Grainger, March 29, 1750, *Selected Letters of Samuel Richardson*, ed. John Carroll [Oxford: Clarendon Press, 1964], 153).

Similarly, according to Richardson, except for the right to refuse to marry Mr. Solmes, Clarissa had no choice but to obey Mr. Harlowe's commands:

> Tho' the parental authority should be deemed sacred, yet Parents should have reason in what they do (i:87).
> It is better for a good Child to be able to say, her Parents were unkind to her, than that she was undutiful to them (iii.25; see also i:125).
> A good Child will be careful of making a party against even harsh and severe Parents (vii:212). *Clarissa*, (1751), 8:365–67.

References to volumes here in small Roman numerals are those included in Richardson's quotations as printed in this edition.
16. *Grandison*, 6:148.
17. *Pamela*, 3:263.
18. *Clarissa*, (1751), 8:188.
19. *AVM*, 84.
20. For instance, Richardson worried about the timing of books against deism that were issuing from his press:

> St. John, as you most properly call him, has raised against his Work many Writers. I almost wish, that they had been left to the noble Discourses of Sherlock, so seasonably publish'd (tho' not levelled at their Author) and to Leland; for the Sale is far from answering the sanguine Expectations of their Boutefeu Editor, and I am afraid that so many Tracts on them will add to his Profits, by carrying into Notice Works that would have probably otherwise sunk under the Weight of their dogmatical Abuse & Virulence. I imagine, that these Works of the quondam Peer, so far as they favour the Cause of Infidelity, rather abound with Objections against the Christian System, that he thought New, than were really so. He seems to have been willing to frame a Religion to his Practices. Poor Man! He is not a doubter now! (Richardson to Thomas Edwards, December 30, 1754. [Carroll, 316–17])

Richardson deliberately delayed the publication in 1753 of *The History of Sir Charles Grandison* to avoid confusion with another novel by a similar name—*Memoirs of Sir Charles Goodville and his Family, In a Series of Letters to a Friend*. Similarly, he postponed the printing of *A Collection of Moral Sentiments* in 1755 until after the nearly year-long controversy over the Oxfordshire election was resolved by the House of Commons.

21. See John A. Dussinger, "Debt without Redemption in a World of 'Impossible Exchange': Samuel Richardson and Philanthropy," *The Culture of the Gift in Eighteenth-Century England*, ed. Linda Zionkowski and Cynthia Klekar (New York: Palgrave Macmillan, 2009), 55–75.

22. Second ed. (London: Printed for the author; and sold by J. Roberts, Warwick-Lane, MDCCXXIX [1729]). The following ornaments from Richardson's press according to Maslen's catalogue are as follows: Title page, R306; Advertisement, R162=R137, R493; Dedication, R062, R459; Sig. B, p. 1, R062, R488; Sig. B2 v., p. 4, R141, R488; Sig. E4 v. p. 32, R283; Sig. F, p. 33, R032; Sig. G v., p. 42, R272; and Sig. G2, p. 43, R046 (R332 inset), R449. Yet another book about reforming the system of debtors' prison recently discovered and found to be printed by Richardson is the following: *An Oration on the Oppression of Jailors: which was spoken in the Fleet Prison, on the 20th of February 1730/1 (as advertised in the Daily-Post of that day) and carefully taken in short-hand by one of the audience, who hopes he shall not incur the displeasure of the orator in publishing a thing so manifestly tending to the good of the publick*. (London: Printed for A. Moore, near St. Pa'uls [sic]; and sold at the pamphlet-shops in

London and Westminster, [1731]). Alvan Bregman, curator, discovered this unique copy (not in ESTC) in the University of Illinois Library stacks. It has the Richardson ornaments according to Maslen's catalogue: Sig. A2, p. 3, R243, R468; and Sig. C3, v., p. 22, R383.
23. *Familiar Letters,* 153–54.
24. *The Case of the Unfortunate,* 17.
25. *Grandison,* 5:45.
26. No matter how comical Mrs. O-Hara may seem in converting to Methodism, the mere fact that she becomes serious about religion is meritorious:

> I am sorry that our own Clergy are not as zealously in earnest as they. They have really, my dear, if we may believe aunt Eleanor, given a face of religion to subterranean colliers, tinners, and the most profligate of men, who hardly ever before heard either of the word, or thing. But I am not turning Methodist, Harriet. No! you will not suspect me. (*Grandison,* 6:32)

27. *Grandison,* 5:183.
28. "He [Richardson] evidently favoured the act permitting persons professing the Jewish religion to be naturalized by Parliament and deplored 'the foolish, the absurd Cry' against it; but he thought the Jews themselves would be well advised to ask for its repeal, since they got little by it and it excited popular prejudice against them 'in a Country which they honour for the Liberty of Conscience and the Safety of Property given them in it'" (T.C. Duncan Eaves and Ben D. Kimpel, *Samuel Richardson, A Biography* [Oxford: Clarendon Press, 1971], 549).
29. P. 29, lines 1–18; and p. 31, lines 32–36. I have already argued that this dedication was probably written by Richardson (Dussinger, "Stealing in the Great Doctrines of Christianity," 500–502).
30. Maslen, *Samuel Richardson of London, Printer,* 887–88.
31. P. 29, lines 1–18.
32. The omitted passage is as follows: "And therefore no Man, as it seems to me, has a better Title to the Prescription of Dr. *Willis's Wonderful Cap,* than the Letter-writer and his Abettors," p. 31, lines 32–36.
33. Sale, *Samuel Richardson,* 33.

Chapter Three

Henry Fielding Straddles a Moving Theme

Regina Janes

D—n me, if I don't honour you for [stealing 40 guineas from your Oxford roommate's escritoire]; for, as I hope for Salvation, I would have made no manner of Scruple of doing the same Thing.

—Watson to the Man of the Hill, encountering him in London, *Tom Jones*, VIII.xii.463 [1]

Then let us love, dear love, like as we ought,
Love is the lesson which the Lord us taught.

—Edmund Spenser, *Amoretti* #68 [2]

Surely too much has already been said about Henry Fielding and religion. Certainly there is no argument to be made that religion and Fielding are undiscovered country. Martin Battestin has long insisted that Fielding's views are indistinguishable from those of any Low Church latitudinarian. To understand Fielding, we need only pick up our Barrow, Clarke, and Tillotson, our South and Hoadly, as Fielding intermittently did.[3] Blakey Vermeule closes down a discussion of *Tom Jones* by citing Fielding's situation as a Christian in a Christian culture troubled by the problem of evil, much as certain readers "solve" Gulliver's fourth trip by reference to Swift's profession and the doctrine of original sin.[4] At best, Simon Dickie calls the status of Fielding's beliefs "a minefield," wherein Fielding scholars have long been inclined to blow each other up. Melvyn New claims Aubrey Williams never again spoke civilly to him after Williams read New's "Grease of God."[5] Claude Rawson charges Battestin with laboring for years to make the novels dull, and Battestin ripostes that Rawson put Ronald Paulson up to writing a life that goes wrong whenever it veers from Ruthe Battestin's researches.[6] Cannily skirting questions of "belief," J.H. Plumb observes that Fielding's *"morality* [emphasis added] was conventionally Christian, his philosophy sincerely stoic."[7] Rawson may complain that such practices make Fielding a dull boy, and Paulson may long for Fielding's deist youth, but Fielding certainly colludes with his moral critics.

Joseph Andrews is a brief course in Bible study, from the story of Joseph and Potiphar's wife in Genesis to the parable of the Good Samaritan in Luke. Battestin reports that at Eton students memorized the New Testament and insists the theme of *Joseph Andrews* is charity, St. Paul's great theme in Corinthians.[8] *Tom Jones* hammers away at the Methodists, and their preference for faith and grace over good works and benevolence. *Amelia* brings about its worthless hero's reform by his careful reading, in stir, of Isaac Barrow's sermons (XII.v.511).[9] Capt. Hercules Vinegar in *The Champion* holds out for the immortality of the soul and savages corrupt clergymen, while the magisterial author of *The Covent-Garden Journal* attributes all social evils to the decline of religion, waxing eloquent on the divinity of Christ (nos. 29, 39, 44) and affirming St. Paul to be wittier than Petronius (no. 18).[10] As magistrate, Fielding published a little work on interpositions of Providence in cases of murder that his biographer calls more like Defoe than the "enlightened author of *Tom Jones*,"[11] yet the author of *Tom Jones* assures us that "Providence often interposes in the Discovery of the most secret Villainy, in order to caution Men" (XVIII.iii.920). Revising *Jonathan Wild* (1754), Fielding disambiguates his asterisks (see below). Paired in posthumous publication with the *Journal of a Voyage to Lisbon*, his final defense of revealed religion, *A Fragment of a Comment on L. Bolingbroke's Essays* (1755), replies to that skeptical scalawag Lord Bolingbroke.

Religion the social institution is more conspicuous in Fielding than in any other great comic artist since Chaucer.[12] But this does not make him boring, whatever it does to his critics. Leaving behind the doctrinal disputes of Catholics, Anglicans, and Dissenters that animated Dryden and Swift, Fielding obtruded the classical to ballast the Christian, and struggled with the secularizing idea more than did Defoe, Richardson, or Haywood in a period marked by covert latitudinarian hegemony, enthusiastic revivals, and advancing skepticism (Hoadly, Wesley, and Hume). As Melvyn New argued in "'The Grease of God': The Form of Eighteenth-Century Fiction," the energy of the eighteenth-century novel is its in-betweenness, imbricating the sacred and the secular, affirming the existence, if not the workings, of Providence in a world where only psychology and second causes are visible.[13] For Fielding, religion animates social justice in the period before reform politics became available to perform that function. Within the dialectic of secularization, his religion criticizes the religious. Defining a precarious, enlightened space between the enthusiasts of the seventeenth century and the reforming evangelicals of the late eighteenth, Fielding tangles with both Methodists and deists, affined with and resisting each. This essay re-presents Fielding's religious positions as an integral part of the social panorama Fielding introduces to the English novel, marks his microscopic move toward the evangelicals in his revisions of *Jonathan Wild*, and unveils the scandalous religious allegory of *Tom Jones* in which Allworthy plays the stern Father to Tom's more merciful Son. The impudence of the allegory Fielding insinuates—yet would never confess to—would offend the pious, were it not so outrageous as to be invisible to them, and strike the secular as silly, pointless, or otiose, if they noticed it. The subliminal effect of Fielding's biblical echoes may, however, account for some of the rage Fielding provoked in his contemporary moralists.

Swift's great works provide no overt clues that their author was a clergyman, and barely that he was a Christian (only Gulliver's quarrels with the Dutch in Book III make Christianity explicit, and sympathy lies with the Catholics' trampled crucifix, not the dean's fellow Protestants). Neither cleric nor dean, Fielding is far less circumspect. Religious references percolate through the writings, which are as ostentatious in Christian sympathies as derelict in Pauline prudery or Richardsonian piety or Wesleyan grace. If Fielding studies are divided between those who affirm cheerfully, with Treadwell Ruml II, that Fielding is his own "comical but good-hearted parson" and those who scoff with Paulson at the manifest absurdity of mistaking Fielding "for an Anglican divine," no one denies that Fielding knew his Bible and grew more insistently "orthodox" (for Fielding a pejorative term) as he edged into his forties and magistracy.[14] Whatever the chops and changes of his personal views, he certainly illustrates Bina Gogineni's thesis about the development of the early novel—that it is not secular, but imbued with the immanence of divinity, whether in England or in India.[15] A deistic or secular or "enlightened" Fielding might feel more congenial to the modern reader, but he is not on offer except in re-constructions freed from the tyranny of the author.

Yet Fielding also collaborates with those who would resist stamping IHS across his forehead and filing him under "snug Anglican," after his other labels: "conservative, aristocratic, Augustan," and more currently, "gender-obsessed." To Richardson's friends, Fielding might seem just such a parson as Thomas Rowlandson's *Man of Feeling*, slobbering, his fat paw up the country maid's skirts or in her bosom. Fielding's sympathy with the body and impatience with piety, his guilt-free moralizing and hearty desires, fit no conventional expectations. So Paul Kelleher hopes that male sexuality is Fielding's "source, perhaps the source, of moral judgment and ethical conduct. . . . [I]t is sexual passion that infuses law with spirit and duty with blood."[16] Certainly Fielding imbues his own created characters with the moral and sexual passion earlier religious writers addressed to the persons of God; reuniting sexual and moral energy seems to have been one dazzling project of the early novel. He does not make Butler's and Swift's corrosive jokes about the identity of religious and sexual passion. Rather, he surreptitiously, and inversely, enacts them, sexual passion taking on religious value. So, too, Fielding's classicism seems to challenge religiosity, and he sets literature and religion by the ears in *Jonathan Wild*, better to save both.[17] Fielding straddles, one foot staunchly humanist, the other determinedly Christian.

Religion remains for Fielding what politics has become for us, a scrim through which the world is viewed, an ideological system that enables and limits change, a terrain suffused with the profoundest moral values, with what matters most of all, at the heart's core. Religion (again, like politics) is not a "traditional peace-keeping institution [being displaced] in the modern world,"[18] but a contested space, where evil and good cling and tussle. A Christian in a Christian culture, Fielding finds that by Christian standards his culture is unchristian, with those making the most Christian noises the least Christian in practice. Implicated in "human nature" and institutions, the church and belief are actors, not static figments from the idealized past, when all the great were good.

An integral part of the social landscape that Fielding critiques, religion is as much an object of criticism as a source of value, at once satirized and the source of the frustrated values that motivate the satire. Within that landscape, Fielding's religious positions are so minimalist as to approach deism (a charge persistently leveled against latitudinarian divines), but he obsessively rejects the deist posture as emotionally arid and motivationally defective. Though her logic tempts him, the embrace of skeletal abstraction does not satisfy. Deism demands no action in the world. Although he participated in the transformation of secular institutions as magistrate, Fielding does not imagine institutions as positive sources of social transformation. For him, politics was anti-Jacobite and patronage-seeking, not a rich source of human hope.[19] Conceptually, religion is the only hope; practically, a weak reed.

Mortally deficient in piety, Fielding adheres to religion pragmatically, as a motive for morality via rewards and punishments; ethically, as the source of the highest morality he knows; and hopefully, for its promise of "eternal happiness" (Fielding's preferred phrasing for immortality elides Hell). A protestant of Protestants, his religion is "sola scriptura," but Fielding's scriptures lack miracles, resurrections, voices from on high, garden agonies and passion imagery, doctrines, the learned lumber of *credenda* ("matters of faith," things to be believed, which are not, he points out, to be found in Scripture anyway[20]), all save moral injunctions to love, charity, forgiveness. The one thing needful is the Sermon on the Mount, a "short System of Morality, which is alone a sufficient Proof of the Divine Mission of its

Author" (*Champion*, December 25, 1739, 85). Exceeding the ancients in love, charity, and forgiveness, Christianity's ethics demonstrate that Christianity is not as "old as the Creation" (*Champion*, March 27, 1740, 254), but a new and essential moral revelation.[21]

The closest Fielding approaches a personal Jesus is to observe of the "blessed Person . . . *Jesus* Christ . . . the most perfect Pattern" of good nature, "that he never was once seen to laugh, during his whole Abode on Earth."[22] The Savior's "dying for the Sins of Mankind" may appear more than once in Fielding's oeuvre, but examples are hard to find.[23] The Virgin Birth transmutes to "cho[osing] to be born of the Wife of a Carpenter," so as to supply a "Pattern" of humility (*Champion*, March 29, 1740, 260). In sum, Fielding jettisons Christian narrative mythology (though he adapts its patterns within his own narratives). When Jesus appears, he is either saying something about how people should behave, "*Jesus* says . . .",[24] or a lady is swearing "J—sus" on hearing there is a naked man in a ditch (*Joseph Andrews* [I.xii.52]), or Fanny is falling back in her chair as she cries, "O Jesus" (II.xii.154).[25] By way of contrast, Dryden hymns the Paraclete, and Isaac Watts and Charles Wesley fill their dissenting songs with Jesus's name.[26] The sacraments fare no better, reduced to a form of oath-taking, when Sophia volunteers to "receive the Sacrament" on a vow never to see Tom Jones's face again (XVII.iv.889), or a curse, when Thwackum sends Allworthy to Hell for neglecting him and the sacraments on his deathbed (V.viii.247–48).

Besides his hankering after immortality, Fielding has a passion for the Christian "*Agenda*, or matters of morality," things to be done, which he contrasts with moribund "*Credenda*" (*Champion*, December 25, 1739, 85). Neither orthodox nor doctrinal, his strong positions—those for which he exerts himself to make an argument—combine immortality and morality, and few now disagree with them. Like Locke and Dryden, Fielding is rarely credited with having thrust current commonplaces into the stream of discourse. That all sincere believers, from Turks to Quakers, will be saved;[27] that we will be reunited with loved ones after death;[28] that good works matter more than professions or doctrine; that active, practical generosity separates the good from the self-satisfied and self-absorbed; even that benevolence proceeds from [good]-nature (a premise in evolutionary psychology and primatology): such unexceptionable views are as difficult to applaud as the sun's rising. (It is dark in their absence, as when Buddhist statues are blown up or homosexuals murdered to verses from Leviticus and St. Paul.) Most of Fielding's arguments had recently been versified in the *Essay on Man*, that compendium of commonplaces that set commonplaces in place by fixing them in memory. Nothing is truer—or carries further—than a right rhyme.[29]

In this religion of absences, Fielding situates himself between Square and Thwackum, but with more sympathy for the fornicating philosopher than the self-righteous cleric. Hostile to the pious, whether Methodists or mere prudes or, worst of all, venal, selfish clerics, Fielding never lets a novel go by without converting a deist.[30] Mr. Wilson in *Joseph Andrews* is commonly taken to be a self-portrait of misspent deist youth. Thomas Square's deathbed conversion in *Tom Jones* corresponds to Paulson's suspicion that Fielding's encounters with death in the 1740s (daughter, father, wife) motivated his newly affirming Christianity as a better way to face death, whether one's own or others'.[31] One page of the Gospel, says Square, teaches how to die better than any philosopher and turns death from a dread accepted into a promised good (XVIII.iv.925). In *Amelia,* Billy Booth is helped from passivity relative to his own passions to active choices by Isaac Barrow, his morals amended. Telling a tale of two deists wherein one (Benjamin Franklin) attempts to seduce another's mistress, and the other (James Ralph) takes leave without paying a debt, the Battestins sneer that such are "the friendships of deists."[32] Confirming the Battestins' suspicions, eloping with another man's wife is indeed Mr. Wilson's first clue that his deist friends violate their own Golden Rule of virtue. Yet Thwackum beats on, while Square is capable of a change of heart. Man for man, more Christians commit fornication, adultery, or theft than such lonely deists as Square (Tom Jones, Mr. Fitzpatrick, Mrs. Fitzpatrick's Irish peer, the Man of the Hill, Enderson, Billy Booth, Col. James, et al.). Since Fielding represents no female deists, fornication implicates only daughters of the church (most notably Bridget Allworthy and her pious partners).

Fielding's religion also lacks misery. He seems to have found faith a source of happiness and consolation. No one is ever made depressed, anxious, miserable, or guilty by Christian beliefs or expectations. The Ordinary in *Jonathan Wild* threatens his charges with eternal torments and definitions of "EVERLASTING FIRE" and "the DEVIL AND HIS ANGELS," but Jonathan eludes the sermon with sleep and, later, punch (IV.xiv.178–79). Those who are indeed terrified by the prospect of damnation—felons hanged at Newgate in Fielding's *Journey from This World to the Next*—are pleasantly surprised by being whisked into Heaven, their sins paid in full. A function of the temperament Lady Mary Wortley Montagu praised for enjoying life even in adversity, Fielding's world knows no "castaways" like Cowper's, no fear of death like Johnson's, not even the superstitious anxiety about communion that Bishop Hoadly wrote against (though Sophia's vow suggests superstition).[33] If Fielding rails against Methodists, it is not for their preaching to the poor (he approves of that), nor for their terrorizing the poor with fear of hellfire (a complaint others made of the "poison" of Methodism[34] and condemned in *Jonathan Wild*, but not otherwise alleged against Methodism by Fielding), but for their preference of grace and faith over good works. When Methodism matches works to faith, Fielding applauds by connecting it to a critical plot point that I will discuss in due course. So conducive to happiness is Christian faith that the conviction of their righteousness before

God is one of the chief supports and satisfactions of Fielding's most hypocritical villains, from Blifil *père et fils* in *Tom Jones* to the aspiring young cleric in *Amelia*. As to eternal damnation for the sins of a finite life, that doctrine is handed off to such eminent divines as the Newgate Ordinary and Thwackum. Fielding dislikes the doctrine and evades it as thoroughly as he can, without denying it outright.[35] Like Hercules Vinegar's club, he likes to keep it hanging on the wall, to point to.

As a practical matter, religion sustains and criticizes the social order. It keeps the poor from objecting to the injustice the world so freely offers, while it condemns those who do not alleviate their condition. By the "Laws of Nature," men who refuse charity to those in want are "ROGUES AND ROBBERS OF THE PUBLIC," but a Christian void of charity "is in honest Truth, an Infidel, a Rogue, and a Monster, and ought to be expelled not only from the Society of Christians, but of Men."[36] Such expulsions are rare to the vanishing point. When Fielding argues for the utility of religion, his terms are the same as Hobbes's: it makes men "obedient to government and peaceable to one another."[37] Unlike Hobbes, however, Fielding is concerned for the morals of the poor, and understands, correctly as it happens, that religion can motivate self-transformation when other incentives fail. He anticipates Hannah More and the anti-Jacobins in his *Proposal for Making an Effectual Provision for the Poor, for Amending Their Morals, and for Rendering Them Useful Members of the Society* (1753). As Marx devoutly hoped and even Robespierre feared, denying afterlife rewards and punishments invites social revolution: "Could the Poor become once unanimously persuaded [that the Place which the Rich have allotted them was a mere Utopia and an Estate, according to the usual Sense of the Phrase, *in Nubibus* (in the clouds) only!], what should hinder them from an Attempt in which the Superiority of their Numbers might give them some Hopes of Success; and when they have nothing real to risque in either World in the Trial?"[38] Justice for the poor in the next world relieves Fielding, as well as the poor, from insisting on it in this, but does not prevent them, he points out, from starving in this one throughout the metropolis. So he proposes, explicitly and ineptly imitating Swift's *Modest Proposal*, reinstituting human sacrifice: the poor would be better off dead.

Acutely aware of injustice in the world's distribution of power and wealth, Fielding proposes no social transformations, revolutions, or alterations in the order of his corrupt and unjust world (apart from restoring human sacrifice). Voluntary charity on epicurean principles is prudent for Christians, yet much current public charity is misdirected or obstructed, and requires institutional reform. Beggars are rogues who do not deserve alms, and the foundling and lying-in hospitals demonstrate the sublime heights to which charity currently reaches.[39] Christianity serves a conservative as well as critical function, supporting existing hierarchies and distributions of wealth and power, as well as the order that permits those who possess to enjoy in peace. In sum, although his tone darkens significantly in the *Covent-Garden Journal*, Fielding's Christianity lets him do as he likes, threatens no guilt or shame or mystery, rewards what he most values—benevolence—and promises to make up for the only desideratum deplorably absent from this delightful, amusing, delicious, amorous world: justice.

Turning to the way religion works in Fielding's fictions reveals an active presence rather than a pudding stocked with lumps of sentimental benevolence. When he revised *Jonathan Wild* in 1754, as magistrate, Fielding took a firmer line on God's behalf. In *Tom Jones* an ideal "Religion" is affirmed, embodied in persons and allegorized, covertly, blasphemously, unmistakably, as Old Testament/New Testament in Allworthy and his adoptive son Tom Jones. Such true religion in Fielding is contested not only by the hostility of deists, the indifference of the polite, the venality of the clergy, and the ignorance of the poor, but also by the co-optation of its name and terms for irreligious uses inseparable from a "Christian culture."

Challenging Addison's assertion that faith strengthens morality, the Man of the Hill is a devout Christian who lives a solitary life to which morality is irrelevant.[40] Although he sounds at moments like a deist, he is actually a Christian, whose view of mankind represents Swift's (or Augustine's). Tom answers him not with a religious argument, but an individualist one (the species should be evaluated by its best examples, not the worst or even the average). Then, untheorized, Fielding shows us what is amiss when Mrs. Waters screams, and the Man of the Hill sits still. His sincere faith contributes nothing to moral action, while Tom sets off to make a difference in his world. Articulated, religion does nothing; unarticulated, it acts for social good—and leads directly to Mrs. Waters.

So, too, the Man of the Hill's deceitful friend, Mr. Watson, brims with the verbal faith of a Christian culture. Applauding his friend's theft, a violation of one of the Ten Commandments, Watson invokes his "hope for Salvation . . . D—n me."[41] Characteristically, religion appears in Fielding's fictions in unsavory guise.

In *Jonathan Wild* (1743) Heaven and divines appear early and signify dismally. Wild's ancestor James shifts sides in the civil wars according as "Heaven seemed to declare itself in Favour of either Party," reducing "Heaven" to the fortunes of war or chance or strategy or claim of divine sanction (I.ii.11). Wild's uncle enjoys "a strict Friendship with an eminent Divine, who solicited the spiritual Causes of the said [distressed] Captives [in Newgate]," viz., the Ordinary (I.ii.12). Wild enters the church "baptized by the famous Mr. *Titus Oates*" (I.iii.14). Convocation is likened to a sitting of card sharps. Gamblers hearing the accusation "pickpocket" express the same horror as "the *Conv—n* (whose not sitting of late is much lamented) would express at hearing there was an *Atheist* in the Room" (I.xiii.42). Gamblers:

pickpocket :: convocation: atheist: that is a challenging simile to unpack. Do atheists frequent Convocation as pickpockets the company of gamblers? Is Convocation's horror at atheists merely a horror of having its pocket picked, on Dryden's principle that "the fleece accompanies the flock"? ("The Duty of a Shepherd is not fleecing only," *Champion*, April 19, 1740, 286.) Unlike the gamblers, Convocation has not sat lately. Are those who lament Convocation's not sitting the pickpockets—who want the gamblers' goods—or the gamblers, who want more play? At the very least, the simile places Convocation in a contested situation, between silent, powerful politicians and loud, powerless lamenters.

The religious satire in *Jonathan Wild* is institutional and anticlerical, embodied in the contemptible Ordinary. Marking his shift toward social action a decade later, Fielding will propose that an Ordinary is more needed at Bridewell than at Newgate. Better to reform the morals of those to be released back into the world, than of those soon to be released from it.[42] In 1743, as in 1754, Fielding's Ordinary proves as incompetent to interpret Scripture as to comfort the dying, but in 1754, Wild defends God from the Ordinary, while Fielding continues defending the classics from the cleric. "[T]ruly orthodox," the Ordinary rages against Heartfree's assertion that a sincere Turk might be saved. With "becoming Zeal and Indignation" he damns all who hold such views, and *"so far from a sincere Turk's being within the Pale of Salvation, neither will any sincere Presbyterian, Anabaptist, nor Quaker whatever, be saved"* (IV.i.136). The Ordinary re-enters for a star turn to help Wild face execution (IV.xiv.178–85).

Embodying every objection to the Georgian church, the Ordinary is at once too like an ordinary gentleman (politely greeting a doomed man, "GOOD Morrow. . . . I hope you rested well last Night" [178]) and too like an insufferable pedant explaining what least needs explanation, dividing his discourse, while denying the comforts of religion. Having destined Wild and his audience to *"everlasting Fire, prepared for the Devil and his Angels,"* he sets out to explain "what is meant by EVERLASTING FIRE" and "Secondly, Who were THE DEVIL AND HIS ANGELS," among which angels he sets his interlocutor Wild (178–79). Once the Ordinary praises the unspeakable joys of Heaven (and miseries of Hell) in terms that could come straight from Barrow or Sherlock, Watt or Burnet, the text devolves into Swiftian typographical collapse. Key words and phrases indict the clergy in the terms of the *Champion*'s argument that the clergy, those best informed about God's intentions, should least indulge themselves in vicious and ambitious practices (March 29, 1740, 256–60; April 5, 1740, 266–71; April 12, 1740, 271–78; April 19, 1740, 283–86).

In 1743, Fielding's key words stand out on the page; in 1754, he enables his reader to fill in the blanks in Jonathan's reply to the Ordinary. The reader of 1743 faces this page:

Jonathan
* * * * * * * * * * * * * * * If once convinced
* * * * * * * * * * * no Man * * * * * * *
* * lives of * * * * * * * * whereas sure the Clergy * *
* * * * * * Opportunity * * * * * * better informed
* * * * * * * * * * * all Manner of Vice * * * * *
* * * * *
Ordinary
*are * * Atheist. * * * Deist * * * * *Ari* * * * * * *cinian*
* * hanged * * burnt *roiled * oasted. * * * * * * * *
Dev * * * his An * * * * * * *ell Fire * * * * * ternal
Da * * tion
Jonathan
YOU * * * * to frighten me out of my Wits: But his * * * is, I Doubt not, more merciful than his * * * If I should believe all you say, I am sure I should die in inexpressible Horrour. (IV.xiv.180–81)

Fielding's *Champion* essays suggest words for the asterisks, so that Wild may say, "clergy [have the] Opportunity [to be] better informed [but they are guilty of] all Manner of Vice." Determining whether the Ordinary rages against vicious clergymen or those who call clergymen vicious, Fielding leaves to the reader's discretion.

In 1754 Fielding reclaims God from his ministers. The criminal has a juster sense of religion than the cleric, as Fielding made transparent his more opaque 1743 text. The number of asterisks is reduced across these passages. More pointedly, Fielding adds words. So Jonathan now replies to the Ordinary (italics added to new words), "You * * * [try] to frighten me out of my Wits. But *the good* * * is, I Doubt not, more merciful than his *wicked* * *." The two evenly balanced "his * * *" become the sharply antithetical "the good [G-d] " and "his wicked [servant, clergy, pastor, minister]."[43] Fielding disliked such ministers and reported their sayings wrapped in increasingly strident disapprobation.

In a final fillip—while Wild and the Ordinary await the punch for celebrating Wild's saved soul—the Ordinary inadvertently inverts Erasmus's *Encomium Moriae*, putting Greek philosophy in the place of the cross as "foolishness." In 1 Corinthians Paul embraces the cross and "Christ crucified," which is "to the Greeks foolishness" (1 Corinthians 1:23). The Ordinary takes "*the* Greeks FOOLISHNESS" to refer to Plato's and Aristotle's philosophy, i.e., the Greeks' FOOLISHNESS. This may be the moment Fielding comes closest to the cross (Square converting recurs to the same passage). Very much aware of the cross, he veils it. Plato and Aristotle, with precepts "neither borrowed from Nature, nor guided by Reason; Mere *Fictions,* serv[e] only to evince the dreadful Height of human Pride; in one Word FOOLISHNESS. It may be, perhaps, expected of me, that I should give some Instances from their Works to prove this Charge; but as to transcribe every Passage to my Purpose, would be to transcribe their whole Works [these phrases echo through eighteenth-century controversy], and as in such a plentiful Crop it is difficult to chuse; instead of trespassing on your Patience, I shall conclude this first Head with asserting what I have so fully proved; and what may indeed be inferred from the Text, That the Philosophy of the *Greeks* was FOOLISHNESS."[44] As foolishness Paul defended the cross, so as foolishness Fielding defends Greek philosophy. Yet his Ordinary, who earlier wished for the eloquence of "Cicero and Tully" (like "John and Kennedy" or "Barack and Obama") has it right. It may indeed "be inferred from the text" that Greek wisdom is foolish, since Greek wisdom persuades Greeks that the cross is foolish. Rather than endorsing that inference, Fielding substitutes objects, identifying Christian and Greek, the cross and philosophy, and seeks in effect to reclaim both from the Ordinary's dismissal.[45]

In *Tom Jones*, Fielding moves well beyond but does not abandon the anti-institutional and anticlerical positions of his earlier works—Thwackum embodies the anticlerical satire; as thwackum thwacks 'em, so Fielding thwacks 'em in thwackum. Religion, with its shared beliefs about an invisible world, has been historically the principal means by which people affirm social bonds and group integration, promote and strengthen morality, and account for death and being-in-the-world. Fielding knows and recognizes that, but he also shows religion's failure to produce the desired ends, just as our innate morality fails to achieve the ends proposed for it.

Fielding represents aspirational morality in the novel with an allegory of religion at the apex, in Allworthy and Tom. Battestin's casting the novel's moral dilemmas as Tom's learning prudence and acquiring Sophia (wisdom) has obscured Fielding's slyly wicked allegory, in which Allworthy is the flawed Old Testament Father to Tom's more perfect New Testament Son. That Tom is an adoptive son, conceived out of wedlock, gives the allegory a naughty and Socinian twist. (When Fielding speaks of the Virgin, he turns her into a "Wife," and he knows his Socinianism well enough to make it part of the Ordinary's curse.[46]) The pattern resembles that which Paulson has located in the iconography of Hogarth's *Harlot's Progress*.[47] It is amplified by forgiveness that includes even the devil, and a providence that works only by second causes.

Fielding also equalizes Tom and Sophia as angels of charity and love, respectively, and here he moves toward displacing the love of God with the love of a good woman. When Spenser invites his wife-to-be to love, he inserts her and himself into the love of God. Fielding fits "the biblical story into another world with another story," so that "biblical history [provides] a Christian meaning for events in the secular world."[48] Wrapped in courtly-love rhetoric, Sophia becomes an object in herself, rather than a means to a greater object. No proto–D.H. Lawrence, Fielding has been rightly read as more sympathetic to the body's passions than most canonical authors (Ian

McEwan's *Atonement* and the 1963 film *Tom Jones* make love-in-the-body Fielding's great argument). Neither God nor Love is among the themes discussed in Battestin's *Companion*.

Finally, there is the "Religion" that emerges in the pages of the novel, rarely resembling anything one would wish to see flourish. Fielding's dedication promises only that "nothing prejudicial to the Cause of Religion" (and Virtue, as if they are not quite the same) will be found in his pages, and not that religion, unlike "Goodness and Innocence," will find its interests promoted ("Dedication," 7). So, too, while Virtue's "naked Charms" are alluring, "Religion" enjoys no comparable puff. That is as it should be, for Fielding's protean "Religion" often assumes monstrous shapes.

In the introductory chapter, neither innkeeper nor guest finds any religious condiments, neither pepper nor salt; the appetitive world in which *Tom Jones* begins is entirely secular, and the narrator's introductory chapters rarely mention religion. When it obtrudes on the reader's notice, in capital letters in the second chapter, Allworthy's "Religion" is faulted by his pious neighbors, who know that Heaven is for higher goals than reunions with dead wives (I.ii.35). As to the Christian religion, the baby in Allworthy's bed lacks the odor of sanctity, according to Deborah Wilkins: "Faugh, how it stinks! It doth not smell like a Christian" (I.iii.41). "Religion" and "Christian" enter to define in-groups, reaffirm social bonds, and exclude designated others. These are positive enough objectives, but Fielding associates them with common-garden malevolence, sneering superiority, and the rejection of the helpless. Promoted are uncharitable, unloving, cruel ends: eternal separation from loved ones in favor of God alone, exposure of unwanted infants in baskets on nights that are neither too dark nor stormy (cf. I.v.46, where charity to base-born infants is condemned as "irreligious"). Sunday is a day reserved for shining forth to all the parish in a new gown (I.vi.49); "Church" is a place for appearing "with bare Necks" (I.viii.57), to Miss Bridget's horror; and "Curates" are for being married to learned girls and given a small living (I.vi.50). Religion, its places, persons, and times are part of the world that is, and very far from what even that world thinks ought to be.

Allworthy may have "spent some Minutes on his Knees, a Custom which he never broke through on any Account" before he opened the bedclothes to find the baby, but what he did on his knees is not explained (I.iii.38–39). In his landscape "an old ruined Abbey, grown over with Ivy" makes a pleasant prospect and never another appearance, as Allworthy mulls how to make himself "most acceptable to his Creator, by doing most Good to his Creatures" (I.iv.43). Evoking the decline of an age of faith, the ruined abbey nostalgically ornaments the modern world in which action ("doing . . . Good") has replaced meditation, and a distant "Creator" has replaced Christianity's transcendent and personal divinity. Allworthy lives in an old-fashioned *"Gothick"* house (I.iv.42), but doing Good and recognizing a Creator belong as much to the deist as to the theologian, and arguably more.

When "our Religion" makes its second appearance, the context is once again punitive, censorious, and against loving: Allworthy's sermon against fornication to Jenny Jones. Anticipating his later flawed readings of the law (allowing Partridge's wife to testify against him, committing pregnant Molly to Bridewell, turning Tom Jones out without letting him know the evidence against him and, Fielding notes, for a personal offence against himself), Allworthy attributes to Jesus in the biblical text statements he does not make. Jenny is advised that her violated chastity is an offence to "every Christian, inasmuch as it is committed in Defiance of the Laws of our Religion, and of the express Commands of him who founded that Religion" (I.vii. 51). If the founder of Christianity is Jesus, not Paul or Moses (who does have some words against fornication in the fields), nowhere does Jesus prohibit fornication or enjoin premarital chastity.[49] ("Go look," as Tristram says.) Like homosexuality, fornication is condemned by Paul and in Revelation. As narrator, Fielding marks the distinction with lawyerly precision. Not the founder but the "Religion" delivers such "express Commands." When Mrs. Waters and Tom approach the inn at Upton, the narrator affirms that they had in view "Purposes . . . as expressly forbidden as Murder, or any other horrid Vice, by that Religion which is universally believed in those Countries" (IX.iii.500). The narrator gets it right; Allworthy does not.

Yet religion is not always wrong. Mrs. Bridget, it will be remembered, affects divinity and enjoys religious controversies: "she had read much *English* Divinity, and had puzzled more than one of the neighbouring Curates" (I.x.62). This passion underwrites her attraction to Captain Blifil and leads directly to pregnancy, marriage, and hatred, with love recovered on a tombstone. The Blifil brothers are introduced carefully under the "Appearance of Religion" (I.x.61), and Fielding for the first time separates the true (Religion) from the false (Appearance), though he lacks the "Touch-stone" to make a final determination (the appearance of piety Fielding takes as a sign of hypocrisy, yet the absence of appearance is often genuine indifference). Nor has Fielding forgotten Mrs. Bridget's skill in controversy. When Square and Thwackum disagree over Tom's perfidy in selling Blifil his Bible to support Black George, Mrs. Bridget exonerates Tom, finding "her own Son" equally guilty, "for that she could see no Difference between the Buyer and the Seller; both of whom were alike to be driven out of the Temple" (III.ix.145). In the only distinctive sentence ever heard from Bridget Allworthy, she instructs us that biblical citations may be used to read the fiction and the behavior of its actors.

"Religion" continues to roll from that true "Religion" to be distinguished from "Appearance" through multiple avatars. No religion, the narrator affirms, is as "firmly believed . . . at present" as the ancients' mythology once was (XVII.i.876). Allworthy will forgive Blifil only insofar as his religion obliges him to (XVIII.xi.967). Partridge has a religion in which truth plays no part (XVIII.v.935), and charity stays at home, away from the wars to defend religion and liberty (it is not Christian to shed blood, says Partridge [XII.iii.631]). Partridge's religion also keeps its hands in its pockets when a beggar solicits. So Tom tells Partridge, and the rest of us, "Your Religion . . . serves you only for an Excuse for your Faults, but is no Incentive to your Virtue. Can any Man who is really a Christian abstain from relieving one of his Brethren in such a miserable Condition?" (XII.iv.631). That question, hanging in the air for several hundred years, leaves "really" still looking about it for a definition.

As to the "Religious, or rather Moral Writers, who teach that Virtue is the certain Road to Happiness, and Vice to Misery in this World," the narrator tells them their doctrine is "not true" and denies it "to be Christian" (XV.i.783, 784; Fielding is sharper than Oscar Wilde, who confines the issue to literature: "The good ended happily, and the bad unhappily. That is what Fiction means"[50]). Even Methodism has something good to be said for it. When her landlady turns Methodist, Lady Bellaston loses her pied-à-terre and is forced to meet Tom in her own house, so enabling him to find Sophia. There is an edge: the sort of landlady who turns Methodist is the sort who kept a house used for ill purposes, but at least she backs up her conversion with action (XIII. ix.726). So too Allworthy tells Tom he needs "Prudence and Religion" (V.vii.244), and Tom certainly learns prudence by suffering the consequences of his imprudence (terror of incest, the Bellaston letter's effect on Sophia, the horror he feels when he believes he has killed Fitzpatrick—an episode that treats dueling for honor's sake far more rigorously than Richardson does). But we never see Tom learning "Religion," and indeed Tom instructs Allworthy in the higher religious morality of the New Testament.

At the end of the novel, Fielding plays very deliberately with Allworthy's status as God and not God. So the narrator describes Allworthy as having "the utmost Sweetness and Benevolence in his Smiles [and] great Terrour in his Frowns" (XVII.vii.899). Mrs. Waters alleges Allworthy's goodness has "more of the divine than human Nature" (XVIII.viii.947), and Dowling observes his "Promises of Forgiveness, joined to the Threats, the Voice, the Looks" (XVIII.viii.950). Yet these appearances are qualified by the emphasis on Allworthy's mistreatment of Partridge and his ignorance of the hardship he inflicted on him: "I thought you had left the Country; nay, I thought you had been long since dead" (XVIII.vi.935–36).

Allworthy also echoes those moral (but not religious) writers with whom Fielding disagrees (XV.i.783–84), when he insists on the self-punishment of the vicious: "Villainy . . . is irretrievable," the villain abashed, pursued by shame and guilt, horror and despair (XVIII, x.960). That picture suits Blifil's immediate response to discovery, but from "irretrievable despair" he is long happily recovered at novel's end. It better describes Tom's own feelings when he fears he has killed Fitzpatrick and learns he has been to bed with his own mother. Mrs. Barbauld and others have long objected that Allworthy, wise and good as he seems intended to be, is something of a dupe, frequently erring and often misled. That inadequacy has a source in conventional Christian apologetics.

With Allworthy, Fielding has in mind the Old Testament God who tempers his love and mercy with justice, and who does not always know what's what. How did you know you were naked, the Omniscient asks Adam in the Garden, and later puzzles Cain by asking the whereabouts of his brother, Abel. Fielding is at some pains to point out that the offence that sends Tom out of Paradise is a "personal offence" to the Squire, much like the disobedience that sent Adam and Eve traveling (a joke Fielding makes in *The Journal of a Voyage to Lisbon*). The crime was not the act itself, but its disrespect to the maker of the rule. That literal readings of the Old Testament created such absurdities as the deity's being "subject to Passions," all controversialists knew, from Philo to John Toland.[51]

That Fielding has the Old Testament God in mind could not, however, appear, unless Allworthy were outdone by a more exemplary son in terms defined by Allworthy himself. As, of course, he is. Tom consistently demonstrates a higher degree of mercy and deeper charity than his uncle (or his readers), precisely the areas in which Christians applaud the superiority of their revelation to the old. Conversing with Capt. Blifil, Allworthy restricts true charity to giving from one's necessities, rather than one's surplus (II.v.96). Allworthy never gives from his necessities but always only from the surplus of Paradise Hall. For Allworthy to have necessities would be to redefine him. Tom unselfconsciously and repeatedly surpasses his father by giving from even what he himself needs. As a child he sold his Bible and his pony, raising money to assist Black George. As an adult with almost empty pockets, he gives to the beggar who turns out to have Sophia's pocketbook and to Enderson the highwayman, whom he might have had hanged and whom he continues to assist when he has funds supplied by Lady Bellaston. If Tom's charitable giving proportionately exceeds Allworthy's, so does his practice of forgiveness.

The legitimate extent of forgiveness leads to a sharp disagreement between father/uncle and son/nephew that critics usually resolve in favor of the father by quoting Fielding himself from his reform tracts. When Tom advises forgiving Black George, Allworthy insists such forgiveness is "pernicious to

Society" (XVIII.xi.969). Since Fielding makes precisely that argument in his own person as magistrate, Allworthy must be right, it seems. Yet as Rawson observes, "Fielding's morality transcends his own explicitly formulated socio-legal principles in contexts where the full human situation invited a deeper and larger view."[52] Allworthy's limits appear in his being frequently seconded by Thwackum, and vice versa. If Allworthy tells Tom gently that his broken arm from saving Sophia is "a Visitation for his own Good," Thwackum assures young Tom in the next paragraph that the same broken arm is "a Judgment from Heaven on his Sins" (V.ii.216). Thwackum chides Blifil for carrying forgiveness of enemies "too far" (VI.x.308). Allworthy echoes Thwackum when Tom argues for forgiving Black George; Tom carries "this forgiving Temper too far" (XVIII.xi.969). It is wrong to be so good.

Allworthy's rejection and Tom's forgiveness of Blifil are couched in the terms of the Sermon on the Mount, Fielding's favorite passage in his favorite moral book. When Allworthy says of Blifil, "he knew him not" (XVIII.xi.966), he echoes Matthew 7:23: "I never knew you, depart from me, ye that work iniquity." Yet Tom forgives his enemy Blifil, who despitefully used him, a forgiveness that extends to increasing his pension, and that operates in secret. Tom's actions appear as precepts on the Mount (Matthew 5–7), praised by Fielding as all the proof of divinity anyone needs. "But I say unto you, Love your enemies, bless them that curse you, do good to them that hate you, and pray for them which despitefully use you, and persecute you. (5:44) . . . Take heed that ye do not your alms before men, to be seen of them. . . . But when thou doest alms, let not thy left hand know what thy right hand doeth; That thine alms may be in secret" (6:1–4).

What obscures the Old Testament/New Testament allusion is its scandalous, amusing impudence: the Son wenching? Certainly Work missed it: "Tom Jones, for all his impertinent sermonizing, is for the most part a 'good man' on the purely human level."[53] The "purely human level" is precisely where Fielding would like to see religion acting more than it usually does. If the novel exhibits a "providential order," the narrator insists on acting only by second causes. The ordinary nonfictional course of events is disordered, ugly, and unjust. In that world, Tom Jones is hanged or penniless, Sophia marries Blifil or someone else (XVII.i.875), Jonathan Wild fails to steal the parson's bottle-screw on the scaffold—and the truly great get off. The world's improper, immoral order grounds Fielding's argument for Christianity and immortality in a world where politics offers little and Providence rarely intervenes. If justice existed, if the inner human (and primate) longing for fairness were met, Christianity would be otiose (XV.i.784). The disorder, not the order, of the world promotes it and motivates its adherents.

As to the strangely contrasting fates of Black George and Blifil, the novel's demonic characters, while Tom excuses the former, no one explains or excuses Blifil's conduct, except Fielding's narrative content. Black

George vanishes, and Blifil enjoys an oddly happy ending. Origen-like, the devil is saved; he is also understood. To account for Blifil, Fielding indicates the pull of self, relative to the claims and influence of the group (Blifil's self-centeredness); internal defects in the machine (Blifil's character); genetic endowment (Blifil is his father's son); distortions produced by upbringing, such as a mother's loving or hating the father of her children, or simply preferring one child to another (Bridget relative to Summer and Captain Blifil, to Tom and Blifil). While the narrator never condescends to humanize young Blifil, the narrative supplies irresistible grounds for a neglected, exploited, hated, despised young Blifil to detest Tom Jones with all his heart. Blifil's father dies without ever having paid any visible attention to his son, apart from his interests as heir. Thereafter, Blifil is neglected by Allworthy in favor of Tom, exploited as a pawn by Square and Thwackum currying favor with Bridget, hated by his mother Bridget, and despised by Sophia and the Westerns. The narrator seems to hand off Blifil's behavior to innate character, but his narrative suggests multiple causes for it. The narrator descants on Envy, suggesting that the author knew what the narrative was doing, though the narrator did not disrupt his comic frame with sympathy for Blifil.

The New Testament does not simply supersede the Old; Allworthy and Tom remain engaged in a loving dialogue of difference. In happy families, of which the Trinity ought to be one, the children exceed their parents in goodness or talent, and the parents are happy to be so excelled. Indeed, if Sophia is Lady Wisdom, with God the first of all things, through whom He created the world (Proverbs 8:22–30), then Tom as the Logos and Sophia as Wisdom are indeed one, even before the beginning of the world. Fielding does not go there, of course: he has a different intention—or effect—relative to the love of Sophia and Tom.

When he defines love, Fielding begins from Swift's sect, who discover there is no God (VI.i.268), as if denying one were equivalent to denying the other. God answered for, human Love steps forward as Fielding's concern. In Tom's possessing Sophia, a man uniting with such a woman, the narrator locates the greatest happiness possible on this earth (XVIII.[xiii] chapter the last.979). Sublime in IV.ii, Sophia rises still further in Tom's description to Nightingale: "She is all over, both in Mind and Body, consummate Perfection. She is the most beautiful Creature in the Universe; and yet she is Mistress of such noble, elevated Qualities, that though she is never from my Thoughts, I scarce ever think of her Beauty; but when I see it" (XV.ix.818). When Tom fears losing Sophia, he overworks the decayed idiom of courtly love—perdition, damnation, Hell (XVIII.x.961). Throughout, Sophia is an angel, a superior being, for her beauty and less visible mind, as well as a wise young woman who despises a libertine. She has also set out on her own, in willful flight toward an uncertain good, leaving signs and messages, muffs and pocketbooks, in her wake.

Yet Tom also is wrapped in angelic imagery, reflective of his goodness, principally by the language of Enderson and Mrs. Miller (XIII.x.727), but also by the narrator on behalf of Mrs. Miller, "*Jones*, her good Angel" (XV.x.823). The imagery, sometimes casual discourse, sometimes deeply meant, is worked through to the end of the novel in the language of blessings and reward. Enderson hopes for the angelic Tom that "eternal blessings reward" him (XIII.x.728), and the final sentence of the novel "bless[es] the Day" (XVIII.xiii.982) when Tom marries his Sophia. The social order descends from high to low, neighbors, tenants, and servants, as Tom receives the reward Enderson wished him, and human love displaces the vision of the divine.

Is there any way to reconcile Tom the Son with Tom the Lover, that embodiment of better-directed (Tom the Prudent) sexual energy, within an understanding of Fielding, the freely thinking Christian and novelist? We are not accustomed to such straddlers, with their legs spread wide between camps we regard as incompatible and inconsistent. Looking up, like the Lilliputians marching between Gulliver's legs, Paul Kelleher sees the sexual energy animating Fielding's moral sense and his heroes. Turning more modestly to where Fielding's feet are planted, in religion and literature, we note that the absence of the immediate Christian Persons of the Trinity motivates the embodiment of value in secular persons, in the novel's characters. Fielding's didacticism carries traces of ancient imagery, coexisting delicately with his modern social panorama and his dark, but not despairing account of "Human Nature." In short order, the balance Fielding achieves will be replaced, and a secular politics will define values for secularized characters, simultaneously with religious discourse's co-opting secular reform in evangelicalism. That direction is already visible in *Amelia*, in which Allworthy's and Tom's embodiment of value has been professionalized in Dr. Harrison and Barrow's sermons, and marginalized in Amelia.

In none of Fielding's great heirs, from Frances Burney through Charles Dickens to Mark Twain, does the page produce so many references to religion. Modern readers for the most part read past the pervasive sermonizing, much as they fail to note Evelina's favorite oath: "good God!"[54] Dickens and Twain, a Unitarian-sympathizer and a skeptic, resemble Fielding in their affective and intellectual relationship to Christianity, but both lived within a disciplined, reforming politics that offered very different opportunities for action.[55] Fielding's readers encounter religion poised over one of its important thresholds. Religion remains the dominant ideology to be appealed to for social purposes, providing a vocabulary of reform for individuals, rather than society at large, yet religion is now valued less for its own sake, than for its effects. That we make so much of Fielding's social role as magistrate reveals our desire that the novelist who invented the (English) social reformist, panoramic novel have a social rather than a gospel message. That Western culture's charitable message originates in Leviticus and the gospels, communism in Acts, and liberation in Exodus is a commonplace. In Fielding, intellectual and social historians have the opportunity to watch that evolution as it happens, "to the moment."

NOTES

1. Henry Fielding, *Tom Jones*, ed. Martin C. Battestin, Wesleyan ed. (Oxford: Oxford University Press, 1975), 463. Hereafter cited in text by book, chapter, and page number.
2. Edmund Spenser, *Poetical Works*, ed. J.C. Smith and E. de Selincourt (London: Oxford University Press, 1965), 573.
3. Current discussions begin from James A. Work, "Henry Fielding, Christian Censor," in *The Age of Johnson, Essays Presented to Chauncey Brewster Tinker* (New Haven, CT: Yale University Press, 1949), 139–48, and are carried on by Martin C. Battestin in *The Moral Basis of Fielding's Art* (Middletown, CT: Wesleyan University Press, 1959), his preface to *Tom Jones*, and in Martin. C. Battestin and Ruthe R. Battestin, *Henry Fielding: A Life* (New York: Routledge, 1989), 332–34. See also Battestin, *A Henry Fielding Companion* (Westport, CT: Greenwood, Press, 2000).
4. Blakey Vermeule, *Why Do We Care about Literary Characters?* (Baltimore: Johns Hopkins University Press, 2010), 144.
5. Melvyn New, "'The Grease of God': The Form of Eighteenth-Century English Fiction," *PMLA* 91, no. 2 (1976): 235–44.
6. Flann O'Brien's footnotes in *The Third Policeman* echo faintly in this debate. Simon Dickie, "*Joseph Andrews* and the Great Laughter Debate," *SECC* 34 (2005): 303; Claude Rawson, "Fielding in the Dock," *London Review of Books*, April 5, 1990, 21; Martin Battestin, "Fielding and the Deists," *Eighteenth-Century Fiction* 13, no. 1 (2000): 67–68.
7. "Foreword," Henry Fielding, *The Life of Mr. Jonathan Wild the Great* (New York: New American Library, 1961), xv. Typically for his period, Plumb privileges Christian and Stoic to the detriment of Fielding's Epicurean sympathies. See Neven Leddy and Avi S. Lifschitz, eds., *Epicurus in the Enlightenment* (Oxford: Voltaire Foundation, 2009), 6–7.
8. Battestin, *Life*, 332. Michael McKeon develops the argument at length in *Origins of the English Novel* (Baltimore: Johns Hopkins University Press, 1987).
9. Henry Fielding, *Amelia*, ed. Martin C. Battestin, Wesleyan ed. (Oxford: Oxford University Press, 1983). Hereafter cited in text by book, chapter, and page number.
10. *The Covent-Garden Journal and A Plan of the Universal Register-Office*, ed. Bertrand A. Goldgar (Middletown, CT: Wesleyan University Press, 1988), 184, 229, 246, 125.
11. *Examples of the Interposition of Providence in the Detection and Punishment of Murder*, 1752; Battestin, *Life*, 549.
12. Thomas R. Preston opens his excellent article with Parson Adams's exuberant preference for the cable over the camel as traversing the eye of the needle. His point concerns the audience rather than the author of *Joseph Andrews*, but for all his admirable thoroughness, he finds no comparable example in any other author. "Biblical Criticism, Literature, and the Eighteenth-Century Reader," in *Books and Their Readers in Eighteenth-Century England*, ed. Isabel Rivers (New York: St. Martin's Press, 1982), 97.
13. "'The Grease of God': The Form of Eighteenth-Century Fiction," 236, 242.
14. Treadwell Ruml II, "Henry Fielding and Parson Adams: Whig Writer and Tory Priest," *JEGP* 97, no. 2 (1998): 225; Ronald Paulson, "Henry Fielding and the Problem of Deism," in *Margins of Orthodoxy: Heterodox Writing and Cultural Response, 1660–1750*, ed. Roger D. Lund (Cambridge: Cambridge University Press, 1995), 241. For "orthodox" as ironic and negative, see *Jonathan Wild* in *Miscellanies by Henry Fielding, Esq; Volume Three*, ed. Bertrand A. Goldgar and Hugh Amory (Middletown, CT: Wesleyan University Press, 1997), IV.i.136. Hereafter cited in text.

15. "God and the Novel in India," Ph.D. dissertation, Columbia University, 2011.

16. "'The Glorious Lust of Doing Good': Tom Jones and the Virtues of Sexuality," *Novel* 38, no. 2–3 (2005): 165–92.

17. Fielding habitually intertwines Christian and classical reference, the Epicurean (sexual energy, pleasure) often displacing the Stoic. Ethical arguments start with classical texts and end in Christian reference: "On the Remedy of Affliction" begins philosophically and concludes by misquoting William Sherlock. *The Covent-Garden Journal*, no. 29, after an epigraph from Epicurus, cites Isaac Barrow on the pleasures of doing good, winds through Epicurus again, and concludes with "the divine Founder of our Religion" (184), signed Homer's "Axylus" (183–86). Alternatively, Fielding defends religion from Bolingbroke and ends up amid Ovid, Thales, Tully—and Locke (*Fragment of a Comment on L. Bolingbroke's Essays*, in *The Journal of a Voyage to Lisbon, Shamela, and Occasional Writings*, ed. Martin C. Battestin, Wesleyan ed. [Oxford: Clarendon Press, 2008], 678–80). Similarly, Isaac Barrow and "witty Dr. South" (*Covent-Garden Journal*, no. 57, p. 308; no. 60, p. 327); "excellent Dr. Barrow" and "ingenious Dr. South" (*Covent-Garden Journal*, no. 69, p. 365; no. 12, p. 85); and the always-praised Hoadly march beside Horace and Ovid, Tully and Marcus Aurelius. Recognizing and perhaps sending up this trait, Fielding passes it to the garrulous Mrs. Miller, who applauds a sentiment of Sophia as "worthy of *Seneca*, or of a Bishop" (XVIII.x.962).

18. Michael McKeon, "Fielding and the Instrumentality of Belief: *Joseph Andrews*," in *Critical Essays on Henry Fielding*, ed. Albert J. Rivero (New York: Hall, 1998), 59, rptd. from *Origins of the English Novel*.

19. Thomas R. Cleary has much to say about Fielding's anti-Jacobitism and little about religion, including Catholicism. *Henry Fielding, Political Writer* (Waterloo, ON: Wilfrid Laurier University Press, 1984).

20. December 25, 1739, *Contributions to the Champion*, ed. W.B. Coley, Wesleyan ed. (Oxford: Oxford University Press, 2003), 85. The deist Thomas Chubb made a similar argument in his *True Gospel* and was mocked by Fielding for displacing Matthew's Gospel with "Chubb's Gospel" in the *Covent-Garden Journal*, no. 13, p. 97; James D.G. Dunn credits Chubb as second only to Hermann Reimarus in differentiating "the message of Jesus and the early teachings of Christianity," *Christianity in the Making, Beginning from Jerusalem* (Grand Rapids, MI: Eerdmans, 2009), 2:18.

21. Quoted in Battestin, *Moral Basis*, 74, 76. Fielding recognizes that the "Jewish Dispensation" is as insistent on charitable goodness as the Christian, and he cites it with equal confidence on the point of most importance to him in the year before the unsuccessful Jew Naturalization Bill, 1753 (*Covent-Garden Journal*, May 16, 1752, no. 39, p. 229). Not even Fielding, however, seems to realize that the parable of the Good Samaritan is the only place the New Testament reaches the moral heights of the Old. Jesus and Paul define the high point of Christian ethics with Leviticus 19:18: "Thou shalt love thy neighbor as thyself," but Leviticus 19:36 gives the rule silently acted out in Luke's parable: "The stranger that dwelleth with you shall be unto you as one born among you, and thou shalt love him as thyself, for ye were strangers in the land of Egypt."

22. "An Essay on the Knowledge of Characters of Men," *Miscellanies by Henry Fielding, Esq.: Volume One*, ed. Henry Knight Miller (Middletown, CT: Wesleyan University Press, 1972), 159. Such gravity might make him seem not to be Fielding's type, but the context is an analysis of laughter in Hobbesian terms as cruel and contemptuous, the antithesis of good nature. Fielding probably has the observation from Joseph Addison, *Spectator*, no. 381, May 17, 1712. *The Spectator*, ed. Donald F. Bond (Oxford: Clarendon Press, 1965), III:430.

23. "Characters of Men," *Miscellanies*, I:168.

24. *Champion*, April 5, 1740, 271; "Characters of Men," *Miscellanies*, I:169–73.

25. Henry Fielding, *Joseph Andrews*, ed. Martin C. Battestin, Wesleyan ed. (Middletown, CT: Wesleyan University Press, 1967), 52, 154.

26. Work observes that Fielding frequently mentions "the first and second Persons of the Trinity," as if the third did not count, "Henry Fielding, Christian Censor," 140.

27. Fielding makes that point in *Jonathan Wild* and repeats it in *Joseph Andrews*, I.xvii.82, where Parson Adams also speaks strenuously against the splendor of the church and against Methodism's opposing faith to good works. J.G.A. Pocock suggests that Christology evapo-

rates when the only doctrine necessary to salvation becomes the bare assertion that Jesus was the Messiah ("Within the Margins: The Definitions of Orthodoxy," in Lund, *Margins of Orthodoxy*, 46).

28. Affirmed in *Journey from This World to the Next*, "Of the Remedy of Affliction," and repeated in *Tom Jones*.

29. Alexander Pope, *The Poems of Alexander Pope*, ed. John Butt (New Haven, CT: Yale University Press, 1963):

> For Modes of Faith, let graceless zealots fight;
> His can't be wrong whose life is in the right:
> In Faith and Hope the world will disagree,
> But all Mankind's concern is Charity.
> All must be false that thwart this One great End;
> And all of God, that bless Mankind, or mend. (III. ll.305–10; 535)

Anticipating *Jonathan Wild* (I.i.9) on greatness and "mischief," an attitude Rawson traces from Lucan and Juvenal through Rabelais and Boileau (*Order from Confusion Sprung* [London: George, Allen & Unwin, 1985], 241), Pope remarks that

> Heroes are much the same, the point's agreed,
> From Macedonia's madman to the Swede;
> The whole strange purpose of their lives, to find
> Or make, an enemy of all mankind! (IV. ll.219–22; 542)

Pope's "Universal Prayer" extends from the known world, "Saint . . . Savage . . . Sage, / Jehovah, Jove, or Lord" (ll.3–4; 247–48) to Giordano Bruno's (and Mark Twain's) other worlds (ll.24–25). Fielding does not follow him there.

30. Fielding's anticlericalism resembles Locke's and might be regarded as traditional. See Richard Ashcraft, "Anticlericalism and Authority in Lockean Political Thought," in Lund, *Margins of Orthodoxy*, 73–86.

31. Battestin, *Life*, 196.

32. Battestin, *Life*, 153. Fielding's literary conversions are singularly unpersuasive. He never takes the reader deep enough into the internal debates of the characters to make them plausible; Billy Booth will not even tell his doubts.

33. "[N]o Man enjoy'd life more than he did, tho' few had less reason to do so. . . . I am perswaded he has known more happy moments than any Prince upon Earth. His natural Spirits gave him Rapture with his Cookmaid, and chearfullness when he was Fluxing in a Garret." To Lady Bute, September 22, [1755] (*The Complete Letters of Lady Mary Wortley Montagu*, ed. Robert Halsband [Oxford: Clarendon Press, 1967], 3:87).

34. Pierre Cuppé's translator hoped to halt the "Methodist poison." *Heaven Open to All Men. Or, A Theological Treatise, in which, Without Unsettling the Practice of Religion, Is Solidly Prov'd, By Scripture and Reason, That All Men Shall Be Saved, Or, Made Finally Happy* (London, 1743), xxiv.

35. See Regina Janes, "Henry Fielding Reinvents the Afterlife," *Eighteenth-Century Fiction* 23, no. 3 (2011): 505–6.

36. *Covent-Garden Journal*, no. 39, May 16, 1752, 229, 230.

37. *Proposal for Making an Effectual Provision for the Poor, for Amending Their Morals, and for Rendering Them Useful Members of the Society* (Dublin, 1753), 47–48; Fielding is quoting Archbishop Tillotson and developing his argument. Thomas Hobbes says the same in *Leviathan* I.12.20: "And therefore the first founders and legislators of commonwealths among the Gentiles, *whose ends were only to keep the people in obedience and peace*, have in all places taken care first to imprint . . . a belief that those precepts which they gave concerning religion [did not] proceed from their own device, but from the dictates of some god or other spirit" (*Leviathan* [London, 1651], 57, emphasis added).

38. *Covent-Garden Journal*, no. 11, February 8, 1752, 81.

39. *Covent-Garden Journal*, no. 44.

40. "[Morality and faith] have both their peculiar excellencies, [but] the first has the preeminence in several respects" (*Spectator*, no. 459); for morality's being enhanced by faith, nos. 463 and 465; *The Spectator*, ed. Bond, IV:118, 137, 143.

41. In *Dialogue between The Devil, the Pope, and the Pretender* (London, 1745), 33, the Devil swears, "As I hope to be sav'd," an oath the Pope comments on as "a pretty oath for the Devil."

42. *Provision for the Poor*, 47.

43. *The Life of Mr. Jonathan Wild the Great. A new edition with considerable corrections and additions* (London, 1754), 242–43. IV.xiv.181. For 1754, see *Miscellanies*, III:208. The Wesleyan edition does not count asterisks.

44. This quotation follows the 1754 text; IV.xiv.185, 292.

45. In the *Covent-Garden Journal*, no. 69, Fielding follows his Ordinary, but calls the wisdom that is foolishness the wisdom of this world, not of Plato: "By Wisdom here I mean that Wisdom of this World, which St. Paul expressly tells us *is Folly*" (364).

46. William Sherlock in *A Vindication of the Doctrine of the Holy and Ever Blessed Trinity* (1690) laments Socinianism's implications: "If Socinianism be true, God did not give any son he had before, but made an excellent man, whom he was pleased to call his own begotten son." Still worse, Socinians hold that a good life is necessary to salvation, not belief "in those points that have always been controverted." Quoted in Ronald Paulson, *The Beautiful, Novel, and Strange: Aesthetics and Heterodoxy* (Baltimore: Johns Hopkins University Press, 1996), 36.

47. *The Beautiful, Novel, and Strange*, 11–22. Paulson argues that Plate 1 is a Visitation, Plate 3 an Annunciation, Plate 4 a Flagellation, Plate 6 a Last Supper, with 12 guests, a body, lots of wine, and a son. Plate 3 of *The Stages of Cruelty* is a Taking of Christ in the Garden.

48. The first phrase is from Hans Frei, *The Eclipse of Biblical Narrative* (New Haven, CT: Yale University Press, 1974), 130, quoted in Preston, to whom the second belongs, "Biblical Criticism," 121.

49. To the woman taken in adultery, he says, "Go, and sin no more" (John 8:11), but that is a prohibition of adultery, not fornication. To him who lusts in his heart, he also attributes the sin of adultery, not fornication (Matthew 5:27–28). Fornicators will be locked out of the new world to come, but that is John in Revelation 21:8, 22:15, not Jesus in the gospels. Fornication does appear in the list of vices from the heart that defile, briefly in Matthew: "For out of the heart proceed evil thoughts, murders, adulteries, fornications, thefts, false witness, blasphemies" (Matthew 15:19); more comprehensively in Matthew's source, Mark, "For from within, out of the heart of men, proceed evil thoughts, adulteries, fornications, murders, thefts, covetousness, wickedness, deceit, lasciviousness, an evil eye, blasphemy, pride, foolishness: All these evil things come from within, and defile the man" (Mark 7:21–23).

50. Miss Prism in *The Importance of Being Earnest*, Act II, *The Complete Plays of Oscar Wilde*, ed. H. Montgomery Hyde (London: Methuen, 1996), 244.

51. John Toland, *Christianity Not Mysterious* (London, 1696), 34.

52. Rawson, *Order from Confusion Sprung*, 324.

53. "Henry Fielding, Christian Censor," 147.

54. Frances Burney, *Evelina* (London, 1779), 125, 199, 223, 235, 240. Sir Clement Willoughby also swears by the good God, 126, 128.

55. In *Extract from Captain Stormfield's Visit to Heaven* (New York: Harper's, 1909), Mark Twain proposes a Heaven that welcomes everyone, from serial killers and pirates to Arabs and seven-legged blue beings, a Christian inclusiveness that exceeds and perhaps mocks orthodox Christian charity.

Chapter Four

Samuel Richardson's *Clarissa* and the Problem of Heaven

E. Derek Taylor

Samuel Richardson knew from the start how he would conclude his novel *Clarissa, or The History of a Young Lady* (1747–48)—which may explain, Peter Brooks would tell us, why the end is so long in coming. Having devised the plot for what might well be posited as the singular fictional tragedy of its century—no other literary work from the period generated such an easily followed trail of tears, still evident in letters to the author from agitated readers—Richardson elected to throw the ultimate trump card: Clarissa, abandoned by her family, poisoned and raped by her rakish suitor, dies and goes to Heaven. "I could not think of leaving my Heroine short of Heaven," the author informed Lady Bradshaigh (then posing as "Belfour") in 1748, after receiving her despondent plea for him to change an ending she feared was coming, but had not yet read. In her next letter, the "Catastrophe" reached, Bradshaigh's complaint remained unchanged: "I still think Clarissa should have lived," she baldly insisted.[1] For Bradshaigh, as for many later readers, that "the answer" to Clarissa's many problems "lies in heaven," as Carol Houlihan Flynn puts it, provides "cold comfort to the common reader in the real world."[2]

Whether understood as rhetorical *legerdemain* on Richardson's part or as an artistically successful intermingling of theology and realistic fiction, Clarissa's end is generally treated as a self-evident proposition; we all know what we mean, it would appear, when we insist, or complain, "Clarissa goes to Heaven." This may explain the fact that, while much critical attention has been paid to the skeptical possibilities surrounding the translation, or not, of Clarissa Harlowe into immortal existence, no one has seemed particularly interested in what it means to assume that the heroine *does* find Heaven.

Florian Stuber, for example, focuses on the question of whether or not "God . . . is actually present" in Richardson's self-proclaimed religious novel. In Belford's mind, Stuber explains, "the smile with which [Clarissa] dies 'seemed to manifest her eternal happiness already begun.'" And yet, Stuber notes, "It only *seems*; the reader may believe it or not."[3] For Stuber—really for any skeptical or faithful reader of the novel—the primary interpretive dilemma of *Clarissa* has consisted of choosing whether or not "to leap over" the gap separating religious from irreligious interpretation.[4] I propose a different question: where, exactly, do those readers who choose to leap *land*?

Such a question may not at first seem meaningful. In my own work on Richardson, I have tended to read the conclusion to *Clarissa* in the either/or fashion described above—there is or is not such a thing as Heaven, the protagonist does or does not arrive there, and the rest takes care of itself.[5] I continue to take seriously the artistic, rhetorical, and theological significance of the adjective in Richardson's description of *Clarissa* as a "Religious Novel,"[6] and I continue to think that, for reasons both ethical and aesthetic, readers today would do well to remember that nearly all of Richardson's first readers considered themselves Christians. Nevertheless, a close analysis of the novel and of the intellectual sources surrounding its composition and reception suggest good reasons, I hope to demonstrate, for proceeding cautiously, even when we tread on heavenly ground.

In their comprehensive study, *Heaven: A History* (1988), Colleen McDannell and Bernhard Lang identify the eighteenth century as a site of unique tension in European conceptions of eternal reward—when two understandings, one with strong roots in the century before, one that would blossom in the next, found themselves planted in the same ground. On the one hand, they explain, a "modern view of heaven" was beginning to surface, as defined by "four characteristics":

1. Heaven is immediate—"For the righteous, heavenly life begins immediately after death";
2. Heaven is the perfection and extension of this world, "a continuation and fulfillment of material existence";
3. Heaven is a place of activity, "a dynamic, motion-filled environment"; and
4. Heaven is a setting for human love—including all forms of "communal and familial concerns."[7]

Although McDannell and Lang focus on the writings of Swedish mystic Emanuel Swedenborg (1688–1772), whom William Blake famously satirized in *The Marriage of Heaven and Hell* (1790), as exemplary of this perspective, Elizabeth Rowe (1674–1737) was decades earlier treating English readers to imaginings of Heaven that would seem to qualify as fully "modern." In

Friendship in Death: In Twenty Letters from the Dead to the Living (1728), two editions of which Richardson printed in the early 1740s, Rowe posits Heaven as a place where we wait happily, if sometimes impatiently, for our friends to join us in a perfected and eternal world still recognizably composed of rivers, fields, flowers. "I Leave your fellow-mortals to congratulate your recovery," the spirit of Clerimont writes to the no-longer-sick Leonora, "but I must own 'twas a disappointment to me: You were on the confines of immortality." Clerimont further explains that he "had wreath'd a garland of the fairest flowers that bloomed in the Paradise of God, to crown such early and distinguished virtue," and that, while contemplating the apparently dying Leonora, he "with impatience . . . numbered [her] moments, and expected every one would be [her] last."[8] In Rowe's Heaven, not only do we immediately meet and recognize our lost loved ones ("modern" characteristics 1 and 4)—in one letter, Altamont recounts his rediscovery of the now "divinely fair" Almeria, whose death had preceded his own—but also we ride in an "aethereal chariot" of "sparkling saphire . . . studded with gold" through a landscape composed of "delectable vales and flowery lawns," "myrtle shades and rosy bowers," and "bright cascades and crystal rivulets" ("modern" characteristics 2 and 3).[9]

It is typical of Richardson that, in the same decade in which he was printing Rowe's elaborations of a "modern" Heaven, he was likewise printing James Hervey's *Meditations among the Tombs* (1746); as Keith Maslen has ably demonstrated, any attempt to find clear correspondence between Richardson's personal views and his output as a printer is sure to founder on the shoals of inconsistency.[10] McDannell and Lang point to Hervey's book as illustrative of the persistence into the eighteenth century of a premodern, theocentric view of eternity, according to which "friends, family, change, and human creativity are utterly unimportant."[11] This was the Heaven envisioned by the early Augustine, for whom "a mental, spiritual union with God meant the ultimate human happiness," and of Aquinas in the thirteenth century, for whom the blessed would necessarily concentrate on "*one* thing—the study of God."[12] Indeed, a diverse set of influential Christians on the continent—not only Catholic mystics like Teresa of Avila and John of the Cross, but early reformers like John Calvin and Martin Luther—accepted the basic contours of a theocentric Heaven.[13]

By the middle of the seventeenth century, this view of the afterlife had made significant inroads in England. Puritans such as Richard Baxter in *Saints' Everlasting Rest* (1649) underscored the active and all-consuming love and praise the beatific vision of God would inspire, while Anglicans like Joseph Hall (1574–1656) saw Heaven as a place in which "all social relationships must fade."[14] Perhaps Mary Astell (1666–1731) and John Norris (1757–1712), also Anglicans but with roots in Augustine and in continental followers like Nicolas Malebranche (1638–1715) and Pierre Nicole

(1625–1695), most clearly declare the theocentric perspective in their tellingly titled *Letters Concerning the Love of God* (1695). "[He] that enjoys *GOD* cannot desire any thing out of him, because of the infinite Fulness of *GOD*," Astell writes in one letter; "Divine Love . . . is the Antipast of our Happiness here," she explains in another, "and the full Consummation of it hereafter."[15] Where in 1662, Jansenist Blaise Pascal (1623–1662) wrote on a "slip of parchment sewn into his garment [at death] . . . 'the world forgotten, and everything except God,'"[16] Astell, as she approached death seventy years later, "begged to see no more of her old acquaintance and friends, having done with the world, and made her peace with God." She spent her final two days alone in her room, her coffin by her side.[17]

Where, exactly, did Richardson stand on this question? To which Heaven, put differently, did he send his heroine? These are questions worth asking, I think, largely because we would not be the first to do so. Consider the following moments in Richardson's correspondence, found in three letters from Sarah Chapone, all still buried, unfortunately, in the Forster Collection of Manuscripts held in the Victoria and Albert Museum—the Cambridge Edition of Richardson's correspondence cannot come soon enough.

First, in her letter of December 15, 1750, Chapone eagerly imagines the heavenly reward she feels certain Richardson will receive for his achievement on earth: "When [the] Laws of Precedency shall be adjusted & set right for ever, by the unerring Judge, it may be question'd whether there will be found a more dignified Spirit than the author of Clarissa." She continues by noting that "The Divine Norris seems to think that those who love most in this Life, will be rewarded by Knowing most in the Other."[18] "The Divine Norris" in this case is again John Norris, Astell's correspondent, as noted above, but a prolific author in his own right. Chapone is paraphrasing a section of his essay "An Idea of Happiness, in a Letter to a Friend," wherein Norris argues that "the Blessed" in Heaven are rewarded both in their capacity to desire (the will) and to know (the understanding) through the "*perfect Fruition* of God" in "the *Beatific Vision*." It stands to reason, Norris explains, "*since* God is both Supream *Truth* and infinite *Goodness*, he cannot be entirely possess'd but by the most clear *knowledg* and the most ardent *love*." "Face to Face" with God, denizens of Heaven will discover that they "cannot chuse but love perpetually; and while they perpetually love, they cannot choose but perpetually contemplate."[19] Richardson, Chapone would seem to be suggesting, is sure to experience maximum fulfillment on both counts when finally he encounters divinity.

Later in this same letter, however, Chapone posits a different vision of heavenly existence—one that stresses the persistence of friendship and community. Waxing eloquent on her epistolary relationship with Richardson, Chapone explains that "the Cement [of friendship] is such, that (I trust) it shall not be dissolved, even when Life itself goes out. For all true Lovers of

God, like needles touched by the Load-Stone, not only cleave to him their magnet, but also to one another." Once again, Chapone here borrows from a book by Norris, in this case from his and Astell's *Letters Concerning the Love of God*. Astell concludes her prefacing letter to the collection with rapturous praise for her friend and patron, Lady Catherine Jones, explaining to Norris, "now we have duly stated the Measures, I may venture to say, I love [her] with the greatest Tenderness.... All true Lovers of *GOD* being like excited Needles, which cleave not only to him their *Magnet*, but even to one another."[20] That Astell will now "venture" to express her love reflects her sense that the central dilemma addressed during the course of her correspondence with Norris has been resolved to her satisfaction. Norris had argued that human beings ought to love God not only *above* all creatures, but to their *exclusion*, a point with which Astell had admitted personal, practical qualms in an early letter—"still I find an agreeable Movement in my Soul towards her I love . . . which is a strong Indication of somewhat more than pure Benevolence," she laments.[21] Astell is *not*, then, thinking about the afterlife in the passage Chapone quotes—she is, instead, giving voice to her satisfaction at being able to justify continuing to love with "benevolence" (not, as she and Norris had worked out, with "desire") a particular "creature" here and now.[22] Chapone may not be mis*quoting* Astell, then, but she *is* pushing her magnetic metaphor far beyond its original intent—literally from this world to the next—and in a way that runs directly counter to both the logic and the spirit of Astell's contributions to *Letters*.

Two years later, when Chapone returned to a likeminded line of praise, her wording and emphasis shift away from the social vision of Heaven:

> [I]n the very foremost Rank of this select-exalted Band of Brothers in ingenuity, stands my Honour'd Mr. Richardson, Eminently distinguished by that Love-compelling Goodness, which I am from my soul persuaded shall eminently distinguish him to all Eternity! The Divine Norris says, 'That those who Love most in this Life, shall be rewarded by Knowing most in the next.' What Beatific illuminations—what floods of Light will then fully replenish all the boundless Capacities of your soul! And the rapture of Knowing, shall still add to the Extacies [*sic*] of Loving, 'for God is Love.'[23]

No friendly "cleaving" to the souls of "one another" here; Chapone now envisions "floods of Light" and "Beatific illuminations," a Heaven apparently devoid of love other than divine, of relationship other than with God—that is, a Heaven in keeping both with the theocentric tendencies of Astell and Norris's *Letters* and with Norris's argument in "An Idea of Happiness."

Chapone's vacillations on the nature of Heaven in these two letters provide apt bookends for a concern she expresses in one written in between (December 9, 1751). Here she asks the author a characteristically direct question on precisely the same subject: "Do you think we shall know each other in the next Life?—By many Hints, both in Pamela and Clarissa, you seem to hold that comfortable animating Opinion."[24] Perhaps the most significant point to make about Chapone's question is its being asked at all. Chapone *thinks* she has deciphered Richardson's views in this matter, but she cannot be certain. Furthermore, even in the course of asking the question, her sentences sag with qualifications—her evidence is composed of "hints"; Richardson "seems to hold" an "Opinion" about the social nature of Heaven. Finally, her characterization of the "Opinion" in question—she calls it "comfortable" and "animating"—introduces a psychological dimension to her inquisitiveness. In other words, if the Heaven in which she hopes Richardson believes is *comfortable* and *animating*, how would she describe the alternative? *Uncomfortable? Deadening?*

It is not clear whether or not Richardson shared Chapone's preferred vision—as she thought, or hoped, he did—of Heaven as a place where personal identity and interpersonal relationships endure. No response to either of Chapone's letters exists—either Richardson did not respond, or his response has been lost. As in his debate with Hester Mulso over the rights and responsibilities of daughters and parents respecting marriage—where, once again, Richardson's contributions are missing—we are left to intuit his responses.[25] One almost suspects a prescient Richardson of somehow making disappear from history his most confused letters.

As initial candidates for Chapone's "hints," we might consider the following passages, one from *Pamela*, the other from *Clarissa* (*Grandison* had yet to be published). Toward the end of the first novel, Pamela reflects on her husband's discussion of the settlements he has made on her in the event of his death, and exclaims "Oh! what a poor thing is human Life in its best Enjoyments! . . . This, duly reflected upon, methinks, should convince every one, that this World is not a Place for the immortal Mind to be confined to; and that there must be an Hereafter, where the *whole* Soul shall be satisfy'd." She concludes with a prayer that "I may, with my dear Benefactor, rejoyce in that happy State, where is no Mixture, no Unsatisfiedness; and where all is Joy, and Peace, and Love, for evermore!"[26] For her part, Clarissa contemplates Pamela's "hereafter" as *she* approaches death—"virtue rewarded" indeed. In an encomium to her dearest friend, Anna Howe, whom she will never again meet alive, Clarissa describes the immortality she considers herself on the brink of achieving:

> Oh my dear Anna Howe! How uninterruptedly sweet and noble has been our friendship!—But we shall one day, I hope (and that must comfort us both), meet, never to part again! Then, divested of the shades of body, shall we be all light and all mind—Then how unalloyed, how perfect, will be our friendship! Our love will have one and the same adorable object, and we shall enjoy it and each other to all eternity! (1348)

If these textual moments are indeed what Chapone had in mind, it is little wonder that she elected to press Richardson for clarification. One imagines Chapone seizing eagerly upon Pamela's nonrestrictive clause—"with my dear Benefactor"—as evidence that the author shared her "comfortable, animating Opinion" about the endurance of human relationships in Heaven. But is the experience of "Joy, Peace, and Love" here described a shared one? Does being in Heaven *with* Mr. B., in other words, entail *knowing* he is there? Similarly, if, in an eternal future, the incorporeal spirits of Clarissa Harlowe and Anna Howe will discover "one and the same adorable object" for their "love," what, exactly, becomes of their "noble" friendship? In other words, what does it mean "never to part again" if, as here conceived, all "love" gravitates toward the divine "object"? In what sense does a relationship between Clarissa and Anna, in this scenario, continue to exist?

Such questions suggest that, even as he wrote a novel the major point of which is heavenly reward, Richardson had yet to determine definitively what that reward would entail. In one sense, this is in keeping with his tendencies as a thinker. It is worth recalling John Dussinger's question, mostly playful, partly exasperated, made in the course of discussing the author's utterly inconsistent views on the nature of Adam and Eve's Fall: "Will the real Samuel Richardson please stand up?"[27] No interesting person fails to be inconsistent, of course—but Richardson *does* seem to have been *uniquely* gifted in this respect. For all his efforts, Laurence Sterne, to take one example, was unable (or unwilling?) to put the formal or ideological distance between *Tristram Shandy* (1759) and the ostensibly redemptive *A Sentimental Journey* (1768) that Richardson managed between *Pamela* and *Clarissa*. As for his religious leanings, Richardson has been claimed as a Puritan, a via media Anglican, a Boehmian mystic, and a closet secularist. Politically, Richardson almost certainly leaned, if carefully, in the direction of Jacobites like the Duke of Wharton (1698–1731) during his early days as a printer; later, he would print newspapers supportive of Walpole. No committed feminist has ever been shown so clearly not to have been one. It is just like Richardson, in other words, to take his inconsistencies into the great beyond, even in his most sustained and careful thinking on the topic—even, that is, in *Clarissa*.

Those, like Chapone, eager to discover a "modern" view of Heaven might note the frequency with which the steadily dying title character of that novel imagines an eternal reunion with her loved ones. "And what the consolation attending the sweet hope of meeting again," Clarissa writes to Mrs. Norton, "never more to be separated, never more to be pained, grieved, or aspersed!—But mutually blessing, and being blessed, to all eternity!" (1201). The famous "father's house" letter Clarissa uses to fool Lovelace likewise carries the allegorical suggestion of a social Heaven: "You may in time," she writes (with John 14:2 in mind), "see me at my father's, at least, if it be not your own fault" (1233).[28] But the most pronounced examples of such expressions are found in Clarissa's posthumous letters. Clarissa calls on her mother to imagine "a happy meeting with your forgiven penitent in the eternal mansions" (1372–73). She similarly assures Anna Howe "that a time will come when they shall meet again, never to be divided," and expresses her "trust" to Judith Norton that God "will in his own good time give us a joyful meeting in the regions of eternal blessedness" (1377, 1406). It is easy enough to see how Chapone, or any reader for that matter, would detect in such moments a commitment on Richardson's part to a Heaven defined by community, society, and human love.

Yet in other places *Clarissa* would seem definitively to bespeak an author eager (as Chapone seems hesitantly to suspect) to embrace a theocentric view of eternal felicity. "BUT GOD ALMIGHTY WOULD NOT LET ME DEPEND FOR COMFORT UPON ANY BUT HIMSELF" (1356). These are Clarissa's dramatically accentuated words to Belford as she seeks to discern the meaning of her final days of mortal existence. Not only is the heroine "cut off" from her loved ones as death looms, however; she herself actively seeks (as Astell had done) to avoid her closest friends as she feels their influence wane—and the influence of divinity wax. "And thus by little and little, in such a gradual sensible death as I am blessed with," she explains to Belford, "God dies away in us, as I may say, all human satisfactions, in order to subdue his poor creatures to Himself" (1337). Of her decision not to see Anna Howe or Judith Norton one last time before expiring, Clarissa explains that "*God will have no rivals in the hearts of those he sanctifies.* By various methods he deadens all other sensations, or rather absorbs them all in love of Him" (1338).

It is important to note that Clarissa's love for her friends is not so much *diminished* in her self-description as it is *subsumed*. "The truly friendly love that has so long subsisted between my Miss Howe and her Clarissa," she writes, "has already abated of its fervour; has already given place to supremer fervours" (1342). "Friendly love," Clarissa here makes clear, cannot hope to compete with "supremer" satisfaction—and neither, as two of her posthumous letters make clear, can biological ties. Clarissa signs the letter to her sister, "The forever happy / CLARISSA HARLOWE" (1373), and then, in the next letter, insists to her brother, "I gave up my whole *heart* to a better hope. God blessed my penitence, and my reliance upon Him. And now I presume to say, I AM HAPPY" (1374). Fully happy, her "whole *heart*" consumed with divine love, what need has the now beatified heroine for toadish sisters or spiteful brothers—or, in the final analysis, for truly loving friends?

Using *Clarissa* as evidence, one might even suggest a *third* candidate for Richardson's vision of heavenly existence, one McDannell and Lang do not connect to the eighteenth century, but one fully in keeping with Richardson's

Solomonic instincts when it came to impossible choices. Clarissa's happiness would seem to owe much to the community of truly decent human beings with whom she surrounds herself as she approaches death. Ewha Chung has shown how assiduously the heroine works in her final weeks and days to establish close bonds with this group of otherwise unfamiliar and unrelated men and women.[29] Dr. H. (her doctor), Mr. Smith (her landlord), and Mr. Goddard (her apothecary) are all, in Clarissa's words, "perfectly *paternal*" (1082, 1088). Indeed, as Belford puts it, "she is for finding out something *paternal* and *maternal* in everyone" (1082). For his part, Belford, the friend and confidant of Clarissa's rapist, has become her "warm friend" (1088). When Clarissa insists that Anna Howe love her with a "weaning love"—"I am not what I was when we were *inseparable* lovers, as I may say—Our *views* must now be different"—she is doing so, as she herself puts it, "among honest people" (1088).

Each time they recited the Apostles' Creed, Anglicans professed belief in the "communion of saints." But a *communion* of the blessed does not necessarily equate to the *community* that came to define "modern heaven." In their summary of Hervey's *Meditations*, McDannell and Lang seem to ignore this possibility, and thus diminish a rather crucial aspect of his argument—namely, that while *particular* relationships will not endure in the afterlife, Heaven is nevertheless *social* in nature. Hervey imagines the experience of the recently deceased as follows:

> But who can imagine the delightful Surprize, when they find themselves surrounded by guardian Angels, instead of weeping Friends? . . . Here they sit down with *Abraham, Isaac,* and *Jacob,* in the Kingdom of their Father. Here they mingle with an innumerable Company of Angels, and rejoice around the Throne of the Lamb.[30]

Hervey may not conceive of Heaven as a place "for exchanging sweet memories and renewing old friendships,"[31] but neither is he fully invested in the unequivocally theocentric views of Pascal. Indeed, Hervey's thinking in this matter actually appears to have much in common with the revised understanding of Heaven Augustine himself arrived at late in life, according to which Heaven is a "community," but one wherein "individualized relationships of earth are dissolved." McDannell and Lang's characterization of Augustine's later view of Heaven, in other words, could just as well apply to Hervey: "Since in the city of God there will be no special friendships, there will be no strangers. All special attachments will be absorbed into one comprehensive and undifferentiated community of love."[32]

One might well describe the assortment of people Clarissa gathers around herself in her final days as an "undifferentiated community of love." Richardson goes to some lengths, in fact, to stress the degree to which the human beings surrounding the dying heroine become less and less recognizable to her as discrete individuals, and more and more important to her as a group, as heavenly existence approaches. A few days before her demise, Clarissa's eyes, she tells Belford, have become "misty," and she resorts to "rubbing" them in order better to distinguish between her new friends. Looking "round upon each," Belford explains, "particularly on me—God bless you all, said she! how kindly are you concerned for me!—Who says I am friendless? Who says I am abandoned and among strangers?" (1330). In the moments before she expires, Clarissa has difficulty discerning the difference between Belford and Colonel Morden—between someone with whom she has spent less than a hundred hours and a cousin she has known her entire life: "My sight fails me! . . . Is not this Mr. Morden's hand? pressing one of his with that he had just let go. Which is Mr. Belford's? holding out the other. I gave her mine. God Almighty bless you both" (1362). When, in her final seconds of life, Clarissa "bow[s] her head six several times . . . as if distinguishing every person present," the transformation of "every person" into an "undifferentiated community"—six identical nods for six nameless people—would seem to be complete.

In sum, it is difficult to imagine anyone arriving at certain conclusions about Richardson's view of Heaven from a reading of his "religious novel"—wherein it is posited variously as a place for the beatified to experience God in blissful solitude *and* for renewing old friendships with particular loved ones *and* for joining a community of the anonymous blessed. The ambiguities of Richardson's novelistic "hints" sent Chapone to Mary Astell and John Norris, as we have seen, in framing her questions about the nature of Heaven—an appropriate response, inasmuch as Richardson found in their writings a useful theological touchstone as he composed *Clarissa*.[33] Yet neither Norris nor Astell can provide particular clarity on—or comfort for—the matter at hand.

In her *Serious Proposal to the Ladies* (1694), for instance, Astell allows herself to imagine "Heav'n" as a place where "happy Souls . . . now and then step aside from more general Conversations, to entertain themselves with a peculiar Friend"—but feels compelled to add the rather crucial caveat: "(as some are of opinion)."[34] Norris similarly grapples to reconcile competing impulses—those of head and heart, one suspects—when pondering heavenly existence. A particularly salient (and sorrowful) example of this tension may be found at the conclusion to his *Miscellanies*, in an essay entitled "Concerning the Death of my Dear Neece M. C."[35] Norris here attempts to find consolation for human grief by envisioning immortal coexistence with his loved one, yet his vision is burdened by what seems to register as an unsettling possibility: "'Twill not be long," Norris writes, "e're I shall enjoy the Beatific Vision of God and (if after that the fruition of any Creature can be of any moment) the Society of even this dear person."[36] As in the passage from

Astell's *Serious Proposal*, the parenthetical clause here has the effect of an undertow, unsettling the assertion of a social Heaven even as it is being formulated. As Norris realizes, the logic of the beatific vision would seem to preclude any awareness—any interest, at least—in even our most "dear" human relations and friends.[37] In theory, Norris admits, those who have attained a "near and intimate view" of God "can dispense not only with the *eternal loss* but *damnation* of their *friends* without the least grief or resentment."[38] In practice, Norris cannot imagine not wanting to "enjoy" his beloved niece again.

Even strongly theocentric thinkers of this period like Norris and Astell, in short, were thinking about Heaven in ways that suggest not only *uncertainty*, but at least a hint, to borrow Chapone's word, of *discomfort*. One might almost suggest that Richardson was claiming of his heroine "she went to heaven" just at the moment when Heaven, at least some versions of it, was beginning suspiciously to resemble Hell—and not just for atheists like David Hume.[39]

Elizabeth Carter—Richardson's contemporary and a not uncritical admirer of his novels—offers an apt case in point. Indeed, it is difficult to imagine anyone reading Carter's voluminous correspondence without noticing the frequency with which questions about the afterlife surface—or the insistence with which Carter posits a particular answer, one fully in keeping with the "modern" view of Heaven she had found in the works of an early favorite, Elizabeth Rowe.[40] Heaven, for Carter, is *necessarily* an extension of the pleasures of lived experience. "The longer one lives in the world," she explains to Elizabeth Montagu in a letter of July 4, 1767, "the more strongly one becomes attached to its most reasonable pleasures."[41] Indeed, as she memorably insists to Elizabeth Vesey in a letter of May 4, 1774, pleasure would not *be* pleasure but for a heavenly guarantee: "No pleasure can be capable of giving any real delight to the human mind unless it is connected with immortal ideas! I feel this so strongly that I can scarcely enjoy a rose or a sprig of myrtle, till my imagination transplants it to the walks of Paradise, where it will be secure from fading."[42]

And no pleasure mattered more to Carter, it would appear, than friendship; accordingly, in letters spanning four decades, she insists again and again on "transplanting" (like a "sprig of myrtle") her closest relationships into immortal ground.[43] In a letter of May 21, 1765, to Elizabeth Vesey, Carter underscores "the happiness of meeting one's friends in that universal sejour, where separation will be no more." She writes to Vesey in a similar vein on January 15, 1770: "Adieu, my dear friend, God bless you, and conduct us both to that happy assembly, where the spirits of the just shall dread no future separation." "The best consolation in parting with our friends," she muses nine months later in another letter to Vesey, "is to anticipate the society of Paradise, in which there will be no more separation." And in yet another letter to her (July 26, 1771), Carter reminds Vesey "of that meeting which will not be embittered with the thoughts of any future separation."[44] On first glance, one might suspect that sentiments repeated with such regularity carry concomitantly diminished meaning—that Carter, like many of us, has a favorite off-handed theme or phrase with which she inadvertently lards her correspondence. In this case, however, the opposite explanation seems the better one. Carter's insistence on positing a social Heaven signals not thoughtless confidence but, rather, thoughtful anxiety.

Indeed, far from amounting to theological platitudes, Carter's recurring references to eternal social attachments form part of a mounting *argument* with Vesey, whose doubts about the nature of Heaven Carter felt compelled to address.[45] At stake in this argument, it is worth noting, is less whether Heaven *exists*, more whether we will recognize, or even care to recognize, our loved ones when we take up residence there. "You call every argument for the continuation of our present attachments in a future state a mere exercise of imagination," Carter writes in a letter of 1764 to Vesey. "I do not think this to be the case." She continues by suggesting that, whatever Heaven might be, human beings can rest "contented . . . that all who endeavour to fulfil the circle of their present duties, will, when the task is over, be placed in a condition the most perfect of their nature, and the best adapted to their happiness." At the very least, she admits with uncharacteristic latitude, "[it] will certainly do us no hurt to conclude, that the connections of virtue will be immortal, as the spirits by which they are formed."[46]

If here Carter's argument hinges on what amounts to psychological pragmatism, elsewhere she turns directly to specific scriptural passages as empirical proof for her position—a strategy she had honed in her own private meditations.[47] In a letter of June 1, 1763, Carter writes to, or rather pleads with, Vesey:

> Surely, my dear Mrs. Vesey, there can be no room for the melancholy doubt which you express, that a friendship established upon principles like these, (and no other deserves the name), should ever be dissolved. . . . [A]ttachments formed on the noblest principles and best affections of the soul, must be immortal as itself: and they who have improved, encouraged, and supported each other in the duties of a state of trial, will surely be permitted to rejoice together in the rewards of a world of perfect happiness. Remember, that Heaven is always represented as a society; and read 1 Thess. chap. iv. ver. 13–18; Hebrews, chap. xii. ver. 22–24: and when you have the Bible before you, read the Revelations.[48]

Ten years later (April 25, 1774), Carter continues to blame her friend for giving way to her "melancholy fancies," and essentially combines the two approaches—psychology and Scripture—in her efforts to win Vesey to her side:

[M]y dear friend, why will you suffer your imagination to fix itself on the dismal sound of the passing bell, and the dark chambers of the grave, instead of teaching it to wander through the regions of light and immortality, amidst the great community of happy spirits? You love society: take a view of that brilliant assembly described by an author (Heb. xii. 22, &c.) who gives such excellent rules for securing an admission to it: and when any painful ideas of separation deject you, let it comfort your heart.[49]

Vesey should accede to Carter's view of Heaven, in other words, both because the Bible says so *and* because she will feel better if she does.

Vesey appears to have remained unconvinced—"the unmanageable Vesey never did practice any of the lessons" friends like Carter provided, Deborah Heller writes.[50] In a note Vesey included in the packet of Carter's letters she returned in December of 1774, and which Montagu Pennington (Carter's nephew and the editor of her correspondence) includes in his prefacing "ADVERTISEMENT," Vesey concludes with a cleverly conditional reference to Carter's eventual ascension to *"those happy regions where I wish I could deserve to meet you."*[51] Reverend Pennington, writing in 1817 as Vicar of Northbourn in Kent, must have felt an explanation was necessary—though his attempt at clarification results in precisely the sort of uncertainty that had ruffled Chapone. He writes, "In those 'happy regions' it is hoped, and may upon Christian principles be believed, that Mrs. Carter is now indeed receiving her reward, and perhaps sensible of the grateful affection of her amiable friend."[52] As before, the question is not whether Carter is in Heaven, but whether her "reward" includes being "sensible" of her "amiable friend." Pennington's is a very loud "perhaps," in other words, but one fully in keeping with his general editorial defensiveness with respect to his aunt's conception of Heaven. "Mrs. Carter had no doubt," he writes as if he himself might, "that, in the glorified state, souls will be conscious of, and will renew the pure and innocent attachments which they have begun in this life."[53]

It is important to note that Carter's interest in these questions is neither limited to a specific moment in time nor to interactions with a particular friend. Letters to Elizabeth Montagu (noted above) and Isabella Sutton, for instance, contain like-minded descriptions of (or claims for) friendship beyond the grave.[54] And years before she had even met Vesey, Carter was already debating the matter at hand with Catherine Talbot—who seems to have proved a less consistent, and more thoughtful, foil to her earnest friend. In a letter of July 26, 1748, Talbot quotes Pascal on the importance of not loving any particular person—"as is by some friendly and affectionate hearts and lively imaginations thought due to the poor insect here"—and concludes: "But as for those who make idols of their friends, I think they deserve no more toleration than you would allow to those who treat, and kiss, and talk to their dogs and cats as if they were *christians.*"[55] Talbot clearly knew Carter well enough to cut carefully, painfully close to the bone—without seeming to cut at all, of course. (She's simply reporting what someone *else* wrote.) Carter answered in kind ten days later: "[Pascal] seems to have founded his notions of duty rather on the basis of a severe and gloomy temper," she writes, "than on the cheerful, social, good-natured spirit of the Gospel." She then turns to the offending "passage in question" and responds in French ("wretched French," as she herself characterizes it) for two full paragraphs, less to Talbot than to Pascal himself. "It does not follow from Mr. Pascal's reckoning that friendship is unreasonable," she explains. "Most of the violence that we do to the constitution of human nature, and to society's obligations," Carter complains, "seems to be born from the idea that some pious visionaries have formed from a *speculative* love of God, which consists of a distrust of virtues and a withdrawing from the commerce of people like them, like miserable and stunted beings." At which point she begins her peroration:

> The best representation that we can make for ourselves of the moral perfection of God is found in its images in the spirit of man—"but it is unreasonable that we form friendships, because we will die!"—to which it is natural to respond: *we will live again.* . . . A friendship which does not look beyond the grave would not be worthy of an immortal being. But when we consider the present life, not as a detached state, but as it really is, as a part of eternity, the objection of death doesn't mean anything. We do not look at our friends as lost, but only as those who have arrived first where we will soon follow.[56]

In her response (misdated August 2, 1748), Talbot suggests a détente. "The French paragraph in your last gave me great pleasure," she writes, noting that she and Carter are "too near agreed . . . to carry on a controversial Correspondence." And yet in her magnanimous closing, Talbot essentially takes back her concession even as she offers it: "Perhaps of all the notions of future happiness none is so intelligible to the human mind, and heart, as that of meeting again in joy those dear friends, we either have lost, or may lose, never to part again, and yet undoubtedly even this is low, to what our improved natures will be capable of."[57] That which currently is "intelligible to the human mind," Talbot's logic runs, will "undoubtedly" be superseded by our heavenly capabilities—which leaves us with a version of Norris's dilemma as he ponders the loss of his niece. Unlike her friend, in other words, Talbot (who died of cancer at forty-nine years of age) seems to have been keenly aware of the possibility that what speaks to the "human mind, and heart" *now* may very well fall silent, even if we *do* achieve Heaven—in which case our space for human relationship, for friendship, is necessarily delimited by the grave.[58]

"O no!" John Wesley exclaimed in his final sermon, "On Faith," written in the last months of his long life:

> Had you stood by [a dying parishioner's] bedside when that dying saint was crying out, "I have a father and a mother gone to heaven" (to paradise, the receptacle of happy spirits); "I have ten brothers and sisters gone to heaven; and now I am going to them, that am the eleventh! Blessed be God that I was born!" would you have replied: "What, if you are going to them? They will be no more to *you* than any other persons; for you will not know them." Not know them! Nay, does not all that is in you recoil at that thought? Indeed, sceptics may ask, "How do disembodied spirits know each other?" I answer plainly, I cannot tell. But I am certain that they do.[59]

For Wesley as for Talbot and Carter, for Norris and Astell as for Chapone and Richardson—for a wide spectrum of eighteenth-century Christians, in short—the transition to the social, "modern" view of Heaven was at best messy, at worst painful. Philip C. Almond suspects that shifting attitudes about the afterlife may be explained in part by "changing patterns of human relationships" (the rise of "companionate marriage," for example) during the seventeenth and eighteenth centuries.[60] One thinks too of anxieties generated by Locke's disembodied account of personal identity and the challenge it represented to orthodox notions of bodily resurrection.[61] Christians of this period were hardly the first to struggle with the difficulty of reconciling personality to immortality, of course; Dante, who allows Beatrice one final glance before she turns back to God,[62] would surely have sympathized with Richardson's attempt to give artistic voice to the theological incoherencies of his particular moment. But it does seem likely that the concurrence of intellectual and cultural factors giving birth to so many "histories" focused *on* individuals in eighteenth-century Britain would likewise give a particular urgency to the question of what happens *to* individuals after death.

This is not to diminish the enormous difference between even the "modern" reading of *Clarissa*'s Heaven and the Spiritualist view of the afterlife that would develop in the next century, where, to take just one wonderful example, "similarities with earthly life included the availability of whisky sodas and cigars."[63] Indeed, I suspect it is unwise to attempt to separate out the particular strands of heavenly imagining in Richardson's novel, although clearly that is exactly the approach I have taken throughout this essay. Doing so may well bespeak that all too human desire, the irritable reaching after fact and reason that Keats identifies as the surest way to vitiate the type of truth-telling available only in works of human artistry. Put differently, we might say that in his "negatively capable" willingness to resist the instinct toward closure and certitude, Richardson invites his readers to embrace the mystery and doubt at the heart of any truly faithful expression of Christianity; at the same time, of course, he tempts them—us—to closure and certainty, knowing that however diligently we might strive for divine openness and indifference, we inevitably land in the utterly human world of closed opinion and conviction.

If we were evolutionary biologists, we might consider *Clarissa*, with its multifarious conceptions of Heaven, as a member of a "transitional species"—a whale with legs, as it were, one on the track that leads not to Nietzsche but to Kierkegaard. It should go without saying that such wonderfully bizarre creatures are worth studying in part because they offer a snapshot of the environmental pressures that surrounded—and produced—them.

NOTES

1. Anna Laetitia Barbauld, ed., *The Life and Correspondence of Samuel Richardson*, 6 vols. (London, 1804), 4:217, 244. Richardson's letter is included in John Carroll, ed., *Selected Letters of Samuel Richardson* (Oxford: Clarendon Press, 1964), 104.
2. Carol Houlihan Flynn, *Samuel Richardson: A Man of Letters* (Princeton: Princeton University Press, 1982), 255.
3. Florian Stuber, "*Clarissa:* A Religious Novel?," *Studies in the Literary Imagination* 28, no. 1 (1995), 119. See Samuel Richardson, *Clarissa, or The History of a Young Lady*, ed. Angus Ross (Harmondsworth: Penguin, 1985), 1362. Hereafter cited in the text.
4. See Stuber, "*Clarissa:* A Religious Novel?," 120.
5. "The flood of all human plots necessarily channels into a single stream—death—and from thence into one of two strictly delimited (and eternal) oceans: heaven or hell" (E. Derek Taylor, *Reason and Religion in* Clarissa [Burlington, VT: Ashgate, 2009], 144).
6. Richardson uses this descriptive phrase in his letter of October 26, 1748, to Lady Bradshaigh (Carroll, *Selected Letters of Samuel Richardson,* 92).
7. Colleen McDannell and Bernhard Lang, *Heaven: A History* (New Haven, CT: Yale University Press, 1988), 183.
8. Elizabeth Rowe, *Friendship in Death; in Twenty Letters from the Dead to the Living* (London, 1745), 40.
9. Rowe, *Friendship in Death*, 7.
10. Maslen warns against the "bias of seeing the printer only through the author" in his splendidly thorough *Samuel Richardson of London Printer: A Study of His Printing Based on Ornament Use and Business Accounts* (Dunedin, NZ: University of Otago Press, 2001), 37.
11. McDannell and Lang, *Heaven*, 178. Hervey's text—"one of the most widely read devotional works of its time," as McDannell and Lang put it (176)—saw ten editions, beginning in 1746 and ending in 1753, and Richardson's press was responsible for each of them, albeit with some slight theological reservations on Richardson's part. He expresses his misgivings about Hervey's inclinations toward "the enthusiastic part of Methodism" in a letter to Lady Bradshaigh (March 31, 1750; Barbauld, *The Life and Correspondence of Samuel Richardson*, 6:13).
12. McDannell and Lang, *Heaven*, 57, 90. "In a sermon," McDannell and Lang explain, "Augustine imagined someone asking about human activities in eternal life: 'What will I do? There will be no work for our limbs; what, then, will I do?' The bishop answered simply: 'Is this not activity: to stand, to see, to love, to praise [God?]'" (59). "In heaven, according to Aquinas, there will be no more active life; only contemplation will continue" (89).
13. McDannell and Lang, *Heaven*, 157, 147–48.
14. McDannell and Lang, *Heaven*, 172, 173.
15. Mary Astell and John Norris, *Letters concerning the Love of God*, ed. E. Derek Taylor and Melvyn New (Burlington, VT: Ashgate, 2005), 115, 130. Cf. non-juror William Law's influential *A Serious Call to a Devout and Holy Life* (London, 1729), where Law explains that whether "*in* the body, or *out* of the body, in *heaven*, or on *earth*, [human spirits] must have every degree of their greatness and happiness from God alone" (493).
16. McDannell and Lang, *Heaven*, 167–68.

17. See Ruth Perry's excellent biography, *The Celebrated Mary Astell* (Chicago: University of Chicago Press, 1986), 323. The quotation is from a letter written by Astell's friend Lady Elizabeth Hastings.
18. See the Forster Collection of Manuscripts in the Victoria and Albert Museum (48E5–48E10), XII, 2, f. 9.
19. John Norris, *A Collection of Miscellanies* (London, 1687; New York and London: Garland, 1978), 412, 415, 412.
20. Astell and Norris, *Letters concerning the Love of God*, 66–67.
21. Astell and Norris, *Letters concerning the Love of God*, 80.
22. This distinction is first broached by Astell in letter VII—and Norris eagerly seizes on it in his response. Astell and Norris, *Letters concerning the Love of God*, 100 and 103–9.
23. Letter of June 4, 1752. Forster Collection, f. 75.
24. Forster Collection, ff. 36–37.
25. See my account of this debate in *Reason and Religion in* Clarissa, 63, and Tom Keymer's analysis in *Richardson's* Clarissa *and the Eighteenth-Century Reader* (New York: Cambridge University Press, 1992), 120–22. Mulso's letters are reprinted in vol. 1 of *The Works of Mrs. Chapone*, 4 vols. in 2 (Boston, 1809).
26. Samuel Richardson, *Pamela, Or Virtue Rewarded*, ed. Thomas Keymer and Alice Wakely (New York: Oxford University Press, 2008), 496.
27. John A. Dussinger, "'Stealing in the Great Doctrines of Christianity': Samuel Richardson as Journalist," *Eighteenth-Century Fiction* 15, no. 3–4 (2003): 485n15.
28. John 14:2 recounts Jesus's soothing words to the disciples before his arrest and crucifixion: "In my Father's house are many mansions: if it were not so, I would have told you. I go to prepare a place for you."
29. Ewha Chung has been particularly attentive to this aspect of the novel. See her "Samuel Richardson's *Clarissa*: Defining the 'Sacred' Community and Defending Religious Education," *English Language and Literature* 42 (1996): 813–26; also see her *Samuel Richardson's New Nation* (New York: Peter Lang, 1998).
30. James Hervey, *Meditations among the Tombs* (Bath, 1746), 38–39.
31. McDannell and Lang, *Heaven*, 176.
32. McDannell and Lang, *Heaven*, 64.
33. See my *Reason and Religion in* Clarissa.
34. Mary Astell, *A Serious Proposal to the Ladies Parts I & II*, ed. Patricia Springborg (London: Pickering & Chatto, 1997), 37.
35. See Richard Acworth's account of this "most moving document" in *The Philosophy of John Norris of Bemerton (1657–1712)* (New York: Georg Olms Verlag, 1979), 77–78.
36. Norris, *A Collection of Miscellanies*, 464.
37. Cf. Aquinas, *Summa Theologica*: "The blessedness of those who are beatified is God alone" (*Aquinas: Summa Theologica, Questions on God*, ed. Brian Davies and Brian Leftow [Cambridge: Cambridge University Press, 2006], 285).
38. Norris, *A Collection of Miscellanies*, 462. Norris is giving voice to a version of what F.W. Farrar called the "abominable fancy"—namely, as Philip C. Almond puts it, that the "joys of the righteous were heightened by the vision across the great divide of the torments of the wicked" (*Heaven and Hell in Enlightenment England* [Cambridge: Cambridge University Press, 1994], 97; see Farrar, *Eternal Hope* [London, 1878], 66). D.P. Walker has a thorough section on this notion as well in *The Decline of Hell: Seventeenth-Century Discussions of Eternal Torment* (Chicago: University of Chicago Press, 1964), 29–32.
39. See James Boswell's famously nonplussed account of Hume's famously non-nonplussed death in *Boswell in Extremes: 1776–1778*, ed. Charles McC. Weis and Frederick A. Pottle (Yale University Press, 1931; New York: McGraw-Hill, 1970), 11–15.
40. See *Memoirs of the Life of Mrs. Elizabeth Carter*, ed. Montagu Pennington, 2 vols. (London, 1825; New York: AMS Press, 1974), 64–69. Carter wrote an elegy for Rowe on her death in 1737—and her father both praised the poem and warned against Rowe's "tincture of enthusiasm" (1:65–66). The poem is reprinted in vol. 2 (30–31).
41. *Letters from Mrs. Elizabeth Carter to Mrs. Montagu*, ed. Montagu Pennington, 4 vols. (London, 1817; New York: AMS, 1973), 1:336.

42. *A Series of Letters between Mrs. Elizabeth Carter and Miss Catherine Talbot*, ed. Montagu Pennington, 4 vols. (London, 1809; New York: AMS, 1975), 4:108–9.

43. Carter never married, and her closest relationships were with women. Sylvia Harcstark Myers reads her "refusal to marry and her reliance on the friendship of women" as the result of her awareness that "marriage involved a power relationship in which men dominated women, whereas the friendships with women involved a more trustworthy relationship between equals" (*The Bluestocking Circle: Women, Friendship, and the Life of the Mind in Eighteenth-Century England* [Oxford: Clarendon Press, 1990], 111). More recently, Susan S. Lanser has found in the writings of Bluestockings in general, and "Carter in particular," a range of "free-floating homoerotic desire" ("Bluestocking Feminism and the Economies of Desire," in *Reconsidering the Bluestockings*, ed. Nicole Pohl and Betty A. Schellenberg [San Marino, CA: Huntington Library Press, 2005], 272–73). In either reading, Carter's closeness with women remains a crucial aspect of her biography.

44. *A Series of Letters*, 3:256, 207; 4:25, 34.

45. Carter apparently was not alone in this endeavor. Myers summarizes a letter from Elizabeth Montagu to Vesey (October 24, 1773) in which she attempted to "reassure her" of "the life hereafter, in which all friends were to meet" (253).

46. *Memoirs*, 2:400–401. The letter is anonymous as presented in *Memoirs*. Pennington elected not to include it in *A Series of Letters*, but it is gathered in *Memoirs* with others addressed to Vesey in *A Series of Letters*.

47. In "On Good Friday / A Fragment," Carter provides a fascinating reading of Christ's death that stresses the implications of His social nature for a proper understanding of Heaven:

> To all who believe the Gospel it must give an inexpressible delight, that those sentiments of affection to which we owe our most exquisite pleasure, were sanctified by many instances in the history of Him, whose whole conduct is proposed for our unerring example; who, amidst the suffering of a violent and painful death, felt all the tenderest sensibilities of social love, and employed some of the latest moments of expiring life in expressing his concern for a parent, and his confidence in a friend. . . . Amidst all those delightful contemplations which the hopes of immortality inspire, it is impossible for a heart devoted to particular attachments, not to feel the most exquisite pleasure in the prospect of improving and perpetuating these sentiments. (*Memoirs*, 2:405–6)

48. *A Series of Letters*, 3:217. Each of the scriptural passages here referenced (and much of Revelation, of course) envisions the second coming of Christ as an event that reestablishes the community of all Christians—both the living and the dead.

49. *A Series of Letters*, 4:105.

50. Deborah Heller, "Elizabeth Vesey as the Sylph in Bluestocking Correspondence," in *Reconsidering the Bluestockings*, 231.

51. *A Series of Letters*, 3:211.

52. *A Series of Letters*, 3:211–12.

53. See Pennington's note in *Letters from Mrs. Elizabeth Carter to Mrs. Montagu*, 2:366. Carter's letter of July 9, 1776, to Elizabeth Montagu, to which Pennington is responding, reads in part, "I very sensibly feel the kindness of what you say of our friendship. May it continually improve our mutual virtue, and our mutual happiness, till both are completed in that world where neither will receive any interruption" (3:365–66). The elaborate footnote—it is one of the longest Pennington included in the many volumes of material he edited on behalf of his aunt—suggests that anxieties on this point among believers (certainly, at least, for this believer) continued well into the century that saw the development of Spiritualism. Indeed, Georgina Byrne notes, "[S]ome thought that spiritualism might rekindle the Christian faith, and in particular the belief in life after death. Thomas Colley, a convinced spiritualist who became Archdeacon of Natal, speaking in 1875, criticized the Church's grey and gloomy religion, preferring the possibility of birdsong, flowers and sunshine after death" ("'Angels Seen Today:' The Theol-

ogy of Modern Spiritualism and Its Impact on Church of England Clergy, 1852–1939," in *The Church, the Afterlife and the Fate of the Soul*, Studies in Church History 45, ed. Peter Clarke and Tony Claydon [Rochester, NY: Boydell & Brewer, 2009], 367).

54. In a letter of October 27, 1762, to Sutton, Carter writes,

> Was every prospect to be limited by the grave, what inexpressible horrors must one feel, at the thought of quitting such a system of creation, as engages the attention by every form of variety, strikes by every wonder of magnificence, and charms with every grace, and every elegance of beauty! How terrible to close one's eyes upon the flower earth and radiant sun, to 'leave the warm precincts of the cheerful day,' and sink into a cold, dark, eternal night! Then to think of losing all sense of intellectual pleasure, all the tendernesses of affection, and all the excellencies of virtue.
> From this dreadful extinction, God be praised, we are graciously secured (*Memoirs* 1:416–17).

55. *Series of Letters* 1:281–82. Talbot provides the quotation from *Pensées*: "Il est injuste qu'on s'attache, quoi qu'on le fasse avec plaisir, et volontairement: je tromperois ceux en qui je farai naître ce desir, car je ne suis la fin de personne, et n'ai de quoi le satisfaire. Ne suis je pas prête à mourir? et ainsi l'objet de leur attachemont mourra donc?"

56. *Series of Letters*, 1:286 87. Carter's original reads as follows:

> Ainsi il ne s'ensuit pas du raisonnement de Mons. Pascal qu'il soit injuste qu'on s'attache.... La plus part des violences que l'on fait a la constitution de la nature humaine, et aux devoirs de la societé semble naître de l'idée que quelques visionaires pieux se sont formés d'un Amour *speculatif* de Dieu, qui consiste dans un mepris des vertus, et un éloignement du commerce de leur semblables, commes des êtres chétifs, et miserables.... La meilleure representation que nous pouvons nous faire des perfections morales de Dieu, se tire de leur images dans l'esprit de l'homme—'Mais il est injuste que l'on s'attache, par ce que nous mourrons!'—cela se respond fort naturellement par—*nous revivrons*.... Un attachement qui ne porteroit pas ses vues plus loin que le tombeau, seroit indigne d'un être immortel. Mais lorsque l'on considere la vie presente, non pas comme un état détaché, mais comme elle est effectivement, comme une partie de l'éternité, l'objection de la mort ne fait rien. On ne regarde pas ses amis comme perdus, mais seulement arrivéz les premiers ou nous devons bientôt les suivre. (1:286–87)

I am grateful to Wade Edwards (Longwood University) and to his student Kelly James for the English translation.

57. *Series of Letters* 1:289–90, 292.

58. Celia Barnes Rasmussen notes that "Talbot's letters are full of . . . ups and downs, new beginnings and pledges that come out of a profound fear of time's eternal march." In "negat[ing]" Talbot's "obsession, her fear of wasting time—and of wasting away—in the face of death," Carter's remembrances of her friend, Rasmussen argues, reconstruct her life and death as "the lesson that teaches Carter what she already knows," namely that "death is not the end" ("'Speaking on the Edge of My Tomb': The Epistolary Life and Death of Catherine Talbot," *Partial Answers: Journal of Literature and the History of Ideas* 8 [June 2010]: 263, 272).

59. John Wesley, "On Faith," in *The Works of John Wesley*, vol. 4 (Nashville: Abingdon Press, 1987), 196.

60. Almond, *Heaven and Hell in Enlightenment England*, 104–5.

61. On this point, see Lucia Dacome, "Resurrecting by Numbers in Eighteenth-Century England," *Past and Present* 193 (November 2006): 73–110.

62. In canto 31 of *Paradiso*, Beatrice bestows one last smile on Dante ("sorrise e riguardommi") before turning toward the eternal fountain ("poi si tornò a l'eterna fontana").

63. Byrne, "'Angels Seen Today,'" 364.

Chapter Five

The Intellectual Background to Johnson's *Life of Browne*

A Study of Johnsonian Construction

Robert G. Walker

Construction: The act of arranging terms in the proper order, by disentangling transpositions; the act of interpreting; explanation.

—Johnson's *Dictionary*

In 1756 Samuel Johnson wrote a biography of the seventeenth-century polyglot Sir Thomas Browne to serve as an introduction to a second edition of Browne's posthumously published *Christian Morals* (1716). In the month that Johnson died, December 1784, one of his earliest biographers, Thomas Tyers, commented, "There is indeed too much Latin in [Johnson's] English. He seems to have caught the infectious language of Sir Thomas Brown [*sic*], whose works he read, in order to write his life."[1] Little did anyone suspect that Tyers would set the pattern for almost all comments regarding the Browne biography over the next two centuries.

These comments are invariably short, usually link the biography with Browne's and Johnson's writing styles, and frequently are dismissive, either implicitly or explicitly. Thus, although James Boswell professes not to avail himself much of Tyers's biographical sketch because Tyers "was not sufficiently attentive to accuracy,"[2] he nonetheless yokes Johnson's work about Browne to stylistic issues: after listing Johnson's "original essays" in 1756, he comments, "In all these he displays extensive political knowledge and sagacity, expressed with uncommon energy and perspicuity, without any of those words which he sometimes took a pleasure in adopting, in imitation of Sir Thomas Browne; of whose 'Christian Morals' he this year gave an edition, with his 'Life' prefixed to it." To be fair to Boswell, he ends by referring to the work as "one of Johnson's best biographical performances" (*L of J*, 1:307–8). However, despite Boswell's praise, occasionally echoed in a similarly brief manner over the years, and despite a competent and interesting essay devoted to the *Life of Browne* by James Lill in 1983, it seems accurate to quote Walter Jackson Bate's evaluation from his magisterial biography of Johnson as representative of the dominant view: "[Johnson] revised an older edition of Sir Thomas Browne's *Christian Morals* and prefixed to it a 'Life' of Browne, which tends to be rather testy and is remembered now largely for its perceptive remarks on Browne's style."[3] In this essay I will reconsider Johnson's *Life of Browne* with special attention on how it was constructed; by examining its intellectual milieu, especially but not exclusively its theological context, I hope to extend and modify Lill's assessment and establish Boswell's evaluation over Bate's as the more valid.[4]

How neglectful Johnsonians have been of the *Life of Browne* is probably curious to Browne scholars. With the exceptions just noted—Lill's essay and mentions of stylistic affinities—the work has had no extended study. Meanwhile, Brownean Daniela Haverstein has recently asserted that "Johnson's importance for the reputation of Browne cannot be exaggerated. . . . Johnson . . . wrote the single most influential piece of criticism on Browne, the *Life of Sir Thomas Browne*."[5] And Jonathan Post has opined,

> There can be no denying [the *Life*'s] importance, both as an independent critical document and as a landmark in the history of Browne criticism. Before its publication, Browne was a noted scientist, physician, and antiquarian. He had been the subject of some brief biographical sketches, often defending or denying his religious orthodoxy, and portions of his works were occasionally quoted and commended by purveyors of good taste like Addison. After Johnson's "life," it was possible to think of Browne as an author—as someone with a substantial corpus of works, varying in significance, purpose, and originality, who could be valued for his thought as well as his linguistic attributes.[6]

Johnson's accomplishment and the motives for his efforts are both worthy of further examination.

The title page of the 1756 edition provides the reader, both then and now, with a good indication of what to expect: *Christian Morals: by Sir Thomas Browne, of Norwich, M.D. and Author of Religio Medici. The Second Edition. With a Life of the Author, by Samuel Johnson.*[7] We find Johnson near the midpoint of his literary career: the *Life of Browne* is considered too late by some Johnsonians to be grouped with his "Early Lives," including the anonymously published *Life of Savage* (1744)—and the publication of his

Dictionary the previous year had made his name now marketable enough to be prominently displayed here. Browne is associated with his first (and most famous) work, *Religio Medici*, to which Johnson will frequently turn in his biography as he places Browne, both because of his writings and his behavior, firmly in the Anglican tradition, albeit more a mid-eighteenth-century Anglicanism than a mid-seventeenth-century one.

Johnson's frequent quotation from *Religio Medici*, from Browne's other works, and from works about Browne, especially that of Browne's longtime friend Rev. John Whitefoot, can be disconcerting to the contemporary reader, who may react by skimming over such sections in haste in order to return to what Johnson himself is saying. For instance, emphasizing Johnson's dire financial straits at the time of the composition of the *Life of Browne*—he was, about this time, briefly imprisoned for debt—Robert DeMaria Jr. writes, "Johnson's moderate appraisal of Browne's style is interesting . . . but *most of the biography is so highly derivative* that Johnson's remarks on the life of writing must be read as gratuitous expressions of his own state of uneasiness and anger."[8] Rather than dismissing or ignoring those sections of the work derived from previously printed sources, however, I will here try to demonstrate how several of them contribute to Johnson's depiction of Browne's Anglicanism. Such passages are far more than the padding they at first may seem to be.

One of the pleasures of reading the *Life of Browne* comes from recognizing the unifying elements Johnson has employed in composing it. Sometimes these are relatively minor, like his pithy recapitulations. Here, for example, is his comment on Browne's focus on trivial matters in the *Garden of Cyrus*—I quote only the first and final sentence of a lengthy paragraph: "Some of the most pleasing performances have been produced by learning and genius exercised upon subjects of little importance. . . . To this ambition, perhaps, we owe the Frogs of *Homer*, the Gnat and the Bees of *Virgil*, the Butterfly of *Spenser*, the Shadow of *Wowerus*, and the Quincunx of *Browne*" (xxiv–xxv). This epic catalogue of literary trivia has its charm, as does the traveler's précis in the following example. A few pages after enumerating the various foreign countries to which the youthful Browne traveled, and lamenting that he left no written record of his observations abroad, Johnson offers Browne's famous comment from *Religio Medici*, that "[h]is life has been a miracle of thirty years; which to relate, were not history but a piece of poetry, and would sound like a fable" (xi), and observes, "A traveller has greater opportunities of adventure [than a scholastic]; but *Browne* traversed no unknown seas, or Arabian desarts: and, surely, a man may visit France and Italy, reside at Montpellier and Padua, and at last take his degree at Leyden, without any thing miraculous. What it was, that would, if it was related, sound so poetical and fabulous, we are left to guess; I believe, without hope of guessing rightly" (xii). The passage reminds us concisely of the previously described travels, renews the gentle indictment of his failure to write about them, but also highlights the example of Browne's sloppy use of *miracle*; that Johnson lights on a theological miscue to make his point seems not without significance.

Browne's choice of words had indeed come under Johnson's scrutiny in a passage immediately preceding this, where Browne, admitting theological errors from rhetorical excesses in *Religio Medici*, cites as an example "of this liberty of thought and expression: 'I could be content . . . to be nothing almost to eternity, if I might enjoy my Saviour at the last'" (x). As is clear in the full version of the passage, not cited by Johnson, the self-charged error is the heresy, advanced by so-called Arabian philosophers and defeated by Origen, that the soul perished with the body at death and was recalled to life at the last day. Here Johnson exonerates Browne by suggesting that his sagaciousness precludes taking literally his inexact diction: "He has little acquaintance with the acuteness of *Browne*, who suspects him of a serious opinion, that any thing can be 'almost eternal,' or that any time beginning and ending is not infinitely less than infinite duration" (x–xi). A year later Johnson would employ the same logic to refute in devastating fashion an author who had little metaphysical understanding of *eternity* and *infinity*. To cite two illustrations of many in his review of Soame Jenyns' *Free Inquiry into the Nature and Origin of Evil* (1757):

> That every being not infinite, compared with infinity, must be imperfect, is evident to intuition; that whatever is imperfect must have a certain line which it cannot pass, is equally certain. But the reason which determined this limit, and for which such being was suffered to advance thus far and no further, we shall never be able to discern.
>
> [Jenyns] has told us of the benefits of evil, which no man feels, and relations between distant parts of the universe, which he cannot himself conceive. There was enough in this question inconceivable before, and we have little advantage from a new inconceivable solution.[9]

Johnson was much more "testy" (to borrow Bate's term) toward Jenyns than toward Browne, but I would draw attention especially to the nature of the words Johnson singles out for attention. *Miracle*, *eternity*, and *infinity* are concepts neither to be taken lightly nor used loosely in Johnson's world.

The *Life of Browne* occupies sixty-one pages in the 1756 edition of *Christian Morals*; one-third through occurs the first extensive interpolated quotation, a passage of two pages from Browne's *Hydriotaphia, Urn-Burial, or a Discourse of Sepulchral Urns* (1658). Johnson finds Browne's work dazzling in its detail and learning and virtually useless otherwise: "It is, indeed, like other treatises of antiquity, rather for curiosity than use; for it is of small importance to know which nation buried their dead in the ground, which threw them into the sea, or which gave them to birds and beasts" (xxi). Johnson goes on, however, to draw a sharp contrast between the subject matter of *Hydriotaphia* and an observation by Browne within it, which he quotes at length: "Of the uselessness of all these enquiries, *Browne* seems not to have been ignorant; and, therefore, concludes them with an observation which can never be too frequently recollected" (xxi). This "observation" deserves a closer look, not only as an example of the basis of Browne's belief in a Christian afterlife, a basis here wholeheartedly endorsed by Johnson, but also as an anticipation of similar sentiments that were soon to recur in one of Johnson's most famous works, *The History of Rasselas* (1759).

The passage begins, "All or most apprehensions rested in opinions of some future being, which ignorantly or coldly believed, begat those perverted conceptions, ceremonies, sayings, which christians pity or laugh at" (xxi–xxii). Browne's syntax may be a bit obscure to a modern reader, but by "opinions of some future being" he means, simply, varying ideas of life hereafter. Browne continues with a common distinction between the classical view of immortality, dependent solely on reason, and that of the Christian: "Happy are they, which live not in that disadvantage of time, when men could say little for futurity, but from reason; whereby the noblest mind fell often upon doubtful deaths, and melancholy dissolutions" (xxii). Browne's (and Johnson's) audience would have understood the implicit contrast here between pagan reason and Christian Revelation as sources for a belief in immortality—one dubious, the other certain. Next Browne predicates an argument for man's immortality on the principle that God does nothing in vain, and he advances that argument mainly on psychological grounds: "It is the heaviest stone that melancholy can throw at man, to tell him he is at the end of his nature; or that there is no further state to come, unto which this seems progressional, and otherwise made in vain: without this accomplishment, the natural expectation and desire of such a state, were but a fallacy in nature" (xxii). The desire for immortality planted in man by a just God supports belief in an afterlife; otherwise, God would be unjust and man would be better off as part of the (lower) animal kingdom:

> unsatisfied considerators would quarrel the justice of their constitution, and rest content that *Adam* had fallen lower, whereby, by knowing no other original, and deeper ignorance of themselves, they might have enjoyed the happiness of inferior creatures, who in tranquillity possess their constitutions, as having not the apprehension to deplore their own natures; and being framed below the circumference of these hopes or cognition of better things, the wisdom of *God* hath necessitated their contentment. (xxii–xxiii)

Browne concludes, "But the superior ingredient and obscured part of ourselves, whereto all present felicities afford no resting contentment, will be able at last to tell us we are more than our present selves; and evacuate such hopes in the fruition of their own accomplishments" (xxiii).

Johnson was to illustrate in fiction the complex argument Browne makes here, demonstrating that it was indeed an observation that "can never be too frequently recollected," when he reprises it in *Rasselas*. Here our focus is on the *Life of Browne* and why Johnson singled out particular passages in his writings, so there is no need to rehearse again the view I posited years ago that *Rasselas* may be most satisfyingly understood within the context of contemporary discussions of the doctrine of immortality.[10] Suffice to say, the theme appears in *Rasselas* early and late. In the second chapter Prince Rasselas, inexplicably dissatisfied in the Happy Valley where all his wants are supposedly supplied and

> having for some time fixed his eyes upon the goats that were brousing among the rocks, began to compare their condition with his own. "What," said he, "makes the difference between man and all the rest of the animal creation? Every beast that strays beside me has the same corporal necessities with myself; he is hungry and crops the grass, he is thirsty and drinks the stream, his thirst and hunger are appeased, he is satisfied and sleeps; . . . I am hungry and thirsty like him, but when thirst and hunger cease I am not at rest; I am, like him, pained with want, but am not, like him, satisfied with fulness. . . . Man has surely some latent sense for which this place affords no gratification, or he has some desires distinct from sense which must be satisfied before he can be happy."[11]

That the place affording man "no gratification" is not narrowly the Happy Valley but widely the created world becomes clear in the final third of the work, dominated by *memento mori* and punctuated symbolically by visits to the pyramids and the catacombs. At the latter site a discussion on the immateriality (and thus the immortality) of the soul ends with Imlac (here Johnson's voice) remarking, "That [the soul] will not perish by any inherent cause of decay, or principle of corruption, may be shown by philosophy; but philosophy can tell no more. That it will not be annihilated by him that made it, we must humbly learn from higher authority" (174).

The passage from *Hydriotaphia* that Johnson copies into the *Life of Browne*, then, manifests a co-incidence between Johnson and Browne, both in their recourse to the Christian doctrine of immortality and in their several arguments based on justice and animal existence. To Christian Revelation Johnson and Browne—among many others—add what I termed an argument from desire in support of immortality. Man's uniqueness among animal creation, his infinite yearnings and inability to be satisfied in even the most desirable of places in this world, coupled with the assumption of a just God who does nothing in vain, all join to support a belief in immortality that permeates all Johnson's writings. Finding a resonance in Browne of what he considered a core element in his Christian faith, Johnson would naturally call it to specific notice. In *Rasselas* it is the "scene of mortality . . . and mansions of the dead" (174), in *Hydriotaphia*, the sepulchral urns themselves, that trigger parallel movements of thought in both writers, from last things to lasting ones.

Certainly Johnson need not have read Browne at all to have instilled in *Rasselas* the theme of man's immortality; he had a myriad of other possible sources for these ideas, sources closer to what appears in *Rasselas* than what Browne wrote in *Hydriotaphia*.[12] But that Johnson elsewhere in the *Life of Browne* previews ideas he would repeat in subsequent writings gives additional credence to the connection with *Rasselas*.[13]

The second extensive interpolated quotation used by Johnson takes up eight pages and occurs two-thirds through the text. Johnson probably found his source, John Whitefoot's "Some Minutes for the Life of Sir Thomas Browne," in the *Posthumous Works of Browne* mentioned above. Whitefoot's work is included in both the 1712 and 1722 editions, and Johnson reproduces virtually all of it. He omits the first four paragraphs, except for one phrase that he uses to justify his extensive quotation: Whitefoot remarked that he considered it "an especial favour of *Providence*, to have had a particular acquaintance with [Browne] for two thirds of his life" (xli). Johnson, then, depends on Whitefoot for his "character" of Browne, with its depiction of "those minute peculiarities which discriminate every man from all others" but which are "soon forgotten" and "irrecoverably lost" "if they are not recorded by those whom personal knowledge enabled to observe them" (xl). Johnson here rehearses his well-known theory of biography, which he expressed at greatest length in *Rambler* 60 (October 13, 1750):

> [T]he business of the biographer is often to pass slightly over those performances and incidents, which produce vulgar greatness, to lead the thoughts into domestick privacies, and display the minute details of daily life, where exterior appendages are cast aside, and men excel each other only by prudence and by virtue.
>
> [T]he incidents which give excellence to biography are of a volatile and evanescent kind, such as soon escape the memory, and are rarely transmitted by tradition.[14]

In addition to the opening paragraphs, Johnson omits four paragraphs from the middle of Whitefoot, but these he had largely used earlier. Another paragraph omitted but not used elsewhere is Whitefoot's treatment of Edward

Browne, Thomas's son. Johnson had already summarized Edward's life immediately before this character section, in a more extended fashion over two pages (xxxviii–xl). Johnson's mini-biography of Edward, by the way, is the only part of the *Life* that is truly digressive.[15]

Although it does not, strictly speaking, concern us here, Whitefoot's prose style is not without interest. He (like Johnson) has a knack for just the right learned allusion, such as when he describes the physician Browne's comfortable, but not opulent, financial situation: "He might have made good the old saying of Dat Galenus opes, had he lived in a place that could have afforded it" (xlvii). Burton, in his *Anatomy* (I, 2, 3, 15) renders the poetic epigram:

> The rich Physician, honor'd Lawyers ride,
> Whilst the poor Scholar foots it by their side.
> [*Lat.*, Dat Galenus opes, dat Justinianus honores,
> Sed genus species cogitur ire pedes.][16]

The saying pre-dates Burton, and Johnson was much at home with the layered, allusive, seventeenth-century style of Burton, Browne himself, and Whitefoot. Still, it was not Whitefoot's style but rather his defense of Browne's religious beliefs that most appealed to Johnson, and that primarily motivates the lengthy inclusion.

Whitefoot highlights Browne's specifically Anglican beliefs, both as expressed in his writings and as reflected in his behavior: "In his religion he continued in the same mind which he had declared in his first book, written when he was but thirty years old, his *Religio Medici*, wherein he fully assented to that of the church of England, preferring it before any in the world, as did the learned *Grotius*" (xlvi). Browne's church attendance, his taking of the sacrament whenever available, and his sermon reading are mentioned, as is the fact that he "delighted not in controversies" (xlvi), and the context makes clear that sectarian controversies are meant. The links Whitefoot forges here between Browne, the avoidance of controversy, the Church of England, and the noted Dutch jurist Hugo Grotius (1583–1645) must have greatly appealed to Johnson, who was outspoken in his admiration for Grotius's *De Veritate Religionis Christianae* (1627), sometimes referred to as the first work of Protestant apologetics.[17] Maintaining that disagreements among Christian religions were destructively counterproductive, Grotius focused his polemics on non-Christians, especially pagans, Jews, and Muslims. One of his followers, the Swiss theologian Jean Le Clerc (1657–1736), published an edited version of *De Veritate* (1709; translated into English, 1711). Le Clerc not only added a book of his own to the six that made up Grotius's work, but also appended to it "Testimonies concerning Hugo Grotius's Affection for the Church of England," several of which make the case "that this very great Man had the highest Opinion of the Church of *England*, and would most willingly have lived in it, if he could."[18] In one such letter the Laudian Ambassador to France John Scudamore wrote, "Body and Soul He professeth himself to be for the Church of *England*, and gives this Judgment of it, that it is the likeliest to last of any Church this Day in being."[19] A brilliant scholar with an explicit interdenominational (albeit solely Christian) approach and with historical affection for the English church, Grotius was a quintessential example for the type of intellectual Anglicanism that Browne and Johnson practiced, making Whitefoot's mention of him something Johnson surely would want to echo in his *Life of Browne*.

Some of the "testimonies" in Le Clerc's collection report that Grotius's death from injuries incurred in a shipwreck prevented him from joining the Anglican communion; Browne, certainly, had no such untimely death. According to Whitefoot, Browne's dying provides a fitting exemplum, exhibiting as it does Christian patience rather than Stoic pride:

> In his last sickness, wherein he continued about a week's time, enduring great pain . . . with as much patience as hath been seen in any man, without any pretence of Stoical apathy, animosity, or vanity of not being concerned thereat. . . . His patience was founded upon the christian philosophy, and a sound faith of *God's Providence*, and a meek and humble submission thereunto. (xlvi–xlvii)

Whitefoot's recounting of Browne's last days fits the century's pattern of rendering the passing of a notable person as a public phenomenon, at least so long as it provided evidence in support of orthodox Christian beliefs.[20] Nowhere could the practicality of Browne's Anglican beliefs be better demonstrated than in the comfort they apparently provided him during his last days.

Johnson viewed Browne's religion as both pious and practical and thus worthy of emulation. Immediately after quoting the Whitefoot passage, he seizes on and repeats one of its phrases: "It is observable, that he who in his earlier years had read all the books against religion, was in the latter part of his life *averse from controversies*" (xlix, my emphasis). As Johnson continues, it is tempting, and perhaps correct, to see his remarks as particularly pertinent to himself as much as to Browne:

> To play with important truths, to disturb the repose of established tenets, to subtilize objections, and elude proof, is too often the sport of youthful vanity, of which maturer experience commonly repents. There is a time, when every wise man is weary of raising difficulties only to task himself with the solution, and desires to enjoy truth without the labour or hazard of contest. There is, perhaps, no better method of encountering these troublesome irruptions of scepticism, with which inquisitive minds are frequently harrassed, than that which *Browne* declares himself to have taken [in *Religio Medici*]. (xlix)

Browne's method of dealing with "troublesome irruptions of scepticism" (one of Johnson's most piquant, but seldom-cited phrases, in my opinion) is to "forget them; or at least defer them, till my better settled judgment and more manly reason be able to resolve them" (xlix). This offers an opportunity to remind ourselves of another similarity between Browne and Johnson: both were wont to offer the wisdom of an old sage at a young age—Browne was thirty when *Religio Medici* was published and Johnson in his mid-forties when he wrote the *Life of Browne*.

Amid all the similarities, however, we should not forget a nice distinction made by one of Johnson's most perceptive readers, W.B.C. Watkins: "Johnson . . . never achieved the beautiful serenity of Pascal, nor even the philosophic equanimity of his great favorite, Sir Thomas Browne, who pondered with insatiable wonder the curious involutions and convolutions of existence. He did not have that rare faculty for perplexing and unperplexing the soul."[21] In the last year of his life we find Johnson still dealing with the irruptions that troubled both him and Browne, and dealing with them, as he typically did, with a prayer for God's grace:

> O Lord, . . . enable me to drive from me all such unquiet and perplexing thoughts as may mislead or hinder me in the practice of those duties which thou hast required. . . . [G]ive me Grace always to remember that thy thoughts are not my thoughts, nor thy ways my ways. . . . [T]each me by thy Holy Spirit to withdraw my Mind from unprofitable and dangerous enquiries, from difficulties vainly curious, and doubts impossible to be solved.[22]

Rather than the great controversialist always talking for victory, the Johnson we see in the *Life of Browne* is the one whom Boswell depicts on several occasions, eliding distinctions among Christian sects:

> For my part, Sir, I think all Christians, whether Papists or Protestants, agree in the essential articles, and that their differences are trivial, and rather political than religious. (*L of J*, 1:405)

> [A]ll denominations of Christians have really little difference in point of doctrine, though they may differ widely in external forms. There is a prodigious difference between the external form of one of your Presbyterian churches in Scotland, and a church in Italy; yet the doctrine taught is essentially the same. (*L of J*, 2:150)

> He repeated his observation, that the differences among Christians are really of no consequence. "For instance, (said he,) if a Protestant objects to a Papist, 'You worship images;' the Papist can answer, 'I do not insist on *your* doing it; you may be a very good Papist without it: I do it only as a help to my devotion.'" I said, the great article of Christianity is the revelation of immortality. Johnson admitted it was. (*L of J*, 3:188)

And the Johnson we see in the *Life of Browne* is the one that at least two recent scholars have seen as the Johnson of the *Dictionary*, published the year before. Robert DeMaria Jr. finds that "an unwillingness to take sides in intramural religious disputes is characteristic of all of Johnson's religious pronouncements, but he seems to have taken special care to avoid such presumptions in the *Dictionary*." Howard D. Weinbrot agrees, arguing that Johnson's selection and use of illustrative quotations from religious divines is a type of "theological pacifism": "on commercially prudent and intellectually communal grounds, Johnson avoided rather than courted [religious] controversy" in the *Dictionary*.[23] Perhaps due to the practical piety of the dual motives Weinbrot mentions, when Johnson concludes his defense of Browne, we discover him employing unusually close editing to rub the rough edges from Browne's rhetoric as he places him in the familiar Anglican position of middle ground, this time between nonbelievers on the one hand, overly zealous Christians on the other.

Before that conclusion, however, Johnson establishes further credibility as a somewhat disinterested biographer by citing, and agreeing with, a rather serious criticism of Browne by Isaac Watts: "It is charged upon *Browne* by Dr. *Watts*, as an instance of arrogant temerity, that, after a long detail of his attainments, he declares himself to have escaped 'the first and father-sin of pride'" (l).[24] The comment is rather incidental in Watts, but it provides Johnson an opportunity to measure Browne by his own words and to draw a moral: "A perusal of the *Religio Medici* will not much contribute to produce a belief of the author's exemption from this *Father-Sin*: pride is a vice, which pride itself inclines every man to find in others, and to overlook in himself" (l). At times Browne may have overestimated his courage as well as his humility, Johnson suggests, but he seems to have passed the final test on that score: "the time will come to every human being, when it must be known how well he can bear to die; and it has appeared, that our author's fortitude did not desert him in the great hour of trial" (li).

Johnson further accentuates the use to which he is putting Browne's death, that is, as evidence of the sincerity of his Christian beliefs, by quoting a commonplace associated with Browne: "It was observed by some of the remarkers on the *Religio Medici*, that 'the author was yet alive, and might grow worse as well as better:' it is, therefore, happy, that this suspicion can be obviated by a testimony given to the continuance of his virtue, at a time when death had set him free from danger of change, and his panegyrist [Whitefoot] from temptation to flattery" (li–lii). This "remarker" was the French physician and literary figure Guy Patin, in a letter from Paris dated April 7, 1645. Johnson could have come across Patin's witticism in several places, but the most likely source, although not credited here, is *Biographia Britannica*.[25]

Although Johnson's observations about Browne's style have garnered virtually all previous critical attention devoted to the final nine pages of the *Life*, this section has other, even more interesting aspects. One shows Johnson at his "derivative" best. He seems to be directing our attention once more away from Browne's life and toward his writings:

> But it is not on the praises of others, but on his own writings, that he is to depend for the esteem of posterity; of which he will not easily be deprived, while learning shall have any reverence among men. . . . His memory supplied him with so many illustrations, parallel or dependent notions, that he was always starting into collateral considerations: but the spirit and vigour of his persuit always gives delight; and the reader follows him, without reluctance, thro' his mazes, in themselves flowery and pleasing, and ending at the point originally in view. (lii–liii)

I do not believe it has been pointed out previously that Johnson's memory had turned to Browne's *Vulgar Errors* (*Pseudodoxia Epidemica*) for this observation. There Browne had written,

> [A]dventures in knowledge are laudable, and the assayes of weaker heads afford oftentimes improveable hints unto better . . . although in this long journey we misse the intended end, yet are there many things of truth disclosed by the way: And the collaterall verity, may unto reasonable speculations, some what requite the capitall indiscovery.[26]

We know Johnson had this passage in mind relatively recently, since he had used its first part in the *Dictionary* to illustrate the word *improveable*. Here he softens Browne's *collaterall verity* into *collateral considerations*, but then gives his distinctive style more credit than Browne himself claimed for reaching his intended end. We are thus encouraged, once again, to link Browne's writings with his life in their shared teleology. In other words, Johnson finds Browne's "flowery and pleasing" mazes not at all Miltonic (like the fruitless philosophy of the fallen angels in "wandering mazes lost") but instead Popean ("a mighty maze but not without a plan").

Johnson's final defense of Browne reaches back once more to the man as well as his writings. Johnson tells us,

> There remains yet an objection against the writings of *Browne*, more formidable than the animadversions of criticism. There are passages, from which some have taken occasion to rank him among Deists, and others among Atheists. It would be difficult to guess how any such conclusion should be formed, had not experience shewn that there are two sorts of men willing to enlarge the catalogue of infidels. (lv)

Johnson then proceeds to distinguish between the two sorts, atheists, on the one hand, bigots on the other. It is perhaps to be expected that Johnson would arrange his defense by establishing Browne in a middle position, attacked by extremists from opposite directions. I have deliberately avoided using John Henry Newman's term, via media, to describe the Browne / Johnson / Anglican position on the theological spectrum, not only because it would be anachronistic but also because it may suggest a stasis of the players across time that did not, in fact, exist. The most consistent Anglican tendency was its attempt to occupy the middle—regardless of who was on either end—and those extremities often changed due to secular politics rather than doctrinal reinterpretation. Thus Phillip Harth can define the Anglican Rationalism of the late seventeenth and early eighteenth century as "a middle way between these two extremes [deism and fideism] pursued by those who adopted the third attitude, which was equally opposed to each of the other two views," and proceed immediately to locate Anglican Rationalism in a small number of Puritans, including Richard Baxter, as well as the mainstream tradition of the Catholic and Anglican churches.[27] And thus Johnson himself, in a letter of May 28, 1768, to Frederick Barnard, librarian to George III, as the latter prepared to travel to Europe on a book-buying expedition:

> You are going into a part of the world divided, as it is said, between bigotry and atheism. Such representations are always hyperbolical, but there is certainly enough of both to alarm any mind solicitous for piety and truth. Let not the contempt of Superstition precipitate you into infidelity, nor the horrour of infidelity ensnare you in superstition.[28]

Although Johnson understands that atheists lack the motive of Christians to proselytize (no one has urged them to go into all the world to preach the anti-gospel), he recognizes their psychological need to do so: "[i]n proportion as they doubt the truth of their own doctrines, they are desirous to gain the attestation of another understanding; and industriously labour to win a proselyte, and eagerly catch at the slightest pretence to dignify their sect with a celebrated name" (lvi). At this point Johnson's footnote quotes four lines from "Davies":

> Therefore no hereticks desire to spread
> Their wild opinions like these epicures.
> For so their stagg'ring thoughts are computed,
> And other men's assent their doubt assures.

Though given only the author's surname, Johnson's readers would have recognized the reference to Sir John Davies's *Nosce Teipsum* (1599), a work better known in the eighteenth century as *A Poem on the Immortality of the Soul*.[29] In the selection of these lines Johnson is careful with sectarian labels:

clearly the "epicures" in Davies's poem correspond to the atheists he is deploring. Heretics are within the faith, at least from their own point of view, while atheists lie outside.

The second sort of men who would place Browne in the camp of the enemy, the "bigots," have "become friends to infidelity only by unskilful hostility: men of rigid orthodoxy, cautious conversation, and religious asperity." These men, attacking Browne and others like him, "make in their heat concessions to Atheism, or Deism, which their most confident advocates had never dared to claim or to hope" (lvi). In a single sentence Johnson notably contrasts the relative triviality of the zealots' reasons for objecting to "infidelities" with the enormity of the result: "A sally of levity, an idle paradox, an indecent jest, an unseasonable objection, are sufficient, in the opinion of these men, to efface a name from the lists of *Christianity*, to exclude a soul from everlasting life" (lvi). Like a dog with a juicy bone, Johnson now has his teeth into the overly scrupulous Christian, and he writes some of the best prose in the biography before letting go:

> Such men are so watchful to censure, that they have seldom much care to look for favourable interpretations of ambiguities, to set the general tenor of life against single failures, or to know how soon any slip of inadvertency has been expiated by sorrow and retractation; but let fly their fulminations, without mercy or prudence, against slight offences or casual temerities; against crimes never committed, or immediately repented. (lvii)

Johnson is at pains to point out the irony of the position of hypercritical Christians, and does so again with reference to the two sorts of men: "The Infidel knows well, what he is doing. He is endeavouring to supply, by authority, the deficiency of his arguments; and to make his cause less invidious, by shewing numbers on his side. . . . But the zealot should recollect, that he is labouring, by this frequency of excommunication, against his own cause; and voluntarily adding strength to the enemies of truth" (lvii).

In a paragraph that begins with the same sentiments Johnson would later express several times to Boswell (see p. 104), Johnson defines Christianity by means of its highest, and most radical, virtue:

> Men may differ from each other in many religious opinions, and yet all may retain the essentials of *Christianity*; men may sometimes eagerly dispute, and yet not differ much from one another: the rigorous persecutors of error, should, therefore, enlighten their zeal with knowledge, and temper their orthodoxy with *Charity*; that *Charity*, without which orthodoxy is vain; *Charity* that "thinketh no evil," but "hopeth all things," and "endureth all things." (lviii)

The biblical quotation, of course, is from St. Paul's first letter to the Corinthians, with its most famous of all definitions of Christian love. Johnson abstains, however, from quoting the verse most pertinent to those whom he is attacking—"Charity . . . rejoiceth not in iniquity"—thus exhibiting the very virtue he is celebrating.[30]

The *Life of Browne* concludes with a highly selective pastiche from the first part of *Religio Medici*. A brief transition disposes finally of the two camps of Browne's detractors: "Whether *Browne* has been numbered among the contemners of religion, by the fury of its friends, or the artifice of its enemies, it is no difficult task to replace him among the most zealous *Professors* of *Christianity*" (lviii). And replacing him on that pinnacle is exactly what Johnson does, using Browne's own words. His first three quotations are found in the opening two pages of Browne's first published work:[31]

> It is, indeed, somewhat wonderful, that *He* should be placed without the pale of *Christianity*, who declares, that "he assumes the honourable stile of A *Christian*," not because it is "the religion of his country," but because "having in his riper years and confirmed judgment seen and examined all, he finds himself obliged, by the principles of *Grace*, and the law of his own reason, to embrace no other name but this." (lix)

Until the end of the penultimate paragraph of the *Life*, Johnson continues in this, for him, unusual fashion, stringing together key phrases and short sentences from Browne's work. Despite frequently skipping pages, he almost always moves in parallel with Browne's text, although at one point he jumps backward from page 14 to page 10, then ahead to page 21.[32] Why Johnson worked this way becomes clear, I believe, when we examine the nature of the material that he elided.

Browne stakes out virtually the same middle ground that Johnson would assign him a century later, but either his contentiousness or the contentiousness of his era results in concrete references to religious differences that Johnson systematically removes. When Browne emphasizes the role that Christian charity plays in minimizing his participation in religious strife, he hardly sounds ecumenical: "neither doth herein my zeal so far make me forget the general charity I owe unto humanity, as rather to hate than pity Turks, Infidels, and (what is worse) Jews" (2). Here is his justification of the Protestant Reformation, with its implicit criticism of Catholicism:

> I am of that reformed new-cast religion . . . of the same belief our Saviour taught . . . but by the sinister ends of princes, the ambition and avarice of prelates, and the fatal corruption of times, so decayed, impaired, and fallen from its native beauty, that it required the careful and charitable hand of these times to restore it to its primitive integrity. (3)

Browne writes of his indifference to what he considers unimportant forms of Catholicism—"holy water and crucifix (dangerous to the common people) deceive not my Judgment" (5)—and stresses how he translates such forms into authentic Christianity: "whilst therefore they directed their devotions to [Mary], I offered mine to God, and rectified the errors of their prayers by rightly ordering mine own" (7). He finds dubious ceremonies "in Greek, Roman, and African churches" (7), and shows none of the lexical squeamishness of twenty-first-century political correctness when he maintains that, even after being excommunicated and termed a heretic by the Bishop of Rome, "yet can no ear witness I ever returned him the name of Antichrist, Man of Sin, or Whore of Babylon. It is the method of charity to suffer without reaction" (10–11). Although both Luther and Calvin are named and rejected as sources of belief, the Roman church bears the brunt of Browne's harsh diction, and all this is excised by Johnson in his edited version.

What remains of Browne's words in Johnson's text establishes the former as a firm Anglican of the eighteenth-century sort, with a belief dependent on "the principles of *Grace*, and the law of his own reason" (lix), "Who, tho' 'paradoxical in philosophy, loves in divinity to keep the beaten road'" (lx), and who observes a particular hierarchy among the underpinnings of belief: "To whom 'where the Scripture is silent, the Church is a text; where that speaks, 'tis but a comment;' and who uses not 'the dictates of his own reason, but where there is a joint silence of both'" (lx). Despite the attempt by Dissenters to deny that grace had a primacy in the established church, it remained for all Anglicans the sine qua non on man's road to salvation, and, concomitantly, the subordination of unassisted human reason both to Scripture (Revelation) and to the Church (Tradition) forms an important constituent of Anglican belief in the eighteenth century. Johnson has no truck with arguments among Christian sects about forms, provided that the essential beliefs of Christianity (like individual immortality) are maintained.

The final occasion of Johnson quoting Browne in the *Life* is somewhat puzzling: "Nor can contempt of the positive and ritual parts of religion be imputed to him, who doubts, whether a good man would refuse a poisoned eucharist; and 'who would violate his own arm, rather than a church'" (lxi). Most of this is straightforward, as Johnson dips back to page 6 in *Religio Medici* (from page 22) and continues the same editorial practice we have been outlining. Browne had written, "I should violate my own arm rather than a church, nor willingly deface the name of saint or martyr" (6); Johnson omits the more inflammatory anti-Catholic phrase. Browne's words recall generally the English Civil War and specifically the desecration of his Norwich Cathedral that occurred almost contemporaneously with the publication of *Religio Medici*.[33] But for the remark about the willing acceptance of a poisoned communion cup assigned to Browne by paraphrase, Johnson jumps to *Vulgar Errors*, a work otherwise hardly mentioned in the *Life*, except as discussed above.[34] Moreover, the expression is sufficiently elliptical to require further explanation, although Johnson offers none. Exactly what is on his mind here?

To drink knowingly a poisoned Eucharist may be one of the most conspicuous testaments to a belief in the preeminence of life after death over life in this world, with the afterlife virtually assured by the ultra-timeliness of the infusion of God's grace from the consecrated wine. That the cup is accepted willingly, as it was by Christ, separates this act from other numerous instances of poisoning by holy cup found in popular literature and legends. Best known among the willing recipients is St. John the Evangelist, who is so depicted in medieval legend and iconography, where the poison in the cup is represented by a serpent. Also medieval but closer to home, William Comyn or Cumin, Bishop of Durham (*d. c.*1160), according to the fourteenth-century historian John Fordun, drank knowingly and fatally of a communion cup poisoned by his priests. (St. John, naturally, fared better.)[35] But in *Vulgar Errors*, Browne comes to the idea of a willing acceptance of the poisoned cup only as an afterthought, having begun with an unwitting victim, Emperor Henry VII:

> I hope it is not true, and some indeed have probably denied, what is recorded of the Monke that poysoned Henry the Emperour, in a draught of the holy Eucharist. . . . I will not say what sinne it was to act it; yet may it seeme a kinde of martyrdome to suffer by it: For, although unknowingly, he dyed for Christ his sake, and lost his life in the ordained testimony of his death. Certainely, had they knowne it, some noble zeales would scarcely have refused it, rather adventuring their owne death, then refusing the memoriall of his.[36]

Johnson certainly knew that the interpretation of the sacrament of the Eucharist had been, and continued to be, perhaps the most contentious issue among differing Christian sects; yet he invokes it here, after deliberately avoiding or downplaying the contentiousness he found elsewhere in Browne's writings. And he invokes it in a manner that without doubt is meant to credit Browne's respect for the importance, and one assumes, efficacy of this sacrament. Granted, Browne had used the word "memorial," the general Protestant code that signaled how their interpretation differed from the Roman Catholic and in some ways the Lutheran. But Browne and by inference Johnson seem clearly to regard the grace conferred by cup, albeit poisoned, to be worth the risk of one's life, a nonsensical position sans a belief in personal immortality.

Maurice J. Quinlan is correct, I believe, when he reads Johnson's Eucharistic sermons straightforwardly and accepts the description given in Sermon 9 that the communicant receives "the supernatural and extraordinary influences of grace, and those blessings which God has annexed to the due use of means appointed by himself."[37] Furthermore, Quinlan, although he devotes only a single paragraph to the *Life of Browne*, comes closest to the heart of the matter, as I see it, when he maintains that, although Johnson never specified what he meant by the essentials of the Christian faith, "the nearest he came to doing so was in his *Life of Thomas Browne*" (151). Quinlan's view seems a precursor to the one I have argued above, that Johnson recognized the roots of his eighteenth-century Anglicanism in the beliefs of seventeenth-century Protestant Christians like Browne and Grotius; that he believed that learned men across recent centuries in fact had provided him a body of knowledge alternative to that generated by the Catholic church over a longer and earlier span of time; and that he was confident that this body of knowledge could be espoused and relied upon, especially if troublesome rhetorical harshness was omitted from it.

The last paragraph in the *Life of Browne* is, so far as I can tell, all Johnson's. It begins with yet another reference to the twin sources of information about his subject that Johnson has examined: Browne's own words and the writings of others about him. Students of Johnson, familiar with his view that the degree of certainty one may have about anything is dependent both on the nature of the evidence and on the nature of the subject studied, will recognize that this lies behind his reference to the degree of certainty he has obtained regarding the sincerity of Browne's Christianity:[38]

> The opinions of every man must be learned from himself: concerning his practice, it is safest to trust the evidence of others. Where these testimonies concur, no higher degree of historical certainly can be obtained; and they apparently concur to prove, that *Browne* was *A zealous adherent to the faith of CHRIST*, that *he lived in obedience to his laws, and died in confidence of his mercy*. (lxi)

Johnson's ultimate judgment about Browne here can be seen within both a doctrinal and personal context. First there is the Anglican unwillingness to presume the certainty of anyone's salvation, in sharp contrast to the doctrine of the elect emphasized by other Christian sects. Second is Johnson's reluctance to make such a determination himself, perhaps nowhere better illustrated than in the humble and deliberately tentative words found at the end of an entry in his *Prayers and Meditations* (August 17, 1767). Johnson writes of taking communion, "the sacrament preparatory to her death," with Catherine (Kitty) Chambers, a servant of his mother and her family for over forty years and now in her final illness: "I have communicated with Kitty, and kissed her. . . . Kitty is, I think going to Heaven."[39] The final clause in the *Life of Browne*, with its conspicuous typographical emphasis, fairly thunders in comparison.[40]

NOTES

1. *Johnsonian Miscellanies*, ed. G.B. Hill (1897; New York: Barnes & Noble, 1970), 2:351.
2. *Boswell's Life of Johnson*, ed. G.B. Hill, rev. L.F. Powell (Oxford: Clarendon Press, 1934–50), 3:308; hereafter cited in text as *L of J*.
3. James Lill, "A Lesson in Futurity: Johnson's *Life of Sir Thomas Browne*," *Notre Dame English Journal* 15 (Winter 1983): 39–50; W. Jackson Bate, *Samuel Johnson* (1975; Washington, DC: Counterpoint, 1998), 329.
4. Although limited in space by his format and choosing to emphasize the issue of prose style in the space he has, Pat Rogers at least regards the *Life of Browne* as "one of [Johnson's] most accomplished short biographies." See his *Samuel Johnson Encyclopedia* (Westport, CT: Greenwood, 1996), 56. Donald Greene groups the work among middle biographies "unjustifiably neglected" and finds specifically that it "has always been somewhat of a disappointment to students of Johnson" due to the author's supposed lack of enthusiasm for his subject (*Samuel Johnson: Updated Edition* [Boston: Twayne, 1989], 72, 74).
5. Daniela Haverstein, *Democratizing Sir Thomas Browne* (Oxford: Oxford University Press, 1999), 184.
6. Jonathan F.S. Post, *Sir Thomas Browne* (Boston: Twayne, 1987), 152.
7. (London, 1756); hereafter cited in text. I have silently converted small caps to italics throughout.
8. *The Life of Samuel Johnson: A Critical Biography* (Cambridge, MA.: Blackwell, 1993), 183; my emphasis.
9. I quote Johnson's review from *Samuel Johnson, A Commentary on Mr. Pope's Principles of Morality, or Essay on Man*, ed. O M Brack Jr. (New Haven: Yale University Press, 2004), 403, 418. Lill (41) has previously noted the similarity between passages in the *Life of Browne* and the review of Jenyns. Lill is a perceptive reader, but I disagree in general with his emphasis on the differences between Browne's faith and Johnson's, which I find strikingly similar in their most important elements.
10. Robert G. Walker, *Eighteenth-Century Arguments for Immortality and Johnson's Rasselas*, (Victoria, BC: University of Victoria, ELS Monograph Series, 1977).
11. *Samuel Johnson: Rasselas and Other Tales*, ed. Gwin J. Kolb (New Haven: Yale University Press, 1990), 13; hereafter cited in text.
12. See Walker, *Eighteenth-Century Arguments*, and Gwin J. Kolb, "The Intellectual Background of the Discourse on the Soul in *Rasselas*," *Philological Quarterly* 54 (1975): 357–69.
13. Johnson so "previews" at least two other times. The first, noted by James Lill (44–45), is his description of the disparate energy of Browne's style later echoed in his famous definition of the wit of the metaphysical poets. The second occurs as Johnson discusses the history of the papers that appeared as Browne's *Posthumous Works*, which were "found in his closet" and published in two collections, "one by Dr. *Tennison*, the other . . . by a nameless editor." Johnson speculates that the tracts "might, without [these editors'] interposition, have, perhaps, perished among other innumerable labours of learned men, or have been burnt in a scarcity of fuel like the papers of Pereskius" (xxvii–xxviii). Three years later, in *Idler* 65 (July 14, 1759), we find Johnson observing, "The papers left in the closet of Peiresc supplied his heirs with a whole winter's fuel" (*Samuel Johnson: Idler and Adventurer*, ed. W.J. Bate, J.M. Bullitt, and L.F. Powell [New Haven: Yale University Press, 1963], 202; the Yale editors state that "Johnson apparently refers to the account of Gilles Ménage," and also point out the *Life of Browne* passage [202n4]). The mention of Pereskius in conjunction with Browne's papers was Johnson's addition, but the passage otherwise is dependent on the following from a work Johnson cites specifically in three other places in the *Life*—pages 5, 32, and 35—but not here, *Biographia Britannica*: "[Browne] thought and wrote with the utmost freedom, illustrating every subject he touched, by such new and nervous remarks, as charmed every attentive reader, and has occasioned more care to be taken of the papers he left behind him, than has usually happened to the remains of learned men, a circumstance singular in itself, and which reflects on his memory the highest honour" (*Biographia Britannica* [London, 1748], 2:998). It is tempting

to speculate that Johnson's reference to Browne's papers being found "in his closet" is a further influence of the Pereskius anecdote, as I have not found the closet mentioned as the specific location in any of the earlier biographies of Browne.

14. *Samuel Johnson: The Rambler*, ed. W.J. Bate and Albrecht B. Strauss, 3 vols. (New Haven: Yale University Press, 1969), 1:321, 323.

15. Immediately following the entry for Thomas Browne in *Biographia Britannica* (2:1000–1003) is an entry for his son Edward, from which Johnson may have gotten all the material he includes in his short biography of Edward within the *Life of Browne*.

16. Or as when he describes Browne's habitual clothing: "He ever wore a cloke, or boots, when few others did. He kept himself always very warm . . . though he never loaded himself with such a multitude of garments, as Suetonius reports of *Augustus*, enough to clothe a good family" (xli), from Suetonius, *Life of Augustus*, 82.

17. For Johnson's admiration of Grotius, see Robert G. Walker, "Johnson in the 'Age of Evidences,'" *Huntington Library Quarterly* 44 (1980): 27–41, esp. 34–35; and Robert DeMaria Jr., *Samuel Johnson and the Life of Reading* (1997; Baltimore: Johns Hopkins University Press, 2009), 117–21.

18. *The Truth of the Christian Religion. In Six Books by Hugo Grotius. Corrected and Illustrated with Notes, by Mr. Le Clerc*, trans. John Clarke (London, 1719), 328; italics reversed. One must keep in mind, of course, that Anglicans laying claim to Grotius were not disinterested, nor alone. As William Orme wrote, "The religion of Grotius must have been of a very equivocal kind, for as many sects seem to have contended for him, as cities about the birth of Homer" (*Life and Times of Rev. Richard Baxter* [1830; Boston, 1831], 2:215).

19. *The Truth of the Christian Religion*, 334.

20. For a description of this pattern and how it changed later in the eighteenth century, see Robert G. Walker, "Public Death in the Eighteenth Century," *Research Studies* 48 (1980): 11–24; and, more recently, Stephen Miller, *Three Deaths and Enlightenment Thought: Hume, Johnson, Marat* (Lewisburg, PA: Bucknell, 2001).

21. Watkins, *Perilous Balance: The Tragic Genius of Swift, Johnson, and Sterne* (Princeton: Princeton University Press, 1939), 82.

22. *Samuel Johnson: Diaries, Prayers, and Annals*, ed. E.L. McAdam Jr. with Donald and Mary Hyde (New Haven: Yale University Press, 1958), 383–84; entry for August 12, 1784.

23. DeMaria Jr., *Johnson's Dictionary and the Language of Learning* (Chapel Hill: University of North Carolina Press, 1986), 223; Weinbrot, "What Johnson's Illustrative Quotations Illustrate: Language and Viewpoint in the *Dictionary*," in his *Aspects of Samuel Johnson* (Newark: University of Delaware Press, 2005), 55. Weinbrot cites DeMaria on p. 59. See also Weinbrot's "Johnson and the Moderns: The Forward Face of Janus," in *Johnson after 300 Years*, ed. Greg Clingham and Philip Smallwood (Cambridge: Cambridge University Press, 2009), 55–72: "Johnson admired Robert South's energetic prose, but not its verbal and theological violence, which he often deleted when citing South in the *Dictionary*" (64).

24. See I[saac] Watts, *Reliquiæ Juveniles: Miscellaneous Thoughts in Prose and Verse* (London, 1734), 133.

25. *Biographia Britannica*, 2:995nG. Patin himself credits the remark's origin to Philip de Comines, speaking of Francis de Paula.

26. *Sir Thomas Browne's Pseudodoxia Epidemica*, 6.12, ed. Robin Robbins (Oxford: Clarendon Press, 1981), 1:530.

27. Harth, *Swift and Anglican Rationalism* (Chicago: University of Chicago Press, 1961), 23. Still helpful on this issue is L. P. Curtis, *Anglican Moods of the Eighteenth Century* ([Hamden, CT]: Archon Books, 1966), esp. 31–34.

28. *The Letters of Samuel Johnson*, ed. Bruce Redford (Princeton: Princeton University Press, 1992), 1:314.

29. See, for instance, Thomas Sheridan's edition under that name (Dublin, 1733), one of several editions of the poem published during the first sixty years of the century. Johnson's two slight misquotations, *wild* for *light* and *computed* for *comforted*, may indicate that he is quoting from memory, highly likely given his familiarity with the poem. "Johnson's knowledge of Sir John Davies' poetry is confined almost entirely to one poem, *Nosce Teipsum*, but that he read

and reread and greatly admired. His admiration . . . began before 1750 and lasted until his death" (W.B.C. Watkins, *Johnson and English Poetry before 1660* [1936; New York: Gordian Press, 1965], 74).

30. 1 Corinthians 13:4–7. Perhaps coincidentally, Johnson mentioned earlier in the *Life* (xxx) Browne's letter concerning "the cymbals of the Hebrews," a reference to this same chapter (13:1).

31. In this comparison—in order to cite a text with pagination similar to the one Johnson may have had in hand—I use the 10th ed. for *Religio Medici* (Edinburgh, 1754); hereafter cited in the text. A modern scholarly edition is found in vol. 1 of *The Works of Sir Thomas Browne*, ed. Geoffrey Keynes (Chicago: University of Chicago Press, 1964).

32. Here are the page numbers of the quotations from *Religio Medici* in the order Johnson uses them: 1, 2, 2, 3, 3, 13, 13–14, 10, 10, 21–22, 22, 6.

33. For a good recent study of Browne's response in print to the image controversy, see Kevin Killeen, *Biblical Scholarship, Science and Politics in Early Modern England* (Farnham: Ashgate, 2009), esp. 202–4.

34. I assume Johnson did not have *Vulgar Errors* in front of him, hence the paraphrase. He may not have looked into it since finishing the *Dictionary*, where it is quoted far more than any other Browne work. That Johnson does not quote or paraphrase *Christian Morals* once in the *Life* may seem curious, since the biography was written to preface that work. I suspect that Johnson viewed *Christian Morals* as a relatively minor work by a major author, a view endorsed by modern Browne scholars.

35. For St. John, see Beth Williamson, *Christian Art: A Very Short Introduction* (New York: Oxford University Press, 2004), 59–60. Even though Fordun's identification of the legend with William Comyn was accepted through the early nineteenth century, he probably confused this William with St. William, Archbishop of York. To complicate things further, R.A. Coffin takes pains to disassociate William of York from the legend in *Lives of the English Saints: St. William Archbishop of York* (London, 1844), 52–54. Finally, although both Browne and Johnson ignore the issue, the willing acceptance of a poisoned cup could represent sinful suicide, as an early Browne annotator, Matthew Wren, pointed out: see *Pseudodoxia Epidemica*, 7.19; 2:1143.

36. *Pseudodoxia Epidemica*, 7.19; 1:607.

37. Quinlan discusses Sermons 9 and 22 in *Samuel Johnson: A Layman's Religion* (Madison: University of Wisconsin Press, 1964), 96; hereafter cited in text. For the quotation from Sermon 9, see *Samuel Johnson: Sermons*, ed. Jean Hagstrum and James Gray (New Haven: Yale University Press, 1978), 99. Nicholas Hudson recently disputed Quinlan's view of this passage, and maintained that "Communion, a mere material act, was simply an instrument by which the worthy communicant received special grace directly from God" (*Samuel Johnson and Eighteenth-Century Thought* [Oxford: Clarendon Press, 1988], 219–20). Johnson certainly stresses the communicant's need to be a worthy recipient (thus following closely the emphasis of the Book of Common Prayer), but I find nothing anywhere in Johnson to suggest he would view Communion as "a mere material act"—just the opposite, in fact.

38. For Johnson on the certainty issue see Robert G. Walker, "Johnson, Tillotson and Comparative Credibility," *Notes & Queries* 24 (1977): 254–55, and "Johnson in the 'Age of Evidences,'" 28–34.

39. *Diaries, Prayers, and Annals*, 115.

40. Although he takes a different tack from mine about the *Life of Browne*, Henry Hitchings writes tellingly, "The *Life* ends with a strange capitalized section which has the look of a monumental inscription. . . . Johnson's explication of Browne's Christian values looks like a statement of his own essential beliefs" ("Samuel Johnson and Sir Thomas Browne," *New Rambler* E:8 [2004–5]: 52).

Chapter Six

"But Philosophy Can Tell No More"

Johnson's Christian Moralism and the Genre of Rasselas

Patrick Müller

"Religion?"
"The fashionable substitute for Belief."
"You are a Sceptic."
"Never! Scepticism is the beginning of Faith."

—Oscar Wilde, *The Picture of Dorian Gray*

Like any other academic discipline, literary history relies on generalizations for its didactic purposes, especially in order to characterize an author's intellectual allegiances or determine the formal nature of the works under discussion. To this end, the scholar or critic can choose from a set of signifiers—labels, that is, which are conventionally employed in such categorizations. Samuel Johnson's religious views and his "tale" *Rasselas* are both cases in point here, as studies devoted to each reflect the difficulty inherent in this procedure, as well as the restricted range of all critical tags. Johnson is thought by some to have converted to evangelicalism shortly before his death, and his religion has been described in general terms as "Augustinian Christian gospel morality," "Christian Epicureanism," "Christian Stoicism," or as a via media between fideism and Dissent, to name but a few examples. In terms of literary genre, *Rasselas* is labeled either a philosophical novel, an apologue, an oriental tale, a parable, a potential *Bildungsroman*, or an ironic oriental romance, and variously divided into two, three, four, or six parts. Even if these views are not always mutually exclusive (although some of them are), what they demonstrate is that it is important to define carefully the terms we use to categorize an intellect or its product and thereby support the conclusions we draw. Otherwise, the critic who tries to come to terms with Johnson's mind and his most famous text will inevitably embark upon a quixotic endeavor. I would contend that the obvious failure of conventional terminology to capture the essence of an author for whom "thinking is a process without conclusion, an unresolved dialectic"[1] can offer a significant clue for our understanding of Johnson's religious thought and convictions, and no less so for our understanding of *Rasselas* and its structure.

One of the common denominators in characterizations of the "English Socrates"[2] is that he was a moralist. To emphasize the religious dimension of Johnson's writings in general, and the periodical essays in particular, he is sometimes called a "(Judeo-)Christian" or "Anglican" moralist.[3] The difficulty here is that the epithet "moralist" is never used with precision, either by modern critics or by Johnson himself. But while the eighteenth-century writer may be forgiven for his terminological imprecision, we might expect more conscientious usage from academics. Above all, the term will raise different expectations in readers, depending merely on their nationalities. Continental European readers will see it in the context of French moralism and the unorthodox treatment there of the *conditio humana*, couched in innovative forms by writers such as Montaigne, Pascal, La Rochefoucauld, or La Bruyère. The reception of these authors throughout mainland Europe gradually turned moralism into a continental phenomenon. After being identified as such in the early nineteenth century,[4] this tradition spawned a rogue wave of secondary literature that differentiates moralistic writings from philosophical and literary texts, with regard to both form and to content. Johnson had read the authors today regarded as French moralists: he revered Pascal's *Pensées* and admired the psychological observations of La Rochefoucauld. It seems clear that his admiration for some of the French writers shaped the aphoristic concision of much of his prose.

By contrast, British and American readers tend to adopt a unilateral perspective, concentrating on moralism as a hermetically British development ever since the umbrella term "British moralism" was established to denominate the moral philosophy of the long eighteenth century. "British moralism" has inspired anthologies and monographs in which an experimental author like Shaftesbury can be lumped together with disciplined thinkers such as Cudworth, Butler, or Berkeley. These latter writers are in fact "(moral) philosophers," whose ethical theories are accordingly presented in a systematic form.[5] The essayists Addison, Steele, and Johnson should also be excluded from this philosophical group. Nonetheless, they have come to be styled the "great moralists," their contribution to ethics consisting not so much in carefully reasoned ethical theories but in unsystematic reflections on *mores* and miscellaneous moral questions. There seems to be a tacit consensus among scholars that there *is* a fundamental difference between the British moralists (as moral philosophers) and the essayists; the exact nature of that difference, however, remains unclear.

Given these different traditions, to what extent can we speak of Johnson as a moralist? It is clear that he thought of his authorial self primarily in moralistic terms. The essays abound with meditations on the moralist's task, and his own definition of the noun (which he derives from the French *moraliste*) speaks of "One who teaches the duties of life."[6] The didactic implications of this definition are obvious: the question for us is just how far Johnson in actuality "teaches" or even "preaches" the duties of life. It was his express aim, as a writer of moral essays, to impersonate the moralist "whose precepts are intended chiefly for those who are endeavouring to go forward up the steeps of virtue."[7] On the face of it, Johnson does not employ the terminology of moralism in any distinctive sense, but the gap he perceived between the moralist and the moral philosopher can be deduced from his writings. For him, the difference consists in the foundation of precepts and their potential to provide reliable guidelines. He regards the moralist as a participant himself in everyday life, as an observer of human actions and the mind behind them, someone whose psychological monitoring leads to moral statements culled from the workings of the human psyche; the maxims, then, are based on empirical observation and evidence. The moral philosopher's precepts are "laid down in solitude, safety, and tranquillity," whereas the moralist's task is infinitely more difficult:

> The speculatist is only in danger of erroneous reasoning; but the man involved in life, has his own passions, and those of others, to encounter, and is embarrassed with a thousand inconveniences, which confound him with variety of impulse, and either perplex or obstruct his way.

The moral philosopher practices "pure science, which has to do only with ideas"; the moralist tests "the application of its laws to the use of life." The Rambler reminds us that moral judgment has to allow for "the influence of accidents" and for the "many impediments [that] obstruct our practice" (*Rambler* 14, 3:75–76). Johnson summarized this attitude aphoristically in his review of Soame Jenyns's *Free Inquiry*: "Life must be seen before it can be known," or in explicitly moral terms, "evil must be felt before it is evil."[8]

In ethics, Johnson was a perennial critic of the unempirical a priori reasoning practiced by those he tauntingly called "speculatists," men "not versed in the living world, but accustomed to judge only by speculative reason" (*Rambler* 70, 4:4). Even in his hortatory sermons Johnson avoided metaphysical speculation.[9] What he regarded as the "speculative reasoner's" chief fault was that he "examines every thing rather than his own state."[10] It is, then, Johnson's moral empiricism that helps us understand the tension underlying much of his writing. In an age that Hume alerted to the fundamental difference between "is" and "ought," Johnson intuitively shunned the ready-made "ought" of the several philosophical schools: *nullius in verbis magistri*. Although he believed that moral philosophers present us with an "idea of perfection" necessary for moral progress (*Rambler* 14, 3:75), he was at the same time convinced that these precepts had to stand the test of life. The moral precept never attains the status of dogma in Johnson—it is always counterbalanced by the moral "is," the facts of human life as transmitted by experience. As a moralist, he was indeed "an unsystematic and anti-systematic thinker,"[11] and as nearly all of his writings in general and *Rasselas* in particular show, Johnson was deeply suspicious of moral philosophy's pretensions to a system.

It is precisely this distinction or tension between "is" and "ought" that underlies one influential definition of *moralism*: Hugo Friedrich's claim that the moralist (in his case the essayist Montaigne) does not attempt to form his readers' morals, but only to characterize them.[12] The moral philosopher's aim is normative, that of the moralist merely descriptive. While this distinction is very (even perhaps far too) schematic, in conjunction with recent research on the nature of moralism it does promise to shed new light on Johnson as a moralist. As these studies have shown, the moralist appeals to experience in order to counter the claims of static dogma. Moreover, he eschews metaphysics, concentrating instead on human nature.[13] If we refine Friedrich's basic definition of *moralism* with these additional characteristics, we can more easily position Johnson within the moralistic tradition. He is not only a moralist because his writings address practical moral questions, but also in this more profound sense, which takes into account the rationale behind most of his writings.

To adopt such a broad perspective is not a symptom of hair-splitting; the implications will help us reach, it is hoped, a deeper understanding of Johnson's thought. One further characteristic of the moralist may be mentioned here. According to Friedrich, the moralist's texts are hybrids between philosophical tracts and *belles lettres*; the moralist "rides the borders," as it were. Moralists were important for the further development of literary forms such as the aphorism (La Rochefoucauld) or character writing (La Bruyère). Another example, one more pertinent here, is the genre that emerged with Montaigne and Bacon as eminently suitable for the expression of moralistic intent, a literary form at which Johnson, choosing it as the principal vehicle for his moralism, excelled: the essay.

Johnson experimented with many genres, but his reputation as a moralist is primarily based on his contribution to the development of the essay. The "initial impulse" of the essay "was away from genre altogether, in the direction of formlessness,"[14] and this tendency naturally makes any concise definition impossible. Johnson himself offers four different descriptions, the latter three of which are the most interesting: he defines the noun "essay" as either "A loose sally of the mind; an irregular, indigested piece; not a regular and orderly composition"; as a "trial; an experiment"; or as a "first experiment."[15] The experimental nature of the essay and its irregularity accentuate its progressive character—it is not static, but rather a *perpetuum mobile*. Johnson thought of the human mind in very much the same terms: "we desire, we pursue, we obtain, we are satiated; we desire something else, and begin a new pursuit" (*Rambler* 6, 3:35). Given this conviction, that "natural flights of the human mind" (*Rambler* 2, 3:10) are from hope to hope, it becomes clear why Johnson inclined to the essay. It provided the ideal platform for moral observations based on psychological insight and on an empirical study of human nature.[16] As a literary mode not tied to any one discipline (in the sense of either form or content), one that "does not aim at system at all,"[17] the essay lends itself naturally to the moralist's unsystematic observations. The essayist examines the authority of others but does not offer his own views as normative correctives. As an author of moral essays, Johnson exhibits "an isolated self confronting a world of which nothing is known for certain."[18] The very names of the periodicals and the characters they suggest point to his searching attitude: the Rambler, bound, to borrow a phrase from Pope, to "[e]xpatiate freely o'er all this scene of Man";[19] the Idler, who "is always inquisitive" (*Idler* 1, 12:5); and the daring Adventurer.

This is not to say that Johnson thought of the essay form in terms of lawlessness or structural anarchy. Writing, he declared, is a means to discipline the natural stream of consciousness:

> To fix the thoughts by writing, and subject them to frequent examinations and reviews, is the best method of enabling the mind to detect its own sophisms, and keep it on guard against the fallacies which it practices on others: in conversation we naturally diffuse our thoughts, and in writing we contract them; method is the excellence of writing, and unconstraint the grace of conversation. (*Adventurer* 85, 2:416)

Consequently, what is typical of Johnson's handling of the form is the tension between "the pursuit of normative ethical judgments" and "the skeptical, empirical, aspect," between moral precept and psychological observation.[20] This friction is reflected in the structure and rhythm of most of the essays: he would customarily begin by "setting up a general assertion to be examined meticulously and in detail, challenging it from various points of view, and finally—having either accepted or rejected it—attempting to provide the result with some universal significance or application."[21] These universal applications, however, are tempered by the skeptical implications of Johnson's empiricism, which are "well expressed in the periodical essay as a form which interrogates an opening proposition, 'sees more,' and modifies or complicates it, without pretence to finality or system."[22] The genre has been associated from the start with skepticism, Montaigne's "Apology for Raimond Sebond" being *the* manifesto of philosophical and religious doubt of the Renaissance. Like Montaigne's, Johnson's skepticism is not out and out philosophical, as the disposition to doubt that is congenial to the formal freedom afforded by the essay is of a less dogmatic nature. Johnson was a searcher, looking for hidden motives in order thereby to explain human conduct. The essay's form tends toward a skeptical attitude that "is spontaneous and unsystematic, and accepts its *occasional*, even accidental nature,"[23] another factor that I believe appealed to Johnson. He saw the essay's potential for giving suitable expression to his epistemological views and was attracted to the self-critical didacticism it allowed. It enabled him to steer a middle course between formulating moral precepts and qualifying them at the same time.

There can be no doubt that Johnson's essays *are* didactic, but the question is *how* the advice is given. It is once again an example from his moral thought that illustrates this point most effectively. Johnson adopted the ordinary opposition between reason and the passions, the regulation of which he regarded as the chief trial of human life: the "disturbers of our happiness, in this world, are our desires, our griefs, and our fears" (*Rambler* 17, 3:92). This urge to do credit to our reputation as rational animals, the "moral discipline of the mind" (*Rambler* 8, 3:42), was for Johnson the essence of God's law (see *Rambler* 32, 3:178–79). However, at the same time he saw the limits the human condition imposed on this moral and religious imperative. Paradoxically, by advising readers that they should always keep the possible in mind, the empirical pragmatist in him works both ways, as a check to immoderate desires and as a reminder that reason has its limits in conditioning the self.

There is, then, an analogy between Johnson's moralist thought and his theory of writing. This latter he saw as a rational activity that permits a more detached look at human passions and follies. Being a product of the human mind, however, writing underscores the same limitations: its precepts or "universal applications" can only approximate an ideal "truth" to which it has ultimately no access. Similarly, the essay writer's mitigated skepticism "makes a claim to truth, but not permanent truth."[24] There is always a delicate balance between *is* and *ought*—the passions and reason are constantly at odds. This is exactly the challenge to which classical Skepticism responded in its attempt to create "an appropriate inner state that would prevent the vicissitudes of life from penetrating the soul of the practitioner," that is, to construct a via media between Epicureanism, which "recommended the pursuit of simple and undemanding pleasures," and Stoicism and its "passionless pursuit of ends set by the divine order."[25] In Johnson these two poles are not different versions of a moral imperative but different expressions of a tension inherent in human life. His empirical psychology accounts for the psychological facts, man's journey from desire to desire, and these are counterbalanced by a Swiftian view of man as *animal rationis capax*. Like the early Skeptics, Johnson constantly sought "inner peace" in his life. But while the Skeptics attempted to achieve this "through withholding assent to any dogma about what the realities are, and recognizing the incapacity of human reason to determine them,"[26] Johnson sought refuge in a realm that transcends the province of moralism: that of religion.

Fideism is the religious corner in the triangle that holds together Johnson's epistemological views. The significance of the relation between his empiricism, skepticism, and fideism seems to me not to have been sufficiently illuminated. Fred Parker's work has enhanced our understanding of the skeptical implications of Johnson's art, while David F. Venturo and Blanford Parker have established the importance of fideism in Johnson's thought. None of them, however, has realized that there are, as in the case of empiricism and skepticism, close affinities between these two intellectual attitudes. At first sight, fideism is a doomed attempt to reconcile two disproportionate views: "For faith surely consists in, or at least involves, beliefs about transcendent realities, whereas Skepticism casts doubt on our beliefs in everyday facts."[27] It is an epistemological position usually associated with Protestant thought, and at its core is the relation between faith and reason; as such, it stands at the intersection of religion and philosophy, a dichotomy that informs much of Johnson's writing. The fideists' God is a *deus absconditus*, who is not only not knowable but also in this world "an *absence* rather than a *presence*,"[28] which "seems to be a strong proof for His presence in another."[29] According to the fideist, the world is merely a stopping place on the human pilgrimage to another realm, to one which, however, "must be taken on faith."[30] It is therefore in the question of death and the afterlife that the theologian's faith reigns supreme over the philosopher's reason.

Death was certainly the most pressing issue in Johnson's life and thus is frequently dealt with in his prayers and meditations as well as, albeit more enigmatically, in his essays. *Rambler* 102 combines these fideistic elements in an allegorical dream vision—exemplary and Bunyanesque—on the journey of life. After having stumbled across Seneca's analogy of life as a voyage, the Rambler falls asleep and embarks on a visionary journey across the ocean of life. The allegory is designed to undeceive the multitude of those who think themselves safe on that journey toward their inevitable death. Despite the helping hand offered by reason, most pilots steer their vessels blindly into the "Gulph of Intemperance" or onto the "Rocks of Pleasure." The possible cure offered by religion, or God, is sensed as an absence in the allegory. In the end, "some unknown Power" reminds the dreamer of his own danger before he finally wakes up (4:179–84). The essay shows that the most pressing questions haunting Johnson throughout his adult life were the four last things: death, judgment, Heaven, and Hell. Significantly, the narrative ends on a gloomy note: waking, the Rambler has just seen the "Gulph of

Intemperance" opening before him. Johnson does not and cannot offer a more salutary vision. All the Rambler knows is that he is in danger on his journey, and that reason offers a way to avoid imminent destruction. How to find the proper course remains a mystery.

Death is clearly the *leitmotif* of the essay. The allegorical journey reveals the several psychological mechanisms that block out awareness of impending death: "they all had the art of concealing their danger from themselves." Again, Johnson combines these reflections with his psychology of human motivation, holding that the multitude put their trust in "Hope, who was the constant associate of the voyage of life" (4:182). The very term *hope* excludes certainty: it "is, indeed, very fallacious, and promises what it seldom gives" (*Rambler* 67, 3:354). Given the certainty of death, Johnson saw a contradiction in these coping mechanisms: constantly aspiring to ephemeral goods in our present state, we unreasonably create imaginary evils consequent on this vicious circle of wishful thinking when we should, instead, be preparing for the afterlife. Yet, nothing "can so much disturb the passions, or perplex the intellects of man" as death (*Rambler* 78, 4:47). It is characteristic of Johnson's thought that he would regard death as the prime irrational force in the cycle of human life. As he wrote a week after his mother's death: "Reason deserts us at the brink of the grave, and can give no further intelligence" (*Idler* 41, 2:130). The inevitability of this sway of unreason over mankind is expressed in the claim that "no man is pleased with his present state" (*Rambler* 63, 3:335). Consequently, "it seems to be the fate of man to seek all his consolations in futurity" (*Rambler* 203, 5:291). Johnson thus transfers his own empirical theory of the human mind, with its longing for perpetual satisfaction, to the expectations nourished by the doctrine of futurity: "Futurity is the proper abode of hope and fear, with all their train and progeny of subordinate apprehensions and desires" (*Rambler* 8, 3:45). Since Johnson thought of human conduct in circular terms, with all its different strategies and plots for achieving happiness, the prospect of eternal felicity must appeal to the human psyche to an extraordinary degree, becoming a potent source of immoderate desires and exaggerated hopes. This prospect, however, has the potential to interrupt the cycle of wishful thinking, eschatology adding a teleological dimension to life. Therefore, future felicity should be the principal psychological factor informing all human endeavor.

When Johnson writes about futurity, however, he usually does so with regard to our desire for an amelioration of our present state. The reason for this caution is that the future state is unknown. Not only is its nature uncertain, but also its very existence. It is at this crucial juncture that Johnson becomes a *Christian* moralist. He "flies at last to the shelter of religion" (*Idler* 2, 2:278) and, to use the words of *The Vanity of Human Wishes*, its medium faith, "that panting for a happier seat."[31] Death and other calamities "are the great occasions which force the mind to take refuge in religion:

when we have no help in ourselves" (*Idler* 2, 2:130). His "first full-blown moral essay,"[32] *Rambler* 2, revolves around futurity, and here Johnson declares that Heaven is among the "subjects too solemn for my present purpose" (3:11). At this transitional point between moralism and religion, Johnson's thought is again shaped by the tension inherent in his moral essays between didacticism and skepticism. Later, he will take the leap from present to future hopes to convince his readers that virtue will be rewarded hereafter, a leap necessitated by his fideistic awareness that God's hand in the present world cannot be understood: "one evidence of a future state is the uncertainty of any present reward for goodness" (*Rambler* 52, 3:284). Nevertheless, the empirical Johnson had doubts stemming from the fideistic logic of repentance and regeneration. The letter that accompanies John Taylor's collection of proofs for a future state and the soul's immortality was written after Johnson had told him "that he would prefer a state of torment to that of annihilation."[33] Many of Johnson's writings betray this unease, or rather profound disturbance in the face of unfathomable death. In his prayers, he more often than not implores God to support him in his resolution to live a virtuous life and asks that He grant eternal happiness.[34]

Since fideists advocate a pragmatic theodicy, informed by their doubts as to whether God interferes in human affairs, they have to accept that the experience of evil is a necessary aspect of life, "allotted to us by providence" (*Rambler* 32, 3:176). This attitude enabled Johnson to adopt, at least in many of his essays, a seemingly matter-of-fact attitude toward the calamities of the present state, and to dissect their psychological causes and uses. At the same time, this attitude caused him considerable anxiety, since he saw that salvation and thus our advancement to "that state in which evil shall be no more" (*Idler* 89, 2:278) are uncertain. As his private records show, Johnson himself was only able to take the leap after much greater difficulty than he wanted his readers to believe. The psychological factor that explains his problem is a religious fear that tends to overrule the hope for eternal happiness. In analogy to the dream that ends with the Rambler seeing a vision of the "Gulph of Intemperance," human beings are afraid of divine punishment, which "has always burdened the human mind" (*Rambler* 110, 4:221), and which is consequently the greatest cause of unease: "the fear of death has always been considered as the great enemy of human quiet, the polluter of the feast of happiness, and embitterer of the cup of joy" (*Sermons*, 263). Behind this anxiety, then, stands yet another epistemological problem: man's inability to know for certain that there will be a future state that will compensate for the moral imbalance of the present.

In a memorable passage from *Rambler* 78, death is introduced as "an entrance into a state not simply which [man] knows not, but which perhaps he has no faculties to know" (4:47). For Johnson, this is a confession of the limits of human reason and so of philosophy, but not of religion. He regarded the knowledge of God's existence as the "origin of philosophy" (*Rambler* 10, 4:221). Combined with faith, reason is quite capable of providing *sufficient* proof:

> If, instead of wandering after the meteors of philosophy which will fill the world with splendour for a while, and then sink and are forgotten, the candidates of learning fixed their eyes upon the permanent lustre of moral and religious truth, they would find a more certain direction to happiness. (*Rambler* 180, 5:186)

Here lies the possible source for the tension between the didactic usefulness of precept and the empirically informed skepticism that informs Johnson's art of the essay. The *Rambler* essay abstractly proposes scriptural "instructions which fortify the heart" as the proper alternative to the "unnecessary speculations" of philosophy (5:186). In the essays, however, Johnson could not discuss such theological niceties at length, whereas in the hortatory sermons it was natural to appeal to the flock's enlightened self-interest; he could speak there of revelation as imparting "certain knowledge of a future state, and of the rewards and punishments, that await us after death" (*Sermons*, 107). The homilies naturally provided ample space for an investigation of religious "truths" and so we find in them most of the religious rationale that shaped the moral essays. What religion had to achieve was a reconciliation of Johnson's pragmatic empiricism and psychological acumen with his eschatological doubts. Given our insatiable desire for happiness, it was important to show that, for the moral agent, its apotheosis, eternal bliss, is a likely prospect.

Johnson was steeped in arguments brought forth by both philosophers and theologians in favor of the soul's immateriality and immortality. As his friend John Taylor wrote (or, more probably, Johnson himself, as the Yale editors seem to suggest), "some philosophers, men capable of the most abstruse ratiocination," could "by the mere light of reason, even without assistance from, or knowledge of, revelation" illustrate these points (*Sermons*, 321–22). We have seen that Johnson was generally suspicious of such abstract speculation, not least because he thought it was inaccessible to the greater part of mankind. This is precisely the argument of the famous Sermon 25, written on the occasion of his wife's death. Superficially, Johnson adopts Samuel Clarke's metaphysical argument, which derives the immortality of the soul from its immateriality.[35] These, however, are the logical deductions of a philosopher with "leisure and capacity, not allowed in general to mankind." The findings of the philosophers were therefore "confined to a small number, without any benefit to the unenlightened multitude." This critique of philosophical thought allows Johnson to ascribe to religion the democratization of such knowledge. In order to achieve this, he introduces an empirical argument: "the constitution of mankind is such," he writes, "that abstruse and intellectual truths can be taught no otherwise than by positive assertion, supported by some sensible evidence." God chose an efficacious didactic method and sent the mediator Christ to cater to our need for "sensible evidence."[36] In this way, God provides sufficient reasons to believe in a future state, the example of Christ's resurrection having "more force than the arguments of a thousand reasoners" (*Sermons*, 264–65). Revelation satisfies the needs of both faith and reason.

The language of the essays, in which Johnson softened the theologian's normative rigor, is less apodictic. The message, however, is the same. In existential questions, "Philosophy may infuse stubbornness, but religion only can give patience" (*Idler* 41, 2:131). Johnson's reservations against philosophy strengthen his ties to the moralist tradition that he believed had more to offer than the metaphysical speculations of the philosophical schools. Moralism is the proper compromise between philosophy and religion. On the basis of an empirically minded reading of Scripture, the Christian moralist Johnson can explain the transition from man's penchant for the factual (the *is*) to his need for sound moral advice (the *ought*). He interprets divine precepts, designed to open up the prospect of eternal felicity, as supported by experience. It is in his essayistic practice, especially in the more solemn pieces of the *Idler*, that this moralistic pathway from a philosophical proposition to its religious application is met in its most concise form. For example, *Idlers* 41 and 89 turn to religion's salutary message only after denouncing philosophy's failure to give adequate reasons for the evils of the human condition. Like any good spiritual doctor, Johnson first diagnoses and then administers the medicine: man's desire for happiness is eventually to be satisfied with the prospect of everlasting felicity. Unfortunately, however, the essays' conclusions remain nothing but hopes. Johnson shared John Tillotson's view that "for any man to urge that tho' men in temporal affairs proceed upon moral assurance, yet there is greater assurance required to make men seek Heaven and avoid Hell, seems to me to be highly unreasonable."[37] The essays in which Johnson is speaking as a Christian moralist appeal to his readers' enlightened self-interest in the face of the vicissitudes of life. Knowledge he cannot offer, only a greater good to appease the mind's desires. The essays offer good reasons for having faith, but they conclude nothing. This is the privilege of God.

And this brings us, finally, to *Rasselas*. After a spate of interest in genre in the second half of the twentieth century, triggered largely by the recovery of Bakhtin, by the work of Wayne Booth, and by Northrop Frye's *Anatomy of Criticism,* theoretical attention has again seemed to have waned in the past decade. Yet questions of literary form and the related analysis of structural components are extremely important from an epistemological point of view—for both author and reader. First, the choice of genre affects an author's ordering of materials. As Irvin Ehrenpreis points out, questions of genre and structure are interdependent from a positivistic point of view if, that is, by "structure" we mean "a design conceptually prior to the completion of the work under examination, and established in such a way that both the author and the reader may know it."[38] Needless to say, the importance of structure for a text's interpretation could not escape a critic of Johnson's caliber. As he observes in *Idler* 85, "Truth like beauty varies its fashions, and is best recommended by different dresses to different minds" (2:265). Johnson's knowledge of classical rhetoric facilitated his attempt to determine whether or not a writer had made the proper choice of a rhetorical device to support the proposed "truth." Second, all readers will approach a comic novel, a didactic poem, or a sentimental comedy with a set of preconceived expectations. But while it is universally agreed that *Tom Jones* is a comic novel, *An Essay on Man* a didactic poem, and *The Conscious Lovers* a sentimental comedy, the genre of *Rasselas* remains, so to speak, a mystery.

The title page of the first edition identifies *Rasselas* as "A Tale," but the two definitions of the noun in the *Dictionary* cast some doubt on Johnson's veneration for the genre. It is either a "narrative; a story. Commonly a slight or petty account of some trifling or fabulous incident" or an "Oral relation." In fact, it is clear that in *Rasselas* Johnson is toying with the fashionable "oriental tale" or "romance." His fascination with the East is well documented, but I am not interested here in how far *Rasselas* should be seen as "a deflation of the ordinary eastern tale"[39] (although I agree with this view). In my view, any examination of the work promises more concrete results if we approach the question of genre within the context of Johnson's general *Weltanschauung* as outlined above. Johnson had already produced allegorical episodes in an easterly vein in *Ramblers* 65 and 204/5. These earlier pieces helped prepare the way for *Rasselas*. *Rambler* 65 allegorizes once more the journey motif, Obidah's aimless meanderings through the plains of Indostan being another quest on which "the care of omnipotence" (3:349) is the only reliable companion. The two later essays are even more interesting as precursors. In 204, the mighty Ethiopian lord Seged retires "for ten days from tumult and care, from counsels and decrees" (5:297), only to learn that the human mind irresistibly flies from desire to desire, and that to interrupt this perpetual striving is the privilege of death. The vision is much bleaker than that of Obidah's tale with its glimmer of religious hope. Religion is absent from the secular story of Seged, and this is why there is no consolation after his daughter's death, only the sobering experience "that no man hereafter may presume to say 'This day shall be a day of happiness'" (*Rambler* 205, 5:305). Unaided by religion, the human mind is left alone to struggle with its circularity. Thrown back on reason, all man can learn is that happiness is ephemeral, even radically so: "when we have no help in ourselves," death is the only certainty—there is nothing beyond. One could say that the two allegorical episodes illustrate the different degrees of consolation to be drawn from a purely philosophical plan of life as opposed to a religious or spiritual one. Both Obidah and Seged are searching for life's meaning; the answers are to be found between the poles of faith and reason.

Two interesting formal aspects of these essays are the way in which Johnson interweaves a narrative element (the quest motif), as well as his use of the rhetorical mode of allegory. For the English reader, its oriental setting detached *Rasselas* not only spatially from the worlds of Fielding's "Histories" or of the epistolary novels "edited" by Richardson; both of these authors create, albeit by widely differing strategies, the illusion that their fictions have a profound footing in reality. This gap between fiction and "reality" is much wider in *Rasselas*. It has been argued that the raison d'être of the tale's Ethiopian background consists in the country's "unique and ancient Christianity."[40] With the exception of the penultimate chapter, however, this Christian substrate does not make itself felt. Eternity enters the text with the pyramids and the question as to how far the pharaohs succeeded in their "method of eluding death."[41] The religious dimension of the quest, on the other hand, which revolves around the "choice of life," is apparent as soon as the subject of death is broached. It is at this point that some sense of teleology complements the hitherto circular structure of the text. The dialogue between Imlac and the astronomer on the immortality of the soul is part of the dialogue that Johnson himself held intermittently throughout his oeuvre[42] with contemporary philosophers and theologians, especially Locke and Clarke. This colloquy is always staged as a diatribe between philosophy and religion. This is why Imlac ends the dispute as follows:

> That [the soul] will not perish by any inherent cause of decay, or principle of corruption, may be shown by philosophy; but philosophy can tell no more. That it will not be annihilated by him that made it, we must humbly learn from higher authority. (*Rasselas*, 174)

It is this dialogue between philosophy and religion, between reason and faith or revelation, and ultimately between life and death, that helps us understand how far the text is "speaking otherwise." In *Rasselas*, as in the essays, life is stuck in an endless cycle of unfulfilled wishful thinking. Of this cycle the allegory reminds us when it points beyond the narrative surface which represents the contingency of a life without faith. This allegorical dimension of *Rasselas* stands in the tradition of scriptural allegory, which distinguishes between the spiritual and physical worlds. In Johnson, the temporal happiness to be had in the physical world must yield to the lasting promises of the spiritual.

This brings us to the structure of *Rasselas*. Carey McIntosh has argued that "several different pictures of its structure are valid."[43] Along with this observation, the telltale remark that "*tale-telling* is not the talent"[44] of the author of *Rasselas*, made by Johnson's contemporary Owen Ruffhead, or later critical caveats about the work's "episodic impatience"[45] help us understand why the text has proven immune to categorization. The significance of such remarks becomes clearer once we see that the structure of the work is determined by Johnson's empirical psychology.[46] The point made almost ad nauseam in the essays, that the human mind is determined to hasten from wish to wish, informs the quest motif. Rasselas and Nekayah are eager to find the only true source of happiness. What they learn is that there is no such entity. This negative enlightenment as to the possibilities of finding happiness in this life determines first of all the rhythm, or structure, of the text, in a way reminiscent of the periodical essays: time after time, new schemes and propositions collapse and necessitate the "tale's" continuation.[47] Second, it explains the text's moral and religious meaning, as well as its allegorical layers. This moral, tempered as it is by Johnson's fideism, appears in a book closed by a chapter "in which nothing is concluded" (*Rasselas*, 175).

Much has been written about this paradoxical anticonclusion. But what can it tell us about the generic matrix of *Rasselas*? If we regard the Happy Valley as a *chiffre* for paradise,[48] a state in which there are no material needs and where "the blessings of nature were collected, and its evils extracted and excluded" (*Rasselas*, 9), the moral unfolds its full irony.[49] Read in this way, the principal characters' final plan "to return to Abissinia" (176) can be read as a resolution to reform their lives in order to achieve eternal felicity. But what the characters wish to return to is a place they once tried desperately to escape because, as Rasselas characterizes life in the valley, "possessing all that I can want, I find one day and one hour exactly like another, except that the latter is still more tedious than the former" (16). *Rasselas* actually reflects human life as a vicious circle. But the Happy Valley is a product of the human imagination, a place in which all the earthly, physical desires of its inhabitants are gratified without giving spiritual contentment. As the prince intimates very early in the text, "Man has surely some latent sense for which this place affords no gratification, or he has some desires distinct from sense which must be satisfied before he can be happy" (13). This is the profoundly spiritual, Christian vision of the text. Like any allegorical vision, however, and this is the limit of the human imagination Johnson accepts, it does not impart any certainty. His text refuses to cut the Gordian knot of human life. Paradoxically, the teleological structure of *Rasselas* is at the same time circular, but it nevertheless becomes clear that the fulfillment of life lies beyond the physical, secular realm embodied by the Happy Valley. The skeptical upshot of Johnson's fideist vision transcends the abilities of human thought and thus the scope of art. We should have known all along, because *Rasselas* predicts at the outset that it will give no simple answers.

Johnson's Christian moralism enables him to uphold a skeptical epistemology that combines a (secular) empirical psychology with a (spiritual) fideistic eschatological vision. An essayistic structure is the form best suited for the expression of such a worldview. Robert Spector speaks of "the chameleon-like trail of the essay as it enters into the various other genres that Johnson employs."[50] In fact, *Rasselas* mirrors Johnson's view of human life as a series of essays to achieve happiness; only faith can break this structure and add a teleological dimension in order to impart a sense of closure. Graham Good points out that "despite its non-fictional status, the essay has a strong affinity with the novel."[51] It is Johnson's adherence to the inherent requirements of the "formless" essay-genre, on which he imposes an episodic plot based on his psychology, that may account for some of the critical confusion surrounding *Rasselas*. The nature of the work is perhaps most aptly illustrated by one of the quotations Johnson used to define a "tale," from *Macbeth*, V.ii.24–28: "Life's ... a tale / Told by an idiot, full of sound and fury, / Signifying nothing." In the Christian moralist's art it is the epistemologically precarious realm of religion, with its promise of a future state, that provides a sense of closure and shoulders the burden of meaning.

NOTES

1. Fred Parker, "Johnson's Conclusiveness," *Scepticism and Literature: An Essay on Pope, Hume, Sterne, and Johnson* (Oxford: Oxford University Press, 2003), 238.
2. Bernard Knieger, "The Moral Essays of Dr. Samuel Johnson," *The Personalist* 42 (1961): 361.
3. See Melvyn New, "*Rasselas* in an Eighteenth-Century Novels Course," in *Approaches to Teaching the Works of Samuel Johnson*, ed. David R. Anderson et al. (New York: Modern Language Association of America, 1993), 122; Graham Good, "Johnson: The Correction of Error," in *The Observing Self: Rediscovering the Essay* (London: Routledge, 1988), 66; and Thomas M. Curley, "The Spiritual Journey Moralized in *Rasselas*," *Anglia* 91 (1973): 39.
4. That is, with Amaury Duval's *Collection de Moralistes français* (first edition, 1820; see Margot Kruse, "Die französischen Moralisten des 17. Jahrhunderts," *Beiträge zur französischen Moralistik* [Berlin: de Gruyter, 2003], 1).
5. Lawrence E. Klein speaks of the "expository mode" that dominated seventeenth- and eighteenth-century British philosophy (*Shaftesbury and the Culture of Politeness: Moral Discourse and Cultural Politics in Early Eighteenth-Century England* [Cambridge: Cambridge University Press, 1994], 52).
6. *A Dictionary of the English Language* (1785), II, *s.v. Moralist*.
7. *Rambler. The Yale Edition of the Works of Samuel Johnson*, vols. 3–5 (New Haven: Yale University Press, 1969), *Rambler* 70, 4:4.
8. *Review of 'Free Inquiry.' The Yale Edition of the Works of Samuel Johnson*, vol. 17 (New Haven: Yale University Press, 2005), 407 and 401.

9. According to James Gray, Johnson saw "the futility . . . of probing hidden causes and abstruse connections that lay outside human perception" (*Johnson's Sermons: A Study* [Oxford: Clarendon Press, 1972], 132).

10. *Idler and Adventurer. The Yale Edition of the Works of Samuel Johnson*, vol. 2 (New Haven: Yale University Press, 1963), *Idler* 41, 2:129.

11. Fred Parker, "'We Are Perpetually Moralists': Johnson and Moral Philosophy," in *Samuel Johnson after 300 Years*, ed. Greg Clingham et al. (Cambridge: Cambridge University Press, 2009), 15. Parker does not distinguish between "moralism" on the one hand and "moral philosophy" on the other.

12. See Hugo Friedrich, *Montaigne* (Bern: Francke, 1949), 12.

13. See Hans Peter Balmer, *Philosophie der menschlichen Dinge: die europäische Moralistik* (Bern and Munich: Francke, 1981), 11–12.

14. Good, "The Essay as Genre," in *The Observing Self: Rediscovering the Essay* (London: Routledge, 1988), 1.

15. *Dictionary of the English Language*, s.v. *Essay*.

16. See Robert D. Spector, *Samuel Johnson and the Essay* (Westport, CT: Greenwood Press, 1997), 2: "Johnson's very approach to literature is that of an essayist, not simply in any narrow generic sense . . . but . . . in the qualities of mind that lead naturally enough to the creation of what are commonly regarded as essays."

17. Good, "The Essay as Genre," 3.

18. Good, "The Essay as Genre," 4.

19. "An Essay on Man," in *The Poems of Alexander Pope: A One-Volume Edition of the Twickenham Text with Selected Annotations*, ed. John Butt (Bungay: Methuen, 1985 [1963]), 503, line 5.

20. See Good, "Johnson: The Correction of Error," 55 and 60.

21. Spector, *Samuel Johnson and the Essay*, 2.

22. Parker, "Johnson's Conclusiveness," 238.

23. Good, "The Essay as Genre," 4.

24. Good, "The Essay as Genre," 4.

25. Terence Penelhum, *God and Skepticism: A Study in Skepticism and Fideism* (Dordrecht: D. Reidel, 1983), 4.

26. Penelhum, *God and Skepticism*, 4–5.

27. Penelhum, *God and Skepticism*, 2.

28. David F. Venturo, "Fideism, the Antisublime, and the Faithful Imagination in *Rasselas*," in *Samuel Johnson after 300 Years*, ed. Greg Clingham et al. (Cambridge: Cambridge University Press, 2009), 95.

29. Blanford Parker, *The Triumph of Augustan Poetics: English Literary Culture from Butler to Johnson* (Cambridge: Cambridge University Press, 1998), 190.

30. Venturo, "Fideism," 96.

31. *Poems. The Yale Edition of the Works of Samuel Johnson*, vol. 6 (New Haven: Yale University Press, 1964), 6:108, line 363.

32. Parker, "We Are Perpetually Moralists," 18.

33. *Sermons. The Yale Edition of the Works of Samuel Johnson*, vol. 14 (New Haven: Yale University Press, 1978), 14:317–18.

34. *Diaries, Prayers, Annals. The Yale Edition of the Works of Samuel Johnson*, vol. 1 (New Haven: Yale University Press, 1958), 76.

35. Robert G. Walker discusses the sources for Johnson's views on immortality: *Eighteenth-Century Arguments for Immortality and Johnson's* Rasselas (Victoria, BC: University of Victoria, ELS Monograph Series, No. 9, 1977), 9–34.

36. The editors of the sermons have pointed out Johnson's possible debt to Tillotson (16:265). Tillotson thought that "the evidence of the senses, particularly sight and hearing, gives the highest assurance of anything one has in this world" (Henry G. van Leeuwen, *The Problem of Certainty in English Thought, 1630–1690*, with a preface by Richard H. Popkin [The Hague: Martinus Nijhoff, 1970], 36). See also his conviction that "things of a Moral nature, [are to be prov'd] by Moral Arguments, and Matters of Fact by credible Testimony. And though none of these be strict Demonstration, yet we have an undoubted assurance of

them, when they are prov'd by the best Arguments that the nature and quality of the thing will bear" (*The Works of the Most Reverend Dr. John Tillotson* [London: Printed for B. Aylmer and W. Rogers, 1707], A3r).

37. "The Wisdom of Being Religious," *Works*, 29.

38. Ehrenpreis, "*Rasselas* and Some Meanings of 'Structure' in Literary Criticism," *Novel: A Forum on Fiction* 14 (1981): 108.

39. Gwin J. Kolb, "The Structure of *Rasselas*," *PMLA* 66 (1951): 711.

40. Sheridan Baker, "*Rasselas*: Psychological Irony and Romance," *Philological Quarterly* 45 (1966): 249.

41. *Rasselas. The Yale Edition of the Works of Samuel Johnson*, vol. 16 (New Haven: Yale University Press, 1990), 16:169.

42. Adam Potkay's observation that *Rasselas* is indebted to ancient dialogue, is indeed a "dialogic" text, suggests interesting parallels to Socratic skepticism; see *The Passion for Happiness: Samuel Johnson and David Hume* (Ithaca, NY: Cornell University Press, 2000), 209 and 215.

43. *The Choice of Life: Samuel Johnson and the World of Fiction* (New Haven: Yale University Press, 1973), 187–88.

44. Quoted in Kolb, "The Structure of *Rasselas*," 713. The remark is from Ruffhead's review of *Rasselas* in the *Monthly Review* 20 (May 1759).

45. New, "*Rasselas* in an Eighteenth-Century Novels Course," 123.

46. Some of my assumptions are shared by Fred Parker who, however, adheres to the traditional view that *Rasselas* is an oriental tale ("The Skepticism of Johnson's *Rasselas*," *The Cambridge Companion to Samuel Johnson*, ed. Greg Clingham [Cambridge: Cambridge University Press, 1997], 127–42).

47. An observation for which I am indebted to Rudolf Freiburg's unpublished "Habilitationsschrift": *"Short Flights Frequently Repeated": Studien zur Essayistik Samuel Johnsons* (Göttingen: University of Göttingen, 1991), 529–37.

48. Paul Fussell argues that "*Rasselas* takes place in that secular wasteland lying between *Paradise Lost* and *Paradise Regained*" (*Samuel Johnson and the Life of Writing* [London: Chatto and Windus, 1971], 227).

49. Ehrenpreis regards "comic irony" as the cement that binds the text's structure ("*Rasselas* and Some Meanings of 'Structure' in Literary Criticism," 113–14).

50. Spector, *Samuel Johnson and the Essay*, 45.

51. Good, "The Essay as Genre," 9.

Chapter Seven

Johnson's Fallen World

Steven Scherwatzky

If one were to compile a list of the most social English writers of stature, Samuel Johnson would surely rank among them. From his admonitions against solitude to his love of London, Johnson famously cherished good company and urban living. His preference was always to be among people and their productions. From books to buildings, Johnson found comfort in the mark humans impress on the world. He grew uneasy if left alone amid a pristine natural setting, or indeed if left alone at all, especially alone with his God. "Society is necessary to the happiness of human nature," he remarked.[1] But despite Johnson's love of society and much that it has created, he found the world deeply flawed, perhaps beyond correction. The world, for Johnson, was fallen, mired in the legacy of an original sin that forever challenged the hope for salvation. The idea of a fallen world permeates his thought with powerful urgency. When this idea is granted its central status in his worldview, much else about Johnson falls into place. Yet for Johnson the misery of the fallen world is also mankind's greatest gift, because without it we might not turn our eyes toward God.

To say that Johnson considered the world fallen might seem a commonplace observation. Howard Weinbrot has listed Johnson's conviction that "man was fallen" among "sensible conclusions that by now are obvious to all."[2] In response to the attention showered upon Johnson's gloomy tendencies, Weinbrot rightly reminds us to recall "Smiling Sam" and not just "Sad Sam," as each are "integral parts of his life" (17).[3] Noting Johnson's penchant for good fun, Weinbrot emphasizes his love of laughter and joy. Adam Potkay also insists upon the "social nature" of Johnson's "passion for happiness."[4] However much weight we might properly attach to Johnson's sober observation in "Life of Collins" that "man is not born for happiness," it would be misleading to say that Johnson was always miserable.[5] The happiness Johnson experienced, he experienced with others. But Potkay also adds that "[a]s a Christian, Johnson's eudaimonism is, like Augustine's, always centered on a telos, the love of God, that is not of this world" (73). This is not to say, as we shall see, that Johnson would ever recommend a turning away from the world; on the contrary, as Potkay puts it, Johnson believes we must live in the world, "steadily pursuing the goals dictated by appropriate (i.e., moderate, benign) passions" (75). Weinbrot too reminds us that, despite its challenges, Johnson "sees life as a continuing process of trying to make progress, in which inevitable failure is part of the price of success" (14). But Johnson's sense of the "inevitable failure" attendant on all human pursuits reflects his inner burden, namely the sense that in a fallen world the quest for happiness is transient and even misleading, a distraction at best from a more lasting state that awaits us. However, most discussions of the relationship between Johnson's religious convictions and his sense of happiness overlook the link he establishes between original sin and the prospect of redemption.[6]

Johnson's conviction that the world is fallen was no secret to those who knew him, as evident in the following exchange reported by Boswell: "'Lady MacLeod asked if no man was naturally good.' JOHNSON: 'No madam, no more than a wolf.' BOSWELL: 'Nor no woman, Sir?' JOHNSON: 'No, Sir.' Lady MacLeod started at this, saying in a low voice, 'This is worse than Swift.'"[7] But though Johnson no doubt enjoyed shocking Lady MacLeod, those who knew him best would not be surprised to learn that, when it came to original sin, Swift had little on Johnson. Few knew Johnson as well as Hester Lynch Piozzi, who remarked, "The natural depravity of mankind and remains of original sin were so fixed in Mr. Johnson's opinion, that he was indeed a most acute observer of their effects."[8] When Boswell asked for a definitive statement on the topic of original sin, Johnson responded: "With respect to original sin the inquiry isn't necessary; for whatever the cause of human corruption, men are evidently so corrupt, that all the laws of heaven and earth are insufficient to restrain them from crimes" (*Life* 4:123). While in the Hebrides, Boswell reports that Johnson informed him that "original sin was the propensity to evil, which no doubt was occasioned by the fall."[9] With what must have been a heavy heart, Johnson told Boswell, "Sorrow is inherent in humanity" (*Tour* 5:64).

It was not in conversation alone that Johnson expressed his concern for the fallen world. The idea permeates his writings, but it finds particularly powerful expression in his periodical essays and, not surprisingly, his sermons. "Misery is the lot of man," laments *Adventurer* 120,[10] while *Sermon* 23 bemoans "the miseries of our present state" (*Sermons*, 237). Johnson considered the misery of a fallen world to be an incontrovertible consequence of original sin. "That the life of man is unhappy," he remarks, "that his days are not only few, but evil, that he is surrounded by dangers, and oppressed by calamities, requires no proof. This is a truth, which every man confesses, or which he, that denies it, denies against conviction" (237). In lines that echo *The Vanity of Human Wishes*, Johnson states, "If we cast our eyes over the earth, and extend our observations through the system of human beings, what shall we find but scenes of misery and innumerable varieties of calamity and distress, the pains of sickness, the wounds of casualty, the gripings of hunger, and the cold of nakedness" (207). In *Rasselas*, Nekayah goes so far as to ask what "is to be expected from our persuit of happiness, when we find the state of life to be such, that happiness itself is the cause of misery."[11] If Lady MacLeod would simply open her eyes to the world around her, Johnson might say, she would see the naïveté of her question.

But however much Johnson might have enjoyed startling Lady MacLeod, his view of the nature of man and his relationship to the world and others is in fact more despairing than his tart rejoinder suggests. *Adventurer* 120, for example, goes so far as to state that we deceive ourselves about the joy in our lives far more than we care to admit. "The world," he observes, "in its best state, is nothing more than a large assembly of beings, combining to counterfeit happiness which they do not feel, employing every art and contrivance to embellish life, and to hide their real condition from the eyes of one another" (*Idler and Adventurer*, 468). Not surprisingly, Johnson's comments on going to the theater in *Idler* 18 are emblematic of his view of happiness in general: "the fiction of happiness is propagated by every tongue, and confirmed by every look, till at last all profess the joy which they do not feel, consent to yield to the general delusion; and when the voluntary dream is at an end, lament that bliss is of so short duration" (58).

If we turn to his *Dictionary*, we see that Johnson can hardly conceive of the words *fall* and *world* without viewing them in tandem.[12] He initially defines *to fall* as "to drop from a higher place." But he soon adds "to apostatize; to depart from faith or goodness." He then defines *world* first as a "great collective of all bodies" but follows with "the present state of existence," "a secular life," and, perhaps most significantly for our purposes, "business of life, trouble of life." Perhaps that is why his definitions of *world*, regardless of how secular they might seem, are often followed by illustrative quotations that offer religious instruction. From the Reverend John Rogers he cites, "By the world, we sometimes understand the things of this world, the variety of pleasures and interests which steal away our affections from God." From John Dryden, he offers, "Christian fortitude consists in suffering for the love of God, whatever hardships can befall in the world." In keeping with his policy of choosing quotations that exemplify the "precept of prudence or piety," these selections suggest that even when Johnson offers secular definitions he cannot conceive of the "world" without invoking a theological framework. A "secular life" in the "world" is typically one consumed by the temptations that turn us from faith and goodness, that lure us from God in much the same way as Adam and Eve. In addition, his definitions of *worldly* largely focus on inattention to a "future state," devoid of any of the positive connotations (such as urbanity) found in the word today.

But what makes the "misery of the world" a distinctly theological matter for Johnson? What does Christian ontology offer that is missing from other possible explanations for the pain and suffering of the world? The roots of Johnson's conception of original sin run deep, beginning with Paul's injunction to the Romans (5:12), "Wherefore, as by one man sin entered into the world, and death by sin; and so death passed upon all men, for that all have sinned." Yet it is Augustine, the primary architect of original sin, who provides the sense of personal struggle that most closely approximates Johnson's view of the matter. For Augustine, original sin manifests itself in two distinct ways: first, from concupiscence, that is, the direct transmission of sin from person to person, generation to generation, through sexual intercourse; second, from our own weakness, the misdirection of our will as it succumbs to temptation and chooses vice over virtue. Augustine's sense of sin as both inherited and chosen, places the propensity toward evil both within us and without us. In his *Miscellany of Questions in Response to Simplician*, Augustine remarks:

> For willing itself is in our power since it is close at hand, but the fact that doing the good is not in our power is part of the deserts of original sin. For nothing remains of this first nature of humankind but the punishment of sin, through which mortality itself has become a kind of second nature, and it is from this that the grace of the Creator frees those who have submitted to him through faith.[13]

Given the dual nature of sin, Augustine understands that free will alone might not be strong enough to resist the temptations of the world and our own prideful desires. The resulting struggle defines us as divided beings. As Augustine puts it in *Sermon* 182.6, "Either you don't know what to do, and you go wrong, you fall into error; or else you know what should be done, and you are overpowered with weakness. So every human evil is error and weakness" (qtd. in Kelley, 30).

Augustine's unflinching embrace of original sin, in all its tension regarding the power of free will and the weakness of individual choice, found a welcome home in the Protestant Reformation. Alan Jacobs states, "The Protestant Reformation did not bring about any substantially new teaching regarding original sin."[14] According to Jacobs, Luther, Calvin, and Cranmer "all clearly endorsed and reinforced the Augustinian view" (107). In the English eighteenth century, Wesley identifies the "sin in our members" as inherited at birth (qtd. in Jacobs, 130), a conviction shared by Whitefield, who offered the admonition, "If you have never felt the weight of original sin, do not call yourselves Christians" (qtd. in Jacobs, 133). But it is the inclusion of "original sin" among the Thirty-Nine Articles of Religion in the Book of Common Prayer that testifies to the orthodoxy of the Augustinian viewpoint in England. Article IX states:

> Original sin standeth not in the following of Adam, (as the Pelagians do vainly talk;) but it is the fault and corruption of the Nature of every man, that naturally is engendered of the offspring of Adam; whereby man is very far gone from original righteousness, and is of his own nature inclined to evil, so that the flesh lusteth always contrary to the Spirit; and therefore in every person born into this world, it deserveth God's wrath and damnation.

While the direct influence on Johnson of Augustine or any of the Continental shapers of the Protestant Reformation can be difficult if not impossible to determine, that of English divines such as Cranmer and Hooker, and indeed the Book of Common Prayer itself, cannot be overstated. The concerns of Article IX, with its attention to "the fault and corruption of the Nature of every man" and his "inclin[ation] to evil," provide the basis for a belief that manifests itself throughout Johnson's writings and conversation. But Johnson himself admits, more generally, that his views have been shaped by the wisdom of the early church fathers, for whom the "general and indiscriminate distribution of misery," as *Adventurer* 120 observes, "has provided one of the strongest arguments for a future state" (*Idler and Adventurer*, 469). He continues by arguing, "It is scarcely to be imagined, that Infinite Benevolence would create a being capable of enjoying so much more than is here able to be enjoyed . . . if he were not designed for something nobler" (469).

Yet despite his admiration of the early Church fathers as well as the Protestant reformers, there is little evidence beyond what is quoted above that Johnson held a strictly Augustinian view of original sin. In some respects Johnson's view of original sin resembles John Locke's reflections on the topic in *On the Reasonableness of Christianity*. Like Johnson, Locke emphasizes the necessary relationship between sin and redemption. Locke begins, "'Tis obvious to anyone who reads the New Testament, that the Doctrine of Redemption, and consequently of the Gospel, is founded upon the supposition of Adam's fall."[15] "What Adam fell from," Locke argues, "was the state of perfect obedience" (6). In contrast to Augustine's conception of original sin as transmitted through concupiscence, Locke suggests that humans sin because Adam has sinned, not necessarily because they inherited a genetic predisposition to transgress; once cast outside of Eden, humans entered a world of mortality and suffering that heightened the possibility of sin. As Greg Foster and Kim Jan Parker put it, "Locke affirms that human beings are radically sinful, such that they cannot attain the standard of moral perfection that God rightly sets for them, and thus the saving work of Christ is necessary if anyone is to be spared from eternal condemnation."[16] Locke's view seems to fall somewhere in between that of Augustine, who sees original sin as deeply ingrained within the very nature of our being, and the Pelagians, who rejected the idea of original sin outright. Indeed, Johnson comes closest to expressing Locke's view when, in "Life of Milton," he says, "We all, indeed, feel the effects of Adam's disobedience; we all sin like Adam, and like him must all bewail our offences" (*Lives* 21:194). To "feel the effects" of Adam's sin might not be the same as inheriting a genetic predisposition to sin; however, Johnson's failure to specify his understanding of the nature of original sin might suggest a sense that the prevalence of sin provides more compelling evidence than any theological speculation.

For Johnson, the evidence of original sin was everywhere; its precise nature, however, especially given Scripture's lack of clarity in this matter, remains in the realm of speculation. This is perhaps why, in response to Boswell's request for a statement on original sin, Johnson says, "with respect to original sin, the inquiry isn't necessary." To *inquire*, as Johnson defines the word in his *Dictionary*, is "to ask questions; to make search; to exert curiosity on any occasion." Johnson most likely saw little reason to speculate regarding whether or not Augustine or Locke best understood its nature and origin. To side directly with either one would make Johnson guilty of exactly what he condemns in Soame Jenyns, namely the attempt to explain beyond what we can see or understand in a fallen world. "We see but in part," Johnson reminds Jenyns, as he warns against deciding "too easily . . . upon questions out of the reach of human determination."[17]

This response to Jenyns indicates what Blanford Parker has identified as Johnson's fideism, which he links with a "Pauline and Augustinian conception of the injured perceptive faculties, but still surviving inner voice."[18] Fideism, as Parker understands it, involves the apprehension of God's "absence" from the earthly city but suggests His presence in a heavenly one. This fideism might explain Johnson's uneasiness in response to Boswell's queries regarding the evidence for God and the prospect of salvation. When discussing the evidence in support of Christian truth, Johnson admitted to Lord Lyttleton, "I would like to have more" (*Life* 4:298). In the absence of a purely rational basis for the existence of God, Johnson felt the power of faith. While the evidence of the senses tells us much about the nature of our physical experience (the *locus classicus* for Johnsonians being the famous stone-kicking refutation of Bishop Berkeley), it ultimately tells us nothing regarding what lies beyond. Refuting Berkeley by kicking a stone might seem to complicate any idea of Johnson as fideist, as he seems to trust the senses as a key to truth rather than any philosophical conception of an immaterial reality. Yet Johnson had faith that the propensity to sin promised the prospect of redemption, however unlikely that prospect might have seemed to him during his dark nights of the soul. Johnson's sense of his own unlikely redemption could be read as an indication of the humility he found essential to beings living in a fallen state. The problem with the Augustinian conception of original sin, as many Protestant Reformers were well aware, is that, arguably, it frees us from responsibility for our actions; if original sin is a genetic predisposition, then what chance is there that we can struggle against it? Johnson, however, never understood his Christian humility as an acceptance of his inevitable status as a sinner. In the manner of Richard Allestree's *The Whole Duty of Man*, Johnson believes that proper moral instruction can serve to inculcate an ideal of virtue that, if honestly pursued, might prove pleasing to God, however short of that ideal we might ultimately—and inevitably—fall.

But neither fideism in general nor the writings of Augustine, the early Church Fathers, the Protestant reformers, or John Locke, would be likely to persuade Johnson if the evidence of his experience did not confirm their teachings. In *Sermon 5*, Johnson reminds his readers that, according to Scripture, God created mankind for happiness, but that happiness was "dependent upon choice, and to be preserved by his own conduct" (*Sermons*, 55). The lesson imparted by Scripture, Johnson insists, is that man is responsible for the "breach" where "physical and moral evil entered the world together" (55). This sense of the relationship between the burden of sin and its impact upon humanity finds eloquent expression in *Idler* 89, which states, "Religion informs us that misery and sin were produced together" (*Idler and Adventurer,* 275). The essay offers a grim depiction of the world, where "innocence and happiness" are "remote" and "where our senses assault us and our hearts betray us" (276). Yet, when all seems lost, the essay takes a surprising turn, as Johnson identifies the positive benefits of misery. Rather than simply a malign consequence of sin, Johnson argues that misery serves a beneficial purpose. It becomes the mechanism that turns us toward God. Without misery, our inclination to evil would run rampant. In other words, feeling miserable is not merely a consequence of, or punishment for, our misdeeds. If not for misery, Johnson remarks, we would "pass on from crime to crime, heedless and remorseless" (276). Misery reminds us that this fallen world is not the only world. "None would fix their attention on the future," he insists, "but that they are discontented with the present" (277). Similarly, in *Adventurer* 120 Johnson says, "If our present state were one of a continued succession of delights, or one uniform flow of calmness and tranquility, we should never willingly think upon its end" (470). In this sense, misery is as much a gift as a punishment. We might feel as though it brings us down, but, for Johnson, when properly understood, misery lifts us up. "Godliness, or piety, is the elevation of the mind towards the supreme being," he writes, "and extension of the thoughts to another life" (277). For Johnson, this "elevation of the mind" would be unlikely without misery to guide us.

In his sermons, Johnson acknowledges misery as the legacy of our first disobedience. But that legacy does not absolve us from responsibility for our actions. When we sin, we sin through no fault but our own. Johnson will not excuse sin on the grounds of its inevitability in a fallen world, nor will he accept that, in the face of the "universality of misery," God must have abandoned the world. He remarks, "Though the world be full of misery and disorder, yet God is not to be charged with disregard of his creation. . . . [I]f we suffer, we suffer by our own fault" (*Sermons*, 55). For Johnson, the Divine Presence diligently watches over each of us, fully aware of our actions and their consequences. "He who traces his troubles to their source," he says, "will commonly find that his faults have produced them. And he is then to consider his sufferings as the mild admonitions of his heavenly Father, by which he is summoned to timely penitence" (166). Perhaps this sense of a God who "still continues to superintend and govern" (172) creation helps explain the discomfort Johnson felt in solitude, when left most exposed and vulnerable. In his prayers Johnson acknowledged that he sought "the peace which the world cannot give" (*Idler and Adventurer*, 45), but curiously enough he seemed least at peace when at prayer.

Prayer, for Johnson, was an act of solitude, often composed after one of his many sleepless nights, when agonies of mind and body kept him awake. In 1773 he remarks, "My nights are now such as give me no quiet rest,"[19] an observation repeated throughout most of his adult life. Rather than bringing comfort in the wake of his torments, prayer often added to his misery as he reflected on his own failings.[20] As one reads through Johnson's prayers, a sense of inevitable repetition occurs. Time after time, he catalogues the same failings and chastises himself for not living up to his previous resolutions. Over a period of many years of prayer, again and again Johnson resolves to rise early; to avoid indolence and sensuous thoughts; to calm his wayward imagination; to work harder; to read more, especially in Scripture; to attend church regularly (despite his difficulty in hearing the services); to keep track of his life and weigh his improvements and deficiencies; and, of course, to repent of his sins and express gratitude for what he sees as his infrequent virtues. The cumulative effect of the prayers, like his more public writings, enacts a sense of the vanity of human wishes, a vicious cycle of promises made and broken, despite the best intentions. Perhaps this is why, in his rejection of Soame Jenyns's blithe optimism, Johnson castigates those who "imagine that we are going forward, when we are only turning round" (*Free Inquiry*, 418). Despite his worldly accomplishments, Johnson, especially in the second half of his life, feels inescapably trapped in a cycle of sin and fears the harsh judgment of God. Rather than a source of comfort or consolation, prayer becomes a painful but necessary reminder of his fallen nature. Prayer, for Johnson, provides a sober confirmation of his sinfulness in a corrupted world, instead of a tranquil bulwark against it. Regardless of his many goals, happiness remains elusive and misery prevalent: as he remarks in a supplication of 1764, "I have now spent fifty-five years in resolving, having from the earliest time almost that I can remember been forming schemes of a better life. I have done nothing" (*Diaries*, 81).

Yet however much Johnson advocates prayer, he also warns against the dangers of excessive solitude, especially forms of solitude that have traditionally been privileged as conducive to piety. Imlac advises Rasselas, "He that lives well in the world is better than he that lives well in a monastery," while the hermit in *Rasselas* remarks, "The life of a solitary man will be certainly miserable, but not certainly devout" (165 and 83). Virtue, according to Johnson, must be tested in a field of social activity and civic duty. From the hermit preparing for his return to society to the equation of isolation with uselessness in *Idler* 19, Johnson's wariness of solitude is well known. "Man may indeed preserve his existence in solitude," Johnson admits in *Adventurer* 67, "but can enjoy it only in society" (*Idler and Adventurer*, 389). But the rationale behind Johnson's objections to solitude becomes more apparent when viewed in relation to the challenges posed by the fallen world. In *Sermon* 3, for example, Johnson remarks of those who have chosen a monastic existence, "But surely it cannot be said that they have reached the perfection of a religious life; it cannot be allowed that flight is victory; or that he fills his place in the creation laudably who does no ill, only because he does nothing" (*Sermons*, 33). The benefit of a fallen world is that it allows us to demonstrate faith through virtuous action. As Religion observes in the allegorical dream vision of *Rambler* 44, "Society is the true sphere of human virtue."[21] Faith should not be "confined to cells and closets, nor restrained to sullen retirement" (*Rambler*, 242). *Rambler* 44 argues that we need to confront the inevitable difficulties of life and struggle against the challenges and temptations that conspire to turn our hearts from God. To be tested, of course, surely does not mean that we will always pass. A merciful God, as Johnson explains in *Sermon* 1, neither expects "uniform regularity" nor "unfailing virtue" (*Sermons*, 8). We won't always be able to act virtuously at all times or in all places. "Who can pass undefiled through a polluted world?" Johnson asks in *Sermon* 3 (34). But, paradoxically enough, it is through confrontation with the misery of the world that we can find our happiness, if only through a patient awareness that God knows we have met a challenge and have done our best. Johnson elaborates upon this point in response to Soame Jenyns: "The religion of man produces evils, because the morality of man is imperfect; that he may be justly a subject of punishment: he is made subject to punishment, because the pain of part is necessary to the happiness of the whole; pain is necessary to happiness, no mortal can tell why or how" (*Free Inquiry*, 431).

We should not, however, allow these firm injunctions against solitude to suggest that Johnson did not also believe in the need to turn our attention, periodically, away from the world. *Rambler* 7, for example, argues that "a constant residence amidst noise and pleasure inevitably obliterates the impressions of piety," and warns that "our regard for an invisible state would grow every moment weaker" if we focus too exclusively on the world (*Rambler*, 39). Consequently, Johnson emphasizes the need to "weaken the temptations of the world, by retreating at certain seasons from it" (40). These moments of retreat provide opportunity for the reflection and self-scrutiny that Johnson considers essential for a proper rendering of one's soul. Thus he also seems to encourage and maintain a balance between private contemplation and social activity. The measure of one's soul, for Johnson, reflects the degree of virtue present in his worldly engagements. "The great art therefore of piety, and the end for which all the rites of religion seem to be instituted," he advises, "is the perpetual renovation of our motives to virtue" (40). It is no surprise, therefore, that Johnson concludes *Rambler* 44 with the exhortation, "Return from the contracted views of solitude, to the proper duties of a relative and dependent being" (242).

"Virtue," as Johnson states in *Sermon* 5, "is a consequence of choice" (*Sermons*, 56). This claim, however, does not suggest that we have absolute control over our destiny. *Adventurer* 120, for example, chastises those "swelling moralists" who believe that "every man's fortune [is] in his own power" and who mistakenly advise that "happiness is the unfailing consequence of virtue" (*Idler and Adventurer*, 468). However, the fact that we do not determine our own destiny does not absolve us from making the most virtuous choices possible. If we choose solitude, for example, we choose to remove ourselves from the challenge of abiding by God's commandments and putting our talents to proper use. This of course is not always easy, and Johnson was painfully aware of the difficulty of putting his own to use. Johnson remained mindful of the parable of the talents from Matthew 25. He cites the chapter in *Sermons* 19 and 27 (*Sermons*, 212, 297), and in private prayed that God would "render up at the last day an account of the talent committed to me" (*Diaries*, 50). He also expressed to Boswell his impatience with those who dismiss good works and believe that faith alone is all that is necessary for salvation. To reject good works, he argues, is "utterly incompatible with civil and social security" (*Life*, 2:126). In Johnson's estimation, we must struggle to use our talents to improve the world, not in spite of its fallen nature but because of it. Yet he is also careful to insist that we are each responsible for ourselves and must avoid the temptation of measuring our degree of virtue in relation to others. *Rambler* 28 warns against "those who regulate their lives, not by the standard of religion, but the measure of other men's virtue; who lull their own remorse with the remembrance of crimes more atrocious than their own, and seem to believe that they are not bad while another worse can be found" (*Rambler*, 154). Nor, as he argues in *Idler*

19, should we ever be pleased with our own degree of virtue. For Johnson, God is the true and only judge, and His judgment, unlike ours, is not comparative.

Rambler 7 insists that "the great art therefore of piety, and the end for which all the rites of religion seem to be instituted, is the perpetual renovation of the motives to virtue" (*Rambler*, 40). In his *Dictionary*, Johnson defines *rite* as "a solemn act of religion; external observance." Despite his own infrequent church attendance (largely because he could not hear what was said), Johnson insisted on the value of public worship. He believed that, in a fallen world, the shared rituals of public worship, as enshrined in the Book of Common Prayer, offered consolation amid ceaseless flux. The first illustrative quotation of the word *rite*, drawn from Richard Hooker's *Laws of Ecclesiastical Polity*, testifies to the value Johnson found in public worship, sanctified by time; Hooker is thus quoted: "The ceremonies, we have from such as were before us, are not things that belong to this or that sect, but they are the ancient rites and customs of the church." As Johnson understood it, the Anglican Church provided a secure balance between Roman Catholicism and dissenting Protestantism, the classic via media between what he saw as dogmatism and enthusiasm. But despite his passionate Anglicanism, Johnson believed that virtue derives from a commitment to Christian truth broadly understood. "All Christians," Boswell reports him as having said, "whether Papists or Protestants, agree in the essential articles, and that their differences are trivial, and rather political than religious" (*Life*, 405). Or, as Johnson puts it in *Idler* 37, "Religion may regulate the life of him to whom the Scotists and Thomists are alike unknown, and the asserters of fate and free-will, however different in their talk, agree to act in the same manner" (*Idler and Adventurer*, 117).

In a fallen world, Johnson believed that the most secure path to virtue is to make intentional choices guided by the common bond of shared rituals. The structure provided by Anglicanism and the Book of Common Prayer— which Johnson had by heart—offered him consolation amid the vicissitudes of life. This is why the end of *The Vanity of Human Wishes* directs its readers toward Heaven. After advising the prayerful to pursue the Pauline virtues of "Love," "Patience," and "Faith," Johnson concludes, "With these Celestial wisdom calms the mind / And makes the happiness she does not find."[22] Here, Johnson departs from Juvenal's classical model that argues happiness can be achieved on earth through a rational pursuit of virtue and self-sufficiency. The subject of the verb *makes* is "celestial wisdom," not "happiness." In his *Dictionary*, Johnson defines "Celestial" as "relating to the superior regions" and the "blessed state." The conclusion is consistent with the rest of the poem in indicating that we cannot ourselves create lasting happiness in the here and now; "celestial wisdom" cannot calm us enough to "find" something that is not here. Perhaps the assurance that prayer "calms" the mind seems in direct contrast to the anguish of Johnson's own prayers. But ultimately prayer, for Johnson, directs our thoughts to Heaven, which he sees as their proper focus. Happiness for Johnson, as David Venturo argues, cannot be found through empirical search; to attempt to do so, as Rasselas does, mires us in this inferior earthly region rather than in contemplation of the superior heavenly one, leaving us in a wretched rather than a blessed state.[23] *Wisdom*, as Johnson defines it, is "sapience; the power of judging rightly," which, according to the illustrative quotation from William Temple "gives a man advantage of counsel and direction." For Johnson, this counsel and direction comes from God, as evident in the lines, "Still raise for good the supplicating voice, / But leave to heav'n the measure and the choice" (351–52). The "goods . . . the laws of heav'n ordain" that we enjoy on earth are essences, derived from God, "who grants the pow'r to gain" (365–67), and are best put to use when they direct our attention to "a happier seat" (363).[24]

In response to *The Vanity of Human Wishes*, Boswell inquired regarding what Johnson might have meant in identifying *misery* as "being the 'doom of man' in this life." After enumerating several instances of activities pursued upon "the supposition of happiness," such as "grand houses," "fine gardens," and "splendid places of public amusement," Johnson responds dismissively, much as Imlac had done in response to the Egyptian pyramids, by stating, "these are all only struggles for happiness" (*Life*, 3:198–99). For Johnson, the mutability of quotidian experience provides the evidence we need to focus our thoughts on the more lasting value of eternity. Robert G. Walker has identified this position as the "argument from desire" for a future state.[25] Walker cites Boswell's reflections on *Rasselas* as exemplifying Johnson's acknowledgment of original sin and the attendant necessity, in a fallen world, to focus our thoughts upon the immutable. Boswell remarks:

> To those who look no further than the present life, or who maintain that human nature has not fallen from the state in which it was created, the instruction of this sublime story will be of no avail. . . . Johnson meant, by shewing the unsatisfactory nature of things temporal, to direct the hopes of man to things eternal. (*Life*, 1:341–42)

Early in the narrative, Rasselas in the Happy Valley questions the value of his immediate state, despite the pervasive efforts to have all his desires satisfied. The empirical world simply cannot satisfy his emotional needs: "Man has surely some latent sense for which this place affords no gratification, or he has some desires distinct from sense which must be satisfied before he can be happy" (*Rasselas*, 13). This desire for contentment in a future state is expressed later in the tale, when Rasselas and his companions encounter the Old Man. Despite having lived a moral life, the Old Man remains dissatisfied, viewing his life as a series of vain efforts. In words that recall Johnson's own personal reflections, the Old Man acknowledges, "My retrospect of life recalls to my view many opportunities of good neglected, much time squandered upon trifles, and more lost in idleness and vacancy" (*Rasselas,* 156). But the value of these reflections, however sobering, is that he continues "to hope to possess in a better state that happiness which here I could not find, and that virtue which here I have not attained" (156). These lines recall *Idler* 41, where Johnson remarks, "Rational tranquility in the prospect of our own dissolution, can be received only from the promises of him in whose hands are life and death, and from the assurance of another and better state, in which all tears will be wiped from the eyes" (131).

Rather than advocate a stoic acceptance of mortal vanity, Johnson directs our thoughts to a transcendent realm, free from the misery unleashed by original sin. Johnson expands upon this idea in distinctly Augustinian terms in *Sermon* 12, inspired by Ecclesiastes 1:14: "I have seen all the works that are done under the sun; and behold, all is vanity and vexation of spirit":

> When the present state of man is considered, and when an estimate is made of his hopes, his pleasures, and his possessions; when his hopes appear to be deceitful, his labours ineffectual, his pleasures unsatisfactory, and his possessions fugitive, it is natural to wish for an abiding city, for a state more constant and permanent, of which the objects may be more proportioned to our wishes, and the enjoyments to our capacities; and from this wish it is reasonable to infer, that such a state is designed for us by that infinite wisdom, which, as it does nothing in vain, has not created minds with comprehensions never to be filled. (*Sermons,* 135)

Johnson's language here—which displays many parallels with that of *The Vanity of Human Wishes*—reminds his audience that the prospect of lasting happiness lies beyond this fallen world, in the heavenly city alone. As the connections with the poem make clear, Johnson is not simply tailoring his words to suit an occasional sermon. As Michael Suarez puts it, *The Vanity of Human Wishes* advocates "an understanding rooted in the higher truths of revelation and religious tradition." Suarez suggests that *Rasselas* "also lends itself (as Boswell also believed [*Life,* 1:341–44]) to the interpretation that it is only in the hereafter that our hopes for fulfillment can be satisfied."[26] *Idler* 101 concurs: "Terrestrial happiness is of short continuance" (*Idler and Adventurer,* 309). As a final example, Johnson's review of Jenyns states, "Though the production of happiness is the essence of virtue, it is by no means the end; the great end is the probation of mankind, or the giving them an opportunity of exalting or degrading themselves, in another state, by their behavior in the present" (*Free Inquiry,* 68).

Johnson's faith in the promise of virtue recalls Locke's admonition in *On the Reasonableness of Christianity*: "The view of heaven and hell, will cast a slight upon the short pleasures and pains in this present state; and give attractions and encouragement to virtue, which reason, and interest, and the care of ourselves, cannot but allow and prefer. Upon this foundation, and upon this only, morality stands firm" (39). The idea of virtue guided by religion leads Johnson, in *Sermon 5*, to the most unabashed expression of hopefulness to be found in his writings. Here he imagines a virtuous and civilized community, where citizens share a bond of mutual friendship and devotion to the common good, where the care of each individual is the concern of all, and where hardship is eradicated, poverty eliminated, and persecution unknown. In anticipation that these sentiments will seem inconsistent with the miseries of the world, Johnson advises his audience:

> Let no man charge this prospect of things, with being a train of airy phantoms; a visionary scene, with which a gay imagination may be amused in solitude and ease, but which the first survey of the world will shew him to be nothing more than a pleasing delusion. Nothing has been mentioned which would not certainly be produced in any nation by a general piety. To effect all this, no miracle is required; men need only unite their endeavours, and exert those abilities, which God has conferred upon them, in conformity to the laws of religion. (*Sermons*, 62)

At first glance, the utopian vision of *Sermon 5* sounds somewhat like the dreams of a theist doomed to awaken a skeptic. Indeed, one would be hard pressed to find so glorious a celebration of mankind's potential elsewhere in Johnson's writings. But despite this celebration, Johnson feared he had not reached his potential and would eventually be "sent to Hell" for his sins and "punished everlastingly" (*Life*, 4:299). And not only does Johnson fear for his sins in this world, but for the prospect of those in the next as well: he admits to Boswell that, even in Heaven, "We have no reason to be sure that we shall then be no longer liable to offend against GOD. We do not know that even the angels are quite in a state of security; nay, we know that some of them have fallen" (*Life*, 3:200). Nonetheless, the sentiments expressed in *Sermon 5* are wholly consistent with Johnson's faith in the human capacity for virtue. As Johnson sees it, if we cannot live up to the ideals of our faith, we have only ourselves to blame. So since reason rarely guides the stubborn choice, sin and misery will continue to shape our lives and our experience of the world. Yet, for Johnson, our present misery keeps us in mind of God, the creator of a world now fallen, but also of a greater one beyond.

NOTES

I would like to thank Matthew Davis, Melvyn New, and David Venturo for their helpful advice with this essay.
1. *Sermons*, ed. Jean H. Hagstrum and James Gray, vol. 14 of *The Yale Edition of the Works of Samuel Johnson* (New Haven: Yale University Press, 1978), 3. Hereafter cited in text as *Sermons*.
2. Howard D. Weinbrot, Review of Leopold Damrosch Jr., *Samuel Johnson and the Tragic Sense*, in *Eighteenth-Century Studies* 7 (Summer 1974): 508.
3. Howard D. Weinbrot, "Samuel Johnson: Process, Progress, and the Beatus Ille," *Johnsonian Newsletter* 60 (March 2009): 7–17.
4. Adam Potkay, *The Passion for Happiness: Samuel Johnson and David Hume* (Ithaca, NY: Cornell University Press, 2000), 65.
5. *The Lives of the Poets*, ed. John H. Middendorf, vols. 21–23 of *The Yale Edition of the Works of Samuel Johnson* (New Haven: Yale University Press, 2010), 23:1330. Hereafter cited in text as *Lives*. It is worth noting, as Weinbrot reminds us, that we can go too far in equating Johnson's misery with madness. The equation of misery with madness nonetheless finds expression most recently in Jeffrey Meyers's *Samuel Johnson: The Struggle* (New York: Basic Books, 2008). For correctives to such a view, see (aside from Weinbrot above) Donald Greene, "'A Secret Far Dearer to Him Than His Life': Johnson's 'Vile Melancholy' Reconsidered," *Age of Johnson* 4 (1991): 1–40; Samuel T. Joeckel, "Narratives of Hope, Fictions of Happiness: Samuel Johnson and Enlightenment Experience," *Christianity and Literature* 53 (Autumn 2003): 19–38; and Thomas Kass, "Morbid Melancholy, The Imagination, and Samuel Johnson's *Sermons*," *Logos: A Journal of Catholic Thought and Culture* 8 (2005): 47–63.
6. The most influential discussion of Johnson's Augustinianism remains Donald Greene, "Augustinianism and Empiricism: A Note on Eighteenth-Century English Intellectual History," *Eighteenth-Century Studies* 1 (Autumn 1967): 33–68. Curiously enough, Greene never cites Augustine directly, nor does he engage in depth with Johnson's own writings. Instead, he offers mostly general observations. The best study of Johnson's religion remains Maurice Quinlan, *Samuel Johnson: A Layman's Faith* (Madison: University of Wisconsin Press, 1964), though Augustine receives only two brief mentions and Locke three references. Similarly, Chester Chapin, in *The Religious Thought of Samuel Johnson* (Ann Arbor: University of Michigan Press, 1968), barely notes Augustine other than to quote Sir John Hawkins as having written that Johnson's faith "had a tincture of enthusiasm, arising, as it is conjectured, from the fervour of his imagination, and the perusal of St. Augustine and the other fathers" (13).
7. *Boswell's Life of Johnson*, ed. George Birkbeck Hill and L.F. Powell, 6 vols. (Oxford: Clarendon Press, 1934), 5:211. Hereafter cited in text as *Life*. See also Isobel Grundy, "'This Is Worse Than Swift': Johnson as Speaker of the Unacceptable," *Johnsonian Newsletter* 58 (March 2007): 6–17.
8. *Anecdotes of the Late Samuel Johnson, LL.D.* (London, 1786), 268. For a useful discussion of Johnson and the cultural context of original sin, see Nicholas Hudson, *Samuel Johnson and Eighteenth-Century Thought* (Oxford: Clarendon Press, 1988), 203–15.
9. *The Tour of the Hebrides* in *Boswell's Life of Johnson*, ed. Hill and Powell, 5:88. Hereafter cited in text as *Tour*.
10. *The Idler and the Adventurer*, ed. W.J. Bate, John M. Bullitt, and L.F. Powell, vol. 2 of *The Yale Edition of the Works of Samuel Johnson* (New Haven: Yale University Press, 1963), 466. Hereafter cited in text.
11. *Rasselas and Other Tales*, ed. Gwin Kolb, vol. 16 of *The Yale Edition of the Works of Samuel Johnson* (New Haven: Yale University Press, 1990), 129. Hereafter cited in text.
12. *A Dictionary of the English Language*, 2 vols. (London, 1755). All subsequent quotations from the *Dictionary* are from this edition.
13. Quoted in Joseph T. Kelley, *Saint Augustine of Hippo: Selections from Confessions and Other Essential Writings* (Woodstock: Skylight Paths, 2010), 39. Hereafter cited in text.
14. Alan Jacobs, *Original Sin: A Cultural History* (New York: HarperCollins, 2008), 107. Hereafter cited in text.

15. John Locke, *On the Reasonableness of Christianity*, ed. John C. Higgins Biddle (Oxford: Oxford University Press, 1999), 5. Hereafter cited in text.

16. Greg Foster and Kim Jan Parker, "'Men Being Partial to Themselves': Human Selfishness in Locke's *Two Treatises*," 2006 Annual Meeting of the American Political Science Association, Philadelphia, August 21, 2006, 8.

17. "Review of Soame Jenyns, *A Free Inquiry into the Nature and Origin of Evil*," ed. O M Brack Jr., vol. 17 of *The Yale Edition of the Works of Samuel Johnson* (New Haven: Yale University Press, 2004), 398. Hereafter cited in text as *Free Inquiry*. The best analysis of Johnson's review of Jenyns's *Free Inquiry* can be found in Richard B. Schwartz, *Samuel Johnson and the Problem of Evil* (Madison: University of Wisconsin Press, 1975).

18. Blanford Parker, *The Triumph of Augustan Poetics: English Literary Culture from Butler to Johnson* (Cambridge: Cambridge University Press, 2006), 231. See also David Venturo, "Fideism, the Antisublime, and the Faithful Imagination," in *Johnson after 300 Years*, ed. Greg Clingham and Philip Smallwood (Cambridge: Cambridge University Press, 2009), 95–111.

19. *Diaries, Prayers, and Annals*, ed. E.L. McAdam, with Donald and Mary Hyde, vol. 1 of *The Yale Edition of the Works of Samuel Johnson* (New Haven: Yale University Press, 1958), 139. Hereafter cited in text as *Diaries*. Hester Lynch Piozzi reports that "nothing was more terrifying to him than the idea of retiring to bed, which he never would call going to rest, or suffer another to call so. 'I lie down,' (said he), 'so that my acquaintance may sleep; but I lie down to endure oppressive misery, and soon rise again to pass the night in anxiety and pain'" (*Anecdotes of the Late Samuel Johnson, LL.D.*, 231).

20. For a full discussion of the inability of prayer to provide Johnson relief from distress, see Max Byrd, "Johnson's Spiritual Anxiety," *Modern Philology* 78 (May 1981): 368–78. Byrd states, "Plainly, Johnson's religion brought him none of that 'calmness, caution, and moderation' that he expected it should." The reference to "calmness, caution, and moderation" is from Johnson's Sermon 7, 76.

21. *The Rambler*, ed. W.J. Bate and Albrecht B. Strauss, vols. 3–5 of *The Yale Edition of the Works of Samuel Johnson* (New Haven: Yale University Press, 1969), 3:241. Hereafter cited in text.

22. *Poems*, ed. E.L. McAdam Jr. with George Milne, vol. 6 of *The Yale Edition of the Works of Samuel Johnson* (New Haven: Yale University Press, 1964), 108–9. All subsequent quotations will be indicated by line numbers.

23. My discussion of Johnson's perspectives on empiricism, stoicism, and Pauline theology in *The Vanity of Human Wishes* is indebted to David Venturo, *Johnson the Poet: The Poetic Career of Samuel Johnson* (Newark: University of Delaware Press, 1999), 126–34.

24. In a response to the implications of a "happier seat," which dismisses, implicitly, the "argument from desire," Donald Greene remarks, "this is hardly the same as saying that your present predicament is so gloomy that we are obliged to believe in a future life." See "Augustinianism, Authoritarianism, Anthropolatry," *Eighteenth-Century Studies* 5 (Spring 1972): 456–66.

25. Robert G. Walker, *Eighteenth-Century Arguments for Immortality and Johnson's Rasselas*, ELS Monograph Series 9 (Victoria, BC: University of Victoria, 1977), 35–63.

26. Michael Suarez, "Johnson's Christian Thought," in *The Cambridge Companion to Samuel Johnson*, ed. Greg Clingham (Cambridge: Cambridge University Press, 1997), 206.

Chapter Eight

Aesthetics and Theology in Samuel Johnson's *Life of Isaac Watts* and *Prayers and Meditations* (1785)

Katherine Kickel

Throughout his career, Samuel Johnson equated his literary efforts and ambitions—from the *Rambler* and *Idler*, to the *Dictionary*, and ending with his *Lives of the Poets*—with his quest for spiritual regeneration. In a sermon that echoes Philippians 2:12, he wrote: "The business of life is to work out our salvation,"[1] —a sentence in which *work* is less an abstract, discursive effort to understand God's promise of a future world and more a concrete, literal determination to practice acts of virtue by means of one's special talents. In the tradition of St. Francis de Sales's motto—*laborare est orare*—"prayer reinforced by work, or rather work which is inspired by prayer" is the basis of Christian salvation.[2] In Johnson's life in particular, poetic vocation and critical appraisal were the very serious business of saving one's soul by what one did during the trial period between birth and death; the Jewish concept of *mitzvoth*, or good deeds, comes to mind.

In his *Lives of the Poets*, Johnson frequently insisted on the necessity of putting one's virtues to work; it was the measure he applied to the lives of his subjects, even while he was judging himself, often harshly, by the same rule. Judgment could prove particularly vexing and complicated because, for Johnson, most writers inhabited two spaces: public and professional on the one hand, private and personal on the other. Each offered itself for moral examination, and each contained opportunities for the practice of virtue or for a collapse into error and sin. For example, in the *Life of Milton*, Johnson condemns the author's personal life because of political and religious practices that he considers misguided, yet he praises Milton's literary contribution, for although he was "of no church . . . his studies and meditations were

147

[in themselves] an habitual prayer."[3] In this case, what Milton achieves as a poet, a public role, richly compensates for what he fails to accomplish in his private space. Ultimately, then, Milton is judged to have fulfilled the vocational application of his talent in this world, and for Johnson that seems to have been enough to deem the man, despite apparent personal failings, a responsive recipient of divine grace. The laudatory conclusion of the *Life of Milton* is somewhat unusual in this regard. Occasionally, in the cases of notably accomplished craftsmen like Pope, Dryden, Butler, and Waller, Johnson turns to the achievement of the poet's public work in order to ameliorate some failure in his private life. In most of the lives, however, Johnson's cataloguing of personal insufficiencies in a poet is mirrored by a weakness in his professional qualities, a failure most often confirmed by poor writing, a "fallen" rhetoric that, for Johnson, meant a language that failed as art—and as truth. Poor writing was a sign of an ill-applied practice of one's vocation and an indication of ill-used talent, and it was relatively rare for Johnson to find the poet's personal life and his professional practice in disharmony with one another. To Johnson's credit, when he did encounter such a disjuncture, as in the case of Milton, his fervent desire to practice his vocation as a responsible critic alleviated what might otherwise be considered mere prejudice. Johnson's literary judgments strike us as honestly and painstakingly arrived at, even when we might—in hindsight—disagree with them.

This correspondence between a poet's personal and professional lives is a recurring theme in *Lives of the Poets*. Inveterate critic that he is, however, Johnson almost never issues a positive review of both the author's private and public endeavors. The great exception is in the *Life of Isaac Watts*, which, although not entirely uncritical, is considered by most readers to be a highly idealized portrait of both the man *and* the writer. Key passages in this biographical account reveal what Johnson admires in Watts's devotional practices and religious compositions. Thus, the unusually acclamatory estimation of these two realms in Watts's life offers insight into Johnson's own intertwining of aesthetic and religious practice. The *Life of Watts* epitomizes Johnson's insistence on finding concord between private and public ends. There is no disparity, he seems to insist, between Watts's personal life and public practice (both as a preacher and a writer). For Johnson, such an agreement signals a universal ideal of spiritual commitment and reward, aptly manifest in every facet of Watts's biography.

In recounting Watts's successful public and private careers, Johnson specifically emphasizes the lived experience, extemporaneity, and emotional affect that inspire spiritual recommitment in an individual. This Watts accomplished by means of a rhetoric that Johnson characterizes as "expressing" and "enforcing" in its appeal to the twin (if somewhat problematic) doctrines of faith and works. Watts is described as adhering to a theological aesthetic that tilts toward faith over works, the private over the public, but only insofar as an intensely personal attitude toward religious devotion and practice is ultimately manifested in virtuous professional discourse. And this, I would argue, closely mirrors Johnson's own practical theology of faith and works and, most especially, his concept of private prayer, as it is illustrated in his *Prayers and Meditations* (1785).

The *Life of Watts* is distinguished by the fact that it was chosen by Johnson, and not by the publishers, for inclusion: "The Poems of Dr. Watts were by my recommendation inserted in the late Collection; the readers of which are to impute to me whatever pleasure or weariness they may find in the perusal of Blackmore, Watts, Pomfret, and Yalden" (4:105). This admission, at the text's beginning, highlights Johnson's preference for the poet and draws the reader's special attention to the life that follows. In shaping Watts's biography, Johnson follows the tripartite structure typical of the collection, opening with some domestic particulars of Watts's upbringing (that is, where he lived, what he studied, whom he worked for). After these details, Johnson resorts to Dr. Thomas Gibbons's account of the financial and emotional patronage Watts received.[4] Gibbons is Johnson's primary source on Watts, and his incorporation in the life signals (in its matter-of-fact approach) the most conventional passage of the biography.

The second section, though, provides Johnson's explanation for Watts's inclusion in the canon, why he had earned his place in the pantheon. Here, Johnson emphasizes Watts's particularly effective and even august use of language, despite his Dissenting affiliation: "He was one of the first authors that taught the Dissenters to court attention by the graces of language. Whatever they had among them before, whether of learning or acuteness, was commonly obscured and blunted by coarseness and inelegance of style. He shewed them, that zeal and purity might be *expressed* and *enforced* by polished diction" (4:107; my italics). In this passage in particular, and in *Lives* more broadly, religious expression is far more than a measure of rhetorical acuity: it is also an important indicator of individual grace and, in the case of a poet, a measure of one's application to virtuous works in the world. Despite the alluring "zeal and purity" of Dissenting worship, Johnson finds its measure "commonly obscured and blunted" when it does not conform to traditional conventions of rhetorical elegance, epitomized by the Anglican church's reliance on the collect. Where in many of the biographies, the poet's personal life detracts from a full realization of poetic achievement, Watts stands alone in the collection, not only in his exemplary personal conduct, but also in Johnson's favorable estimation of his contribution to religious composition—despite his Dissenting sympathies.

In *The Ordering of the Arts in Eighteenth-Century England*, Lawrence Lipking identifies the middle portion of the individual lives, or what he calls the character study, as comprising much of the innovation that *Lives* offered to eighteenth-century literary criticism: "In his reliance upon the character,

Johnson surpasses all predecessors. Formally speaking, the originality of the *Lives* consists in a new weight placed upon the central section, which is both clearly distinct from the rest of the Life and flexibly employed for a variety of purposes."[5] Successfully blending biography, aesthetics, and criticism, Johnson's malleable employment of the central section is particularly apparent in the *Life of Watts*. Here Johnson outlined the pertinent characteristics of a successful personal life and interlaced them with the contours of a notable devotional aesthetic. Significantly enough, his account closely echoes features in his own prayer collection, published posthumously in 1785.[6] Clearly, however, the distinguishing trait of Watts's story, which differentiates it from all the other lives in the collection, is Johnson's admiration for Watts's unparalleled promotion of a noteworthy religious expression. Johnson recognized in his compositions, particularly in his religious writings, a significant use of a poetic rhetoric, characterized, as already indicated, by both "expressing" and "enforcing" the doctrines he wanted to inculcate simultaneously in himself and in his audience. What Johnson approves in Watts's writing is a version of the venerable Anglican axiom *lex orandi lex credendi*, meaning that "there is a correspondence between the beliefs of those who pray and the articulate form their prayers take."[7] Johnson observes in Watts's writing a form of theological speech that not only affirms what can or cannot be reasonably said about a religious issue, but also reiterates a literal and figurative "grammar of believing," ultimately moving beyond the words themselves (3). Watts's religious writing allows his lay audience to grasp a profound spiritual union initiated, cultivated, and disciplined by language, but one that transcends language at the same time. What Johnson is affirming in Watts is the invocation of, and subsequent experience with, a distinguished sanctified language.

Greg Clingham has demonstrated that the concept of "nature" operates adversely in Johnson's estimation of the metaphysical poets because, "[a]lthough Johnson is able to *imagine* the poem 'philosophically' in this way, and to formulate its unrelatedness, he clearly does not like or value the *accompanying feeling*."[8] So too here Johnson contests any kind of ephemeral, curious, or elaborate religious expression (despite its "zeal" or "purity") that cannot summon the requisite affective feelings. However, it is important to remember that the type of affect that Johnson admires in Watts's religious writing is very different from the affect of the ruling passion as he defines it in the *Life of Pope* (4:44–45). Whereas in the former, an individual's affect is awakened by, and placed in service to, a prayerful contemplation that inspires virtuous behavior, in the latter, an individual's affect is distracted by a beguiling cant that impedes change. In this sense, Johnson believes that language structures an individual's reality; thus, it must necessarily adhere to an exquisite and disciplined expression. As a moralist and a critic, Johnson is always alive to acknowledging the gaps between principle and practice, but as a faithful and sincere Christian, he is also intent on reconciling them, both in himself and in his observation of others.

In the seventeenth and eighteenth centuries, the terms *regeneration* and *restoration* were used interchangeably to refer to the spiritual rebirth that the soul experienced both in baptism and over the course of one's life. Based primarily on Paul's Epistle to the Romans (see 3:10, 3:20, 3:23–24, and 8:29–30), the concept of regeneration and the subsequent affective states that the soul underwent in its process (that is, election, calling, justification, adoption, sanctification, and glorification) outlined a spiritual paradigm that was widely accepted by English Protestants across the spectrum.[9] Central to regeneration is a "profound concern with the interior life, and [an] emphasis upon the conversion experience" that can be monitored by way of an emotional excavation throughout one's life.[10] Not surprisingly, in both Catholic and Protestant traditions, private prayer and meditation acted as one of the most reliable options for the depth of self-examination necessary to gauge one's progress on the path to salvation. In the tradition of the Pauline model, Johnson's "feeling" or Watts's "affective theological reasoning" demands a specific type of scrupulous self-examination that includes inventorying, analyzing, and cataloguing not only one's emotions but also one's prior and subsequent behaviors. In this paradigm, one's works, one's talents, can never be ignored. They must be evaluated with the same rigor that one applies to one's inner spiritual state.

Thus in the *Life of Watts* and elsewhere in the *Lives*, the truest religious composition (whether in the form of homiletic oration, extemporaneous conversation, private prayer/meditative application, or philosophical treatise), like the sincerest ethical behavior, is constituted in simple rhetorical expressions that eschew the artifice and distraction of poetic device. At times, such simplicity may sacrifice nuance, but it also discourages idiosyncratic reflection. Johnson, due to his particular abhorrence for idiosyncrasy, is uncomfortable with the idea of contemporary sacred poetry, whether by Watts or Waller or any other poet of his time. Johnson's critical view of Waller, for instance, goes beyond a mere objection to the author's politics. It ultimately rests on the idea that the aesthetic aspirations of any contemplative verse must fail to achieve what, for Johnson, constitutes the basis of religious worship: a substantive apprehension and application of religious ideas to everyday existence—to the virtuous works that we are called on to perform, as well as the theological realizations that we might generate along the way (2:53).

In this sense, reflection on lived experience plays an important role in the mental inventorying necessary to gauge one's spiritual journey. Echoing *Adventurer* 126's cautionary proclamation, "Piety practiced in solitude, like the flower that blooms in the desert, may give its fragrance to the winds of heaven, and delight those embodied spirits that survey the works of God and the actions of men; but it bestows no assistance upon earthly beings, and however free from taints of impurity, yet wants the sacred splendor of beneficence," Johnson looks to Watts to render a practical model of Christian living rather than an unrealistic abstraction.[11] In the *Life of Watts*, as in *Prayers and Meditations*, the prosaic details of everyday experience, the opportunity of the extemporaneous moment, and the role of affect in personal reflection form the devotional aesthetic that Johnson not only approves in others but also employs in his own practice.

In *Prayers and Meditations*, Johnson's practice of private prayer illustrates a blend of formal and informal meditative types borrowed from both the Catholic and Protestant traditions. This is not surprising given Johnson's Anglican affiliation as well as his long-standing admiration for the primitive Church and its fathers. In "Johnson's Christian Thought," Michael F. Suarez explains how Johnson's affinity with Arminian theology in particular reconciled the doctrines of faith and works for him and other Protestants in the eighteenth century:

> If Calvinism views salvation as a definitive and irreversible act of God, then Arminianism regards salvation as a provisional outcome dependent upon how humans accept and cooperate with the grace that God freely bestows. Opposing predestination and its implications, Arminianism emphasizes individual moral freedom and the conditional nature of salvation. The sinner seeking salvation must engage in constant self-examination, perform interior and exterior labors of repentance, and be strongly committed to charitable works. While Calvinists examined themselves to discover signs of God's favor and election, Arminians scrutinized the quality of their Christian living in order to determine whether or not they had done their duty and, thus, rendered their lives acceptable to God.[12]

The system of belief that Suarez describes, the mid-century influence of William Law, and Johnson's particular emphasis on the parable of the talents (Matthew 25:14–30) represent the primary forces determining Johnson's spiritual development; all three support the notion that prayer involves an active as well as a reflective component, and all three lend equal weight to deed and thought.

Generally speaking, Protestant meditative tradition, including eighteenth-century Anglican practice, promoted two types of mental or meditative prayer practice—"Occasional" and "Deliberate." The second, derived from the Ignatian tradition, was the formal method; it usually took its starting point from a biblical event, sermon, or doctrine, rather than drawing on a prior emotion or lived experience. Its counterpart, Occasional meditation, usually involved a myriad of semi-contemplative topics, including "brief spiritual reflections and daily devotions on such topics as awakening, dressing, the lighting of candles, taking meals, retiring, Christ's passion, God's providences, the last things, walking in the fields and observing the creatures, [and] the various circumstances developing in the course of an illness."[13] Occasional meditation was the preferred Protestant practice, in large part because of its emphasis on lived experience, affect, and extemporaneity. In *Protestant Poetics and the Seventeenth-Century Religious Lyric*, Barbara Kiefer Lewalski highlights the main difference between the Catholic and Protestant approaches:

> The manner of application to the self in Protestant meditation also distinguishes it from Ignatian or Salesian meditation. In these continental kinds, the meditator typically seeks to apply himself to the subject, so that he participates in it; he imagines a scene vividly, as if it were taking place in his presence, analyzes the subject, and stirs up emotions appropriate to the scene or event or personal spiritual condition. The typical Protestant procedure is very nearly the reverse: instead of the application of the self to the subject, it calls for the application of the subject to the self—indeed for the subject's location in the self. (149)

Thus, in contrast to Catholic meditative theory, which asked its subjects to locate the meditative topic via an imaginative immersion in, for example, the Passion stories, Protestant practice demanded the application of those stories to a particular lived experience. One might say that in place of the *compositio loci* that anchored Catholic practice, Protestant practice domesticated long-standing abbatial methods of mental prayer by insisting that the lived experience of the meditator serve as the context for whatever spiritual content one's prayers might contain. In this tradition, experience was both paramount in prayer practice and central to the process of regeneration, with its dual basis in private reflection and public action.

Since Johnson frequently looks to his vocation for inspiration in his *Prayers and Meditations*, his meditative practice may be said to be far more Occasional than Deliberate, especially when the 1785 collection is taken as a whole.[14] In virtually every New Year's Eve and New Year's Day entry, in his annual birthday and Easter accounts, and in his descriptions of his miscellaneous vocational pursuits, often shaped as collects in his early years (e.g., "Study of Tongues" [1768] and "On the Study of Religion" [n.d.]), Johnson returns to his work as writer and scholar, weighing his performance as the determining factor of his possible regeneration.[15] In addition to the emphasis placed on vocation, there is also evidence of the importance of domestic detail and social exchange; together, they constitute a decidedly task-oriented, here-and-now vision of salvation.

The year 1760, or thereabouts, marks the period when Johnson's concerns about his lived experience in *Prayers and Meditations* shift somewhat from the vocational objects and career aspirations of his youth to a more intense, discursive self-examination, centered on keeping house, reading the Bible, rising early, avoiding idleness and ill thoughts, going to church, maintaining a journal, and caring for his health. Following the Pauline model as well as the Ignatian colloquy, the prayers and meditations of Johnson's middle years assign more weight and specificity to reflection on a wider variety of lived experiences than previously, although he still relies on vocation. Now, all of Johnson's experiences are invoked in order to measure accurately his progress toward salvation. Thus, Johnson records, among many other resolutions, recommitting his daily life to Christ (e.g., Easter Eve, 1761, and Easter Day, April 22, 1764), organizing his household (e.g., April 20, 1764, and September 18, 1764), rising early (e.g., September 18, 1760, and Easter Day, April 7, 1765), avoiding ill thoughts (e.g., April 21, 1764, and Easter Day, April 15, 1770 [one o'clock in the afternoon]), journaling his life (e.g., September 18, 1764 [seven in the evening] and September 18, 1766), and managing his melancholy (e.g., September 18, 1768 [at night]).[16] Here, domestic life and its diurnal reflection acquire a rich symbolism that facilitates the plotting of an individual's spiritual journey.

As Johnson's prayer practice becomes more domestic, it also becomes less stylized, more customary and poetically balanced yet simplified and compressed; in doing so, it simultaneously echoes many of the features that Johnson admired in Watts's style. Most notably, Johnson applauds Watts's employment of "familiar visits and personal application" to "stated and publick instruction," along with his advice "to lay aside the scholar, the philosopher, and the wit, to write little poems of devotion, and systems of instruction, adapted to their wants and capacities, from the dawn of reason through its gradations of advance in the morning of life" (4:108). Indeed, it is Watts's considerate communication with his different lay audiences, both children and adults, that Johnson highlights when he describes Watts as a "teacher of a congregation" rather than its "Doctor of Divinity" (4:107).

In the *Life of Watts*, Johnson is ostensibly mapping the contours, in person, in practice, and in profession, of the devotional aesthetic that is illustrative in large part of his 1785 prayer collection. In this sense, whereas much of *Lives* is concerned with distinguishing the features of a particular literary aesthetic and considering its merit and abuse, the character study passages of the *Life of Watts* are intent on recording an aesthetic of devotion and articulating a corresponding theology of prayer for its readers. This devotional aesthetic is invested with its own criteria of lived experience, extemporaneity, and affect, and it forms a basis, then, for Johnson's critical assessment of all religious writing: it undergirds both Johnson's favorable evaluation of Watts's life and work and his critical dismissal of most other religious verse.

Indeed, Johnson had little regard for religious verse as a genre. For him, the only true results of pious meditation are "Faith, Thanksgiving, Repentance, and Supplication," and these "cannot be invested by fancy with decorations"; in fact, for one to do so only corrupts prayer by detracting from its perfect simplicity (2:53). This does not mean, however, that there is no value in technically ornate or sophisticated language; rather, in the *Life of Watts*, Johnson suggests that religious language serves a different purpose than secular rhetoric. Religious language is intended for deeply personal communion or, in the tradition of the Ignatian meditation, a colloquy with God rather than a detached testament to God's omnipotence. In this tradition, language and experience live in each other in a nuanced way; both inspire a particular form of reflection, which, when operating correctly, actually allows for theological content and insight. Rarely, however, does Johnson find this union in contemporary poetry. Poetry alone, it seems, is unable to approach the ends of religion, as he would define them. To describe the typical incompatibility of poetry and prayer (and thus of literary and devotional aesthetics), Johnson famously writes in the *Life of Waller*:

> The doctrines of religion may indeed be defended in a didactick poem; and he who has the happy power of arguing in verse, will not lose it because his subject is sacred....
>
> Contemplative piety, or the intercourse between God and the human soul, cannot be poetical. Man admitted to implore the mercy of his Creator, and plead the merits of his Redeemer, is already in a higher state than poetry can confer. (2:52–53)

In making this distinction, Johnson is insisting on recognition of the individual and transcendent aspect of the human being's relationship with God. For Johnson, this communication is only hindered by the ornate conventions of verse; rather, in order for communion to occur, the colloquy must already be operating on a plane that exceeds the limits of our most elevated poetic expression. How human language can embody transcendence is perhaps an unfathomable mystery, but Johnson turns to Watts precisely to understand how it might occasionally happen.

The conjunction of form and function that Johnson appreciates in Watts's religious writing and in his practices of piety, then, is that his language not only expresses God's grandeur by means of a succinct and unadorned personal address—in homily, in theology, in catechism, and (at times) in poetry—but that it also enforces its effect through the emotional impact its personalization has on the listener, the conversant, or the reader. In Johnson's judgment (aesthetic or theological), Watts is able to summon the appropriate affective feelings (that is, to *express*), and, as a result of the emotional experience that he inspires, to call individuals to right action, indeed to move them to it (that is, to *enforce*).

Johnson observes this model two-part structure in Watts's preaching by paying particular attention to his employment of the extemporaneous moment to heighten the didactic effect and the subsequent resolve that occurs in the auditor. He describes the rhetorical movement of Watts's sermons thus: "Such was his flow of thoughts, and such his promptitude of language, that in the latter part of his life he did not precompose his cursory sermons; but having adjusted the heads, and sketched out some particulars, trusted for success to his extemporary powers" (4:108). What is interesting here is that success points in two directions: first, the successful rhetorical organization that he is able to impose on his own impromptu thoughts, and, second, the implication of a successful mastery of his congregation, success being, always, the ability to move his listeners to right conduct. For Watts and for Johnson, an aphoristic or gnomic genre is only as sound as it is ultimately action-oriented. Significantly, then, the dual capacity for a swift organization of impromptu thoughts and the subsequent reflection or call to action that they inspire is not only what Johnson admiringly observes in Watts, but also what he aspires to demonstrate in his solemn addresses in *Prayers and Meditations*.

In many of Johnson's most famous private meditations, the extemporaneous moment leads directly to an organized and formal composition, which, in turn, creates and bolsters a resolve that he seems not to have been capable of committing to before constructing the prayer. The effective persuasion to act more virtuously is the most important aesthetic component Johnson identifies in the writings of Watts, yet critics have long agreed that it is also a signal characteristic of many of Johnson's writings, and particularly of those reflecting his own sense of weakness and sinfulness in need of reform—that is to say, in his *Prayers and Meditations*. Take, for example, Johnson's Easter meditation on April 4, 1779 (205–9). The entry begins with a typical invocation of his domestic events, problems, and challenges (a nod to lived experience); he then organizes this experience into a traditional invocation of grace, both as dispensation for his sins and a calming of his mind; and he concludes with his "Purposes" or resolutions ("To rise at eight, or as soon as I can / To read the Scriptures / To study religion") followed by a formal prayer (207–9). In this prayer entry, as in many others, Johnson is able to invoke his lived experience, to summon the extemporaneous language, to reflect on its consequent affect (we might call it "empowerment" in the jargon of our age), and to resolve to do better both informally in a resolution list as well as formally in an occasional prayer. Taking into consideration the process of prayer evident in this particular entry, as well as the process he approvingly observes in the *Life of Watts*, it is clear that Johnson's approach, like Watts's, aptly *expresses*" via its aesthetic, and affects and *enforces* via its emotional reflection and performatory resolution.

Let no reader be fooled, however; Watts's extemporaneous style in preaching and prayer is predicated on the lifetime of theological study that Johnson had already sketched for his reader. His style is carefully demonstrated to be a "method of study," characterized, for example, "by interleaving [books] to amplify one system with supplements from another" (4:105). Watts's poetry and preaching alike pay heed to their classical antecedents, whether they be the *glyconick* verse of the Greeks or the liturgical rhythms of the primitive Church as preserved in the Book of Common Prayer. In that sense, what appears informal and extemporaneous is, in reality, formalized by a mind that has already obsessively attended to its own improvement, so much so that Johnson pays heed to Watts's attainment of the honorary degree of "Doctor of Divinity" (4:109).

Significantly, when Johnson comments on Watts's diminutive physical stature in the pulpit, it is only by way of contrast to the majestic scope of his ideas. There is in Watts's writing an abundance of theological cultivation on the one hand, and of lived experience on the other, that sets it apart from the rhetorically attractive but empty zeal that Johnson alludes to, for example, in the *Life of Butler*.[17] Moreover, in much the same fashion as Watts's religious compositions are marked by their simple "expressive" form and a corresponding "enforcing" effect that distinguishes them from the usual ornate style of Dissenters, so too is Watts's character delineated as superior to the typical human being in its dedicated pursuit of Christian virtue.

Illustrating Watts's nature, Johnson writes, "By his natural temper he was quick of resentment; but, by his established and habitual practice, he was gentle, modest, and inoffensive" (4:108). Like all human beings, Watts was prone to a particular temperament and a particular personal failing, but unlike others, according to Johnson, he overcame his disposition by its careful improvement. Again and again in the *Life of Watts* the qualities of cultivation, discipline, and habit take center stage in Johnson's characterization in order to explain the transformation of a good writer into a better or a solid preacher into a stellar. Watts's life becomes a model of the self-reforming process that any person might willfully and fruitfully undergo. For all his intellect and integrity, Watts cannot compare to the genius of a Pope or the craft of a Milton; still, he offers the reader of the *Lives* something more accessible than either in terms of his virtuous melding of his person and his profession. Johnson clearly values this achievement, and if we cannot finally agree with his assessment of Watts's poetry, at least we can attempt to understand his reasoning in reaching it.

In one of the most telling compliments in the *Lives,* Johnson assesses Watts thus: "As his mind was capacious, his curiosity excursive, and his industry continual, his writings are very numerous, and his subjects various.... It was not only in his book but in his mind that *orthodoxy* was *united* with *charity*" (4:108). The twin concepts of "orthodoxy" and "charity" are important for Johnson because, in the tradition of William Law and others, they suggest religious action in this world, uniting faith and works. This union, which is so well reflected in Watts's personal life, mirrors the reconciliation of "expression" and "enforcement" in his religious writing. For Johnson, the only weakness in Watts's nature is in the sheer diffusion of his talent in the world (for example, "he has left neither corporeal nor spiritual nature unexamined; he has taught the art of reasoning and the science of the stars" [4:109]). This "failing" indicates an inclination to do "too much," to serve his fellow human beings in too many ways, to the detriment (and underdevelopment) of his art. In particular, Johnson complains of the "paucity" of his devotional poetry. Johnson takes pains, then, to exculpate this lack of productivity by offering one of his most muted—and perhaps most self-mirroring—compliments: "It is sufficient for Watts to have done better than others what no man has done well" (4:110).

Ultimately, Johnson pays supreme tribute to Watts's life by metaphorically illustrating it in the orchestrated urging to prayer, meditation, and reflection that all of his work encouraged in others and in himself:

> whatever he took in hand was, by his incessant solicitude for souls, converted to Theology. As piety predominated in his mind, it is diffused over his works: under his direction it may be truly said, *Theologiae Philosophia ancillatur*, philosophy is subservient to evangelical instruction; it is difficult to read a page without learning, or at least wishing, to be better. The attention is caught by indirect interest, and he that sat down only to reason is on sudden compelled to pray. (4:109)

Teaching occurs subtly and expressively here, and it is regularly "enforced" by heightening the reader's self-reflection. In every page of Watts's writing, the eye is formulaically pointed toward God; the indifferent heart is surprised by what initially seemed nothing more than of "indirect interest"; and the spirit is led to divine communion by the grace of happenstance and the power of a scrupulous, affective reflection that awakens and compels the individual's resolve to do better.

When Johnson famously dismisses religious verse in the *Life of Waller* by writing that the "ideas of Christian Theology are too simple for eloquence, too sacred for fiction, and too majestick for ornament; to recommend them by tropes and figures, is to magnify by a concave mirror the sidereal hemisphere," he employs the word *simple* to mean a type of perfection that cannot be rhetorically approximated (2:53–54). Conversely, when he uses the metaphor of the concave mirror to illustrate the absurdity of magnifying the sky in order to better see the stars, he captures the insufficiency of any poetic device to insinuate that which is already perfectly represented and intuitively apprehended. Last, when he implies the distorting effect that the heavens can have on human consciousness, he illustrates how easily sense perception can be distracted and how easily the capacity of the senses can overwhelm even the finest of human intentions, including a sincere and prayerful colloquy with God. Prayer and religious expression involve both an invocation of the awe of sublimity and the careful use of reason; however, affect (awe) can go too far, as when it descends into the realm of religious enthusiasm or, worse, into a predominance of one's passionate desire for sublimity over a careful, modest, and humble application of reason. In the *Life of Watts* and *Prayers and Meditations*, the appropriate devotional aesthetic is a carefully disciplined spiritual exercise that is guided by reflection on lived experience, infused with an extemporaneous, but customary and personal expression, and ultimately concluded by a sustained recommitment to "works" in the everyday world.

This is a devotional aesthetic that relies on both the Anglican custom of invoking customary prayer forms (epitomized by Johnson's reliance on the collect and the language of the Book of Common Prayer in his own prayers and meditations), as well as a personal theology of prayer that inspires an emotional thrust in the individual that personalizes salvation and compels change. And if Johnson's assessment of Watts's approach to prayer and religious writing is indicative, to any extent, of changing attitudes toward prayer in the eighteenth century, it suggests (in keeping with Charles Taylor's recent work on the rise of secularism) a religious expression that is only slightly less institutional or customary in its form, and only guardedly more affective and personalized in its function.[18]

Thus, both Johnson's *Prayers* and Watts's devotional and professional practices tend to reflect eighteenth-century Anglicanism's moderate and inclusive view toward other denominations, originally initiated by John Tillotson, the late seventeenth-century Archbishop of Canterbury. Generally speaking, eighteenth-century Anglicanism successfully posited a pragmatic religious practice that not only allowed for an increased broad-mindedness toward other beliefs but at the same time worked to sustain an intense piety in its own believers. This paradox might be said to have characterized both Dissent, represented by Watts's "affectionate religion" and Anglicanism, represented by Tillotson's tolerance. Johnson's approval of Watts's theology, and his paralleling of it in his prayers and meditations, is a very strong indication, I believe, that eighteenth-century Christian theology had absolutely no intention of losing its intensity when it suggested the reasonableness of its faith.

In *Reason, Grace, and Sentiment: A Study of the Language of Religion and Ethics in England, 1660–1780*, Isabel Rivers characterizes Watts's devotional aesthetic as modulating the philosophical tensions between rationalism's intellectual argument and evangelism's fiery passion. She observes in Watts's writing and preaching two different styles, one being "the cold rational language of philosophical argument, which is intended to work demonstratively on the reader's intellect," a second being "the warm affectionate language of evangelical preaching, which is aimed at arousing the passions."[19] In Watts's personal life and in his professional career, Johnson observes this same paradoxical interaction between "affective" and "reasonable" appeals, between "expressing" and "enforcing" doctrines. Indeed, it is Watts's successful negotiation between these opposing tendencies that may well have reinforced Johnson's notions concerning, first, the importance of simplicity and sincerity in all religious writing, and second, the use of devotional writing to promote not merely one's own spiritual well-being, but that of the community to which such writings had to be addressed. The capacity to reform one's community through one's preaching and writing bespoke the success of one's own Christian reformation.

Ultimately, Watts is exemplary to Johnson not only for what he had actually accomplished, but, more important, for cultivating the person God intended him to become, through a multifaceted personal and professional religious application. As a religious writer who disciplined nature via reflection on lived experience, who married learned and extemporaneous expression, and who invoked "affect" and "reasoning," Watts fused oppositional realms, including Dissenting and Anglican orientations, to produce a religious expression that Johnson himself employs in his prayer practice: "expression" and "enforcement" work in tandem in their solemn religious compositions and their personal prayer applications.

NOTES

1. Quoted in Michael F. Suarez, S.J., "Johnson's Christian Thought," in *The Cambridge Companion to Samuel Johnson*, ed. Greg Clingham (Cambridge: Cambridge University Press, 1997), 200. Cf. *Sermons*, eds. J.H. Hagstrum and J. Gray, vol. 14 of *The Yale Edition of the Works of Samuel Johnson* (New Haven: Yale University Press, 1978), 161.
2. S.v. "Prayer (necessity of)," in *The Catholic Encyclopedia*, vol. 12 (New York: Robert Appleton Company, 1911), 347.
3. Samuel Johnson, *The Lives of the Most Eminent English Poets; With Critical Observations on Their Works*, ed. Roger Lonsdale, 4 vols. (London: Clarendon Press, 2006), 1:275–76. Hereafter cited in text.
4. Gibbons published *Memoirs* of Watts in May of 1780. Additionally, Johnson recorded meeting with Gibbons to consult on the Watts material. See Lonsdale's notes on the composition history of the life of Watts: Johnson, *Lives of the English Poets*, 4:378–79.
5. Lawrence Lipking, *The Ordering of the Arts in Eighteenth-Century England* (Princeton: Princeton University Press, 1970), 421.
6. The intended publication of the *Prayers and Meditations* is an issue of contention in Johnson criticism. It is unclear whether or not Johnson intended its release. What is known is that Johnson entrusted the manuscript to the clergyman George Strahan, who later became its editor and was ultimately responsible for shepherding it through to publication. For more information on Strahan's role in the public appearance of the text and his subsequent editorial presentation of Johnson's devotional life, see Michael Bundock, "The Making of Johnson's

Prayers and Meditations," *The Age of Johnson: A Scholarly Annual* 14 (2003): 77–97; and J.D. Fleeman, "Some Notes on Johnson's Prayers and Meditations," *The Review of English Studies* 19 (May 1968): 172–79.

7. Introduction to Charles Hefling and Cynthia Shattuck, eds., *The Oxford Guide to the Book of Common Prayer: A Worldwide Survey* (New York: Oxford University Press, 2006), 3.

8. Greg Clingham, "Life and Literature in Johnson's *Lives of the Poets*," in *The Cambridge Companion to Samuel Johnson*, ed. Greg Clingham (Cambridge: Cambridge University Press, 1997), 172.

9. Barbara Kiefer Lewalski, *Protestant Poetics and the Seventeenth-Century Religious Lyric* (Princeton: Princeton University Press, 1979), 14–15.

10. Lewalski, *Protestant Poetics and the Seventeenth-Century Religious Lyric*, 148.

11. *Adventurer* 126 in *The Idler and The Adventurer*, eds. W.J. Bate, J. Bullitt, and L.F. Powell, vol. 2 of *The Yale Edition of the Works of Samuel Johnson* (New Haven: Yale University Press, 1963), 475.

12. Suarez, "Johnson's Christian Thought," 199–200.

13. Lewalski, *Protestant Poetics and the Seventeenth-Century Religious Lyric*, 151.

14. For a full discussion of Johnson's meditative practice and theory in the *Prayers*, see my essay, "'Occasional Observance and the Quiet Mind': Meditative Theory and Practice in Samuel Johnson's *Prayers and Meditations* (1785)," *The Age of Johnson: A Scholarly Annual* 20 (2010): 35–55.

15. Samuel Johnson, *Prayers and Meditations, Composed by Samuel Johnson, LL.D. and Published from His Manuscripts by George Strahan, A.M. Vicar of Islington, Middlesex; and Rector of Little Thurock, in Essex* (Dublin: Printed for Mess. White, Byrne and Cash, 1785), 89, 264. The "Study of Tongues" was transcribed in 1768 but written earlier, and "On the Study of Religion" does not contain a composition date. Instead, it is included in the miscellany after the last chronological entry. I have decided not to use the Yale edition of the *Prayers and Meditations* because it intersperses the annals and fragmentary manuscripts among the 1785 prayer collection. Due to this juxtaposition, the biographical elements often overwhelm the design of the collection's devotional aesthetic.

16. Johnson, *Prayers and Meditations*, 45–48, 57–61, 53, 43–44, 65–71, 54–55, 109–12, 62–64, 76–78, and 90–91. This is just a sampling of some of Johnson's more famous resolutions. Hereafter the collection will be cited in text.

17. Johnson writes,

> It is scarcely possible, in the regularity and composure of the present time, to image the tumult of absurdity, and clamour of contradiction, which perplexed doctrine, disordered practice, and disturbed both publick and private quiet, in that age, when subordination was broken, and awe was hissed away; when any unsettled innovator who could hatch a half-formed notion produced it to the publick; when every man might become a preacher, and almost every preacher could collect a congregation. (*Lives of the English Poets*, 2:8)

18. See Charles Taylor, *The Secular Age* (Cambridge, MA: Belknap Press of Harvard University, 2007).

19. Isabel Rivers, *Reason, Grace, and Sentiment: A Study of the Language of Religion and Ethics in England, 1660–1780*, vol. 1, *Whichcote to Wesley* (New York: Cambridge University Press, 1991), 175.

Chapter Nine

Providence, Futurity, and Typology in Oliver Goldsmith's *The Vicar of Wakefield*

Nicholas Seager

> Good and bad are no longer positively black and white; the art of the moralist is out of fashion in fiction. But Goldsmith not only believed in blackness and whiteness; he believed—perhaps one belief depends upon the other—that goodness will be rewarded, and vice punished. It is a doctrine, it may strike us when we read *The Vicar of Wakefield*, which imposes some restrictions on the novelist. . . . One advantage of having a settled code of morals is that you know exactly what to laugh at.

—Virginia Woolf[1]

> Such as mistake ribaldry for humour, will find no wit in his harmless conversation; and such as have been taught to deride religion, will laugh at one whose chief stores of comfort are drawn from futurity.

—Oliver Goldsmith[2]

The literary reputation of *The Vicar of Wakefield* (1766) seems to rise in direct proportion to the diminution of its author's sincere religious goals. Goldsmith can be a "true genius" for Robert Hopkins only because he shows Dr. Primrose to be disingenuous—in this reading, the story is an irreverent satire on clerical hypocrisy embodied in the eponymous vicar.[3] Goldsmith fits into the development of the novel for Ronald Paulson as a "missing link" between Fielding and Austen, because *Vicar* is an exploitation of narrative irony through a self-consciously unreliable narration that mocks the vicar's pious values.[4] As Marshall Brown states it, in a teleological and taxonomical argument that places *Vicar* at the historical moment when the novel moves from didacticism to aestheticism, "Primrose's failure is the novel's triumph."[5] The revisionist, "ironic" readings of *Vicar* that first arrived in the 1960s were a corrective to a long-standing critical tradition—from early reviewers to Virginia Woolf—that emphasized the novel's sincerity and what Henry James called its "incomparable amenity," but regarded *Vicar* as either poorly organized or artistically restricted by its fidelity to a moral code.[6] The revisionists thus extended New Critical attention to the novel's unity of pattern and theme offered by critics like Curtis Dahl, Morris Golden, and Michael Edelstein by seeking rhetorical strategies that complicated an apparently too-simple work.[7] In turn, assertions of *Vicar*'s concomitant artistic *and* religious coherence appeared during the 1970s and 1980s.[8] An undoubted highlight here was Thomas Preston's contextualization of Goldsmith's novel amid popular homiletic, apologetic, and exegetical practices of the time, which showed that the novel is a "moral progress" toward "worldly detachment," with Primrose as its hero.[9] Interest then shifted with the New Historicism to intersecting questions of politics, family, and law, readings that tend to overlook theology.[10]

The state of play for theological readings of *Vicar of Wakefield* is well illustrated by two articles published since the turn of the millennium by Henry N. Rogers III and Preston, respectively. Rogers's reading is commonsensical and accepts the Vicar's values prima facie, but hence appears reductive. He argues the somewhat self-evident point that Goldsmith believed in Providence, and he explains the sudden plot reversals as a way of drawing attention to divine design.[11] If accepted in this form, his reading makes Goldsmith seem remarkably unsophisticated, especially alongside a providential plotter like Fielding. Making Goldsmith seem considerably more sophisticated, on the other hand, Preston revises his earlier reading and reverses Rogers's conclusion. He invokes Derridean deconstruction and sees *Vicar* drawing attention to chance and randomness in a universe no longer presided over by God (or Goldsmith). The vicar is the author of an "antiparable about the Christian moral life" that shows the fatuousness of drawing ethical lessons from experience. *Vicar*, in Preston's view, reflects the larger historical shift away from religious perfectibilism (typified in this period by the Methodists), toward moral relativism, and away from delusory didacticism toward the aesthetic.[12] It makes Goldsmith less pious and thus, perhaps, more pertinent, more relevant to current critical complexities. But even this reading comes at the expense of what can be garnered from Goldsmith's actual aims, which was at least the objective of Hopkins. Hopkins's reading is fundamentally unacceptable, because it leaps too eagerly from noting the comic irony at Primrose's expense to labeling the whole novel a satire, ignoring the self-evident (Primrose is more admirable than condemnable), the theological contexts that Preston's earlier essay had outlined, and the actual operation of irony, whereby Primrose is frequently the vehicle rather than the target of satire. He narrates retrospectively and judges his less enlightened earlier self by precisely the values that Hopkins thinks are being held up to general ridicule.

The larger points are, first, that the critical history of *Vicar of Wakefield*, like that of the Age of Johnson more generally, has been polarized into seemingly discrete sects of scholars who pronounce either endemic secularization or enduring religiosity. Second, that the former camp has had more success in discerning complexity in *Vicar*, the latter in finding coherence, partly because it looks to value systems deemed still quite stable. We can trace the matter back a step further by recalling another critical disagreement, this one in the 1970s, over precisely how Goldsmith uses the Book of Job to organize the novel's action, given the heated theological debates about Job that were raging at the time. Against the ironic reading of Goldsmith exemplified by Hopkins, Martin Battestin in 1974 urged the necessity of reading *Vicar* in light of "the aesthetic and theological assumptions implicit in the Augustan mode" and illustrated how Goldsmith employs "parabolic" narrative techniques typical of that mode, how Dr. Primrose exemplifies fortitude and patience in imitation of his biblical prototype, and how this supports "the doctrine of a particular Providence: that every event in life, good or evil, happens by divine permission."[13] James Lehmann, five years later, attempted to correct Battestin on the significance of Job for Goldsmith by suggesting that *Vicar* actually reflects a "detheologized" conception of Job. Some mid-eighteenth-century theologians had denied the divine provenance of this book, studying it instead as a primarily literary work. This chapter in the development of historical criticism of the Bible and the rise of the aesthetic, particularly the irreligious sublime, is "fundamentally secularizing."[14] Essentially, Lehmann suggests that Battestin is wrong to think that "analogical" structures of thought persist into the 1760s; people were already giving up the ghost on religion.

I will return to the so-called Job controversy in a moment as part of my effort in this essay to explain the theological meaning of *Vicar* without privileging either side of the secular/religious divide that has dominated scholarship. It has become the new orthodoxy to restate the everyday importance of religion to eighteenth-century men and women, just as it was once customary to seek signs of its eclipse in the Age of Reason.[15] Interpretations that perpetuate the secular/religious divide come at the expense of the necessary effort to reconstruct Goldsmith's preoccupations and intentions.[16] Revisiting Goldsmith's "advertisement" to the novel, from which the second epigraph to this essay has been taken, and to which he signed his own name, offers a different approach. Goldsmith asserts, to paraphrase another apologetic preface, that of Defoe's *Moll Flanders*, that the novel is intended for those who know how to use it, that "such as have been taught to deride religion, will laugh at one whose chief stores of comfort are drawn from futurity." As with *Pilgrim's Progress*, generating a correct readerly response is part of the authorial effort. Goldsmith implies that his book has been written in defense of religious tenets in a milieu that is more and more perceptibly resistant to them. In short, Goldsmith seems to have conceived his writing such a novel as similar to Primrose preaching in prison, prepared to endure having his wig disarranged, his spectacles stolen, himself showered with spit, and his sermon switched with "an obscene jest-book." Primrose is undeterred: "However I took no notice of all that this mischievous groupe of little beings could do; but went on, perfectly sensible that what was ridiculous in my attempt, would excite mirth only the first or second time, while what was serious would be permanent. My design succeeded, and in less than six days some were penitent, and all attentive" (4:148). What makes us laugh is temporary, even temporal, and though humor may sweeten the pill, we are to imbibe the solemn, supernal messages as well. Virginia Woolf, in my other epigraph, is among the last generation of innocents, who still knew where we were supposed to be laughing. However, her inkling that moral systems inhibit fiction is echoed in postmodernist definitions of the novel as a basically secular form.

Melvyn New addresses the secularization narrative customarily applied to the rise of the novel in the eighteenth century, and he supplies a perspective the usefulness of which has rarely been applied. Notwithstanding the conventional claims in early prose fictions that the order of Providence is both endorsed and reflected in the plot, these works are evidently written at a transitional cultural moment when belief in divine design was becoming more fraught.[17] I suggest, then, that the defense of Providence in the early novel is to some degree reactionary. Michael McKeon's concept of "explicitation," though he introduces it in a quite different context, is helpful here. For McKeon, the moment when political absolutism is rendered explicit in Sir Robert Filmer's *Patriarcha*, written during the Civil War but published during the Exclusion Crisis, is paradoxically the moment at which that ideology is starting to wane. Previously, it existed as "tacit knowledge," implicitly accepted because not yet subjected to discursive interrogation.[18] This seems to work for theodicy: the fact that Milton feels the need to "justify the ways of God to men" suggests that something has changed and that there is a new need to "assert eternal Providence." Subsequent to Milton, the eighteenth-century novel is the space in which Providence is made, in McKeon's term, *explicit* at the level of both form and theme, which suggests its interrogation in the wider culture. Leopold Damrosch has written a study of how "man's stories" assayed to reflect "God's plot," though he stops with Fielding, and concentrates more on how prose fiction was a vehicle for challenging traditional doctrine.[19] Goldsmith, I will suggest, was a reactionary in this process.

Goldsmith vindicates a providential order that appears unequal in its earthly distribution of happiness by looking to futurity; he even reasons, in Primrose's prison sermon, that those who suffer now are lucky, because they will be better able to appreciate the hereafter:

> Thus providence has given the wretched two advantages over the happy in this life, greater felicity in dying, and in heaven all that superiority of pleasure which arises from contrasted enjoyment. And this superiority, my friends, is no small advantage, and seems to be one of the pleasures of the poor man in the parable; for though he was already in heaven, and felt all the raptures it could give, yet it was mentioned as an addition to his happiness, that he had once been wretched and now was comforted, that he had known what it was to be miserable, and now felt what it was to be happy. (4:162)

Hugh Kelly, in an early response to the novel, found this sentiment especially praiseworthy:

> It is a fine observation of the very learned and ingenious Doctor Goldsmith, in the Vicar of Wakefield, an excellent novel, with which he has lately obliged the public, that though the poorer part of mankind may in this world suffer more inconveniences than the rich, still, upon their entrance into another life, the joys of hereafter will be enhanced by contrast, in proportion to their afflictions here; and that consequently there can be no room to suppose the least partiality in Providence, since sooner or later those who are entitled to it's benignity are certain of meeting with an equal degree of favour from it's hand.[20]

Suggestively for my purposes here, Kelly relates *Vicar*'s message to attacks on Providence by "modern infidels," and I will suggest that the deists are also in Goldsmith's sights.[21] Primrose illustrates his point with an allusion to the parable of Lazarus and Dives (Luke 16:19–31), and *Vicar* frequently draws on biblical parables. Indeed, the novel itself is presented as a series of exemplary episodes designed to illustrate moral universal truths derived from Scripture.

However, the novel that rises in the eighteenth century is usually considered a genre that replaces the tendency to typify human experience with a preference for particularizing it. This is the eclipse of allegory by realism, and the eclipse of religious faith by individualistic epistemologies derived from the new philosophy and new science. Its literary correlative is realism. "For all of us," Jorge Luis Borges once wrote, "the allegory is an aesthetic error," redressed by the realistic novel.[22] The shift from allegory to realism, for Borges, was under way by the time of Chaucer, and though most novel critics would bring that forward to the seventeenth or eighteenth century, the same teleology prevails. The shift has, certainly, an explanatory power, helping us get from John Bunyan to George Eliot. It becomes difficult, however, not to read future developments back into earlier texts. Retaining New's vocabulary, Goldsmith's moment is "transitional," and we should resist the desire to determine whether or not he inhabits a religious or secular *weltanschauung*. *Vicar of Wakefield* certainly has affinities with the allegorical moral progress prototyped by Bunyan a century earlier. Primrose concludes, having finally learned that pride comes before a fall in the first half, and having passed some stern tests in the second, that "it now only remained that my gratitude in good fortune should exceed my former submission in adversity" (4:184). The lesson in worldly detachment shows Primrose that he can enjoy the things of this world precisely because he has also renounced them—including eventually his own family, with which Bunyan's story began. Goldsmith's novel is also realistic, seeking reconciliation between divine order and the apparent disorder of ordinary experience, concerned as much with authentically depicting a socially recognizable milieu as with imparting universal truths. I will try to explain why and how this novel "tried to hold together two conflicting visions of life in their moment of transition."[23]

Just as the story of the novel's rise is bound up with that of allegory's demise, historians of biblical interpretation have similarly seen a decline of allegorical exegetical habits during the course of the eighteenth century. Specifically, following the gradual breakdown of fourfold interpretation after the medieval period, literalism and allegoresis sat comfortably together until the turn of the eighteenth century.[24] The question came down to whether or not the Bible's stories were literally true and historical, or allegorical and therefore fictional, whereas past generations had been content to maintain they were both historical *and* allegorical, in the tradition from Augustine to Aquinas. Typology, or figuralism, which discerns the gradual revelation of God in Scripture, culminating in Christ and his church in the gospels, becomes an essential part of this debate; it understood Old Testament events to be prefigurations or types of Christ, the antitype, who fulfilled messianic prophecies in the Hebrew Bible. As Erich Auerbach has demonstrated in his survey of the topic, figural or typological interpretation maintained both type and antitype as historical events.[25] So, for example, Jonah was actually swallowed by a whale at the same time that his three days in its belly allegorically prophesized the three days spent by Christ in the earth before the Resurrection. The validity of typology was mainly established by the Church Fathers, but it is also sanctioned by the New Testament. Starting in the later seventeenth century, what Frei calls the unified hermeneutic of typology starts to sever, as heterodox writers, particularly deists, questioned the divinity of Christ, the central role accorded to revelation, the fulfilment of Old Testament prophecies, and the manifestation of God through miracles and special Providence. Paul Korshin's literary history of typology emphasizes the emergence of "abstracted typology," tantamount to a secular view of intertestamental unity, as in the application of Scripture to postbiblical history, and the divestiture of spiritual significance.[26]

In both Frei's and Korshin's accounts, the developments I am summarizing are facilitated by or reflected in realistic prose fictional narrative. Frei sees the same urge to subject the Bible to "realist critique" also producing the novel; as such, novels go against a prefabricated Christian schema. "Novels were not moral tales," Frei claims, "but renderings of a temporally connected world in which interpersonal and social experience was related to moral existence in a way that was as intimate as it was ambiguous."[27] To my mind, however, *Vicar of Wakefield* is both of these worlds. Battestin and Lehmann each adduce the controversy about Job—a crucial stage in the revaluation of Scripture that Frei traces—in order to identify Goldsmith's relationship to contemporaneous theology and thus determine whether or not his values are ultimately sacralized or secular. I suggest that Goldsmith justifies the divine order in part as a response to contemporaneous theological debates, particularly those over scriptural prophecy and Providence. But Goldsmith is, in fact, only briefly in direct dialogue with polemical divinity, and the story, we will see, goes back further than Warburton, Sherlock, and Lowth on Job; it also concerns Primrose's model for his principle of clerical monogamy, the Arian and biblical literalist, William Whiston, famed for his exegetical debates with heterodox writers.

First, a brief summary of the mid-century controversy about Job will be useful.[28] In *The Divine Legation of Moses* (1738–1741), William Warburton set himself the task of confuting the deist position that the doctrine of futurity—rewards and punishments in the next world—was a "pious fraud" contrived to maintain temporal priestly power. He reasoned that Moses was able to keep the Israelites obedient to the law without mentioning futurity; hence, Christianity was the true faith to be gradually revealed by God. God's extraordinary Providence, His direct intervention, made the doctrine of futurity temporarily unnecessary in the Exodus from Egypt. The deists were wrong, Warburton stated, to downplay revelation and wrong to dismiss an afterlife of rewards and punishments. However, Job presented a problem to this thesis, because he appears to invoke futurity and to predict the salvific sacrifice of Christ at Job 19:25–26, the verses used by Handel in *Messiah* (1742). Warburton, however, argued that Job was written much later and was not history but rather an allegory about the Jewish Captivity and hence about temporal deliverance only. Thomas Sherlock in 1725 had supplied a contrary, more traditional reading of Job, emphasizing Providence and futurity, and basically following the tradition of Simon Patrick and Matthew Henry. Battestin finds Goldsmith's view of Job close to that of Sherlock,[29] while Lehmann looks instead to another divine, Robert Lowth, whose *Prælectiones in Sacra Poesi Hebræorum* (1753) had come to a diametrically opposite conclusion about Job to that of Warburton. Lowth affirms the historical sense of Job, but to the extent, says Lehmann, that Warburton's allegorical sense is totally compromised. As Frei would have it, this debate attests to the wider breakdown of figural hermeneutics; even if one is content to think of Job as both allegorical and historical, the symbiosis of these modes is no longer tacitly accepted. As Frei puts it, speaking of literal and figural senses, "the point to realize is not that they had been conceived to be in harmony with each other but that they had not even been generically distinct issues."30

Lehmann overstates the case for putting Goldsmith in Lowth's camp, as well as the extent to which Lowth represented a new "secularizing" view of Scripture; he then wrestles unconvincingly with Goldsmith's text in order to make it fit his thesis. What is at stake, as previously suggested, is whether Goldsmith sided with the forces of theological conservatism in the service of Augustan aesthetics, or with the vanguard of thought that was emptying biblical stories of their theological import. More specifically, Lehmann contends that Goldsmith uses the Job story playfully, even parodically, because Providence is not at stake in Job. Goldsmith's direct comments on the controversy are revealing. They come in a 1759 *Critical Review* essay, in which Goldsmith lukewarmly praises William Hawkins's opposition to deism but bemoans in general the proliferation of paper in theological controversy. After condemning the heterodox positions that had occasioned disputes within Anglicanism, and affirming that revelation is required for salvation (against the claims of natural religion and deism), Goldsmith strikes a conciliatory note. He commends Hawkins for coming down on the "safe side," which is Sherlock's; he hints that "though [Hawkins] loses his cause he may gain a vicarage" (Goldsmith picks up on Hawkins's careerism in a later number); and he says, "we must really acknowledge ourselves sceptics in the debate." The tone is one of weariness with controversy: "We could wish our divines would therefore rather turn their arms against the common enemy; and while infidelity is at the gate, not waste their time in civil altercation."31

Goldsmith evidently had little time for disputes within the Anglican clergy over what he considered fine points of doctrine. Disputing with the heterodox is dangerous business enough, as Primrose's son Moses finds out when he challenges the "free-thinker" Thornhill's assertion that "priestcraft" is "but an imposition, all a confounded imposture" (4:44, 42). Moses's refusal to "submit to such heterodox doctrines" (4:43) partly parodies his father's self-destructive obstinacy. It also trivializes theological debate, a process that continues when Primrose's daughter Olivia claims: "I have read a great deal of theology. I have read the disputes between Thwackum and Square; the controversy between Robinson Crusoe and Friday the savage, and I am now employed in reading the controversy in Religious courtship" (4:45). The last reference is to Daniel Defoe's 1722 pamphlet, which warns against marriage for social ambition and against marriages between partners of different religious congregations; it is a bit of irony on Goldsmith's part, because despite Primrose's assertion that "no freethinker shall ever have a child of mine" (4:44), this is exactly what his wife and daughter desire and what comes to pass. The two other allusions also bring orthodoxy and heterodoxy into view. The disputatious positions of both the deistic philosopher and the hypocritical Anglican theologian from *Tom Jones* are obviously mocked; more subtly, Goldsmith alludes in all likelihood to Friday's inquiry of his religious preceptor, "why God no kill the Devil," challenging Crusoe's neat theodicy, but allowing Defoe to argue against deists, as Timothy Blackburn astutely demonstrates, that natural religion based on reason is inadequate for salvation without divine revelation.[32] These moments also suggest that Goldsmith, however playfully, even scornfully, was still aware that the new forms of prose fiction were, from the beginning, participating in the debate with heterodoxy.

The most significant theological dispute within *Vicar of Wakefield* is, of course, Primrose's falling out with his eldest son's prospective father-in-law, Mr. Wilmot, over the non-issue of whether widowed clergymen can remarry in good conscience—just as Wilmot is lining up his fourth wife! The authority for Primrose's principle is William Whiston and his project to restore "primitive Christianity."[33] Something of its triviality is indicated by Primrose's account of his debate with Wilmot: "It was managed with proper spirit on both sides: he asserted that I was heterodox, I retorted the charge: he replied, and I rejoined" (4:24). More troubling is the way that the sharper, Jenkinson, is able to play on the pride of the "courageous monogamist" and "glorious pillar of unshaken orthodoxy" (4:73) to swindle Primrose out of the price of a horse. This pride—which builds in the novel's first half, culminating in the ill-fated family portrait, wherein the Vicar presents his Whistonean sermons to his wife dressed as the pagan love goddess Venus, while the polygamist Thornhill makes up to his daughter dressed as an Amazon (4:83)—is purged during the novel's second half, so that Primrose can declare, "I now condemned that pride which had made me refractory to the hand of correction" (4:95), before a few minor relapses and his more complete final humility: "There is no pride left me now, I should detest my own heart if I saw either pride or resentment lurking there" (4:154). Nevertheless, the precise significance of Whiston's place in the novel has divided opinion along lines—religious and secular—similar to those we have already seen. Hopkins argued that through the association with Whiston, "Goldsmith marks the religious orthodoxy of his narrator as suspect to the discerning eighteenth-century reader."[34] Eighteenth-century readers, however, were evidently undiscerning, and it took two centuries and a reader with Hopkins's penetration to note this. As such, Oliver Ferguson suggests that Primrose shares more with Whiston than a whimsical predilection for clerical monogamy; Whiston was held in high esteem for his piety, honesty, and unworldly adherence to principle (his nontrinitarianism cost him his Cambridge professorship), which brings him into accord with Goldsmith's clerical ideal embodied in Primrose.[35] Howard Weinbrot and Eric Rothstein pursued this insight by explaining why the Primroses leave Wakefield, arguing that "the Whistonean controversy, my last pamphlet, the archdeacon's reply, and the hard measure that was dealt me" (4:72) are all connected to the "neighbouring clergyman, who was a dignitary in the church" (4:23), Wilmot. Primrose's falling out with Wilmot is the real reason he accepts "a small Cure of fifteen pounds a year ... in a distant neighbourhood, where I could still enjoy my principles without molestation" (4:25). Whiston's place in the novel, for Weinbrot and Rothstein, is primarily thematic rather than doctrine-specific, though Goldsmith does "share in the Whistonian theme of the primary or the primitive."[36] John Irwin Fischer, however, disagrees with this positive spin, saying that Primrose is associated with Whiston's "very seductive, but violently reductionist and unChristian, view of the relationship between reason and faith, this world and the next."[37]

Again it may be seen that analysis is divided between seeing Primrose as the sincere ideal or the impious butt of Goldsmith's treatment. To take a different tack, and to connect Whiston with the Job controversy, we have to return to Whiston's writings on the fulfillment of scriptural prophecy, which is the debate, I believe, Goldsmith's readers would have remembered, rather than Whiston's incidental attack on clerical remarriage. In *The Accomplishment of Scripture Prophecies* (1708), Whiston attempted a systematic and stridently literalist demonstration of scriptural prophecy, insisting that Old Testament predictions were fulfilled precisely, in Christ, as reported in the New Testament. The flavor of Whiston's millenarian views and rhetoric can be garnered from his listing of hundreds of fulfilled prophecies, all signifying "the design of God's Providence, which was the reinstating the ruin'd Affairs of faln Men, and the destruction of that wicked but potent Empire which the Devil had set up, by the coming of the promis'd Messias, and the gradual advancement of His Kingdom."[38]

Whiston had mounted a defense of Christianity, *contra* deism, based on the providential fulfillment of prophecies, but he drew the immediate ire of the deist Anthony Collins, when he went beyond conventional apologetics to claim that where Old Testament prophecies and gospel fulfillments did not jibe, there was evidence that the Jews had corrupted Scripture in an attempt to disprove Christianity. Whiston proposed to restore the texts, and this "primitive Christianity" led him, on principle, to reject the Holy Trinity as a postapostolic accretion. Collins's *Discourse of the Grounds and Reasons of the Christian Religion* (1724) roundly mocked the proposed "Whistonian Bible," and asserted that Christ fulfils Old Testament prophecies typically or allegorically, not literally, perfectly illustrating Frei's point that literal and allegorical interpretations become ruptured at this time.[39] Collins's *Discourse* is a sustained attack on the argument from prophecy, which, he says, cannot prove Christianity. At this point, Thomas Sherlock's *The Use and Intent of Prophecy* (1725) supplied a defense, less literal and more trinitarian than Whiston's account, of the argument from prophecy, which aimed to confute Collins. This is, of course, the perspective that Goldsmith calls the "safe side" amid the furor caused by Warburton. My contention in the remainder of this essay is that the interwoven discourses of Providence and futurity in *The Vicar of Wakefield* are affirmed through a typological structure that is informed by a prophetic understanding of Job in response to historical scriptural criticism representing the deist challenge. It would be speculative to suggest that Goldsmith specifically had these chapters in Whiston's career in mind when he modeled Primrose on him, but the issues opened by writers like Whiston and Collins evidently continued into the middle of the century and informed the controversies that have also been found to inform Goldsmith's novel.

As has already been noted, Goldsmith structures *The Vicar of Wakefield* on the biblical prototype of Job, and Korshin has shown how Goldsmith draws on a standard typological understanding of Job as a type of Christ.[40] This, of course, is what Thomas Sherlock had asserted in 1725, but what Warburton's reading denies, on the grounds that futurity was unknown to the ancient Hebrews. Lowth—despite Lehmann's setting him against Sherlock as embodying a newer, secular, historical biblical scholarship—also endorses the argument from prophecy. Lehmann connects Lowth to the breakdown in typological reasoning mapped by Frei, and he finds his evidence negatively, in Lowth's avoidance of Christology in talking about allegory.[41] This is his argument despite Lowth's quite explicit use of figuralism, his outline of how typology works, the Christological bent of his interpretations of Psalms 2 and 72, and the very evident awareness of Lowth's later annotator, Johann David Michaelis, that Lowth is writing about messianic prophecy.[42] Lehmann contends that "Goldsmith plays a good deal with the Biblical story; the Biblical paradigm is often invoked only to be toyed with," but this is markedly less persuasive than Battestin's demonstration of Goldsmith's concerted analogical use of Job.[43] If Lehmann's notion of parodic typology fails to stick, his larger argument, that new ways of reading Scripture had taken hold, might well suggest not that Goldsmith endorsed a new valuation of the Bible but rather that he was well aware of the shift chronicled by Frei, and that *Vicar* is his counterargument. The case ought to rest on textual evidence.

We have seen that Primrose's pride in the first half of the novel is subjected to ironic treatment, and that Battestin connects this to contemporaneous readings of Job's "spiritual pride."[44] When Primrose reports that "there were three strange wants at Wakefield, a parson wanting pride, young men wanting wives, and ale-houses wanting customers" (4:22), the self-congratulatory tone is evident. This mild complacency is reflected in his view of "those little rubs which Providence sends to enhance the value of its favours" (4:19); theologically correct as it is, Primrose's appreciation will be strengthened by being tested. Again, when Primrose quotes Psalm 37:25 to his son, George ("I have been young, and now am old; yet never saw I the righteous man forsaken, or his seed begging their bread"), he privileges faith in divine Providence, again establishing a thesis to be tested. His basic goodness is indicated by his charity toward Burchell, whose own charitable acts have left him short of cash, and from this early stage, Burchell, "the poor Gentleman that would do no good when he was young, though he was not yet thirty," is associated with Christ (4:39). That he is the noble Sir William Thornhill has been revealed to the reader by a pronomial slip (4:30), but not to Primrose: that revelation will come later. Praising his children for their hospitality in accommodating Burchell, Primrose's biblical allusions clearly but unwittingly make the connection: "The beast retires to its shelter, and the bird flies to its nest; but helpless man can only find refuge from his fellow creature. The greatest stranger in this world, was he that came to save it" (4:39). The first sentence alludes to Christ's teaching at Matthew 8:20 and Luke 9:58, and indeed Burchell is a traveler, a Christlike figure, telling parabolic stories about himself as an example of uncontrolled benevolence.[45]

We start to worry about the way things are going at the start of chapter 10, which pledges in its headnote to teach us "the miseries of the poor when they attempt to appear above their circumstances." Though the chapter titles control our response on the level of discourse, Primrose's own didactic authority on the level of story is slipping: "I now began to find that all my long and painful lectures upon temperance, simplicity, and contentment, were entirely disregarded" (4:56). A vicar who is "tired of being always wise" (4:57) is one whose authority is slipping. Mr. Thornhill is entertained despite his rakish reputation and his freethinking—Moses says that "heaven will never arraign him for what he thinks, but for what he does" (4:44). But "what he does" is precisely the problem with Thornhill, and now he is being courted as a possible husband for Olivia. His passing off two "ladies of the town" as fit companions for the Primrose girls, occasions a dispute with Burchell, who now "is found to be an enemy; for he has the confidence to give disagreeable advice" (4:68). Burchell is rejected by the world he has come to save; he will later tell Primrose with Godlike majesty and mercy: "I partly saw your delusion then, and as it was out of my power to restrain, I could only pity it" (4:164–65). After Burchell's banishment, the fortune that "seems resolved to humble the family of Wakefield" manifests itself in rather trivial "mortifications," notably those occasioned by Deborah Primrose's desire to maintain a show of respectability, but most crucially by the double machinations of the rogue, Jenkinson, who will later appear to undo his ill deeds after Primrose forgives him. The gross of green spectacles neatly symbolizes moral blindness at the same time that it represents the baleful exchange of husbandry, represented by the colt, for speculation in useless commodities. The spectacles are retained nevertheless by Primrose, as is the disastrous family portrait, both reminders of frivolity and pride. Raymond Hilliard is right to talk about a crisis of paternal authority at this point: the enmeshed roles of head of family, priest, and husbandman are all being neglected by Primrose.[46] Hilliard's astute reading identifies a redemption of fatherhood being undertaken in the novel's second half, particularly through Primrose's association first with Job and then, along with Burchell, with Christ.

Burchell's words prior to his banishment are a reassurance to the reader and an unheeded warning to Primrose: "Providence seems kindly our friend in this particular, thus to debilitate the understanding where the heart is corrupt, and diminish the power where there is the will to do mischief" (4:79–80). Primrose seems to see through Thornhill to some degree, disapprovingly observing his rakish use of playhouse language (4:81) and noting that his words to Olivia have "more of love than matrimony in them" (4:85–86), but he distressingly calls Thornhill "our benefactor," he allows Thornhill to impinge on the family portrait, and he acquiesces in his wife's plot to use Williams to stoke the Squire's jealousy. Williams's independence from the squire's power, markedly unlike his namesake in *Pamela*, pointedly contrasts with Primrose (4:86). Olivia's elopement, "the first of our real misfortunes" (4:92), is where Primrose's identification with Job begins in earnest. Like Parson Adams in *Joseph Andrews* when he hears of his son's drowning, Primrose's fortitude initially fails him; he seems at first more eager to indulge his misery than to act. When Moses reproves him, he is then ready to act vengefully with pistols, until his wife instructs him: "the bible is the only weapon fit for your old hands now. Open that, my love, and read our anguish into patience" (4:91–92). This is the first of several times that Primrose's instruction comes from his family, who act as his comforters, a twist on rather than inversion of Job. Adapting Job's patience, Primrose states: "Blest be his holy name for all the good he hath given, and for all that he hath taken away" (108; see Job 1:21). Primrose, armed with Bible and staff, sets out to reclaim his daughter.

It is not a coincidence that, after political debate with the servant Wilkinson and after being reunited with George and hearing of his adventures, Primrose finds Olivia at the exact moment he resigns himself to God's will, "sending a sigh to heaven to spare and forgive her" (4:124). The parable of the prodigal son (Luke 15:7) provides the moral lessons that see the repentant Olivia restored to the family's fold as Primrose begins to claw back his clerical and paternal authority: "The kindness of heaven is promised to the penitent, and let ours be directed by the example. Heaven, we are assured, is much more pleased to view a repentant sinner than ninety nine persons who have supported a course of undeviating rectitude" (4:132). Primrose's monogamist principles come to the fore when Thornhill seeks approbation for his marriage, adulterous in Primrose's eyes (4:153), with Miss Wilmot; the implication is that complaisance in the earlier dispute with Mr. Wilmot could entail a further compromise of principle here, until marriage is ultimately reduced from a holy sacrament to a mere temporal form.[47] To his family's pleas that he relent, Primrose replies "why will you thus attempt to persuade me to the thing that is not right!" (4:139), associating him further with his biblical prototype (see Job 33:27, 42:7–8).

Primrose's imprisonment does not mark the end of his trials: complete humility and detachment from the world are required. Primrose's patience is being constantly tested through fresh sufferings, which break in just as consolation has seemed to prevail. The bleak view of divine order represented in *King Lear* seems to win out when news of Sophia's abduction follows on the heels of the greatly exaggerated report of Olivia's death. "What! not one left! not to leave me one!" (4:156). Again, his wife's and Moses's comfort assuages Primrose's despair, partly with misinformed news of George's prosperity. Now, Goldsmith puts Providence and its promise of a future state of reward and punishment in the dock. "I thank providence," exclaims Mrs. Primrose, when she thinks that her aggravating letter to George has miscarried: "I will now confess that though the hand of heaven is sore upon us in other instances, it has been favourable here. . . . Providence has been kinder to us than we to ourselves" (4:156–57), echoing words with which Primrose had comforted the despoiled Olivia (4:129). On cue, George's bloodied body is dragged in and it appears that Job's lesson of patience amid suffering is being inflicted on the sympathetic reader as well as Primrose. George delivers the last piece of rebounded instruction to Primrose—his youngest two have just schooled him in the lesson of trusting to futurity (4:154)—when he states: "You have often charmed me with your lessons of fortitude, let me now, Sir, find them in your example" (4:159). Primrose's response indicates that his moral journey is complete: "I am now raised above this world, and all the pleasures it can produce. From this moment I break from my heart all the ties that held it down to earth, and will prepare to fit us both for eternity" (4:159). The alternation of consolation and misfortune in the presermon prison scene, as well as being especially Joblike, shows that Goldsmith is neither blithely rubber-stamping Providence nor subversively parodying it: he takes its opponents very seriously, but controls narrative action and reader response in ways that ultimately vindicate an embattled doctrine.

I would argue that Primrose's prison sermon on the equal dealings of Providence and the consolations of futurity is not only sincere but is the climax of the novel's instruction, and that this instruction is in dialogue with skeptics. To my knowledge, despite Primrose's averring that "philosophy is weak; but religion comforts in an higher strain" (4:161), David Hume's writings against particular Providence, futurity, and prophecy have not been considered as contexts for *The Vicar of Wakefield*. Hume mounts an attack on the argument from design, suggesting that the cause posited by theists (a controlling deity) exceeds that which can be inferred from the effect (an ordered world).

> All the philosophy, therefore, in the world, and all the religion, which is nothing but a species of philosophy, will ever be able to carry us beyond the usual course of experience, or give us measures of conduct and behaviour different from those which are furnished by reflections on common life. No new fact can ever be inferred from the religious hypothesis; no event foreseen or foretold; no reward or punishment expected or dreaded, beyond what is already known by practice and observation.[48]

Hume here extends, with epistemological skepticism, earlier deist attacks on the doctrine of futurity. James Force has shown that Hume exploded the model of biblical interpretation favored particularly by Whiston, which was based on a carefully balanced intersection of messianic prophecy, miracles, futurity, and the synthesis of general and special providences, all designed to confute deism.[49] As Frei notes, with reference to Sherlock, typology and Providence were part of a "circular argument" that made them mutually supporting.[50] The typological conclusion, in which Sir William and Primrose are each revealed as figurations of Christ, similarly upholds the orthodox position on Providence and futurity that was under renewed assault by Hume. Having resigned himself to Providence, Primrose is vindicated through narrative machinery that shows its effects.

As Korshin notes, the typological patterns in *Vicar* are fully visible; in fact, he calls it "the most simple as well as most affecting typological story in an eighteenth-century novel."[51] We have had the ground prepared for the parallel *imitatio Christi* of both Primrose and Burchell. "The hero of this piece," we hear of Primrose, "unites in himself the three greatest characters upon earth; he is a priest, an husbandman, and the father of a family" (4:14). Primrose finally lives up to these three Christological roles. He will take Olivia's guilt upon himself (4:126), he advises his followers to submit to civic authority when arrested, and in prison "he undergoes his own version of the trials and death of Christ."[52] Primrose's final words before his sermon, about being above this world, allude to Christ's message to the apostles before his betrayal (John 17:11). The Christology, moreover, is not confined to Primrose; the revealed Sir William Thornhill, "with a countenance open as the sun" (4:180), enters as *deus ex machina* to ensure that justice is done. Through the disguise motif, Goldsmith portrays the encryption of God and now His revelation through Christ and His church. The worldly dispensation of justice does not controvert the spiritual message: "[t]emporal evils or felicities being regarded by heaven as things merely in themselves trifling and unworthy its care in the distribution" (4:151). The vicar's end, like Job's, is rewarded with a return to prosperity, because he has manifested fortitude; it prefigures an afterlife of rewards and punishments.

Most essentially, *Vicar of Wakefield* tries to show that there is a moral reality behind a world of appearances. The Book of Job is significant because it illustrates a message about submission and because its providential and prophetical dimensions illustrate the point that this world is a passage to a more complete state. This is precisely what Hume denied:

> But what must a philosopher think of those vain reasoners, who, instead of regarding the present scene of things as the sole object of their contemplation, so far reverse the whole course of nature, as to render this life merely a passage to something farther; a porch which leads to a greater, and vastly different building; a prologue, which serves only to introduce the piece, and give it more grace and propriety.[53]

Goldsmith's statement on this matter, which serves as a guide to reading *Vicar* in emblematic and typological ways, could be a direct rejoinder: "Almost all men have been taught to call life a passage, and themselves the travellers. The similitude still may be improved when we observe that the good are joyful and serene, like travellers that are going towards home; the wicked but by intervals happy, like travellers that are going into exile" (4:135). In defiance of Hume, and the deistic thinking he represents, in Goldsmith's novel life is very precisely portrayed as a pilgrimage toward Heaven.

Goldsmith, I believe, used his fiction to intervene in theological questions about Providence, prophecy, and futurity. He seems to have found an unlikely ally in Whiston, who provided a model for the unworldly Primrose, because Whiston's arguments from prophecy and design bolstered the providential order of the world that Goldsmith wished to portray. Goldsmith's orthodoxy operates at the level of both theme and form in *The Vicar of Wakefield*, as emblematic, parabolic, and typological structuring enforces the moral message of Job and Christianity. We see here an episode in the history of the early novel's attempt to both justify and help do the work of the Anglican Church, the authority of which Goldsmith and his age felt to be declining. I take this effort, however, less as a sign of wholesale secularization, more as a reaffirmation of belief and its articulation. Through his fiction, Goldsmith supplies religious instruction against the claims of natural religion, benevolism, and skepticism. His criticism does not fall on religious ethics as some critics have claimed, but occasionally on aspects of the social order still primarily organized by religion. However, from the somniferous squire who naps through Primrose's sermons at the start (4:19), we see a union forged between the landed interest and the clerical order at the novel's close. The eighteenth-century Anglican Church was once condemned by

R.H. Tawney as "a servile appendage to a semi-pagan aristocracy."[54] I suspect that this is exactly what Goldsmith, loyal to both interests, is trying to assuage. Ultimately, religious values are not simply residual; questions of doctrine are not secondary to questions of polity as they perhaps are in Trollope's *Chronicles of Barsetshire*. Religion was not necessarily dictating what people thought in the Age of Johnson, but it was certainly shaping how they thought.

NOTES

1. Virginia Woolf, "Oliver Goldsmith" (1934), in *The Captain's Death Bed and Other Essays* (London: Hogarth Press, 1950), 13–14.
2. Oliver Goldsmith, *The Vicar of Wakefield*, in *Collected Works*, ed. Arthur Friedman, 5 vols. (Oxford: Clarendon Press, 1966), 4:14. Hereafter cited in text.
3. Robert H. Hopkins, *The True Genius of Oliver Goldsmith* (Baltimore: Johns Hopkins University Press, 1969), 166–230.
4. Ronald Paulson, *Satire and the Novel in Eighteenth-Century England* (New Haven: Yale University Press, 1967), 269.
5. Marshall Brown, *Preromanticism* (Stanford: Stanford University Press, 1991), 151.
6. G.S. Rousseau, ed., *Oliver Goldsmith: The Critical Heritage* (London: Routledge and Kegan Paul, 1974), 44–47, 65–69.
7. Curtis Dahl, "Patterns of Disguise in *The Vicar of Wakefield*," *ELH* 25 (1958): 90–104; Morris Golden, "The Family-Wanderer Theme in Goldsmith," *ELH* 25 (1958): 181–93; Michael E. Adelstein, "Duality of Theme in *The Vicar of Wakefield*," *College English* 22 (1961): 477–91.
8. Because I will cite these articles in the course of my essay, I will forbear listing them here.
9. Thomas R. Preston, "The Uses of Adversity: Worldly Detachment and Heavenly Treasure in *The Vicar of Wakefield*," *SP* 81 (1984): 229–51.
10. Inter alia: John Bender, "Prison Reform and the Sentence of Narration in *The Vicar of Wakefield*," in *The New Eighteenth Century: Theory, Politics, English Literature*, ed. Felicity Nussbaum and Laura Brown (New York: Methuen, 1987), 168–88; John Zomchick, *Family and the Law in Eighteenth-Century Fiction: The Public Conscience in the Private Sphere* (Cambridge: Cambridge University Press, 1993), 154–76; Cates Baldridge, *The Dialogues of Dissent in the English Novel* (Hanover, NH: University Press of New England, 1994), 21–39; J.A. Downie, "New Wine in Old Bottles? The 'New' Historicism and the Eighteenth Century," in *Talking Forward, Talking Back: Critical Dialogues with the Enlightenment*, ed. Kevin L. Cope and Rüdiger Ahrens (New York: AMS Press, 2002), 265–80; James P. Carson, "The 'Little Republic' of the Family: Goldsmith's Politics of Nostalgia," *Eighteenth-Century Fiction* 16 (2004): 1–24.
11. Henry N. Rogers III, "God's Implausible Plot: The Providential Design of *The Vicar of Wakefield*," *Philological Review* 28 (2002): 5–17.
12. Thomas R. Preston, "Moral Spin Doctoring, Delusion, and Chance: Wakefield's Vicar Writes an Enlightenment Parable," *Age of Johnson* 11 (2000): 274.
13. Martin C. Battestin, *The Providence of Wit: Aspects of Form in Augustan Literature and the Arts* (Oxford: Clarendon Press, 1974), 198.
14. James H. Lehmann, "*The Vicar of Wakefield*: Goldsmith's Sublime, Oriental Job," *ELH* 46 (1979): 97, 114.

15. See W.M. Jacob, *Lay People and Religion in the Early Eighteenth Century* (Cambridge: Cambridge University Press, 1996), 11; Jeremy Gregory, "Christianity and Culture: Religion, the Arts, and the Sciences in England, 1660–1800," in *Culture and Society in Britain, 1660–1800*, ed. Jeremy Black (Manchester: Manchester University Press, 1997), 117.

16. For some suggestive theoretical and methodological points on this, see Kevin Seidel, "Beyond the Religious and Secular in the History of the Novel," *New Literary History* 38 (2007): 637–47.

17. Melvyn New, "'The Grease of God': The Form of Eighteenth-Century English Fiction," *PMLA* 91 (1976): 235–44.

18. Michael McKeon, *The Secret History of Domesticity: Public, Private, and the Division of Knowledge* (Baltimore: Johns Hopkins University Press, 2005), 13.

19. Leopold Damrosch Jr., *God's Plot and Man's Stories: Studies in the Fictional Imagination from Milton to Fielding* (Chicago: University of Chicago Press, 1985).

20. Hugh Kelly, *The Babler*, no. LXXVI (Saturday, July 10, 1766), reprinted in *The Babler: Consisting of Original Essays, on the Most Interesting and Familiar Topics*, 2 vols. (London, 1770), 2:51.

21. See Goldsmith, *Collected Works*, 3:154–55. Primrose, I believe, typifies the more emotive style of preaching Goldsmith calls for in this piece for *The Lady's Magazine*, which ends by enjoining the clergy to decline disputes with deists.

22. Jorge Luis Borges, "From Allegories to Novels" (1949), in *Other Inquisitions, 1937–1952*, trans. Ruth L.C. Simms (1964; rpt. London: Souvenir Press, 1973), 154.

23. New, "'The Grease of God,'" 243.

24. See Victor Harris, "Allegory to Analogy in the Interpretation of Scriptures," *PQ* 45 (1966): 1–23; Hans W. Frei, *The Eclipse of Biblical Narrative: A Study in Eighteenth and Nineteenth Century Hermeneutics* (New Haven: Yale University Press, 1974).

25. Erich Auerbach, "Figura" (1944), trans. Ralph Manheim, in *Scenes from the Drama of European Literature* (1959; rpt. Manchester: Manchester University Press, 1984), 53.

26. Paul J. Korshin, *Typologies in England, 1650–1820* (Princeton: Princeton University Press, 1982).

27. Frei, *The Eclipse of Biblical Narrative*, 148.

28. See A.W. Evans, *Warburton and the Warburtonians: A Study in Some Eighteenth-Century Controversies* (Oxford: Oxford University Press, 1932), 67–70, 246–57, 294–306; Jonathan Lamb, *The Rhetoric of Suffering: Reading the Book of Job in the Eighteenth Century* (Oxford: Oxford University Press, 1995).

29. Thomas Sherlock, *The Use and Intent of Prophecy* (1725), 5th ed. (London, 1749), 206–47. Sherlock calls Job 19:25 "a Prophecy of the Office and Character of Christ Jesus" (228). Writing before Warburton, Sherlock is challenging Grotius's solely temporal reading of Job and Collins's exclusively allegorical reading of Scripture. Sherlock denies that Job is "a mere *poetical Fiction*" and affirms that it "must be founded in *History*, and not in Invention" (245–46).

30. Frei, *The Eclipse of Biblical Narrative*, 56.

31. Goldsmith, *Works*, 1:199–201, 225.

32. Timothy C. Blackburn, "Friday's Religion: Its Nature and Importance in *Robinson Crusoe*," *Eighteenth-Century Studies* 18 (1985): 361.

33. William Whiston, *Memoirs of the Life and Writings of Mr. William Whiston* (London, 1749), 467. Clerical monogamy is rather buried in this seven-hundred-page tome.

34. Hopkins, *The True Genius of Oliver Goldsmith*, 175.

35. Oliver W. Ferguson, "Dr. Primrose and Goldsmith's Clerical Ideal," *PQ* 54 (1975): 327–29.

36. Howard D. Weinbrot and Eric Rothstein, "*The Vicar of Wakefield*, Mr. Wilmot, and the 'Whistonean Controversy,'" *PQ* 55 (1976): 232.

37. John Irwin Fischer, "'Yet Will I Trust in Him': Goldsmith's *The Vicar of Wakefield*," *South Central Review* 1 (1984): 13.

38. William Whiston, *The Accomplishment of Scripture Prophecies* (London, 1708), 30–31.

39. Anthony Collins, *A Discourse of the Grounds and Reasons of the Christian Faith* (London, 1724), 225.

40. Korshin, *Typologies in England*, 255–60.
41. Lehmann, "*The Vicar of Wakefield*: Goldsmith's Sublime, Oriental Job," 116–17n15.
42. Robert Lowth, *Lectures on the Sacred Poetry of the Hebrews* (1753), trans. George Gregory (Boston, 1815). This edition contains Michaelis's "principal notes," which he added to his 1758–1762 reprint of Lowth. In Lectures X ("Of Allegory") and XI ("Of the Mystical Allegory"), respectively, Lowth outlines what he means by allegory (fiction representing truth) and typology (or mystical allegory), in which both events are literally true. Two representative claims are these: "The very words which express the one in the plain, proper, historical, and commonly received sense, may typify the other in the sacred, interior, and prophetic sense" (147) and "The Divine Spirit . . . has in a manner appropriated to its own use this kind of allegory, as peculiarly adapted to the publication of future events, and to the typifying of the most sacred mysteries" (148). See Michaelis's notes to 151–54; he is in little doubt that Lowth is talking about the Messiah. Contra Lehmann, Lowth speaks explicitly of messianic prophecy (e.g., 260). It is fair to say that Lectures XXXII–XXXIV, all on Job, agree that it upholds the doctrines of futurity and Providence, and that nothing in Lowth contradicts the argument from prophecy. For a helpful discussion that also restates the traditionalism of Lowth's use of scripture, and which in general qualifies the suddenness of the hermeneutical shift Frei describes, see Stephen Prickett, *Origins of Narrative: The Romantic Appropriation of the Bible* (Cambridge: Cambridge University Press, 1996), 113–17.
43. Lehmann, "*The Vicar of Wakefield*: Goldsmith's Sublime, Oriental Job," 103.
44. Battestin, *The Providence of Wit*, 203.
45. See Goldsmith's short oriental fable, "The Proceedings of Providence Vindicated," in *Works*, 3:58–65.
46. Raymond F. Hilliard, "The Redemption of Fatherhood in *The Vicar of Wakefield*," *SEL* 23 (1983): 465–80.
47. See Robert H. Hopkins, "Matrimony in *The Vicar of Wakefield* and the Marriage Act of 1753," *SP* 74 (1977): 322–39.
48. David Hume, "Of a Particular Providence and of a Future State" (1748) in *Enquiries*, ed. L.A. Selby-Bigge, 3rd ed. (Oxford: Clarendon, 1975), 146.
49. James E. Force, *William Whiston: Honest Newtonian* (Cambridge: Cambridge University Press, 1985), 121–55.
50. Frei, *The Eclipse of Biblical Narrative*, 73.
51. Korshin, *Typologies in England*, 255.
52. Hilliard, "The Redemption of Fatherhood," 476. See the Christological parallels drawn by Hilliard, who correctly states that Primrose sees and applies the Job parallels himself, but not the Christ ones.
53. Hume, "Of a Particular Providence," 141.
54. R.H. Tawney, *Religion and the Rise of Capitalism: A Historical Study* (London, 1926), cited in Jeremy Gregory, "The Church of England," in *A Companion to Eighteenth-Century Britain*, ed. H.T. Dickinson (Oxford: Blackwell, 2002), 225.

Chapter Ten

Divine and Human Love

*Letters between John Norris and Mary Astell,
Laurence Sterne and Eliza Draper*

Geoff Newton

During the course of precisely one year, John Norris, the vicar of Bemerton near Salisbury, corresponded with Mary Astell, now recognized as one of the most important of the early feminist writers. This correspondence, from September 21, 1693, to September 21, 1694, was subsequently published as *Letters Concerning the Love of God, between the author of the Proposal to the Ladies and Mr John Norris*. Seventy-three years later, during the nine months from January to November of the last full year of his life, 1767, Laurence Sterne corresponded with a young married woman, Eliza Draper; only Sterne's letters survive. During this period, he also entered his feelings for Draper in a journal and, in tandem, under the inspiration derived from his relationship with her, wrote his last work, *A Sentimental Journey*.[1]

Similarly Astell, while corresponding with Norris, was writing the first part of her *Serious Proposal to the Ladies*, which, published shortly after the correspondence ended, Norris included in the title of the published letters.[2] In this essay I will compare the two sets of correspondence, each of which has love for its theme, focusing on the way in which both Norris and Sterne sought to give spiritual expression to sexual longings in a Neoplatonic idiom. I also will compare Sterne's and Astell's approaches to human love and the way each sought to absorb, translate, and displace that love through their reading of Norris. Astell's engagement with Norris's ideas is plain to see through their correspondence, while Sterne's engagement with them, although less plain, is quite discernable in his letters, journal entries, and *ASJ*.[3]

Norris's attraction to Astell is evident and can be summarized as that of an older scholar for an independent and intelligent young woman, prepared to challenge him but ultimately to use his ideas to develop her own; clearly she had no basic disagreement with him. Sterne, on the other hand, could not think of Eliza Draper as independent, since she was both a wife and a mother, and destined to soon return to her husband in India; nor, if he were fairly assessing her, as intelligent—she was certainly not in Astell's league. However, once she departed England, he could idealize her at will, creating his own image of what the woman might be. While Norris was, I believe, probably sexually stimulated by the thought of Astell, as can perhaps be deduced from his extravagant compliments to her, he rationalized this attraction, spiritualizing these sexual desires quite out of existence. Sterne, in contrast, openly confronted his sexual feelings, pouring them into a prefabricated image of Draper that became increasingly separated from reality as the distance between them increased. Both Norris and Sterne were inclined to the mystical in love, given to flights of ecstatic writing to express their love, at times in quite explicit sexual terms. However, there are significant differences as well: Norris generalized and displaced whatever human sexual feelings he may have had onto a completely spiritualized being, the image of the divine Jesus; Sterne, on the other hand, displaced his ardor for a very human woman he was in love with onto a particularized idealization, spiritualizing her as a last resort in place of a longed-for bodily presence. Both place human love at the heart of their religious expression, and religious expression at the service of human love.

The full title under which Norris published his correspondence with Astell—retained in its entirety in all three editions—is revealing, and it pinpoints the similarities and variations between their understanding of the love of God and Sterne's: *Letters concerning the Love of God, Between the Author of the Proposal to the Ladies and Mr John Norris: Wherein his late Discourse, showing that it ought to be intire and exclusive of all other Loves, is further cleared and justified.*[4] The text Norris uses to support his key claim that the love of God must be "intire and exclusive of all other Loves" is the *Shema* of Judaism, embedded at its heart since the Deuteronomic reformation and repeated frequently in Jewish rituals. Prefaced by "Hear O Israel: the Lord our God is one Lord," it declared: "thou shalt love the Lord thy God with all thine heart, and with all thy soul, and with all thy might" (Deuteronomy 6:5), to which was added, eventually, the injunction taken from a phrase included in a list of tribal rules and regulations in Leviticus 19:18: "thou shalt love thy neighbour as thyself." This basic religious requirement was endorsed by Jesus as recorded in the Gospels (Matthew 22:37–39). Bishop Arthur Lake's sermon, from which Norris quotes at length in *Letters*, is devoted to this "great Commandment" and becomes a point of reference in Norris's concluding discussion (100 and 105). For Lake and Norris, the love of God is the prior and originating love, without which human love would not even exist; without God, human love is warped into a rival love of whatever is not God.

In his introductory "To the Reader," Norris sets out his basic premise. After commending Astell, whom he describes as "a Gentlewoman, and to add to thy Wonder, a young Gentlewoman" he quickly turns away from her and toward "the *Love of GOD.*" He views this love as a mystical experience rather than a rational deduction or item of dogma, both of which tend toward wrangling about "abstruse Theories" (56). In this emphasis on the pursuit of the mystical over argument and dogma, Norris was expressing the view of his latitudinarian church—adopted following the religious conflicts of the seventeenth century—which favored compromise and tolerance regarding those things that cannot be proved or disproved by rational argument. For this stance he finds support in selected passages from the Bible, but most particularly the often-cited 1 Corinthians 13:12: "we see him but in a Glass darkly" (56);[5] and he adds a passage from Exodus 33:23, wherein Moses is discovered, in his search for God, not to be allowed to see His "Face" but only His "Back parts" (57). Norris then follows with texts in praise of love: "Neither Tongues, nor Prophecy, nor Knowledge, nor Faith, nor Alms, nor even Martyrdom it self signifie anything without Charity" (a summary of 1 Corinthians 13) and: "GOD is Love, and he that dwelleth in Love dwelleth in GOD and GOD in him" (1 John 4:16). To these scriptural texts, Norris adds the testimony of Christian mystics, past and present: St. Augustine, St. Teresa of Ávila, Thomas à Kempis, Pierre Corneille, Pierre Jurieu, and last, Bishop Lake. Like them all, Norris argues for a sensual approach to God, one that can be adequately described only in the erotic language of sexual love. Corroboration for this observation he finds in a love poem included in the canon: "*my Love, my undefiled is but one*" (Song of Solomon 6:9) (58), which he reads allegorically, as did most in his time, as Christ's words to his bride, the Church. This spiritual/erotic tone can be discerned throughout the correspondence, reaching its climax, perhaps, in his concluding letter:

> *Make me sweetest Lord to love thee, and through the Desire of thee to lay down the weight of all carnal Desires, and the most heavy load of earthly Concupiscences, which fight against and weigh down my miserable Soul . . . kindle me all over with thy Fire, with the Love of thee, with thy Sweetness, with thy Joy, with thy Pleasure and Concupiscence, which is holy and good, chaste and clean, quiet and secure, that being all full of the Sweetness of thy Love, all on fire with the Flame of thy Charity, I may love thee my* GOD *with my whole Heart, and with all the Power of my inward Parts, having thee in my Heart, in my Mouth, and before my Eyes, always and every where, that so there may be no Place in me open to adulterous Loves.* (124)

There could be no clearer expression of the displacement of sexual desire—which he basically views as a negative, and with which he seems, despite his marriage, to have difficulties—onto a mystically conceived image of God. Taking his cue from Augustine, he uses an erotic diction that we might suspect was stimulated by Astell's youthful admiration, but he immediately displaces these feelings onto a spiritualized Jesus. Of course, since his theory of love was formulated before Astell's correspondence (indeed, she was responding to that theory), we can suggest that she reawakened his defenses and reinforced his strategy for dealing with human sexuality.[6]

Astell joins forces with Norris, and like him is suspicious of human sexuality, displacing it onto a safer spiritual realm while, at the same time, expressing reservations, recognizing there is something in human passion itself that uniquely expresses divine love:

> Our Passions (although they have both their Use and Pleasure, yet) as we usually feel them are blended with so much Pain, that 'tis hard to determine whether the good or evil they do us be the greater, and a Man sometimes overpays for his Mirth, by that Sting of Sorrow which attends it. However, I am not for a *Stoical Apathy*. I would not have my Hands and Feet cut off lest they should sometimes incommode me. . . . If we make *GOD* the Object of our Desire, our Hopes will neither delude, nor our Joys forsake us; there is no Serpent lurks in this Grass, all is calm and pleasing, secure and entertaining. (*Letters*, 99)

Like Norris she is concerned with her "own Hearts Lust, and . . . our own Imaginations" (114), describing human love as "a Heart groveling on the Earth, cleaving to little dirty Creatures." Like Norris, also, she displaces her desire onto "the Love of *GOD* . . . so vast . . . it must needs stretch it self to receive the Fullest Draught that ever it can" (116). Yet throughout, she struggles with desire, recognizing the strength, rightness, and inevitability associated with the sensual; it is "glew'd to the Creature" and as integral a part of us as a "Leopard's Spots" or "Negro's Skin." Yet she also writes that, finding the "Propension so early and so strong, we imagine that Nature not Custom is the Author of it, which certainly is a very gross Mistake" (117). Clearly for Astell, this was an unresolved and continuing concern.

For Sterne, on the other hand, this recoil from human passion was problematic, perhaps the most important difficulty of his adult life. Where Norris and Astell—reluctantly, perhaps, but avidly and ultimately successfully—abandon human sexual love as hopelessly of the earth and corruption (what Norris's wife thought of this is unknown), in their pursuit of their love of God, Sterne tried to embrace it, merging sexual appetite with divine love precisely because he could not abandon his physical urges, yet was unwilling to assign those urges to perdition; his reading of Norris moved him toward a reconciliation with himself.

Astell, of course, had her own reservations regarding Norris's ideas. She perceptively perceives an important discrepancy between his two fundamental premises: *"That* GOD *is the Efficient Cause of our Sensations,* Pain as well as Pleasure"; and the conclusion he draws from them: *"And that he is the only Object of our Love"* (70). As Taylor and New point out, Astell pinpoints a "glaring logical inconsistency in Norris's argument, and . . . took direct aim in her first letter" (*Letters,* 23). Astell argues that if God is the efficient cause of both our pleasure and our pain, is God not also, and necessarily, the object both of our love, as the cause of our pleasure, and "of our Aversion," as the cause of our pain. She continues: "it is as natural to avoid and fly from Pain, as it is to follow and pursue Pleasure"; hence, "something else does us Good, besides what causes Pleasure" (70). Wanting to support Norris rather than criticize him, however, she proposes an interesting extension of his argument that responds with some validity to the difficulty she had raised; it was a "solution" that Norris would eventually accept. Taylor and New summarize Astell's disagreement and Norris's response:

> Norris's initial response is fumbling, and reads mainly as an exercise in avoidance; in a 'Postscript' to letter 2, however, he sets aside his previous rebuttals and grasps the line Astell had subtly thrown him: "If as to the present Life, the pain that *GOD* inflicts upon us here, is only Medicinal, and in order to our greater good, and consequently from a Principle of Kindness . . . there will be no more pretence for not loving or hating *GOD* for this, than for hating our Physician or Surgeon for putting us to pain in order to our Health or Cure" [75–76]. We should love God fully, Norris now realized, not because he is the author of our pleasure, but because he is the author of our Good.
>
> One can only imagine Astell's satisfaction at having an established philosopher accept the efficacy of her corrective. (*Letters,* 24)

A second reservation focuses on the way in which human love relates to divine love. As Taylor and New point out, "Norris had been developing since the beginning of his authorial career . . . his neoplatonic conviction that God is 'the Proper and Principal end of Man, the Center of our *Tendency*' and 'the Object which alone can satisfy the appetite of the most Capacious Soul (*Miscellanies,* 409). . . . [H]e had already developed his Thomist distinction between Love as *desire,* '*A* simple Tendency of the Soul to good' which necessarily implies self-love and indigence, and Love as *benevolence,* a selfless desire for the good of others . . . (*Theory and Regulation of Love,* 11–12, 14, 31, 50–51, etc.)" (*Letters,* 22). For Norris (and this is central in understanding his appeal to Sterne), our love of God cannot be the love of benevolence, because wishing or doing good for God is impossible; He needs nothing and is already perfect. Hence, our love of God must be the love that desires.

Astell could not accept this distinction without expressing her unease regarding its practice, raising her reservations toward the end of her second letter, with sentiments one feels Sterne would have fully understood:

> [A]las, *sensible* Beauty does too often press upon my Heart, whilst *intelligible* is disregarded. For having by Nature a strong Propensity to friendly Love, which I have all along encouraged as a good Disposition to Vertue, and do still think it so if it may be kept within the due Bounds and Good-will: But having likewise thought till you taught me better, that I need not cut off all Desire from the Creature: . . . I have contracted such a Weakness . . . by voluntary Habit, that it is a very difficult thing for me to love at all, without something of Desire. . . . And though I have in some measure rectified this Fault, yet still I find an agreeable Movement in my Soul towards her I love, and a Displeasure and Pain when I meet with Unkindness, which is a strong Indication of somewhat more than pure Benevolence. (80)

And she concludes, tartly, that Norris's distinction is "too nice for common Practice" (80). Norris responded rather weakly:

> [Y]ou are to distinguish between the Movements of the Soul and those of the Body, the Movements of the Soul ought not to tend but towards him who only is above her, and only able to act in her. But the Movements of the Body may be determined by those Objects which environ it, and so by those Movements we may unite our selves to those things which are the natural or occasional Causes of our Pleasure. (86)

This seems too easy a solution from Norris and does not satisfy Astell. She knew that soul and body could not so easily be separated.

From this exchange forward, the correspondence deals with this issue and provides its culmination. The crux of Astell's reservation continues to revolve around human desire, the extent to which it could be considered natural and thus welcomed. Her demur comes across as remarkably clear and unequivocal. Perhaps encouraged by Norris's capitulation to her earlier opening argument she now, almost cheekily, in her penultimate letter, suggests that she can correct him:

> I have heard some Object against your Account of the first and great Commandment, *that it is prejudicial to the second*, and because I am of a quite contrary Opinion, and think nothing does more effectually secure and improve it, I will therefore offer to your Consideration and Correction such Meditations as I have had about it.
>
> It were I confess a strong Prejudice against your Way of stating the Love of *GOD*, if it were in any Measure injurious to the right Understanding and due Performance of the Love we owe to our Neighbour. . . . [I]f I can't make over the whole of my Desire to *GOD*, without taking from him that Portion of Love he has assigned my Neighbour, I must of Necessity . . . find out some other

Medium to interpret the first and great Commandment. But there's no Necessity for this: So far is your Account of the Love of *GOD* from being prejudicial to the Love of our Neighbour, that (if I think right) 'tis the only solid and sure Foundation it can rest upon. For if I may lawfully bestow any Share of my Desire on my Neighbour, why not on the rest of *GOD*'s Creatures that are useful and beneficial to me, provided my Love be not inordinate, but contain it self within those Bounds that Reason and Religion have prescribed? . . . [T]he Divine Nature is an inexhaustible Ocean of Felicity, in which every one of us may satisfie his most inlarged Desires, without the least Diminution of its Fullness! (100–101)

Repeatedly, Astell refers to the inescapable realities of her physicality and the implications arising from her conviction that it is right to enjoy the simple physical functions of life: by appealing to her own "nature" she seems to insist that because creation preceded the Fall some quality inheres in natural objects and people independent of God's direct and unmediated influence, a residue that allows His influence to function.

In her final letter Astell is even more forthright, strongly suggesting that Norris's reference to the immediacy of God's influence as *"the only efficient Cause of all our Sensation . . .* renders a great Part of *GOD*'s Workmanship vain and useless," which "does not well comport with his Majesty" (131). She writes of a *"sensible Congruity,"* namely that God produces our sensations *"mediately* by his Servant Nature" as distinct from *"immediately* by his own Almighty Power" (132). Norris's final response is lengthy (133–38), closely argued, and reads in some places like a teacher putting down a tiresome student. He is clearly stung by her argument and forcibly rejects the idea of any natural congruity without God's immediate influence: "I deny that there is any such thing as a sensible Congruity. . . . I utterly disclaim it as an absurd and unphilosophical Prejudice" (137).

Astell does not pursue Norris further, and instead closes the correspondence, but she insists, at the same time, that it be dedicated to her friend and lifelong patron, Lady Catherine Jones (53 and 55): "One whom . . . I may venture to say, I love with the greatest Tenderness. . . . All true lovers of *GOD* being like excited Needles, which cleave not only to him, their *Magnet*, but even to one another" (66–67). This statement is followed (in the original) by several pages glowingly describing Lady Catherine's qualities. For Astell, the love of human friendship is vital and real, and cannot be excluded from her love of God, however much she says she agrees with Norris that it should be exclusive of all other loves. After the correspondence they pursued their different ways. Norris continued his isolated, academic, and mystical ministry at quiet Bemerton, but he also published numerous works of abstract philosophy and practical theology, works often reprinted to the end of the eighteenth century.[7] Astell embarked on a much more engaged and controversial course, leading her to be dubbed, in our century, the first English feminist.

The differences between Norris and Astell, on the one hand, and Sterne, on the other, in their attitude toward human and divine love and how they might be related to one another is instructive. Norris seems able to make a smooth transition from his desire for another human being to his eroticized passion for the invisible spiritual entity he calls God; Astell seems finally to achieve this as well, but less happily, and with some metaphysical sleight of hand and psychological unease. Sterne also makes the transition, but only after considerable mental gymnastics, by which he attempts to square the circle without abandoning an iota of his sexual appetite, indeed embracing it by demonstrating the unfailing presence of body in everything he wrote and in every affair he contemplated. While Sterne is closer to Astell's position, he shares with them both a Neoplatonic emphasis on the importance of the senses in his understanding of God.

As noted, Astell was disturbed by the thesis *"that* GOD *is the only efficient Cause of all our Sensations"* (69). Sterne, on the other hand, was willing to accept Norris's sentiments regarding the senses, giving utterance to them in an ecstatic and lyrical passage in *ASJ*, one that Norris would surely have found compatible with his own thoughts:

> —Dear sensibility! source inexhausted of all that's precious in our joys, or costly in our sorrows! thou chainest thy martyr down upon his bed of straw—and 'tis thou who lifts him up to HEAVEN—eternal fountain of our feelings!—'tis here I trace thee—and this is thy divinity which stirs within me—not that, in some sad and sickening moments, *"my soul shrinks back upon herself, and startles at destruction"*—mere pomp of words!—but that I feel some generous joys and generous cares beyond myself—all comes from thee, great—great SENSORIUM of the world! which vibrates, if a hair of our heads but falls upon the ground, in the remotest desert of thy creation. (*ASJ*, 6:155)

If this passage was inspired by Eliza Draper, as I believe to be the case, it can be compared to those passages in *Letters* where Norris waxes eloquently and erotically, in correspondence with a woman, about the sensations created in him by the thoughts of Jesus: *"sweet Christ, good Jesus, my* GOD, *my love, kindle me all over with thy Fire, with the love of thee, with thy Sweetness, with thy Joy, with thy Pleasure and Concupiscence"* (*Letters*, 124).

Sterne's depiction of God as a hugely magnified "SENSORIUM" reflects his keen appreciation of the real pleasure he derived from the senses within an exalted idea of God as the supreme reality, made even closer to human passions through Jesus, to whose words he refers (Matthew 10:29–31). Commenting on this passage the Florida editors make a connection with Platonism:

The argument of Sterne's entire passage would seem to be that God's "sensibility," manifested as providential care for the weak and the pitiful, is a model for human "sensibility." Hence, God (as Christ, the "sensorium of God" in Christian platonism) is projected as the seat of "sensibility." (*ASJ*, 6:376)

J.T. Parnell links the same passage specifically to Norris:

> No small part of what makes Sterne's sentimentalism "unreadable" for twentieth-century readers is that its theological underpinnings are almost entirely lost to us. While we can recover, from eighteenth-century sermons, part of the religious context that gave it meaning we can never, perhaps, reconstruct the belief that made it sincere. However, when Norris argues that "there is nothing in Scripture so pathetically expressed as the Tenderness and Mercy of God," or when he cites Christ's human soul as the supreme instance of "Sympathy and Mercy," we are reminded of the centrality of pity within the Christian tradition.[8]

This "centrality of pity" valorizes the senses for both Norris and Sterne. In this ultimately philosophical perception, Norris borrows heavily from the ideas of Nicolas Malebranche; as Taylor and New observe, "it would be difficult to overestimate the importance of Malebranche" (13–14). He is cited in the first and second letters (71, 85–86) and quoted extensively in the third (94–95). Malebranche had set out his ideas in *Méditations Chrétiennes et Métaphysiques* (1683), translated as *Dialogues on Metaphysics and on Religion* (1688), and Norris's attraction to him can be traced to Malebranche's merging of the Platonic involutions of Descartes with the mystic immediacy of Augustine. Norris used Malebranche to buttress his argument that while we know our bodies through ideas—that is, through measurement, extension, and mathematics—we can only know our souls (our essential selves, spirit, and being) through sentiment, sense, and experience: "he can never know it till he feel it" (96).

For both Malebranche and Norris only the assertion that "GOD is the only efficient Cause" of sensations, and that there are no secondary causes can do full justice to the Pauline theme that "in God we live and move and have our being" (Acts 17:28).[9] Norris returns to this argument, as we have seen, at the end of his correspondence with Astell, at one point affirming a consequent marked difference between two forms of knowledge: "there is a vast Difference between knowing by *Sentiment* and knowing by *Idea*" (134), a distinction that finally terminates the correspondence:

> I doubt not but that if you carefully read over Mr. *Malbranch, Touchant l'efficace attribuée aux Causes second*s, you will find to hold as true as to all things else. I mean that *GOD* is the only true efficient Cause, and that his *servant Nature* is but a mere Chimera. (138)

What Norris can achieve by spiritualizing the physical world, Sterne can also achieve, applied specifically to human sexuality. His sensual/sexual vocabulary merges with the Neoplatonic tendency he absorbed from or shared with Norris—both men, through their reading of Neoplatonic writers, eschewing late Augustinian (and Roman Catholic Thomistic) rejection of the body as evil; Cartesian dualism is thus also discarded.[10]

Sterne clearly displaces his sexual longings for Eliza Draper within a spiritual dimension, but his spirituality seems much more solidly anchored in the physical than the metaphysical. He begins with a bodily woman, albeit one whose accessibility may perhaps be only in his mind, and he weaves a web of mystical and spiritualized desire around that image—an image nonetheless tinged with explicit sexuality. Norris, on the other hand, begins with his abstract thesis that God only is to be loved, and then allows (whether easily or in a struggle, we will perhaps never know) his desire for Astell to be subsumed and sublimated into that thesis—one that directs its own explicit sexuality toward Christ. Norris (or Neoplatonism more generally) taught Sterne something about spiritualizing his desires, but Sterne could have taught the theologian something about allowing human desire to speak for itself.

For Sterne, there could be little argument about the way in which the love of God was related to human love, no disconnect between the two parts of the great commandment; to love God was the same moral act as loving one's fellow human being. Consequently, when confronted (like Norris) with a young woman to whom he was attracted (and he was attracted by many, it would seem) he had little qualm about equating his love of God with love for the creature, and it would have been incomprehensible to him, I believe, to seek Eliza "for his good" and yet not "love her as his good." For him, this would certainly have been "too nice for common practice." Desire was seen not as leading necessarily to "mischief and malice," but rather as an incentive to greater "charitableness," an openness and toleration toward others that he seems, in the last year of his life, to associate particularly with his love for Eliza Draper, and, conversely, God's love for the human creature. The love of God was not exclusive of all other loves, but was to be found, and indeed fulfilled, in expressions of care toward one's neighbor, and if one's neighbor was an attractive woman, he refused to be moralized out of his desire. The need to justify one's sexual desire to God, I might add, is not an indication of hypocrisy, as many have argued, but of religious faith.

The editors of Sterne's *Sentimental Journey* identify two qualities that characterize Sterne, first, the prioritizing of "heart over head," and, second, the urge toward conciliation:

without doubt, he had preached, early and late, the importance of the heart over the head, by which he seems to have meant primarily a kind and charitable disposition toward others, even against one's own self-interests. It was a notion he almost certainly believed he had found in the life and teachings of Jesus, one that he did not need the Earl of Shaftesbury to teach him.

. . . Sterne seems to have equated that same "heart," or "sentiment," or "sensibility," not only with charity and kindness directed toward neediness, but with tolerance toward the different lives and actions of others. . . . [H]e wanted to extend that kindness, charity, and tolerance toward all those human beings—including himself—who had been unable to rise to sainthood, or even to chastity and a uniformly virtuous and disciplined existence, those who could never, during their all too human days and nights, unplait the various strands of appetite, lust, dalliance, devotion, commitment, and love into separate and distinct threads. . . . Sterne's guiding idea in *A Sentimental Journey* and *Bramine's Journal* is to conciliate the ways of a very imperfect humankind to God. (*ASJ*, lii–liii)

Conciliation—synthesis and the merging of disparate ideas, notions, genres, and disciplines—is of the essence of Sterne's genius. As an Anglican sermonizer and again in *Tristram Shandy*, Sterne had already committed himself to an attempt to justify the ways of men to God.[11]

The dominance of heart over head in Norris's Neoplatonic mysticism, as noted above, surely was one of his attractions to Sterne. However, the way in which Sterne thought of the priority of feeling was quite different. Norris grounds his argument in a spiritual and mystical theology, while Sterne grounds his in his own lived experience. Norris's attempted separation of physical (sexual) feelings from the sensuous feelings he attached to his perception of divinity was anathema to Sterne.[12] Far from separating out and excluding his love of Eliza from his love of God, he tried to see her as a Beatrice, a Laura, that is, an elevation of the actual into the ideal, but always rooted in the perception of a sensual beauty that awakens real appetite.[13] Norris, lamenting the lack of divine love in the world, contrasts it with the prevalence of sensual love—clearly, to him, meaning sexual love:

> O divine Love whither art thou fled. . . . How charming and ravishing are thy Pleasures, and yet how very few hast thou inamoured by them! While in the mean time . . . sensual Love is continually spreading its Victories, and leading in triumph its inglorious Captives. (*Letters*, 62)

For Sterne, sensual love's victories certainly led him in triumph but were in no way "inglorious" in his eyes. Indeed, sensual love seems to have had for him a powerful and positive transformative influence. He tried to integrate his world of desire into a world in which God's love for His creatures encompassed, indeed generated, the love they had for one another. Norris, to the contrary, sees sexual attraction and erotic love as rivals to the love of God rather than a way toward it, and in his "Postscript to the Preface," refers to the "*Corruption of the Heart*" and its inclination to "*fill that Emptiness which she [the soul] feels in herself by the Possession of Creatures*" (68).

Sterne had a gift for friendship and like Astell saw something crucial in companionship, especially as it was exemplified and intensified in sexual relationships. Arthur Cash records an anecdote about Sterne that provides an unusually clear picture of this gift, referred to by Cash as "a knack for intimacy":

> His behaviour to a comparative stranger, Allessandro Verri, the Italian historian, was described by Verri after he had called upon Sterne in Bond Street in January 1767. "He gave me some chocolate, and a thousand caresses," Verri told his brother: "he took off my coat wet with the rain and spread it over a chair; he embraced me, he pressed my hand and led me to the fire." When Sterne saw Verri a few days later at a public assembly, he stepped up to him, embraced him, and began a conversation whispered in his ear.[14]

This pleasure of Sterne in the companionship of others became, perhaps, more intense than usual in his relationship with Eliza; his ill health, his loneliness (Elizabeth Sterne and their daughter Lydia were in France), her youth and obvious infatuation with him,[15] and, finally, the brevity of their acquaintance and her return to India, all contributed to the passionate desire for her presence evident on every page of the *Bramine's Journal*, described by Sterne as "a Diary of the miserable feelings of a person separated from a Lady for whose Society he languish'd" (*BJ*, 169). Amanita Forrna in her recent novel writes: "People are wrong when they talk of love at first sight. It is neither love nor lust. No. As she walks away from you, what you feel is loss. A premonition of loss."[16]

Years before, Sterne had written a sermon, "The Levite and His Concubine," justifying the importance of companionship within sexual relationships; he included it in the second installment of his publication of sermons, a year before meeting Eliza in January 1767, and it was probably among those he gave her to read when they first met. In it, Sterne took a brutal story from the Old Testament and turned it into a lesson in compassion, one stressing the necessity and innocence of sexual companionship. At first, he assumes the traditional stance of the moralists who would condemn the Levite for "taking a concubine" but then challenges this stance, condemning instead those who rush to judgment. Rather, he emphasizes a compassionate tolerance of the human need for sexual companionship, the universal need to

> fill up that uncomfortable blank in the heart in such a situation; . . . Yet still, "*it is not good for man to be alone:*" . . . Nature will have her yearnings for society and friendship;—a good heart wants some object to be kind to—and the best parts of our blood, and the purest of our spirits suffer most under the destitution.
> Let the torpid Monk seek heaven comfortless and alone——God speed him! For my own part, I fear, I should never so find the way: let me be wise and religious——but let me be M A N: wherever thy Providence places me, or whatever be the road I take to get to thee——give me some companion in my journey, be it only to remark to, How our shadows lengthen as the sun goes down;——to whom I may say, How fresh is the face of nature! How sweet the flowers of the field! How delicious are these fruits! (*Sermons*, 4:169–70).[17]

In this beautiful passage, Sterne reveals his strongly held conviction that Norris's way to God was not his. Whatever it was that led him to love God, it was not exclusive of all other loves, but rather through them. Also, this love was not just one of companionship but included and became exquisitely intensified and concentrated in a love affair. For Sterne, the "companion" of the sermon became one particular companion, and with a modicum of familiarity with Sterne's biography we can certainly find in it his own self-justifying cry from the heart: "give me a companion." It was a prayer we assume he had answered for himself several times in the course of his life, but the time we know most about is, of course, his love affair—however brief, however imagined—with Eliza Draper.

In the *Bramine's Journal*, Sterne compares Eliza with his wife, from whom he imagines a separation by mutual consent, and having glanced at the "Duty & Submission" (*BJ*, 6:205) that is sending Eliza back to India and her husband, he soon rejects both for what we might perceive as his notion of an even higher moral obligation:

> What a stupid, selfish, unsentimental set of Beings are the Bulk of our Sex! by Heaven! not one man out of 50, informed with feelings—or endow'd either with heads or hearts able to possess & fill the mind of such a Being as thee, with one Vibration like its own. . . . [A]t this moment, my heart glowes more warmly as I think of you—& I find myself more your Husband than contracts can make us. (6:206–7)

Here, it is Eliza who triggers a vibration between kindred spirits, one that foretells the "SENSORIUM" passage from *Sentimental Journey*, quoted earlier: "great SENSORIUM of the world! which vibrates, if a hair of our heads but falls upon the ground, in the remotest desert of thy creation" (*ASJ*, 6:155). The clear echo of the providential verse of Matthew 10:29–31 parallels the close and loving care between human beings that Mary Astell describes as "sensible" and "vital" contiguity, the unresolved problem in her correspondence with Norris. For Sterne, this contiguity becomes an indication of an inevitability that bespeaks a providential God:

> when will the like [times together] return?—tis hidden from us both, for the wisest ends—and the hour will come my Eliza! when We shall be convinced, that every event has been order'd for the best for Us—Our fruit is not ripend—the accidents of times & Seasons will ripen every Thing *together* for Us. (*BJ*, 6:190)

If God is Eliza-like in His providential companionship with human beings, valorized by Astell as a "sensible contiguity," then the obverse works as well, and Sterne allows his imagination to turn Eliza into a goddess. Imagining the room at Shandy Hall that he is preparing for her, he promises to enter it

> ten times a day to give thee Testimonies of my Devotion———Was't thou this moment sat down, it w^d be the sweetest of earthly Tabernacles—I shall enrich it, from time to time, for thee—till Fate lets me lead thee by the hand into it—& then it can want no Ornament. . . . Oh my Eliza!—I shall see thee surely Goddesse of this Temple,—and the most sovereign one, of all I have—& of all the powers heaven has trusted me with———They were lent me, Eliza! only for thee—& for thee my dear Girl shall be kept & employ'd.—You know *What rights* you have over me. (*BJ*, 6:197)

Likening the room to a "Tabernacle" and "Temple," with Eliza as its "Goddesse" is a daring (if not quite original) application of the Old Testament's vision of the particular place where God's holy presence could be felt. This temporary and movable "Tabernacle"—when as nomads, the Israelites wandered in the desert—became a permanent "Temple" in Jerusalem once they settled in the Promised Land (see Exodus 25–27, 1 Kings 8ff).

Lest we think this merely a rash effusion of the moment, Sterne returns to the image three weeks later, in a fascinating journal entry that intertwines the real woman with the holy presence, his "Goddesse" in her Temple equipped with petticoats, gowns, and bandboxes:

> I have made you, a sweet Sitting Room (as I told You) already—and am projecting a good Bed-chamber adjoining it, with a pretty dressing room for You, which connects them together—& when they are finishd, will be as sweet a set of romantic Apartments, as You ever beheld—the Sleeping room will be very large—The dressing room, thro' wch You pass into y^r Temple, will be little—but Big enough to hold a dressing Table—. . . wth spare Room to hang a dozen petticoats—gowns, &c—& Shelves for as many Bandboxes –Y^r little Temple I have described—& what it will hold—but if ever it holds You & I, my Eliza—the Room will not be too little for us—but We shall be *too big* for the Room. (*BJ*, 6:209)

The mystic's "imitation of Christ" (whereby identification with God is the path to righteousness, and hence to Oneness with the divine), certainly one of the most important of theological concepts for both Norris and Astell, is suggested by Sterne's "We shall be *too big* for the Room,"[18] but far more specifically in an earlier journal entry where one is almost compelled to feel a parallel to the Christian's communal act by which oneness with God is achieved:

> You must teach me fortitude my dear Bramine—for with all the tender qualities wch make you the most precious of Women—& most wanting of all other Women of a kind protector—yet you have a passive kind of sweet Courage wch bears You up—more than any one Virtue I can summon up in my own Case—We were made with Tempers for each other, Eliza! & You are blessd with such a certain turn of Mind & reflection—that if Self love does not blind me—I resemble no Being in the world so nearly as I do You—do you wonder that I have such friendship for you? (*BJ*, 6:198)

That Eliza has now become fully merged with the divine in Sterne's mind, is perhaps suggested by the term "Being," Sterne's consistent and frequent synonym for God in his sermons. However, even without that linguistic turn, the merging of lovers here envisioned comes very close indeed to those mystically erotic passages in Norris's responses to Astell, wherein he abandons all philosophical, much less rational discourse, and soars in ecstasy: "*Fill always (I beseech thee) my Heart with an unquenchable Love of thee, with a continual Remembrance of thee, that so as a burning Flame, I may burn all over in the Sweetness of thy Love, which may not be quenched even by many Waters,*" etc. (*Letters*, 124). Significantly, Norris is not inventing this outcry in some enthusiastic trance, but rather copying the words of Augustine. Sterne has thus arrived, it would seem, at the same place as Norris, although perhaps he is a bit more honest (as was Augustine) about the sexual passions prompting his spiritual ecstasies.

Even the end of the affair, inherent in its beginning, allows Sterne one final opportunity to spiritualize the relationship:

> ——And now Eliza! Let me talk to thee——But What can I say, of What can I write—But the Yearnings of heart wasted with looking & wishing for thy Return—Return—Return! my dear Eliza! May heaven smooth the Way for thee to send thee safely . . . to us, & sojourn . . . for Ever. (*BJ*, 6:225)

In thus concluding his journal and his affair Sterne has recourse to his religion and to its apocalyptic hope, expressed in the closing verses of Revelation with which the New Testament ends. The Christian's hope for the return of Jesus to bring human history to its end is combined with the rapture of reunion between the saints and their beloved Lord and Saviour. The belief in a second coming (Acts 1:11), after centuries of disappointment, had evolved into hope projected into an indeterminate future time. Sterne brings his *Journal* to its conclusion, just as the Bible concludes, with a repeated appeal to "Return," mirrored by the repeated cry from the "Spirit and the bride" to the believer to "Come" and partake in a mystic lover's reunion with Jesus (Revelation 22:17). For Sterne, however, this mystic reunion was with the human but now quite distant and totally spiritualized Eliza.

The correspondence of Norris and Astell in 1694 and that of Sterne and Eliza Draper seventy-three years later are inextricably linked by a mystical Christian tradition in which the language of human relationship—friendships, marriages, sexual couplings, or romantic yearnings—is fully echoed in the fundamental relationship between the human and the divine. Norris, to be sure, tries to establish his uncompromising position that the love of God brooks no competition and must be entire, excluding all other loves. Astell's questioning, in the name of a friendship she could not separate from her love of God, opens the door, perhaps, to Sterne's quite uninhibited yielding to human love as a mode of caring for others, modeled after both the human Jesus, as chronicled in the Gospels, and the divine Christ, who is, doctrinally, not only God incarnate, but the path by which human beings can be reconciled, made whole, brought finally to oneness with the Infinite. The atonement for sin (at-one-ment) that Christ heralds is for Sterne a unique opportunity to wish for Heaven despite his sinful appetites (surely he was not totally self-deluded), while at the same time it enables him to embody those appetites in his own version of incarnate being, the woman he loved, spiritualized. This combination of devout faith with a strong humanitarian instinct, supported with a warm companionable personality, and a mystical, sentimental disposition, directed Sterne into a relationship best described as an amalgam of human and divine love; we may be skeptical, but I would suggest that Laurence Sterne was not.

A brief coda: I would suggest that Sterne's faith in his own vision of love is supported by the insights of the influential Protestant theologian, Paul Tillich. For Tillich, all the experiences of life—including sexual appetite—were to be treated as good and natural phenomena, with their origins in the goodness of creation: "God is neither alongside nor even 'above' them [that is, phenomena]; he is nearer to them than they are to themselves. He is their creative ground, here and now, always and everywhere."[19] In his work on the theology of love, Tillich invokes the concept of a *new being* at the heart of Christianity, expressed by a love that overcomes dividedness. He works on a principle of correlation, much the same as Sterne's conciliation, and he aims to synthesize what might seem to be disparate ideas.

However, it is the element of *eros* that gives Tillich's thought its peculiar inner power and tension. For him, infinity reveals itself in the finite without absorbing the concreteness of the finite; it makes the finite whole, restoring it to meaningfulness. Just as Sterne refuses to separate human love and divine love, so Tillich speaks of a love that unites one with oneself, saving the self from despair, making us whole again, and making us real so that we are able to unite "the separated 'I' with the 'Thou' of one's neighbour." Tillich does not separate, as did Norris, one love from another, the one directed toward God, the other directed toward one's neighbor. Rather, he treats them as facets of one divine command: "In the great commandment the word love is combined with the imperative 'thou shalt' and demands of everyone total love of God and total love of one's neighbour." Significantly, the different aspects of love that have been identified and labeled in the long course of history—*eros* (by Plato); *epithymia, philia*, and *agape* (by Christianity); *libido* (by Freud)—Tillich maintained are singularly present in "every act of love."[20]

It is *epithymia*, or desire, that brings Tillich's thought closest to Sterne's, and indeed to Norris's. *Epithymia*—considered the lowest form of love in orthodox Christian dogma and identified with sexual, sensual fulfilment—is rehabilitated by Tillich. If separation is the true nature of sin, then union, the aim of all love, the desire embodied in *epithymia*, is absolutely necessary for the religious life. Without the desire—the passion—to know the truth (that is, God and His manifestations), theology would not exist. Furthermore, the rejection of *epithymia* or *eros* in one's love of God leads to a love shaped by obedience; but obedience, for Tillich, is not love, and can easily become its opposite, as when religion becomes the acting out of an obedience designed to *please* or *satisfy* God's commands.[21] As Norris had noted two centuries earlier, there is nothing the human being can do to enrich God through action; only the love that passionately desires to be reunited with its origin is meaningful as a spiritual response to the original separation; in this, Norris, Astell, Sterne, and Tillich all seem to be in absolute agreement, although for each the object of that desire, the precise nature of that separation, may be in dispute. Difference of opinion, dread of isolation: they are, after all, what first inspired the young Mary Astell to question John Norris, and the wasted Laurence Sterne to turn to Eliza Draper.

NOTES

1. Sterne refers to the *Journey* in *Bramine's Journal* and to Eliza Draper in *Journey*. That the former was inspired by his affair with Eliza is suggested in the entry for June 3: "Cannot write my Travels, or give one half hours close attention to them, upon Thy Acct, my dearest friend—Yet write I must, & what to do with You, whilst I write—I declare I know not—I want to have you ever before my Imagination—& cannot keep You out of my heart or head" (*A Sentimental Journey and Bramine's Journal*, ed. Melvyn New and W.G. Day, vol. 6 of *The Florida Edition of the Works of Laurence Sterne* [Gainesville: University Press of Florida, 2002], 194). Hereafter cited in text as *ASJ* and *BJ*.

2. Interestingly, both *A Serious Proposal to the Ladies* and, sixty-five years later, the first two volumes of *Tristram Shandy* sold well and gave rise to much comment. The first "burst upon London in 1694 and was read and talked of from Pall Mall to Grub Street" (Ruth Perry, *The Celebrated Mary Astell* (Chicago: University of Chicago Press, 1980), 99; the second, within days, was the subject of conversation in all the London coffee shops.

3. Cf. Introduction to *ASJ:* "we have made a case for the significant appearance in *Journey* of England's first critic of *Essay concerning Human Understanding*, John Norris of Bemerton, whose place in Sterne's thinking is just beginning to be adequately explored" (1). New repeats his assertion of the unexplored importance of the influence of Norris on Sterne in a more recent essay: "That Sterne would be particularly attracted to Norris' Christian mysticism seems to me worth even more exploration and explication" ("Reading the Occasion: Understanding Sterne's Sermons," in *Divine Rhetoric: Essays on the Sermons of Laurence Sterne,* ed. W.B. Gerard (Newark: University of Delaware Press, 2010), 118.

4. See Mary Astell and John Norris, *Letters concerning the Love of God,* ed. E. Derek Taylor and Melvyn New (Burlington, VT: Ashgate, 2005), 53–54. Hereafter cited in text as *Letters.*

5. Taylor and New comment: "it is surely one of his favorite texts, as it was for many of the Cambridge Platonists" (*Letters,* 139).

6. See, for example, *Theory and Regulation of Love* (1693), included in his *Miscellanies,* and hence often reprinted.

7. For the most recent account of his career and a bibliography of his writings, see W.J. Mander, *The Philosophy of John Norris* (Oxford: Oxford University Press, 2008).

8. J.T. Parnell, "'A Story Painted to the Heart?' *Tristram Shandy* and Sentimentalism Reconsidered," *The Shandean* 9 (1997): 126.

9. Nicolas Malebranche, *Dialogues on Metaphysics and on Religion,* ed. Nicholas Jolley, trans. David Scott (Cambridge: Cambridge University Press, 1997), xxii.

10. Plotinus, for example, firmly associates sensual and even sexual passion with divine resonance: "Once the soul has received an 'outflow' coming to her from the Good, she is excited and seized with Bacchic madness, and filled with stinging desires. Thus love is born. . . . Once . . . a 'warmth' from the Good has reached her, she is strengthened and awakened, she becomes truly winged and although she is seized with passion for what is close to her, nevertheless she is lifted up, as if by memory, towards a different object" (*The Enneads,* IV.7.22, 8–21; quoted from Pierre Hadot in *Plotinus: or the Simplicity of Vision,* trans. Michael Chase (Chicago: University of Chicago Press, 1993), 52.

11. One strong impression gained when reading the sermons alongside *Tristram Shandy* is that his intention evolved to conciliate and balance the diverse activities of life, and set all of them within a spiritual and hence, for him, Christian context. This is described by Joshua Pederson as "when two speech genres—two distinct voices—interact positively in such a way as to produce unexpected new composite voices and propitious effects," ("Gnostic Mantra: Reading Religious Syncretism in Alan Ginsberg's 'Plutonian Ode,'" in *Religion and Literature* 41 (Autumn 2009): 41).

12. Cf. the often-remarked opening of "The house of feasting and the house of mourning described"; after announcing his text, "It is better to go into the house of mourning, than to the house of feasting" from Ecclesiastes 7:2–3, he declares: "That I deny—but let us hear the wise man's reasoning upon it—*for that is the end of all men, and the living* will *lay it to* his *heart: sorrow is better than laughter*—for a crack'd-brain'd order of Carthusian monks, I grant, but not for men of the world" (*Sermons,* ed. Melvyn New, vol. 4 of *The Florida Edition of the Works of Laurence Sterne* [Gainesville: University Press of Florida, 1996], 12).

13. See Sterne, *Letters,* ed. Melvyn New and Peter de Voogd, *The Florida Edition of the Works of Laurence Sterne,* vols. 7–8 (University Press of Florida, 2009), 8:564 (to Eliza): "We shall fish upon the banks of Arno," and 566n4, where the editors compare it to another allusion to the Arno in the *BJ,* and suggest the intertwining of Petrarch's idealized mistress and Sterne's own probable bawdry in his allusions.

14. Arthur H. Cash, *Laurence Sterne: The Later Years* (London: Methuen, 1986), 318, citing Giovanni Rabizzani, *Sterne in Italia* (Rome, 1920), 34–37.

15. Since her correspondence during this period has not survived, Eliza's state of infatuation is based solely on the impressions we receive from Sterne's account; it is difficult to believe, however, that he would have so totally deceived himself as to their shared interest, and so we assume reciprocation on her part. Beyond that, it would be folly to speculate.

16. Amanita Forma, *The Memory of Love* (London: Bloomsbury, 2010), 1.

17. Sterne's: "let me be wise and religious but let me be M A N" seems to echo David Hume's "Be a philosopher, but amidst all your philosophy, be still a man" (*Enquiry concerning Human Understanding*, ed. Tom L. Beauchamp [Oxford: Oxford University Press, 1999], I.6.90); see my scholia to the Florida edition in *Scriblerian* 41 (Autumn 2008): 96. For a discussion of Sterne and Hume see my doctoral dissertation *A Moral Preceptor: The Sermons of Laurence Sterne in the Light of His Fiction and of Contemporary Thought*, (Exeter University, 2007), 180–89.

18. That Sterne is not the first Christian, nor even the first Anglican cleric to inextricably entwine the language of human and divine love is perhaps suggested by the echo here of Donne's famous lines: "For love, all love of other sights controls, / And makes one little room, an every where" ("The Good Morrow," ll. 10–11). Whether Sterne had read Donne has not been determined.

19. Paul Tillich, *Systematic Theology*, 2 vols. (Chicago: University of Chicago Press, 1961–1963), 2:8.

20. Tillich, *Love, Power, and Justice: Ontological Analysis and Ethical Application* (Oxford: Oxford University Press, 1954), 10, 24–25.

21. Tillich, *Love, Power, and Justice*, 29–31.

Chapter Eleven

Tristram Shandy and the Devil

Ryan J. Stark

The best way to drive out the Devil, if he will not yield to texts of Scripture, is to jeer and flout him, for he cannot bear scorn.

—Martin Luther

There may be right opinion of God without either love or one right temper toward Him. Satan is a proof of this.

—John Wesley

The Devil regularly appears in *Tristram Shandy*. Old Nick.[1] Old Harry. Old Gooseberry. He is "the great disturber of our faiths in this world" (9.22.777), Tristram reminds us, and "he never lies dead in a ditch" (8.28.712). Throughout the satire, we confront "temptations and suggestions of the devil" (3.31.258), not to mention suspicions about him: for example, *"Ferdinand de Cordouè* was so wise at nine—," we are told, "'twas thought the devil was in him;——and at *Venice* gave such proofs of his knowledge and goodness, that the monks imagined he was *Antichrist*" (6.2.494). An early reviewer imagined that Sterne was Antichrist, but for different reasons.[2] The book's central riddle—the question of Tristram's paternity—contains within it a sly reference to the Cloven Hoof, one that anticipates Yorick's cock-and-bull pun at the end of Book 9: "I can not (making two syllables of it) imagine, quoth my father, who the duce he takes after" (6.18.526). And it is not just The Enemy per se who accounts for *Tristram Shandy*'s eerie-melancholic-preternatural atmosphere, but also the "FIFTY thousand pannier loads of devils" (5.26.457), the "imps, with their hammers and engines" (8.2.657), and the "little party-colour'd devils" (1.8.13). Tristram alludes to Satan and his horde more frequently than he does to John Locke, or to anyone else for that matter, save the other main characters. The "arch-jockey of jockeys" sits not exactly at the center of the Shandean universe, but rather runs alongside—and perhaps astride—nearly every notable scene (4.20.356). And even when he is not there, he is there:

> Quicker still, cried Margarita.
> Fou, fou, fou, fou, fou, fou, fou, fou, fou.
> Quicker still, cried Margarita.
> Bou, bou, bou, bou, bou, bou, bou, bou, bou.
> Quicker still—God preserve me! Said the abbess—They do not understand us, cried Margarita—But the Devil does, said the abbess of Andoüillets. (7.25.614)

Coleridge saw all of this and decided that Sterne dallied with the Devil.[3] I doubt it, as I doubt Blake's and Shelley's assertion that Satan is the tragic hero of *Paradise Lost*.

But that Sterne shows an unusual preoccupation with the Devil seems clear. Why? To what end? Is he inventing gothic fiction before Horace Walpole? Are we to read *Tristram* as an eccentric commentary on Ephesians 6:12—our struggle is not against flesh and blood but against wicked spirits in heavenly places? Or is it that Sterne performs an "exorcism, most un-ecclesiastically," by drawing to the surface and then lampooning the many demonic thoughts that Christians have (9.4.744), a comic version of the *Thesaurus Exorcismorum*? The answer to all of these questions, I believe, is yes, and emphatically yes to the last one. Sterne uses the Devil to cast profane shadows on various foibles and schemes, enthusiasms, pedantries, and tartufferies of every denomination. His aim in doing so is not to demolish the human being, an image bearer of God, but rather to discourage the vice, and the Father of Vices, in a way that usually leads to redemptive laughter. In other words, the Devil functions as the butt of the ontological joke in *Tristram Shandy*, as he does in all righteous Christian satire. Indeed, the Devil as ultimate target is precisely what differentiates classical from Christian satire. Satan will often laugh at the former but never at the latter. In classical satire, motives vary considerably, are often eclectic, prove sometimes cruel, and sometimes not. In Christian satire, "there is only one" target, to quote the old priest from *The Exorcist*, as he tries to explain to the young, contemporary, inexperienced priest that the possessed girl does not suffer from multiple personality disorder. In similar fashion, there is only one satirical target in Sterne's masterpiece.

Once we restore the Devil to his proper role in *Tristram Shandy*, that of thwarted arch villain, some long-standing interpretive debates take new shape—and new root sources for key scenes become visible for the first time. The Toby-and-the-fly incident, for example, appears as a poetic retelling of 2 Kings 1. The blank page explicates Matthew 5:27–28. The list goes on. But why fight the Devil with bawdy prose satire in the first place? Would not Sterne's talents have been better spent writing more sermons, or—God help us—a prolegomena to any future metaphysics? Sterne's contemporary and imitator Richard Griffith rightly replied to this query, "a tale may catch him who a sermon flies."[4] He alludes to George Herbert's *The Temple,* although he truncates the phrase and obscures the full meaning of the couplet in which it appears: "A verse may find him who a sermon flies, / and turn delight into a sacrifice." *Sacrifice* is not a word often used in relation to the copious delights of reading *Tristram Shandy.* Beyond a commitment of time and attention, the book seems not to require a sacrifice, unless we read *Tristram* alongside the related sermon "The Pharisee and Publican in the Temple." Here, Sterne distinguishes between the congregant full of spiritual pride and the one who quietly begs God for mercy, head bowed: "the most acceptable sacrifice we can offer [God] is a virtuous and upright mind" (*Sermons,* 4:64). In the Shandean universe, of course, this sentiment is slightly worrying and beautifully hilarious.

First, a brief comment on Sterne's demonological framework may be useful. From the early Reformation until the end of the seventeenth century, exorcisms were legally banned in England, because they smelled of Catholicism.[5] The Anglican Church closed its office of exorcism in 1550, but, unsurprisingly, clandestine procedures of various sorts continued throughout the early modern era.[6] Most Christians living in York, and everywhere else in Christendom, accepted that the Devil exerted influence on people, either directly via possession or indirectly through instruments such as witches and corrupt priests. On the topic of possession, the commonplace perception among intellectuals and nonintellectuals alike was certainly not that of Hobbes, who wrote in a contorted sentence, "That there were many Daemoniaques in the Primitive Church and few Madmen, and other such singular diseases, where as in these times we hear of, and see many Madmen, and few Daemoniaques, proceeds not from the change of Nature, but of names."[7] Hobbes sounds as skeptical as any philosopher could sound, arguing that demonic possession is a matter of mere terminology rather than metaphysics. Nor would the broader conversation about Hell between James Boswell and Lord Kames have garnered widespread agreement a century after Hobbes: Boswell told Kames that the idea of Hell's torments harmed the world, and Kames replied, "Nobody believes it."[8] By "nobody," Kames meant himself and a few close friends, not the vast majority of thinkers who lived in the Age of the Sermon, also called at times "the Age of Johnson."[9]

Much closer to the mainstream of the period's religious thought about the Devil was William Whiston, successor to Newton in the Lucasian chair of mathematics at Cambridge. He argued that demonic possessions are "no more to be denied, because we cannot, at present, give a direct solution of them, than are Mr. Boyle's experiments about the elasticity of the air, or Sir

Isaac Newton's demonstrations about the power of gravity, to be denied, because neither of them are to be solved by mechanical causes."[10] Whiston restated for an Enlightenment audience Thomas Browne's well-known position in *Religio Medici* (1642), one that encapsulated the early modern Anglican attitude toward demonry: "The devil doth really possess some men; the spirit of melancholy others; the spirit of delusion others."[11] How might we distinguish among melancholy, delusion, and demonry? Therein lies the rub.

For Sterne, the Devil exists, not as pure allegory, which is how Walter views Satan (5.16.448), but rather as sentient being. One of the best indicators appears in a candid letter that Sterne writes to his friend John Hall-Stevenson, wherein he addresses his own infidelity: "I do not know what is the matter with me, but I am sick and tired of my wife more than ever—and I am possessed by a Devil who drives me to town."[12] This is not a remark about a figurative Devil, nor is it a bland abstraction, shared witticism, or whatever else might be said in an effort to explain away the existential reality of Satan and of Sterne's reference to him. In the sermons, Sterne also and predictably often mentions the Devil, either straightforwardly or obliquely, but nowhere more convincingly than in sermon 28, "Temporal Advantages of Religion": "As the deceiver of mankind thus began his triumph over our race—so has he carried it on ever since by the very same argument of delusion.—That is, by possessing men's minds early with great expectations of the present incomes of sin" (*Sermons*, 4:268). We do ourselves and Sterne a disservice if we try to mythologize what is so obviously an ontological theme in his letters, sermons, and fiction: the Devil tempts us often and to great effect. The Devil cajoles us, just as he "and all the devils in hell" cajoled John de la Casa, the priest who held that Satan took an exceptional interest in distinguished religious men (5.16.447).[13] My sense is that the Devil takes a keen interest in all of us, and by "the Devil," Tristram, Sterne, and I mean the Father of Lies, the defiant presence in the universe that seeks our ruin. Mr. Scratch; the Son of Perdition (2 Thessalonians 2:3–4); the Crooked Serpent (Isaiah 27:1); the Angel of Light (2 Colossians 11:14); the Father of Curses (3.11.212); the Father of Confusion (3.31.257)—behind all these titles is the basic Christian perception that we are part of an ongoing struggle between good and evil, and that evil has a champion.

The Devil plays an important role throughout *Tristram Shandy*, but perhaps nowhere more dramatically than in the sentimental crescendos, three of which are especially worth calling to attention: Le Fever's death, Toby and the fly, and the address to Jenny in the last volume of the work:

> I will not argue the matter: Time wastes too fast: every letter I trace tells me with what rapidity Life follows my pen; the days and hours of it, more precious, my dear Jenny! than the rubies about thy neck, are flying over our heads like light clouds of a windy day, never to return more——every thing

presses on——whilst thou art twisting that lock,——see! it grows grey; and every time I kiss thy hand to bid adieu, and every absence which follows it, are preludes to that eternal separation which we are shortly to make.——
——Heaven have mercy upon us both! (9.8.754)

Time does waste too fast. What intensifies the passage, however, is not the ticking of the clock but rather Tristram's unexpected reference to "eternal separation," a phrase that carries a quite negative undertone. It is not, clearly, the anticipatory vision with which Christians view Heaven's banquet, as for example, the "eternal inheritance" Sterne invokes in sermon 43, on the efficacy of prayer, explaining what awaits the righteous person at death (*Sermons*, 4:407). For readers steeped in the Bible—including most of his eighteenth-century audience and a handful of twenty-first-century scholars—the expression strikes a Book of Revelation chord, 20:10 and 21:8, if not also Matthew 25:41 and 25:46: the second death, everlasting loneliness, where the unbelieving "shall have their part in the lake which burneth with fire and brimstone."

This is not the first time Tristram brings us down such dark paths: "The Popish doctors," we discover in volume 4, made it plain that Luther was destined to die "cursing and blaspheming," sailing "into the lake of hell fire" via the wind of his own rhetoric (4.S.T.310–11). Lessius, Tristram tells us in volume 7, calculated that "one Dutch mile, cubically multiplied, will allow room enough, and to spare, for eight hundred thousand millions, which he supposed to be as great a number of souls (counting from the fall of Adam) as can possibly be damn'd to the end of the world" (7.14.594). These other examples, of course, are parodies of scholastic Hell theory, some of the book's blackest comedy, which makes Tristram's heartfelt articulation of damnation anxiety all the more noticeable. By uttering "eternal separation" in the way that he does, Tristram invokes the pit of Tartarus, and simultaneously foregrounds the worst kind of human pride, the despairing idea that one has transgressed in such a way, or so persistently as to be out of God's reach.[14] Macbeth suffers from a similar form of despondency, the Macbeth who sleeps no more and declares the end of grace: "There's nothing serious in mortality: All is but toys: renown and grace is dead" (II.iii.93–94). Marlowe's Faustus, too: "now I die eternally," he laments, after kissing the Helen-demon (V.ii.4). Had Sterne ended the passage in this way, with intense damnation anxiety, then we would have an entirely different episode, a *No Exit Tristram Shandy*. But rather than sounding the Macbethean infernal hiss—words, words, words, "signifying nothing"—Sterne, the orthodox priest, in an astonishing moment of theological and artistic virtuosity, has Tristram pray: "Heav'n have mercy on both of us!" Heaven have mercy on all of us. This ejaculation changes the tenor and cosmology of the passage, because we hear in the background the faint sound of the repentant thief on the Cross, the one who cries out, "Jesus, remember me when you come into your kingdom." Tristram makes the same gesture, as Sterne stages the incident. Writing in his study, surrounded by his books of bawdry on the one hand, serious theology on the other, Tristram has a moment of clarity, and in this moment humbles himself before God, thus reinforcing the work's overall argument that divine grace is the only true remedy for our brokenness. We cannot fix ourselves, and the Great Instauration's new technologies will also fail to deliver us from evil (for example, innovative forceps, universal language schemes, Tristrapedias). What can we do? We can fall seven times a day (illustrated, perhaps, in the mocking one-sentence chapter that follows the prayer to Jenny), and we can offer "a hopeful petition before the seat of Judgment," possibly New's most discerning description of what goes on in *Tristram Shandy*.[15]

The Toby-and-the-fly episode presents the demonic in a different way from the address to Jenny, and in a manner more obscure:

> —Go,——says he, one day at dinner, to an over-grown one which had buzz'd about his nose, and tormented him cruelly all dinner-time,—and which, after infinite attempts, he had caught at last, as it flew by him;——I'll not hurt thee, says my uncle *Toby*, rising from his chair, and going a-cross the room, with the fly in his hand,——I'll not hurt a hair of thy head:——Go, says he, lifting up the sash, and opening his hand as he spoke, to let it escape;——go poor Devil, get thee gone, why should I hurt thee?——This world surely is wide enough to hold both thee and me. (2.12.130–31)

Toby's reference to "poor Devil" hardly seems pregnant with meaning. On the contrary, it reads like a mere colloquial and thoughtless apostrophe. I would suggest, however, that it is not, for although Sterne has a light touch at times, he also likes to hide things in plain sight. In this case, Sterne uses "poor Devil" in order to disguise the obvious by flaunting it, much as he does with the reference to "the duce" in Walter's acknowledgment that he cannot imagine "who the duce" Tristram takes after: Yorick, Mrs. Shandy, and the Devil make three. By means of the fly episode—and through the character of Toby more broadly—Sterne attempts a poetic retelling of the first chapter of 2 Kings. After severely damaging his groin by falling through a lattice in his fortress, King Ahaziah of Israel sends messengers to the Philistine city of Ekron to ask Beelzebub, Lord of the Flies, if and when he will heal: "Go inquire of Beelzebub, the god of Ekron, whether I shall recover from this injury."[16] That the king did not seek Yahweh's council displeased the God of Israel, and Ahaziah never healed, dying a wounded man, unable to get past his injury.

The same can be said of Toby, who also never heals, as suggested most pertinently by his failed courtship with the Widow Wadman. And also exactly like Ahaziah, Toby shows too much deference to Beelzebub, not only in this homage to the fly, but also at the end of Dr. Slop's reading of Ernulphus's curse, which gives us a fuller sense of Toby vis-à-vis the Devil:

> I declare, quoth my uncle *Toby*, my heart would not let me curse the devil himself with so much bitterness.——He is the father of curses, replied Dr. *Slop*.——So am not I, replied my uncle.——But he is cursed, and damn'd already, to all eternity,——replied Dr. *Slop*.
> I am sorry for it, quoth my uncle *Toby*. (3.11.212)

That Toby is "sorry for it," for the Devil's damnation, signals a misunderstanding of the ontological order, a confusion born out of pride and indiscriminate sentimentality. The man of feeling is one thing, and the man of feeling toward the Devil quite another. Toby is of the latter sort, and as such falls into the heresy of Origen and Gregory of Nyssa, both of whom advo-

cated apocatastasis and—of more particular relevance—the salvation of Satan. The Council of Constantinople 2 declared the idea heretical, and heretical it has remained ever since.[17] Sterne's purpose, I would argue, in both the Toby-and-the-fly episode and at the end of the excommunication scenario, is to show how unrestrained sentimentality in an age of personal conscience might subtly curve in on itself and become a vice, not a virtue. Sometimes we need to swat flies, in other words. As it turns out, the world is *not* big enough for Toby and the pestilence: Beelzebub always returns, and there is no peace to be bargained, or truce to be made, although the Devil would have us believe otherwise.

The problem of Toby, Beelzebub, and apocatastasis never found its way into *Tristram Shandy* criticism, perhaps because the scene appeared early on in the hugely successful *Beauties of Sterne* (1782), under the category "Mercy," of which Toby shows much. Almost from the start, Toby became emblematic of venerable sentimentality,[18] which makes examining the demonic dimensions of his character all the more difficult. When we do, however, we might discover an entirely different fiction from the one we thought we were reading.

The Devil makes a more obvious appearance in the scene depicting Le Fever's death, where Toby, in a moment of poignant denial, swears by God that Le Fever will not die, an oath that triggers a pro forma demonic response:

> ——He shall not die, by G—, cried my uncle *Toby*.

—The ACCUSING SPIRIT which flew up to heaven's chancery with the oath, blush'd as he gave it in;—and the RECORDING ANGEL as he wrote it down, dropp'd a tear upon the word, and blotted it out for ever. (6.8.511)

The episode alludes to the Book of Deeds from Revelation 20:12, as New notes, but Tristram also refers explicitly and more affectionately to Isaiah 43:25, where God declares, "I, even I, am he that blotteth out thy transgressions for mine own sake, and will not remember thy sins."[19] In other words, God's grace has a smudging effect on the Book of Deeds, making any quantitative approach to sinning highly problematic. God forgives and forgets.

Many critics have called the Le Fever episode sublime, and rightly so, but it also comes with an interpretive temptation worth exploring. Why does the Accusing Spirit (Job 1–2, Revelation 12:10) blush with embarrassment as he reports Toby's inappropriate oath—his swearing by God's name in vain? Since demons have a reputation for not blushing, ever, the blush here invites us inappropriately to see the demon as a sensitive soul, a fiend with a soft side who presumably knows that the sin in this context is to be expected; he is surely not surprised by it, but neither does he seem delighted. Indeed, we are tempted to see the demon experiencing relief when the angel behaves mercifully, and seemingly behind God's back. On such a reading, the demon blushes out of embarrassment for an inflexible God, or shame for a legalistic theology that buries believers in technicalities and unreasonable expectations. But Tristram's reference to Isaiah changes everything, making such an interpretation both difficult and undesirable. The demon's blushing is better explained by the desperate situation in which he operates. By trying to indict uncle Toby in this sad case, he grasps at straws, and on some instinctive level detects his own foolishness in making the accusation in the first place. Put differently, the war against Heaven does not go well, and the blush shows that the demon catches a glimpse in the mirror of his own ragged visage.

If there is a modicum of demonic success to be discussed in one of *Tristram Shandy's* several death scenes, it is not Le Fever's but rather Bobby's that should have our attention, or—more precisely—Walter's response to it.[20] On hearing about his son's death, Walter performs for Toby a strange oration, quoting various ancient authorities on the topic of death. "Philosophy has a fine saying for every thing.—For death it has an entire set" (5.3.419), Tristram notes, and Walter proves. The demonry, here, is in Walter's invocation of stoic pride, which some people incorrectly or euphemistically call "stoic calm." Juxtaposed against Trim's few words on Bobby's death aimed point blank at the heart, and punctuated by a dropping hat, Walter's mechanical speech achieves what most demonic rhetoric achieves: a rhetorical chill. Walter acts more like a machine than a man, or, worse still, like a man possessed by the ghost of Epictetus past.[21] In *On the Sublime*, Longinus has a word for this type of eloquence: *psychrotita* (ψυχρότητα), often translated as "failed sublimity" or "false wit." The word literally means "frigidity" and in Greek rhetoric connotes the cold conveyances of grandiose speakers.[22] Walter fits the description. Sterne also probably had in mind Erasmus's critique of stoicism when he created Walter's untimely speech on death. As Folly observes, the stoics invented a "marble statue of a man, utterly unfeeling and quite impervious to all emotion," "a man who is completely deaf to human sentiment," "something that cannot even be called human."[23] Walter is such a statue, or becomes one, and Sterne uses him and his chilling rhetoric as a foil to intensify the emotional force of the satire's warm eloquence and also, simultaneously, to lampoon various aspects of "stoical stupidity," to use a phrase from Sterne's sermon on Job's expostulation (*Sermons*, 4:145).

The eighteenth-century poet William Cowper noted that Sterne was "a great master of the pathetic; and if that or any other species of rhetoric could renew the human heart and turn it from the power of Satan unto God," he knew of "no better writer qualified to make proselytes to the cause of virtue."[24] Sadly, however, the compliment is backhanded, because Cowper goes on in the same paragraph to suggest that, in point of fact, no species of rhetoric can renew the human heart. Like other fundamentalists, he forgets what Luther understood so well: the Holy Spirit is the greatest rhetorician of all.[25] But on a positive note, Cowper gets one crucial point right: he places the question of Sterne's wit in its proper theological-chronological-enigmatical framework (*TS*, 1.21.72), that is, the spiritual battle between God and Satan.

Sterne brings the Devil to bear on many of *Tristram*'s pages, including—perhaps surprisingly—the oddest ones: black, marbled, and blank. The blank page is the most demonic of all, but there are elements of demonry in the others. In volume 3, for example, Tristram calls the black page "the black one," a conventional nomenclature for the Devil, as in "bo melas" from the *Epistle of Barnabas* (3.36.268).[26] And in volume 5, he connects the blackness to acts of "MALICE" (5.38.568), which fatally wounded Yorick and, in a thinly veiled autobiographical sense, also wounded Sterne.[27] Exactly what else lies "mystically hid under the dark veil of the black one" remains a point of some conjecture, but we can easily imagine more gloom. Tristram no doubt hears the persistent derogatory chatter in town that blackens Yorick's remembrance, and he endures the vapid inkhorn rhetoric at Yorick's tombstone, the rehearsals of *Hamlet*'s graveyard scene by bad actors who are only slightly acquainted with the gentle priest and the Bard of Avon. Add to these problems Walter's own off-stage cuttlefish eloquence on various aspects of Tristram's breeches, and we arrive at a place of multilayered rhetorical darkness. But like everything else Shandean, there is a twist. The black page also amuses—macabre humor in this case. Using its blackness, Sterne foreshadows his own death, and portends as well the interpretive confusion surrounding his Rabelaisian wit.[28] Bordering on the slapstick (as does the graveyard scene in *Hamlet*), Sterne's black page is absolutely literal, yet interrupts any desire on the reader's part for a purely somber mood. It is difficult not to write satire.

The black page provides one of those scenes in *Tristram Shandy* that illustrates what James Joyce meant when he said, "I am trying to build as many planes of narrative [as possible] with a single esthetic purpose. Did you ever read Laurence Sterne?"[29] But how many planes of narrative intersect under the dark veil? If we believe Wilbur Cross that Sterne got the idea from Robert Fludd's *Utriusque Cosmi* (1617), which also has a black page, then the answer might be twenty-two, the number of tiers Fludd postulates in his metaphysical coil, stretching from the mushrooms to the angels in a pattern that looks a lot like Trim's swirling stick (9.4.743).[30] Regardless, what we know for certain is that Sterne neither aims at nor achieves the one-dimensional rhetoric sought after by the faux sages in Swift's Laputa, men who communicate using objects (for example, ladles, cucumbers, slabs of marble), not words. Nor does he limit himself to the dim literalism of Robert Ferguson, who—in *The Interest of Reason and Religion* (1675)—proclaims, "No Text hath any more than one determinate Sense, otherwise it could have no sense at all."[31] On the contrary, Tristram's veil produces meaning in several directions, calling attention to the existence of some overt motives as it simultaneously hides many others, leaving readers in a state of bemused curiosity. A word aptly spoken is like apples of gold in settings of silver, Solomon says in Proverbs 25:11, and Maimonides echoes in *The Guide of the Perplexed*.[32] Words darkly spoken give us the black page.

Where is the Devil in the marbled page, the "motly emblem" of Tristram's satire (3.36.268)? Perhaps the best way to find Satan there is to search for the biblical scene to which Sterne alludes via the marbling. This may seem provisional as a method (that is, to ask about the Bible), but we should keep in mind that Sterne refers to more than one thousand passages of Scripture in his sermons, and editors of the fiction have discovered hundreds of biblical allusions and quotations.[33] There are many more to discover, including in the marbled page a seemingly loud echo of Matthew 23:27, where Christ chastises the Tartuffes of the world via a memorable simile: "Woe unto you, scribes and Pharisees, hypocrites! for ye are like unto whited sepulchers, which indeed appear beautiful outward, but are within full of dead men's bones, and of all uncleanness." This is the sixth of Christ's seven woes against impostures, and the one most relevant to Tristram's undecorated, dappled, piebald marble: Tristram's sepulcher, and Sterne's. In the same way that Shakespeare literalizes on stage the memento mori of Yorick, Sterne literalizes his and Tristram's tome as a tomb (that is, marble/marbling), thus making *The Life and Opinions* the world's longest epitaph. That *tome* and *tomb* are homonyms in early modern England simply intensifies the spectacular visual pun of the marble, which functions as part of Tristram's larger tomb motif, from "the tomb stone of Lucian" (3.19.225) to the "*tomb of the lovers*" (7.31.629), and all the graveyards and all the "alas, poor *Yoricks*" in between. "To what end are such great tomes [tombs]?," asks Robert Burton in *The Anatomy of Melancholy*.[34] Sterne poses the same question and implies a humble answer via the marble's raw presentation. Sterne knew that he—like all of humanity—was full of uncleanness, what the Calvinists call absolute depravity and others call original sin, the inheritance of ash going all the way back to the Old Serpent. But rather than deploring the human condition or masking it (as he believed that critics of volumes 1–2 would have preferred),[35] Sterne examines it, providing a Momus window of sorts through which we might view "the soul stark naked," or at least more naked than most souls we view (1.23.82). By writing such an ironic and confessional epitaph, Sterne, of course, makes quite impossible for himself the sort of saccharine epitaph that Pope satirizes in the *Dunciad*, "the Sepulchral lies, our holy walls to grace"; or that Matthew Prior earlier satirized with Bishop Matthew Parker in mind, a man who took great care while alive to see that all aspects of his grave were properly managed:

> Then take Matt's word for it, the sculptor is paid,
>   That the figure is fine pray believe your own eye,
> Yet credit but lightly what more may be said,
>   For we flatter ourselves and teach marble to lie.[36]

Critics might say what they will about Sterne's infidelities, his sentimental and not-so-sentimental romances, but he does not hide behind a whited sepulcher. He does not teach his marble to lie.

The blank page on which we are to imagine the Widow Wadman contains more than enough demonry to fill it, but critics have focused on other matters. The most persistent type of claim about the page is summarized by Peter de Voogd, who describes it as "witness to the impossibility of perfect communication in language"—but that can be said about almost every word and object in *Tristram Shandy*.[37] In a more whimsical direction, Elizabeth Harries calls the blankness "aesthetic foolery," an extreme instance of the *non finito*.[38] It might very well be, but it is also more than that. Here is how C.A. Patrides characterizes the blank pages in Hartmann Schedel's *Nurnberg Chronicle* (1493):

> The Nurnberger Chronik follows the traditional pattern, commencing with the creation and dividing history into Six Ages. There follows a description of the Last Judgment with appropriately terrifying illustrations ingeniously introduced by six folio pages left totally blank. This very blankness constitutes an obvious invitation to readers to take inventory of their lives before the horrid end.[39]

Sterne's blank page functions in almost exactly the same way, inviting us to take a moral inventory of our lives. It does so, however, with mischievous mirth. Patrides's "horrid end" mutes precisely that type of cosmic laughter invoked by Sterne's dark wit.

And the standard by which we are to take this inventory is part of the black comedy: "Sit down, Sir, paint her to your own mind——as like your mistress as you can——as unlike your wife as your conscience will let you" (5.38.566). Conscience is the proposed yardstick, and this should immediately cause disquiet, given Yorick's insightful sermon on the subject (2.17.142–64) and Tristram's earlier remark—pointed with a manicule—about the dangers of carrying around personal measuring sticks: "A dwarf who brings a standard along with him to measure his own size—take my word, is a dwarf in more articles than one" (4.25.375), which is both a bawdy comment and simultaneously an indictment of spiritual pride.[40] Humorously, yet with serious intent, Sterne also quietly alludes to another standard by which we might take inventory of our mental lives, Matthew 5:27–28, where Christ memorably redefines adultery: "Ye have heard that it was said by them of old time, Thou shalt not commit adultery: But I say unto you, That whosoever looketh on a woman to lust after her hath committed adultery with her already in his heart." Seldom is this scriptural verse read in a comic context, but Sterne's literary universe functions by an unexpected set of rules. Tolstoy's does not. He fretted over this biblical passage, used it as the epigraph for *The Kreutzer Sonata* (1889), and argued for celibacy.[41] Sterne reaches no such conclusion, but provides in his sermons deeper insight into the blank page's dilemma. In "The House of Feasting and the House of Mourning," for example, we hear that "in those loose and unguarded moments the imagination is not always at command—in spite of reason and reflection, it will forcibly carry [us] sometimes whither [we] would not—like the unclean spirit, in the parent's sad description of his child's case, which took him, and at times cast him into the fire to destroy him" (*Sermons*, 4:16).[42] That is, the demonic imagination takes on a life of its own and is oftentimes difficult to stop, until we are in the middle of the woods with demon lovers. A second example: in the apocalyptic "Description of the World" sermon, after referring to 2 Peter 3:10 and 1 Thessalonians 5:2 (the thief-in-the-night verses), Sterne remarks, "[W]e are standing upon the edge of a precipice, with nothing but the single thread of human life to hold us up;—and that if we fall unprepared in this thoughtless state, we are lost, and must perish for evermore" (*Sermons*, 4:290).[43] In short, we are wise to be mindful of how we arrange our mental lives, which—in essence—is the sermonic point of the blank page.

Dante said that the most sensitive readers of *The Divine Comedy* were those who regularly read the Bible and the Church Fathers. I believe him, insofar as authors can be trusted to say anything intelligent about how to read their works. A similar type of claim may be made for *Tristram Shandy*, if by "sensitive readers" we mean those interested in the work's nuances, inevitably present when a traditional Anglican priest like Sterne, the Bible and Prayer Book on the tip of his tongue, writes a satire so obviously ironic and layered, and, as he labeled it, wise, if only readers would allow it to be (*Letters*, 8:645–49).[44] At the end of his "Preface" to the *Notes on the Sermons*, New provocatively addresses this topic of reading Sterne's fiction in light of, or in spite of, his theology:

> Clearly, [Sterne] might have written *Tristram Shandy* without thinking very much about his Christian beliefs; as suggested, one fundamental insight of his religion is that people rarely live by their faith. Still, it might behoove readers of *Tristram* and *A Sentimental Journey* to entertain, at least for one moment, the possibility that the author of these fictions did not consistently hold beliefs that the author of the sermons would consider heretical, damnable, and quite simply wrong. In that moment of vacillation and oscillation, our own and Sterne's, we might discover an entirely different fiction from the one we thought we were reading. (xx)

The second suggestion of New's statement certainly rings true—the part about Sterne as a self-conscious religious author. But the first suggestion, clearly offered with ironic intent, the idea that Sterne might have ignored his Christianity while writing *Tristram*, seems untenable, given the sheer number of scriptural allusions and theological motifs in the satire, starting with the Devil's key role as arch nemesis. Indeed, the work overflows with well-crafted spiritual themes, so many, in fact, that it is difficult not to hear Sterne the priest underneath the harlequin's coat. The burden of proof in this case falls heavily on the shoulders of those who try to dissociate *Tristram Shandy* from the world of Christian literature, where it naturally belongs, alongside *In Praise of Folly* and *Tale of a Tub*. We should therefore, without qualifiers and caveats, phrase questions about Sterne's Christian narrative strategies, Christian rhetorical techniques, and Christian satirical impulses: a Christian Sterne, much as we read a Christian Fielding or a Christian Richardson. The alternative, Sterne the pagan who disguised himself as a sometimes fretful, sometimes triumphant Anglican priest, makes too little sense.

 The Devil believes in *Tristram Shandy*'s critics, even if *Tristram Shandy*'s critics do not believe in him. I think it fair to say that most do not, probably to the detriment of studying the book's ontological-existential aura. More to the present point, Sterne believed in the Devil and wrote a satire accordingly, defending authentic Christianity, grace-filled Christianity, against various manifestations of the demonic, but especially the pretense and prudery that comes with self-righteousness. *Tristram Shandy* is a counterstatement to Hell's gravity. It is an informal exorcism ritual designed—successfully—to laugh away the foul fiend, the proud spirit who cannot endure to be mocked.

NOTES

1. Sterne, *Tristram Shandy*, 1.19.62. All citations to Sterne's works are from *The Florida Edition of the Works of Laurence Sterne* (Gainesville: University Press of Florida, 1978–2009).
2. Anon., "Attack on Sterne and the Methodists," in *The Critical Heritage*, ed. Alan B. Howes (New York: Routledge, 1974): "The profane history of *Tristram Shandy* is as it were anti-gospel, and seems to have been penned by the hand of Antichrist himself" (100).
3. "Sterne," in the *Literary Remains of Samuel Taylor Coleridge*, ed. Henry Nelson Coleridge (London: Pickering, 1836), 1:141.
4. Richard Griffith, "Sterne's Appeal to Pit, Box, and Gallery," in *The Critical Heritage*, ed. Alan B. Howes (New York: Routledge, 1974), 142.
5. Lennard Davis finds that "demonic possession was legally banned"; it is more difficult to prohibit possession. *Obsession, A History* (Chicago: University of Chicago Press, 2008), 13.
6. Ryan Stark, *Rhetoric, Science, and Magic in Seventeenth-Century England* (Washington, DC: Catholic University of America Press, 2009), 28.
7. Hobbes, *Leviathan*, ed. C.B. MacPherson (1968; rpt. London: Penguin, 1985), 114.
8. Boswell, *Private Papers of James Boswell*, ed. Geoffrey Scott and Frederick Pottle (n.p., 1932), 15:299, cited in Keith Thomas, *The Ends of Life* (Oxford: Oxford University Press, 2009), 232.
9. See Jack Lynch, "Reading and Misreading the Genres of Sterne's Sermons," in *Divine Rhetoric*, ed. W.B. Gerard (Newark: University of Delaware Press, 2010), 84.
10. Whiston, *An Account of the Daemoniacks, and of the Power of Casting Out Daemons* (London, 1737), 74.
11. Browne, *Religio Medici* (London, 1642), 57.
12. Arthur Cash, *Laurence Sterne: The Later Years* (London: Methuen, 1986), 105–6. Cash translates Sterne's letter, which is written in Latin.
13. Elizabeth Kraft suggests that "Sterne's own narrative preference, of course, is to give in to the devils" (*Laurence Sterne Revisited* [New York: Twayne, 1996], 74). I would phrase it differently.
14. "Tartarus" appears in the Septuagint: Job 40:20 and 41:21. The Greek verb *kata-tartaroo* ("throw down to Tartarus") appears in 2 Peter 2:4.
15. New, "Laurence Sterne," in the *Cambridge Companion to English Novelists*, ed. Adrian Poole (Cambridge: Cambridge University Press, 2009), 74. See also Sterne's sermon on pride: "Survey yourselves, my dear Christians, a few moments in this light—behold a disobedient, ungrateful, intractable and disorderly set of creatures, going wrong seven times in a day" (*Sermons*, 4.232); cf. Proverbs 24:16: "For a just man falleth seven times, and riseth up again."
16. "Beelzebub," an onomatopoetic name, literally translates as "Lord of the Flies," and in Christian terms is one of Hell's princes (e.g., see *Pilgrim's Progress, Paradise Lost*). See also *Notes to Tristram Shandy*, 3:438.
17. See Pierre Batiffol, "Apocatastasis," in the *Catholic Encyclopedia* (New York: Robert Appleton Company, 1907), http://www.newadvent.org/cathen/01599a.htm. Like Catholic theologians, traditional Anglican theologians dismiss the idea of Satan's salvation.
18. Kraft includes the scene in her chronology of important events in Tristram's life, one of three incidents listed for the twenty-year span between 1720 and 1740 (*Laurence Sterne Revisited*, 49).
19. See also Acts 3:19: "Repent ye therefore, and be converted, that your sins may be blotted out, when the times of refreshing shall come from the presence of the Lord."
20. This is an episode that "deserves a chapter to itself," Tristram suggests, "and a devil of a one too" (5.3.418).

21. Judith Hawley notes that Walter often behaves like an automaton. "Tristram Shandy, Learned Wit, and Enlightenment Knowledge," in *Cambridge Companion to Laurence Sterne*, ed. Thomas Keymer (Cambridge: Cambridge University Press, 2009), 36.

22. James Arieti and John Crossett translate "psychrotita" as "false wit," but they clarify the term in their annotations to *On the Sublime* (Lewiston, NY: Edwin Mellen Press, 1985): "Literally, the word means 'coldness,' and is applied to snow, air, and dead things; by extension it is applied to a cold-hearted person, and then to one who is flat, lifeless, insipid" (25). Notably, Tristram rejects "cold conceits" and advises readers to study Longinus (4.10.337). On Sterne's admiration of Longinus, see *Notes to Tristram Shandy*, 3:306–8; *Notes to the Sermons*, 5:417–28.

23. Erasmus, *In Praise of Folly*, 2nd ed., trans. Clarence Miller (New Haven: Yale University Press, 2003), 45–46.

24. Cowper, "Letter to Joseph Hill," in *The Critical Heritage*, ed. Alan B. Howes (New York: Routledge, 1974),173.

25. Luther, *Martin Luther Werke*, 66 vols. (Weimer: Böhlaus, 1883–1966), vol. 40, pt. 3, 59–60. Cited in Debora Shuger, "Foundations of Sacred Rhetoric," *Rhetorical Invention and Religious Inquiry*, ed. Walter Jost and Wendy Olmsted (New Haven: Yale University Press, 2000), 61.

26. See Jeffrey Burton Russell, *The Devil: Perceptions of Evil from Antiquity to Primitive Christianity* (Ithaca, NY: Cornell University Press, 1987), 247; Richard Macksey, "'Alas, Poor Yorick': Sterne Thoughts," *MLN* 98 (1983): 1015; Frank Brady, "*Tristram Shandy*: Sexuality, Morality, and Sensibility," *Eighteenth-Century Studies* 4 (1970): 56. The black page could be read as oblique commentary on 2 Corinthians 3–4, where faith in God lifts the Devil's dark veil and allows us to see clearly.

27. On Sterne's description of Yorick's death as autobiographical, see *Notes to Tristram Shandy*, 3:73–74.

28. Scholars have taken as axiomatic the idea that the black page somberly memorializes Yorick. This interpretation has a long genealogy, as Peter de Voogd shows: "the 1779 Dublin edition of *Tristram Shandy* has placed the phrase 'Alas, poor Yorick!' in the black page, thus turning it into a perfect tombstone" ("*Tristram Shandy* as Aesthetic Object," in *Laurence Sterne's Tristram Shandy: A Casebook*, ed. Thomas Keymer [New York: Oxford University Press, 2006], 111). But Tristram calls the black page a veil, not a tombstone, not a memorial, and he borrows the dark-veil-of-allegory idea from Peter Anthony Motteux's preface to Rabelais's works; see *Notes to Tristram Shandy*, 3:269–70.

29. *James Joyce: Two Decades of Criticism*, ed. Seon Givens (New York: Vanguard Press, 1948), 11–12.

30. Cross, *The Life and Times of Laurence Sterne*, 3rd ed. (New Haven: Yale University Press, 1929), 147.

31. Ferguson, *Reason and Religion* (London, 1675), 308.

32. Maimonides, *The Guide of the Perplexed*, vol. 1, ed. Shlomo Pines (Chicago: University of Chicago Press, 1974), 11–12. Maimonides cites Proverbs 25:11 when explaining allegorical veils, which both Rabelais and Sterne produce and parody.

33. New, preface, in *Notes to the Sermons*, 5:xiii. While casting the Newian Lot (i.e., opening the *Notes to Tristram Shandy* and reading for inspiration), I found Bible verses time and again.

34. Burton, *Anatomy of Melancholy* (New York: NYRB Classics, 2001), 366.

35. We know from the mottoes to volumes 5–6 that the charge of clerical hypocrisy rankled Sterne. The marbled page confronts this charge preemptively with a bit of Scripture aimed directly at the critics of his bawdry, whom Sterne saw as the real hypocrites.

36. *Literary Works of Matthew Prior*, ed. H. Bunker Wright and Monroe K. Spears (Oxford: Oxford University Press, 1959), 409.

37. de Voogd, "Sterne and Visual Culture," in *Cambridge Companion to Laurence Sterne*, 145.

38. Harries, "Sterne's Novels: Gathering up the Fragments," *ELH* 49 (1982): 38.

39. Patrides, *The Grand Design of God: The Literary Form of the Christian View of History* (London: Routledge, 1972), 47.

40. Matthew 7:3: "And why beholdest thou the mote that is in thy brother's eye, but considerest not the beam that is in thine own eye?"

41. Chaucer's Wife of Bath reads Christ's admonition as opening the possibility of divorce and remarriage based on the stipulation of Matthew 5:31–32.

42. Sterne alludes to Mark 9:25–26, where Christ casts out a demon from a boy: "When Jesus saw that the people came running together, he rebuked the foul spirit, saying unto him, I charge thee, come out of him, and enter no more into him. And the spirit cried, and rent him sore, and came out of him." In Mark 16:9, Christ casts seven devils out of Mary Magdalene.

43. I read "perish for evermore" as dramatic hyperbole, but Sterne might have meant it: eternal versus conditional salvation is the issue.

44. On *Tristram Shandy* and genre, see New, *Laurence Sterne as Satirist* (Gainesville: University of Florida Press, 1969). See also Robert Folkinflik, "*Tristram Shandy* and Eighteenth-Century Narrative," in *Cambridge Companion to Laurence Sterne*, 49–63.

Chapter Twelve

Methodists on the Move in *The Spiritual Quixote*

Brett C. McInelly

At the base of a statue of John Wesley that sits in front of the Methodist leader's City Road chapel in London is an inscription that reads, "The world is my parish." The words are Wesley's own and encapsulate his attitude regarding the scope of his ministry. Wesley saw his religious call reaching well beyond the relatively restricted confines of a parish community, and the extent of his travels is impressive. He traveled throughout England, Wales, and Scotland while attending to the societies in his connection, made several excursions to Ireland, and one voyage to the American colonies. Wesley's friend and associate George Whitefield likewise traveled widely, including multiple journeys to America. Both men remained active even in old age—Whitefield died while on a preaching tour in America at the age of 55, and Wesley toured and preached until his death at the age of 87. Both were determined to carry their message of salvation to as many places and people as possible.

Wesley expected this same expansive and relentless activity from his followers, dispatching itinerant preachers throughout Great Britain and America. Early Methodists also circulated within their own communities, visiting the sick, ministering to condemned felons, and attending the class and band meetings requisite for membership in the Methodist societies. Wesley's need for lay ministers similarly ensured that Methodism would provide opportunities for social as well as geographic mobility. Men *and* women from the lower and middle ranks served as band and class leaders, and they even preached, albeit under Wesley's strict supervision. As Paul Chilcote states, "Those who stood on the fringe of English society often found their way to the center of the Wesleyan revival."[1]

219

Activities like itinerant preaching and lay ministry, of course, flew in the face of eighteenth-century social and ecclesiastical convention. Nonetheless, Wesley and his followers overcame their anxieties regarding the propriety of their religious involvement by claiming a spiritual witness, or what Wesley referred to as an "extraordinary call."[2] Regarding the controversial practice of using women preachers, Wesley declared, "God owns them in the conversion of sinners, and who am I that I should withstand God."[3] But what the Methodists perceived as divine sanction, the anti-Methodists labeled enthusiasm. Methodists, they claimed, imagined spiritual motions or impulses. Thus, anti-Methodist writers set out to neutralize the perceived threat of Methodism by attributing Methodist activity to an agitated mental and emotional state. The seeming restless energy that drove Wesley and his followers confirmed such claims, inasmuch as energetic and seemingly immoderate religious involvement could, in the eighteenth century, be interpreted as a symptom of lunacy. In *Observations on the Nature, Kinds, Causes, and Prevention of Insanity, Lunacy, or Madness* (1782), for example, Thomas Arnold classifies enthusiasm as one of the causes of "Pathetic Insanity": "Enthusiasm not only originates, for the most part, from religious *distress*; but is often interrupted by *intervals of depression*, is at best ardent and *restless*; and not infrequently *tumultuous*, and *turbulent*."[4]

Perhaps no anti-Methodist publication connects the irregular activities of the Methodists with the supposedly irregular mental state of the devotee more emphatically than Richard Graves's *The Spiritual Quixote*. Graves, an Anglican clergyman who had firsthand knowledge of the Methodists,[5] was initially goaded into writing the novel by the incursion into his parish of a traveling Methodist preacher; this occurred in 1757, though he would not complete the novel until 1773. While Graves's tone is at times conciliatory and lighthearted, he takes serious aim at the Methodists by detailing the effects of enthusiasm on self and society. Once his mind is agitated by Methodist teachings, the novel's protagonist, Geoffry Wildgoose, abandons an ailing mother and his country estate to pursue the life of a self-appointed traveling preacher. Besides exposing him to emotional and physical harm, Wildgoose's adventures demonstrate the ways Methodism allegedly promoted private and public immorality, along with social and ecclesiastical insubordination, as misguided itinerant preachers zealously propagated unsound theological tenets. Graves effectively counteracts Methodist mobility—whether the rank-and-file's presumption in rising above their station, women neglecting their wifely and maternal duties, or lay preachers sauntering from place to place spreading heretical notions—by associating the movement of Methodists through physical and social space with the irregular motions and impulses of the protagonist's mind. That is, Graves makes the psycho-emotional state of the Methodist believer a matter of public concern and the root of the Methodist problem.

The novel's title, of course, acknowledges Graves's debt to Cervantes, and the novel as a whole "reflects the pervasive influence of Quixotism in the eighteenth-century [English] novel."[6] Graves's more immediate predecessors were Fielding and Smollett. Like *Tom Jones* or *Humphry Clinker*, *The Spiritual Quixote* is episodic, peopled by an array of characters, and digressive, moving alternately between plot and subplot. The targets of Graves's satire likewise include a wide array of people, behaviors, and social institutions. However, unlike Fielding and Smollett, whose critiques of Methodism represent one of many tangents from the main trajectory of their narratives, the main plot in Graves's novel centers on Methodism, and his tangents aim at other targets.[7]

While *The Spiritual Quixote* is generally regarded as a relatively minor novel, it does represent the most sustained literary attack on Methodism in the century, encompassing in its original edition three volumes and nearly one thousand pages. Charles Jarvis Hill refers to *The Spiritual Quixote* as "the literary monument to anti-Methodism."[8] Graves, however, deviates from the tenor of most anti-Methodist publications, which tend to be unequivocal in their contempt for Methodism, by presenting a more qualified portrait of the revival. Indeed, much of the scholarly debate surrounding *The Spiritual Quixote* centers on Graves's seemingly ambivalent attitude toward the movement and its leaders, most notably Whitefield and Wesley, both of whom make appearances in the novel.

Most scholars agree that Graves reserves his harshest commentary for Whitefield, whose florid preaching style, fund-raising activities, and Calvinist leanings aroused suspicion.[9] Frans De Bruyn states, "Graves's low opinion of Whitefield is easily the harshest note he strikes in his critique of Methodism";[10] and Michael Rymer labels Whitefield "the real villain of the novel."[11] Other assessments of Graves's satire emphasize what Susan Auty refers to as the novel's "quiet and gentle style." "The motivating anger at Methodism," she claims, "results not in satire but a slight jest aimed at the sect and a pleasant novel that occasionally mocks Methodist extravagance."[12] Rymer challenges this view, as well as the tendency by critics to read the novel biographically, by approaching *The Spiritual Quixote* as a straightforward attack on Methodism, contending that Graves's genial style subtly contributes to his satiric technique.[13] Other critics account for the novel's seeming ambivalence by claiming that Graves approved of the Methodists' motives but not their methods,[14] or by dissociating Methodist belief from practice. Noting the ways Methodism empowered members of the lower ranks, De Bruyn suggests that "Graves's differences with the Methodists are political rather than theological";[15] and Paul Goring argues that Graves, who presents the Methodists' passionate way of preaching as an antidote to the dispassionate preaching style of most Anglican preachers, asserts that religious reform was "not a matter of theology but rather of the physical presentation of that theology."[16]

There is little doubt that Graves's view of Methodism was more nuanced than most anti-Methodist writers, but characterizing his satire of Methodism as mere "jest" ignores the perspective of early Methodists, the targets of his so-called genial reproof. Graves, after all, characterizes Methodists as enthusiasts, a word with strong negative connotations in the eighteenth century and the most common charge leveled at the Methodists.[17] In its most extreme sense, enthusiasm denoted religious madness and was perceived as a threat to political and social order. As Roy Porter argues, "Methodistical madness struck real fear into the polite and propertied, alarmed lest a popular religion of the heart should foment civil disorders, as in the bad old times of the Civil War."[18] Enthusiasm's more mild definitions included religious whim and "a vain belief of private revelation."[19] From the point of view of individuals firm in their religious convictions, the label of enthusiast cavalierly dismissed the sincerity of those convictions. As Charles Wesley emphatically states in one of his hymns, "Ye prudent fools, be not so proud, / Suspend your idle scorn; / . . . / Ye fain would judges be, / and make us think there is no light / Because you cannot see."[20]

As to separating theology from practice, Graves may at times be more critical of one than the other, as De Bruyn and Goring argue, but Graves simultaneously acknowledges throughout the novel that Methodist theology naturally informed religious practice and that in criticizing one, we criticize the other. The key to understanding *The Spiritual Quixote*'s treatment of Methodism, I would suggest, is to recognize the comprehensive nature of Graves's critique. Wildgoose's irregular behavior in religious matters is motivated by a mind corrupted by fallacious doctrine. Though Graves's tone may not be quite as vitriolic as that of many of his contemporaries, his novel touches on all the conventional charges leveled at Methodists in the anti-Methodist literature; there are personal attacks on Whitefield, and to a lesser degree Wesley, and a pervasive satiric treatment of Methodist polity *and* doctrine, from lay preaching to salvation by faith alone. It is on these grounds that we can declare *The Spiritual Quixote* "the literary monument to anti-Methodism." As Hill states, "In no other publication of the kind have the errors of that particular species of enthusiasm been so extensively . . . played upon."[21]

Of all the "errors" Graves identifies, he is most unequivocal in condemning itinerant preaching. As the putative "editor" states in the preface, "But they are the practices of their itinerant preachers, rather than the general principles of the people in question, which [the author] thinks exceptionable."[22] Despite Wildgoose's best intentions, his rambling tour is portrayed as nothing more than a "wild goose chase," and Graves characterizes his undertaking as both unnecessary and illogical: "our modern itinerant reformers . . . are planting the gospel in a Christian country" (40).

Graves makes clear, however, that the senselessness of Wildgoose's "ramble" is precipitated and then paralleled by the equally senseless spiritual musings that ultimately motivate his itinerancy. Following a disagreement with the local minister, in which he is publicly embarrassed, Wildgoose falls into a state of melancholy and turns his attention to "a miscellaneous collection of godly discourses, upon predestination; election, and reprobation; justification by faith; grace and free-will, and the like controverted points of divinity." Wildgoose finds satisfaction in such "trash" because these works include "bitter invectives against the regular clergy, and the established church" (19). Corrupted by such doctrinal disputes, he sets out to rouse the negligent clergy and revive primitive Christianity, an undertaking as foolish as the *new* doctrines he is now ready to believe and propagate.

Wildgoose justifies his ministry on the same grounds Wesley justified lay preaching: that is, he does not believe that people have the "right to break through the restraints of society," *except* in the event of "extraordinary occasions" (377), in this instance, the inward motions of the spirit that hasten his preaching tour. Wildgoose's language, of course, reiterates Wesley's belief in an "extraordinary call" and indicates that Graves's critique centers on perhaps the most fundamental feature of Methodist religiosity—the spiritual witness that confirmed Methodists in their faith and justified unconventional religious practice.

Indeed, the anti-Methodists scrutinized the viability of the "extraordinary call" from the outset of the revival. In one of the most well-known anti-Methodist tracts produced during the eighteenth century, *The Nature, Folly, Sin and Danger of Being Righteous Over-much* (1739), Joseph Trapp explains, "By *enthusiasm* is meant a Person's having a strong, but false Persuasion, that he is *divinely inspired*; or at least, that he has *the Spirit* of God *some* way or *other*; and This made known to him in a *particular* and *extraordinary* Manner." Modern enthusiasts, Trapp contends, "*make void* Reason *through* Christianity," and he claims that enthusiasm in religion necessitates "dethroning the higher Power of the Soul, *Judgment*; and setting up the lower Faculty, *Fancy*, or *Imagination*, in its room." What most vexes Trapp is that Methodists offer no "*Evidence*" or "*Proof*" to validate a supernatural witness.[23]

In his well-publicized response to Trapp, Whitefield raises the obvious question: "*What Proof do they give?* Says the Writer: What Sign would they have?" Whitefield goes on to argue, "This Writer . . . tells us, it is against *Common-Sense to talk of the Feelings of the Spirit of God*: Common-Sense . . . was never allow'd to be a Judge yet; it is above its Comprehension, neither are, nor can the Ways of God be known by Common-Sense." The spirit of God, Whitefield insists, must be felt: "Religion consists not in external Performance, it must be in the heart."[24] For Trapp, then, an extraordinary call defies reason; for Whitefield, religious experience occurs outside the scope of rational inquiry. What becomes clear when surveying their exchange is that both men ground their arguments in two competing epistemologies and that neither Trapp nor Whitefield would ever be able to offer "evidence" that met the demands of the other's conceptual system.

Nonetheless, the debate between Trapp and Whitefield illustrates a more salient point: anti-Methodists vied with Methodists over the interpretation of their religious experiences. Both parties describe an internal shift or movement of the Methodists' faculties that precipitates precisely the physical movement through geographic space and across social boundaries that characterizes evangelical activity. Moreover, both groups were acutely aware of the ways participation in the revival defied social convention. Many Methodists were themselves reluctant to pursue a public ministry but could not resist the call to an active Christian life. Regarding her anxieties about public preaching, one Methodist woman claimed, "I had rather be obscure. But I dare not."[25] The anti-Methodists agreed that the Methodists experienced inward motions, though they chose to credit those motions to unholy sources, such as the devil, or to a disturbed mental state.

Since the idea of an extraordinary call defied reason, and since some Methodists expressed their religious convictions in highly emotional ways, critics could, naturally enough, diagnose Methodists as enthusiasts and madmen. As Porter observes, "In common parlance, people were typically called 'mad' when impassioned beyond moderation and 'reason.'"[26] Foucault similarly argues in *Madness and Civilization* (1965) that unreason in the eighteenth century was generally associated with madness, a move that effectively silenced seemingly irrational expressions.[27] While later historians have challenged Foucault's claim that madness was subjected to a rigorous physical confinement during the period, forms of behavior that ran counter to nature and reason were effectively relegated, if not to an asylum, at least to the periphery of eighteenth-century society. Graves and other anti-Methodist writers effectively confined the Methodists, at least symbolically, by portraying them as devoid of reason and common sense. Graves, however, is careful to suggest that Wildgoose is only mad in religion; in all other matters, he represents one of the most sensible of Graves's characters, a point that serves as a stinging indictment of Methodism, since its doctrines turn the brain of an otherwise reasonable man.

Whether some Methodists actually experienced madness as a result of their religious convictions[28] is less important than what was ultimately at stake. When assessing the anti-Methodist literature, it becomes clear that the most contested feature of the revival was the psycho-emotional state of the believer, since every other aspect of the movement—whether itinerant preaching, social insubordination, or the spread of supposedly heretical doctrines—was inevitably rooted in the extraordinary call. To some extent, the Methodists themselves invited scrutiny of their mental and emotional faculties by insisting on a deeply personal kind of religious experience, beginning with the New Birth. Wesley and Whitefield both preached the absolute necessity of a spiritual rebirth as the gateway to a Christian life and salvation. Before experiencing this New Birth, Wesley claims, a person "is a dead Christian," having "no knowledge of God, no intercourse with him," and he insists, as did Whitefield, that such knowledge cannot be acquired through one's physical senses. Rather, when a person is born again, "he feels, is inwardly sensible of, the graces which the Spirit of God works in his heart."[29] In making internal experience the essential mark of the Christian life, and religious activity a manifestation of that experience, Wesley and Whitefield inadvertently made the inner life of the believer the central target of anti-Methodist literature in general, Graves's novel in particular.

Citing the Methodists' "restless impatience and insatiable thirst of *Travelling*" and their "*Spirit of rambling*," George Lavington, in *The Enthusiasm of Methodists and Papists Compar'd* (1749), claims that "this only shews the natural *unsettled* humour, the rapid motion of *Enthusiastic* heads."[30] Both Graves and Lavington deploy spatial metaphors to describe the Methodists' shifting mental state—the mind is "moved" or "transported" by enthusiasm. Methodism, Graves writes, "quite unsettled Mr. Geoffry's mind; and filled his head with such a farraginous medley of opinions, as almost turned his brain" (20). Moreover, Cervantes provides in the form of the Quixote figure the perfect model to link Wildgoose's "Summer's Ramble" to a mind transported from sanity to the threshold of insanity, at least in religious matters. Once Wildgoose's "fancy became entirely possessed with . . . enthusiastic ideas," he sets out "like a true 'Spiritual Quixote' . . . in imitation of Mr. Whitefield and his associates . . . by turning missionary; and publishing his religious notions in every part of the kingdom" (29). Tugwell, the Sancho Panza of the novel, likewise is "worked up to a pitch of Spiritual Quixotism; and grew impatient to set out" on their adventures (39). Graves and Lavington suggest that checking the Methodists' "insatiable thirst" for spiritual adventures requires that they be diagnosed, labeled, and treated for mental derangement, a process eventually realized in Graves's novel.

Graves emphasizes the link between Wildgoose's mental state and the senseless futility of his undertaking by satisfying Wildgoose's masochistic desire to be persecuted for the gospel's sake, the only intended outcome of his preaching tour realized in the novel: "Mr. Wildgoose was ambitious of emulating . . . [the] spiritual adventures [of the early Reformers], and even burnt with zeal to imitate them in their sufferings; and wished for nothing so much as to be persecuted for the sake of his religion" (29). Christians, at least since Pauline times, have interpreted persecution as a sign of divine commission, and many early Methodists interpreted anti-Methodist hostility in such terms. "Grant, Dearest Redeemer," a Methodist proclaimed to a fellow believer, "that we may rejoice when we are counted worthy to suffer shame for thy sake."[31] But Graves and other anti-Methodists portray such desires as evidence of religious enthusiasm, inasmuch as Methodist suffering is both relished and self-inflicted. As Lavington writes, "That when *Enthusiasm* comes in . . . and Men fancy they are upon *God's work*, and entitled to his *rewards*; they are immediately all on fire for rushing into sufferings and pain; and *sorrow is turned into joy before them*."[32] Each instance of persecution, including the blow to Wildgoose's head that precipitates his "cure," confirms Wildgoose in the righteousness of his cause, while simultaneously demonstrating the absurd and reckless nature of his endeavors. While Wildgoose's preaching fails in every case to produce its desired effect—the conversion of sinners—he nearly always encounters the hostility of an unreceptive audience, and he is anxious "when . . . persecuted in *one City*," as Lavington observes of enthusiasts, "[to] fly unto another."[33]

Besides threats to Wildgoose's wellbeing, Graves indicates that his protagonist's zealous undertaking "would necessarily be productive of disorder and confusion" in British society (377). Graves is particularly concerned with the spread of antinomianism resulting from untrained laypersons preaching faith to the exclusion of works. Though neither Whitefield nor Wesley approved of antinomianism, and despite their disagreement regarding works righteousness, they both insisted on faith as the principal requirement for salvation. Graves and others, however, worried that such an emphasis could warp in the minds of lay preachers and naïve devotees. Wildgoose becomes so fixated on faith that he develops "contempt for . . . formal devotions and good works." He explains that "a man might fast and pray, and give all his goods to feed the poor; and yet not have true Christian *charity*, or what Saint Paul calls Faith working by Love" (351–52).

In denigrating works not motivated by faith, Wildgoose concurs with, though in a perversely exaggerated form, an attitude propagated in the Methodist literature. Whitefield, in fact, refers to good works as "filthy Rags," claiming that "*you are justified before God, without any respect to your Works past, present or to come.*"[34] Even Wesley, who espoused the necessity of works righteousness, contends that "'works done before justification are not good,' in the Christian sense, 'forasmuch as they spring not of faith in Jesus Christ. . . . [Y]ea, rather for that they are not done as God hath willed and commanded them to be done, we doubt not' (how strange soever it may appear to some) 'but they have the nature of sin.'"[35] Although Whitefield and Wesley intended, in all likelihood, only to emphasize the centrality of faith in a Christian life and to give credit to God for an individual's righteousness, they so often articulated a disparaging attitude toward virtuous conduct not motivated by faith that their statements easily devolved into outright antipathy for good works in the minds of their antagonists—and in Wildgoose's enthusiastic mind, as well.

Because of his contempt for good works, Wildgoose, along with other Methodists he encounters on his journey, justify obvious cases of immorality and unlawfulness. In a motif made popular by Samuel Foote's *The Minor* (1760), Wildgoose meets a Mrs. Placket, who, like Foote's Mrs. Cole, shamelessly keeps a brothel while professing to be a devout Methodist: "I make my poor Lambs read the Bible every Sunday, and go to church in their turn; and, in short, though their bodies may be polluted, I take great care of their souls" (256). Wildgoose later observes that the Barber he leaves in charge of his society at Gloucester "was still in a state of Grace," although his circumstances cause him to turn highwayman (319). Of course, neither Wesley nor Whitefield would have condoned prostitution or robbery, and most Methodists were far from being antinomians. But Graves effectively discredits the doctrine of faith without works as well as the means by which it was promulgated—itinerant preaching—by exaggerating the lengths to which the doctrine might be taken in an enthusiast's mind.

Graves registers his particular concern regarding the Calvinist leanings of many Methodists, most notably Whitefield. The movement, in fact, splintered in 1739 when Wesley published his sermon on *Free Grace*, in which he denounced the doctrines of predestination and election, and Whitefield responded by advocating a pro-Calvinist view.[36] Though the two men remained friends, they never reconciled their theological differences, and the Methodist societies split along Arminian and Calvinist lines. Like Wesley, Graves worried that the doctrine of election promoted arrogance among "the Elect" and an indifferent attitude toward good works. Thus in the novel, we are told regarding one profligate preacher: "One Roger Ball asserted, 'that the Elect had a right to all women'" (451). Lyons suggests that Graves reserves his sharpest commentary for Whitefield because, unlike Wesley, who was a gentleman, Whitefield was a "social upstart."[37] I would suggest, instead, that doctrine, not social status, accounts for the severity of the satire directed at Whitefield. Graves detested the Calvinist doctrines Whitefield espoused.[38]

Whitefield's manner of preaching, coupled with such doctrines, might even nudge his followers into other moral quandaries. When Graves tells the reader that Wildgoose "had thoroughly imbibed [the Methodists'] manner and style of eloquence, which consists chiefly in a figurative application of the most luscious expressions and sensual ideas to spiritual subjects" (74), he refers to a style of preaching made famous, or infamous, by Whitefield. In his sermon *Christ the Best Husband*, Whitefield characterizes the relationship between Christ and the believer as a relationship between lovers. Although there is biblical precedent for the metaphor—Christ refers to himself as the bridegroom (Matthew 25:1)—Whitefield's language pushes the comparison to uncomfortable extremes, at least in the minds of some contemporaries, including Graves. In what probably appeared more like a love letter than a sermon to some, Whitefield explains how "your souls pant and long for [Christ]"; he goes on to admonish believers to "embrace Christ in the arms of your dearest love."[39] Such language effectively sexualizes spirituality,[40] and we should not be surprised that Graves and other critics accused Methodists of confusing sexual and spiritual feelings.[41]

In addition to the commonplace charge that Methodist preachers use their rhetorical gifts to seduce female converts (283–84), Graves intimates that Methodists, when worked into an enthusiastic state, are particularly susceptible to sexual indiscretion. The meetings of one Methodist society are described in language laden with sexual innuendo, thus intimating that more than spiritual communion is transacted among believers at Methodist gatherings:

> [W]e have such *soul-searching* teachers! Such *ravishing* ministers! They come so close to the point; and does so *grapple* with the sinner! They probe his sores to the very quick; and *pour in such comfortable balsam*! And (as Twangdillo told us last night) though it may pain; yet, like physics in the bowels, it pains us to some purpose;—and, to be sure, as he said, Conversion follows Conviction, as naturally as Thread does the Needle. (142–43)

Anti-Methodists were particularly suspicious of Methodist watch-night services and love feasts, meetings generally held well after dark. As Graves writes, the parents of a Methodist girl "did not approve of those late nocturnal vigils, which were frequently solemnized by the warmer devotees" (294). Again, the innuendo is unmistakable, Graves strongly implying that enthusiasm warms both the spiritual and sexual passions, and that the same spiritual motions or impulses propelling a person on an aimless preaching tour well might lead that person down a path of sexual transgression.

This path, Graves indicates, also leads to social confusion. As a gentleman-turned-preacher, Wildgoose is an inversion of the stereotypical itinerant preacher who rises from the lower and middle ranks to presumptuously preach without the proper authority. As Graves explains, these preachers "who, with a view of raising themselves above their fellow-plebeians, without any other apparatus than a long cravat and a demure pertness of countenance, together with a little common-place jargon (picked up from their weekly assemblies), forsake their lawful callings, and commence reformers and teachers of their brethren" (31). The mobility encouraged by Methodism, through preaching or mere participation in the societies, allegedly lured people from their respective and proper places, resulting in an unproductive and chaotic social scene. When hearing that Wildgoose intends to preach, an old Taylor leaped nimbly off his board; and, leaving a suit of cloaths which he had promised to finish that evening . . . immediately ran and communicated this intelligence to a Blacksmith, his next neighbor, who leaves the Farmer's horses half-shoed, and with like speed acquaints the Farmer's wife, who . . . leaves her cows unmilked, and her child dangerously ill in the cradle; and, with half a dozen more, who, upon spreading the alarm, had left their several employments, joined the devout cavalcade. (280)

Ironically, Wildgoose, who zealously pursues a calling unsuited to his own circumstances, becomes Graves's spokesperson for a stratified social order. When Tugwell laments the unequal distribution of wealth, and proposes a more balanced socioeconomic system, wherein people throughout the kingdom are given "each an hundred pounds a-year, and no more," Wildgoose responds by suggesting that each man would then have to make his own clothes, grow his own food, and build his own house, since no one would be willing to perform such tasks. Under such a system, "every man must work ten times harder than the poorest man now does." This, Wildgoose concludes, "shews the unavoidable necessity of that inequality amongst mankind" (311). A quack doctor Wildgoose encounters, who is no more qualified to practice medicine than Wildgoose is to preach, makes a similarly ironic observation when condemning Wildgoose for preaching without the proper credentials: "Let the Parson keep to his church; the Farmer to his plough; and the Cobler to his stall" (358). While the hypocritical nature of the doctor's comment certainly creates comic effect, the underlying point is one Graves took quite seriously. As one of Graves's minor characters observes, "I am for proper subordination, and would have people keep to their *ranks* in life" (376).

In addition, Methodism disrupts the domestic order by luring women away from their homes and familial responsibilities. Many contemporaries, in fact, believed that Methodism attracted predominately female followers. William Fleetwood claimed that the majority of Wesley and Whitefield's followers were merely "silly *Women,*"[42] and the ex-Methodist James Lackington observed, "that by far the greatest part of [Wesley's] people are females."[43] In actuality, women did outnumber men by two to one in some Methodist societies. Noting the preponderance of women in early Methodism, David Hempton suggests that Methodism was, in fact, a women's movement.[44] At a time when women were becoming more and more valued for the work they did in the home in propagating religious and moral values,[45] Graves and many of his contemporaries worried that Methodism's appeal to women might disrupt the domestic and, by extension, the social order. The Wednesbury Riots (1743), to which Graves alludes (324), were reportedly caused by a woman who abandoned her husband and children, and was found at a Methodist meeting.[46] Similarly, one of Graves's minor characters explains "that [the Methodists] had *convarted* [*sic*] his wife . . . who used to mind her knitting, and bustle about. . . . But, since these Methodists had come about, and *convarted* her, she minded nothing but reading and praying, and singing Psalms, from morning to night" (361). Graves also suggests that some Methodist men are distracted from their duties as they "run about from one Meeting to another, and take no care of their wives and families at home" (254). Indeed, the only real obstacle to Wildgoose's union with Miss Townsend and domestic tranquility, the happy conclusion to which Graves brings his narrative, is Wildgoose's enthusiasm and rambling spirit.

Graves juxtaposes Methodism's perceived challenge to British domesticity with two paragons of eighteenth-century womanhood, Mrs. Rivers and Mrs. Forester, women who, by diligently attending to their domestic duties, represent the most potent religious forces in the narrative. Graves's depiction of these women represents a trend Ruth Bloch observes in eighteenth-century Anglo-American culture, in which "fictional and religious literature began attributing to women not only a commendable piety but also the primary power to enforce religious and moral standards."[47] When Wildgoose meets Mrs. Rivers for the first time, sitting in her home and surrounded by her children, she is described as "the divinity of the place" (186); Mrs. Forester similarly represents the religious and moral center of the Forester estate and the neighboring community. She refers to her constant concern for her children's physical and spiritual well-being as her "devotion to heaven" (372), and she does not indulge her own private interests until, first, her family's needs are met, and, second, her poor and ailing neighbors are attended to. Both women follow the maxim espoused by the man who affects Wildgoose's cure, Dr. Greville, namely, "to enforce the practice of Religion in [their] own famil[ies], and amongst [their] neighbors" (469). The efficient and consequential effects of these ladies' efforts within a relatively narrow sphere of action contrast with the extensive but aimless and ineffectual nature of Wildgoose's preaching tour.

Graves, then, casts Methodism as a "potentially revolutionary" force that encourages social insubordination and outright rebellion.[48] Such rebellion might take the form of women resisting the authority of their husbands—one man is "deprived of his conjugal claims" because of his wife's involvement in Methodism (296)—or it might manifest itself in political unrest. As Susan Staves suggests, "Graves is particularly anxious to show a connection between the mid-seventeenth century Puritans as rebels and usurpers and the Methodists as political subversives who teach the lower classes contempt for legitimate authority" (199). Indeed, Methodists were regularly compared to Cromwellian Puritans, whose religious zeal fomented revolution and civil war. The puritanical writings that turn Wildgoose's brain, we are told, were written "in the time of Cromwell's usurpation" (19); curiously, Graves also alludes to the 1715 and 1745 Jacobite rebellions (24, 360), both motivated by political *and* religious concerns.

It probably was neither fair nor accurate to suggest that Methodists were political subversives. Wesley in particular held conservative political views and publicly opposed the American Revolution. But fully to appreciate the revolutionary implications of eighteenth-century Methodism as Graves and others perceived it, we should keep in mind that the theology that justified lay ministry and the restless activity of early Methodists was, in fact, revolutionary in nature, not necessarily as politics or theology but in a personal sense to those who took it seriously and acted on spiritual impulses. Spiritual conviction gave these individuals the courage (or "enthusiasm") to transcend restrictive social norms. As one woman claimed of her ministry, "Persecution will not affright me, neither any distress prevent me attending to my duty both to God and my fellow creatures who have a claim upon me."[49] At the same time, it is easy to see how Graves and the anti-Methodists might have felt threatened by Methodist zeal and mobility.

Reining in Wildgoose, and thereby counteracting Methodism, involves not just regulating his movements through the physical and social world, but regulating his thinking, an event brought about by a blow to his head that fittingly brings his preaching tour to an end and leads to his acquaintance with Greville near the end of the novel. Greville encourages a "degree of Enthusiasm" but warns, "I would not have your zeal transport you so far, as to hurry you into any irregularities, which only expose you to danger and ridicule, and can never answer any really useful purpose" (453). Greville, who serves as Graves's mouthpiece in the novel, establishes the normative values of *The Spiritual Quixote* by advocating moderation in all things, particularly in religious matters; and eighteenth-century Methodism, in many ways, was anything but a moderate religion. In addition to emphasizing extraordinary religious experience and demanding relentless activity on the part of its members, Methodist practice encouraged its followers to live lives of disciplined—perhaps excessive—sobriety. Some Methodists thus accepted the possibility that devotees might have to forsake family and friends for Christ's sake. Wesley even advocated celibacy, fearing that love for one's spouse might surpass one's love for God.[50] In the eighteenth century, merely living what Wesley and other Methodist preachers taught could land the pious devotee in a madhouse. Whitefield records in his journal the circumstances under which one man was committed: "I . . . went and talked with his sister, who gave me the three following Symptoms of his being mad. *First*, That he fasted for near a Fortnight. *Secondly*, That he prayed so as to be heard four Story high. *Thirdly*, That he had sold his Cloaths, and given them to the Poor." Whitefield goes on to explain that the man sold his clothes after reading in the Bible that Christ had instructed a man to do likewise.[51] "To Georgian churchmen this was crazy," Porter explains, "once it would have been holy."[52] While this episode represents an extreme case, less fanatical kinds of behavior appeared equally immoderate to many outside observers.

While Wildgoose abandons an ailing mother, believing that true faith requires him to shun family commitments for God's sake, Greville explains "that no doctrine, no religious opinion, can be true, that contradicts the tenderest feelings of human nature, the affection and duty which we owe to our parents" (448). Greville is similarly critical of the Methodists' means of rousing a supposedly negligent clergy. He acknowledges that some among them may be remiss in fulfilling their duties, but he asks, "Does this warrant every ignorant Mechanic to take the staff out of the hands of the Clergy, and set up for Reformers in Religion?" (450). Regarding itinerant preaching, Greville admires the devotion that undergirds the desire to preach, but suggests that this too is an extreme and potentially harmful form of religious expression. He concurs that Christians have "a divine call . . . to revive the practice of true Christianity," but only "within the sphere of their own neighbourhood." "No one," Greville argues further, "has a right to break through the regulations of society, merely from the suggestions of his own fancy, and unless he can give some visible proof of a supernatural commission" (449).

Ironically, Wildgoose advocates a similar kind of moderation while narrating "the particulars of Sir William K_____'s unhappy affair" (397). While the story is delivered in casual conversation, it represents Wildgoose's best sermon. As one listener observes, "We are obliged to the Gentleman for his story—and for a sermon into the bargain" (402). The "sermon" details a sexual liaison that destroys a man and his marriage and, according to Wildgoose, demonstrates "the dreadful consequences of irregular indulgences" (397). While Wildgoose refers specifically to sexual indulgences, it is clear at this point in the novel that his own irregular indulgences are likely to produce their own dreadful consequences. Thus, Wildgoose's best sermon indirectly, and ironically, condemns his religious ramblings, and represents the most pointed instance in the narrative when Wildgoose talks sense.[53]

As a clergyman himself, Graves appreciated and accepted sincere Methodist devotion, but like so many of his contemporaries, he worried that even sensible people might fall prey to Methodist enthusiasm. Once moved by the spirit, early Methodists were compelled to action and moved through physical and social space with relative fluidity. And since the Methodists justified themselves by claiming an extraordinary call, the anti-Methodist literature inevitably went to the core of the Methodists themselves, namely the mental and emotional states of those who responded to the call. An experience that was intensely private thus became a matter of public concern when it was externalized through itinerant preaching and other public activities. For early Methodists, the consequences of responding to a divine calling were clear: damned if you do, damned if you don't, as both the anti-Methodists and God contended for the Methodist's mind and soul. While Graves was perhaps not as mean-spirited in his treatment of Methodism as some of his contemporaries, he was certainly as thorough, if not more so, in portraying Methodist beliefs and practices, and the psycho-emotional state behind them—at least to the extent of his own perception of their erroneous ways.

NOTES

1. Paul W. Chilcote, *She Offered Them Christ: The Legacy of Women Preachers in Early Methodism* (Eugene, OR: Wipf and Stock, 1993), 34. See also 22.
2. See John Wesley, Letter XLV, *The Works of the Reverend John Wesley* (New York: B. Waugh and T. Mason, 1835), 6:656.
3. Zechariah Taft, *Biographical Sketches of the Lives and Public Ministry of Various Holy Women* (Leeds: H. Cullingworth, 1828), 1:ii–iii.
4. Thomas Arnold, *Observations on the Nature, Kinds, Causes, and Prevention of Insanity, Lunacy, or Madness* (Leicester: G. Ireland, 1782), 235 and 236–37.
5. Besides the run-in with the Methodist preacher that provoked Graves into writing his novel, Graves became acquainted in the mid-1730s with members of the Oxford "Holy Club," which sparked the Methodist movement. He may have even been a fringe member of that group with his brother, Morgan. He did know and interact with Charles Wesley. Charles Casper Graves, another brother, actually became a Methodist preacher and eventually experienced a mental breakdown as a result of his intense religious feelings, and some scholars have speculated that Wildgoose is, at least in part, modeled after Charles Casper. See Clarence Tracy, *A Portrait of Richard Graves* (Toronto: University of Toronto Press, 1987), 40–47.
6. Frans De Bruyn, "Richard Graves," *Dictionary of Literary Biography*, vol. 39, ed. Martin C. Battestin (Detroit, MI: Gale Research Company, 1985), 240.
7. Charles Jarvis Hill also notes Sterne's influence on Graves; see "The Literary Career of Richard Graves," *Smith College Studies in Modern Languages* 16, nos. 1–3 (1935): 46.
8. Hill, "The Literary Career of Richard Graves," 16.
9. Whitefield was, in fact, the recipient of the most cutting of anti-Methodist attacks. See Albert M. Lyles, *Methodism Mocked: The Satiric Reaction to Methodism in the Eighteenth Century* (London: Epworth Press, 1960), 127.
10. De Bruyn, "Richard Graves," 243.
11. Michael Rymer, "Satiric Technique in *The Spiritual Quixote*," *Durham University Journal* 34 (1973): 62. See also Hill, "The Literary Career of Richard Graves," 23.
12. Susan G. Auty, *The Comic Spirit of Eighteenth-Century Novels* (Port Washington, NY: Kennikat Press, 1975), 87–88. See also Tracy, *A Portrait of Richard Graves*, 136.
13. Rymer, "Satiric Technique in *The Spiritual Quixote*," 56. Nicholas Lyons challenges Rymer's claim, in part, by invoking biographical data. See Nicholas Lyons, "Satiric Technique in *The Spiritual Quixote*: Some Comments," *Durham University Journal* 35 (1974): 266–77. See also Hill, "The Literary Career of Richard Graves," and Tracy, *A Portrait of Richard Graves*, for biographical readings.
14. Hill, "The Literary Career of Richard Graves," 35.
15. De Bruyn, "Richard Graves," 244.
16. Paul Goring, "Anglicanism, Enthusiasm, and Quixotism: Preaching and Politeness in Mid-Eighteenth Century Literature," *Literature and Theology* 15 (December 2001): 338.
17. Of course, poets like William Collins and James Thomson applied the term in a more positive sense in relation to poetic expressions, anticipating Romantic sensibilities, but enthusiasm, at least when applied in religious contexts, continued to include primarily negative associations throughout the eighteenth century.
18. Roy Porter, *Madmen: A Social History of Madhouses, Mad-Doctors, and Lunatics* (Stroud, UK: Tempus, 2004), 86.
19. Samuel Johnson, *A Dictionary of the English Language* (1755).

20. John Wesley, Preface to *A Collection of Hymns for the Use of the People called Methodists*, in *The Works of John Wesley*, ed. Franz Hilderbrandt and Oliver A. Beckerlegge (Nashville: Abingdon Press, 1983), 7:198.

21. Hill, "The Literary Career of Richard Graves," 16.

22. Richard Graves, *The Spiritual Quixote, or the Summer's Ramble of Geoffry Wildgoose*, ed. Clarence Tracy (London: Oxford University Press, 1967), 3. Hereafter cited in text.

23. Joseph Trapp, *The Nature, Folly, Sin, and Danger of Being Righteous Over-much* (London: S. Austen, 1739), 39, 16–17, 43, 41.

24. George Whitefield, *The Folly and Danger of Being Not Righteous Enough* (London: C. Whitefield, 1739), 9–10, 7–8. Wesley did not discount reason entirely. While faith was ultimately produced by feeling, he believed that reason could assist an individual in making sense of spiritual impulses. See Isabel Rivers, *Reason, Grace, and Sentiment: A Study of the Language of Religion and Ethics in England, 1660–1780*, 2 vols. (Cambridge: Cambridge University Press, 1991), 1:208. See also Richard E. Brantley, *Locke, Wesley, and the Language of English Romanticism* (Gainesville: University Press of Florida, 1984).

25. Bathsheba Hall, *The Diary of Bathsheba Hall*, in *Her Own Story: Autobiographical Portraits of Early Methodist Women*, ed. Paul W. Chilcote (Nashville: Kingswood Books, 2001), 105.

26. Porter, *Madmen*, 35.

27. Michel Foucault, *Madness and Civilization: A History of Insanity in the Age of Reason* (New York: Vintage Books, 1965).

28. I've already observed in note 5 that Graves's brother experienced a mental breakdown as a result of his religious convictions, and there are documented cases of other Methodists who experienced mental illness. I discuss this issue in more detail in "Method or Madness: Methodist Devotion and the Anti-Methodist Response," *Religion in the Age of Reason: A Transatlantic Study of the Long Eighteenth Century*, ed. Kathryn Duncan (New York: AMS Press), 195–210.

29. John Wesley, "The New Birth," *John Wesley's Sermons*, ed. Albert C. Outler and Richard P. Heitzenrater (Nashville: Abingdon Press, 1991), 339, 340.

30. George Lavington, *The Enthusiasm of Methodists and Papists Compar'd* (London: J. and P. Knapton, 1749), 26, 27.

31. T. Mitchel to William Seward, April 26, 1739, The John Rylands University Library, Letters of William Seward, DDSe 40.

32. T. Mitchel to William Seward, April 26, 1739, 39.

33. T. Mitchel to William Seward, April 26, 1739, 30.

34. Whitefield, *The Folly and Danger of Being Not Righteous Enough*, 28.

35. John Wesley, "Justification by Faith," *John Wesley's Sermons*, 117.

36. John Wesley, *Free Grace* (Bristol: S. and F. Farley, 1739); George Whitefield, *A Letter to the Reverend Mr. John Wesley; in Answer to his Sermon Entitled Free Grace* (London: W. Strahan, 1741).

37. Lyons, "Satiric Technique in *The Spiritual Quixote*: Some Comments," 272.

38. This is not to suggest, however, that Graves is wholly favorable in his portrait of Wesley, as some critics suggest. The Wesley that appears in the novel is certainly more dignified and sincere than the caricature of Whitefield; nonetheless, it is Whitefield who serves as Graves's mouthpiece when he decries the most controversial theological maxim advocated by Wesley, the doctrine of perfection, the belief that people can be free of sin in this life. In response to one Methodist's claim that he "has not committed sin these five years," Graves's Whitefield responds (quoting 1 John 1:8), "If we say that we have no sin, we deceive ourselves" (242).

39. George Whitefield, "Christ the best Husband: Or an Earnest Invitation to Young Women to Come and See Christ," *The Works of the Reverend George Whitefield* (London: Edward and Charles Dilley, 1772), 5:67, 70.

40. For discussions of this phenomenon, see Henry D. Rack, *Reasonable Enthusiast: John Wesley and the Rise of Methodism*, 3rd ed. (London: Epworth, 2002), 251–69; Boyd Stanley Schlenther, *Queen of the Methodists: The Countess of Huntingdon and the Eighteenth-Century*

Methodists on the Move in The Spiritual Quixote   235

Crisis of Faith and Society (Durham, NC: Durham Academic Press, 1997), 133–42; and Henry Abelove, *The Evangelist of Desire: John Wesley and the Methodists* (Stanford: Stanford University Press, 1990).

41. See, for example, *The Story of the Methodist-Lady: Or the Injur'd Husband's Revenge* (London: John Doughty, 1770).

42. William Fleetwood, *The Perfectionists Examin'd; Or, Inherent Perfection in This Life, No Scripture Doctrine* (London: J. Roberts, 1741), 2.

43. James Lackington, *Memoirs of the Forty-Five First Years of the Life of James Lackington* (London: J. Lackington, 1791), 68.

44. David Hempton, *Methodism: Empire of the Spirit* (New Haven: Yale University Press, 2005), 149–50.

45. See Nancy Armstrong, *Desire and Domestic Fiction: A Political History of the Novel* (New York: Oxford University Press, 1987), 80; Marlene LeGates, "The Cult of Womanhood in Eighteenth-Century Thought," *Eighteenth-Century Studies* 10 (1976): 21–39; Catherine Hall and Leonore Davidoff, *Family Fortunes: Men and Women of the English Middle Class, 1780–1850*, 2nd ed. (London: Routledge, 2002).

46. See *Some Papers Giving an Account of the Rise and Progress of Methodism at Wednesbury and Staffordshire* (London: J. Roberts, 1744), 21–22.

47. Ruth H. Bloch, *Gender and Morality in Anglo-American Culture, 1650–1800* (Berkeley: University of California Press, 2003), 52.

48. De Bruyn, "Richard Graves," 244.

49. Dorothy Ripley, *An Account of the Extraordinary Conversion and Religious Experience of Dorothy Ripley*, in *Her Own Story: Autobiographical Portraits of Early Methodist Women*, 143.

50. John Wesley, *Thoughts on a Single Life* (London: Foundery, 1765), 5.

51. George Whitefield, *A Continuation of the Reverend Mr. Whitefield's Journal, from His Arrival at London, to His Departure from Thence to Georgia* (London: James Hutton, 1739), 98.

52. Porter, *Madmen*, 28.

53. The question might be asked, does Graves follow his own advice? Can his satire of Methodism be viewed as moderate? As indicated at the outset of this essay, modern scholars often characterize Graves's satiric technique as just that. But while his tone is relatively conciliatory, I have tried to show that his satiric treatment of Methodism is both thorough and hard hitting, though perhaps not as vicious as most anti-Methodist publications. Even Graves suggests that anti-Methodist accounts might exaggerate the truth. When Wildgoose arrives in Bath, his landlord explains: "There was one [Methodist] at Gloucester, (as a gentleman's servant told me that very morning) caught in bed with a Millener's prentice but last week; nay, and one of them is in Gloucester Gaol at this time, for setting fire to the Cathedral." Wildgoose, who has just come from Gloucester, assures the landlord that the stories are fallacious and reminds him of "the malignity of the world, and the absurdity of those popular stories, which are so freely propagated by the vulgar part of mankind" (141–42).

Chapter Thirteen

"A Very Agreable Way of Thinking"

Devotion and Doctrine in Boswell's Religion

Paul Tankard

Even by some of those who admire his literary achievements, James Boswell is frequently regarded as a trifler, a man of neither notable intellect nor serious principles. His major work, *The Life of Samuel Johnson* (1791), is of course taken very seriously, attracting both scholarly attention and extra-scholarly devotion, but it is regarded as something of a comic epic in prose, albeit a nonfictional one, and insofar as it has many serious qualities and themes, these are conventionally attributed to the book's hero, not its author.[1] Unlike Samuel Johnson, Boswell is not regarded as a thinker, and certainly not a religious thinker. As more than one of my colleagues has remarked to me about the subject of this essay, Boswell has no obvious place in a consideration of literature and theology.

However, Boswell left behind him another major work, of which the world is becoming increasingly aware: I mean, the letters and journals that constitute his vast and miscellaneous "Private Papers," of which the editing and publication is still ongoing; they are (almost uniquely) being treated by scholars as a huge and undigested single classic work of autobiography and self-fashioning. The modes of reading and analysis to which the Private Papers may be subject will one day be at least as complex and profound as those pertaining to any more traditional work of literature. Careful reading in and of his Private Papers, and a number of scholarly studies,[2] make it clear that it is not ludicrous to consider Boswell as a man of religious faith. His faith was, furthermore, not merely complacent conformity to conventional public piety, and his religious allegiance not simply an aspect of his sociopolitical loyalties; Boswell's faith was an abiding aspect of his psychology and self-perception. Certainly, Johnson did not think it ludicrous to write of him, in a letter of introduction to John Wesley, "I think it very much to be wished that worthy and religious men should be acquainted with each other."[3] Boswell characteristically put this letter into the *Life of Johnson*,[4] and for over two hundred years, it must have made a great many readers smile. But Johnson was not easily fooled. The central concerns of religion greatly exercised Boswell's mind, emotions, and imagination.

To have particular and identifiable religious convictions that one willingly articulates and defends in both public and private, is prima facie evidence of a serious cast of mind. An even greater degree of religious seriousness or conscientiousness is usually assumed of those who convert from one religious stance or allegiance to another. Boswell's seriousness about—and lifelong preoccupation with—religion is indicated by, among other clues, the early shifts in his religious allegiance. Soon after he first met Samuel Johnson, as he records, "I then told my history to Mr. Johnson which he listened to with attention. I told him how I was a very strict Christian & was turned from that to Infidelity. But that now I had got back to a very agreable [sic] way of thinking[;] That I believed the Christian Religion; tho' I might not be clear in many particulars."[5] His "history," according to this account, is not his educational, medical, or amatory history, but his religious history; and this account in fact represents a very short version of the various religious positions he had already moved through by the tender age of twenty-two. A longer and far more specific account may be constructed, based on his journals and other accounts—in particular, a written "Sketch" of his early life that he prepared by way of introduction to Rousseau in 1764.[6]

Boswell was brought up in Edinburgh according to a strict and narrow version of Calvinism, as promulgated by the Presbyterian Church of Scotland, and as reinforced at home by his mother, who was loving and devout, but seems in all innocence to have instructed him in the church's most difficult doctrines. As a young man, he recalled of his childhood, the "dreary tolboothkirk ideas, than which nothing has given me more gloomy feelings,"[7] and that "my tender mind was lacerated with infernal horror" (*London Journal*, 61; December, 22, 1762). For four years from the age of eight, he was tutored at home by John Dun, a minister of more liberal views (*Ébauche*, 359n11), of whom he recorded gratefully, "At last my governor put me in love with heaven, and some hope entered into my religion" ("Sketch," 3). Boswell retained a fondness for Dun, and decades later subscribed generously to his published *Sermons* and mourned his death (Sher, 33). When Boswell was twelve years old, Dun was appointed as Auchinleck parish minister, and a new tutor named Joseph Ferguson was appointed (*Ébauche*, 359n21), of whom Boswell wrote, "He was a dogmatist who never doubted. He felt and acted according to system" ("Sketch," 3). The term *system* was also used in this negative (and unusual) way by Johnson; as Boswell records, Johnson said of an argument that he regarded as based not on thought or observation, but simple consistency with the author's presuppositions, "That is system, Sir" (May 20, 1783; *Life*, 4:210). Mr. Ferguson was not prepared to entertain sincere sceptical questions on religious subjects, or to give them sensible answers.

From 1753, Boswell attended the University of Edinburgh, and pursued courses in arts and law. In 1757, aged sixteen, he suffered a religious crisis, brought on (he said) by the study of logic and metaphysics, which, as his biographer Frederick Pottle describes, "forced him to think about the problem . . . of God's foreknowledge and man's free will." According to Pottle, "The suspicion that Necessity governed all his actions" destroyed forever "the foundations of his peace" (*EY*, 32). Boswell told Rousseau that, in reaction to this disturbance, he "became Methodist" ("Sketch," 4; *Ébauche*, 360n31). Pottle argues that this should not be seen as a conversion to Methodism, which movement did not at that stage have an institutional presence in Edinburgh, but rather that Boswell developed a sympathy for the emotional faith endorsed by such preachers as George Whitefield (*EY*, 33–34). He suffered a nervous collapse, and was sent by doctors to take the waters at Moffat, where he came under the influence of a man he described as "an old Pythagorean"—a self-educated shepherd named John Williamson (*Ébauche*, 360n33). He briefly became a vegetarian and "looked upon the whole human race with horror" ("Sketch," 4).

In 1759, Boswell's father Lord Auchinleck had him change his place of study from Edinburgh, where he was too much involved with theatrical company, to the University of Glasgow. The most dramatic change in doctrine and allegiance came when, as he wrote, "At eighteen I became a Catholic" ("Sketch," 4). After seven months in Glasgow, he ran away to London and once there—so the evidence suggests (and Pottle argues)—was formally received into the Roman Catholic Church, admitted to communion, and thought of becoming a priest or monk. Some have trivialized this conversion, as it seems to have been in part a result of his having had for a time a Catholic lady friend (an actress named Mrs. Cosway). But Boswell would not have undertaken conversion lightly, since being a Catholic would have had at the time serious consequences for his social or professional ambitions (*EY*, 46).[8] His seriousness may be indicated by the presence of a number of Catholic publications in his 1770 list of his books.[9]

His father requested their Ayrshire neighbor, Lord Eglinton, who was a Scottish member of the House of Lords and kept a London residence, to find the young Boswell and take him under his wing. Eglinton's influence and the fashionable society to which he introduced Boswell led to the period of "infidelity" that he mentioned to Johnson; to Rousseau he said that Eglinton "made me a deist" ("Sketch," 4), and he later described himself as being freed "from the gloom of superstition, although it led me to the other extreme."[10] Calvinist, Methodist, Pythagorean, Catholic, and deist—all before the age of twenty-two. In addition, by the time Boswell was in London in 1762 for his second and most famous visit he was, at least when in England, mainly attending Anglican worship—to which he had been introduced in Edinburgh in 1755 by his lifelong friend, the future clergyman William Johnson Temple. In Scotland he was a member of—and acted professionally as a lawyer for—the Church of Scotland, for reasons of civic duty and family tradition; but privately he always objected to its theology and politics.[11]

Boswell's conversions, if this is an appropriate word, certainly bear no relation to conversion as, for instance, described by William James, in his *Varieties of Religious Experience*. Boswell does not seem to have been subject to mystical experiences. On the other hand, when he makes notes in his journal concerning his life as a religious being (apart from recording where he went to church), they almost always concern his feelings.

Although Boswell was not at all unaware of the movements between doctrinal positions that are implied by his changing religious allegiances or professions, from 1762 his main interest in his religious experiences, whether worship at church, theological reading, or religious conversation, seems solely to have been how they made him feel. During the nine-and-a-half months of his famous second sojourn in London, the one documented in the *London Journal*, he records regular Sunday churchgoing (as well as attendance at occasional midweek festivals), and the feelings aroused by it, as if he were carrying out an experiment on himself. The reader of this journal is struck by the remarkable variety of places of worship that Boswell attends during this period: he treats the church (in the broad sense of the word) not as a mystical body to which he belongs, but as a series of places or venues that he visits. At this stage in particular he is quite explicitly behaving as a connoisseur. For example, on Sunday, December 26, 1762, having been at the service at Whitehall Chapel, he records, "I took a whim to go through all the churches and chapels in London, taking one each Sunday" (*London Journal*, 65). While he did not fully achieve this, he did quite well: there were another thirty-one Sundays until he left London for Holland the following August. In that time he missed church (or neglected to record his attendance) on eleven Sundays; on the remaining twenty Sundays, he attended twenty different churches, chapels, or religious meetings.[12] What exactly was he looking for? He seems not to be assessing the churches and congregations he visits for sound teaching, liveliness of worship, challenging preaching, or warm Christian fellowship, as a modern-day churchgoer might; he is certainly not looking for a parish or church community into which to settle—to attend regularly, sign up for the planned giving program, and perhaps be elected to vestry.[13]

What Boswell particularly wants to experience or enjoy from attending to his religious duties is the feeling he calls "devotion"; he carefully records when this feeling comes upon him in church. On Sunday, November 21, for example, two days after arriving in London, he attended Anglican worship at the Mayfair Chapel and records with satisfaction, "heard prayers & an excellent sermon. . . . I was in a fine frame. . . . I have now & then flashes of devotion, & it will one day burn with a steady flame" (8–9). Reviewing his life in his journal on December 11, he envisages himself at his ancestral home and resolves that there "will I end my days in calm devotion" (40). The following Sunday, December 19, at St. John's Chapel, he "heard a tollerable sermon on humility. I was not so devout as I could have wished" (54). At Spring Garden Chapel in Charing-Cross, on March 6, 1763, "I felt a calm delight in again being at divine service" (165), and later that month, March 20, "I was at St. Clement's Church, which gave me very devout ideas" (177). On Good Friday (April 1), he says, "I endeavoured to excite in my mind a devout & solemn frame" (187). Two days later, he spent Sunday socializing with his friend Temple (who was to become a clergyman), the two of them "so pleasingly forgetfull of every thing . . . that we did not go to church, altho' it was Easter day[,] that splendid Festival." He was afterward somewhat contrite at having neglected the occasion, as he recorded in his journal: "At night, at home, I read the Church service by myself with great devotion" (189–90). He goes to the Temple Church on April 10, where he "heard a very good sermon . . . [which] with the Music & the good building put me into a very devout frame, and after service my mind was left in a pleasing calm state" (194–95). On May 22 at St. Andrew's Holborn, he says, "I was in an excellent frame, & heard Service with true devotion" (227); the following Sunday he experienced "much devotion" at Westminster Abbey (233). On his last Sunday before leaving London, he went to St. Paul's, where he "was very devout" (297). His preferences were not narrowly ritualistic: he also enjoyed the simplicity of Quaker worship. But he was on both of these grounds dissatisfied with the faith of his fathers: as Mary Stewart describes, "the Presbyterian Church had neither a quiet devotional atmosphere nor a dignified ritual."[14]

He assesses the churches, or to be more precise the services, that he attends by their effect on his feelings. An unsatisfactory church service or any other disagreeable attention to religion may bring on for Boswell an opposite state to devotion, which is "gloominess." On Sunday, May 15, as he records, he has to attend three churches in order to get satisfactory sensations:

> I was in an excellent calm and serious mood. I attended divine service in Ludgate-church with patience and satisfaction and was much edified. I then dined at honest Cochrane's, after which He & I and two other Gentlemen went

> to Dr. Fordyce's meeting in Monkwell Street, and heard Doctor Blair preach.[15] I thought this would have done me good. But I found the reverse. Blair's new-kirk delivery and the Dissenters roaring out the Psalms sitting on their Backsides[,] together with the extempore prayers & in short the whole vulgar idea of the Presbyterian worship made me *very gloomy*. I therefore hastened from this place to St. Paul's, where I heard the conclusion of service, and had my mind set right again. (219; my italics)

After worshipping the following Sunday, May 22, at St. Andrew's Holburn, he noted in his journal that the church was "a very fine building. At one end of it is a window of very elegant painted glass" (227). A considerable portion of Boswell's religious feeling is his pleasure in the aesthetics of the church in which he finds himself, and of the service offered there. When he attended Westminster Abbey (April 12, 1772), he wrote, "The solemnity of the grand old building, the painted glass windows, the noble music, the excellent service of the church, and a very good sermon, all contributed to do me much good."[16] The week after this, it was Easter, and he attended a Roman Catholic chapel, and again, "The solemnity of high mass, the music, the wax lights, and the odour of frankincense made a delightful impression upon me" (*Defence*, 134). He is sensitive to the aesthetic character of the church architecture, other visual features such as the lights and windows, the music, the language of the liturgy, the smell of incense (when he can get it)—all sensual pleasures—and he includes in one of these catalogues "a very good sermon." We can, I think, extrapolate that his pleasure in sermons is aesthetic as well: he appreciates a reasonable approach, careful choice of words, genteel delivery, and the doctrinal content orthodox and unexceptional. In this he remained a disciple of his old tutor John Dun, who wrote concerning his own *Sermons* (two volumes, 1790) that he hoped that "by something *not gloomy* . . . I might lead the lively genius, and man of taste, into serious thoughts" (quoted in Sher, 34; my italics).

However irrelevant the finer points of Christian doctrine may seem to Boswell's life as a religious being ("I might not be clear in many particulars"), he records having been exposed very early to theological ideas, and having been mostly repelled by what he learned. As James Caudle observes, Boswell's objections to the teaching of the Church of Scotland were both "pedagogical and psychological" (122): he was compelled to learn by rote the Westminster *Shorter Catechism* and found its lessons incomprehensibly abstract; what he did understand he found gloomy and indeed terrifying.

Boswell told Rousseau that his mother taught him about "the eternity of punishment [, which] was the first great idea I ever formed" ("Sketch," 2). Because it was an idea accompanied by strong imagery, it took a powerful possession of his young imagination: "How it made me shudder! Since fire was a material substance, I had an idea of it" (2). His mother, who "was of that sect which believes that to be saved, each individual must experience a strong conversion" ("Sketch," 2), was keen for him to make a personal response to his religious instruction. He was given stories to read of dramatic religious conversions of toddlers. In an unfinished early draft of the *Ébauche*, only recently published for the first time, Boswell mentions other abstract dogmas in which he was instructed, including the Fall of Man and Original Sin (*Ébauche*, 362). His early tutor, John Dun, countered the severity of these teachings by emphasizing to him the blessings of Heaven ("Sketch," 3). I have already mentioned his profound disturbance, when he came to understand them, over deterministic teachings, whether secular or religiously based. When Boswell writes about any of these doctrines, he does so in a biographical and narrative way; that is, he does not discuss them as intellectual constructs to be assessed according to reason and in the light of Scripture and experience, but as reported conversations and the feelings invoked by them.

With this background, it is not surprising that questions of religion should (as we have seen) form the major part of his self-presentation to both Johnson and Rousseau; it is clear that despite describing his various conversions as troubling and requiring counsel, he is also rather proud of them, and considers that they make him particularly interesting to the philosophers he wants to cultivate. Religious issues arose in conversation between Boswell and Johnson within weeks of the two having met. After Boswell had described his shifts in religious position to Johnson, and perhaps seemed to invite Johnson's determination on matters of denominational allegiance, he reports himself "agreeably surprized" when Johnson told him, "For my part, Sir, I think all Christians, whether Papists or Protestants, agree in the essential articles, and that their differences are trivial, and rather political than religious" (June 25, 1763; *Life* 1:405; cf. *London Journal*, 250). Boswell proceeded on another occasion to raise with Johnson the doctrine of purgatory and other specifically Catholic doctrines,[17] and although he voices objections to Johnson's responses, he is of course pleased that Johnson thinks that most of those teachings are more rather than less of what is required of a Christian, and seems to consider them as, at worst, harmless.

In her pioneering survey of Boswell's religious views, Margaret M. Stewart frames the issues—perhaps as much for rhetorical purposes as anything else—as "Boswell's Denominational Dilemma." For all the thoroughness and accuracy of that essay, I think the title overstates the case. From the time of the first of these conversations, Boswell seems not to have troubled himself about religious differences; he felt under no impulse to decide among the claims of the various churches and certainly did not seem to believe that disputes among churches over matters of doctrine in any way vitiated the essential truth of the Christian religion. Indeed, it may be that Johnson unwittingly licensed Boswell's ecclesiastical connoisseurship. Writing in 1767 to Temple, Boswell recalled Johnson's distinction, and counseled Temple not to be discouraged in his faith by what he found in the history of the Church. He says, "I conf[e]ss that it is not in ecclesiastical Histo[ry] that we find the most agreable Account of Divines [i.e., men in holy orders]. Their Politics their Ambitions their art and their cruelty are there displayed. But remember Temple You are there reading the vices of only Political Divines, of such individuals as in so numerous a body have been very unworthy Members of the Church, and should rather have been employed in the rudest secular concerns."[18] "Political divines" are those clergymen whose chief interest seems not to be their priestly duties or the central truths of religion, but whose preaching and activities are mostly directed at advancing their own careers, and the interests of their own party in the church.

In the second of these conversations, Boswell introduced the subject of predestination; he was clearly—at least, in the privacy of his journal—not impressed with Johnson's replies, and said to himself that Johnson, who recommended a course of reading, "avoided the question" (*Search*, 352; October 26, 1769). Boswell argues that with regard to doctrine generally, and the doctrine of predestination in particular, the Church of England is no different from the Presbyterian. Johnson takes the line that the Church of England's supposed position was "political," arguing that the doctrine is mentioned, without emphasis, in the Articles of the Church only because it was "part of the clamour of the times" (*Search*, 351). In reply, Boswell addresses the substantive issue and asserts that if God is all-knowing there can be no free will, and prayer can be of no use. Johnson recommends some books that Boswell should read, and Boswell abandons the topic, but remains unconvinced that it is anything but a real and practical difficulty. Of course, when Boswell had attempted to raise the subject on another occasion, a few weeks earlier, Johnson made his best-known remark on the subject: "we *know* our will is free, and *there's* an end on't" (October 10, 1769; *Life* 2:82, Boswell's emphasis; cf. *Search*, 336). This commonsense view was for Johnson very forceful; he recognizes the conundrum and the force of the various arguments against free will, without seeming to be much troubled by them, summarizing his view on another occasion: "All theory is against the freedom of the will; all experience for it" (April 15, 1778; *Life* 3:291). Boswell shows himself quite adept at formulating the predestinarian arguments, but is satisfied with Johnson's conclusion, and expresses his pleasure at finding Johnson on this occasion prepared to discuss the question with frankness and equanimity.

It does seem as if Boswell presses the arguments for necessity, not out of conviction, but rather as a devil's advocate, and perhaps because a certain degree of doubt was necessary for the exercise of his religion. As his one-time romantic interest, the Dutch bluestocking Isabella van Tuyll van Serooskerken ("Belle de Zuylen"), observed of him, "The fact is you do not love conclusions; you love problems which can never be solved" (*Holland*, 357). His older friend and adviser, David Dalrymple, Lord Hailes, wrote in similar terms (regarding exactly the same topic), telling him, "I find you infatuated with Fatality" (*Holland*, 88). But Boswell could abandon his infatuation and be quite Johnsonian on the subject when it suited the circumstances. When defending the sheep-stealer John Reid, in the case which has subsequently become one of the best known of his legal career, Boswell described how, when facing the prospect of execution, Reid "expressed his willingness to submit to what was *foreordained* for him." Boswell told him firmly, "this would not have been *foreordained* for you if you had not stolen sheep, and that was not *foreordained*. GOD does not foreordain wickedness"; and he read to Reid from the New Testament, James 1:13–14. In his journal, he went on to observe sagely that "people in his [Reid's] situation are very apt to become predestinarians" (August 20, 1774; *Defence*, 288); that is to say, the doctrine of predestination has a particular appeal to people who have some powerful reason for wanting not to believe themselves responsible for the consequences of their actions. Certainly such a divided creature as was Boswell, so powerfully swayed by contradictory impulses, would often find himself in this situation. He goes on to record a grimly amusing story of a condemned man who was so infected by the doctrine of predestination that he "was positive that the crime he had committed was decreed by his Maker," and from the scaffold began to "harangue the people upon this subject." His argument was ended prematurely when the attending clergyman (who told Boswell the story) impelled the executioner to proceed with his task, before the man could inflict any more troublesome nonsense on his parishioners; there, indeed, was "an end on't."

We may surmise that Johnson's seemingly firm (if somewhat defensive) insistence on the freedom of the will derives from both his sense of his own ability decisively to manage his life, as well as a powerful sense of his own failures: both the ability to act and the sense of failure to act testify to the freedom of the will. Johnson's fragmentary diaries record a succession of reiterated resolutions for self-management, framed within a devotional setting.[19] Boswell's instructions to himself, familiar to all readers of his journals, to "be" other people or (with greater frequency) to exercise some reserve or restraint ("be retenu"; see *London Journal*, xxxix, and passim) are of a different character.

In the public space of the text of the *Life of Johnson*, Boswell also appears as a defender of the orthodox position on free will; he addresses the subject on his own authority, outside the diegesis, in two footnotes. The first is prompted by his account of a conversation in which a nonconformist minister, Dr. Henry Mayo, asks if Johnson has read Jonathan Edwards on grace (3:291; April 15, 1778); Johnson had not, but Boswell had (although Frederick Pottle wonders when),[20] and he pursues the subject, allowing Johnson to conclude with his assertion that "all experience" is for free will. In his footnote (3:291n2), Boswell addresses "any of my readers who are disturbed by this thorny question," and recommends they read one of the *Persian Letters* of Montesquieu and John Palmer's answer to Dr. Priestley. The dissenting theologian and scientist Dr. Joseph Priestley was a particular target for Boswell, and when his name again makes its way into Boswell's narrative (September 1783), in one of a series of anecdotes supplied by William Bowles (in which Johnson's own comments about Priestley are unexpectedly conciliatory), Boswell glosses it with a four-paragraph footnote of his own, saying of him, "I know of no writer who has been suffered to publish more pernicious doctrines" (4:238n1). Boswell mentions three "pernicious doctrines" in particular: materialism, necessity, and doubts about the blessedness of any future state.

As these occasional asides suggest, at certain periods at least theology was surprisingly high on Boswell's reading list. As a student in Holland, writing from Utrecht to Temple in November 1763, he declared, "I am going to read Butler's Analogy, Grotius on the Truth of Revelation and Locke on the same Subject" (*Boswell-Temple Corresp.*, 75–76).[21] These three works were of a similar tendency: works of apologetics, and opposed to deism. True to his word, in December he notes that he is taking Butler to read on a jaunt to The Hague (*Holland*, 92). The *Analogy of Religion* (1736) was the most famous book by churchman and philosopher Joseph Butler (1692–1752); it aimed to counter deistic thought by showing that both nature and Scripture reveal the same divine and rational ordering of the universe. Although there is no further mention of Boswell's actually reading or having read the book, he held Butler in esteem, and many years later he extracted from his friend Lord Kames an account of Kames's admiration for Butler, and of his seeking and making Butler's acquaintance in London; Boswell made a careful record of this in his journal (*Applause*, 22–23). I find no evidence that Boswell read Grotius's pioneering and much-reprinted work of Protestant apologetics, although he notes occasions, before and after this resolve, when Johnson praises and recommends him (*London Journal*, 230, 293; *Life*, 5:69). In Holland he instructed himself, in his journal (May 23, 1764), to "Swear Locke's Christianity" (*Holland*, 247), which appears to suggest a very strong affirmative response to the approach to Christianity that John Locke recommended. It may be said, however, that such resolutions and recommendations as these are all very well, and that it is interesting that what one very seldom finds in Boswell's journals are any notes on his actual reading: simple accounts of what or how much he has read, or summaries or discursive reflections on his reading. I do not mean to suggest that he did no such reading, but simply that if he did, the experience did not impel or equip him to pursue this sort of discourse himself.[22] It is as if it is sufficient for him to know that such cogent intellectual defenses as these books represent may be mounted, by men of intelligence and integrity; he feels under no obligation to engage critically with their reasonings and speculations.

The theological writer who "could indeed be considered Boswell's favorite"[23] was Dr. Samuel Ogden, whose *Sermons on the Efficacy of Prayer and Intercession* (1770) he famously mentions on a number of occasions, particularly in the *Journal of a Tour to the Hebrides*. The chief interest for Boswell in theological reading is always the question of "necessity," and he rejects any writer who proposes or defends a view of the subject that is consistent with the Calvinism of his childhood, which taught "double predestination": that is, the view that holds that God's choosing or foreknowledge of those who are saved must imply His foreknowledge or choosing of those who are damned. He describes one of Ogden's sermons as "much superior" to those of Blair, who (he writes) "showed his opinion that prayer *doth not avail* with our Heavenly Father, and that man is indeed fatally carried on. Such a system is dreary and dispiriting, and I am convinced is not true."[24] Here we find Boswell again deploying the word *system* to mean an intellectual position taken to a relentlessly logical but ridiculous or disagreeable conclusion.

It is interesting also to consider the relationship between his two assertions here about Blair's "system": the order of his thoughts suggests that his conviction that it is untrue is a conclusion he draws from his emotional reaction. If this is the case, I suggest that we should see Boswell's faith not so much—or at least as not only—governed by a hedonistic search for particular feelings (that is, "devotion"), as by a strong conviction that true Christian faith should inspire happiness and hope, rather than gloom and terror. In an essay of March 1782, no. 74 in his periodical series called "The Hypochondriack" (1770–1782), he says that by Religion he means,

> a belief in a great and good power, the supreme fountain of intelligence and felicity, joined with an habitual devotion or pious endeavours to direct all the powers of the soul towards that divine object, and, as much as may be, to approach to a similitude with what we conceive of the amiable nature of God.

Such a belief opens the mind to "magnificent and permanent views," to "the contemplation of immensity and eternity"; it is so "grand" and "honourable" that even if "Religion were altogether a fiction," every person of nobility and spirit would want to preserve it.[25] The "evidences of Religion" are not exactly irrelevant to him, but he very early reached a point at which he was sufficiently convinced on those issues, and they ceased to address his condition.

The theological works that Johnson suggested to Boswell that he read with regard to predestination (*Search*, 352; October 26, 1769) were "Dr. Clarke, and Bishop Bramhall on liberty and necessity, and . . . South's sermons on Prayer." I find no evidence that Boswell ever read Bramhall or Robert South (the latter of whom was a favorite of Johnson, and is frequently quoted in the *Dictionary*). But Johnson had earlier recommended the work of the latitudinarian theologian Samuel Clarke (*London Journal*, 230; May 24, 1763), and Boswell read quite deeply in his work when he was in Holland in 1763–1764. Clarke (1675–1729) was best known for his two consecutive series of Boyle lectures (1704–1705), published first as *A Demonstration of the Being and Attributes of God: More Particularly in Answer to Mr Hobbes, Spinoza and Their Followers, wherein the Notion of Liberty is Stated, and the Possibility and Certainty of It Proved, in Opposition to Necessity and Fate* (1704) and *A Discourse Concerning the Unchangeable Obligations of Natural Religion, and the Truth and Certainty of the Christian Revelation* (1705), and thereafter frequently published together.[26] Boswell was reading the combined book in November 1763 and recommended it to Temple (*Boswell-Temple Corresp.*, 75); in January 1764 he told his Edinburgh friend John Johnston that he had "read, this winter, Dr. Clarke's *Evidences of natural and revealed religion* a book which I earnestly recommend to you. It has given me a very strong conviction of the truth of Christianity, which is a constant support to the soul."[27] In his journal (December 30, 1765) he told himself that "Dr. Clarke's argument for one great first cause is most noble and convincing."[28]

However, always bubbling just beneath the surface of expressions like these was Boswell's awareness of the limitations of Clarke, of theology, indeed of all discourse of an abstract and theoretical kind. Writing to Temple in March 1775, from an inn at Grantham, he tries to excuse his lifelong sexual promiscuity, asking "Why did our Saviour never say a word against it?" and he continues with a quotation from Edward Young: "A fever argues better than a Clarke." This passage, in Young's *Satire* no. 4, depicts an atheist driven to prayer not by logical or theological considerations, but by ill-health. Boswell glosses this in a way that Young would probably not approve—but which is, as he points out, equally reasonable—namely, that "this handsom maid" (named Matty) who attends to his room at the inn, by her mere presence and appearance "argues better than—whom you please."[29] Reason is fine, but is easily rendered powerless by strong feelings engendered by immediate circumstances and experiences.

By 1768, Boswell has reached what was for him a satisfactory accommodation with religion. Though he was subject to periods of doubt and skepticism, as well as gloom and melancholy, these moods seem never in his adult life to have been religiously induced, and Boswell remained on the whole a defender of orthodox religion in public, and a striver after piety of a kind in private. In the preface to the third edition (1768) of his *Account of Corsica*, he writes, probably in response to published criticism from John Wilkes,

> To those who have imagined themselves very witty in sneering at me for being a Christian, I would recommend the serious study of Theology, and I hope they will attain to the same comfort that I have, in the belief of a Revelation by which a SAVIOUR is proclaimed to the world, and "life and immortality are clearly brought to light."[30]

Although I have emphasized Christian doctrines that Boswell disliked, with Boswell I think it was less a matter of disliking particular doctrines than of disliking *all* doctrines. If this seems unfair or perhaps flippant, it can at least be said that for Boswell doctrine of any kind seems always to imply—or necessarily lead to—"system," and thus to be at risk of pursuing its own logic at the expense of contradicting the comforting, agreeable, and life-giving central tenets of Christianity.

In September 1774 he spent an evening with his uncle Dr. John Boswell, who was a member of the Glasites, a fundamentalist sect (known later, and particularly in America, as Sandemanians) that taught "That the bare death of Jesus Christ without a thought or deed on the part of man, is sufficient to present the chief of sinners spotless before God."[31] As Pottle describes him, the eccentric Dr. Boswell "demonstrated his antinomianism practically by frequenting bawdy houses, and was excommunicated by his sect, who (as Boswell says) were very strict in enforcing morality though they did not admit any efficacy in it" (*EY*, 21). As they concluded the evening, Boswell says of his uncle, "by the road he disputed warmly for his particular tenets as to the Christian religion: salvation by faith alone, etc." Boswell continues, reflecting on this dispute, "I felt some pain when I found how ill I could argue on the most important of all subjects, and cold clouds of doubt went athwart my mind" (*Defence*, 336). A few weeks later he had a discussion on religious subjects with his friend Alexander Wood, a surgeon: "Wood got into a disagreeable kind of sceptical conversation about the soul being material, from all that we could observe. It is hard that our most valuable articles of belief are rather the effects of sentiment than of demonstration. I disliked Wood because he revived doubts in my mind which I could not at once dispel" (*Defence*, 342). In other words, being compelled to reason of itself made him doubt.

When in 1770 Boswell embarked on a series of topical newspaper columns, which he signed with the name "Rampager," his approach to the serious and mainly political issues that he discussed was to treat them as jokes.[32] There are two "Rampagers" of 1774 that concern the so-called

Feathers Tavern petitioners, a group of clergy who met at the Feathers tavern in the Strand and who were opposed to the requirement that those ordained to the Anglican priesthood subscribe to the Thirty-Nine Articles. The movement took in a variety of Protestant viewpoints: some who simply opposed vows as offending against the Christian freedom of conscience, some who believed the Articles dictated more than was warranted by Scripture, and others more radical who rejected the doctrine of the Trinity. There was certainly enough in such topics for an aspiring religious controversialist to get his teeth into, but Boswell simply commends those who have attempted to answer them on the substantial issue (with, as he says, "the Seriousness which becomes its Importance"), then goes on to parody Dr. Priestley ("whose Name is like a Contrast to his Principles") and the petitioners' meeting place, using an array of feather-related images and allusions.[33]

After a correspondent signing himself "A Feather's Man" wrote in to the *Public Advertiser* to suggest that serious issues should be written about seriously,[34] in the next "Rampager" letter, Boswell tries to put the issue into perspective, by arguing (in effect) that the issue is not religious, but broadly political:

> Far be it from me to censure any Man who takes Revelation itself for his sole Rule in Matters of Religion. The modest and humble Christian, be his Opinions ever so different from the Standard of the Church of England, shall have my best Wishes; but I cannot help feeling an Indignation to see Men forming themselves into a regular Body to attack a respectable Establishment, by which our holy Religion hath been carried on with Dignity and Beneficence for Ages. I am for an Indulgence sufficiently liberal: but every regular Society has surely a Right to prescribe its own Terms; And are these to be abolished because certain Individuals do not like them, when those Individuals need not be of the Society unless they chuse it?[35]

One can, in Boswell's view, be a "humble Christian," however unorthodox one's religious opinions (be they "ever so different from the Standard of the Church of England"); but if such persons choose to belong to a particular church they are thereby obliged to keep their opinions to themselves. Presumably Boswell is here describing his own practice, taking advantage of "an indulgence sufficiently liberal," keeping to himself unorthodox doubts as well as unorthodox opinions. In this "Rampager" he proceeds to recommend that the Feather's Man read a recent publication, *An Essay on the Clergy* by his friend Temple; he then goes on to defend the strategy of mockery, quoting from the Old Testament book of 1 Kings, where Elijah mocks the priests of Baal, and in conclusion renews his barrage of puns and ad hominem attacks.

In 1762, with the self-centeredness of youth but also with surprising insight into the operations of his own mind, he wrote in his journal:

I see too far into the system of things, to be much in earnest. I consider Mankind in general, & therefore cannot take a part in their quarrels when divided into particular states & nations. I can see that after a war is over and a great quantity of cold & hunger & want of Sleep and torment endured by mortals, things are upon the whole, just as they were. I can see Great People, those who manage the fate of Kingdoms are just such beings as myself: Have their hours of discontent and are not a bit happier. This being the case I am passive rather than active in life; it is difficult to make my feeling clearly understood. I may say, I act passively. That is[,] not with my whole heart & thinking this or that of real consequence; but because so & so things are established & I must submit. Meditating calmly & finding myself situated in this sublunary system, I do not know what to make of it. (*London Journal*, 37)

In this remarkable passage, Boswell figures his inability or disinclination to participate earnestly in contests of ideas as something of a virtue. It seems the reflection of a much older man, who has become reconciled to his minor role in the scheme of things, and the ultimate insignificance of his opinions. It is easy to see why, with such a perspective, he might not think it would be worth his trouble to make up his mind about anything other than essentials.

As Boswell grew older, however, he was less inclined to excuse and more inclined to blame himself for not taking seriously the issues that moved so many of his fellows, frequently those of the most worldly eminence, to writing, speaking, and action. On Easter Day 1773 (April 11) he worshipped at St. Paul's Cathedral, and reported in his journal: "I was struck and elevated as usual by the service, and though I did not feel that firm conviction which I have done at different periods of my life, owing I believe to an indolence of mind making me not recollect or feel the importance of settling the truth one way or other, yet my heart and affections were pious, and I received the Holy Sacrament with considerable satisfaction" (*Defence*, 181).

Whether or not it was the result of anything quite as culpable as intellectual laziness ("indolence of mind"), Boswell often confessed that abstract speculation on any subject was not one of his strengths; in May 1779, for example, he advised his friend Temple: "I must candidly tell you that I think you should not puzzle yourself with political speculations more than I do. Neither of us is fit for that sort of mental labour" (*Letters*, ed. Tinker, 2:288). In one of his "Hypochondriack" essays (no. 53: "On Words"; February 1782), he writes that at times "intense inquiry" had "affected [him] even with giddiness and a kind of stupor, the consequence of having one's faculties stretched in vain" (2:150). He told Paoli that (presumably at university) he "had intensely applied myself to metaphysical researches, and reasoned beyond my depth, on such subjects as it is not given to man to know," and had rendered himself melancholy (*Account of Corsica*, 192); many years later, he noted that trying to read Hume's philosophy made him feel dreary and depressed (July 28, 1781; *Laird*, 387). At a conversation over breakfast with friends one Monday morning (Feb. 23, 1784), he was "brought into the distressing perplexity of fate and free will" (*Applause*, 188) and spent a week or more intermittently depressed about the subject. He wrote in his journal the following Monday, "I had an abhorrence at metaphysical speculation, while I perceived that it sickened my perceptions of real life" (189). He was not psychologically equipped to think through from first principles issues religious or otherwise.

For Boswell, the most "agreeable way of thinking" about a good many matters, including theological ones, was if possible not to think at all. But all readers of Boswell know that his most attractive and indeed endearing quality was and remains his candor. Those who share his faith will hope that if his "heart and affections were pious," God might overlook his inability to be in earnest about more abstract and purely intellectual issues. And even pious folk of a more dogmatic persuasion will be able to sympathize with his heartfelt belief that Christianity is best recommended not as an intellectual "system," but as a (true) source of hope and happiness.

NOTES

An early version of this essay was presented as a paper at the "Global Scots" Symposium at the University of Otago in February 2011. I am grateful for the interest and feedback it received on that occasion, and particularly to John Stenhouse for his comments then and subsequently. Thanks also to Chris Ackerley and Paul Sorrell for reading over my work.

1. With the virtual extinction of the educated general reader, views of this kind are now expressed more seldom than in the past—and scholars have never quite expressed themselves this way. But a representative expression may be that of Moray McLaren: those who "smile at or pity his [Boswell's] follies, weaknesses and sins can salute the *Life* with veneration"; *Corsica Boswell: Paoli, Johnson, and Freedom* (London: Secker and Warburg, 1966), 18. There are many collections of Johnson's "wit and wisdom"—and they are usually deeply in Boswell's debt—but there are no collections of the wit and wisdom of Boswell.

2. These include four essays from the 1960s by Mary Margaret Stewart, to be referred to shortly. More recent work is James J. Caudle, "James Boswell and the Bi-Confessional State," in *Religious Identities in Britain, 1660–1832*, ed. William Gibson and Robert G. Ingram (Aldershot: Ashgate, 2005), 119–46; Murray Pittock, "Boswell and Belief," chapter 5 of his *James Boswell* (Aberdeen: AHRC Centre for Irish and Scottish Studies, University of Aberdeen, 2007), 81–93; Richard B. Sher, "Scottish Divines and Legal Lairds: Boswell's Scots Presbyterian Identity," in *New Light on Boswell: Critical and Historical Essays on the Occasion of the Bicentenary of* The Life of Johnson, ed. Greg Clingham (Cambridge: Cambridge University Press, 1991), 28–55; and Robert G. Walker, "Boswell's Use of 'Ogden on Prayer' in *Journal of a Tour to the Hebrides*," in *The Age of Johnson: A Scholarly Annual* 19 (2009): 53–68.

3. Letter to John Wesley, May 3, 1779, in *The Letters of Samuel Johnson*, ed. Bruce Redford, 5 vols. (Princeton: Princeton University Press, 1992–1994), 3:162.

4. James Boswell, *The Life of Samuel Johnson, LL.D.*, ed. George Birkbeck Hill, rev. L.F. Powell, 6 vols. (Oxford: Clarendon Press, 1934–1964), 3:394.

5. James Boswell, *London Journal, 1762–1763*, ed. Gordon Turnbull (London: Penguin, 2010), 250; June 25, 1763 (hereafter cited in text as *London Journal*). Cf. *Life* 1:404–5. The text of this new edition of the *London Journal* differs from that of the only previous edition, Frederick Pottle's much-reprinted text of 1950, in that it "restores Boswell's original (sometimes erratic) spelling, punctuation and paragraphing" (lvii).

6. A translation of Boswell's "Sketch" for Rousseau is given as the first chapter of Frederick A. Pottle's *James Boswell: The Earlier Years* (New York: McGraw-Hill, 1966), hereafter cited in text as *EY*, 1–6. The original French text, with the title *Ébauche*, together with an outline, an unfinished first draft, and other related authorial documents, is given as appendix 2 in James Boswell, *The Journal of His Swiss and German Travels, 1764*, ed. Marlies K. Danziger (Edinburgh: Edinburgh University Press, 2008). The editorial notes to the various texts in this second source have been drawn on in the account that follows. The English version and French original will be cited in the text as "Sketch" and *Ébauche* respectively.

7. The Tolbooth Church occupied the southwest end of the chief church of Edinburgh, St. Giles', which during the Reformation was partitioned into four places of worship. Boswell's uncle Dr. Alexander Webster, with whom he enjoyed a convivial friendship, was a minister there, and Boswell often attended his Sunday service.

8. For Pottle's frankly speculative account of this episode, see *EY*, 45–54; see also *EY*, 569–74 for an appendix in which Pottle presents and assesses the evidence for his interest in Catholicism. He argues that "Boswell's conviction as regards the claims of Rome could not have gone very deep, and it is probable the whole Roman-Catholic episode . . . was in part inspired by a wish to be different from other people, especially his father" (52). On the other hand, Murray Pittock argues that the importance of this conversion is indicated by the fact that such a candid and open man as Boswell was subsequently so unforthcoming about it (82).

9. Boswell's 1770 booklist includes the following Catholic titles (the dates given are those of Boswell's editions): Msgr. Michele Casati, *Compendio della Dottrina Cristiana di Genova* (n.d.); Richard Challoner, *The Grounds of the Old Religion: Also the Touchstone of the New Religion* (1751); Jacques Bénigne Bossuet, *Doctrine de l'Eglise Catholique* (1751); Fr. Paul Segnery, *True Wisdom* (1751). See *A Catalogue of Books Belonging to James Boswell, Esq.*, ed. Eleanor Terry Lincoln, rev. Su Jing-fen (typescript, 2010), 58, 64, 65. (This text courtesy of the Yale Boswell Editions office.)

10. *Boswell in Holland, 1763–1764*, ed. Frederick A. Pottle (London: Heinemann, 1952), 260: entry for June 2, 1764.

11. For an account of his relationship with the Scottish Presbyterian church, see Mary Margaret Stewart, "James Boswell and the National Church of Scotland," *Huntington Library Quarterly* 30:4 (August 1967): 369–87.

12. This figure does not actually represent attendance at a different place of worship each Sunday: Boswell worshipped at St. Paul's on three occasions and Westminster Abbey on two; on the other hand, one Sunday he attended three places of worship (as described below), and two on two other Sundays.

13. In Sept. 1774 he was invited by an Edinburgh minister, Rev. Dr. Daniel Macqueen, "to be an elder in his parish, the Old Kirk, but I told him that I did not think myself fit for the office" (*Ominous Years*, 7).

14. Mary Margaret Stewart, "Boswell's Denominational Dilemma," *PMLA* 76, no. 5 (December 1961): 503–11, vid. 504.

15. James Fordyce and Hugh Blair were notable Church of Scotland ministers; Blair was also well known as a literary critic and professor of rhetoric and was from 1758 a minister at the New Kirk, in St. Giles', which was the Edinburgh church that Boswell most often attended.

16. *Boswell for the Defence, 1769–1774*, ed. William K. Wimsatt and Frederick A. Pottle (London: Heinemann, 1960), 114.

17. *Boswell in Search of a Wife, 1766–1769*, ed. Frank Brady and Frederick A. Pottle (London: Heinemann, 1957), 352: entry for October 26, 1769 (cf. *Life*, 2:104–5).

18. Letter of February 1–8, 1767, *The Correspondence of James Boswell and William Johnson Temple, 1756–1795*, vol. 1, *1756–1777*, ed. Thomas Crawford (Edinburgh: Edinburgh University Press, 1997), hereafter cited as *Boswell-Temple Corresp.*, 163; my interpolation.

19. In the Yale compilation, Samuel Johnson, *Diaries, Prayers and Annals*, ed. E.L. McAdam, with Donald and Mary Hyde (New Haven: Yale University Press, 1958), there are, by my calculation, thirty or more sets of resolutions. My work on this subject is part of an ongoing project.

20. *Boswell in Extremes, 1776–1778*, ed. Charles McC. Weis and Frederick A. Pottle (New York: McGraw-Hill, 1970), 289.

21. That is: Joseph Butler, *The Analogy of Religion, Natural and Revealed, to the Constitution and Course of Nature* (1736); Hugo Grotius, *De Veritate Religionis Christianae* (1627); and John Locke, *The Reasonableness of Christianity as Delivered in the Scriptures* (1695).

22. Among Boswell's papers at Yale are a number of manuscripts, mainly scraps and single leaves, of miscellaneous notes concerning his reading. This material, which consists of short extracts, notes and summaries from works of literature, history, the law, and travel, is worthy of closer study; but among the sixty books and manuscripts mentioned (not including periodicals) there is only one religious work: Priestley's *Institutes of Natural and Revealed Theology*, 3 vols. (1772–74). See Marion S. Pottle, Claude Colleer Abbott, and Frederick A. Pottle, *Catalogue of the Papers of James Boswell at Yale University*, 3 vols. (Edinburgh: Edinburgh University Press; New Haven: Yale University Press, 1993), 1:107–13.

23. Walker, "Boswell's Use of 'Ogden on Prayer,'" 54.

24. April 20, 1780; *Boswell, Laird of Auchinleck, 1778–1782*, ed. Joseph W. Reed and Frederick A. Pottle (New York: McGraw-Hill, 1977), 202.

25. James Boswell, *The Hypochondriack*, ed. Margery Bailey, 2 vols. (Stanford: Stanford University Press, 1928), 2:156–57.

26. A 1728 edition of the book is listed in Boswell's 1770 *Catalogue of Books*, 40.

27. *The Correspondence of James Boswell and John Johnston of Grange*, ed. Ralph S. Walker (London: Heinemann, 1966), 118.

28. *Boswell on the Grand Tour: Italy, Corsica, and France, 1765–1766*, ed. Frank Brady and Frederick A. Pottle (London: Heinemann, 1955), 268–69.

29. *Letters of James Boswell*, ed. Chauncey Brewster Tinker, 2 vols. (Oxford: Clarendon Press, 1924), 1:215.

30. James Boswell, *An Account of Corsica, the Journal of a Tour to That Island, and Memoirs of Pascal Paoli*, ed. James T. Boulton and T.O. McLoughlin (Oxford: Oxford University Press, 2006), 18. The verse quoted is 2 Timothy 1:10.

31. This famous formulation of the sect's teaching is found on the tombstone of Robert Sandeman, who was the son-in-law of the sect's founder, John Glas. See James Ross, *A History of Congregational Independency in Scotland* (Glasgow: n.p., 1900), 30.

32. These twenty essays were published sporadically between 1770 and 1782 in the London daily, the *Public Advertiser*. They received little attention at the time, and their authorship was unknown until the recovery of Boswell's private papers in the twentieth century. They have not hitherto all been identified, very few were ever reprinted, and the series has never been collected. They will be included in *Facts and Inventions: Selections from the Journalism of James Boswell*, ed. Paul Tankard (forthcoming from Yale University Press).

33. *Public Advertiser*, no. 12955 (February 23, 1774), 2 (lead article).

34. *Public Advertiser*, no. 13005 (April 23, 1774), 2.

35. *Public Advertiser*, no. 14001 (August 16, 1774), 1 (lead article).

Chapter Fourteen

Bluestockings and Religion

Deborah Heller

Scholarly work on the Bluestockings has, over the past dozen years or so, increasingly turned our attention to the challenge of situating the Blues within the broader context of the Enlightenment. Variously using the analytical frameworks of the Habermasian public sphere, the rise and development of commercial society and its institutions, and the proliferation of knowledge, this new scholarship has opened important avenues of historical inquiry.[1] Most recently, some theorists have posited a peculiarly religious or Anglican Enlightenment in Britain, and this religious emphasis has influenced writings on the British Bluestockings. For example, in the wake of scholars such as J.G.A. Pocock and B.W. Young, who have argued for a "decidedly clerical" English Enlightenment, several writers have applied a theological explanation to the Bluestocking phenomenon.[2] In particular, Karen O'Brien and Mary Hilton—within their broader-ranging studies treating eighteenth-century British women's relationship to the Enlightenment and to education, respectively—have introduced the thesis of a specifically latitudinarian "Bluestocking theology," arguing that the Bluestockings' personal adherence to a "latitudinarian" religious viewpoint opened the way for their characteristic advocacy for women's education and social activism: in short, that their theological commitments produced their Bluestockingness.[3]

Because it had never before occurred to anyone (to my knowledge) to suggest that there was a peculiarly Bluestocking religion, and because O'Brien's and Hilton's shared thesis includes the strong suggestion of an "indissolubly determinist link" (to use B.W. Young's term) between "religious and philosophical options" and political and social outcomes,[4] I will in this essay examine the merits of this emerging view, posing two questions in particular: first, can the claim that the Bluestockings are latitudinarian be justified; and, second, can the larger but related claim that the British Enlightenment was a religious one in the sense that theological commitments determined—or even tracked with—enlightened practice, be equally validated?

I feel certain that the Bluestockings would have been surprised to hear themselves called latitudinarians. No Bluestocking, with one insignificant exception, ever used the word *latitudinarian*—or *latitude*—in reference to herself or to anyone else.[5] Indeed the term, as applied to the eighteenth century, seems to be a category created by later church historians. It was in fact rarely used during the eighteenth century, and when it was used, it was predominantly pejorative. In any event, far from being in any straightforward sense latitudinarian, the Blues were a diverse lot confessionally: Eva Garrick, for example, was a practicing Roman Catholic; Elizabeth Vesey, though the daughter of an Irish bishop, appears to have been a lifelong religious doubter; and Bluestocking affiliates like Sarah Chapone, Anne Donnellan, and Mary Delany were followers of the High-Church Hutchinsonian movement.[6] Additionally, Elizabeth Carter and Catherine Talbot would have been shocked and offended at being called latitudinarians. Not only were the pejorative and politically charged connotations of the word not apt, but as close associates of Archbishop Thomas Secker (Talbot spent her entire life from childhood in the Secker household; Carter was a close friend of Talbot and a particular protégée of Secker), both would have instinctively rejected the label as applied to themselves or to Archbishop Secker. As used in the eighteenth century, *latitudinarian* would connote—if not heterodoxy ("one who departs from orthodoxy," as Johnson defines *latitudinarian* in his *Dictionary*)—at least one who was lax in doctrinal commitments, as well as one who espoused a merely "moral religion." These connotations would suit neither the High Church archbishop nor his Bluestocking friends.[7] As a matter of fact, as I will show in what follows, all of the Bluestockings treated by Hilton and O'Brien held to a remarkably orthodox set of religious beliefs.

Hilton's and O'Brien's claims for a latitudinarian "Bluestocking theology" (O'Brien, 56; Hilton, 49) cannot be squared with the evidence. The Bluestockings as a group were far too diverse to fit into any theological category—and it must be pointed out as well that "theology" is not an apt word to apply to the Bluestockings, whose religious expression would more accurately be classified as "lay piety" rather than "theology" (though Carter could be argued to have produced "religious writings"). The Blues simply were not female philosophers and theologians who cobbled together "ideas of ethics and epistemology hospitable to the rational and moral agency of women," or who had a "role . . . in the advancement of the (mainly Whig) Latitudinarian English Enlightenment" (O'Brien, 35–36). And even if we restrict our arguments to Carter, Montagu, Talbot, and Chapone (the only Blues recognized by Hilton and O'Brien), the "latitudinarian Bluestocking" thesis still cannot stand. Starting with a critique of their definition of latitude as an "ideological wing of the Anglican Church" with its own distinctive intellectual tenets featuring rationalism and secularizing ethics (O'Brien, 35) and continuing with a rebuttal of their argumentative methodology, this essay will argue against Hilton and O'Brien that theological doctrines and propositions did not play a significant role in producing the Blues' "Bluestockingness" (gentry women's progressive innovations in education and social activism). Instead, I will argue that their valorization of reason and education, and their engagement in philanthropy and projects of social and cultural improvement, were products of secular "public sphere" institutions and assumptions. At the same time, I will complicate the picture by arguing that religion did indeed provide, as it were, the "drive belt" for the Blues' social activism and progressivism—not through theological propositions but through the influence of the traditional, deeply enculturated Christian principles of charity and salvation history.

The sociological thesis of secularization dies hard. Many scholars of eighteenth-century Britain are now claiming to oppose secularization theory (the notion that the so-called demise of religion correlates with societal modernization), arguing that theology was not merely neutral or an ideological reflex of political or economic causes, but was itself instrumental in producing the progressive aspects of modernization. It seems to me, however, that they can redeem their bid to uncouple modernization and secularization theory only by retaining a hidden *rationalization* theory within their treatment of religion. The theory of rationalization, well known from Max Weber's disenchantment thesis, holds that modernization is inevitably accompanied by the dismantling of traditional religious belief through reason. Subjected to the steady assault of critical reason, so the theory goes, religions progressively lose their power and cogency.

Some scholars, as I have said, resist the coupling of modernization and secularization theory, arguing that the English Enlightenment was instead played out in the arena of religion and theology. Thus, although Hilton and O'Brien argue that the "Latitudinarian English Enlightenment" was the "ideological wing" of the Anglican Church (O'Brien, 35–36) and that it produced the societal and cultural improvement formerly thought to result from innovations in secular institutions and ideas, I believe they continue to tacitly rely on the rationalization thesis: latitudinarianism is progressive (it is assumed) only insofar as its commitment to reason penetrates the theological core of Anglicanism and trumps its fundamental Christian doctrines. My imputation of a hidden rationalization thesis is confirmed by their treatment of evangelicalism as a counter-Enlightenment force. As they would have it, evangelicalism at the end of the century reversed latitudinarian progress, a regression to prerational and unenlightened thinking. As a corollary, so their theory suggests, Hannah More, second generation Blue and author of the Bluestocking "anthem" *Bas Bleu*, cannot be counted a Bluestocking because of her allegedly atavistic religious commitments.

My essay has, then, a specific hermeneutical task. Seeking to demonstrate that the Bluestockings were not latitudinarians in Hilton's and O'Brien's sense of the word, I want first to define what that sense is, and second to place their definition within the larger inquiry of what exactly was eighteenth-century latitude. Some recent historians believe that latitudinarianism was a distinct "theological position, even a movement, with definable doctrines and principles," while others believe that it was "a state of mind" or "a temper rather than a creed."[8] As a temper, latitude is described by scholars as irenic, that is, a desire to comprehend within the Church as many as possible of those Protestants who, differing little in essential doctrine, had been driven out by the legislation of 1662. Such irenic latitudinarians valued *peace* over *polemics*. They were essentially conservative in matters of church polity and church doctrine (orthodox in matters of original sin, human corruption, needful repentance, the atonement of man's sin by Christ's sacrifice); their goal was to preserve intact the constitutional arrangements of church and state, to preserve and expand the communion between the *catholic* Anglican Church and the English state, its citizens and their minds and morals. They were motivated by Christian charitableness and toleration, not by intellectual propositions. More specifically, *reason* for them was not a battle cry or *machine de guerre*. Latitudinarian insistence on the reasonableness of Christianity arose during the troubles of the civil wars, when reason as a public standard of *consensus* was thought a promising antidote against the fever of enthusiasm. And in the eighteenth century also, irenic latitudinarians, while never doubting the *truth* of their Christian beliefs and never releasing their hold on doctrinal orthodoxy, nevertheless were loath to place their *claim* to truth in front of unity-seeking peace.

Scholars who endorse this definition of latitude as an irenic *temper* and not a creed include Patrick Müller and Melvyn New. Müller speaks of "a distinctive *theological spirit*," and New of "the *essential spirit*, irenic and anti-systematical of latitudinarianism." Both see the irenic latitude of the eighteenth-century church as a continuation of seventeenth-century latitudinarianism, resembling it in being orthodox doctrinally and conservative in ecclesiology. Latitudinarianism possessed, according to them, neither a rationalistic nor a secularizing tendency. Müller emphasizes (1) that it maintained no doctrine of human benevolence; (2) that it upheld a firm belief in eschatology; and (3) that it maintained a belief in voluntarist ethics. These points also held true for seventeenth-century latitudinarians, according to scholars like W.M. Spellman, Gerard Reedy, Gordon Rupp, John Spurr, and others, who have emphasized the traditional Christian orthodoxy of the seventeenth-century latitudinarians and have challenged the uncritical assumption of an alliance between Enlightenment rationalism and the rational theology of the Restoration divines.[9]

The other main approach to defining *latitude*—which could be called *ideological*—tends to see latitudinarianism, not as a widespread temper but as an ideological wing of the Anglican Church that eventually would place the claims of reason *above* considerations of unity and peace. Taking the Reformation principles of *sola scriptura* and the right of individual conscience to a level of importance never envisioned by seventeenth-century rational divines, these ideological latitudinarians were ready to question the church's right to an authority independent of the state, or its right to impose any doctrine "which is not *clearly* and *expressly* contain'd and *declared to be necessary* in the Gospel."[10] These *ideological* latitude men were willing to press the claims of individual reason against the authority of the church, as did Benjamin Hoadly in the Bangorian controversy and Francis Blackburne in his *Confessional* and subsequent Feathers Tavern Petition.

Ideological latitude's eruption into political activism arose from its "enlightened emphasis on truth above all things," as Martin Fitzpatrick points out,[11] but it must also be pointed out that it depended on a new Enlightenment concept of reason as well. Enlightenment reason can be characterized as both critical and discursive. Robert Voitle explains the latter: "*reason becomes merely reasoning or ratiocination*, and, since it is now an operation of mind rather than a faculty of the soul, it loses the character of an entity, a *thing*, and becomes an activity, a calculating process dependent upon the data of sense and reflection."[12] The metaphysically grounded reason (*recta ratio*) of the Cambridge Platonists, where the mind of man can mirror exactly the eternal and immutable truth in the mind of God, is replaced with individual reasoning, and thus no longer serves as a secure foundation for religious (and political) consensus.

Historians who promote the ideological interpretation of latitude (and here we include Hilton and O'Brien) see latitudinarianism as akin to, and leading into, Rational Dissent and political radicalism.[13] This view probably derives from eighteenth-century sources like Theophilus Lindsey, son-in-law of Blackburne and convert to Unitarianism, who provides a genealogy linking Unitarianism to seventeenth-century latitude via Clarke, Hoadly, Blackburne, and others: "O ye *Tillotsons, Patricks, Burnets, Tennisons*, could ye have been now recalled from your long quiet repose in the grave, . . . how different a part would ye have acted! . . . had ye enjoyed those lights concerning the equal rights of men, and the incompetency of human authority in the things of religion, with which the world hath been blest since your time, by the labours of Locke, Hoadley, Blackburne, Law."[14] Such political consequences of free reasoning in matters of religion, let me add parenthetically, would be vigorously condemned by the Bluestockings. Elizabeth Montagu's opinion of Lindsey puts the Bluestockings' view in a nutshell:

> A Mr Lindsay who had for 30 years been Pastor of a parish near one of my Estates in Yorkshire told his Parishioners that the opinions in which they had lived & many of their Neighbours had dyed were all wrong, were so wicked, he must abandon his Living on which his subsistence depended, rather than longer maintain those doctrines which he had inculcated into them. That Jesus was really a Human Person & the Son of a Carpenter. . . . [H]e kindly advised them to beware of all established doctrine & appointed Teaching and to think for themselves.[15]

The Bluestockings do not fit into the political tendency of ideological latitudinarianism. Nor do they adhere to a "Bluestocking theology" commensurate with ideological latitude; yet this is what Hilton and O'Brien try to show.

Hilton and O'Brien use three modes of argument: first, from ties of personal association; second, from reading habits; and third, from quotations taken from writings of Carter, Montagu, Talbot, and Chapone. The first category of argument is perhaps the most important. Both Hilton and O'Brien begin with personal ties, making, I believe, extremely speculative and, at times, far-fetched arguments. Hilton's allegation, for example, that Talbot became latitudinarian because of her association with the "renowned latitudinarian bishop" Thomas Secker backfires when it is pointed out that Secker was anything but latitudinarian, in Hilton's and O'Brien's sense. And at any rate, it is never made clear why a close personal tie necessarily denotes a philosophical or theological discipleship as well. Hilton further tells us that

> Elizabeth Carter was the daughter of the scholarly Nicolas Carter, curate of Deal, who was the friend of Sir George Oxendon MP, a close associate of the Prime Minister Sir Robert Walpole, who appointed several latitudinarian bishops. It is not surprising that, immersed in this theological milieu, these highly intellectual women began to use for themselves the discourses of the latitudinarian "religion of reason." (49)

This chain of association, in which Carter is five times removed from the allegedly latitudinarian bishops, is, needless to say, too tenuous to be taken seriously.

Reading habits are also no dependable indicator of theological allegiances. If the young Elizabeth Montagu (then Robinson) once read Samuel Clarke with approval in 1741, as O'Brien points out (56), that does not make her a "Clarkist," any more than Hannah More's recommendation of Joseph Butler's *Analogy* to her female readers to strengthen their reasoning abilities makes her a "Butlerian."[16] Reading habits in the eighteenth century were notoriously eclectic, and they do not necessarily track with ideological commitments. Both Talbot and More, who (according to Hilton and O'Brien) stood at opposite extremes theologically, read and admired the writings of the Port Royal authors; and More, the alleged foe and destroyer of the supposed Bluestocking "latitudinarian ideology," puts into the mouth of Mr. Stanley (her ideological spokesman in *Coelebs*) high praise for the sermons of seventeenth-century latitudinarians Isaac Barrow and John Tillotson.[17]

Finally, Hilton's and O'Brien's practice of selective quotation is virtually *required* by their argument: in order to argue that Bluestocking religious views had enlightening effects on Bluestocking practice, they must paradoxically make those views as secular as possible. The "latitudinarianism" they fashion for the Blues becomes "a largely moral religion based on reason" (Hilton, 50)—in fact, it leans toward being a rationalistic religion that teaches that "men and women have reason enough to decipher the laws of nature and discover the truths of religion for themselves" (O'Brien, 57). Human nature retains enough of its prelapsarian perfection of reason and will to enable it to decipher on its own the principles of morality and to act accordingly. Additionally, so the Bluestockings are alleged to believe, human beings are essentially benevolent and sociable. The effect of these theological premises on Bluestocking practice is supposed to be twofold: first, the Blues realized the importance of reason for women and therefore advocated improved women's education; second, they were disposed to be outward-looking and sociable instead of inward and self-searching, and thus they were encouraged to work out their own salvation through good works in society and through cultivation of their own manners.

To attribute this rationalistic and secularizing "latitudinarianism" to the Bluestockings requires a practice of selective quotation from their writings. One must exaggerate their commitment to "reason" and autonomous morality, and one must underplay their adherence to the biblical doctrines of original sin (or corruption of human nature) and the redemption of mankind through Christ's sacrifice. It is my belief that the Bluestockings can only be made into "latitudinarians" (in Hilton's and O'Brien's sense)—and Hannah More can only be made into a "Counter-Enlightenment" figure—by ignoring, or discounting, a substantial portion of their religious statements. If those statements are also considered, writings of Carter, Talbot, Chapone, and Montagu begin to resemble more and more the religious writings of their Bluestocking comrade, Hannah More. All five Bluestockings then conform to what I might dare to call "orthodox Anglicanism."

In an important review article, Jonathan Sheehan lays out the *malgré soi* secularizing logic of the new attempts to wed Enlightenment and religion:

> Although recent scholarship has tried hard . . . to detach the Enlightenment from irreligiosity, the story of Enlightenment secularization proves very difficult to shed. On the one hand, the presence of religion seems to diminish the power of the Enlightenment. On the other, the resulting Enlightenment still retains a fundamentally secularizing power.[18]

One attempt to resolve this dilemma and get the oil and water of religion and Enlightenment to mix, while retaining the full powers of both, has been the revival of Isaiah Berlin's idea of a "Counter-Enlightenment"; an example is Brian Young's unearthing of a British "Counter-Enlightenment" that raised its dogmatic, irrational, and superstitious head against the antidogmatic, rational, and progressive clerical Enlightenment in England. "In all these cases," Sheehan says, "the Counter-Enlightenment allows its authors both to tell a story of an eighteenth-century religion untarnished by the patina of decay and also to salvage the traditionally rationalist idea of enlightenment from the challenge of religion."[19] This attempted solution (or emulsion) of the seemingly insoluble elements of religion and Enlightenment has the advantage of a tidy simplicity: two opposing religious currents, a good and a bad, now wash through the British eighteenth century, the good bringing progress and secularization, the bad threatening reversal of all social and political improvement brought about by its opponent. In the case of Hilton and O'Brien, "latitudinarianism" is the rational, good religious movement bringing Enlightenment; evangelicalism is the evil sibling bringing Counter-Enlightenment.

As "a largely moral religion based on reason," both writers ultimately see latitude as tending toward the development of a secular ethics—a development well known from studies of the British moralists, and one that minimizes the principle of moral obligation as *founded on* obedience to the will of God. According to J.B. Schneewind, "during the seventeenth and eighteenth centuries established conceptions of morality as obedience came increasingly to be contested by emerging conceptions of morality as self-governance."[20] O'Brien makes this emphasis on human moral self-sufficiency explicit when she applies the technical theological term *anti-voluntarist* to the Bluestockings:

> They all constructed for themselves a non-dogmatic, anti-voluntarist kind of Christianity. It was serious but flexible; it was less important to adhere to the orthodox doctrine of the Trinity, for example, than to believe that men and women have reason enough to decipher the laws of nature and discover the truths of religion for themselves. (57)

O'Brien stresses that the Blues *constructed for themselves* not merely a "practical, socially oriented kind of piety" but a "theology" (57), and this theology was "anti-voluntarist"— by which she means a theology according to which moral obligation is based on the individual's ability to discern God-independent moral principles and to motivate his or her action accordingly, rather than on God's will and His capacity to reward and punish. Moreover, human reason is able to "discover the truths of religion" for itself.

Both O'Brien and Hilton see this anti-voluntarist and secularizing "theology" as based on a rejection of Christian notions of original sin and original human corruption. If human nature is not incapacitated by original corruption, it follows that there is no need for Christ's redeeming sacrifice; if moral behavior is motivated by the autonomous self and not by God's will, one need not worry about reward or punishment in the afterlife. Both authors tend to ignore passages in Bluestocking writings having to do with these topics— systematic omissions and distortions that can be grouped under three rubrics: (1) reason and its limitations; (2) sin and redemption; and (3) the afterlife.

Reason and Its Limitations: Did the Bluestockings hold "that men and women have reason enough to decipher the laws of nature and discover the truths of religion for themselves?" O'Brien adduces as evidence two series of letters by Elizabeth Carter to unknown correspondents; the first to a certain "Vittoria," the second to an unnamed correspondent, probably Elizabeth Vesey. Carter tries through "rational" arguments to bring Vittoria, who has apostatized from the Christian religion, to recognize and accept the truth of the Gospel; to her second correspondent, she responds to the demand for rational proof of the truth of Scripture. In these letters Carter does indeed admit that we are "reasonable creatures, whose assent is to be determined by reasonable arguments,"[21] but, despite that, she is far from being a rationalist in the Enlightenment sense. In one letter, she addresses her correspondent thus: "You say that it appears to you, 'that it is the business of the head to bring to trial the authority of the facts upon which we receive a revelation.' Very true; but let us consider what are the previous dispositions necessary to our entering upon such a trial" (Pennington, 615). In the first place, she says, to make a serious examination of the Gospel, "yet entirely with a confidence in our own understanding, is not having a proper sense of human weakness." If we wish to judge Scripture rationally, we must first "endeavour to form not only our outward behaviour, but the whole internal frame of our mind, with reference to [God's] approbation":

> Those who sincerely wish to make his will the first object of their choice, who submit their understanding to his direction, and implore and depend on his assistance to guard them from error, his goodness will never suffer to be fatally misled; and they will enter on their enquiry with a full security of obtaining every degree of conviction which is necessary to their virtue and their peace. So true I believe is the position that conviction depends on the heart. (616)

Religion, according to Carter, is not so much a matter of the head but of the heart: "[It is] not so much a matter of speculation to the understanding as an object of the affections of the heart" (622).

Gerard Reedy, in his study of Scripture, reason, and seventeenth-century divines, gives us a way of understanding how an apologist could claim to use "reason" to prove the Christian faith and yet not be a rationalist—indeed, like Carter, could be a voluntarist with a strong orientation toward obedience to God's will antecedent to any reasoning. According to Reedy, "rational divines" like Edward Stillingfleet and John Tillotson (Reedy avoids the label "latitudinarian") used the word "reason" in their rational arguments for the truth of Scripture in two senses: reason in the narrow sense "is the reason of philosophy that operates strictly on its own first principles"; reason in a wider sense "is reason that is informed not only by its own laws but by the matter it is investigating. . . . [T]his definition means that reason is disposed toward a full acceptance of the full contents of Scripture." Reason thus admits "as a constituent object of rational inquiry, the possible existence of an external principle that guarantees Scripture's truth irrespective of its rational content":

> Reason in this wider sense thus holds, in its core, an abiding affection for a source of truth that is not rationally verifiable in all its operations; such a commitment is not the result of a persuasion but of some deeper human act that has always been called, in spite of the divines' attempt to broaden the category, specifically religious faith.

It is "the divines' reticence in speaking of their prerational bias," argues Reedy, that has "encouraged subsequent use of the term 'rationalism' to describe their project." In a similar way, though less clandestinely, when Carter speaks of eliciting persuasion through reason, she is ultimately basing her conviction on religious faith—on a disposition of the heart, not of the head. To make Carter an Enlightenment rationalist in her approach to Scripture is to ignore the apologetic tradition—found earlier in Tillotson, Stillingfleet, and others—that bases its polemics for the reasonableness of scriptural Christianity on "reason" in a double sense.[22]

One could cite many instances of the nonrationalistic religious views of Bluestockings, but space permits only one more example. In 1753 Hester Chapone contributed "The Story of Fidelia" to the *Adventurer*. Fidelia, having lost her mother at the age of twelve, was raised by her freethinking father and led by his teaching to reject revealed religion. Instead, she relied on the "pride of reason" and on her rationally calculated virtuous behavior. Basing her actions on "motives which had no necessary connexion with immortality," she "was not led to consider a future state either with hope or fear."[23] When her father dies, at her age of twenty, she is called on to put to the test the deistic and freethinking philosophy she had learned from him. Her fortunes steadily decline: she plunges into poverty, is seduced by Sir George Freelove, and, finally, attempts suicide. Providentially rescued by an elderly clergyman and his wife, Fidelia stays in the parsonage and eventually undergoes a conversion:

> Here, with the assistance of the clergyman . . . I have studied the Holy Scriptures, and the evidences of their authority. But after reading them with candour and attention, I found all the extrinsic arguments of their truth superfluous. The excellency of their precepts, the consistency of their doctrines, and the glorious motives and encouragements to virtue which they propose, together with the striking example I had before my eyes of their salutary effects, left me no doubt of their divine authority. (Chapone, 4:77)

Fidelia here is persuaded of the truth of the Scriptures, not through rationalism in the narrow sense, but through a broader reasoning that relies, indeed, on the evidence of internal consistency, but on the evidence of felt experience as well. Though Chapone is a ferocious reasoner in other contexts (see, for example, her *Letters on Filial Obedience*), we see here a reasoning quite distinct from the Enlightenment rationality that would test religion not by the heart but by the head.

Sin and Redemption: In an attempt to separate the theological tenets of Hannah More from the other Bluestockings, Hilton and O'Brien claim that More's evangelicalism placed an emphasis (almost Calvinistic) on original sin and human depravity, but that the "latitudinarian" Bluestockings stressed rather an intact and benevolent human nature, capable of cultivation and right direction: "The rise, from the 1780s, of Evangelical Christianity placed a parallel emphasis upon man's helplessness in this world and deliberately tried to put an end to the diluted, amiably benevolent Latitudinarian Anglicanism of the eighteenth century" (O'Brien, 223). This is to misrepresent both More's evangelicalism, which stressed man's ability to work out his own salvation through grace, and the Blues' theological beliefs, which resembled More's both in their Arminian tendency and in their acceptance of the orthodox Christian doctrines of original corruption and Christ's redemptive power. Typical of the Bluestocking position on original sin and redemption is Catherine Talbot's comment in *Reflections*: "We are to acknowledge, that of ourselves we are able to do nothing as we ought: . . . We are to trust and hope alone in the Merits and Intercession of our blessed Redeemer; and to own ourselves 'less than the least of God's mercies.'"[24]

Passages with such explicit mentions of sin and redemption are generally omitted by O'Brien and Hilton. A striking instance is Hilton's quotation from Chapone's *Letters on the Improvement of the Mind*:

> The great laws of morality are indeed written in our hearts, and may be discovered by reason; but our reason is of slow growth; very unequally dispensed to different persons; liable to error, and confined within very narrow limits in all. [Therefore the Scriptures should be regarded as] a particular revelation of [God's] will. (56)

Hilton has docked the quotation after the words "narrow limits in all." The actual passage continues at that point thus:

> If therefore, God has vouchsafed to grant a particular revelation of his will—if he has been so unspeakably gracious, as to send his son into the world to reclaim mankind from error and wickedness—to die for our sins—and to teach us the way to eternal life; surely it becomes us to receive his precepts with the deepest reverence.[25]

The allusion to the darling passage of rational moralists—Romans 2:15, that the work of the law is written in the Gentiles' hearts—Chapone (in the full passage) carefully places into its proper Pauline context (cf. Romans 3:23–24: "For all have sinned, and come short of the glory of God; Being justified freely by his grace through the redemption that is in Christ Jesus").

It is equally clear that Elizabeth Carter regarded Stoicism as vastly inferior to the Christian revelation, because Stoicism's view of human nature omitted original sin and redemption: "Far differently the Christian System represents Mankind: . . . as created in a State of improveable Virtue and Happiness: Fallen, by an abuse of Free Will, into Sin, Misery, and Weakness; but redeemed from them by an Almighty Saviour."[26]

The Afterlife: Hilton and O'Brien assure us that the Bluestockings, on the force of their "theology," were principally concerned with personal and social improvement in the here and now. O'Brien writes: "[The Bluestockings] rejected schemes of philosophy or theology which demanded . . . an eschatological concern for the next life" (59). Two examples will suffice to show that this is false. First, there is a letter of Montagu to her friend Elizabeth Vesey, whose husband had died some months earlier. Vesey was suffering from what today we would call clinical depression, and she would not stop weeping. Montagu counsels her:

> oh my Friend! your obstinate grief may affect your bliss in the life eternal, which shall have no end. . . . You take a sort of pleasure in the indulgence of weeping, but is it so delightfull that you wish rather to have your eternal life with that Society where there is incessant weeping & gnashing of teeth, than in the state where all tears are wiped for ever from all eyes?[27]

Second, we read in Chapone's *Improvement* the following passage on the four last things:

> What a tremendous scene does the gospel place before our eyes of the *last day*? When you, and every one of us, shall awake from the grave, and behold the Son of God, on his glorious tribunal, attended by millions of celestial beings, of whose superior excellence we can now form no adequate idea:—When in presence of all mankind, of those holy angels, and of the great judge himself, *you* must give an account of your past life, and hear your final doom, from which there can be no appeal, and which must determine your fate, to all eternity.[28]

Clearly, Bluestockings did not reject an eschatological concern for the afterlife, nor did they reject the voluntarist ethics that it implied.

It was virtually *required*, as stated above, that Hilton and O'Brien adopt the strong hypothesis that the "latitudinarian" Blues explicitly or implicitly rejected the fundamental biblical doctrines of sin, redemption, and afterlife. Had they held that the Blues did not emphasize these doctrines but did not reject them, then the results they imagined to have flowed from Bluestocking doctrinal premises would not have followed. The alleged Bluestocking belief in the natural benevolence of humankind would not follow, because it would conflict with the belief in original sin; their alleged this-worldly orientation would not follow, because it would contradict the doctrine of the afterlife; and, finally, their alleged commitment to a secularized ethics would contradict orthodox voluntarist Christian ethics, grounded on reward and punishment in the afterlife and enmeshed with the doctrine of original sin and Christ's necessary redemption. As a corollary, the alleged result, that Bluestockings promoted reason and education for women, would also not follow from any theological premises, if the Blues did not firmly hold to the position that reason was the test of faith and therefore the sovereign instrument for discerning religious and ethical duties.

Let us look at the results that are proposed by Hilton and O'Brien to have issued from theological premises. They fall roughly into the following categories: (1) reason and education for women; (2) this-worldliness; and (3) natural benevolence. The first category is indeed characteristic of Bluestockingness as I and everyone else would define it. The second, however, is simply wrong; the Blues did indeed have a commitment actively to do good *in* the world, as enjoined in the Gospel—but without being *of* the world. Chapone makes the point with distinct clarity: "It is with the rules of the gospel we must compare ourselves, and not with the world around us; for we know . . . that we must not be 'conformed to the world.'"[29] Similarly, the third category, natural benevolence, does not hold, for the Blues did not as a group espouse any doctrine of natural human benevolence; instead, they felt that the heart and affections must be governed according to the precepts of Scripture—a point Chapone also clearly formulates: "You must *form* and *govern* your *temper* and *manners*, according to the laws of benevolence and justice; and qualify yourself, by all means in your power, for an *useful* and *agreeable* member of society" (3:262).

The characteristics of Bluestockingness—as I define them—might be summarized as both the cultivation of reason and education for women, on the one hand, and the active and charitable engagement of women in society, on the other. These are not the *result* of any specific Bluestocking theological propositions, latitudinarian or otherwise. Instead, we can attribute them to two background causes, neither, perhaps, fully apparent to the Blues themselves: published discourses—and pragmatic assumptions underlying them—of certain "public sphere" institutions; and second, the deeply enculturated principles of Judeo-Christian piety. Before returning to this question of causality, however, it is worth demonstrating that Hannah More did not differ from the first-generation Blues in her "Bluestockingness," because if she did not, the alleged differences in their theological premises would be moot since the *results* could not then be shown to have been different.

Cultivation of female reasoning was an important issue for More, both before and after her conversion to evangelicalism. Shortly after moving to London in her younger years (before her conversion), she reports a Bluestocking assembly at Montagu's where she was delighted to find "a diversity of opinions, which produced a great deal of good argument and reasoning."[30] Similarly, in *Bas Bleu: or, Conversation* (1783) she celebrated the "rational entertainment" (as the Bluestockings liked to call it) of Bluestocking conversation, which featured "Polemics, really seeking truth" (1.179).[31] Later, as an evangelical, she wrote in *Strictures*: "I mean not here to recommend books which are immediately religious, but such as exercise the reasoning faculties, teach the mind to get acquainted with its own nature, and to stir up its own powers." She then proceeds to recommend "Watts's or Duncan's little book of Logic, some parts of Mr. Locke's Essay on the Human Understanding, and Bishop Butler's Analogy."[32]

Further, there was no Bluestocking more involved in promoting and practicing women's social activism than More. Indeed, she seems not a deviation from, but the very pinnacle of the Bluestockings' project for women's active engagement in philanthropic and educational enterprises. Why, then, argue that she broke with the Bluestockings? The facts are simply otherwise. From her arrival on the scene in 1774, More was a public intellectual of the Bluestocking group, and she remained a Bluestocking. Furthermore, she continued to engage in salon activity even after she began her antislavery and Sunday school projects. She regularly visited Elizabeth Montagu in the summers at Sandleford and, up until Montagu's death in 1800, routinely attended Montagu's winter sessions in London. The two women were linked by their role as public intellectuals, but also by their shared commitment to doing good to body and soul of the poor. In fact, Montagu was the first to start a

Sunday school and may have inspired More in this, rather than vice versa. In the antislavery campaign, it was Elizabeth Carter who especially shared More's fervent commitment. Writing to her in June 1787, More expects the anti–slave-trade bill to be brought before Parliament in the spring and urges Carter to solicit votes: "My dear friend, be sure to canvas every body who has a heart."[33]

My argument thus far has endeavored to undermine both ends of the theory undergirding the notion that latitudinarianism (mistakenly defined as ideological and therefore rationalizing and secularizing) either caused or resulted in social and political activities. On one hand, this so-called latitudinarianism, with its allegedly progress-promoting theological premises, has been shown *not* to hold for the Bluestockings. On the other, the alleged differences in results supposed to have flowed from Hannah More's evangelicalism, as opposed to "latitudinarianism," have also been shown not to be valid. How much, we may finally ask, do theological propositions in general influence progress or regression in matters social and political? Do they have any influence at all? It turns out that More's evangelicalism was at least *not incompatible* with her social and political activism and with her promotion of female reason and education—values often associated with the Enlightenment. More positively, one could point out that her evangelicalism was certainly not Calvinistic but Arminian on the questions of election and the cooperation of individual efforts and divine grace, and that it embraced postmillennialism and therefore allowed an optimistic belief in the possibility, indeed duty, of initiating change and improvement in society. May we then speak of a fusion of evangelical theology and Enlightenment—of a penetration of Enlightenment premises into theological foundations? Anne Stott has recently opined that More's evangelicalism should be seen as part of a "British Christian Enlightenment": "Hannah More's Christianity was infused with Lockean principles and wider Enlightenment values and these impacted strongly on her theory and practice of education."[34]

I believe we are quite unjustified in speaking of either an "enlightened Christianity" or "Christianized Enlightenment," most especially when "Enlightenment" implies the penetration of reason and its operations into the foundations of Christian theology, and when the resulting theological propositions are thought to be causative of social and political actions. Such actions are never caused by theological or philosophical propositions—if by causation we mean logical entailment.[35] Second, the notion of a Christian Enlightenment seems based on mistaken understandings of both the Christianity of the era and "Enlightenment." *Christianity*, in this mistaken view, seems to refer not to a set of rituals or practices, or to institutions or faith communities, but exclusively to a set of propositions, mistakenly labeled latitudinarian, when what is meant is rationalism; and the term *Enlightenment* is also generally used to embody ideas rather than practices and institutions.

I would suggest that the relationship between religious *faith* and Enlightenment *reason* is similar to that between oil and water. The very word *faith*—and its cognates in the biblical languages, Greek *pistis* and Latin *fides*—implies, not a cognitive relationship between a knower and an object of knowledge, but rather a relationship of trust or "faithfulness" between two or more persons. The same is true of the Hebrew *'ĕmûnāh* ("faithfulness").[36] Faith, then, essentially refers to an intersubjective relationship of trust and solidarity—an ethical concept rather than a cognitive one. Enlightenment reason, on the other hand, asks questions about the truth or falseness of propositions. To be sure, divines like Stillingfleet and Tillotson, as noted above, were willing and able to describe faith as "a *rational* and *discursive Act* of the mind" (Stillingfleet), and as "a Perswasion of the mind concerning any thing; concerning the truth of any Proposition, concerning the Existence, or Futurition, or Lawfulness, or Convenience, or Possibility, or Goodness of any thing, or the contrary" (Tillotson).[37] But, as Reedy has shown, these divines were using the word "reason" and its related cognates in a double sense: reason in a strict, narrow sense; and reason in a wider sense, which virtually collapsed reason into the concept of faith. In the eighteenth century, as we saw in the case of Elizabeth Carter, Christian apologists also used the notion of reason in an ambiguous sense: "reason" was a useful tool of persuasion, but it never became (for writers like Carter) the criterion of faith.

Enlightenment reason is essentially opposed to, and corrosive of, traditional religious belief. If we imagine Enlightenment reason, following Jürgen Habermas,[38] to be a procedural, critical reason, where justificatory answer follows challenging questions in a public forum, then we can never expect to reach a position where God-given "right reason" corresponds exactly to eternal, immutable, and necessary truth, as with the Cambridge Platonists. Instead, the "leaven of reason," in the words of evangelical Joseph Milner, "a spirit of religious investigation, which exerts itself independently of revealed truth," "threatens to leave neither root nor branch."[39] If we imagine Enlightenment reason, again following Habermas, as permission for any and all persons to question accepted, traditional truths and to demand of an interlocutor justificatory reasons, we can also see in our mind's eye a traditional faith under siege. From a phenomenological point of view, a unified, traditional worldview is a body of unquestioned beliefs that may then be subjected to rational challenge. As the challenge goes on, there always exists a shared body of accepted, unchallenged belief behind the backs of the interlocutors. This, I suggest, constitutes the body of primitive, original Christian assumptions that drove the self-concept and actions of the Bluestockings. Untouched by sectarian controversies, these beliefs—the fundamental Christian doctrines of charity and salvation history—were the "drive belt" of Bluestocking social consciousness.

I make here a distinction between these fundamental doctrines, which were deeply enculturated into all British men and women of our period, and theological doctrines that might be argued about and might even create sectarian factions. The fundamental assumptions of Christian charity and salvation history are deep-seated in the mentality of the West and are shared by religious and nonreligious alike. They unconsciously provide, perhaps, much of the motivational background of even secular, progressivist movements. I am suggesting, however, that these assumptions formed *more than an unconscious energy* of motivation for the Bluestockings. The Blues openly embraced these elements of their religious heritage in their drive for improvement of manners, propagation of the faith, and social progress generally.

The universalism of Christianity and its belief in the equality of all human souls form an ethical basis for the West more fundamental than Enlightenment discourses of natural law, rights, and equality. Specifically, *charity*, the command to love God and to love each other—the sum of the law and the prophets, as we read in the gospels (Matthew 22:40, 7:12)—is, as Hester Chapone tells her niece in *Improvement*, "that part of scripture, which is the most important of all."[40] This fundamental Christian principle was the great motor of Bluestocking charitable activities, such activities as formed (together with Enlightenment-driven aspirations) at least half of Bluestockingness.

In addition, there is *salvation history*. Christianity is a religion rooted in history, and oriented toward a future kingdom of righteousness, in which all the faithful will be saved from sin and misery. The stages of this progression toward salvation—the "history of salvation"—include many apparent setbacks, where suffering or catastrophe stir the faithful to remember and retell God's promises and his faithfulness in the past, in the hope of getting the salvific journey back on track. According to David Spadafora, this aspect of salvation history played a decisive role in the eighteenth-century idea of progress: "This pattern of thought—the sense of living in times of religious trouble, accompanied by the dream of a far better future brought about by redoubled human effort working in concert with the divine plan—has been called the 'afflictive model of progress.'"[41] Such an "afflictive model" became apparent in times of perceived crisis, especially at the century's beginning and end, when it was resorted to as a communal source of solidarity across the spectrum of theological and political opinion. The Society for Promoting Christian Knowledge (SPCK), for example, was founded at the century's start by a surprisingly multipartisan group of men; the century's end saw a similar increased effort in religious education and reform of manners at the hands of More and others coming from quite diverse ideological positions.[42]

The Bluestockings responded to this Christian source of ethical solidarity in their self-definition. Salvation history provided a sense of the crucial importance of each irreplaceable individual—a sense almost of vocation, of calling. Each tried to do her part to fulfill her purpose in God's overall plan and to earn heavenly approbation. Typical of the Bluestocking attitude is that expressed to More by William Weller Pepys: "Oh could I but look back upon a life spent as yours has been, in the service of God, and the promotion of the eternal welfare of my fellow creatures how happy should I now feel at the conclusion of my task!"[43]

The Bluestocking phenomenon, however, was not driven solely by these two Christian motivations, charity and salvation history. Without their Enlightenment setting, these women would never have become what they became: upper-ranking women who secured for themselves a role in the public sphere, not only through their philanthropic efforts but also through their accomplishments in multiple intellectual and artistic venues—including salon conversation, epistolary exchange, and publication in genres ranging from novels to literary criticism to translation. I take this "Enlightenment setting" not as a set of ideas or philosophical propositions but rather as opportunities newly offered in the realm of the public sphere. In the neutral communicative space of the literary public sphere, Bluestocking women enjoyed a position of freedom, equality, and reciprocity that was denied them in the official political realm.[44]

As fully entitled participants in the arena of public opinion, the Bluestockings expressed their views freely on many subjects, including religion. They did not, however—as I have argued in this essay—subject the basic theological tenets of Christianity to a critical, rational scrutiny; and, most importantly, they remained faithful to, and driven by, the basic Christian motives of charity and salvation history. As a result, we do not see with the Bluestockings a "Christian Enlightenment." The two factors—traditional Christianity on one side, and Enlightenment reasoning on the other—did not mix, but mingled only in temporary suspension. Thus we see two different sides to the Bluestockings: instead of an Elizabeth Carter who could both translate Epictetus and make a pudding, we have a Carter who could both publish books and personally undertake a rescue mission for illegitimate infants. In a fascinating unpublished letter, Elizabeth Montagu reports to Elizabeth Vesey on the charitable efforts of Carter and Lord Dartrey (Thomas Dawson): "Is there an Alley where they have not made an Assignation to relieve their mutual passion? their passion to relieve distress. ... As to Mrs Carter, she has children in every poor Court & Alley, all spinster as she is, & truely I believe her the Mother of above an hundred illegitimate infants."[45] In Carter we see a woman who combined the ancient Christian principles of human solidarity and hope for a better future with the capability of acting in public as a worker of heart and head. She was a reasoner without being a rationalist, a worker in the world without being a secularist. She was motivated not by the intellectualistic propositions of a new theology, but rather by a practical piety, a religion of the heart. This is perhaps the epitome of the Bluestockings, a model followed by Hannah More and many others, including Anglicans, Dissenters, and the nonreligious: different shades of blue, but all Blue.[46]

NOTES

1. Deborah Heller, "Bluestocking Salons and the Public Sphere," *Eighteenth-Century Life* 22 (May 1998): 59–82; *Women, Gender and Enlightenment*, ed. Sarah Knott and Barbara Taylor (Houndmills, UK: Palgrave Macmillan, 2005); Elizabeth Eger, *Bluestockings: Women of Reason from Enlightenment to Romanticism* (Houndmills, UK: Palgrave Macmillan, 2010); Deborah Heller, "Bluestocking Studies: The State of the Field—and into the Future," *Literature Compass* 8, no. 4 (2011): 154–63, doi: 10.1111/j.1741-4113.2011.00789.x.

2. On "clerical" Enlightenment, see J.G.A. Pocock, "Clergy and Commerce: The Conservative Enlightenment in England," in *L'età dei Lumi: Studi storici sul settecento europeo in onore di Franco Venturi*, 2 vols., ed. R. Ajello, E. Contese, and V. Piano (Naples, 1985), 1:523–62; and B.W. Young, in *Religion and Enlightenment in Eighteenth-Century England: Theological Debate from Locke to Burke* (Oxford: Oxford University Press, 1998), 3.

3. Karen O'Brien, *Women and Enlightenment in Eighteenth-Century Britain* (Cambridge: Cambridge University Press, 2009), 56; Mary Hilton, *Women and the Shaping of the Nation's Young* (Aldershot, UK: Ashgate, 2007). Hereafter cited in text.

4. Young, *Religion and Enlightenment*, 6.

5. The one exception is Hannah More, whom O'Brien and Hilton do not even consider to be a Bluestocking—precisely *because* of her evangelical (and thus, in their sense, antilatitudinarian) theology. More applies the term "latitudinarian" ironically to herself in her preface to *Practical Piety; or, The Influence of the Religion of the Heart on the Conduct of the Life*, 6th ed., 2 vols. (London, 1811), 1:ix. Because she is writing in a "Catholic spirit" of "moderation" and doctrinal "candour," she says, she fears being accused by one class of readers—the strict dogmatists—of being "latitudinarian," that is, of being solely concerned with morality and practice and remaining indifferent to, or noncommittal about, specific doctrines of the Christian faith.

6. Lady Augusta Llanover, *The Autobiography and Correspondence of Mary Granville, Mrs. Delany*, 6 vols. (London, 1861–1862), 1st series: "Sally [Chapone] is a Hutchinsonian. Mrs. A. Donnellan is deep that way, Miss Sutton too. . . . I am struck with their scheme, but don't know enough to talk on the subject" (3:94).

7. On Secker, see Robert Ingram, *Religion, Reform and Modernity in the Eighteenth Century: Thomas Secker and the Church of England* (Woodbridge, UK: Boydell Press, 2007). Secker was a ferocious defender of orthodoxy and a believer "in the necessary role of the visible and apostolic church in the nation's life" (Ingram, 77). He believed that "[o]ur clergy have dwelt too much upon mere morality, and too little on the peculiar doctrines of the Gospel" (qtd. in Ingram, 78).

8. John Walsh and Stephen Taylor, "Introduction: The Church and Anglicanism in the 'Long' Eighteenth Century," in *The Church of England, c.1689–c.1833: From Toleration to Tractarianism*, ed. John Walsh, Colin Haydon, and Stephen Taylor (Cambridge: Cambridge University Press, 1993), 36. Gerald Cragg described latitude as "a temper rather than a creed": *From Puritanism to the Age of Reason* (Cambridge: Cambridge University Press, 1950), 81.

9. See Patrick Müller, *Latitudinarianism and Didacticism in Eighteenth-Century Literature: Moral Theology in Fielding, Sterne, and Goldsmith* (Frankfurt am Main: Peter Lang, 2007), 42 (my emphasis); and Melvyn New's finely chiseled article, "Benjamin Whichcote's Aphorisms and the Importance of Latitudinarianism," in *1650-1850: Ideas, Aesthetics, and*

Inquiries in the Early Modern Era 4 (1998): 95 (my emphasis). For Müller on benevolence, eschatology, and voluntarism, see 103, 139, 149. On those arguing against the old view (still espoused by Isabel Rivers, on whom O'Brien and Hilton heavily depend) of an alliance between Enlightenment rationalism and latitudinarianism, see the useful review article by James Bradley in *Albion* 26 (Spring 1994): 153–59.

10. John Jackson, *The Grounds of Civil and Ecclesiastical Government* (London, 1718), 38.

11. Martin Fitzpatrick, "Latitudinarianism at the Parting of the Ways: A Suggestion," in Walsh, Haydon, and Taylor, *The Church of England*, 216.

12. Robert Voitle, "The Reason of the English Enlightenment," *Studies on Voltaire and the Eighteenth Century* 27 (1963): 1751.

13. See especially John Gascoigne, "Anglican Latitudinarianism, Rational Dissent, and Political Radicalism in the Late Eighteenth Century," in *Enlightenment and Religion: Rational Dissent in Eighteenth-Century Britain*, ed. Knut Haakonssen (Cambridge: Cambridge University Press, 1996), 219-40; and Fitzpatrick, "Latitudinarianism at the Parting of the Ways." Hilton and O'Brien have been much influenced by Isabel Rivers's treatment of latitudinarianism, which leans toward a vision of latitude as rationalizing and ethically secularizing. For example, she writes: "There are essentially two views of reason: as a divine implantation, and as a faculty of ratiocination. . . . [T]here is a definite shift in the period away from right reason towards reasoning as the primary meaning" (*Reason, Grace, and Sentiment: A Study of the Language of Religion and Ethics in England, 1660–1780*, 2 vols. [Cambridge: Cambridge University Press, 1991, 2000], 1:63). In volume 2 of her magisterial study, Rivers traces the shift toward secular ethics as a reflex of religious developments. Despite her subtle treatment of religious language during the period, Rivers's bottom line on latitude remains this: "The central tenets of latitudinarian Christianity are the rational basis of religion and the happiness of the moral life" (1:87). On the kinship of latitude and Rational Dissent, see O'Brien, 5.

14. Theophilus Lindsey, *Vindiciae Priestleianae: An Address to the Students of Oxford and Cambridge* (London, 1788), 26–28.

15. Elizabeth Montagu to Elizabeth Vesey, June 8, [1780], ALS, Huntington Library, MO 6540.

16. Hannah More, *Strictures on the Modern System of Female Education* . . . , 5th ed., 2 vols. (London, 1799; rpt., Cambridge Library Collection, 2010), 1:183.

17. *A Series of Letters between Mrs. Elizabeth Carter and Mrs. Catherine Talbot* . . . , ed. Montagu Pennington, 4 vols. (London, 1809; rpt., AMS Press, 1975), 1:280, 282; William Roberts, *Memoirs of the Life and Correspondence of Mrs. Hannah More*, 4 vols. (London, 1834), 3:234. On More's supposed antilatitudinarianism, see Hilton, 143: "[B]y the end of the century, More was working hard and effectively to reverse the latitudinarian ideology of Hester Chapone." For Barrow and Tillotson, see Hannah More, *Coelebs in Search of a Wife* (London, 1808), ed. Patricia Demers (Peterborough, ON: Broadview, 2007), 178, 226.

18. Jonathan Sheehan, "Enlightenment, Religion, and the Enigma of Secularization: A Review Essay," *American Historical Review* 108 (October 2003): 1069.

19. Sheehan, "Enlightenment, Religion, and the Enigma of Secularization," 1068. On English "Counter-Enlightenment," see Young, *Religion and Enlightenment*.

20. J.B. Schneewind, *The Invention of Autonomy: A History of Modern Moral Philosophy* (Cambridge: Cambridge University Press, 1998), 4.

21. Matthew Pennington, *Memoirs of the Life of Mrs. Elizabeth Carter* (London: 1807), 621. Hereafter cited in text.

22. Gerard Reedy, S.J., *The Bible and Reason: Anglicans and Scripture in Late Seventeenth-Century England* (Philadelphia: University of Pennsylvania Press, 1985), 35–37.

23. Hester Chapone, *The Works of Mrs. Chapone*, 4 vols. (London, 1807), 4:44.

24. Catherine Talbot, *Reflections on the Seven Days of the Week* (London, 1770), in *Bluestocking Feminism: Writings of the Bluestocking Circle, 1738–1785*, gen. ed. Gary Kelly, 6 vols. (London: Pickering & Chatto, 1999), 3:62.

25. Hester Chapone, *Letters on the Improvement of the Mind* (London, 1773), in Kelly, *Bluestocking Feminism*, 3:265.

26. Introduction, *All the Works of Epictetus* (London, 1758), in Kelly, *Bluestocking Feminism*, 2:25.

27. Elizabeth Montagu to Elizabeth Vesey, October 11, [1785], ALS, Huntington Library, MO 6602.
28. Chapone, *Improvement*, in *Bluestocking Feminism*, 3:279.
29. Chapone, *Improvement*, in *Bluestocking Feminism*, 3:287.
30. Roberts, *Memoirs of the Life and Correspondence of Mrs. Hannah More*, 1:63.
31. *Selected Writings of Hannah More*, ed. Robert Hole (London: William Pickering, 1996), 30.
32. More, *Strictures on the Modern System of Female Education*, 1:183.
33. On More and Montagu, see Roberts, *Memoirs of the Life and Correspondence of Mrs. Hannah More*, 3:87; on More and Carter, 2:71.
34. Anne Stott, "Education and Enlightenment: The Educational Agenda of Hannah More," in *Educating the Child in Enlightenment Britain: Beliefs, Cultures, Practices*, ed. Mary Hilton and Jill Shefrin (Farnham, UK: Ashgate, 2009), 42–43.
35. For an interesting attempt to test logically Jonathan Clark's thesis that anti-Trinitarian theology "entailed" the demise of the ancien régime, see A.M.C. Waterman, "The Nexus between Theology and Political Doctrine in Church and Dissent," in Haakonssen, *Enlightenment and Religion*, 193–218.
36. I thank my husband, Dr. Steve Heller, for advice on the biblical languages.
37. Qtd. in Reedy, *The Bible and Reason*, 30–31.
38. Jürgen Habermas, *The Structural Transformation of the Public Sphere: An Inquiry into a Category of Bourgeois Society*, trans. Thomas Berger, with Frederick Lawrence (1962; Cambridge, MA: MIT Press, 1989). See also Deborah Heller, "Bluestocking Salons and the Public Sphere," 22 (1998): 59–82.
39. Joseph Milner, *Gibbon's Account of Christianity Considered* (York, 1781), 250–53, qtd. in Rivers, *Reason, Grace, and Sentiment*, 2:332.
40. *Bluestocking Feminism*, 3:277.
41. David Spadafora, *The Idea of Progress in Eighteenth-Century Britain* (New Haven: Yale University Press, 1990), 101.
42. Cf. Craig Rose, "The Origins and Ideals of the SPCK 1699–1716," in Walsh, Haydon, and Taylor, *The Church of England*, 172–90.
43. *A Later Pepys: The Correspondence of Sir William Weller Pepys*, ed. Alice C.C. Gaussen, 2 vols. (London: John Lane, 1904), 2:397.
44. See Heller, "Bluestocking Salons."
45. Elizabeth Montagu to Elizabeth Vesey, July 26, 1775, ALS, Huntington Library, MO 6449.
46. For the practical piety of More, Anna Barbauld, and Harriet Martineau, see the fine article by R.K. Webb, "Rational Piety," in Haakonssen, *Enlightenment and Religion*, 287–311.

Chapter Fifteen

"Through a Glass Darkly"

Edmund Burke, Political Theology, and Literary Allusion

Frans De Bruyn

The presence of theological ideas and their play in eighteenth-century literary texts can be strikingly explicit and close to the surface. A case in point is Henry Fielding's *Joseph Andrews* (1742), in which the characters of the clergymen encountered by Joseph and Parson Adams in their journey are deftly and economically delineated by the opinions they express on the doctrine of justification: whether faith alone or good works is the key to salvation. Another (admittedly extreme) example is Thomas Amory's *The Life of John Buncle, Esq.* (1756), in which Buncle's anti-Trinitarianism, expressed in numerous learned disquisitions, is a central feature of the story—including Buncle's romantic courtships of a succession of beautiful young women. These and other instances imply a level of theological literacy and interest on the part of eighteenth-century readers now largely lost on twenty-first century audiences, as well as a conception of literary form and aesthetic pleasure that would not have found the structural presence of abstract theological ideas in works of imaginative literature either incongruous or rebarbative.

By eighteenth-century lights, Edmund Burke was as much a literary writer as Fielding or Amory, making use of the same rhetorical and cultural resources as they.[1] And yet, in works of intellectual prose produced by him on aesthetics, politics, and history, in which a present-day reader might expect to find theological questions, when they arise, to be addressed directly, such issues are approached with considerable circumspection and are expressed with a concomitant measure of literary indirection, rhetorical art, and allusive subtlety. In this essay I propose to explore briefly the reasons for Burke's theological reticence and then to inventory some of the literary resources he characteristically deploys when he discusses political problems that present a theological dimension, particularly, the interrelated questions of religious toleration and the legitimacy of church establishments. These were two recurrent subjects of debate where religion and politics inevitably intersected and sometimes collided. Burke's strategic use of allusion in his interventions on these questions illustrates how he prefers to engage with the often partisan and dogmatic arguments of opponents (such as Anglican high churchmen or Dissenters) without disputing directly the premises of their arguments. In so doing, he reframes controversial issues of political theology to make a broader, more universal argument—a justification not associated with a particular denominational affiliation—for the social and political necessity of established religion.

Explanations for Burke's caution in religious debate are not difficult to find. His own background as an Irishman whose father was Anglican in profession but whose mother and many other relatives remained Roman Catholic can be adduced as a reason for his customary care in pronouncing on doctrinal issues. More broadly, as a practicing politician with a keen sense of history, Burke was acutely aware of the destructive power of dogmatic positions dogmatically held. The English Revolution of the mid-seventeenth century and the country's continuing denominational divisions in the eighteenth served as a cautionary historical lesson in the former case and as a prudential consideration in the latter.

The cautionary lesson seemed to him obvious. Even to invoke the memory of the religious discord of the previous century struck him as profoundly unwise. Although, as he affirms in *Reflections on the Revolution in France*, "In history a great volume is unrolled for our instruction," it may, nonetheless, "in the perversion, serve for a magazine, furnishing offensive and defensive weapons for parties in church and state, and supplying the means of keeping alive, or reviving dissentions and animosities."[2] When the dissenting preacher Richard Price took to the pulpit on November 4, 1789, where he invoked the Glorious Revolution of 1688 as a splendid precedent for events then unfolding in France, Burke deplored the occasion, arguing that "politics and the pulpit are terms that have little agreement. No sound ought to be heard in the church but the healing voice of Christian charity. The cause of civil liberty and civil government gains as little as that of religion by this confusion of duties" (*Writings*, 8:62). Though Burke does not pursue the point further, J.C.D. Clark suggests plausibly that he must have held a similar distaste for political anniversary sermons, "the Anglican convention of preaching learned polemical sermons at the state services of 30 January, 29 May and 5 November, a genre particularly valued by High Churchmen."[3]

In the 1790s, when Burke sought analogues or historical precedents to account for the political convulsions of the French Revolution and the driving energy of a speculative "theoretic science" of the "rights of men," he found them amply in the religious wars that had torn Europe apart not long since (*Writings*, 8:82–83). "A theory concerning government," he declares in *An Appeal from the New to the Old Whigs* (1791), "may become as much a cause of fanaticism as a *dogma* in religion."[4] If the French Revolution was proving to be "*a Revolution of doctrine and theoretick dogma*," the same point could be made about the religious conflicts of the preceding centuries: indeed, Burke maintains that the "last Revolution of doctrine and theory which has happened in Europe, is the Reformation."[5] The lesson to be drawn from this historical analogy is that in both instances arguments based on abstract principles, whether of political philosophy or theology, are bound to furnish a treacherous basis for political action. In short, Burke's general reluctance to argue from theoretical (or hypothetical) first principles in political debate extended to a disinclination to invoke theological or doctrinal tenets, even in political discussions touching on specifically ecclesiastical issues.

Prudential considerations equally counseled against the political wisdom of wearing one's religious convictions too plainly on one's sleeve. As a member of the Rockingham Whigs, whose grandees controlled Burke's access to political influence, Burke found himself making common cause with political allies, such as the Foxite Whigs, whose views on religion did not necessarily square with his own. More generally, despite the continuing hegemony of the Anglican establishment in the eighteenth century, England was a country marked by divided religious allegiances, with important constituencies of Methodists, Dissenters of various persuasions, Roman Catholics, and persons of heterodox opinion, branded as freethinkers and deists. Beyond England's borders, the broader constituencies of Scotland and Ireland, to say nothing of the growing empire overseas, further fractured the political community over which members of Parliament were called on to preside. A prudent politician (such as Burke), responsible for deliberating and legislating on behalf of this diverse body politic, would clearly find it expedient not to draw unnecessary attention to doctrinal and theological principles that underwrote conflicting claims of religious authority and political power.

For these and other reasons Burke was notably reticent about proclaiming his personal faith or creed, explaining to an unknown correspondent in 1791 that "My particular religious sentiments are not of much importance to anyone but myself."[6] This should not, however, prompt the conclusion that he regarded religion as a matter of indifference to the statesman. He took it as axiomatic that human beings are fundamentally religious by nature, that the "best privilege and prerogative of human nature [is] that of being a religious animal."[7] The instinct for religion is a universal psychological fact of human experience, which implies for Burke the existence of an underlying providential order that has ordained this state of things. F.P. Lock summarizes Burke's position succinctly: "To use a modern idiom, Providence has 'hardwired' man to be a 'religious animal.'"[8] Providentially ingrafted, the religious impulse is a prime regulator of human behavior, spurring productive conduct and restraining destructive and selfish passions. In these circumstances the statesman has a solemn responsibility to foster religion through civil society, the latter being the second great gift of Providence for the promotion of human virtue and felicity.

Thus outlined, Burke's political theology, if it can be called that, is a purely natural theology, with little room for dogmatic insistence on the primacy of one mode of belief over another. The *Reflections* articulates this irreducible position: "The body of all true religion consists . . . in obedience to the will of the sovereign of the world; in a confidence in his declarations; and an imitation of his perfections. The rest is our own" (*Writings*, 8:208). This formulation, as Lock points out, is one that a deist might feel comfortable with, but deism, a worldview incompatible with a belief in Providence and divine revelation (and many proponents of which Burke suspected of disguised atheism), was distasteful to him, if not abhorrent. Instead, as Lock, Clark, and others have argued, the basis of his conviction was what might be termed an Anglican latitudinarian perspective that regards questions of creed, liturgy, and church government as of less moment than the fundamentals of Christianity, which impart consolation, give hope for the life to come, and spur the believer to virtue and charitable action. He himself was a lifelong adherent to Anglicanism, as he affirms in the same letter of 1791, but his broader attachment, as he puts it there, was "to Christianity at large; much from conviction; more from affection."

However one may parse the often opaque evidence of Burke's religious beliefs and theological opinions,[9] there is no doubt of religion's centrality to his political conceptions or of the necessity, over his political career of some thirty years, to address religious issues at repeated junctures. Among these were the debate in 1772 occasioned by the Feathers Tavern Petition, an application submitted by ordained Anglican clergymen who sought to relax the terms of compulsory clerical subscription to the Thirty-Nine Articles; a Toleration Bill presented to the Commons in the same year and again in 1773 on behalf of Dissenting clergy and schoolmasters (also concerned with subscription requirements); measures introduced at the end of the 1770s for the relief of Roman Catholics; three motions successively presented in 1787, 1789, and 1790 to repeal the Test and Corporation Acts; and a bill introduced in 1792 by Charles James Fox to extend the benefits of the Toleration Act to non-Trinitarians (chiefly the Unitarians). Finally, the French Revolution, though obviously not a matter specifically of parliamentary legislation, elicited from Burke his most extended statements on the relation between religion and civil society, and on the legitimacy of established religion, chiefly in his *Reflections on the Revolution in France*.

Burke's early parliamentary speeches on toleration, given on April 3, 1772, and March 17, 1773, during debates on a bill before the House of Commons to exempt Dissenting preachers and schoolmasters from the requirement to subscribe "thirty-five articles and a half, which are not peculiar to the Church of England"[10] illustrate his characteristic approach on questions susceptible to doctrinal or theological modes of argumentation. His speech in March 1773 took as its point of departure the position that the proposed measure posed no danger to the established Church. The "walls, bulwarks, and bastions" of the Church are constructed, he asserts, "upon the principles of true fortifications built up by the strong and stable matter of the Gospel of liberty, true, constitutional, legal establishment."[11] This statement exemplifies his preferred grounds of argument, which are legal and constitutional, and it articulates these arguments in a distinctively Burkean fashion, by way of metaphor, a turn designed to appeal over the heads of his hearers to their hearts. As will appear, the interconnected metaphors of architecture and military fortification employed here are a central means of embodying Burke's conviction that religion and civil society are interdependent.

Burke follows the statement just quoted with a declaration that the established Church has other powerful resources with which to defend herself, but these are not the recourse of the politician: "Sir, she has other securities, she has the security of her own doctrines, she has the security of the piety, the sanctity of her own professors. Their learning is a bulwark to protect her, she has the security of the two Universities not shook in any single battlement, in any single pinnacle" ("Speech on Toleration," *Writings*, 2:382). In affirming the unassailable security of the Anglican establishment by means of metaphors of architecture and fortification, Burke engages with High Church polemicists on the subject without actually saying anything about them. A favorite strategy of those who periodically raised the cry of the "Church in danger" was to characterize her as besieged, her foundations sapped, her buttresses undermined.[12] By employing the same language to make the opposite point, Burke answers opposing views without addressing them directly and entangling himself needlessly in polemic.

A central doctrinal bulwark for the Church of England was the doctrine of the Trinity, especially its affirmation of the coequal divinity of Christ and the Holy Spirit. Evidence of the centrality of this belief for eighteenth-century Anglicans can be seen in the Act of Toleration of 1689, which excluded from the benefits of the Act "any person that shall deny in his Preaching or Writeing the Doctrine of the Blessed Trinity," and in the Blasphemy Act (1698), under which denial of the Trinity was the first of four specified grounds for prosecution. Christ had instituted the Church and ordained the sacraments, and the continuing authority the Church claimed on this basis in after ages derived its validity, it was thought, from the affirmation that Christ was divine and that the Holy Spirit remained a continuing presence in the Church. Anglican attacks against religious enthusiasm—the belief, in particular, that Christ and the Spirit are actively present in individual believers—were similarly motivated by the need to justify the institutional authority of Church and State over that of the individual.

Burke sidesteps such arguments as these in his writings and speeches on toleration and established religion. He also demurs on the view that the Bible provides a sufficiently clear standard to regulate belief, as proposed by those who sought to abolish Anglican clerical subscription to the Thirty-Nine Articles. The Scriptures are, to be sure, divinely inspired: they "contain the words of eternal life, and certainly furnish every thing necessary to salvation. Yet the bible is one of the most miscellaneous books in the world and exhibits by no means a regular series of dogmas, or a summary of religion proper . . . to be subscribed by a publick teacher. . . . Some clergymen will explain a passage in the figurative and some in the literal sense; and upon this foundation they will build the most heterogeneous doctrines."[13]

To ground the established position of Anglicanism in Britain on a theological argument or a biblical interpretation would be to invite endless controversy, a return to "the dissensions and animosities, which had slept for a century." Only legislative supremacy can confer the legitimacy that a religious establishment requires in order to be of service to the nation, for only "the legislature, representing the people" can determine the doctrines and mode of worship that are "most agreeable to their general sense."[14] Burke is convinced that established religion contributes to civil peace and social stability, yet these benefits can be derived only from an establishment that enjoys legal sanction and broad public support. Hence proceeds his bold and rather startling assertion that the "gospel" upon which the church establishment in England is founded is "the Gospel of liberty, true, constitutional, legal establishment."

Thus, when Burke argues in support of religious establishment, he prefers a figurative over a ratiocinative mode of argument, as he shows in his reaffirmation of the English Church toward the end of his speech on toleration in March 1773, which reverts to the previously introduced imagery of architecture and fortification:

> I wish to see the established church of England great and powerful, I wish to see her foundations laid low and deep that she may crush the giant powers of rebellious darkness. I would have her head raised up to that heaven to which she conducts us. I would have Her open wide her hospitable Gates by a noble and Liberal comprehension; but I would have no breaches in Her Wall. ("Toleration," in *Writings*, 2:388)

A striking feature of this and many other such passages, given the caution voiced by Burke about the use of Scripture to authorize one's assertions, is the extent to which their power nevertheless derives from the language of the Bible, which, like musical overtones, echoes allusively throughout. The deep-laid foundations of the Church are those ordered for the Second Temple at Jerusalem in Ezra 6:3 ("let the foundations thereof be strongly laid"); the powers of rebellious darkness against which the Church contends are those described by Paul in his Epistle to the Ephesians 6:12 ("we wrestle . . . against powers, against the rulers of the darkness of this world, against spiritual wickedness in high places"); and the Church's head raised up to Heaven, together with her wide and hospitable gates, recalls the apostrophe in Psalm 24:7, addressed by the Psalmist to the city gates of Jerusalem when the Ark, symbol of the covenant between God and the people of Israel, was brought into the city ("Lift up your head, O ye gates; and be ye lift up, ye everlasting doors; and the King of glory shall come in"). By a process of rhetorical alchemy, the biblical allusions, drawing on a common linguistic, religious, and cultural heritage, become verbal equivalents of the stones from which the fortress of the established Church is built.

These allusive echoes are apt in the sense that any listener who caught the specific biblical contexts Burke draws on would be able to appreciate the applicability to his argument of references to the Temple of Jerusalem, the apocalyptic struggle of good against evil, and the ancient Jewish symbol of divine presence. But drawing out such inferences is easier for a reader with the leisure to reflect on a written or printed text than for an audience hearing Burke's words in passing. The very density of the allusions further militates against the likelihood of their being unpacked in this way by an assembly of hearers (as opposed to readers). He seeks rather to forge an emotional bond with his audience, a bond that can transcend denominational difference. J.T. Boulton has pointed out how this allusive style enacts Burke's early observation in *Philosophical Enquiry into the Sublime and Beautiful* that words operate in general without raising distinct pictures or ideas in the mind: "when words commonly sacred to great occasions are used, we are affected by them even without the occasions." Poetry and rhetoric, as Burke further explains, aim "to affect rather by sympathy than imitation; to display rather the effect of things on the mind of the speaker, or of others, than to present a clear idea of the things themselves."[15]

Burke's use of biblical language is governed by his recognition that the Bible, though divinely inspired, is fundamentally a generically mixed literary text, "a collection of an infinite variety of Cosmogony, Theology, History, Prophecy, Psalmody, Morality, Apologue, Allegory, Legislation, Ethics, carried through different books, by different authors, at different ages, for different ends and purposes." The book's heterogeneity accordingly demands of the reader a supremely supple hermeneutic: "It is necessary to sort out what is intended for example, what only as narrative, what is to be understood literally, what figuratively, where one precept is to be controlled and modified by another,—what is used directly, and what only as an argument *ad hominem*,—what is temporary, and what of perpetual obligation."[16] Reading and citing the Bible responsibly is, among other things, an act of literary criticism.

It is therefore noteworthy in this regard that Burke almost never cites the Bible directly. To do so would too much resemble the practice of adducing proof texts to support a doctrinal position, a procedure likely to provoke division rather than consensus, and one fraught with difficulty, moreover, since all too frequently it misleadingly ignores or effaces the context that gives meaning to the passage in question. Instead, by invoking *allusively* the language of the King James Bible (a translation itself originally designed to bridge religious differences), he achieves a rhetorical texture that can stir his audience at the deepest strata of collective cultural memory embedded in the English language. It is the Bible as a linguistic, literary, and cultural touchstone, as a shared heritage of all English-speaking people, that Burke seeks foremost to evoke in his political utterances.

A key instance of this strategy is the brief peroration to Burke's *Speech on Conciliation with America* (1775), which affords, in the words of his nineteenth-century editor E.J. Payne, a striking "illustration of the manner in which Burke in his more impassioned appeals, refunds his 'rich thievery' of the Bible and the English poets."[17] These concluding paragraphs are a dense tissue of allusion that incorporates more than half a dozen readily recognizable biblical references, and other echoes besides. The final sentence of the speech—the words with which he formally moves his resolution for conciliation—is itself a capstone biblical allusion: "I now (*quod felix faustumque sit*) lay the first stone of the Temple of peace."[18] Here, as is typical of Burke, the allusion is composite, with the chief biblical echo recalling the declaration in Romans 10:15: "How beautiful are the feet of them that bring the gospel of peace."

I have argued elsewhere that Burke uses this Protestant, biblical idiom in the *Speech on Conciliation* as a way of reaching out beyond the House of Commons to an American audience largely composed of Dissenters.[19] The same can be observed of his speeches on toleration, which, while defending the established position of the Church of England, seek also to connect with the broader religious community, whose continued well-being is, paradoxically, essential to the survival of the established church itself: "The Cause of the Church of England is included in that of Religion, not that of Religion in the Church of England" ("Toleration," in *Writings*, 2:389). Indeed, the "best part of Christianity," the doctrine by which the Church of England most securely merits its established position, is a generous toleration of all genuine religious belief. The biblical texture of Burke's language unites his listeners of all religious persuasions in common cause against freethinkers, atheists, and infidels, who are "outlaws of the constitution not of this country but of the human Race" (2:388).

Perhaps the most memorable iteration in Burke's writings of a metaphorical structure of architecture and fortification, erected on a foundation of biblical and classical allusion, and designed to embody linguistically his political conviction of the indissolubility of religion and civil society, is the solemn evocation of Windsor Castle in *A Letter to a Noble Lord* (1796). The passage in question is framed by the assertion that

> as long as the well compacted structure of our church and state, the sanctuary, the holy of holies of that ancient law, defended by reverence, defended by power, a fortress at once and a temple, shall stand inviolate on the brow of the British Sion . . . so long . . . we are all safe together. . . . Amen! and so be it: and so it will be,
> Dum domus Aeneae Capitoli immobile saxum
> Accolet; imperiumque pater Romanus habebit.[20]

The biblical context invoked here is Mount Zion in Jerusalem, first mentioned in 2 Samuel 5:7 as the site of a citadel and subsequently the site of the Hebrew Temple. Burke exploits the double association of fortress and temple (quoting Tacitus in a footnote as confirmation that the Temple was built like a citadel[21]), which finds its modern antitype in the "British Sion" of Windsor Castle, to clothe metaphorically the central tenet of his political theology that no just and enduring society can subsist without incorporating into its constitution a reverence for religion.[22] But as the concluding citation from Virgil's *Aeneid* signals, Burke reaches beyond the Judeo-Christian horizon of modern Europe to generalize his insight into a universal principle of political theory. Rome too, as Virgil indicates in naming the "Capitol's unshaken rock" as the dwelling place of Aeneas's descendants, placed religion at the center of its social order, for the Capitoline Hill was, likewise, both a citadel and a temple.

This shift from the Bible to the classics is evident in *Reflections on the Revolution in France*, Burke's most extended defense of England's Anglican religious establishment.[23] As J.C.D. Clark notes, Burke cites an array of Roman authors, rather than, as might be expected, quoting Scripture or invoking the works of Anglican apologists: "the proof-texts in the *Reflections* were rarely drawn from Scripture . . . and never from works of political theology, but overwhelmingly from the classics" (Clark, 93). In conspicuous contrast with his use of the Bible, which appears not in direct quotation but woven into the affective linguistic texture of his discourse, Burke cites classical sources directly, and when they are deployed allusively the context and the source in question are usually recalled explicitly. Clark identifies several clusters of such references, including a series that underscore the dangers of reckless rhetoric and oratory and highlight "the presumption of literary men" whose speculative philosophies affront the gods (93–94). The cluster of chief interest in the present context, however, is a series of no fewer than seven references that punctuate Burke's most extended argument in defense of established religion, which occupies over twenty-five pages (132–58) of the text published in 1790 (*Writings*, 8:140–54).

Burke begins with the axiom "that religion is the basis of civil society, and the source of all good and of all comfort," a premise he supports with a footnoted passage from Cicero's *De Legibus*, II.vii:

> So in the very beginning we must persuade our citizens that the gods are the lords and rulers of all things, and that what is done, is done by their will and authority; that they are likewise great benefactors of man, observing the character of every individual, what he does, of what wrong he is guilty, and with what intentions and with what piety he fulfils his religious duties; and that they take note of the pious and the impious.[24]

This citation also articulates the second theological premise that underpins Burke's argument, namely, that the gods are providential, that they mark "the character of every individual" and "take note of the pious and impious." This affirmation of Providence is a key to the reader's understanding of the famous passage that follows a few pages on, in which Burke affirms that "Society is indeed a contract ... a partnership in all science; a partnership in all art; a partnership in every virtue, and in all perfection ... a partnership not only between those who are living, but between those who are living, those who are dead, and those who are to be born" (*Writings*, 8:147).

This passage is often noted by readers of Burke, but what often goes unnoticed is its placement at the center of his defense of religious establishments. It begins with a statement that John Locke would have subscribed to, but with its characterization of the social contract as a partnership, which echoes Aristotle's definition of the state in his *Politics* as a partnership "formed with a view to some good," Burke moves beyond Locke to emphasize the teleological character of the contract.[25] That teleological dimension is then quickly extended beyond Aristotle's conception of it, for the final cause of the social partnership is affirmed as the work of divine Providence: "Each contract of each particular state is but a clause in the great primeval contract of eternal society ... according to a fixed compact sanctioned by the inviolable oath which holds all physical and all moral natures, each in their appointed place" (*Writings*, 8:147). By alluding to Aristotle at this juncture, Burke signals that the Providence he is describing is not special or particular to Protestant Britain or to the Christian world but operates generally in societies throughout history. Though he is concerned to defend the legitimacy of the Anglican establishment in England, he does so in terms that vindicate all legitimate establishments.

An observation at the outset of Burke's discussion of the principle of establishment signals how the series of classical allusions that punctuate his argument are intended to be understood. He commends the wisdom of the Romans, "who, when they wished to new-model their laws, sent commissioners to examine the best constituted republics within their reach" (*Writings*, 8:142). Burke's allusions can be read as a virtual or simulated undertaking of such a tour of inquiry. He notes the necessity of religious awe as a check to the exercise of power in an arbitrary, tyrannical, or self-serving manner. Such a check, he insists, is even more crucial in societies where the people enjoy a share in the exercise of sovereignty, for if individuals who abuse power can be punished or subjected to infamy, the same cannot be done to correct the abuses of the many. This proposition, which might reasonably be anticipated to encounter objection, is authorized with a reference to Lucan's *Pharsalia*, V, 260, "Quicquid multis peccatur inultum": "For their mere numbers had dispelled their fears and made them bold; the sin of thousands always goes unpunished."[26] Without the salutary caution imparted by a sublime sense of the state as a consecrated institution, a reformation of its defects or corruptions may too readily lapse into wholesale destruction: "By this wise prejudice we are taught to look with horror on those children of their country who are prompt rashly to hack that aged parent in pieces, and put him into the kettle of magicians, in hopes that by their poisonous weeds, and wild incantations, they may regenerate the paternal constitution, and renovate their father's life" (*Writings*, 8:146). Burke's apprehension of the peril courted by those, whether well-intentioned or not, who propose theoretical, utopian schemes to new-model the political order is vivified here with a graphic allusion to the story recounted in Ovid's *Metamorphoses* of the children of Peleus, who dismembered their father in order to rejuvenate him.[27]

The capstone classical allusion in Burke's argument also comes from Cicero, whose "antient truth" that "nothing of all that is done on earth is more pleasing to that supreme God who rules the whole universe than the assemblies and gatherings of men associated in justice, which are called States" is quoted in the text to introduce a climactic tribute to religious establishments.[28] This "tenet of the head and heart" is grounded in "the common nature and common relation of men" and demands to be celebrated in ceremonies of homage to the divine "institutor, and author and protector of civil society":

> He who gave our nature to be perfected by our virtue, willed also the necessary means of its perfection—He willed therefore the state—He willed its connexion with the source and original archetype of all perfection. They who are

convinced of this his will, which is the law of laws and the sovereign of sovereigns, cannot think it reprehensible, that this our corporate fealty and homage, that this our recognition of a seigniory paramount, I had almost said this oblation of the state itself, as a worthy offering on the high altar of universal praise, should be performed, as all publick solemn acts are performed, in buildings, in musick, in decoration, in speech, in the dignity of persons, according to the customs of mankind, taught by their nature; that is, with modest splendour, with unassuming state, with mild majesty and sober pomp. (*Writings*, 8:148)

This passage introduces a concluding argument in Burke's defense of establishments, justifying the provision of a portion of the nation's wealth in support of its state religion. Having made the case for religious establishments, Burke argues logically that they must be nurtured materially and celebrated by means of all the arts—architecture, eloquence, music, spectacle—at the state's disposal. As many readers have noted, however, the celebratory language in which he makes his point draws its inspiration from a different quarter. The cadences of this passage are those of the Anglican Book of Common Prayer, a point especially evident in the phrase, "this oblation of the state itself, as a worthy offering on the high altar of universal praise," which recalls the moment in the Communion service prayer of consecration when the atoning sacrifice of Christ—"his one oblation of himself once offered"—is invoked.

I have argued that Burke has been careful, throughout his discussion, to make what might be termed a generic case for establishment; indeed, a number of those who took issue with him, including Thomas Paine, pointed out that his "continual choruses of . . . 'Church and State'" do not designate "some one particular church, or some one particular state, but any church and state."[29] Yet the allusion to the Prayer Book in the passage above raises an interesting question: whether Burke's views in the 1790s on church and state, as on other long-held political positions, shifted materially in the direction of what his opponents at the time derided as an apostate Toryism. Joseph Priestley scoffed that Burke's conception of the social contract in the *Reflections*, which only the direst "necessity paramount to deliberation" could revoke, entailed forever the existing religious order in England: "On these principles, the *church*, or the *state*, once established, must for ever remain the same. This is evidently the real scope of Mr. Burke's pamphlet, the principles of it being in fact, no other than those of *passive obedience* and *non-resistance*, peculiar to the Tories and the friends of arbitrary power, such as were echoed from the pulpits of all the high church party, in the reigns of the Stuarts, and of Queen Anne."[30]

Priestley's accusation and others like it can fairly be dismissed as gross polemical exaggerations, but readers of Burke have continued to wonder whether his writings in the 1790s marked something more than merely a shift in emphasis. Nigel Aston, who has investigated this problem in some detail, argues that "an overriding emphasis on the Christian character of the polity has nothing like the same prominence in his earlier speeches and writings and constitutes a major reordering of his thinking."[31] He points by way of example to Burke's extensive defense in the *Reflections* of the property, rights, and privileges of the established church, yet the question remains, as Aston himself notes, whether this restatement marks "an enhanced appreciation of the religious truths distinctively conveyed by the Church of England or of its primitive Episcopalian character" (Aston, 94). It might also be argued that the new emphasis here is tactical, impelled by a rapidly shifting political context that threatened a concerted assault on establishments both at home and abroad. In this view, Burke can be seen as making explicit the logic of his long-held view of the value and necessity of religion to the state: the legitimacy of establishments in general justifies the conferral of a portion of wealth and privilege on the existing, broadly accepted English establishment. "It is for the man in humble life," Burke writes, "and to raise his nature, and to put him in mind of a state in which the privileges of opulence will cease, when he will be equal by nature, and may be more than equal by virtue, that this portion of the general wealth of his country is employed and sanctified" (*Writings*, 8:148–49).

I do not pretend to resolve this conundrum here; it appears to me a question we will never be able to answer definitively. I would suggest, however, by way of conclusion, that we can detect Burke's own hesitation on the issue in his allusion to the Prayer Book in the passage quoted above. His bold characterization of religious worship as an enactment of the "oblation of the state itself, as a worthy offering" is introduced with the qualifying words, "I had almost said"—by which means he both proffers the metaphor of the state as a sacramental offering and draws back from it. Perhaps this represents an implicit acknowledgment that a figurative comparison of the state, duly consecrated by religion, with the atoning sacrifice of Christ may be read as bordering on blasphemy. In the context of the allusive pattern I have been tracing here, however, the words "I had almost said" can be seen to mark the point where Burke stops short in his endorsement of the Anglican establishment as intrinsically superior to all other religions, particularly other forms of Christianity. The oblation of the state, it would appear, remains for him an act of religious worship that can take many forms. This political conviction coexists with his personal commitment to Anglicanism and his broader allegiance to Christianity as revealed truth. For Burke, the cause of the Church of England continued to be bound up with that of religion at large.

NOTES

1. See Frans De Bruyn, *The Literary Genres of Edmund Burke: The Political Uses of Literary Form* (Oxford: Clarendon Press, 1996).
2. Edmund Burke, *Reflections on the Revolution in France*, in *The Writings and Speeches of Edmund Burke*, gen. ed. Paul Langford (Oxford: Oxford University Press, 1981), 8:189. Hereafter cited in text as *Writings*.
3. J.C.D. Clark, ed., "Introduction" to Burke, *Reflections on the Revolution in France* (Stanford: Stanford University Press, 2001), 30. Hereafter cited in text as Clark.
4. Burke, *An Appeal from the New to the Old Whigs*, in *The Works of the Right Honourable Edmund Burke*, Bohn's Standard Library, 8 vols. (London: George Bell and Sons, 1876–77), 3: 98. Hereafter cited in text as *Works*.
5. Burke, *Thoughts on French Affairs*, in *Writings*, 8:341.
6. Burke, "To Unknown—26 January 1791," in *The Correspondence of Edmund Burke*, ed. Thomas W. Copeland et al., 10 vols. (Cambridge: Cambridge University Press, 1958–1978), 6:215.
7. Burke, "Speech on Toleration Bill, 17 March 1773," in *Writings*, 2:388. See also *Reflections*, 8:142: "We know . . . that man is by his constitution a religious animal; that atheism is against, not only our reason but our instincts."
8. F.P. Lock, "Burke and Religion," in *An Imaginative Whig: Reassessing the Life and Thought of Edmund Burke*, ed. Ian Crowe (Columbia: University of Missouri Press, 2005), 20.
9. A number of scholars have written of late on the complex and elusive subject of Burke and religion. Besides Lock and Clark (in his "Introduction" to his edition of the *Reflections*, esp. 23–33), see Nigel Aston, "A 'Lay Divine': Burke, Christianity, and the Preservation of the British State, 1790–1797," in *Religious Change in Europe, 1650–1914: Essays for John McManners*, ed. Nigel Aston (Oxford: Clarendon Press, 1997), 185–211; Michael W. McConnell, "Establishment and Toleration in Edmund Burke's 'Constitution of Freedom,'" *Supreme Court Review* (1995): 393–462; and Frederick Dreyer, "Burke's Religion," *Studies in Burke and His Time* 17 (1976): 199–212. These scholars agree on the broadly latitudinarian complexion of Burke's religious outlook, but differ in their emphases. Aston argues that Burke's identification with mainstream Anglicanism was genuine, with his commitment growing stronger in the 1790s, and Clark concludes that his churchmanship was "orthodox in its Trinitarian theology," whereas Lock points to the evidential difficulty in pinning down Burke's profession of religious faith. At the extremes of these positions lies the view argued by Conor Cruise O'Brien that Burke was covertly Catholic, and the opposing opinion expressed by Harvey Mansfield that there are grounds for doubting whether his belief in a personal "God and His providence are specifically Christian" at all. See O'Brien, *The Great Melody: A Thematic Biography and Commented Anthology of Edmund Burke* (Chicago: University of Chicago Press, 1992), passim; and Harvey C. Mansfield Jr., *Statesmanship and Party Government: A Study of Burke and Bolingbroke* (Chicago: University of Chicago Press, 1965), 230–35.
10. This is Burke's own summary of the issue in a speech on the same proposal delivered a year earlier. The articles excluded from the subscription requirement for Dissenters were xxxiv, xxxv, xxxvi, and part of article xx; these deal with matters of Church government particular to Anglicanism. See "Speech on Toleration Bill, 3 April 1772," in *Writings*, 2:369.
11. Burke, "Speech on Toleration Bill, 17 March 1773," in *Writings*, 2:382.
12. A relatively restrained example of such discourse can be found in Bishop Samuel Horsley's pamphlet *A Review of the Case of the Protestant Dissenters; with Reference to the Corporation and Test Acts* (London, 1790), 74–75: "But buildings have been known to fall, while the foundations have been unimpaired. And how long our National Church should stand, if these two buttresses [the Corporation and Test Acts] should be taken away, would depend upon the zeal and cunning of the Non-conformists, to improve the opportunity of its gradual ruin."
13. Burke, "Speech on Clerical Subscription, 6 February 1772," in *Writings*, 2:362.

14. This argument appears in notes prepared by Burke for his speech of February 6, 1772, published as "Speech on the Acts of Uniformity" in a collection of "Fragments and Notes of Speeches" in *Works*, 6:97.

15. Burke, *A Philosophical Enquiry into the Origin of Our Ideas of the Sublime and Beautiful*, in *Writings*, 1:311, 317. See also J.T. Boulton, *The Language of Politics in the Age of Wilkes and Burke* (London: Routledge & Kegan Paul, 1963), 110.

16. Burke, "Fragments and Notes of Speeches" ("Speech on Clerical Subscription," February 6, 1772), in *Works*, 6:102.

17. Burke, *Select Works*, ed. E.J. Payne (Oxford: Clarendon Press, 1892), 1:327.

18. Burke, "Speech on Conciliation with America," in *Writings*, 2:166.

19. Frans De Bruyn, "William Shakespeare and Edmund Burke: Literary Allusion in Eighteenth-Century British Political Rhetoric," in *Shakespeare and the Eighteenth Century*, ed. Peter Sabor and Paul Yachnin (Aldershot, UK: Ashgate, 2008), 88–89.

20. Burke, *A Letter to a Noble Lord*, in *Writings*, 9:172–73. The citation is from the *Aeneid*, 9.448–49: "so long as the house of Aeneas shall dwell on the Capitol's unshaken rock, and the Father of Rome hold sovereign sway." The translation is from Virgil, *Aeneid VII–XII, The Minor Poems*, Loeb Classical Library, trans. H. Rushton Fairclough (Cambridge: Harvard University Press, 1986), 143.

21. Burke's note reads, "Templum in modum arcis. Tacitus on the Temple of Jerusalem" (*Writings*, 9:172). See Tacitus, *Histories*, v.xii.

22. For an extended analysis of this key passage in *A Letter to a Noble Lord*, see De Bruyn, *Literary Genres*, 89–98.

23. A similar pattern of classical allusion is also present in Burke's speech of May 11, 1792, opposing an extension of religious toleration to non-Trinitarians. See *Works*, 6:113–26.

24. Burke, *Writings*, 8:141. The translation is from Cicero, *De Re Publica, De Legibus*, Loeb Classical Library, trans. Clinton Walker Keyes (Cambridge: Harvard University Press, 1952), 389.

25. Aristotle's *Politics* begins, "Every state is as we see a sort of partnership, and every partnership is formed with a view to some good. . . . It is therefore evident that, while all partnerships aim at some good, the partnership that is the most supreme of all and includes all the others does so most of all, and aims at the most supreme of all goods; and this is the partnership entitled the state, the political association" (I.i.). The translation is from *Politics*, Loeb Classical Library, trans. H. Rackham (Cambridge: Harvard University Press, 1977), 3.

26. Burke, *Writings*, 8:144. The translation is from Lucan, *The Civil War [De Bello Civili]*, Loeb Classical Library, trans. J.D. Duff (Cambridge: Harvard University Press, 1957), 257–59.

27. See *Metamorphoses*, VII, 297–349.

28. Burke cites this from memory in Latin (*Writings*, 8:148). The passage comes from Cicero's *De re publica*, VI: xiii; Loeb translation, 265–67.

29. Thomas Paine, *Rights of Man* (London: J. Johnson, 1791), 76.

30. Joseph Priestley, *Letters to the Right Honourable Edmund Burke, Occasioned by His Reflections on the Revolution in France* (Birmingham, 1791), viii.

31. Aston, "A 'Lay Divine,'" 186.

Chapter Sixteen

The Bible in the Dock

Thomas Erskine, Thomas Paine, and the Trial of
The Age of Reason

Roger D. Lund

The essays in this collection all point to the continuing importance of Christianity as an enabling presumption of English society in the long eighteenth century. Many of these essays concern themselves with manifestations of private belief in works of literature, philosophy, and so on. This essay considers the relation between religion and the law, specifically as it appears in the trials of Thomas Paine's *Rights of Man* (1792) and *The Age of Reason* (1797), trials that provide a unique perspective on the public role of religion in eighteenth-century England. These trials are significant because Thomas Erskine (1750–1832), the barrister who defended the printer of *The Rights of Man*, also prosecuted the printer of *The Age of Reason,* suggesting that the desire to preserve the religious establishment from the corrosions of Paine's skeptical wit was so powerful that it could induce perhaps the most notable defender of press freedom to argue that where Anglican Christianity was at issue there were some opinions that should never be expressed.

Born the youngest son of the impoverished tenth earl of Buchan, the young Thomas Erskine attracted the attention of Lord Mansfield, who persuaded him to enter the Inns of Court. Called to the bar in 1778, Erskine had grown famous by successfully defending a series of sensational clients, including Admiral Keppel on a charge of incompetence in the face of the enemy and Lord Gordon, instigator of the No Popery riots of 1780. Erskine gained even greater notoriety for his successful defense of Thomas Hardy, Horne Tooke, and John Thelwall, radicals who had all been accused of treason. In 1783 he was made a King's Counsel and in 1791 attorney general to the Prince of Wales. Perhaps Erskine's greatest contribution to English jurisprudence was his decades-long struggle with his early sponsor Lord Mansfield over the responsibilities of juries in libel trials. Mansfield had maintained that it was the prerogative of the judge to determine if the defendants' statements were libelous, while it was the jury's responsibility only to determine if the work in question had been written or published by the defendant. Erskine had argued that the intent of the writer needed to be considered before guilt could be determined and that the jury had the right to decide the whole matter in libel cases and to weigh matters of law as well as matters of fact. Erskine won the argument, and this final principle was embodied in Fox's Libel Act of 1792.[1]

There is no small irony in the fact that Erskine's defense of the printer of *The Rights of Man* failed in part because the jury assumed precisely the prerogatives that Erskine had earlier defended. Indeed, the jury was so outraged by Paine's radicalism that they didn't even retire to consider their verdict. The foreman simply instructed the attorney general that they did not need to hear his rebuttal of Erskine's evidence; Paine was guilty.[2] Their premature certainty did not hinder Erskine, however, from delivering a grand peroration in defense of *The Rights of Man,* a speech that has come to be seen as one of the landmarks in the defense of press freedom.

As everyone recognized, there was never any question that the printer of *The Rights of Man* would be convicted, since in anticipation of the trial Paine had written directly to the attorney general, from the relative safety of France, taking responsibility for having written *The Rights of Man* and expressing profound contempt for the whole proceeding. "Whether you go on with the prosecution, or whether you do not, or whether you obtain a verdict or not, is a matter of the most perfect indifference to me as an individual," he writes. "If you obtain one (which you are welcome to—if you can get it), it cannot affect me, either in person, property, or reputation, otherwise than to encrease the latter."[3] Paine had never been given to understatement, and he makes no effort to amend that pattern here. He repeats the claim, made earlier in the *Rights*, that "the government of England is as great, if not the greatest perfection of fraud and corruption that ever took place since governments began."[4] While Paine dared the attorney general to read the letter aloud in court, Erskine tried, and failed, to have the letter excluded from evidence. Paine knew his conviction (or more specifically the conviction of his printer) was a foregone conclusion. And because he was in France, with no intention of returning to England, Paine argued that proceeding with the prosecution would show that the real target of the prosecution was the "people of England" for it is "against *their rights*, and not against me, that a verdict or sentence can operate at all."[5] So it is that Erskine attempts to transform Paine's trial into a discussion of the freedom of Englishmen more generally.

Although he decries Paine's letter to the attorney general, Erskine agrees that the central issue in the trial of *The Rights of Man* is nothing less than "*the nature and extent of the liberty of the English Press*" (*CS*, 12). In words that would return to haunt him, Erskine insists that any person

> seeking to enlighten others with what his own reason and conscience, however erroneously, dictate to him as truth, may address himself to the universal reason of a whole nation, either upon the subject of governments in general, or upon that of our own particular country: that he may analyze the principles of its constitution, point out its errors and defects, examine and publish its corruptions, warn his fellow citizens against their ruinous consequences. . . . All this every subject of this country has a right to do, if he contemplates only what he thinks its happiness, and but seeks to change the public mind by the conviction which flows from reasonings dictated by conscience. (*CS*, 13)

Here Erskine establishes the principle that all Englishman have the right, sincerely and conscientiously, to question the principles of the government under which they live. And he introduces into evidence passages from other writers who expressed sentiments indistinguishable from Paine's but which had not attracted the attention of the prosecutor. Erskine quotes William Paley to the effect that "no usage, law, or authority whatever, is so binding, that it need or ought to be continued, when it may be changed with advantage to the community," sentiments not fundamentally different from those expressed by Paine. The only difference, Erskine suggests, is that Paley has a better reputation: "the Attorney General will say, these are the grave speculative opinions of a friend to the English government, whereas Mr. Paine is its professed enemy—what then?—the principle is, that every man, while he obeys the laws, is to think for himself, and to communicate what he thinks—The very ends of society exact this licence" (*CS*, 38). Of course Paine had been vilified in the press as a republican monster, and therefore Erskine sought to make his arguments seem as consistent with the traditional constitution as possible.

Erskine quotes Paine: "The end of all political associations is the preservation of the rights of man, which rights are liberty, property, and security; that the nation is the source of all sovereignty derived from it." According to Erskine, this is an unexceptionable agenda; Paine's "rights of man" are the same rights which all governments defend, "but which he thinks (no matter whether right or wrong) are better to be secured by a republican constitution than by the forms of the English government" (*CS*, 14–15). According to Erskine, Paine had instructed him to make it clear that he was not a rebel: once government had been established no persons without rebellion could withdraw their obedience, and that "no private opinion, however honestly inimical to the forms or substance of the law, can justify resistance to its authority" (*CS*, 14–15). Erskine insists that his reason for reviewing this argument has been only to show that there is nothing new in Paine's opinions that would "lead you to think he does not *bona fide* entertain them, much less when connected with the history of his life." The great question still remains unanswered, however: "Had he a right to promulgate these opinions?" Erskine's answer is unequivocal. He quotes Lord Loughbourough: "Every man may publish at his discretion his opinions concerning forms and systems of Government. . . . If they be wise and enlightening, the world will gain by them; if they be weak and absurd, they will be laughed at and forgotten; and, if they be *bona fide*, they cannot be criminal, however erroneous" (*CS*, 51).

Erskine insists that the government ought to respect the search for truth, no matter how false or foolish, as long as that search is sincere. It is not enough merely to condemn opinions with which we disagree, or which happen to be unfashionable at the moment. We must consider intent: "the *bona*, or *malafides*, as lawyers express it, must be examined: for a writing may undoubtedly proceed from a motive, and be directed to a purpose, not to be deciphered by the mere construction of the thing written" (*CS*, 11). This is an important argument, one central to the revision of libel law in 1792. Traditionally, all trials for libel had depended primarily upon a careful examination of individual passages drawn from the texts under indictment with particular attention to what the "innuendoes" in those texts might suggest. But as Erskine argues, this is not enough; we must also consider the motives of the writer, and by this standard *The Rights of Man* is not libelous, for while Paine may be mistaken, he is "sincerely" mistaken.

Context was a particularly troublesome issue where Paine was concerned because of his reputation, his involvement in the American Revolution, and his other writings (frequently radical and intemperate), not to mention the fact that he was now serving as a delegate in the French Assembly. In short, Erskine could not have imagined a less attractive figure to defend, and he stresses that Paine is being tried, not because of the sentiments expressed in *The Rights of Man*, sentiments that had also been expressed by writers as established as John Milton and David Hume, but because of factors of personality, and political behavior occurring beyond the pages of the text in question. Therefore, Erskine attempts to redirect the jury's attention from Paine's reputation and behavior back to the words on the page, reminding the jurors that Paine was being tried only for libel. "I come to defend his having written this book. The record states nothing else: the charge of sedition in the introduction is notoriously paper and pack thread, and the innuendoes cannot enlarge the sense, or natural construction of the text" (*CS*, 11–12). In sum, Erskine argues, Paine's "opinions indeed were adverse to our system; but I maintain that *opinion* is free, and that *conduct* alone is amenable to the law" (*CS*, 19).

This argument undergoes a transformation in Erskine's prosecution of the second part of Paine's *Age of Reason* (1797), a trial for "blasphemous" libel in which it was not merely the state, but God Himself who had seemingly been offended. Part 1 of *The Age of Reason* had appeared in 1794 without much fanfare. Indeed, Paine's publisher, Thomas Williams, might have remained unmolested by the courts had not Part 2 of *The Age of Reason* attracted the attention of Richard Watson, Bishop of Llandaff, whose *An Apology for the Bible, in a Series of Letters Addressed to Thomas Paine, Author of a Book Entitled, The Age of Reason* (1797) quickly became the most frequently reprinted of all the attacks on *The Age of Reason*, one so influential that the transcript of Williams's trial explicitly cites Watson's pamphlet as the initial inspiration for the prosecution itself. An indictment was preferred against Thomas Williams, and Thomas Erskine was chosen for lead counsel. If nothing else, Erskine's powerful arguments for free speech in the previous trial of *The Rights of Man* made him an odd choice to insist that while Paine might question his government, he was not allowed to question the authenticity of the Scriptures. In an early-day version of the Scopes trial, the Court of King's Bench suddenly found itself arbitrating the question of whether the Bible was the inspired word of God and whether a citizen was even allowed to question that belief.

Had he known how his sentiments would be used against him in the trial of *The Age of Reason*, in which he was now prosecutor, Erskine might have wished to moderate his enthusiasm for free speech in his defense of Paine's *Rights of Man*. For whenever he can, Stewart Kyd, the attorney for the defense, echoes Erskine's earlier arguments insisting on "the right of every individual, fairly and honestly to discuss a subject confessedly of the first importance to mankind," and to publish the result of his inquiries "whether that result be *right* or *wrong;* in *favour* of the prevailing system, or *against* it."[6] In the trial of *The Rights of Man,* the prevailing system in question was the constitutional structure of the British government. But in *The Age of Reason*, the system in question was the Church of England, the Christian religion, and the biblical account upon which this establishment was founded. Kyd alludes to Erskine's role in transforming English libel law, and as often as he can, Kyd repeats Erskine's earlier claims in the *Rights of Man* trial that Paine's guilt or innocence needed to be determined not merely by the words on the page but by the whole context surrounding his remarks. It is now "happily established," argues Kyd, "that from the mere fact of publication a jury are not to convict; they are to look, not only to the nature of the publication, its composition and its spirit, but to the *intention* of the defendant; whether he be the author or publisher; and from their opinion of the moral guilt or innocence of that intention, to convict or to acquit" (*ST,* 672). As Paine insisted, his intention was entirely sincere and within the limits of a free press. Even Bishop Watson, Paine's severest critic, had given him "credit" for his "sincerity" when he swears that "the Christian religion is not true."[7] According to Paine, he had done nothing more than exercise his right to question whether the Bible was actually true. But as Erskine would argue, it was not at all clear whether an Englishman actually had this right.

In an open letter to Erskine, written after the trial, Paine rehearses what to him were its key arguments. He insists that he sought merely to redress the historical errors of those who claimed that the Bible was the inspired word of God, an assertion clearly undermined by the plethora of inconsistencies one finds in the text. Paine points out that the first two chapters of Genesis contain different accounts of the creation obviously written by two different writers, an assertion that would eventually come to be accepted by even the most orthodox scholars. "If this, then, is the strange condition, the beginning of the Bible is in, it leads to a just suspicion, that the other parts are no better, and consequently it becomes every man's duty to examine the case. I have done it for myself, and am satisfied, that the Bible is *fabulous*."[8] For Paine, an even more telling proof that the Bible was not written by God was the wretched style in which it is written. "What!" he asks, "does not the Creator of the Universe, the Fountain of all Wisdom, the Origin of all Science, the Author of all Knowledge, the God of Order and Harmony, know how to write?" (*Letter*, 13). The deists had always argued that the truths necessary to salvation were clear even to the meanest capacities, and Paine scoffs at those who would attempt to explain the "seemingly contradictory passages of the Bible." The fact that the Bible needs to be explained or interpreted "is one of the first causes to suspect it is NOT the word of God" (*Letter*, 13).[9] Paine laughs about the discovery of the law of Moses by Hilkiah the priest, some thousand years after Moses's demise, a discovery "which much resembles that of poor Chatterton finding manuscript poems of Rowley the Monk in the Cathedral Church at Bristol, or the late finding of manuscripts of Shakspeare in an old chest, (two well-known frauds)" (*Letter*, 16). Paine argues that the *Age of Reason* was written "to shew from the bible itself, that there is abundant matter to suspect that it is not the word of God, and that we have been imposed upon, first by the Jews, and afterwards by priests and commentators" (*Letter*, 19). Despite his ironic tone, Paine insists that he is completely sincere. "For my own part, my belief in the perfection of the Deity, will not permit me to believe that a book so manifestly obscure, disorderly, and contradictory, can be his work. . . . This disbelief in me proceeds from my belief in the Creator" (*Letter*, 18).

Paine's attorney repeats this assertion that Paine's rejection of the Bible is the result of a "sincere" examination of its text. Of the passages selected for prosecution, he argues, four out of the five that have been read in evidence afford the strongest proofs of the chastity of the author's mind, of the benevolence of his heart, of the general philanthropy of his disposition, and of the correctness of his moral sense.—He may be wrong, . . . in drawing the conclusions that he does, against the authenticity of the Bible as containing the word of God—If he is wrong, his error is involuntary; it is the erroneous application of principles, honestly assumed as the foundation of his reason. (*ST*, 681)

Kyd insists that if the jury had actually read the Old Testament, even they would have been forced to admit that it was full of stories "which if found in any *other* book, you would justly have denominated obscene," not to mention descriptions of "voluptuous debaucheries" described "as having taken place under the immediate direction of the Deity" (*ST*, 682). Kyd then cites a long list of such "debaucheries," including Lot's incest with his own daughters, the story of Judah and Tamar, the solicitation of Joseph by Potiphar's wife, the saga of Samson and Delilah, the story of Amnon debauching his sister Tamar, the tale of Absalom debauching his father's concubines, and the story of David debauching Bathsheba. Apparently overcome by all this biblical debauchery, Lord Chief Justice Kenyon, abruptly halted the proceeding to say, "I do not know how far I ought to sit here, and suffer a gentleman at the bar to bring forward parts of the Bible in this way" (*ST*, 683). In effect, Kenyon concedes Paine's point: so offensive are the biblical accounts themselves, that merely to quote them is to engage in virtual burlesque. It certainly points to the dilemma of insisting that the Bible, all of it, is the divinely inspired word of God, when one cannot abide to hear it read in open court.

Indeed, Paine's attorney argues, if the court were brave enough to consider the actual events of the Old Testament, their own faith in the divine authorship of the Bible might also be tested. Quoting from the *Age of Reason*, Kyd asks when we read of the Israelites' destruction of "whole nations of people . . . that they put all those nations to the sword, that they spared neither age nor infancy; that they utterly destroyed men women and children; expressions that are repeated over and over again with exulting ferocity; are we sure these things are facts? Are we sure the creator of man commissioned these things to be done? Are we sure that the books which tell us so, were written by his authority?" (*ST*, 686). Paine's attorney argues that while "the author goes too far when he represents the Bible as containing 'scarcely anything else but a history of the grossest vices, and a collection of the most paltry and contemptible tales,'" his argument is true, at least in part. "It will not be denied, that a considerable part of it is a history of the grossest vices. . . . [I]t contains tales which, if found in any *other* book, you would consider as paltry and contemptible. The author, then, refuses his assent to the divine authority for the Bible, not from a malevolent intention towards mankind, but from the reverence he feels for the creator" (*ST*, 685). This is a reasoned argument, Kyd concludes, "such argument as I believe a rational man will find some difficulty to resist" (*ST*, 686).

Erskine had no difficulty resisting this argument. He was forced, however, to shift the focus from the truth of Paine's assertions concerning the status of Scripture to questions of whether they were offensive to Christian sensibilities. Paine's attorney had argued that one could not find a single passage in *The Age of Reason* that was inconsistent with the chastest morals, including the assertion that "it would be more consistent" if we called the Bible "the Word of a Demon, than the Word of God. It is an history of wickedness that has served to corrupt and brutalize mankind" (*ST*, 699). Erskine insists that he is willing to "rest the whole cause upon the possible good faith of this sentence" that the defense has quoted, and to "waive all the protections of the law as it has been delivered in the most solemn judgments of our courts, if you can believe that the author wrote this as his *honest, conscientious opinion, and belief*" (*ST*, 699). It seems clear that Erskine simply cannot understand how anyone could deny the validity of Scripture as Paine has done. He argues that nobody who has read *Common Sense* "can refuse to acknowledge his masculine understandings." Such a writer "cannot ask credit for believing, that the crimes of the Jewish nation before the period of the gospel, which he himself admits was preached to correct and stigmatize, and to deliver the world from their contagion and example, was nevertheless published to brutalize the world by their record" (*ST*, 699). Paine's attorney points out, however, that even Bishop Watson, who initially inspired the prosecution, does not condemn Paine's conclusions as "absolutely and certainly false." Even he "supposes it possible that they may be just; he expresses with becoming modesty, his opinion that they are erroneous, but he leaves it to the Author of all truth to pardon the author if they be" (*ST*, 675). In his letter to Erskine following the trial, Paine points out that Erskine was simply incapable of accepting the fact, that "there is such a thing as a *sincere* and *religious* belief that the Bible is not the word of God. This is my belief," Paine argues. "It is not infidelity, as Mr. Erskine prophanely and abusively calls it. . . . It is a pure religious belief, founded on the idea of the perfection of the Creator. If the Bible be the word of God, it needs not the wretched aid of persecution to support it; and you might with as much propriety make a law to protect the sunshine as to protect the Bible, if the Bible, like the sun, be the work of God" (*Letter*, 25).

According to Paine the case comes down to a simple matter of demonstrable fact. "Is the book called the Bible the word of God or is it not? If it can be proved so, it ought to be believed as such; if not, it ought not to be believed as such" (*CS*, 19). In his defense of *The Rights of Man*, Erskine had argued that if it was true, a work could not be libelous. Here Paine challenges the prosecution using its own logic. He argues that in *The Age of Reason* he has presented evidence that the Bible "is not the word of God." Therefore, "those who take the contrary side, should prove that it is," something they either cannot or will not do (*Letter*, 19). Defenders of Christianity against the onslaught of modern deism and infidelity routinely argued that because it was founded in truth, the Christian religion could "stand the test of reason, the more it is examined, the more firmly will it be established in the minds of men" (*ST*, 690). As Paine's attorney stated the case, however, prosecution for blasphemy was a mute concession that the Bible could not be defended in these terms, that "To punish men for disputing the truth of Christianity, is almost to admit that it will not bear the test of a rigid examination" (*ST*, 691).

This is not good enough for Erskine, however. Let us suppose, he argues, "that though he gave full credit to the pure morals of our Saviour, he nevertheless believed the Bible to be an infamous book. Would it therefore follow that he might publicly maintain it in print?" Here Erskine is forced to ignore the arguments laid down in his own defense of *The Rights of Man*—"that *opinion* is free, and that *conduct* alone is amenable to the law" (*CS*, 19). As we have seen, the law drew a distinction between ideas and behavior. But opponents of deism and freethinking had consistently clouded this distinction, arguing, for example, that because "freethinking" led inexorably to "free-living," freethinking ought therefore to be suppressed. In much the same fashion, Erskine concludes that certain heterodox ideas must never be expressed because they presumably *lead* to criminal conduct in much the same fashion as lewd thoughts lead to sexual aggression. Suppose a man were to conclude that "there was no crime in adultery and lewdness," Erskine argues. "Would that mean that he might lie with our wives and daughters without being brought to an account?" Of course, this ignores the possibility that one may have lewd thoughts without actually acting on them, just as he ignores the fact that the law is designed to respond to actions rather than to the thoughts that presumably inspired them.

Like many eighteenth-century opponents of a free press or free ideas, Erskine is forced to argue that some ideas are more dangerous than others. "In fact intellectual differences of opinion are respected," he says, "and great latitude ought to be allowed to writings, whether they regard religion or government; but not when they are obviously intended to strike *at the very foundations of both*" (*ST*, 701). Here Erskine falls back on the argument made by countless defenders of the Anglican establishment, that questioning one article of belief was tantamount to undermining the very "foundations" of Anglican Christianity itself. Paine insists that he has no interest in overthrowing institutions (here Paine's sincerity is open to question), only in seeking the truth. This was the kind of argument, however, with which Erskine refused to engage. Ignoring Paine's question regarding the truth of the Scriptures, Erskine rather grandly asserts that "I shall call for reverence to the sacred Scriptures, not from their merits, unbounded as they are, but from their *authority* in a Christian country—not the obligations of conscience, but from the rules of law" (*ST*, 661). Understandably, Paine scoffs at this conclusion. As for such acts of Parliament, he sneers,

> there are some that say, there are witches and wizards; and the persons who made those acts (it was in the time of James the first) made also some acts which call the Bible the holy scriptures or word of God; and as these acts of parliament makers were wrong with respect to witches and wizards, they may also be wrong with respect to the book in question." (*Letter*, 18–19)

As Paine points out in his letter following the trial, charges of blasphemy are not dependent upon eternal truth, but upon the definition of words. "In this prosecution, Mr. Erskine admits the right of controversy; but says the Christian religion is not to be abused. This is somewhat sophistical, because, while he admits the right of controversy, he reserves the right of calling that controversy, abuse: and thus, lawyer-like, undoes by one word, what he says in the other" (*Letter*, Introduction). Paine's attorney had made much the same point, arguing that the terms "blasphemously, impiously, and profanely," included in the charges against Paine, were essentially terms of abuse. While a Christian might call a Turk "blasphemous, impious and profane, for maintaining the divine mission of Mohammed, and ascribing his actions to the immediate influence of God," a Turk would "speak of the Christian in the same terms, for denying that mission, disputing the divine authority of the Koran, and ridiculing and reviling its doctrines" (*ST*, 674). In effect, blasphemy was in the eye of the beholder.

> The promoters of the present prosecution assume it as a first principle, which must not be controverted or discussed, that the Bible was written under the immediate direction of authority of the Deity, and that it contains the special revelation of his will to mankind. They will, therefore, justly, *according to that assumed principle*, brand with the epithets of blasphemous, impious, and profane, the man who shall doubt the authenticity of the Bible, deny that it contains the word of God, or speak of it in a disrespectful or irreverent manner. (*ST*, 674)

In effect, Kyd argues, Paine has been prosecuted for denying the authenticity of the Bible, a belief that Erskine claims to be foundational, but which Paine insists, is merely a matter of opinion.

Stewart Kyd, Paine's attorney, quoted lengthy passages from *The Age of Reason* to prove that "the author expresses the most reverential awe of the Great Author of the universe" (*ST*, 679), a figure who was not to be confused with the author of the Bible. Having exercised his own reason and formed his own "ideas of the justice, benevolence, and other attributes of God" from the "contemplation of his works," Paine had merely asserted "the right of examining by the standard of those ideas" the book presented to him as "containing the oracles of God, and having been written under his immediate inspiration." Having discovered things in the book which attribute to the Deity actions inconsistent with Paine's ideas of God's dignity, it is little wonder that he should conclude those who assert that the Bible is "the word of God, and the actions related in it were done by his immediate direction" are themselves "blasphemous, impious, and profane" (*ST*, 674). Just as he had done in *The Rights of Man*, Paine had merely engaged in the free exercise of his God-given reason. While Christians might take offense at Paine's response to the Bible, there were not sufficient grounds for trying him in a court of law. Kyd quotes Bishop Watson to the effect that if this was Paine's intent, "the *author* ought not, and of course the *publisher* ought not to be amenable to a human tribunal."[10] Seeking, as Erskine had done in the first Paine trial, to define the issues in terms of the inalienable liberties of Englishmen, Paine's attorney insisted that "The real question is not, whether you or his lordship approve the book? . . . Not whether you are of the same opinion with the author; but *whether at the time when he wrote the book he felt as he wrote, and expressed himself as he felt?*" without any "WANTON AND MALEVOLENT INTENTION TO DO MISCHIEF?" (*ST*, 674).

Paine argues that if Erskine denies the right to examine a series of ancient Hebrew texts, many of which had found their way into the Christian Scripture, "he had better profess himself at once an advocate for the establishment of the Inquisition, and the re-establishment of the Star Chamber" (*Letter*, Introduction). This mention of the Star Chamber was a not a garden-variety slur, for in a sense Erskine was involved in just such a prosecution. Originally the province of the Star Chamber, responsibility for ferreting out seditious and blasphemous libels after the Restoration devolved variously on the Stationers' Company, the Houses of Parliament, and the courts of common law, most notably the court of King's Bench,[11] which assumed the jurisdiction of the Star Chamber as a "censor morum," punishing indecency, ribaldry, and blasphemy. The common law courts also assumed the jurisdiction of the ecclesiastical courts and punished the publication of heterodox ideas as tending to sedition and as undermining the "foundations of the Christian faith."[12]

There was one other historical ghost haunting the proceedings: the fact that had it not been for various heretics and dissenters at signal points in British history, the liberty so loudly boasted of in both of Paine's trials would never have come about. In the first Paine trial, Erskine had insisted that the evolution of English liberty was in large measure dependent upon a series of challenges like those issued in *The Rights of Man*. Were it not for "private opinion, however honestly inimical to the forms or substance of the law," the English would not have enjoyed the liberties earned by their forebears. By definition, every government "*in its own estimation*, has been at all times a system of perfection; but a free press has examined and detected its errors, and the people have happily reformed them" (*CS*, 16). Indeed had it not been for this "unalienable right" to "address the English nation on these momentous subjects . . . how should we have had this constitution which we so loudly boast of? If, in the march of the human mind, no man could have gone before the establishments of the time he lived in, how could our establishments, by reiterated changes, have become what it is?" (*CS*, 15). This was equally the case where religious liberty was concerned. Erskine points out that once the political power had joined forces with the church, there began "the corruptions both of religious and civil power . . . ruling by ignorance and the persecution of truth." You will find, Erskine argues, that "in the exact proportion that knowledge and learning have been beat down and fettered, they have destroyed the governments which bound them.—the Court of Star Chamber, the first restriction of the press of England, was erected, previous to all the great changes in the constitution. From that moment no man could legally write without an Imprimatur from the State" (*CS*, 50). In his prosecution of Paine five years later, Erskine elaborates the argument that "A Free and unlicensed Press, in the just and legal sense of the expression, has led to all the blessings, both of religion and government, which Great Britain or any part of the world at this moment enjoys." But, he proceeds, in apparent contradiction to the argument he has just made, "this freedom, like every other, must be limited to be enjoyed and like every human advantage, may be defeated by its abuse" (*ST*, 661).

Erskine is aware of the inconsistency in his argument, and he struggles to explain why some forms of expression ought to be freer than others. "I am well aware," he argues, "that by the communications of a FREE PRESS, all the errors of mankind, from age to age, have been dissipated and dispelled." Certainly, if the books of religious reformers had been suppressed, and "the errors of now exploded superstitions had been supported by the terrors of an unreformed state," the Reformation itself might never have occurred. This is essentially Paine's argument as well, and it seems obvious enough. But Erskine cannot leave the argument here, insisting that we must "examine what are the genuine principles of the liberty of the Press, as they regard writings upon general subjects" (*ST*, 662). Clearly, if there are "genuine principles" of free expression, there must be other forms of expression that are less than "genuine," and Erskine attempts to define which is which. "By such free, well-intentioned, modest, and dignified communication of sentiments and opinions, all nations have been gradually improved, and milder laws and purer religions have been established," he argues. "The same principles which vindicate civil controversies, honestly directed, extend their protection to the sharpest contentions on the subject of religious faiths. . . . The English Constitution, indeed, does not stop short in the toleration of religious opinions, but liberally extends it to practice" so long as the individual "professes the general faith, which is the sanction of all our moral duties, and the only pledge of our submission to the system which constitutes the state" (*ST*, 663). In effect, one can argue in favor of any religious belief as long as one actually believes. Unbelief is a different matter, however. And there can be no necessity "that the law should hold out indemnity to those who wholly abjure and revile the government of their country, or the religion on which it rests for its foundation" (*ST*, 663).

This defense of the Christian religion is not simply an expression of personal preference; it is a reminder to the jury of the reasons why they must convict Paine's publisher, and by extension Thomas Paine. "How any man can rationally vindicate the publication of such a book, in a country where the Christian religion is the very foundation of the law of the land, I am totally at a loss to conceive," Erskine argues. For "how is a tribunal whose whole jurisdiction is founded upon the solemn belief and practise of what is here denied as falsehood, and reprobated as impiety, to deal with such an anomalous defense?" As Erskine reminds the jury, the only reason they are qualified to sit in judgment on Paine is because of the oaths they have taken, and the validity of those oaths is dependent upon the truth of a religion that Paine argues is patently false. Therefore to find Paine not guilty is to admit that as jurors they had no right to try him in the first place. If the Christian religion be "called in question," what "authority has the court to pass any judgment at all of acquittal or condemnation? . . . Under what sanction are the witnesses to give their evidence, without which there can be no trial? Under what obligations can I call upon you, the jury representing your country, to administer justice? Surely upon no other than that you are SWORN TO ADMINISTER IT UNDER THE OATHS YOU HAVE TAKEN" (*ST*, 665). To modern sensibilities this must seem a peculiar argument, but for the eighteenth century it is fundamental. While oaths (or affirmations) remain a part of judicial practice, one suspects that the fear of divine retribution (the "so help me God" of the oath) is less compelling than the fear of a perjury charge. But for Englishmen, for whom such events as the Exclusion Crisis, the rise of Non-Jurancy, or even the persecution of Roman Catholics all turned on the taking of oaths, Erskine's argument would have seemed all too familiar. As he says, "The whole judicial fabric, from the King's sovereign authority to the lowest office of magistracy, has no other foundation" than that God "who has commanded kings to rule, and judges to decree justice" (*ST*, 665).

According to Erskine,

> Every man has a right to investigate, with decency, controversial points of the Christian religion; but no man consistently with a law which only exists under its sanctions has a right to deny its very existence, and to pour forth such

shocking and insulting invectives as the lowest establishments in the graduation of civil authority ought not to be subjected to, and which soon would be borne down by insolence and disobedience, if they were. (*ST*, 663–64)

Here is a key point of difference between Erskine's defense of *The Rights of Man* and his prosecution of *The Age of Reason* only five years later. In the first trial Paine was accused of having questioned constitutional principles that were fair game in an open contest of ideas. But in *The Age of Reason*, Paine sought to destroy the very foundation upon which that constitution was built: the belief in the Christian religion. Erskine insists on the distinction between "the work of an author who fairly exercises the powers of his mind in investigating the religion or government of any country, and him who attacks the rational existence of every religion or government, and brands with absurdity and folly the state which sanctions and the obedient tools who cherish the delusion" (*ST*, 664). Erskine contends that he has no objection to free discussions of Christian doctrine, even works by the deists, because, "An intellectual book, however erroneous, addressed to the intellectual world upon so profound and complicated a subject, can never work the mischief which this indictment is calculated to repress." Such works will only encourage men "enlightened by study to a closer investigation of a subject well worthy of their deepest and continued contemplation" (*ST*, 668). But *The Age of Reason* "has no such object"; it offers no arguments

> to the wise and enlightened; on the contrary, it treats the faith and opinions of the wisest with the most shocking contempt, and stirs up men without the advantages of learning, or sober thinking, to a total disbelief of every thing hitherto held sacred; and consequently to a rejection of all the laws and ordinances of the state, which stand only upon the assumption of their truth. (*ST*, 669)

As Erskine's reference to "men without the advantages of learning" suggests, the purely intellectual objection to Paine's argument is perhaps a blind for a deeper and more frightening apprehension related to the fear of atheism emerging from Jacobin France. Once again Erskine contradicts his own arguments, and once again the cause of this inconsistency is religious. In his defense of *The Rights of Man*, Erskine had argued that the prosecution of the second part of the *Rights* was born of a fear that it might corrupt the lower orders. He points out that no one bothered to prosecute the first part of the *Rights*, because as the attorney general suggests, it circulated "only amongst what he styles the judicious part of the public, who possessed in their capacities and experience an antidote to the poison." The second part, however, deserved prosecution, in part because its circulation "had been forced into every corner of society; had been printed and reprinted for cheapness even upon whited brown paper, and had crept into the very nurseries of children, as a wrapper for their sweetmeats" (*CS*, 19).

In the trial of *The Age of Reason*, however, Erskine adapts the arguments he had rejected in his defense of the *Rights of Man*. Erskine argues that because *The Rights of Man* had been widely circulated amongst the lower orders, Paine now had a ready-made audience among those "who attached themselves from principle to his former works" (*ST*, 677). It is one purpose of his prosecution, "by interrupting the circulation of this detestable book amongst the weak and ignorant, to preserve to them the consolations of religion, and to secure our national morals from the most mischievous and dangerous contamination" (*ST*, 697). We are left with the curious conclusion that while it was acceptable for poorer (and perhaps more radical) readers to consider *The Rights of Man*, it was not acceptable for them to consider *The Age of Reason*, because the sheer numbers of such readers "renders a public attack upon *all revealed religion from such a writer*" far more dangerous.

Erskine is clear as to why a challenge to revealed religion poses such a threat. "The religious and moral sense of the people of Great Britain is the great anchor which alone can hold the vessel of the state amid the storms which agitate the world," he proclaims. "And if the mass of the people were debauched from the principles of religion—the true basis of that humanity, charity, and benevolence, which have been so long the national characteristics," he would feel compelled to flee to "the uttermost corners of the earth, to avoid their agitation" (*ST*, 667). In short, it is not simply the fear of disbelief that so frightens Erskine, but the fear of political dissent unrestrained by the trammels of orthodox Christianity. He would bear the "imperfections and abuses" of the present establishment, or even of the "worst government" on earth "rather than go to the work of reformation" with a mob "who had no other sense of God's existence than was to be collected from Mr. Paine's observations of nature ... which promises no future rewards to animate the good in the glorious pursuit of human happiness, nor punishments to deter the wicked from destroying it even in its birth." With a righteous fervor worthy of a Whitefield or a Wesley, Erskine concludes: "The people of England are a religious people, and, with the blessing of God, so far as it is in my power, I will lend aid to keep them so" (*ST*, 667).

Such sentiments are unequivocal, naïve, and devout; they emerge from a political culture still saturated in Christian ideology. They were no match for the style, the irreverence, and the sheer audacity of Paine's argument, however. Paine simply refuses to play by the rules, to acknowledge the decorum prohibiting all challenges to the authority of the Scriptures because they threatened the establishment in Church and State. Even more troublesome was the sincere and pious quality of Paine's unbelief. According to Bishop Watson, Paine was "the first who ever swore that he was an infidel, concluding [his] deistical creed with—So help me God!"[13] Watson all but throws up his hands in frustration—for what was one to do with a writer who swore by a God he did not believe in? Thomas Erskine had an answer: you could attempt to put the printer in jail. Paine's publisher was condemned to twelve months hard labor and required to provide £1,000 security for his own good behavior for life. Paine, of course, never returned to England to face charges of any kind. Americans tend to speak rather glibly about the establishment of religion, as if the appearance of a Christmas crèche in the public square were a visible threat to the republic. If the two Paine trials tell us nothing else, however, they remind us how the religious establishment really functioned in eighteenth-century Britain, and what a stake the government had in the preservation of a rather limited form of religious belief. Erskine reinforced the principle that at least in England, the sacred Scriptures derived their authority neither from their merit nor from the obligations of individual conscience, but from the rule of law.

NOTES

1. On Erskine's contribution to the debate over the role of juries, see Frederick Seaton Siebert, *Freedom of the Press in England 1476–1776* (Urbana: University of Illinois Press, 1965), 385–92.
2. *The Celebrated Speech of the Hon. T. Erskine, in Support of the Liberty of the Press. Delivered at Guildhall, Dec. 18, 1792* (Edinburgh: A Scott, 1793), 71. All subsequent citations from Erskine's speech are abbreviated *CS* and cited by page number in the text.
3. *The Genuine Trial of Thomas Paine, for a Libel Contained in the Second Part of Rights of Man; at Guildhall, London, Dec. 18, 1792* (London: J.S. Jordan, 1792), 24.
4. *The Genuine Trial of Thomas Paine*, 25–26.
5. *The Genuine Trial of Thomas Paine*, 25.
6. *Proceedings against Thomas Williams for publishing Paine's "Age of Reason;" tried by a Special Jury in the Court of King's-Bench at Westminster, before the Right Honourable Lloyd Lord Kenyon on the 24th day of June: 37 George III. A.D. 1797*. In *A Complete Collection of State Trials*, compiled by Thomas Jones Howell (London: Longman, Hurst et al., 1819), 26:672. All subsequent references are abbreviated *ST* and cited by page number in the text.
7. Richard Watson, *An Apology for the Bible, in a Series of Letters, Addressed to Thomas Paine*, 8th ed. (London: Scratcherd and Letterman et al., 1808), 1.
8. Thomas Paine, *A Letter to the Hon. Thomas Erskine, on the Prosecution of Thomas Williams for publishing The Age of Reason*. In *Poetical and Miscellaneous Works of Thomas Paine*, 2 vols. (London: R. Carlisle, 1826), 1:12–13. All subsequent citations from this letter are marked *Letter* and cited by page number in the text.
9. Paine points out the anachronism of God's instruction to Noah that he should assemble different combinations of clean and unclean beasts, since this distinction was Mosaic Law, which had yet to be formulated. "There were no such things as beasts clean and unclean in the time of Noah," 14.
10. Here Kyd pulls out all the stops, since Richard Watson, Bishop of Llandaff, had been the party who had persuaded Erskine to undertake the prosecution of the publisher of *The Age of Reason* in the first place.
11. The line between outright blasphemy and seditious libel was blurry at best. For a history of the prosecution of blasphemous libels see Leonard Levy, *Treason against God* (New York: Schocken, 1981), 297–330; and Donald Thomas, *A Long Time Burning: The History of Liter-*

ary Censorship in England (London: Routledge & Kegan Paul, 1969), 63–73. See also G.D. Nokes, *A History of the Crime of Blasphemy* (London: Sweet and Maxwell, 1928); Sir William Holdsworth, *A History of the English Law*, 12 vols. (London: Methuen and Co., 1938), 8:333–78; James Fitzjames Stephen. *A History of the Criminal Law in England*, 3 vols. (London: Macmillan, 1883), 2:397–497.

12. Holdsworth, *A History of the English Law*, 8:407.
13. Watson, *An Apology for the Bible*, 104.

Chapter Seventeen

The Novel as the Art of Secular Scripture

Mary Wollstonecraft's Feminist Gospel

Nathalie Zimpfer

Now faith is the substance of things hoped for, the evidence of things unseen.

—Hebrews 11:1

Here we walk by faith, and not by sight. . . . How many are betrayed by traitors lodged in their own breasts, who wear the garb of Virtue.

—Mary Wollstonecraft (*Mary*, 51)

"As Mary Wollstonecraft's feminism came to absorb her mind more fully, her religious convictions retired to the background."[1] Such was the critical view that long prevailed. Recently, however, Barbara Taylor has been instrumental in emphasizing how crucial the religious issue was to the author who is often regarded as the mother of English feminism:[2]

> The religious basis of Wollstonecraft's radicalism is [the] least-explored aspect [of Wollstonecraft's thought], yet it is impossible to understand her political hopes, including her hopes for women, outside a theistic framework. Her contemporaries knew this—they probably took it for granted—but today it is overlooked by most commentators who, if they acknowledge her piety at all, tend to hurry past it to less archaic, more obviously political themes. Most interpretations of the *Rights of Woman* simply obliterate its religious underpinnings. But to secularise Wollstonecraft's radical vision is not only to tear it

from its eighteenth-century context but also to lose its utopian thrust: that unwavering faith in divine purpose that, suffusing her radicalism, turned anticipation of "world perfected" into a confident political stance.

She also argues persuasively that Wollstonecraft's feminism is itself a form of faith in that for her, "women's rights . . . are an essential prerequisite to women's redemption."³

Yet, rather typically, Taylor focuses on Wollstonecraft's most famous nonfictional work. Similarly, when Mary Carpenter suggests that the potentially subversive force of the alternative story of creation offered by the Book of Job—man's coming forth from his mother's womb—is used by Wollstonecraft to counter the myth of woman being born of and for man and to "disorde[r] [the] prisonhouse of language and rational discourse,"⁴ she confines herself to the *Rights of Woman*. Other critics address the question of Wollstonecraft's religion from a historical or biographical perspective, as, for example, Gary Kelly in his biography of her. He analyzes the *feminist*'s religious leanings in quasi-psychoanalytical terms, claiming that "religious resignation played a continuing part in Wollstonecraft's self-identity" and that "religon remained a major compensation for social alienation and inward conflict," though she later came to envisage it in a more philosophical manner, leading to the "integration of philosophy, religion and personal experience [into] her feminism of the 1790s."⁵ As for Daniel E. White, in his study of the link between early Romanticism and religious Dissent, he unsurprisingly places "Wollstonecraft's religion, politics, and aesthetics within the larger field of nonconformist devotion" and goes on to show how much her "lapsed Anglican disposition" owes to both the radical Unitarianism of Joseph Johnson's circle and to "the more affective Dissenting traditions"; "the key to Wollstonecraft's mix of religious nonconformity and political radicalism" thus lies in what he calls her "anti-sectarianism": unless identification with any kind of group was grounded in love or an emotional attachment, be it for family or for nation, it was a prejudice akin to a sectarian attitude.⁶

And indeed, as Wollstonecraft's husband and biographer William Godwin put it: "Mary had been bred in the principles of the church of England, but her esteem for this venerable preacher [Richard Price] led her occasionally to attend upon his public instructions."⁷ The daughter of inactive members of the Church of England, Wollstonecraft was a regular churchgoer for the first twenty-eight years of her life, but a far greater influence, as Godwin suggests, was Price's Unitarian Church, which she attended starting in 1784, when she settled at Newington Green to set up a school and provide a living for herself, her sisters, Eliza and Everina, and her friend Fanny Blood. Her allegiance to Unitarian thinking is obvious in her early works, most notably in their emphasis on the role of reason in the quest for truth, and it is now often argued by theological historians that the various branches of Dissent, from Puritanism to Unitarianism, all played a foundational role in the birth of British feminism.[8] With its emphasis on the democracy of God, for example, Puritanism had long been providing women with a language of spiritual self-assertion by the time Wollstonecraft began her career. Similarly, the Unitarian conception of women and of relations between the sexes, especially the claim that women were as rational as men, that their duties in the domestic sphere did not render them unfit for intellectual and cultural activity, and that they therefore had a right to a liberal education, significantly contributed to the development of feminism in Britain. Such views had pervaded Anglicanism as well, and as early, for instance, as in the thinking of the pious Anglican Mary Astell (1666–1731), who boldly stated that "the Bible is for us, not against us."[9]

More generally, Wollstonecraft's perspective on the French Revolution, like Catherine Macaulay's, exemplifies the British conception of reform by linking it to the demands of the Dissenters, who were also excluded from public life. In that respect, it is worth remembering that Burke's *Reflections on the Revolution in France, and the Proceedings of Certain Societies in London Relative to That Event* (1790) had been triggered by the publication a few weeks previously of Richard Price's *A Discourse on the Love of Our Country* (1790). This was an expanded version of the sermon Price had delivered on November 4, 1790, commemorating the 1688 Revolution in England and claiming that the French Revolution had followed the example of the so-called Glorious Revolution and would in turn serve as a model for the further emancipation of Dissenters in England. Burke's response then prompted Wollstonecraft to assume the role of the female knight-errant and come to Price's rescue; *A Vindication of the Rights of Men* (1790) was the first of at least a dozen pamphlets attacking Burke.

Informative though these historical and biographical approaches may be, they do not do full justice to the importance of Wollstonecraft's religious thought, which I believe best reveals itself in her novels. This may seem a rather paradoxical statement given how relatively little critical attention her fiction has attracted. Though Godwin was confident that her novel *Mary* "would serve, with persons of true taste and sensibility, to establish the eminence of her genius,"[10] Wollstonecraft herself was less than proud of her achievement, writing to her sister in 1797 about the work: "I consider it as a crude production, and do not very willingly put it in the way of people whose good opinion, as a writer, I wish for."[11] It is true that her two novels have, in Claudia Johnson's words, "receive[d] scant attention"[12] from critics: *Mary: A Fiction* (1788) is more often than not ignored, while *Maria, or the Wrongs of Woman: A Fragment*, published posthumously by Godwin in 1798, is treated as little more than a fictionalization of the *Rights of Woman*. Mary Poovey thus characteristically dismisses Wollstonecraft's first novel as "a melodramatic heightening of Wollstonecraft's own love for Fanny Blood, her sense of loss, and the frustrated romantic expectations she had tried to renounce," and regards her second experiment with the genre as an "attempt to fictionalize 'the peculiar Wrongs of Woman'" and to "popularize the insights of *The Rights of Woman* by turning to a genre she felt confident women would read."[13]

One might argue that this lack of critical interest is partly justified, considering that Wollstonecraft was not "a remarkably deft writer"[14] and that the story lines of her novels can hardly be commended for their originality. *Mary* centers on the daughter of a conventional and loveless marriage, who is very much left to her own devices until her brother's death leaves her heir to the family's fortune and she is taught the usual female accomplishments so that she might attract a suitable husband. After being forced into marrying a man she has never met and who leaves immediately for the continent, Mary devotes most of her life to good deeds and to bettering her education, thanks to reading and to the advice provided by her neighbor, Ann. When the latter becomes consumptive, Mary decides to take her to Lisbon, where she meets Henry, who is also trying to recover his health. A platonic love affair ensues and, both having gone back to England, Mary looks after him until his death. On her husband's return, she is forced to live with him, though she cannot bear his touch (the marriage is never consummated), and the novel ends with intimations of the heroine's imminent death.

The in medias res beginning of *The Wrongs of Woman* stages upper-class Maria lamenting her fate after her husband, George Venables, has taken their child away and committed her to a lunatic asylum. But she soon befriends her attendant, lower-class Jemima, who agrees to bring her a few books, some of which have been annotated by Henry Darnford, another inmate, whom Maria eventually meets and with whom she secretly falls in love. From this point, the novel becomes a succession of embedded stories, with Darnford unraveling an existence of debauchery, Jemima recounting the sad story of a life of poverty and oppression (born a bastard, she was made apprentice to a master who beat and raped her, after which she became a prostitute to support herself), before Maria herself relates her own life in the form of a manuscript written for her daughter. It tells of her falling in love with the man who was to become her husband before she realized that he was a libertine. Though pregnant after her husband forced himself on her, she unsuccessfully tried to divorce him, before attempting to flee England with her newborn child, thanks to the fortune that a deceased uncle had left her; her husband, however, had seized the child and imprisoned the mother in the asylum. At this point the manuscript breaks off.

While both novels challenge the delusion of romantic expectations to which most young persons fall prey, they are also very different works. Wollstonecraft's aim in *Mary* was, in her own words, to prove that "a genius will educate itself," an endeavor avowedly and rather immodestly self-inspired: "I have drawn from Nature."[15] But the novel mostly deserves attention for the audacity of Wollstonecraft's groundbreaking attempt at depicting "the mind of a woman who has thinking powers,"[16] an attempt that she sees as standing in direct opposition to the novels of Richardson or Rousseau, which she believes feature women who feel rather than think.[17]

Wollstonecraft's enterprise required an appropriately new genre, hence her rather odd designation *fiction*, a label she abandoned in her second fictional work, plainly called a *novel* in the preface. And while *Mary* is not political, in the sense that it does not generalize its extraordinary heroine's experience, the scope of the *Wrongs of Woman*, on the other hand, is decidedly wider. The "abod[e] of horror" (*Wrongs*, 85), that is to say, the prison-cum-lunatic asylum in which Maria has been imprisoned by her husband, besides clearly pointing to the conventions of gothic fiction, also literalizes the condition of women in eighteenth-century England for which the "mansion of despair" (*Wrongs*, 85) acts as a metonymy: "Was not the world a vast prison, and women born slaves?" (*Wrongs*, 88). The numerous embedded stories of other women's lives, notably that of Maria's warden, Jemima, give a realistic, almost naturalistic quality to Wollstonecraft's aim, as expressed in the preface: "to show the wrongs of different classes of women, equally oppressive, though, from the difference of education, necessarily various" (*Wrongs*, 84).

To be sure, these novels are not masterpieces in the traditional sense of the word. Sometimes brilliant in their insights, they are often clumsy in their overall design as well as in their style, and they are ultimately innovative experiments rather than full-fledged accomplishments. Yet I believe that they are also the best place to discover the fundamental role played by Wollstonecraft's religious beliefs in her feminist thought; as I will attempt to demonstrate, imagination, a key concept in Wollstonecraftian thought, is at the crossroads of both her fiction and her religious beliefs. As a result, not only do these beliefs underpin the entire value system on which the novels are based, but they also inform their aesthetics and narrative technique.

> The best novels that have been written, since those of Smollett, Richardson and Fielding, have been produced by women: and their pages have not only been embellished with the interesting events of domestic life, portrayed with all the elegance of phraseology, and all the refinement of sentiment, but with forcible and eloquent political, theological, and philosophical reasoning.

So argued poet and novelist Mary Robinson, thus anticipating Anna Barbauld's canon-forming claim in *Essay on the Origin and Progress of Novel-Writing* (1810) and, incidentally, Ian Watt's now famous throwaway remark toward the end of *The Rise of the Novel* that most of the novels of the eighteenth century were written by women.[18] True though this assertion may be—a point which in itself would deserve more discussion than the allotted space here allows—it also raises a significant question, one implicitly posed by Wollstonecraft in her preface to *Mary*: if one wants to write about a heroine who is "neither a Clarissa, a Lady G——, nor a Sophie" (*Mary*, 5), how does one avoid being a Samuel, an Oliver, or a Jean-Jacques? In other words, how does one write not as a woman but as a feminist?

To be sure, these novels are not masterpieces in the traditional sense of the word. Sometimes brilliant in their insights, they are often clumsy in their overall design as well as in their style, and they are ultimately innovative experiments rather than full-fledged accomplishments. Yet I believe that they are also the best place to discover the fundamental role played by Wollstonecraft's religious beliefs in her feminist thought; as I will attempt to demonstrate, imagination, a key concept in Wollstonecraftian thought, is at the crossroads of both her fiction and her religious beliefs. As a result, not only do these beliefs underpin the entire value system on which the novels are based, but they also inform their aesthetics and narrative technique.

> The best novels that have been written, since those of Smollett, Richardson and Fielding, have been produced by women: and their pages have not only been embellished with the interesting events of domestic life, portrayed with all the elegance of phraseology, and all the refinement of sentiment, but with forcible and eloquent political, theological, and philosophical reasoning.

So argued poet and novelist Mary Robinson, thus anticipating Anna Barbauld's canon-forming claim in *Essay on the Origin and Progress of Novel-Writing* (1810) and, incidentally, Ian Watt's now famous throwaway remark toward the end of *The Rise of the Novel* that most of the novels of the eighteenth century were written by women.[19] True though this assertion may be—a point which in itself would deserve more discussion than the allotted space here allows—it also raises a significant question, one implicitly posed by Wollstonecraft in her preface to *Mary*: if one wants to write about a heroine who is "neither a Clarissa, a Lady G——, nor a Sophie" (*Mary*, 5), how does one avoid being a Samuel, an Oliver, or a Jean-Jacques? In other words, how does one write not as a woman but as a feminist?

As her advertisement to *Mary* makes clear, Wollstonecraft's ambition was no less than to alter the "models" of femininity depicted in contemporary novels and, beyond that, to change the rules of the fictional game. She did not want to replace the typical novel with another kind of novel that merely told stories which formed "an alternative tale of subjectivity";[20] rather, instead of writing "according to the prescribed rules of art" in order to "gather expected flowers, and bind them in a wreath" (*Mary*, 5), her intention was to use the genre transgressively by writing about a different kind of woman and, in doing so, transform the conventions as well as the aesthetics of a genre that opened a discursive space to women even while it seemed to limit their authority. Indeed, both novels and educational treatises gave women a public platform but also confined them to genres that either were strongly, albeit tacitly, gendered inasmuch as they were related to child-rearing and therefore maternity, or that offered few models of female authority, since they portrayed women as the weak and passive victims of sensuous childishness.[21]

Besides, the numerical increase in female novelists toward the end of the eighteenth century was accompanied by a narrowing of the limits on their expression and by increasingly constraining generic expectations,[22] as is made more than clear, for example, in the conclusion to this review of Charlotte Smith's *Young Philosopher* (1798): "The best of our female novelists interfere not with church nor state. There are no politics in *Evelina* or *Cecilia*."[23] Burney's novels, at least to some, operated as a normalizing paradigm that established the standards of both literary merit and topical decorum, and "like timid sheep, the lady authors jump over the hedge one after the other, and do not dream of deviating either to the right or left" (*Analytical Review*, 92). "The stupid novelists" (*Rights of Woman*, 256), be they male or female, all write novels that "deman[d] the sacrifice of truth and sincerity" by drawing a "fanciful female character" (*Rights of Woman*, 120).[24]

Clearly Wollstonecraft regarded the existing novel as a genre that limited female authority, especially in a society where "sensibility [was] the *manie* of the day" (*Rights of Men*, 8); the popularity of sentimental novels in eighteenth-century Britain was not to be envisaged as a mere trend but as one of the most visible symptoms of a patriarchal society, crippling to both men and women:

> Young women may be termed romantic, when they are under the direction of artificial feelings; when they boast of being tremblingly alive all o'er, and faint and sigh as the novelist informs them they should. Hunting after shadows, the moderate enjoyments of life are despised, and its duties neglected; the imagination, suffered to stray beyond the utmost verge of probability, where no vestige of nature appears, soon shuts out reason, and the dormant faculties languish for want of cultivation; as rational books are neglected because they do not throw the mind into an *exquisite* tumult. The mischief does not stop here; the heart is depraved where it is supposed to be refined, and it is a great chance but false sentiment leads to sensuality, and vague fabricated feelings supply the place of principles. (*Analytical Review*, 19)

That Wollstonecraft considered this a very serious problem is illustrated by the fact that an entire chapter of her most famous opus is devoted to the question of those "writers who have *rendered* women objects of pity, bordering on contempt" (*Rights of Woman*, 147; emphasis added): women are not by nature vapid coquettes but novels have transformed them into such creatures by endlessly *representing* them as such, a representation all the more likely to become a reality as novels were often the only access women had to a public sphere otherwise denied to them.

The deleterious effects of novels are such that one cannot possibly "silently pass over arguments that so speciously support opinions which . . . have had the most baneful effects on the morals and manners of the female world" (*Rights of Woman*, 166). What is at stake is not merely women's freedom, but their moral integrity: "They were made to be loved, and must not aim at respect, lest they should be hunted out of society as masculine" (*Rights of Woman*, 103)—a point reiterated in a slightly different way in the novels:

> When novelists or moralists praise as a virtue, a woman's coldness of constitution, and want of passion; and make her yield to the ardour of her lover out of sheer compassion, or to promote a frigid plan of future comfort, I am disgusted. They may be good women, in the ordinary acceptation of the phrase, and do no harm; but they appear to me not to have those "finely fashioned nerves," which render the senses exquisite. They may possess tenderness; but they want that fire of the imagination, which produces active sensibility, and positive virtue. How does the woman deserve to be characterized, who marries one man, with a heart and imagination devoted to another? Is she not an object of pity or contempt, when thus sacrilegiously violating the purity of her own feelings? . . . Yes; eagerly as I wish you to possess true rectitude of mind, and purity of affection, I must insist that a heartless conduct is the contrary of virtuous. Truth is the only basis of virtue; and we cannot, without depraving our minds, endeavour to please a lover or husband, but in proportion as he pleases us. (*Wrongs*, 144–45)

Novelists or moralists? It is no coincidence that they are yoked together by Wollstonecraft's contempt as allies in a conspiracy intent on perpetuating women's subjection and maintaining them "fettered by the partial laws of society" (*Wrongs*, 146): the latter instruct them to abide by a "false morality," "which makes all the virtue of women consist in chastity, submission, and the forgiveness of injuries" (*Wrongs*, 180), and the former reinforce their alienation by propounding "the glare of lights, the studied inelegancies of dress, and the compliments offered up at the shrine of false beauty" (*Mary*, 8) as the ultimate feminine values.[25]

But if the power of fiction is such that it can turn women into "objects of pity, bordering on contempt," it can also be directed toward opposite ends, foregrounding a different representation of femininity. To do so, however, novels must promote an alternative set of values to the one propounded by the moralists that she condemns. Imagination is the absolute *pharmakon* in Wollstonecraft's paradigm, and that is why novels may be either "those most delightful substitutes for bodily dissipation" (*Mary*, 8) that have the power to "vitiate the taste, and enervate the understanding" (*Rights of Woman*, 166) or, on the other hand, works that improve the mind and make it possible to "advance beyond the improvement of the Age" (Preface to *Wrongs*, 83). Because they allow writers to dispense with "arguing physically about *possibilities*" (*Mary*, 5), novels can open an imaginative space that offers a new perspective on reality, and the genre that has so shrunken women's imagination, causing them to internalize the norms of patriarchal society, might be used, instead, to conjure up "Utopian dreams" (*Rights of Woman*, 105) that will "unfold the[ir] imagination" (110) as a prerequisite to their actual liberation.

Against the cant of philosophers, who are but "self-elected" "would-be oracles" who "fright away fancy, while sifting each grain of thought to prove that slowness of comprehension is wisdom" (*Wrongs*, 114), and also against "the frigid caution of cold-blooded moralists [who] make you endeavour to stifle hopes, which are the buds that naturally unfold themselves during the spring of life" (*Wrongs*, 125), Wollstonecraft asserts the epistemological power of literature. The heroine of the *Wrongs of Woman* casts off the "chain of . . . theory" when her attention "strays" from the "cold arguments" made by "a book on the powers of the human mind" and replaces it with "Dryden's Guiscard and Sigismunda" (*Wrongs*, 94). Firmly anchored in the double theoretical framework of Lockean epistemology and Enlightenment politics, Wollstonecraft harbors the belief that as a tabula rasa, the reader's mind is, almost literally, shaped by his or her reading experience. Her own fictional works, then, may be read not only as an indictment of the kind of sentimentality praised by novelists and moralists alike but also as an attempt to foreground instead "that fire of the imagination, which produces active sensibility, and positive virtue" (*Wrongs*, 144).

What both novels also suggest is that this newly defined sensibility—which is not the mere susceptibility to feeling that always hovers on the brink of overindulgent solipsism and fosters delusions, but an alliance of feeling and reflection that allows for a response to events that is both sympathetic and intelligent, humane and thoughtful—is necessarily a religious sensibility. To the horizontality of a corrupt(ed) imagination that leads women to focus on "grovelling pursuits," both novels oppose the verticality of divinely oriented "flights of the imagination [that] point to futurity" (*Mary*, 46); and to the "sickly sensibility" created by "romance" (*Wrongs*, 176–77) and intensely degrading to women, both novels oppose an authentic religious subjectivity:

> Christianity can only afford just principles to govern the wayward feelings and impulses of the heart: every good disposition runs wild, if not transplanted into this soil; but how hard is it to keep the heart diligently, though convinced that the issues of life depend on it.
> It is very difficult to discipline the mind of a thinker, or reconcile him to the weakness, the inconsistency of his understanding; and a still more laborious task for him to conquer his passions, and learn to seek content, instead of happiness. Good dispositions, and virtuous propensities, without the light of the Gospel, produce eccentric characters: comet-like, they are always in extremes; while revelation resembles the laws of attraction, and produces uniformity; but too often is the attraction feeble; and the light so obscured by passion, as to force the bewildered soul to fly into void space, and wander in confusion. (*Mary*, 61)

"Imagination! Who can paint thy power!" (*Wrongs*, 106). Both *Mary* and *Wrongs* repeatedly underline the power of imagination, but also the potential delusions that it can foster. Maria realizes this toward the end of her life: "Whither did not my imagination lead me," she exclaims (127) when, with the clear-sightedness afforded by hindsight, she becomes fully aware that "the disinterestedness, fortitude, generosity, dignity, and humanity" that she once saw in the man with whom she fancied herself in love were no more than the figments of her imagination (127); in other words: "[Her] fancy had found a basis to erect its model of perfection on" (131).

What is therefore required is a redefinition of the nature of imagination and a disentangling of the relation between gender and genre so that *woman* and *sentiment* are no longer equated—an urgent task when one considers how prostituted the latter term has become.[26] This is precisely what a God-oriented imagination can offer. In his biography Godwin repeatedly emphasizes the rather idiosyncratic nature of his wife's religion, which "was, in reality, little allied to any system of forms; and . . . was founded rather in taste, than in the niceties of polemical discussion," with the result that it was "almost entirely of her own creation." But the most important point in this account remains the central role played by imagination in the feminist's theology:

> Her mind constitutionally attached itself to the sublime and the amiable. She found an inexpressible delight in the beauties of nature, and in the splendid reveries of the imagination. But nature itself, she thought, would be no better than a vast blank, if the mind of the observer did not supply it with an animating soul. When she walked amidst the wonders of nature, she was accustomed to converse with her God. To her mind he was pictured as not less amiable, generous and kind, than great, wise and exalted.[27]

This point is corroborated by Mary Hays's obituary in the *Annual Necrology*, in which she describes Wollstonecraft's God as "a being higher, more perfect, than visible nature," whom she "adored . . . amidst the beauties of Nature, or . . . in the still hour of recollection."[28]

That is not to say that Wollstonecraft's religion was close to that of the decried "Enthusiasts" or had anything to do with the kind of religious superstition exemplified by Mary's mother Eliza, who had "a good opinion of her own merit" because she said "long prayers,—and sometimes read her Week's Preparation [and] dreaded that horrid place vulgarly called hell, the regions below" (*Mary*, 7–8). Nor does it bear any resemblance whatsoever to the meekness of Christian heroism offered as an alternative to traditional heroism that Richardson's Clarissa embodies, as the author himself suggests in a letter to Frances Grainger:

> For is not the Conduct [Clarissa's] laid down for the Pursuit of the Sacred Books. *The Bear and Forbear*, the uncontentious *Giving up the Cloak* also . . . the turning the unsmitten *Cheek*—the *Forgiveness of those that hate us and despitefully use us*. . . . The Christian Meekness—the Affiance in God's Mercy, Power and Goodness, as what shall infallibly reward us thereafter for our Patience and Suffering here. . . . And shall not a Clarissa, shall not a Christian Heroine trust to Heaven for her own Reward?[29]

If "Clarissa was to be an example of suffering virtue, according to the Christian system,"[30] Wollstonecraft's heroines would then embody the admixture of reason and imagination that true religion consists of, as explicitly stated in the *Rights of Woman*, the most detailed statement we have of the author's theology:

> I hope I shall not be misunderstood when I say, that religion will not have this condensing energy, unless it be founded on reason. If it be merely the refuge of weakness or wild fanaticism, and not a governing principle of conduct, drawn from self-knowledge, and a rational opinion respecting the attributes of God, what can it be expected to produce? . . . Men will not become moral when they only build airy castles in a future world to compensate for the disappointments which they meet with in this; if they turn their thoughts from relative duties to religious reveries. (*Rights of Woman*, 184)

Only a religious sensibility makes it possible for women to elevate themselves because it does not take the self as focus; where self is the focus, "selfish principle[s]" take over and "the image of God is lost in the citizen" (*Rights of Men*, 15)—or in the rich rather than in the poor, or again, in men as opposed to women.

The underlying egalitarianism of such a conception of imagination is implicit yet clear: "it [is] not philosophical to think of sex when the soul is mentioned" (*Rights of Woman*, 103). Like men, women possess a God-given, unsexed soul that guides them to "reverence" themselves (*Rights of Men*, 34) and designs them for perfectibility. From this follows the premise that Providence has designed men and women's souls for the same end, and that both sexes should therefore be educated in the same manner. It is the imagination that enables Wollstonecraft to perceive the "mistaken notions that enslave [her] sex" (*Rights of Woman*, 105) and, as woman and as author, to see beyond—and judge differently—the limiting representation of women provided by eighteenth-century society. No longer will she see darkly through the glass of prejudice.

Not only is the Pauline reference repeatedly used in *Mary* and the *Wrongs of Woman*—thus, even young Mary, though she is only fifteen, is able to perceive "that she saw through a glass darkly" and "that the bounds set to stop our intellectual researches" is inherent to our condition, "one of the trials of a probationary state" (*Mary*, 16)[31] —but it is, as well, consistently linked to the condition of women. Both novels are indeed pervaded by a binary opposition between "false morality" (*Wrongs*, 180) and a true virtue that rests on the more or less explicit foregrounding of an alternative referential framework based on divine order rather than "maxims of worldly wisdom" (*Mary*, 46). This so-called wisdom is but a strategy implemented by patriarchal society to perpetuate the subjection of women: "Men, more effectually to enslave us, may inculcate this *partial* morality, and lose sight of virtue in subdividing it into the duties of particular stations" (*Wrongs*, 144–45; emphasis added). That is why "the admiration" for supposedly virtuous women is no more than the gross prejudices of "the misjudging crowd" (*Mary*, 46), which assesses situations according to worldly rather than godly values: "She was chaste, according to the vulgar acceptation of the word, that is, she did not make any actual *faux pas*" (*Mary*, 9); such "chastity," however, is in fact what leads to "the misery and oppression, peculiar to women" since it arises "out of the *partial* laws and customs of society" (*Preface to the Wrongs of Woman*, 83; emphasis added). The clearest expression of this opposition is to be found in *Mary*:

> The same turn of mind which leads me to adore the Author of all Perfection— which leads me to conclude that he only can fill my soul; forces me to admire the faint image—the shadows of his attributes here below; and my imagination gives still bolder strokes to them.... [T]hese flights of the imagination point to futurity; I cannot banish them ...
>
> With these notions can I conform to the maxims of worldly wisdom? can I listen to the cold dictates of worldly prudence and bid my tumultuous passions cease to vex me ... ? My conscience does not smite me, and that Being who is greater than the internal monitor, may approve of what the world condemns ...

> Riches and honours await me, and the cold moralist might desire me to sit down and enjoy them—I cannot conquer my feelings, and till I do, what are these baubles to me? you may tell me I follow a fleeting good, an *ignis fatuus*; but this chase, these struggles prepare me for eternity—when I no longer see through a glass darkly I shall not reason about, but *feel* in what happiness consists. (*Mary*, 46–47)

The "subdivision" of virtue "into the duties of particular stations" and the dictates of the "cold moralist" thus gives way to the alternative framework of Pauline wisdom that, though it must appear as foolishness to the world (1 Corinthians 4:10) and therefore raise a "horse laugh" among men (*Rights of Men*, 7), makes it possible to counter the prevalent secular ideology of male authority and to do away with the notion of specifically "feminine virtues" by collapsing sexual distinctions when it comes to right conduct. Deliberately ignoring the tension within Pauline doctrine itself between the belief in the primacy of the individual conscience and the belief in the divinely ordained subordination of women, Wollstonecraft boldly asserts that it is only "prejudices that give a sex to virtue" (*Rights of Woman*, 76).

In a similar fashion, to the fear and superstition that are inculcated in women—the "dread" that Mary's mother Eliza feels at "that horrid place vulgarly called hell, the regions below," but which fails to make her "a mounting spirit" (*Mary*, 8)—Wollstonecraft opposes an appeal to the inner authority of the individual believer, with obvious political implications, that was at the core of all varieties of enlightened theism—*Intra te quaere Deum*, look for God within thyself. The case made for toleration by the Dissenters, for example, clearly rested on the conviction that "every man ought to be left to follow his own conscience,"[32] and the egalitarian consequences of this belief for women are no less obvious. The affirmation of women's capacity to apprehend the divine was expressed in almost all female writings of the time and was so crucial to women's sense of ethical worth that it must be regarded as one of the founding impulses of feminism. *The Wrongs of Woman* strikingly concludes—and the fact that the conclusion was in all likelihood provisional cannot conceal the strength of the passage—with a juxtaposition of the two as yet incompatible referential frameworks of godly and worldly wisdom:

> While no command of a husband can prevent a woman from suffering for certain crimes, she must be allowed to consult her conscience, and regulate her conduct, in some degree, by her own sense of right. . . . If I am unfortunately united to an unprincipled man, am I for ever to be shut out from fulfilling the duties of a wife and mother?—I wish my country to approve of my conduct; but, if laws exist, made by the strong to oppress the weak, I appeal to my own sense of justice, and declare that I will not live with the individual, who has violated every moral obligation which binds man to man. (*Wrongs*, 180)

This appeal to the wisdom of inner conscience is answered by the voice of patriarchal society as embodied by the judge appointed to examine Maria's petition for divorce:

> The judge, in summing up the evidence, alluded to "the fallacy of letting women plead their feelings, as an excuse for the violation of the marriage-vow. For his part, he had always determined to oppose all innovation, and the newfangled notions which incroached on the good old rules of conduct. We did not want French principles in public or private life—and, if women were allowed to plead their feelings, as an excuse or palliation of infidelity, it was opening a flood-gate for immorality. What virtuous woman thought of her feelings?—It was her duty to love and obey the man chosen by her parents and relations, who were qualified by their experience to judge better for her, than she could for herself." (*Wrongs*, 181)

In the value system established by the novels, however, virtuous women do think of their feelings, because these feelings are not "the fallacious light of sentiment" (*Rights of Woman*, 115) but divinely inspired affections. Wollstonecraft establishes a bold parallel between the love that humans ought to feel for God and the feelings that women should harbor for men. Just as religion is not "a matter of sentiment or taste," unlike what has sometimes been claimed, so relationships between men and women should rest on reason and not solely on feelings: "It were to be wished that women would cherish an affection for their husbands, founded on the same principle that devotion [to God] ought to rest upon. No other firm base is there under heaven—for let them beware of the fallacious light of sentiment; too often used as a softer phrase for sensuality" (115).

> It was particularly the design of the author, in the present instance, to make her story subordinate to a great moral purpose, that "of exhibiting the misery and oppression, peculiar to women, that arise out of the partial laws and customs of society.["]—This view restrained her fancy. . . . It was necessary for her, to place in a striking point of view, evils that are too frequently overlooked, and to drag into light those details of oppression, of which the grosser and more insensible part of mankind make little account. (*Wrongs*, 184)

Such was Godwin's conclusion as the editor of Wollstonecraft's second novel; to it I would add that not only diegetically and thematically, but stylistically as well, her novels are indeed subordinated "to a great moral purpose." As has been emphasized, the advertisements to the novels display the feminist's rhetorical gesture of simultaneously distancing herself from, yet including herself in, the canon; she aligns herself with famous eighteenth-century male writers even as she rejects them, a gesture all the more daring because Richardson was by far the most cited authority in reviews of novels.[33] And if Richardson's concern in "*showing the Distress that may attend the Misconduct both of Parents and Children in Relation to Marriage*" is echoed by Wollstonecraft's wish to "exhibi[t] the misery" of women (*Wrongs*, 83), the former clearly focuses on the personal and the subjective, his novel "*comprehending the most important Concerns of Private Life*," whereas Wollstonecraft presents her aim as far more political in its equation of women's misery with an "oppression" that "arise[s] out of the partial laws and customs of society" (*Wrongs*, 83).

The interior focus of Richardson's novels makes for easier identification on the part of the reader, whereas Wollstonecraft's third-person narratives render distance unavoidable, especially since plot always seems subservient to the didactic. Free indirect speech coexists with passages in which the narrator looks on the characters as an observer, taking on the moral authority of a preacher in order to comment on women's experiences and fate. This voice is accompanied by long disquisitions from the heroines, whose voices are stylistically and ideologically so consonant with the narrator's that they appear less as full-fledged characters of a novel and more as authorial mouthpieces or textual personae. In fact the works constantly oscillate between a novelistic mode and what resembles a homiletic one. It might here be useful to recall the distinction made by theologians between *didache* and *kerygma*, didactic preaching that nurtures the faith of (new) converts and kerygmatic preaching, the aim of which is to convert unbelievers. In Wollstonecraft's novels the emotional response typically elicited by the sentimental novel might be said to be used for kerygmatic purposes in the sense that the story is more often than not ancillary to the purpose of converting the readers to the cause of women. Instances may be found of the heroine's thoughts and feelings being given without any narratorial intervention, for example: "Two months were elapsed; she had not seen, or heard from Henry. He was sick—nay, perhaps had forgotten her; all the world was dreary, and all the people ungrateful" (*Mary*, 57); yet the prevailing narrative mode of the novels is that of the sermonizer resorting to personal stories as mere *exempla* and where free indirect speech is used less to make identification with the heroine possible, more to show the intricacies of the heart, the better to analyze them.

Mary offers an interesting example of the unveiling of the heroine's feelings paving the way for a more general, subtly didactic statement, the two merging seamlessly in the same sentence: "She felt less pain on account of her mother's partiality to her brother, as she hoped now to experience the pleasure of being beloved; but this hope led her into new sorrows, and, *as usual*, paved the way for disappointment" (*Mary*, 13; emphasis added). Another case in point is the following excerpt, quoted at length because it so fully embodies the technique I am identifying as specifically Wollstonecraft's: what might be termed the psychologizing of ethics and of the homiletic message through the subjectivity entailed by the novelistic narrative mode:

> Henry saw her distress, and not to increase it, left the room. He had exerted himself to turn her thoughts into a new channel, and had succeeded; she thought of him till she began to chide herself for defrauding the dead, and, determining to grieve for Ann, she dwelt on Henry's misfortunes and ill health; and the interest he took in her fate was a balm to her sick mind. She did not reason on the subject; but she felt he was attached to her: lost in this delirium, she never asked herself what kind of an affection she had for him, or what it tended to; nor did she know that love and friendship are very distinct; she thought with rapture, that there was one person in the world who had an affection for her, and that person she admired—had a friendship for.
>
> He had called her his dear girl; the words might have fallen from him by accident; but they did not fall to the ground. My child! His child, what an association of ideas! If I had had a father, such a father!—She could not dwell on the thoughts, the wishes which obtruded themselves. Her mind was unhinged, and passion unperceived filled her whole soul. Lost, in waking dreams, she considered and reconsidered Henry's account of himself; till she actually thought she would tell Ann—a bitter recollection then roused her out of her reverie; and aloud she begged forgiveness of her. (*Mary*, 41–42)

The narrator here takes on the voice of the preacher and, significantly, the passage in free indirect speech comes after judgment has been passed, thus precluding any kind of polysemy; what the heroine takes for love is unambiguously termed "delirium" and her feelings are to be put down to ignorance and not, as she believes, to keen sensibility: "she did not know that love and friendship are very distinct." She is also presented as having failed to resort to the kind of introspection that is so much part of the Protestant ethos ("she never asked herself what kind of an affection she had for him") and that would have enabled her to analyze her feelings in order to act righteously.

As a result, Wollstonecraft's novels are not dialogic texts that open up interpretive possibilities, but texts where the narrative voice systematically guides the reader's understanding of them. "As a faithful historian" the narrator's aim is to "tell the truth" (*Mary*, 30, 42), even if that entails showing a character in an unfavorable light, as is made clear by the uncompromising manner in which Mary is introduced: "Her understanding was strong and clear, when not clouded by her feelings; but she was too much the creature of impulse, and the slave of compassion" (*Mary*, 12). Similarly, the heroines are, again, less characters in a story than *exempla* that preachers might use to illustrate their point. In this respect, chapter IV of *Wrongs* is particularly interesting, since its very structure recalls that of a sermon. The opening generalization, for example—"Pity, and the forlorn seriousness of adversity, have both been considered as dispositions favourable to love, while satirical writers have attributed the propensity to the relaxing effect of idleness" (*Wrongs*, 104)—plays the role of the scriptural subject-text of the traditional sermon, and is followed by a portrait of Maria, whose mode is didactic from the outset, since the first sentence then continues: ". . . effect of idleness; what chance then had Maria of escaping, when pity, sorrow, and solitude all conspired to soften her mind, and nourish romantic wishes, and, from a natural progress, romantic expectations?" (*Wrongs*, 104). The chapter thereafter consists of a constant alternation between specific observations about Maria ("There was a simplicity sometimes indeed in her manner, which bordered on infantine ingenuousness" [104]) and much longer didactic generalizations:

> There are mistakes of conduct which at five-and-twenty prove the strength of the mind, that, ten or fifteen years after, would demonstrate its weakness, its incapacity to acquire a sane judgment. The youths who are satisfied with the ordinary pleasures of life, and do not sigh after ideal phantoms of love and friendship, will never arrive at great maturity of understanding; but if these reveries are cherished, as is too frequently the case with women, when experience ought to have taught them in what human happiness consists, they become as useless as they are wretched. Besides, their pains and pleasures are so dependent on outward circumstances, on the objects of their affections, that they seldom act from the impulse of a nerved mind, able to choose its own pursuit. (104)

The ancillary dimension of the narrative becomes still more obvious when the narrator's voice turns into the moralistic *we*: "We mean not to trace the progress of this passion" (*Wrongs*, 105).

Even more arresting are the passages in which the plot becomes a mere excuse for the expression of strong anti-Catholic feelings typical of "the antipopery long sheltered in the national psyche,"[34] and bearing more than a little resemblance to similar sentiments expressed in the sermons still preached in Wollstonecraft's time on November 5, to commemorate the discovery of the Gunpowder Plot, and January 30, to remember the "martyrdom" of Charles I. Such is the case in the chapters narrating Mary's visit to Lisbon, where an extremely virulent denunciation of monastic life, "In short, when [the nuns] could be neither wives nor mothers, they aimed at being superiors, and became the most selfish creatures in the world: the passions that were curbed gave strength to the appetites" (*Mary*, 34–35), is immediately followed by a striking statement at the outset of the next chapter:

> The Portuguese are certainly the most uncivilized nation in Europe. Dr. Johnson would have said, "They have the least mind." And can such serve their Creator in spirit and in truth? No, the gross ritual of Romish ceremonies is all they can comprehend: they can do penance, but not conquer their revenge, or lust. Religion, or love, has never humanized their hearts; they want the vital

part; the mere body worships. Taste is unknown; Gothic finery, and unnatural decorations, which they term ornaments, are conspicuous in their churches and dress. Reverence for mental excellence is only to be found in a polished nation. (*Mary*, 36)

This is perhaps the most obvious example of Wollstonecraft's homiletic tone taking over her voice, here pervading her language with the anti-Catholic rhetoric of the period. The epithet "Romish" is characteristic of the presentation of Roman Catholicism as first and foremost a foreign religion, and of Catholics as "Papists" who could not possibly be granted proper toleration since their Church "[was] so constituted that all who enter it *ipso facto* pass into the allegiance and service of another prince,"[35] an argument taken up by countless tracts and sermons throughout the eighteenth century. Equally typical is the denunciation of the artificiality and excess of "Gothic finery." The indictment is then completed by the adjective "unnatural," which implicitly associates Protestantism with civilized behavior the better to emphasize the "uncivilized" barbarity of Roman Catholics, forever those "outlandish" creatures, in the double sense of "bizarre" or "foreign."[36]

Nothing would be more erroneous than to envisage these "disquisitions on God" as "digression[s]" (*Rights of Woman*, 115). They are on the contrary part of both the textual and ideological fabric of the novels; the religious framework acts as a powerful rhetorical strategy that subverts the long-standing metaphor of women as men's satellites—or as "reflector[s] of the most sublime beams" (*Mary*, 5)—and instead represents men themselves as mere satellites in comparison to God. Even more important, the religious emphasis is the essential philosophical basis of Wollstonecraft's feminism, in the sense that relationships between men and women are envisaged as homothetic, always uniting human beings to God. This insistent representation of God as a father figure thus enables Wollstonecraft to debunk the dialectic of women as the natural subordinates of men and to offer instead a feminist gospel that is at its clearest in the striking conclusion to *Mary*: "She thought she was hastening to that world where there is neither marrying, nor giving in marriage" (73).

While the novel as a genre can be said to replace the time-tested values of cultural inheritance with subjective experience, Wollstonecraft's novels, both in their underlying values and in their aesthetics, testify to a (relative) distrust of the subjective, of the self as focus. The transgressive dimension of Wollstonecraft's fictional works rests on the paradoxical joining of the authorial voice of a woman who "wish[es] to speak for [herself]" (*Mary*, 5) with an essentialist form, that of the sermon or morality tale, which emphasizes the universality of human plights and solutions. Her stories do not so much emphasize the individual and the particular as they privilege the exemplary;

even in *Mary*, the less political of the two novels, "the mind of a woman, who has thinking powers" is displayed only to make the didactic point that "the female organs" are not "too weak for this arduous employment" (5). This generalizing tendency appears in the gnomic utterances and quasi-aphorisms that pervade Wollstonecraft's fictional works and lend her heroines a mythic dimension. For Wollstonecraft and most of her contemporaries, negotiations with the image of the woman writer were complex, as was the issue of authorial stance. Women authors were forced to work within the constraints of an authorial image based on a restrictive code of the virtuous woman of feeling. In the scathingly ironic words of the narrator of Charlotte Smith's *Marchmont*, this condemned a woman to "undergo that sort of persecution which has filled so many novels, and either disoblige her only parent and protector, or devote herself for life to a man she detested."[37] Mitzi Myer once commented on the near impossibility of "weav[ing] radical ideology into the fictionalized texture" of female experience as the novel imagined it.[38] I would argue that like Sarah Fielding, Frances Sheridan, or Charlotte Smith before her, Wollstonecraft found creative ways to transcend these constraints in order to reflect the society of her time. Her novels denounce female powerlessness in patriarchal society but also offer a solution to it: unlike "both enthusiasts and cooler thinkers," who have fallen into the "dilemma" of opposing God and man's rules, Wollstonecraft suggests as a paradoxical prerequisite to women's liberation the return to "the wholesome restraints which a just conception of the character of God imposes" (*Rights of Woman*, 115) and foregrounds a utopian thrust that locates a divinely oriented imagination at the core of the transformation of society.

NOTES

1. Jacob Bouten, *Mary Wollstonecraft and the Beginnings of Female Emancipation in France and England* (1922; rpt. Philadelphia: Porcupine Press, 1975), 5.
2. While the word is obviously anachronistic, it will be used throughout this essay for the sake of convenience.
3. Barbara Taylor, *Mary Wollstonecraft and the Feminist Imagination* (Cambridge: Cambridge University Press, 2003), 3–4, 24.
4. Mary Wilson Carpenter, "Sibylline Apocalyptics: Mary Wollstonecraft's *Vindication of the Rights of Woman* and Job's Mother's Womb," *Literature and History* 12, no. 2 (1986): 215–16, 227.
5. Gary Kelly, *Revolutionary Feminism: The Mind and Career of Mary Wollstonecraft* (Houndmills, UK: Macmillan, 1992), 38–39.
6. Daniel E. White, *Early Romanticism and Religious Dissent* (Cambridge: Cambridge University Press, 2006), 115–17.
7. Mary Wollstonecraft, *A Short Residence in Sweden, Norway, and Denmark*, and William Godwin, *Memoirs of the Author of* The Rights of Woman, ed. Richard Holmes (Harmondsworth, UK: Penguin, 1987), 215.

8. Russell E. Richey sees 1760 as the beginning of the final phase of "the transformation of Dissent into Unitarianism," that is, when "the liberal wing of Dissent metamorphosed into Unitarianism under the leadership of Joseph Priestley." While Unitarianism is generally made "an expression of the English Enlightenment or English Liberalism," such a conception leads to losing sight of Unitarianism as a religious movement. That is why, Richey argues, Unitarianism is best envisaged as deriving from Presbyterianism, "from which a significant portion of heterodox leadership and congregations was drawn" and, more generally, from "the social and intellectual base [identified] as Dissent or Nonconformity, the larger community of which Presbyterianism was part." John Spurr emphasizes how the fact that Dissenters became caught up in the Trinitarian controversies of the 1710s would have "horrified earlier Puritans," but suggests that these debates "presage[d] the directions to be taken by eighteenth-century Puritanism" in the sense that they led to a "theological fissure [that] was to reshape Dissent," liberals moving toward Unitarianism, while the more conservative perhaps found their new voice in Methodism. See Richey, "From Puritanism to Unitarianism in England: A Study in Candour," *Journal of the American Academy of Religion* 41 (September 1973): 371–72; Spurr, "Later Stuart Puritanism," in *The Cambridge Companion to Puritanism*, ed. John Coffey and Paul C.H. Lim (Cambridge: Cambridge University Press, 2008), 100. For a similar "theological fissure" across the Atlantic, see David D. Hall, "New England, 1660–1730," in *The Cambridge Companion to Puritanism*, 144.

9. Mary Astell, "Some Reflections upon Marriage" (1700), in Bridget Hill, *The First English Feminist* (Aldershot, UK: Gower, 1986), 84.

10. Godwin, *Memoirs of the Author of* The Rights of Woman, 223.

11. Ralph M. Wardle, *The Collected Letters of Mary Wollstonecraft* (Ithaca, NY: Cornell University Press, 1979), 385.

12. Claudia L. Johnson, "Mary Wollstonecraft's Novels," in *The Cambridge Companion to Mary Wollstonecraft*, ed. Claudia L. Johnson (Cambridge: Cambridge University Press, 2002), 189.

13. Mary Poovey, *The Proper Lady and the Woman Writer: Ideology as Style in the Works of Mary Wollstonecraft, Mary Shelley, and Jane Austen* (Chicago: University of Chicago Press, 1984), 55, 95.

14. Johnson, "Mary Wollstonecraft's Novels," 189.

15. Wardle, *The Collected Letters of Mary Wolstonecraft*, 162.

16. Janet Todd and Marilyn Butler, eds., *The Works of Mary Wollstonecraft*, 7 vols. (London: Pickering, 1989), 1:5; hereafter references to Wollstonecraft's works will be to this edition, cited in the text.

17. The evidence for Richardson's position on gender roles is tentative and highly complex. While some critics claim that "Richardson built into the plot and characterization of the novel [*Clarissa*] a considerable vein of Christian patriarchal authoritarianism," others consider that Richardson's works mostly reveal "the problems and anxieties of gender construction" inasmuch as he "both employs and questions" the conventional model of femininity and therefore is neither totally conservative nor consistently subversive. Lois A. Chaber, "Christian Form and Anti-Feminism in *Clarissa*," *Eighteenth-Century Fiction* 15, no. 3 (2003): 507–8; Tassie Gwilliam, *Richardson's Fictions of Gender* (Stanford: Stanford University Press, 1993), 1, 15.

18. Mary Robinson, *Letter to the Women of England on the Injustice of Mental Subordination; and, The Natural Daughter* (1799), ed. Sharon M. Setzer (Peterborough, ON: Broadview Press, 2003), 84; Ian Watt, *The Rise of the Novel* (1957; rpt. Harmondsworth, UK: Penguin, 1977), 339.

19. Mary Robinson, *Letter to the Women of England on the Injustice of Mental Subordination; and, The Natural Daughter* (1799), ed. Sharon M. Setzer (Peterborough, ON: Broadview Press, 2003), 84; Ian Watt, *The Rise of the Novel* (1957; rpt. Harmondsworth, UK: Penguin, 1977), 339.

20. Wendy Gunther-Canada, *Rebel Writer: Mary Wollstonecraft and Enlightenment Politics* (Dekalb: Northern Illinois University Press, 2001), 4.

21. Not coincidentally the educational treatise was the very first genre at which Wollstonecraft tried her hand as a writer, with her *Thoughts on the Education of Daughters: With Reflections on Female Conduct, in the More Important Duties of Life* (1787).

22. Jane Spencer, "Women Writers and the Eighteenth-Century Novel," in *The Cambridge Companion to the Eighteenth-Century Novel*, ed. John Richetti (Cambridge: Cambridge University Press, 2002), 215.

23. *Anti-Jacobin Review* 1 (1798): 190. Reviews were highly instrumental in defining the nature, function, and proper sphere of the novel; about the constraints that they imposed more specifically on women, see Laura Runge, "Momentary Fame: Female Novelists in Eighteenth-Century Book Reviews," in *A Companion to the Eighteenth-Century English Novel and Culture*, ed. Paula R. Backscheider and Catherine Ingrassia (Oxford: Blackwell, 2005), 286ff.

24. The long-lasting effects of this paradigm appear in Virginia Woolf's ironic remark that "Jane Austen should have laid a wreath upon the grave of Fanny Burney" (*A Room of One's Own*, [New York: Harcourt, Brace, 1929], 113).

25. While the *Christian* virtues of "chastity, submission, and forgiveness of injuries" were also prescribed for men, it was the combination of Christian precepts and the relegation of women to the domestic sphere that contributed to naturalizing the association of women with the Christian, but passive, virtues of meekness and chastity. As Michael McKeon has shown, by the middle of the eighteenth century "inner virtue [was] being established as a particularly feminine trait, increasingly to be associated with the reformative power of domesticity." Michael McKeon, "Historicizing Patriarchy: The Emergence of Gender Difference in England 1660–1760," *Eighteenth Century Studies* 28 (1995): 313.

26. Charlotte Smith, *Marchmont* (London: Sampson Low, 1796), 4:52.

27. Godwin, *Memoirs of the Author of* The Rights of Woman, 215. Wollstonecraft's texts substantiate this claim: while her very first work, *Thoughts on the Education of Daughters* (1787) advocates "fixed principles of religion" (33), in her last book, *Letters Written during a Short Residence in Sweden, Norway, and Denmark* (1796), she remarks, without apparent disapproval, that "on the subject of religion" the Norwegians are "tolerant" and "perhaps here advanced a step further in free-thinking," one writer having even "ventured to deny the divinity of Jesus Christ, and to question the necessity or utility of the christian system" (276).

28. Mary Hays, "Memoirs of Wollstonecraft," *Annual Necrology, 1797–98* (London, 1800), 416.

29. Samuel Richardson, "Letter to Frances Grainger," January 22, 1749/50, in *Selected Letters of Samuel Richardson*, ed. John Carroll (Oxford: Clarendon Press, 1964), 144.

30. Samuel Richardson, "Meditations Collected from the Sacred Books" (1750), in *Prefaces, Postscripts and Related Writings, Samuel Richardson's Published Commentary on Clarissa, 1747–65*, 3 vols., ed. Jocelyn Harris and Tom Keymer (London: Pickering & Chatto, 1998), 1:202.

31. See also *Mary*, 47; *Wrongs of Woman*, 154.

32. Richard Price, *A Review of the Principal Questions and Difficulties in Morals* (1758; Oxford: Clarendon Press, 1974), 180.

33. In *The English Novel, 1770–1829: A Bibliographical Survey of Prose Fiction Published in the British Isles*, vol. 1, *1770–1799*, ed. James Raven and Antonia Forster (Oxford: Oxford University Press, 2000), 34.

34. Michael A. Mullett, *Catholics in Britain and Ireland, 1558–1829* (Houndmills, UK: Macmillan, 1998), 96.

35. John Locke, *Epistola de Tolerantia / A Letter on Toleration* (1689), ed. R. Klibanski and J.W. Gough (Oxford: Clarendon Press, 1968), 133.

36. Colin Haydon, *Anti-Catholicism in Eighteenth-Century England, c. 1714–80: A Political and Social Study* (Manchester, UK: Manchester University Press, 1993), 55.

37. Smith, *Marchmont*, 147.

38. Mitzi Myers, "Unfinished Business: Wollstonecraft's *Maria*," *Wordworth Circle* 11 (1980): 110.

Selected Index

Abelard, 11, 13, 14, 16, 18
abolitionist movement, British, xiii, 2, 22n2
Addison, Joseph, 56; *Cato*, 19
Afterlife: Bluestocking view of, 266–267; Boswell on, 245; Browne's belief in, 94–96; Hume on, 176–177, 178; Johnson on, 94, 120–121, 122, 127, 128n35, 135, 142; in *The Vicar of Wakefield*, 178. *See also* Heaven; immortality
The Age of Reason trial (1797), 293–308; Scriptural authority in, 300, 301, 302–303, 307–308. *See also* Paine, Thomas: *The Age of Reason*
Allegory, 167–168, 172; in *The Rambler*, 124; in *Tom Jones*, 50, 59, 62–63
Allestree, Richard: *The Whole Duty of Man*, 136
Almond, Philip C., 85, 87n38
Amory, Thomas: *The Life of John Buncle*, 277
Anglicanism: Browne's, 93, 98–99, 101, 106; Burke's, 289; church and state in, 258; claims to truth, xiii; customary prayer forms of, 159; decline in authority of, 178; doctrine of the Trinity, 281; inclusiveness of, 159; Johnson's, 141, 152; prayer and belief in, 149; predestination in, 244; rationalism of, 103, 256, 257; salvation in, 108; secularizing ethics of, 256; seventeenth-century roots of, 107; via media of, 4, 103, 141. *See also* Book of Common Prayer; religion, established; Thirty-Nine Articles
anticlericalism Fielding's, 59, 69n30
anti-Methodism, 220–232. *See also* Graves, Richard: *The Spiritual Quixote*; Methodism
antinomianism, 1–2, 4, 7, 10
anti-Trinitarianism, 275n35, 277
Apostles' Creed, Anglican belief in, 79
Aristotle, 15, 286
Arminianism, 152, 227, 265, 269
Arnold, Thomas: *Observations* 220
Astell, Mary, 74, 77, 80, 188, 189, 312; correspondence with Norris, 183–189; feminism of, 189; on human/divine love, 186, 188–189, 195, 196, 198; *Serious Proposal to the Ladies*, 80, 183, 200n2; theocentric Heaven of, 73, 75, 80–81. *See also* Norris, John
Aston, Nigel, 288, 290n9
atheism: charges against Browne, 102, 104; Johnson on, 103, 103–104
Auerbach, Erich, 168
Augustine, Saint: anti-Pelagian texts of, 9; on concupiscence, 134; influence on Johnson, 135, 145n6; Norris's admiration for, 186, 191, 197; on original sin, 134, 135, 136; view of

Heaven, 73, 79, 86n12
Austin, Michael, 4
Auty, Susan, 221

Backscheider, Paula, 4
Bakhtin, Mikhail, 123
Ball, Roger, 227
Bangorian controversy, 10, 259
Barbauld, Anna: *Essay on the Origin and Progress of Novel-Writing*, 316
Barnard, Frederick, 103
Barrow, Isaac, 50, 53, 68n17
Bate, Walter Jackson, 91
Battestin, Martin, 49–50, 53, 59, 165, 173
Battestin, Ruthe, 49, 53
Baxter, Richard, 73, 103
Berkeley, George, bishop of Cloyne, 136
Berlin, Isaiah, 262
Bernard of Clairvaux, 13
Bible. *See* New Testament; Old Testament; Scriptures
Blackburn, Timothy, 170
Blackburne, Francis: *Confessional*, 259
Blair, Hugh, 241, 247–250, 253n15
Blake, William: *The Marriage of Heaven and Hell*, 72
Bloch, Ruth, 230
Blood, Fanny, 312, 313
Bluestockings: belief in salvation history, 256, 270–271, 271–272; charity among, 256, 270–271, 272; Christian assumptions of, 270–272; diversity among, 256, 272; engagement with reason, 261, 263–265, 272; and human benevolence, 267–268; and latitudinarianism, 255–261, 267–268, 269; orthodoxy among, 256, 265; in public sphere, 255, 272; view of afterlife, 266–267; view of redemption, 265–266; view of sin, 265–266, 267; and voluntarism, 262–263, 267; on women's education, 261, 267–268
Bolingbroke, Lord, 50
Book of Common Prayer, 141; Burke's allusions to, 288, 289; Johnson's use of, 159; original sin in, 134–135
Booth, Wayne, 123
Borges, Jorge Luis, 167

Boswell, James: on afterlife, 205, 245; and Church of Scotland, 238, 241, 242, 253n11; conversion to Catholicism, 239; correspondence with Wesley, 237; early religious training of, 238, 242; on original sin, 132, 136; on predestination, 244, 245; on Priestley, 250; on *Rasselas*, 142; religious conversions of, 239–240; and Rousseau, 238, 242, 243; self-representations of, 237, 243; theological readings of, 246–248; theological writings of, 249–251; university education of, 239; on worship services, 240–242, 243, 251
Boswell, James, works by: *Account of Corsica*, 248–249; *Ébauche*, 242, 253n6; "The Hypochondriack", 247, 251; *Journal of a Tour to the Hebrides*, 247; *Life of Johnson*, 100, 237, 252n1, 245; *London Journal*, 240, 253n5; "Private Papers", 237, 254n22; "Rampager" newspaper columns, 249–250, 254n32; "Sketch" of early life, 238, 253n6
Boulton, J.T., 283
Bowles, William, 245
Bradshaigh, Lady Dorothy, 71
Bramhall, Joseph, archbishop of Armagh, 248
Brooks, Peter, 71
Browne, Sir Thomas: Anglicanism of, 93, 98–99, 101, 106; avoidance of controversy, 99–100, 105; belief in afterlife, 94–96; charges of deism against, 102, 104; on Christian charity, 105; critics of, 102, 104; death of, 99; on Protestant Reformation, 105–106, 107; religious sincerity of, 108; similarities with Johnson, 100; Watts's criticism of, 101; writing style of, 91, 93–94, 102, 109n13
Browne, Sir Thomas, works by: *Christian Morals*, 91, 111n34; *Garden of Cyrus*, 93; *Hydrotaphia*, 94–95, 96–97; *Posthumous Works*, 109n13; *Religio Medici*, 92–94, 100, 101, 105, 106; *Vulgar Errors*, 102, 106–107, 111n34
Bunyan, John, 167

Selected Index 335

Burke, Edmund: affirmation of Providence, 286; allusions to Book of Common Prayer, 288, 289; architecture/fortification metaphors of, 281, 282, 285; biblical allusions of, 283–285; classical allusions of, 285–287, 291n23; engagement with Dissenters, 277, 281, 284; on established religion, 277, 280–281, 282, 284, 285–288; Priestley on, 288; religious caution of, 278, 278–279, 283; on Scripture, 282, 283; on social contract, 286, 288; speeches on toleration, 281, 282; theology in writings of, 277–289; use of allusion, 277, 283–287, 291n23

Burke, Edmund, works by: *An Appeal from the New to the Old Whigs*, 278; *A Letter to a Noble Lord*, 285; *Philosophical Enquiry into the Sublime and Beautiful*, 283; *Reflections on the Revolution in France*, 278, 280, 288, 313; *Speech on Conciliation with America*, 284

Burney, Frances, 66, 317

Burton, Robert: *The Anatomy of Melancholy*, 98, 212

Butler, Joseph, 15, 51, 246, 260

Cambridge Platonists, 259, 270
Carpenter, Mary, 312
Carter, Elizabeth: on affections of the heart, 263–264; correspondence with Talbot, 83–84; and latitudinarianism, 256, 260; and More, 268; practical piety of, 272; on reason, 263, 270; view of Heaven, 81–84, 88n53, 89n54

The Case of the Unfortunate Truly Stated (1730), 36

Cash, Arthur, 194

Catholicism: Boswell's conversion to, 239; Browne on, 105–106, 107; in *Mary*, 327–328; meditation in, 153

Caudle, James, 242

Chambers, Catherine (Kitty), 108

Chapone, Hester: on afterlife, 266–267; on charity, 271; on redemption, 265–83

Chapone, Hester, works by: *Letters on Filial Obedience*, 265; *Letters on the Improvement of the Mind*, 265–82, 266–267, 271; "The Story of Fidelia", 264–265

Chapone, Sarah: correspondence with Richardson, 74–76, 77, 80; in Hutchinsonian movement, 256, 273n6; orthodoxy of, 261

Chilcote, Paul, 219

Chubb, Thomas: *True Gospel*, 68n20

Chung, Ewha, 78, 87n29

Church Fathers: Johnson's admiration for, 135, 137, 152; typology of, 168

Church of England. *See* Anglicanism; religion, established

Church of Scotland, Boswell and, 238, 241, 242, 253n11, 254n22

Cicero, 286, 287

Civil War, English, 106, 278

Clark, J.C.D., 275n35, 278, 285

Clarke, Samuel, 15, 16, 122, 125, 260; *A Demonstration of the Being and Attributes of God*, 248

Clingham, Greg, 150

Coleridge, Samuel Taylor, 204

Collins, Anthony: *Discourse of the Grounds and Reasons of the Christian Religion*, 172

Comyn, William, bishop of Durham, 107

Council of Constantinople, 2nd, 209

Counter-Enlightenment, British, 262

Cowper, William, 211

Cross, Wilbur, 212

Curnock, Nehemiah, 28

Damrosch, Leopold, 166

Dante: parting from Beatrice, 85, 89n62; on readers, 214

Dartrey, Thomas Dawson, Lord, 272

Davies, Sir John: *Nosce Teipsum*, 103, 110n29

death: in Johnson's writings, 119–122, 124. *See also* afterlife; Heaven; immortality

De Bruyn, Frans, 221, 222

Defoe, Daniel: Goldsmith on, 170; worldview of, xviii

Defoe, Daniel, works by: *Moll Flanders*, 165; *Roxana*, xv–xvii

deism, 37; afterlife in, 177; Butler on, 246; charges against Browne, 102, 104;

Fielding and, 49, 50, 52, 53; Goldsmith on, 167; Hume's, 178; in *The Infidel Convicted*, 30; Johnson on, 104; in latitudinarianism, 52; Paine on, 298; Richardson on, 31, 34, 47n20; Warburton on, 169; Whiston on, 172
Delany, Mary, 256
DeMaria, Robert, Jr., 93, 101
the Devil: in Christian satire, 204; English belief in, 205; in *Tristram Shandy*, 203–204, 206–212, 213, 215
Dickens, Charles, 66
Dickie, Simon, 49
Diderot, Denis: and Richardson, 2, 21n1, 25n35
Dissent, English: Burke's engagement with, 277, 281, 284; and early Romanticism, 312; in Johnson's beliefs, 113; legislation concerning, 280; political, 295–296, 307; role in reform, 313; toleration for, 323
divines, English: in eighteenth-century fiction, 51; Goldsmith's justification of, 169; influence on Johnson, 135; political, 243; rationalism of, 258, 264; women's apprehension of, 323
Donnellan, Anne, 256
Draper, Eliza, 183; Sterne's love for, 184, 192, 193, 194, 195, 196–197, 199
Dryden, John, 53, 56, 133
Dun, John, 238, 242
Dupré, Louis, 6
Dussinger, John, 77

education: Bluestockings on, 261, 267; More's promotion of, 269; religious, 271; in Richardson's writings, 31; women's, 255, 261, 267–268, 269
Edwards, Jonathan, 245
Eglinton, Alexander Montgomerie, 10th Earl, 239
Ehrenpreis, Irvin, 123
Enlightenment, British: religious aspects of, 255, 257, 261–262, 269–270; women in, 255
enthusiasm, 222, 231, 281. *See also* Methodism
Epistle of Barnabas, 211

Erasmus, Desiderius, 14, 18; critique of Stoicism, 210; on emulation of Christ, 16; *Encomium Moriae*, 58; sacred hermeneutics of, 4
Erskine, Thomas: belief in Scriptural authority, 300, 301, 302; defense of Christianity, 304–306; defense of *The Rights of Man*, 293, 294–296, 300, 301, 306; prosecution of *The Age of Reason*, 293, 297, 300–307
ethics: in Fielding's works, 8, 9, 11–12, 13–14, 16, 17; Johnson's, 115; role in salvation, 7, 9, 10; secular, 256, 262
Eucharist, 106–107, 108
eudaimonism, Johnson's, 131
evangelicalism, eighteenth-century, xi; in Counter-Enlightenment, 262; in *Jonathan Wild*, 50; latitudinarianism and, 257, 265; More's, 265, 269, 273n5
Exclusion Crisis, 166, 305

faith: and Enlightenment reason, 269–270; and good works, 140, 157
Fall of Man: disbelief in, xii; in Johnson's works, 131–144; Richardson on, 77. *See also* sin, original
Feathers Tavern Petition, 249, 259, 280
feminism, British: apprehension of the divine in, 323; Astell's, 189; in fiction, 316; origins of, 312; Wollstonecraft's, 311–312, 316
Ferguson, Joseph, 238
Ferguson, Oliver, 171
Ferguson, Robert: *The Interest of Reason and Religion*, 212
fiction, eighteenth-century: depiction of women, 316–318; divinity in, 51; gothic, 204, 315; Providence in, 50, 166; Quixotism in, 221; realism in, 167–169; Richardson's authority concerning, 324; secularization narrative of, 166; Wollstonecraft's view of, 317–319, 324; women's, 316–317
fideism: Johnson's, 113, 119, 120–121, 126, 136–137; skepticism and, 119; theodicy of, 121
Fielding, Henry: anticlericalism of, 59, 69n30; anti-Jacobitism of, 52, 68n19; on antinomianism, 7; belief in

Selected Index

immortality, 53; Christian narratives of, 53; and deism, 49, 50, 52, 53; grace in works of, 54; on individualism, 18; on Jesus Christ, 53; on latitudinarianism, 10; on Methodism, 23n18, 49, 221; on morality, 52–53, 59; on *Pamela's* theology, 1, 6, 7, 9, 24n31; on piety, 53; Providence in works of, 64; religious beliefs of, 49–66; sexuality in works of, 51; use of Bible, 50, 51, 63, 64, 65; use of Tillotson, 9–10, 69n37

Fielding, Henry, works by: *Amelia*, 53–54, 66; *The Champion*, 50, 58; *The Covent-Garden Journal*, 50, 55; *Dialogue between The Devil, the Pope, and the Pretender*, 70n41; *A Fragment of a Comment on L. Bolingbroke's Essays*, 50; *Jonathan Wild* 50, 54, 56–57, 58; *Joseph Andrews*, 7–14, 16–21, 50, 53, 277; *Journal of a Voyage to Lisbon*, 50, 63; *Journey from This World to the Next*, 54; *Proposal for Making an Effectual Provision for the Poor*, 55; *Shamela*, 8; *Tom Jones*, 50, 56, 56–66, 170

figuralism, 168, 173
Filmer, Sir Robert: *Patriarcha*, 166
Fischer, John Irwin, 171
Fitzpatrick, Martin, 259
Fludd, Robert: *Utriusque Cosmi*, 212
Flynn, Carol Houlihan, 71
Fog's Weekly Journal, 28, 30, 32, 37
Foote, Samuel: *The Minor*, 227
Force, James, 177
Fordun, John, 107, 111n35
Forrna, Amanita, 194
Foster, Greg, 135
Foucault, Michel: *Madness and Civilization*, 224
Fox, Charles James, 280
Francis de Sales, Saint, 147
Franklin, Benjamin, 53
freedom of the press and speech: opponents of, 301; in Protestant Reformation, 304; in *The Rights of Man* trial, 295, 297, 301, 303–304
freethinking, 30, 34
free will: Boswell on, 239; Johnson's belief in, 244, 245

Frei, Hans, 168–169, 172–173, 177
French Revolution, xii, 278, 313
Friedrich, Hugo, 116
Frye, Northrop: *Anatomy of Criticism*, 123

Garrick, Eva, 256
Gibbon, Edward: *Decline and Fall of the Roman Empire*, x
Gibbons, Thomas, 149, 160n4
Glasites (fundamentalist sect), 249, 254n31
Glorious Revolution (1688), xi; and French Revolution, 278, 313
Godwin, William: biography of Wollstonecraft, 320; editing of *Wrongs of Woman*, 324; on *Mary*, 313; on Wollstonecraft's religion, 312
Gogineni, Bina, 51
Goldsmith, Oliver: on Anglican authority, 178; belief in Providence, 164, 167; on Defoe, 170; on deism, 167; on religious disputes, 170–171; *The Vicar of Wakefield* 163–178
Good, Graham, 127
Gordon, Alexander, 27, 28
Goring, Paul, 221, 222
grace, divine: in Fielding's works, 54; Johnson's prayer for, 100; in *Joseph Andrews*, 11, 12, 15, 16, 17–18, 19, 20–21, 25n45; latitudinarian position on, 7; in *Life of Browne*, 106; in natural law, 11; receptivity to, 15, 16, 21. *See also* salvation
Grainger, Frances, 321
Graves, Richard: *The Spiritual Quixote*, 221–232; and Wesley, 221, 222, 234n38; and Whitefield, 221, 222, 227, 234n38
Great Instauration, 207
Green, J. Brazier, 28
Gregory of Nyssa, heresy of, 209
Griffith, Richard, 204
Grotius, Hugo, 98–99; Johnson's admiration of, 98, 110n17

Habermas, Jürgen, xv, xviii, 270; on public/private spheres, xvii, xix, 255; on public religion, xvii

Hailes, David Dalrymple, Lord, 244

happiness: human desire for, 123; in Johnson's works, 99, 125–126, 132–133, 137, 139, 141, 142–143

Harth, Phillip, 103
Haverstein, Daniela, 92
Hawkins, William, 170
Hays, Mary, 320
Haywood, Eliza: *Anti-Pamela*, 8
Heaven: Augustine on, 73, 79, 86n12; in *Clarissa*, 72, 76–78; community in, 74, 77, 78, 87n29; in eighteenth-century thought, 72–73; friendship in, 74, 79; human love in, 72; Johnson on, 120, 141, 144; in *Jonathan Wild*, 56; knowledge in, 74, 75, 75–76; "modern" view of, 77, 81, 85; Richardson's views on, 73, 74–80, 85–86; social vision of, 74–75, 75–76, 77, 79, 80, 81–83, 85; theocentric, 73, 75, 79, 86n12; Wesley's view of, 84–85. *See also* afterlife; immortality
Heaven: A History (McDannell and Lang), 72–73, 78, 79
Hegel, Georg Wilhelm Friedrich, 2, 22n5
Heller, Deborah, 83
Hempton, David, 229
Henry, Matthew, 169
Herbert, George: *The Temple*, 204
Hervey, James: *Meditations among the Tombs*, 73, 79, 86n10
Hill, Charles Jarvis, 221, 222
Hilliard, Raymond, 174
Hilton, Mary, 256–257, 263, 265; on latitudinarianism, 85, 257–258, 259, 260, 260–261, 262
Hoadly, Benjamin, bishop of Winchester, 7, 10, 13, 16, 17, 259
Hobbes, Thomas, 205
Hogarth, William: *Harlot's Progress*, 59
Hooker, Richard: *Laws of Ecclesiastical Polity*, 141
Hopkins, Robert, 163, 164, 165
Hume, David, 81, 87n17, 115, 176–178, 296
Hutchinsonian movement, Bluestockings in, 256, 273n6

Iacobini, Marco, 13

immortality: Christian Revelation on, 96; classical and Christian, 95; Fielding's belief in, 53; persistence of personality in, 85; in *Rasselas*, 94–97, 94, 125; of the soul, 122, 125. *See also* afterlife; Heaven
The Infidel Convicted, deism in, 30
Iser, Wolfgang, 12

Jacobite Rebellions, 230
Jacobs, Alan, 134
James, William: *Varieties of Religious Experience*, 240
Jenyns, Soame: *Free Inquiry into the Nature and Origins of Evil*, 94, 115; Johnson on, 94, 115, 136, 138, 139, 143
Jesus Christ: Fielding on, 53; imitation of, 16, 197; love for, 184; mystical reunion with, 197; sensual imagery concerning, 227; typology of, 173; universalism of, 4
Jewish Naturalization Bill (1753), 38
Job, Book of: allegorical reading of, 169; creation in, 312; historical reading of, 169; Sterne on, 210; typology of Christ in, 173; in *The Vicar of Wakefield*, 165, 169–170, 173, 175–176, 178; Whiston on, 172
Johnson, Samuel: admiration for Church Fathers, 135, 137, 152; admiration of Grotius, 98, 110n17; admiration of Pascal, 114; on afterlife, 120–121, 122, 127, 128n35, 135, 142; Anglicanism of, 141, 152; on atheists, 103, 103–104; belief in free will, 244, 245; Christian moralism of, 113–127; on Christian sects, 100–101, 106, 243; death in writings of, 119–122, 124; definition of Christianity, ix, 104–105; empirical psychology of, 118, 126, 127; essays of, 115, 116–118, 123; on Eucharist, 107, 108; on fallen world, 131–144; fideism of, 113, 119, 120–121, 126, 136–137; on his failings, 138, 147, 154, 156; on Jenyns, 94, 115, 136, 138, 139, 143; on moral philosophers, 115–116; prayers, 100, 138, 146n20, 156; on sacred verse, 154–155, 157, 158; on salvation, 121, 136, 140, 147, 153; similarities with

Browne, 100; on solitude, 139–140; theory of biography, 97; theory of writing, 117, 118; on virtue, 140–141; on Waller, 151; on zealotry, 104–105
Johnson, Samuel, works by: *Adventurer* 132–133, 135, 137, 139, 140, 151; *Dictionary*, 92, 101, 124, 133, 136, 141, 256; *Idler*, 116, 123, 133, 140–141; *Life of Browne*, 91–108; *Life of Butler*, 157; "Life of Collins", 131; *Life of Isaac Watts*, 148–151, 154–155, 157–159; *Life of Milton*, 147; *Life of Pope*, 150; *Life of Savage*, 92; *Life of Waller*, 155, 158; *Lives of the Poets*, 147–151; "On the Study of Religion", 153, 161n15; *Prayers and Meditations*, 108, 149, 151, 154, 156, 158; *Rambler* 115, 116, 119, 121–122, 125, 139–141; *Rasselas* 94, 96–97, 124–127, 132, 139, 141, 142–143; *Sermons*, 107, 122, 132, 137, 139, 140, 143, 144; "Study of Tongues", 153, 161n15; *The Vanity of Human Wishes*, 120, 132, 141, 143
Jones, Lady Catherine, 74, 189

Kames, Lord, 205, 246
Kelleher, Paul, 51, 66
Kelly, Gary, 312
Kelly, Hugh, 167
Korshin, Paul, 168, 169, 173, 177
Kyd, Stewart, 297, 299, 308n10

La Bruyère, Jean de, 114, 116
Lake, Arthur, 184
Langer, Ulrich, 6
Lanser, Susan S., 88n43
La Rochefoucauld, François, 114, 116
latitudinarianism, xx, 25n39; among bishops, 260; Bluestockings' relationship to, 255–261, 267–268, 269; church historians on, 256, 258; and deism, 52; eschatology of, 258; and evangelicalism, 257, 265; Fielding and, 10, 49; ideological, 259–261; in Johnson's *Dictionary*, 256; peace in, 258; pejorative connotations of, 256; position on grace, 7; progressive aspects of, 257; Tillotson's, ix–x, 159; voluntarist ethic of, 258, 267

Lavington, George: *The Enthusiasm of Methodists and Papists Compar'd*, 225
Law, William, 27–28, 46n4, 152, 157
Le Clerc, Jean, 98–99
Lehmann, James, 165, 170, 173
Levinas, Emmanuel, xviii, 13, 24n32
Leviticus, charity in, 66
Lewalski, Barbara Kiefer: *Protestant Poetics and the Seventeenth-Century Religious Lyric*, 152–153
libel, 297–307
Lill, James, 91–92, 109n9, 109n13
Lipking, Lawrence: *The Ordering of the Arts in Eighteenth-Century England*, 149
literature, eighteenth-century, xii–xiii, xx. *See also* fiction, eighteenth-century
Lock, F.P., 279
Locke, John, 246; on original sin, 135–136; on personal identity, 85; *On the Reasonableness of Christianity*, xii, 135, 144; on the soul, 125; in *Tristram Shandy*, 203
Longinus, *On the Sublime*, 210
Loughborough, Alexander Wedderburne, 1st Baron, 295
love, divine, 184–185; in Astell-Norris correspondence, 183–186; and human love, 87n18, 184, 186, 188–189, 190, 198, 324; the mystical in, 184, 185, 189; in Sterne's writings, 192–193; St. Paul on, 105
love, human: companionship in, 194–196, 195; and divine love, 87n18, 184, 186, 188–189, 190, 198, 324; in Fielding, 17, 65; religious expression of, 184; in Sterne-Draper correspondence, 183–184; in Sterne's writings, 186, 192–193, 193, 198. *See also* sexuality
Lowth, Robert, 169–170, 173
Lucan, *Pharsalia*, 287
Luther, Martin, 14, 207
Lyons, Nicholas, 227

Macaulay, Catherine, 313
madness, religious, 30, 32, 38; association with Methodism, 220, 222, 224–226, 231, 234n28
Maimonides, 212

Malebranche, Nicolas, 73, 191
Mansfield, Harvey, 290n9
Mansfield, William Murray, 1st Earl, 293
Marlowe, Christopher: *Doctor Faustus*, 207
Martin, Bernice, xvii
materialism: Boswell on, 245; in literary criticism, xviii, xix; versus spiritualism, xix
Mayo, Henry, 245
McEwan, Ian: *Atonement*, 59
McKeon, Michael, 166
meditation: Catholic, 153; in prayer, 152, 152; Protestant tradition of, 152–153
Methodism, 219–232; association with madness, 220, 222, 224–226, 231, 234n28; Boswell and, 239; desire for persecution in, 225, 231; in Fielding's works, 23n18, 50, 54, 68n27; itinerant preachers of, 219–220, 222, 232; literary attacks on, 221; mobility in, 224, 228, 232; preaching in, 219–220, 221, 222, 232; psycho-emotional state in, 220, 222, 223–226, 231, 232; Richardson on, 37; in *Tom Jones*, 50, 62; women's participation in, 220, 228, 229–231. See also Graves, Richard: *The Spiritual Quixote*
Meyer, Mitzi, 328
Michaelis, Johann David, 173, 181n42
Milner, Joseph, 270
Milton, John, 147, 166, 296
Montagu, Elizabeth, 81, 83, 88n45, 259–260; and More, 268; orthodoxy of, 261; reading habits of, 260; salon of, 268
Montagu, Lady Mary Wortley, 54
Montaigne, Michel de, 114
Montesquieu, Baron de: *Persian Letters*, 245
moral philosophers, British, 114–116
More, Hannah, 55, 260; activism of, 268–269; Arminianism of, 265, 269; educational activities of, 269, 271; evangelicalism of, 265, 269, 273n5; reading habits of, 260; on reason, 268; relationship with Bluestockings, 268

More, Hannah, works by: *Bas Bleu*, 257, 268; *Strictures*, 268
Morgan, Richard, 29–30, 31, 32, 40
Morgan, William, 34–35, 36, 38
Müller, Patrick, 258

Neoplatonism, 18; in expression of sexuality, 183–184, 187; Norris's, 183, 187, 193; self-sufficiency in, 18; Sterne's, 190, 192
New, Melvyn, 166, 191, 210, 258
New Melvyn, works by: "Benjamin Whichcote's Aphorisms", 273n9; "Grease of God" 49, 50; *Notes on the Sermons of Sterne*, 214–215
Newman, Cardinal John Henry, 103
New Testament: evangelical mandate in, xi; in *Tom Jones*, 64, 65
Nicole, Pierre, 73
Norris, John, of Bemerton, 74, 75, 87n22; admiration for Augustine, 186, 191, 197; correspondence with Astell, 183–189; Neoplatonism of, 183, 187, 193; theocentric Heaven of, 73, 80–81
Norris, John, of Bemerton, works by: *Letters Concerning the Love of God*, 74, 87n22, 183–190, 193, 197, 198; *Miscellanies*, 80
Norwich Cathedral, desecration of, 106

oaths, religious basis for, 305
O'Brien, Karen, 255, 257–258, 259–263, 265
O'Brien, Mary, 256, 256–257
Ogden, Samuel: *Sermons on the Efficacy of Prayer*, 247
Old Testament: authenticity of, 299; in *Tom Jones*, 63
Origen, heresy of, 209
Ovid, *Metamorphoses*, 287
Oxford Methodists (student group): charges of Puritanism against, 32–33, 37; charitable works of, 32, 34–36, 37; public perception of, 37; Richardson's defense of, 29; Wesley's account of, 30; zeal of, 39
The Oxford Methodists (pamphlet, 1733), 27–39

Paine, Thomas, 293–303; belief in God, 298–299, 307; and Burke, 288; letter to Erskine, 298, 300, 301–302, 303
Paine, Thomas, works by: *The Age of Reason*, 293, 297–298, 307; *Common Sense*, 300; *The Rights of Man*, 293, 296, 302, 303, 306–307. *See also The Age of Reason* trial; *The Rights of Man* trial
Paley, William, 295
Parker, Blanford, 119, 136
Parker, Fred, 119, 128n11, 129n46
Parker, Kim Jan, 135
Parker, Matthew, 212
Parnell, J.T., 191
Pascal, Blaise, 34, 73, 79, 84, 100, 114
Patin, Guy, 101
patriarchy, 317, 324
Patrick, Simon, 169
Patrides, C.A., 213
Paul, Saint: on Christian love, 105; in *Jonathan Wild*, 58; on original sin, 134; on regeneration, 151; Wollstonecraft's use of, 322–323
Paulson, Ronald, 49, 51, 59
Payne, E.J., 284
peace, Christian, ix–x, xi, xiii, xxi
Pelagianism, 9–10, 11, 20
Pennington, Montagu, 83
Pepys, William Weller, 272
persecution, religious, 225, 231, 305
Piozzi, Hester Lynch, 132, 146n19
Pocock, J.G.A., 68n27, 255
poetry, sacred, 151, 154–155, 157, 158
Poovey, Mary, 313
Pope, Alexander *Dunciad* 212
Porter, Roy, 222, 224, 231
Post, Jonathan, 92
Pottle, Frederick, 239, 245, 249
prayers, 148–153; Anglican, 159; Johnson on, 141, 148, 152; Johnson's, 100, 138, 146n20; solitude in, 138; Sterne on, 207
preaching: didactic, 325; itinerant, 219–220, 222, 232; lay, 223; Methodist, 219–220, 221, 222, 232; to unbelievers, 325; Watts's, 156, 157; by women, 220
predestination, 244–245
Preston, Thomas R., 67n12, 163

Price, Richard, 278, 312; *A Discourse on the Love of Our Country*, 313
Priestley, Joseph, 245; Boswell on, 250; on Burke, 288
Prior, Matthew, 212
prison reform, 36–37, 47n22
progress, eighteenth-century idea of, 271
Providence: in Book of Job, 169; Burke's affirmation of, 286; as cause of social contract, 286; in eighteenth-century fiction, 50, 166; in Fielding, 64; in Goldsmith, 164, 167, 172, 173, 175, 176, 178; Hume on, 176; Warburton on, 169; Whiston on, 178; Whitefoot on, 97; and women's souls, 321
Psalm 137: in *Pamela*, 3–4, 6–7
public sphere, eighteenth-century: Bluestockings in, 255, 272; disjunction with private sphere, xvii; religion in, xvii
Puritanism: charges against Oxford Methodists, 32–33, 37; rationalism of, 103; women's role in, 312

Quinlan, Maurice J., 107, 111n37
Quixotism, in eighteenth-century fiction, 221

Rack, Henry D., 27
rationalism: Anglican, 103, 256, 257; Christian, 269; of English divines, 258; and latitudinarianism, 273n9; theory of, 257; Whitefield on, 223. *See also* reason
Rawson, Claude, 49, 69n29
realism, fictional, 167–168, 172
reason: Bluestocking view of, 261, 263–265, 272; Carter on, 263, 270; Enlightenment, 259; in latitudinarianism, 258; limitations of, 263–265; prelapsarian, 261; in *The Rights of Man*, 302; women's, 267–268, 269, 312. *See also* rationalism
redemption: Bluestocking view of, 265–266; Carter on, 266; Johnson on, 136; sin and, 135
Reedy, Gerard, S.J. ix, xiv, 258, 264, 270
Reformation, Protestant: Browne's justification of, 105–106, 107; Burke

on, 278; freedom of the press in, 304; on original sin, 134–135
regeneration, 151, 153
Reid, John: Boswell's defense of, 244
religion, eighteenth-century: in Age of Reason, 165; concept of progress, 271; displacement by state, xiii; divisions in, 279; effect on morality, 56; and Enlightenment, 255, 257, 261–262; enthusiasm in, 222, 231, 281; Fielding's beliefs concerning, 49–66; impact on education, 30; and the law, 293; in literature, xii–xiii; madness in, 30, 32, 38, 220, 222, 224, 231; Paine on, 293; philosophical affinities of, 255; pleasure in, 33, 35, 54; political issues in, 277; pragmatic, xiii, 52, 55; rewards and punishments in, 52; role in social justice, 50; and sexual passion, 51, 184, 186; in *Tom Jones*, 56, 56–58; utility of, 55. *See also* Methodism
religion, established: in *The Age of Reason*, 115; Burke on, 277, 280–281, 282, 284, 285–288; undermining of, 301. *See also* Christianity; Anglicanism
religion, freedom of, xi; in *The Rights of Man* trial, 303
religion, seventeenth-century: discord in, 278; latitudinarianism, 258; roots of Anglicanism in, 107
resurrection, bodily, 85
Revelation, Book of: Book of Deeds, 210
Revelation, Christian, 95, 96
Richardson, Samuel: authority concerning fiction, 324; as businessman, 34, 37, 39; correspondence with Sarah Chapone, 74–76, 77, 80; defense of Oxford Methodists, 29; on deism, 31, 34, 47n20; depiction of women, 314; on education, 31; on Fall of Man, 77; interior focus of, 325; and "Jew Bill", 38, 48n28; on Methodism, 37; political views of, 77; printing output of, 72, 77, 86n11; on prison reform, 36–37; on Puritanism, 33; religious views of, 77; on religious zeal, 38; views on Heaven, 73, 74–80, 85–86
Richarson, Samuel, works by: *Apprentice's Vade Mecum*, 34; *Clarissa*, 33, 37, 46n15, 71–72, 60–61, 72, 76–78, 79–80, 321; *Familiar Letters*, 31, 36; *Pamela*, 1–7, 20, 33, 76
The Rights of Man trial (1792), 293; defense in, 293, 294–296, 300, 301, 306; freedom of religion in, 303; freedom of the press in, 115, 295, 303–304; free speech in, 297, 301; libel in, 296, 300; Paine on, 294–295; right to dissent in, 295–296. *See also* Paine, Thomas: *The Rights of Man*
Rivers, Isabel, 159, 273n9, 274n13
Robinson, Mary, 316
Rogers, Henry N., III, 164
Rogers, John, 133
Rothstein, Eric, 171
Rousseau, Jean-Jacques: Boswell and, 238, 242, 243; depiction of women, 314; Richardson's influence on, 2
Rowe, Elizabeth, 72, 87n40
Rowlandson, Thomas: *Man of Feeling*, 51
Ruml, Treadwell, II, 51
Rymer, Michael, 221

sacraments: Hoadly on, 10, 16, 24n23, 54; in *Tom Jones* 53
Sale, William, 39, 46n8
salvation: Anglican views on, 108; conditional nature of, 152; dissociation from works, 9; Enlightenment view of, xi; Johnson on, 121, 136, 140, 147, 153; lived experience in, 151; Paine on, 298; role of ethics in, 7, 9, 10; role of self-examination in, 151. *See also* grace
salvation history, Bluestocking belief in, 256, 270–271, 271–272
Sandemanians (fundamentalist sect), 249
Schedel, Hartmann: *Nurnberg Chronicle*, 213
Schneewind, J.B., 262
Scriptures: authority of, 299–300, 301, 302–303, 307–308; Burke on, 282, 283; as cultural touchstone, 284; defense of, 300; Fielding's use of, 50, 51, 59, 63, 64, 65; literary aspects of, 283–284; Paine's questioning of, 297–307; rational judgment of, 263, 264; revelation of God, 168; in Sterne's sermons, 212

Scudamore, John, 98
Secker, Thomas, 256, 260, 273n7
second coming, belief in, 197
sects, Christian: Johnson on, 100–101, 106, 243
sensation, God as cause of, 189, 190, 190–191, 191
Sermon on the Mount, in *Tom Jones*, 64
sermons, Anglican, xiv, xv; anti-Catholic, 327; political anniversary, 278, 327; in popular culture, xix; Sterne's, xiv, 86n11, 197, 207, 210, 212, 214, 216n15
Serooskerken, Isabella van Tuyll van, 244
sexuality: companionship in, 194, 194–195; displaced, 184, 186, 193; expression in religion, 51, 184, 186; in Fielding's works, 51; in Methodist spiritualism, 227–228, 232; Neoplatonic expression of, 183–184, 187; in Norris-Astell correspondence, 184, 186; in Sterne's writings, 186, 192, 193. *See also* love, human
Shaftesbury, Anthony Ashley Cooper, 3rd earl of, 114, 193
Shakespeare, William: *King Lear*, 176; *Macbeth*, 207
Sheehan, Jonathan, 261–262
Shema (Judaism) Norris's use of, 184
Sherlock, William, 68n17, 70n46, 169–170, 173, 177; *The Use and Intent of Prophecy*, 172
Simon, John S., 28, 46n4
sin: atonement for, 198; Bluestocking view of, 265–266, 267; dual nature of, 134; impact on humanity, 137; redemption from, xii; responsibility for, 137
sin, original, 49; Anglican view of, 134–135; Augustine on, 134, 135, 136; Johnson on, 131; Locke on, 135–136; Reformation view of, 134–135; St. Paul on, 134; Swift on, 132. *See also* Fall of Man
skepticism: classical, 118; in essay writing, 118, 122; and fideism, 119; Johnson's, 122
slave trade, British, 5
Smith, Charlotte: *Marchmont*, 328; *Young Philosopher*, 317
Smollett, Tobias, 221

social contract, Burke on, 286, 288
social justice, Fielding on, 50, 55
Society for Promoting Christian Knowledge (SPCK), 271
Socinianism, 1, 2, 10–11, 14, 20; Sherlock on, 70n46; in *Tom Jones*, 59
A Sociology of Religious Emotion, xvii, xviii
solitude: Johnson on, 139–140; piety in, 151
South, Robert, 110n23, 248
Spadafora, David, 271
Spellman, W.M., 11
Spenser, Edmund, 59
Spiritualism, nineteenth-century, 85, 88n53
Star Chamber, libel trials in, 303
Steele, Richard: *The Conscious Lovers*, 19
Sterne, Elizabeth, 194
Sterne, Laurence: charity of, 193; Coleridge on, 204; companionship in writings of, 194–196, 195, 198; conciliatory qualities of, 192, 193; correspondence with Draper, 183–184, 193, 194, 195–197; Cowper on, 211; demonology of, 205, 206, 215, 218n42; divine/human love in writings of, 192–193; gift for friendship, 194; infidelities of, 213; on Job, 210; love for Draper, 184, 192, 193, 194, 195, 196–197, 199; Neoplatonism of, 190, 192; the pathetic in, 211; on prayer, 207; Rabelaisian wit of, 211; reading of Norris, 86n3, 186; on the senses, 190–191; sentimentalism of, 191; sermons of, xiv, 86n11, 197, 207, 210, 212, 214, 216n15; sexuality in writings of, 186, 192, 193; theology in reading of, 214–215
Sterne, Laurence, works by: *Beauties of Sterne*, 209; *Bramine's Journal*, 193, 194, 195–197; "Description of the World", 214; "The House of Feasting and the House of Mirth", 214; "The Levite and His Concubine", 194; "The Pharisee and Publican in the Temple", 204; *A Sentimental Journey*, 77, 183, 192, 195; *Tristram Shandy*, 86n2, 86n11, 203–215, 217n26, 217n28, 217n35, 218n44

Sterne, Lydia, 194
Stevens, Nicholas, 29
Stewart, Margaret M., 243
Stillingfleet, Edward, 264, 270
Stoicism: Erasmus on, 210; Johnson's, 118; self-sufficiency in, 18; view of human nature, 266
Stuber, Florian, 71
Suarez, Michael F.: "Johnson's Christian Thought", 152
Swedenborg, Emanuel, 72
Swift, Jonathan, 49, 65; Christianity of, 51; *A Modest Proposal*, 55; on original sin, 132; on sexuality in religion, 51

Talbot, Catherine, 83–84, 89n55, 256, 260, 261; *Reflections*, 265
Tawney, R.H., 178
Taylor, Barbara, 311–313
Taylor, Charles, 9, 159
Taylor, E. Derek, 191
Taylor, John, 120
Temple, Sir William, 141
Temple, William Johnson, 239, 241, 248; *An Essay on the Clergy*, 250
Test Act, repeal of, 280
theology, eighteenth-century: in "Age of Johnson", xx; in Burke's writings, 277–289; in *Joseph Andrews*, 277; pervasiveness of, xviii; practical aspects of, 277; relationship to literature, xii, 277; in *Rights of Woman*, 321; Sterne's, 214–215
Thesaurus Exorcismorum, 204
Thirty-Nine Articles (Anglicanism), 134–135, 249; compulsory subscription to, 280, 282
Thomas Aquinas, view of Heaven, 73
Tillich, Paul, 198–199
Tillotson, John. archbishop of Canterbury, ix–xi, 123; appeal to reasonableness, x; on faith, 270; in Fielding's works, 9–10, 69n37; on grace, 15, 16; Johnson's debt to, 128n36; latitudinarianism of, ix, xx, 7, 159; rationalism of, 264; on regeneration, 15
tolerance, religious, ix; Burke's speeches on, 281, 282; in English Constitution, 304; legislation concerning, 280

Toleration Acts, 281, 280
Tolstoy, Leo: *The Kreutzer Sonata*, 214
Tom Jones (film, 1963), 59
Trapp, Joseph: *The Nature, Folly, Sin and Danger of Being Righteous Over-much*, 223–224
Trinity: Anglican doctrine of, 275n35, 277, 281
Trollope, Anthony: *Chronicles of Barsetshire*, 178
Twain, Mark, 66
Tyerman, L., 27
Tyers, Thomas, 91
typology, 168, 173; in *The Vicar of Wakefield*, 175, 177, 178

Unitarianism, 312

Venturo, David F., 119, 141
Vermeule, Blakey, 49
Verri, Allessandro, 194
Vesey, Elizabeth, 263; religious doubts of, 256; view of Heaven, 81–83, 88n45
Virgil, *Aeneid*, 285
Virgin Birth, Fielding on, 53
virtue: civic, 139, 144; human capacity for, 144; Johnson on, 139, 140–141, 144, 147
Voitle, Robert, 259

Walker, Robert G., 128n35, 142
Waller, Edmund: Johnson's life of, 151, 155, 158
Walpole, Horace, 204
Warburton, William, 172; *The Divine Legation of Moses*, 169
Watkins, W.B.C., 100
Watson, Richard, bishop of Llandaff, 300, 307, 308n10; and *The Age of Reason*, 297
Watt, Ian: *The Rise of the Novel*, 316
Watts, Isaac, 53, 148, 149, 157; criticism of Browne, 101; devotional aesthetic of, 159; extemporaneous preaching by, 156, 157; Johnson's admiration for, 148–149, 154; religious writings of, 149, 156, 157, 159; theological reasoning of, 151
Weber, Max: disenchantment thesis of, 256

Wednesbury Riots (1743), 229
Weinbrot, Howard D., 101, 145n5, 131, 171
Wesley, Charles, 53, 222
Wesley, John: account of Oxford Methodists, 30; advocacy of celibacy, 231; charitable works of, 35; correspondence with Boswell, 237; death of, 219; on good works, 226; on lay preaching, 223; letter to Richard Morgan, 29–30, 31, 40; on original sin, 134; political views of, 231; in *The Spiritual Quixote*, 221, 222, 234n38; on spiritual rebirth, 224; travels of, 219; view of Heaven, 84–85; and William Law, 28
Wesley, John, works by: *Free Grace*, 227; *Journal*, 28
Wesley, Samuel, Sr., 28, 32, 46n15; *Two Letters from a Deist* 29
Whiston, William, 169, 177; *The Accomplishment of Scripture Prophecies*, 172; on deism, 172; on demonic possessions, 205; on Job controversy, 172; nontrinitarianism of, 171; on primitive Christianity, 171; on Providence, 178
White, Daniel E., 312
Whitefield, George, 1, 13, 38; antinomianism of, 7; *Christ the Best Husband*, 227; death of, 219; in Fielding's works, 7–8; on grace, 10; on original sin, 134; preaching of, 227; pro-Calvinism of, 227; response to Trapp, 223–224; on spiritual enthusiasts, 231; in *The Spiritual Quixote*, 221, 222, 227, 234n38; on spiritual rebirth, 224; travels of, 219; view of rationality, 223
Whitefoot, John: prose style of, 98; on Providence, 97; "Some Minutes for the Life of Sir Thomas Browne", 97, 97–98, 98–99
Wilde, Oscar, 62
Wilkes, John, 248
will, divine, 9, 262, 263; in *Joseph Andrews*, 17
Williams, Aubrey, 49
Williams, Thomas, 297

Williamson, John, 239
Willis's Wonderful Cap, 39, 48n32
Windsor Castle, Burke's metaphor of, 285
Wollstonecraft, Eliza, 312
Wollstonecraft, Everina, 312
Wollstonecraft, Mary: didacticism, 325, 326–327; feminism of, 311–312, 316, 316; fiction, 313–316, 316–319, 321, 324–326; gender relations in, 318, 328; Godwin and, 313; homiletics, 325, 328; indictment of sentimentality in, 319; moral purpose of, 324, 328; Pauline references in, 322–323; religious thought in, 313, 327–328; sermon structure of, 325, 326, 328; Godwin's biography of, 320; imagination in works of, 316, 318–319, 320, 321, 328; radicalism of, 311, 312, 313; religious convictions of, 311–313, 320–323; Unitarian influence on, 134
Wollstonecraft, Mary, works by: *Maria, or the Wrongs of Woman*, 313, 314, 318, 319, 320, 322, 323–324, 326–327; *Mary*, 313–314, 314–315, 316, 320, 321, 322–323, 325–326, 327–328; *Rights of Woman*, 311, 312, 313, 318, 321, 324; *Thoughts on the Education of Daughters*, 330n20, 331n26; *Thoughts Written during a Short Residence in Sweden, Norway, and Denmark*, 331n26; *A Vindication of the Rights of Men*, 313
women, British: in British Enlightenment, 255; education of, 255, 261, 267–268, 269; participation in Methodism, 220, 228, 229–231; in patriarchal society, 317, 324; rationality of, 267–268, 269, 312; religious sensibility of, 319, 321, 323; subjection of, 318, 323. *See also* Bluestockings
Wood, Alexander, 249
Woolf, Virginia, 331n23; on *The Vicar of Wakefield*, 163, 165
Work, James A., 64, 68n26

Young, B.W., 255, 262
Young, Edward, 248

zealotry, Johnson on, 104–105

About the Contributors

Frans De Bruyn is professor of English, University of Ottawa. He has written extensively on Edmund Burke and on numerous other subjects in eighteenth-century studies, including the reception history of Shakespeare and Cervantes, the cultural impact of the South Sea Bubble, and the literature of agriculture. Among his publications are the *Dictionary of Literary Biography: Eighteenth-Century British Literary Scholars and Critics*, ed. De Bruyn (2010) and *The Literary Genres of Edmund Burke* (1996). He is currently editing, with Shaun Regan, a collection of essays on the historical and cultural effects of the Seven Years' War.

John Dussinger, professor emeritus, University of Illinois, Urbana-Champaign, has completed two volumes of the Cambridge Edition of Samuel Richardson's *Correspondence*. His most recent publications have concerned Richardson's role as polemical editor of anonymous books, pamphlets, and newspaper articles that issued from his press.

Deborah Heller is professor of English at Western New Mexico University. She has published extensively on the Bluestockings and on late-eighteenth-century poetry, and she is currently preparing an edition of the complete manuscript letters between Elizabeth Montagu and Elizabeth Vesey. She is also coediting, with Gary Kelly, *Bluestockings Now!*, a collection of essays examining the influence of the Blues in their age and ours. She is on the editorial board of the Montagu Letters Project.

Regina Janes is professor of English, Skidmore College. Recent books are *Edmund Burke on Irish Affairs* (2002) and *Losing Our Heads: Beheadings in Literature and Culture* (2005). Her essay "Beheadings" won the ASECS

Clifford Prize for 1991–1992. Recent articles include "Revisiting García Márquez among the Bananas," *Modern Language Quarterly* (2011) and "Henry Fielding Reinvents the Afterlife," *Eighteenth-Century Fiction* (2011).

Katherine Kickel is associate professor of English and a Women's Studies affiliate at Miami University of Ohio. She is the author of *Novel Notions: Medical Discourse and the Mapping of the Imagination in Eighteenth-Century English Fiction* (2007). Currently she is working on an essay on conceptions of the soul in the British novel.

Roger D. Lund is professor of English at Le Moyne College, Syracuse, New York. He is the author of *Religion, Ridicule and the Politics of Wit in Augustan England* (2012), and editor of *Critical Essays on Daniel Defoe* (1997); *The Margins of Orthodoxy: Heterodox Writing and Cultural Response, 1660-1750* (2005); and *Gulliver's Travels: A Sourcebook* (2006).

Brett C. McInelly is associate professor of English, Brigham Young University. He has published articles on Defoe, Smollett, and the Methodist revival. He is the editor of the annual *Religion in the Age of Enlightenment* (AMS) and is currently working on a book that explores the ways anti-Methodist literature informed Methodist religiosity.

Patrick Müller studied English, German, and philosophy at the Wesfälische Wilhelms-Universität, Münster, and the University of Edinburgh, before joining the Shaftesbury Project at the Friedrich Alexander University, Erlangen-Nuremberg, where he has worked since 2007. His doctoral dissertation, *Latitudinarianism and Didacticism*, was published in 2009, and he has published or forthcoming a number of articles, some connected with Shaftesbury, others focusing on contemporary British and American fiction.

Melvyn New is professor emeritus, University of Florida. He is presently working on volume 9, the *Miscellanies*, the last volume of the Florida Edition of the Works of Laurence Sterne. His most recent essays have appeared in *RES, HLQ, Eighteenth-Century Life, Shandean*, and *The Scriblerian*.

Geoff Newton, independent scholar, Bude, Cornwall, UK, was a Baptist minister and social worker before earning his doctorate at Exeter University in 2008, with a dissertation on Sterne's sermons in the light of eighteenth-century philosophy. He has published essays in *Shandean, Reform* (with Carol Williams), and *Divine Rhetoric: Essays on the Sermons of Laurence Sterne*, ed. W.B. Gerard.

About the Contributors 349

Gerard Reedy, S.J., is University Professor at Fordham University in New York. He has published two books and a number of articles and reviews on the sermon literature of the later seventeenth and early eighteenth century. He shares an interest with Melvyn New in the religious backgrounds to literature of this and later periods.

Steven Scherwatzky is professor of English, Merrimack College. His most recent articles on Samuel Johnson have appeared in *Age of Johnson*. He is currently working on a study of Hobbes, Milton, and seventeenth-century millenarianism.

Nicholas Seager lectures in eighteenth-century literature at Keele University. He has written articles on Defoe, Richardson, Swift, Haywood, and Bunyan, and he has recently completed a guide to criticism on the "rise of the novel," which will be published in 2012. He is now completing a monograph entitled *Daniel Defoe and the History of Fictional Form*.

Ryan J. Stark is an associate professor of English at Corban University. His book *Rhetoric, Science, and Magic in Seventeenth-Century England* was published in 2009. His research on early modern thought has appeared in a variety of journals, including *JHI*, *Studies in Philology*, *Philosophy, and Rhetoric*, and *1650–1850*.

Paul Tankard is senior lecturer in English at the world's southernmost university, the University of Otago in Dunedin, New Zealand. His published scholarship concentrates on nonfictional prose writing and includes work on Samuel Johnson and James Boswell, and C.S. Lewis and his circle. He is publications editor for the Johnson Society of Australia and is preparing for Yale University Press the first-ever edition of Boswell's selected journalistic writings.

E. Derek Taylor is professor of English, Longwood University. His *Reason and Religion in* Clarissa was published in 2009; he has also coedited, with Melvyn New, an edition of Mary Astell and John Norris, *Letters concerning the Love of God* (2005), and with W.B. Gerard and R.G. Walker, *Swiftly Sterneward: Essays on Laurence Sterne and His Times* (2011). His essays have appeared in *Notes and Queries*, *Eighteenth-Century Fiction*, *JHI*, and *Studies in Bibliography*.

Robert G. Walker is senior research fellow, Department of English, Washington and Jefferson College. He is the author of *Eighteenth-Century Arguments for Immortality and Johnson's* Rasselas (1977) and coeditor of *Swiftly Sterneward: Essays on Laurence Sterne and His Times* (2011). He has recently published essays on Boswell in *Age of Johnson*, *English Studies*, and *1650-1850*; an essay on Arthur Koestler in *Sewanee Review*; and also in that journal an essay on Curzio Malaparte.

Donald Wehrs is professor of English at Auburn University where he teaches British eighteenth-century studies, critical theory, postcolonial studies, and comparative literature. He is the author of three books on twentieth-century African fiction, the latest being *Islam, Ethics, Revolt* (2008), and coeditor (with David P. Haney) of *Levinas and Nineteenth-Century Literature* (2009). He is the author of numerous essays on eighteenth-century fiction, critical theory, postcolonial literature, and Shakespeare, appearing in *Poetics Today*, *New Literary History*, *MLN*, *SEL*, *The Eighteenth Century: Theory and Interpretation*, *Comparative Literature Studies*, and elsewhere.

Nathalie Zimpfer wrote her doctoral dissertation on Jonathan Swift and specializes in Anglican homiletics and the links between theology and literature in the Augustan period. She is currently completing a critical translation into French of Mary Wollstonecraft's works. She has published recent essays on the Anglicanism of both Sterne and Swift.